HARVARD HISTORICAL STUDIES

PUBLISHED UNDER THE DIRECTION OF
THE DEPARTMENT OF HISTORY

FROM THE INCOME OF

THE HENRY WARREN TORREY FUND

VOLUME XXXIII

HARVARD HISTORICAL STUDIES

HARVARD UNIVERSITY PRESS
CAMBRIDGE, MASS., U. S. A.

THE
PRESBYTERIAN CHURCHES
AND THE FEDERAL UNION
1861-1869

BY

LEWIS G. VANDER VELDE

University of Michigan

CAMBRIDGE
HARVARD UNIVERSITY PRESS
LONDON: HUMPHREY MILFORD
OXFORD UNIVERSITY PRESS
1932

COPYRIGHT, 1932
BY THE PRESIDENT AND FELLOWS OF
HARVARD COLLEGE

PRINTED IN THE UNITED STATES OF AMERICA

To

MY MOTHER

AND

THE MEMORY OF MY FATHER

PREFACE

AMONG the innumerable works which have been written on the history of the American churches and their individual units only a few represent the point of view of the lay historian. Except for several important studies of recent years, the development of organized religion in America has been interpreted by clergymen whose primary interest is religious rather than by historians whose point of view is detached and objective. This neglect on the part of historians is hard to explain when one considers the unquestioned importance of the influence of the Church in American life. Not only unconsciously have religious groups influenced the course of affairs; present-day Americans need not be reminded that religious denominations have not infrequently considered it their mission to direct public policies as well as to guide individual lives. The problems of the Civil War, vitally concerning each individual as well as the nation as a whole, to a special degree aroused interest and concern in the churches and prompted church action and church advice. Among all of the religious groups the Presbyterians — influential, well-organized, patriotic — were of outstanding importance in the part they played in the national crisis. The story of their activities in connection with the Civil War and Reconstruction is important not only for its own sake, but also for the opportunity it affords of studying a cross-section of the American public in its relation to the great problems of the time.

The written sources of Presbyterian history — thanks to the emphasis placed by Presbyterians upon education and to their love of verbal expression — are almost discouragingly extensive. To the persons in charge of the various depositories in which I consulted these records, I owe the heartiest thanks. The beginnings of the study were facilitated by the wealth of American history material in the Library of Harvard University, and by the richness of the Presbyterian collection of which the Library of the University of Michigan, through the gift of the Tappan Presbyterian Association of Ann Arbor, is in possession. I am particularly grateful to the staff-members of each of these institutions for their courtesy and helpfulness in rendering the resources available to me. I am also especially indebted to Dr. William P. Finney and to Miss Matilda H. Turner of the Library of the Presbyterian Historical Society in Philadelphia for such a welcome to the facilities of their collection — well-rounded, and amazingly complete in the field of periodicals — as librarians seldom accord research students. Dr. Thomas P. Martin of the Manuscripts Division of the Library of Congress was resourceful in directing me to useful materials. In the Libraries of Princeton University, Princeton Theological Seminary, and Union Theological Seminary, I received helpful attention. The heads of other libraries containing large Presbyterian collections in their response to inquiries were generous of time and assistance.

For information with regard to individuals mentioned in this volume I am indebted to Dr. Henry van Dyke of Princeton, New Jersey, to Professor William M. McPheeters of Columbia Theological Seminary, Decatur, Georgia, and to Professor Edward Caldwell Moore of Harvard University. To Mrs. C. H. Van Tyne and to my sisters I owe gratitude for many helpful suggestions as to presentation, and the richly deserved thanks merited by readers of proof.

To Professor A. M. Schlesinger of Harvard University, for guidance in choosing the subject of this study, for an unflagging interest in its development, and for criticisms offered in that unusual manner which stimulates rather than destroys enthusiasm, is due my deepest debt of gratitude.

Lewis G. Vander Velde.

Ann Arbor, July, 1932.

CONTENTS

PART I

THE RISE OF PRESBYTERIANISM IN AMERICA, 1683-1861

PART II

THE OLD SCHOOL PRESBYTERIAN CHURCH AND THE CIVIL WAR

CHAPTER I

The Old School Presbyterian Church Faces a Crisis

CHAPTER II

The Old School Assembly Meets the Crisis

ix

CHAPTER III

The Response of the Church

CHAPTER IV

The Advance of the Old School Assembly, 1862-1864

CHAPTER V

The Voice of the Old School Press

CHAPTER VIII

The Voice of the Old School Pulpit

PART III

THE NEW SCHOOL PRESBYTERIAN CHURCH AND THE CIVIL WAR

PART IV

THE MINOR PRESBYTERIAN CHURCHES AND THE CIVIL WAR

PART V

PRESBYTERIAN PATRIOTISM IN PRACTICE

PART VI

REUNION

STATISTICAL TABLES

PART I

THE RISE OF PRESBYTERIANISM IN AMERICA, 1683-1861

Iᴛ is a curious fact that, while the importance of the Church in colonial times is always recognized, American historians have too frequently assumed that its influence as a force in public affairs disappeared with the American Revolution. Writers in an age when the Church is on the defensive fail to realize that the transformation which has put it in this position is much more a product of the last seventy years than of the previous seventy. In the time of our grandfathers, the Church was still a strong factor in the life of the nation; an institution led by intellectual giants, attended regularly by a large portion of the people, it exerted an important influence upon American life. To be convinced of this, one has but to turn to the newspapers of the middle period of our history, and note the frequent references to the activity of the Church, and the prominent part played by Church leaders in public affairs. Even more convincing is a study of the proportion of the college students of that time who were preparing for the Christian ministry. In 1861, of a total of 5771 students in thirty-nine representative colleges and universities,[1] 1204 were preparing for the ministry; sixty-nine, to be missionaries.[2] Clergymen presided over practically all of the institutions of higher learning.

When it is remembered that in 1860 politics and the Church still offered the greatest professional opportunities, and that in consequence the best minds were to be found there, the ques-

---

[1] Including, for example, several large non-sectarian institutions, such as Yale College and the University of Michigan; and not including many sectarian colleges, such as Oakland College (Mississippi), Center College (Kentucky), and Washington College (Pennsylvania). A complete list of statistics of American colleges, universities, and theological seminaries, would no doubt show that of all the students in American institutions of higher learning, the proportion preparing for the Christian ministry was even greater than that indicated above.

[2] *Cf.* table of statistics, *Presbyterian Banner*, February 23, 1861. The same table is given in the *Presbyter*, February 21, 1861.

tion arises, how did these two professions react on one another? To what degree did politics influence the Church; to what degree did the Church influence politics? These questions are particularly pertinent with regard to the greatest crisis in our

● national life — the Civil War. The interaction between Church and State in this crisis was of importance in the case of each of the large religious denominations; because of certain peculiar conditions it was nowhere of more vital significance than in the case of the Presbyterian Church.

In 1860, Christians in the United States were divided into scores of denominations. The three most important, from the point of view of numbers, were the Methodists, the Baptists, and the Presbyterians.[3] Each of these comprised, besides a

● number of minor bodies, two major divisions. But a most interesting and important contrast lay in this fact: while the Methodist Episcopal Church in 1844, and the Baptist Church in the same year, had been divided geographically into North and South Churches by the slavery question, the split in the Presbyterian Church which had come in 1837 had been caused by questions of church doctrine and church government. Thus in contrast to the " Methodist Episcopal Church," and the "Methodist Episcopal Church, South"; the "Northern Baptists," and the " Southern Baptists," we find the " Presbyterian Church in the United States of America, (Old School)," and the " Presbyterian Church in the United States of America, (New School)," two denominations each having churches scattered over wide areas of the country, with rival congregations existing side by side, not only in the larger cities, but also in many of the smaller communities. Although destined to re-

---

[3] *Cf.* table of statistics on page 5. Note that with but five-twelfths of the church accommodations of the Methodists, and with but five-eighths that of the Baptists, in total value of church property the Presbyterians nearly equaled the record of the former denomination, while they actually exceeded that of the latter. As the types of church property owned by these three denominations did not greatly vary, the total value of church possessions constitutes in their cases a significant and fair basis of comparison. This does not follow in the cases of certain other important denominations. (*Cf. post,* p. 5, note 5.)

STRENGTH OF VARIOUS RELIGIOUS GROUPS
IN THE UNITED STATES, 1860 [4]

Religious Group	Total Church Accommodations	Accommodations in Slave- Holding States	Total Value [5] of Church Property	Value in Slave- Holding States
Methodist	6,259,799	2,788,338	$33,093,371	$10,050,139
Baptist	4,044,220	2,413,818	21,079,104	7,227,123
Presbyterian [6]	2,565,949	943,746	27,840,525	7,044,416
Roman Catholic	1,404,437	266,313	26,774,119	7,387,582
Congregationalist	956,351	....	13,327,511	....
Protestant Episcopal	847,296	287,546	21,665,698	5,151,830
Lutheran	757,637	143,603	5,385,179	915,967
Christian	681,016	273,900	2,518,045	1,017,125
Union	371,899	157,235	1,370,212	....
German Reformed	273,697	26,975	2,422,670	....
Friends	269,084	....	2,544,507	....
Universalist	235,219	....	2,856,095	....
Dutch Reformed	211,068	....	4,453,850	....
Unitarian	138,213	....	4,338,316	....
Jewish	34,412	....	1,135,300	....
Moravian	20,316	....	227,450	....
Adventist	17,128	....	101,170	....
Swedenborgian	15,395	....	321,200	....
Spiritualist	6,275	....	7,500	....
Shaker	5,200	....	41,000	....
Minor Sects	14,150	....	895,100	....
Total	19,128,761		$172,397,922	

[4] This table was compiled from *Statistics of the United States . . . in 1860; compiled from the original returns of the . . . Eighth Census* (Washington, 1866), " Miscellaneous " volume, pp. 352-501. It should be noted that these census returns show the church *accommodations* of each of the various denominations; not the number of church members.

[5] Certain denominations, like the Roman Catholic, Protestant Episcopal, and Lutheran, had considerable property not used primarily for purposes of worship. The value of church property is not, therefore, necessarily an accurate index of denominational strength.

[6] Included in the figures for the Presbyterians are the following for minor sects:

Cumberland Presbyterian	262,978	214,758	$ 914,256	$ 734,506
Reformed Presbyterian...	48,897	....	386,635	....
United Presbyterian......	165,236	....	1,312,275	....

unite in 1869, during most of the period intervening between 1837 and that date, there was an intense rivalry between them. Indeed, each claimed to be the true Presbyterian Church, and for a number of years, the designations " Old School " and "New School " were usually omitted from their records — an omission that has frequently proved to be a stumbling-block to historical workers.[7]

Besides these two major divisions, there were among the Presbyterians several minor groups of varying numbers and importance. The framing of a complete list of Presbyterian denominations at any point in American history is indeed a

[7] Professor W. E. Dodd, for example, in his " The Fight for the North-west, 1860," in the *American Historical Review,* July, 1911, vol. xvi, pp. 774-788, stressing the importance of the Presbyterians in the three states he is considering — Indiana, Illinois, and Iowa — makes no distinction between the two great branches of the Presbyterian Church. He has taken his figures from the *Report* of the Census of 1860, which, although enumerating " Cumberland," " Reformed," and " United " Presbyterians, does not distinguish between the Old School and the New School churches. In his naming of leaders, and in his mention of " ten synods," it is evident that Professor Dodd is familiar only with the Old School in this section. The *Minutes* of the General Assemblies of the two bodies furnish a more reliable and satisfactory source of information with regard to membership than does the Census *Report,* for the latter undertakes simply to give the " church accommodations " of the various denominations. In the three states under consideration, the Old School Church in 1860 had a total of 31,807 communicants; the New School, 16,716 communicants. As churches then had a much larger non-member attendance than now, the number of active church-goers in each branch in these states was no doubt much larger than the figures here given would indicate. Professor Dodd's estimate of the " membership " for this region at 150,000, is obviously much too high; probably the total *attendance* per Sunday for both churches would approximate, on the average, that figure. His statements with regard to the attitude of these 150,000 Presbyterians toward slavery in 1860 may perhaps be accurately applied to the two-thirds of that number who were Old School Presbyterians. His having overlooked the New School element may have considerable bearing on the conclusions set forth in his paper, for the New School Presbyterian Church had been divided on the slavery question in 1857, (*cf. post,* p. 15), and a study of this great group of Presbyterians would have revealed the fact that, when their denomination had been purged of its ultra-conservative Southern element, the people in the New School Church were not backward in their support of the free-soil movement in the Northwest.

daring undertaking. The list below probably approximates accuracy and completeness:

PRESBYTERIAN CHURCHES IN 1861 [8]

Organization	Presby-teries	Minis-ters	Churches	Communi-cants	Benevo-lences	For Cong. Purposes	Total Collected
Presbyterian Church in U. S. A. (Old School)	176	2767	3684	300,874	$736,710	$2,430,715	$3,167,425
Presbyterian Church in U. S. A. (New School)	105	1558	1478	134,760	298,027	....	....
Cumberland Presbyterian Church	97	1150	1250	103,000	140,000	460,000	600,000
United Presbyterian Church of N. A.	43	444	669	57,567	34,071	252,425	286,496
United Synod of the Presbyterian Church	14	116	193	12,934	9,516	57,945	67,461
Reformed Presbyterian Church (General Synod)	7	56	116	10,000	9,523	....	....
Reformed Presbyterian Church (Synod)	9	59	78	6,650	6,000	....	....
Associate Presbyterian Synod of N. A.	4	14	49	1,130	....	....	....
Associate Reformed Synod of New York	2	16	14	1,631	....	....	....
Free Presbyterian Synod	..	41	..	....	....	....	....
Independent Presbyterian Church	..	4	13	1,000	....	....	....
Total	6225	7,544	629,546	$1,233,847			

From these statistics it is apparent that more than two-thirds of the communicants of Presbyterian churches in 1861

[8] Wilson, Joseph M., *ed., Presbyterian Historical Almanac and Annual Remembrancer of the Church,* (Philadelphia, 1859-1868), 1862, pp. 278, 305, 385. The figures given for the Cumberland Presbyterian Church are merely round numbers, as the editor of the *Presbyterian Historical Almanac,* in the absence of official records for the whole Cumberland Church, was forced to rely upon the records of synods and presbyteries, where available; upon statements of publishers of the periodicals of the Church; and upon letters from personal friends. (*Ibid.,* 1862, p. 286, note.) As the same editor gave the total number of communicants in 1857, (with 32 of the 89 presbyteries not reporting), as 48,601, it would seem that in 1861 he over-estimated the size of the Church, when he placed the number of communicants at 103,000. (For the 1857 figures, *cf. ibid.,* 1858, p. 222.) The carelessness of this Church in keeping its records — in contrast to other Presbyterian Churches — is interesting in connection with its laxer educational standards. *Cf. post,* p. 9.

belonged to the two major Presbyterian bodies. Measured in terms of financial strength, their importance would be denoted by a still larger fraction. Actually the relative influence of these two groups in the whole Presbyterian family was far greater than either of these fractions would indicate. In order to appreciate the truth of this statement, it is necessary to be somewhat familiar with the outstanding facts of Presbyterian history in the United States, and particularly with the circumstances which led to the establishment of the various Presbyterian denominations.

As compared with the Anglican and the Congregationalist Churches, the Presbyterians were late in the date of their establishment in the English colonies in America. Although the Puritans of Massachusetts were largely Presbyterians in theory before their emigration from England, various factors prevailed to enable Congregationalism to triumph in Massachusetts.[9] The government of the Connecticut churches, it is true, came to resemble more strongly the Presbyterian system, so that in the eighteenth century they were conscious of their relationship to the Presbyterians of the settlements to the west; yet even in Connecticut the system was essentially closer to the Congregationalist standard than to that of the Presbyterians.[10]

It was not until the first immigration of the Scotch-Irish that Presbyterianism really got under way in America, and not until Francis Makemie arrived in 1683 did organized Presbyterianism begin on this side of the Atlantic. In 1705, when the first presbytery was formed, the roll included but six ministers.[11] From this date on, however, progress was rapid. The table below, including only the main body of the Presbyterians, well illustrates the remarkable growth of the sect:

[9] Thompson, Robert E., A History of the Presbyterian Churches in the United States (American Church History Series, vol. vi, New York, 1895), pp. 13-15; Gillett, E. H., History of the Presbyterian Church in the United States of America (Revised edition, 2 vol., Philadelphia, 1873), vol. i, pp. 2-6.

[10] Thompson, op. cit., p. 15.

[11] Ibid., p. 19.

GROWTH OF THE PRESBYTERIAN CHURCH IN THE
UNITED STATES OF AMERICA [12]

Date	Presbyteries	Churches	Ordained Ministers	Communicants
1789	17	419	177	No report
1799	25	449	266	No report
1803	31	511	322	No report
1810	36	772	434	28,901[13]
1820	129	1,299	741	72,096[14]
1830	...	2,158	1,491	173,329
1840 Old School	...	....	....	126,583
New School	...	....	....	102,060

This marvelous growth of the main body of Presbyterians is all the more striking in view of the fact that this period saw the birth and rapid development of rival Presbyterian denominations. The great revival of 1801, creating an unprecedented demand for preachers, caused the Presbytery of Transylvania (in Kentucky) and the Cumberland Presbytery (in Tennessee) to take the step of licensing as preachers men whose academic training did not meet traditional Presbyterian standards, and whose views on predestination and perseverance were not all that orthodox Presbyterians demanded.[15] The dispute provoked by this action culminated in 1810 in the formation of the Cumberland Presbyterian Church, differing from the older body largely in its less rigorous standards of doctrine and of ministerial training. That the new organization was well adapted to the demands of the times in certain types of settlements is evidenced by the fact that — in spite of its being largely confined geographically to Tennessee, Kentucky, Missouri, Texas, Mississippi, Alabama, and Arkansas, with some strength in southern Illinois, Indiana, and Iowa [16] — by 1861 it had a communicant membership of approximately 100,000.[17] Its position at the outbreak of the Civil War was unique in that it was peculiarly a Border State church. More than one-half

[12] For statistics here given, *cf. ibid.*, pp. 77, 93, 126.
[13] Four presbyteries not reporting.
[14] Three presbyteries not reporting.
[15] *Ibid.*, p. 74; Gillett, *op. cit.*, vol. ii, pp. 192-196.
[16] *Statistics . . . of the Eighth Census*, Misc. vol., pp. 352-501. *Cf.* also, table of church accommodations in the slave-holding states, *ante*, p. 5.
[17] As to the accuracy of this estimate *cf. ante*, p. 7, note 8.

of its strength lay in the three states of Tennessee, Kentucky, and Missouri; more than three-fourths, in slave-holding states.[18]

It has been pointed out that American Presbyterianism is Scotch Presbyterianism twice-tempered: its double transplantation, first to Ulster, and thence to America, has distinctly modified its rigor and lessened its theocratic nature.[19]   This fact is well illustrated in the contrast between the main body of Presbyterians, which was largely of Scotch-Irish and English background, and those lesser bodies which grew up in America following a single transplantation from Scotland.   Such bodies were the Associate Synod and the Associate Reformed Synod, which in 1858 joined to form the United Presbyterian Church. Dissenting minorities in each body reorganized and continued as independent denominations.   To enumerate the points on which these sects agreed is a far simpler task than to name their points of difference.   All agreed in being opposed to oathbound secret societies, hymn-singing, and open communion. More significant items of agreement — from our point of view — were opposition to slave-holding (an issue which had resulted in the separation of the Associate Reformed Synod of the South, in 1821 [20]) and, in general, limitation of the functions of the civil magistracy.[21]   While the reorganized Associate Synod and Associate Reformed Synod remained small, the new United Presbyterian Church, with a membership of nearly 60,000 in 1861,[22] was sufficiently large and compact to be a body of importance and influence.

Other groups owing their origin to direct transplantation from Scotland were two denominations of Reformed Presbyterians, distinguished from one another by the names of their central bodies, the Synod, and the General Synod.   The dis-

---

[18] Total church accommodations of the Cumberland Church in 1860, 262,978; in the slave-holding states, 214,758; in the three states named above, 143, 285. *Cf. ante*, p. 5, note 6; *post*, p. 16.

[19] Thompson, *op. cit.*, pp. 12; 28-29.

[20] *Ibid.*, p. 135.

[21] *Ibid.*, pp. 147-148.

[22] *Cf.* table, *ante*, p. 7.

tinction between them seems to have been largely one of strictness, the former being the stricter of the two.[23]   The Reformed
Presbyterians were often called Covenanters.   Originally
their chief point of distinction had lain in their emphasis upon
" political dissent " — that is, refusal to profess allegiance to
an " immoral government." [23a]   After the American Revolution their "political dissent" against the British government
was transferred to the new Federal Constitution, which, in
failing to recognize the Deity or the Christian religion, was
considered " immoral." [23b]   Gradually the more liberal wing
of the sect abandoned its fidelity to this principle, but the
stricter branch continued scrupulously to observe it.[23c]   The
Reformed Presbyterians held to most of the distinctive principles of the Associate and Associate Reformed churches, but
refrained from joining them in the union of 1858, largely because of adherence to " political dissent " on the part of the
stricter branch, and because of the strong views of the power
of the civil magistrate over the Church on the part of the more
liberal wing.[24]

[23] Thompson, *op. cit.,* p. 149.
[23a] Scouller, James B., *A History of the United Presbyterian Church*
(American Church History Series, vol. xi, pp. 143-255, New York, 1894),
pp. 155-156.
[23b] Thompson, *op. cit.,* p. 102.
[23c] *Ibid.,* p. 147.
[24] *Ibid.,* p. 148.   Other minor Presbyterian bodies were the United Synod
of the Presbyterian Church, composed of units which broke away from the
New School in 1857 on the slavery issue, (*cf. post,* p. 15); the Free Presbyterian Synod, founded in 1847 by the union of a New School presbytery
and part of an Old School presbytery (on the principle of outspoken anti-
slavery sentiment), confined, geographically, for the most part to Ohio and
western Pennsylvania, and destined to join the New School Church in
1862, (*cf. Presbyterian Historical Almanac,* 1862, p. 305; Lyons, John F.,
" The Attitude of Presbyterians in Ohio, Indiana, and Illinois, toward Slavery, 1825-1861," in *Journal of the Presbyterian Historical Society,* June, 1921,
vol. xi, pp. 70-71; 81-82); and the Independent Presbyterian Church, in
South and North Carolina, which had been founded after a secession from
the Presbyterian Church in 1810 on doctrinal grounds.   The last-named
church was always small. (*Presbyterian Historical Almanac,* 1862, p. 305.)

One may thus think of the main body of the Presbyterians (divided into Old School and New School from 1837 to 1869) as being flanked on the left by the Cumberland Presbyterians, with laxer standards of educational qualifications for the ministry, and a less rigid theology; and on the right by a group of stricter bodies of more or less immediate Scottish origin. Among these minor groups to the right, during the first half of the nineteenth century, there was going on a constant process of splitting off and reuniting, a process so involved with arguments on " occasional hearing," " political dissent," and " occasional communion," as to challenge the layman to keep them straight.   Exasperated by the intricacies of these movements, he is inclined to suspect, when he comes across such names as " Reformed Dissenting Presbytery " and " United Secessionists," that the lengthy disputes must at least have served to separate those with no sense of humor from those perhaps more fortunately endowed.   With the formation of the United Presbyterian Church in 1858, about two-thirds of the communicants of these stricter sects had established a really effective union.[25]   The attitude of this whole right wing during the crisis of 1861-1865 is particularly interesting because of the non-political tenets and the anti-slavery views of so many of its members.

Interesting as these lesser groups and their particular views are, however, it may be seen from the foregoing account that, though comprising over one-fourth of the total Presbyterian membership,[26] they were not likely to exert even this proportion of influence in a national crisis.   Their division into many small groups; their reputation with the non-Presbyterians for ultra-strictness, on the one hand, or for lack of erudition of their clergy, on the other; the fact that they tended to become localized in certain sections of the country — all militated against them.   The recognized national Presbyterian Church

[25] *Cf.* table of Presbyterian denominations, *ante*, p. 7.
[26] *Ibid.*

— in spite of the fact that it was divided into two wholly independent branches — was the " Presbyterian Church in the
United States of America."

The history and development of the controversy which in
1837 brought about the division of the Presbyterian Church
into these two branches have a marked bearing on the relation
of each branch to the problems which the Civil War brought
to the churches of the United States. In 1801 the General Association of Connecticut (Congregationalist) and the General
Assembly of the Presbyterian Church, inspired largely by the
religious needs of the rapidly developing West, adopted their
famous Plan of Union. Its terms made the constituent parts
of the two church systems practically interchangeable.
Churches of either body might call a pastor from the
other. In 1808 the Plan was applied to the whole Middle Association of Congregationalists in New York State when that
body accepted an invitation to become a subordinate division
of the Synod of Albany rather than unite with others to form
a State Association of Congregationalists. New York State
became a stronghold of Presbyterians, a considerable portion of
whom had a Congregationalist background. As far as the territory of the West was concerned, the Plan virtually amounted
to an agreement that neither church would invade territory
preëmpted by the other. As the Presbyterians were first in the
field in vast areas of the new West, particularly in western New
York and in Ohio, the hosts of New Englanders who spread
over this territory found churches already established, and
true to their agreement, they joined the Presbyterian fold.

Joining the Presbyterian Church, however, did not necessarily mean giving up preconceived ideas on church government and church doctrine, and the older Scotch and Scotch-
Irish element in the Church began to view with alarm this
Yankeeizing of the Church in the North and West. The membership increased seven-fold between 1810 and 1830.[27] It

----

[27] *Cf.* table on growth of the Presbyterian Church, *ante*, p. 9.

was apparent that much of this increase was due to the influx of Congregationalists.   The anxiety of the older Presbyterian element became particularly acute in the 1830's, as the New England influence came to be more and more powerfully felt in the debates in church councils and in the trend of church action.   To the chagrin of the conservative leaders, in the General Assemblies of 1835 and 1836 the " New School " men had a clear majority.   In 1837, however, a careful counting of strength revealed that the "Old School" party could control the Assembly.   Grasping their opportunity to rid the Church of an element tainted with "diluted" orthodoxy and "infirm" ideas of church government, they precipitately exscinded four synods dominated by the New England element.

Such a step could not be taken, however, without shaking the whole Church.   Presbyterians stand for strongly organized church government, but first of all they believe in independence of judgment on vital matters.   Presbyteries, individual churches, and individual members decided for themselves whether or not they approved of the action of the General Assembly of 1837.   Those who did not usually found their way into the newly organized Presbyterian Church in the United States of America (New School).   All over the country it found its adherents, but naturally its greatest strength lay in the regions settled by Congregationalistic New Englanders.[28]   The records of 1857 show the New School Church with twenty-six synods, twenty of them north of the Mason-Dixon line; and a communicant membership of 139,115, less than one-eighth of which belonged below that line.[29]   On the other hand, fourteen of the thirty-five synods of the Old School

---

[28] The facts cited in this account of the controversy which culminated in the division of the Presbyterian Church in 1837, were taken from Gillett, *op. cit.*, vol. i, pp. 393-396; 437-438; vol. ii, pp. 503-574; Thompson, *op. cit.*, pp. 72, 102-128; the Plan of Union of 1801 is given in Thompson, *op. cit.*, pp. 353-355.

[29] *Minutes of the General Assembly of the Presbyterian Church in the United States of America* (New York, 1838-1869), 1857, p. 554.

Church and considerably over one-third of her 250,000 communicants were in slave-holding states.[30]

The New School Church from its founding, therefore, was predominantly a northern church — not from any stand taken on the great question of slavery, not from anything especially northern in its principles, but simply because its background was principally of Congregationalist origin, and the Congregationalists had settled almost wholly in the North. However, in 1857 it became distinctly a northern church in principle as well as in the geographical location of its membership, for in that year its General Assembly voted decided condemnation of the report of the Lexington (Kentucky) Presbytery on slavery, and as a result, the denomination's six Southern synods, comprising some 15,000 communicants, withdrew from the Church.[31] The New School still had presbyteries in the South, but they were naturally units which felt with their Northern sister-presbyteries on the question which divided North and South.

Thus while the year 1860 found great northern and southern Methodist and Baptist bodies, the two great Presbyterian bodies were a New School Church, distinctly northern in its sympathies, and an Old School, having more than one-third of its strength in the South. Of all these groups, evidently the only one likely to be seriously disturbed by the problem of divided allegiance, in case of a political crisis between North and South, was the Old School Presbyterian Church. In fact, no other church of strength faced so vital a crisis. The Congregationalists had no adherents south of the Mason-Dixon

[30] *Presbyterian Historical Almanac,* 1858-1859, p. 74. *Cf.* also, table, *ante,* p. 5. It must be remembered, however, that in the table the term " Presbyterian " includes both Old School and New School. *Cf.* also, table, *post,* p. 44.

[31] This element organized the United Synod of the Presbyterian Church, (*cf.* table, *ante,* p. 7), and applied for union with the Old School Assembly. The application was declined. After the division of the Old School Church in 1861, however, this southern New School element found its way into the southern wing of the Old School Church. *Cf.* Gillett, *op. cit.,* vol. ii, pp. 556-558; Thompson, *op. cit.,* pp. 135-136.

CHURCH ACCOMMODATIONS OF VARIOUS RELIGIOUS GROUPS IN INDIVIDUAL SLAVE-HOLDING STATES [32]

	Methodist	Baptist	Presbyterian	Cumb. Pres'n	Roman Cath.	Prot. Episc.	Christian	Lutheran
Alabama	212,555	238,055	48,880	16,124	8,000	13,840	6,330	.....
Arkansas	102,000	60,503	19,405	15,490	2,750	1,615	6,450	.....
Delaware	37,695	3,480	12,210	.....	2,770	8,780	.....	.....
Florida	30,360	20,325	9,580	.....	4,350	3,175	.....	600
Georgia	309,079	376,686	48,597	1,500	4,300	8,675	4,150	2,750
Kentucky	228,100	267,860	67,440	31,335	44,820	9,940	104,980	5,400
Louisiana	52,181	47,785	16,550	800	57,600	16,525	950	850
Maryland	165,191	21,775	24,525	.....	43,487	58,344	875	28,200
Mississippi	168,705	172,703	56,973	18,209	5,528	8,175	7,020	2,550
Missouri	150,160	141,515	47,050	30,805	38,826	8,755	54,100	10,905
No. Carolina	328,497	280,341	83,577	.....	3,250	26,695	12,755	40,438
So. Carolina	149,812	170,130	70,525	.....	8,705	30,109	1,200	15,775
Tennessee	288,460	214,381	78,655	81,145	4,305	6,940	35,100	6,350
Texas	103,799	77,435	19,067	19,350	12,772	8,480	15,905	3,510
Virginia	438,244	317,504	117,304	.....	16,650	68,498	24,085	24,675
D. of C.	17,500	3,340	8,650	.....	8,200	9,000	.....	1,600
Total	2,788,338	2,413,818	728,988	214,758	266,313	287,546	273,900	143,603

VALUE OF CHURCH PROPERTY OF VARIOUS RELIGIOUS GROUPS IN THE INDIVIDUAL SLAVE-HOLDING STATES [33]

	Methodist	Baptist	Presbyterian	Cumb. Pres'n	Roman Catholic	Prot. Episcopal	Lutheran
Alabama	$606,270	$495,599	$328,300	$40,200	$230,450	$196,050	$......
Arkansas	185,435	107,595	67,950	37,250	23,300	11,000	......
Delaware	282,000	47,150	254,100	......	51,300	154,900	......
Florida	111,325	47,915	49,450	......	31,200	44,000	500
Georgia	796,138	787,198	442,805	2,200	148,500	211,250	21,150
Kentucky	808,305	888,530	607,225	112,600	695,850	199,100	50,600
Louisiana	336,815	231,945	305,500	1,100	1,744,700	334,000	13,500
Maryland	1,233,850	143,450	518,050	......	1,611,500	1,339,400	311,100
Mississippi	575,770	408,499	280,550	54,401	117,050	136,900	4,295
Missouri	959,125	573,260	727,200	128,125	1,391,632	261,100	92,725
No. Carolina	628,859	481,099	389,670	......	41,300	313,230	49,167
So. Carolina	632,948	699,528	718,885	......	304,300	818,130	153,780
Tennessee	763,655	497,210	478,580	307,200	208,400	165,000	9,550
Texas	319,934	228,030	120,550	47,430	189,900	111,250	20,500
Virginia	1,619,010	1,244,115	901,020	......	329,300	873,120	156,600
D. of C.	190,250	46,000	194,000	......	269,300	183,400	32,500
Total	$10,050,139	$7,227,123	$6,283,835	$734,506	$7,387,582	$5,151,830	915,967

[32] *Statistics* . . . *of the Eighth Census,* Misc. vol., pp. 352-501.
[33] *Ibid. Cf.* statement, *ante,* note 5. Only the groups which were strongest in the South are listed in the above table.

line, nor did the Lutherans have a strong southern contingent, except for some hold on North Carolina, Virginia, Maryland, and Missouri.[34]   While the Christian denomination numbered a considerable portion of its adherents among the people of the South, in numbers and wealth, and especially in their concentration in a few states, they were considerably inferior in importance to the Old School Presbyterians in the South.   One-fifth of the numerical strength of the Roman Catholics, and one-third of that of the Protestant Episcopal Church, was to be found in the slave-holding states, while about one-fourth of the church property of each lay in the same section.[35]   But the form of church organization of these two denominations, with a large degree of autonomy in bishoprics and archbishoprics, lent itself admirably to a fairly quiet, natural separation in the Protestant Episcopal Church when the conflict came, and to the avoidance of a pronouncement on the part of the national organization of the Roman Catholic Church.

The closely-knit character of the Presbyterian organization, with its emphasis on the principle of representation, made the problem of the Old School Church infinitely more critical. Furthermore, while the year 1861 was not a year of meeting of the quadrennial Methodist Episcopal General Conference, the triennial Protestant Episcopal Convention, or for the meeting of any other large denomination in convention, the Presbyterian practice of annual general assemblies in May practically forced upon all the various Presbyterian bodies, at a time when excitement was at its highest pitch, a decision on the question of endorsement of the Union.   For the Old School Presbyterian Church, with its influential Southern wing, the year 1861 was to be, as for the nation itself, a year of crisis.

[34] *Cf.* tables of church accommodations, *ante,* pp. 5, 16.
[35] *Cf.* tables of church accommodations and church property, *ante,* pp. 5, 14, 16.

PART II

THE OLD SCHOOL PRESBYTERIAN CHURCH AND THE CIVIL WAR

CHAPTER I

THE OLD SCHOOL CHURCH FACES A CRISIS

As has been pointed out, the critical turn of political affairs in the winter of 1860-61 was of peculiar importance to the Old School Presbyterian Church. Men were asking, could this historic body, glorying in its record of splendid growth, pointing with pride to its having survived intact while its great rivals were broken asunder on the rock of slavery, weather this mightier storm? Old School Presbyterians were fond of quoting the alleged remark of Cyrus McCormick, that "the two great hoops holding the Union together were the Democratic party and the Old School Presbyterian Church." With the Democratic party rent asunder, might not the Old School Church by holding together now prove to be the salvation of the Union? On the other hand, was it necessary, was it right, even, for the Church to take a stand on the issue dividing the two sides? The President-elect and his advisers insisted that this issue was solely that of the preservation of the Union, since they were pledged not to interfere with slavery in the states. The question at stake in the winter of 1860-61 was thus the question whether federal or state government was supreme. This was a purely political issue—and hence not one for the Church to decide. Or did it after all involve a moral problem? Was not treason sin, and, therefore, was not the matter of first allegiance one that the Church was duty-bound to consider? These were the thorny problems the Old School Presbyterians were trying to solve during the anxious months which intervened between the election of Lincoln and the meeting of the General Assembly in May, 1861.

How they would solve them was of vital interest not only to themselves, but to the whole country. The church was not only the largest Protestant body having considerable strength both North and South; its traditions made it an organization of peculiar power. Its insistence upon a highly educated ministry [1] had given its leaders a well-earned reputation for learning. Its theological seminary at Princeton was the most famous institution of its kind in the land,[2] with some 2500 graduates to its credit.[3] With five other seminaries, twenty-four colleges, and fifty-nine academies under its control,[4] with Congregationalists, Episcopalians, and members of other sects flocking to its seminaries for theological training,[5] the Old School Presbyterian Church could lay claim to intellectual leadership which it would have been difficult for any other denomination — except, perhaps, its New School rival — to challenge. Similarly, the Church had been outspoken in the great political crisis of the American Revolution,[6] and people might naturally expect it to take a correspondingly decided stand now. Presbyterians, indeed, claimed to have a peculiarly intimate interest in the United States government, be-

[1] For the influence of this insistence as a factor in promoting the defection of the Cumberland Presbyterians from the main body, cf. *ante*, p. 9.

[2] *Cf.* interesting estimate of the importance of Princeton Theological Seminary, in an editorial statement in the *Methodist*, quoted in the *Presbyterian*, July 19, 1862: "The Theological Seminary has been surpassed by no one rival in the western world."

[3] From address of Dr. W. B. Sprague at the semi-centennial celebration of the Seminary, quoted in the *Presbyterian*, July 19, 1862.

[4] For these statistics, *cf.* account of the proceedings of the General Assembly at Philadelphia, May, 1861, Philadelphia *Press*, May 18, 1861. These institutions were not all under the control of the central body of the Church; some were under the supervision of individual synods or presbyteries.

[5] Address of Dr. Sprague, *Presbyterian*, July 19, 1862. Dr. Sprague's statistics show that about one-seventh of the 2500 Princeton Seminary graduates were non-Presbyterians.

[6] *Cf.* account of pastoral letter issued by the General Synod (the predecessor of the General Assembly) of 1775, urging Presbyterians to "be careful to maintain the union which now subsists among the colonies", and to respect and encourage the Continental Congress, in Ledoux, Albert R., "The Brick Church and the Nation," American Scenic and Historic Society, *Report*, 1918, xxiii, p. 584. Also, the letter of congratulation addressed to the Church by the General Synod upon the occasion of the acknowledgment of the independence of the United States in 1783, *ibid.*

cause of the close correspondence between its representative features and those of the Presbyterian organization.[7] Likewise, the social position of the Presbyterians lifted them to an important position in the eyes of the people. Except in New England, where they were almost negligible in numbers and influence, they had enviable social prestige. In the South, for the most part, their only serious rivals were the Episcopalians, while in the North and West their long establishment in cities like Philadelphia and Pittsburgh, and the hard-headed, energetic qualities of the Scotch and Scotch-Irish as pioneers, had given them opportunities to amass wealth and influence quite out of proportion to their numbers.[8]

The respect of the public for the Old School Church was perhaps enhanced by its reputation for conservatism. Today the term " conservative " is in some disrepute, and a man *admits* being a conservative. Even the most thorough-going fundamentalist is on the defensive. In spite of evidence on every hand that the majority of Americans are conservatives, they seldom bring themselves to the point of boasting about this point of view. On the other hand, it is amusing to observe how often one hears an arch-conservative proclaim, " I'm a liberal"; sometimes almost pathetic to hear one say, " I try to be a liberal." How amazed we should be if someone should say, " I try to be a conservative"! Yet seventy years ago, in an America which had as yet scarcely found herself, when our land was beset with the strange and often extreme doctrines of multitudes of reformers, when the political future was by no means certain, when the mother-country was still successfully fighting genuine political reform at home, it seemed the part of wisdom to be apprehensive of change. It is not surprising that conservatism should then have been in high regard, and that men should take pride in being conservatives. Certainly Old School Presbyterians loved to boast of their un-

---

[7] One reason for urging support of the Continental Congress was enthusiasm over its democratic and representative features. *Ibid.*

[8] *Cf.* Dodd, *loc. cit.,* p. 781.

swerving, unadulterated conservatism. "It is the most conservative Church in the land," proudly declared one of its leaders in the 1861 General Assembly,[9] and no one, apparently, thought of contradicting the statement. The staunchness with which the Old School Church stood "on her old conservative ground"[10] was boastfully proclaimed. The public, if the press may be used as a criterion, conceded the organization this position.[11] Yet, while boasting of their conservatism, Presbyterians — at least those of the Old School and New School branches — loved to think of themselves as broad-minded, never tiring of pointing out that, in contrast to Baptists and Episcopalians, they practised "open" communion;[12] in contrast to Methodists, they opposed a pronounced degree of regulation by the central authority in matters of conduct, such as dancing;[13] in contrast to Episcopalians, they encouraged coöperation with other denominations.[14] From the point of view of Old School Presbyterians, their Church might be expected to attack a problem in a spirit of broad-minded conservatism, however paradoxical such a point of view may seem to us today. At any rate, with its reputation for learning, support of the government, social prestige, and staunch conservatism, the opinion of this large national denomination was awaited with interest in the crisis of 1860-1861.

The organization's conciliatory attitude on the slavery

[9] Dr. Charles Hodge, as quoted in account of meeting of General Assembly on May 24, 1861, in Philadelphia *Press*, May 25, 1861.

[10] Editorial, *Presbyterian*, June 9, 1860.

[11] *Cf., e. g.*, editorials, New York *World*, May 30, 1861, and June 4, 1861; editorial, Philadelphia *Press*, May 30, 1861.

[12] *Cf.* account of censure of Baptist clergyman for administering communion to a Presbyterian minister, *Presbyterian*, Jan. 25, 1862.

[13] *Cf.* refusal of General Assembly to take over what it considered to be the prerogative of individual church sessions, in this matter, *Minutes of the General Assembly of the Presbyterian Church in the United States of America*, (Philadelphia, 1789-   ), 1860, vol. xvi, p. 21.

[14] *Cf.* letter of Bishop McIlvaine to Canon Carus, relating the censure he experienced for attending a Presbyterian Reunion Convention, Thompson, Robert Ellis, *ed.*, *Life of George H. Stuart*, (Philadelphia, 1890), pp. 219-221.

question and on the problems of the South in general increased
the confidence of that section that now the Old School Church
would remain silent, or at least would take but an equivocal
stand; while to non-Presbyterians and to New School Presbyterians in the North, it made the General Assembly an object
of watchful suspicion.   The Old School Church, anti-slavery
men alleged, had of late been hedging on the slavery question.
In 1818 the General Assembly had declared in a unanimously
adopted report, "We consider the voluntary enslaving of one
part of the human race by another . . . utterly inconsistent
with the law of God . . . and . . . totally irreconcilable with
the spirit and principles of the Gospel of Christ. . . . It is
manifestly the duty of all Christians who enjoy the light of the
present day . . . as speedily as possible to efface this blot on
our holy religion, and to obtain the complete abolition of
slavery throughout Christendom, and if possible, through the
world."   Freely admitting the dangers of immediate emancipation, the report yet exhorted Presbyterians to increase their
exertions for "a total abolition of slavery," and cautioned
against the danger of the demand for delay being used as "a
cover for the love or practice of slavery, or a pretence for not
using efforts that are lawful and practicable to extinguish the
evil." [15]   In 1825, the Assembly commended the increasing
attention in the Presbyterian Church to the religious instruction of the slaves: "No more honored name can be conferred
on a minister of Jesus Christ than that of *Apostle to the American slaves. . . .*" [16]   These actions both came before the
great division of the Church in 1837-38.   It had been apparent
for some time prior to this event that although the anti-slavery
sentiment had strong exponents among Northern Presbyterians
in both groups, it was most manifest among those who were
classed as opponents of a rigid ecclesiastical system and in favor

[15] The text of this report of 1818 may be found in Thompson, *op. cit.*,
pp. 364-368; for an account of the adoption of the report, *cf.* Gillett, *op.
cit.*, vol. ii, pp. 238-241.
[16] Quoted *ibid.*, vol. ii, p. 242.

of voluntary boards — in other words, among those who later were to be found in the New School Church.[17]

It was natural, then, that there should be a pro-slavery trend in the Old School church after the departure of the New School element. In 1845 the Old School General Assembly by a vote of one hundred sixty-eight to thirteen adopted a deliverance upon the subject of slavery, which, although urging the ministers and churches in the slave-holding states to a deeper sense of their obligation to the slaves (with the euphemistic suggestion that every believing master " remember that his master is also in heaven "!) resolved, " That the General Assembly . . . was originally organized, and has since continued the bond of union in the church, upon the conceded principle that the existence of domestic slavery, under the circumstances in which it is found in the southern portion of the country, is no bar to Christian communion." [18]   And then, presumably to cover up the change of front on the question, the General Assembly of 1846 declared that the Church had " always held and uttered *substantially* the same sentiments " on the subject! [19] In 1849, without a division, the General Assembly of the Old School Church voted that it was "inexpedient and improper for it to attempt or propose" methods of emancipation.[20]   In the Assemblies between 1849 and 1861, this decision was strictly adhered to.

The growing influence of the South in the Old School Church is also illustrated by the fact that during the twenty-five years from 1837 to 1861 as many moderators were chosen from the South, in the annual elections, as in the entire preceding forty-seven years of the existence of the Presbyterians as a united national church. Eight of the annual meetings of the General Assembly between 1844 and 1861 were held south of the

[17] *Ibid.,* vol. ii, p. 524.

[18] For the text of this deliverance, *cf.* Thompson, *op. cit.,* pp. 269-272. For an account of the adoption of the deliverance, *cf. ibid.,* p. 136.

[19] Quoted, *ibid.,* p. 136. The account of this action is given in the *Minutes of the General Assembly,* vol. xi, pp. 206-207.

[20] Thompson, *op. cit.,* pp. 136-137.

Mason-Dixon line.[21]   This marked tendency to balance the influence of the two sections in Church affairs is further illustrated by the particular care which was taken to prevent the favoring of the North in the composition of the faculties of the theological seminaries under the control of the General Assembly.[22]

In spite of all this consideration, there had been for several years evidences of dissatisfaction on the part of the Southern churchmen.   For one thing, the South had never been so close to the central organization as the North.   This is best illustrated in the supervision of its theological seminaries.   While the three Northern Old School seminaries were directly under the control of the General Assembly, the same was true of but one of the three Southern seminaries — that at Danville, Kentucky.   The other — and larger — two were each controlled directly by the respective synods in whose territory they lay, entirely outside of General Assembly authority.[23]   Although Southern Presbyterian leaders disclaimed sectional prejudice,[24] for several years many of them had been among the foremost advocates of the right of secession.   Just as an Old School clergyman had first — before McDuffie or Calhoun — advanced the theory that slavery is a positive good recognized by

[21] For these statistics, *cf. Minutes of the General Assembly,* vol. xvi, pp. 840-841.

[22] For illustrations of such caution in the case of appointments in the Danville Seminary, *cf.* speech of Dr. R. J. Breckinridge, as given in report of proceedings of General Assembly of 1858, *Presbyterian,* May 29, 1858; in the case of appointments in the Princeton Seminary, *cf.* Hodge, A. A., *Life of Charles Hodge,* (New York, 1880), pp. 439-446.

[23] The two synod-controlled seminaries were Union Seminary, in Virginia, and Columbia Theological Seminary, in South Carolina. The arguments for synod control were cogently presented in an interesting letter written by Dr. J. H. Thornwell, head of the Columbia Seminary, to Dr. R. J. Breckinridge, head of the Danville Seminary. The letter may be found in the *Breckinridge Papers,* Mss. Division, Library of Congress. The signature has been cut off, but internal evidence, the handwriting, and Dr. Breckinridge's notation on the envelope, prove unmistakably its authorship. The letter was dated January 9, 1860.

[24] *Cf.* letter cited above.

the Scriptures as belonging to the great social system,[25] so in recent years many of the Old School leaders had been among the most ardent champions of secession.[26]   With the southern element strong for local rights in the Church, and politically inclined toward the theory of secession, there was ground for anxiety with regard to the permanence of the Church as a united body.   When the General Assembly meetings of 1860 proved to be free from bitterness between North and South, it provoked astonishment on the part of the older members.[27]

Within the northern element itself, three divisive influences had been for some time apparent: jealousy between the eastern and trans-Allegheny leaders; agitation carried on by an active, though relatively small, anti-slavery group; and propaganda for a reunion of the Old School and New School churches. To a somewhat marked degree, the agitators in these three disturbing influences were the same men: a group of southern Ohioans, with the noisy weekly *Presbyter*[28] as their chief organ of printed expression.   There is no more interesting phase of the story of the Old School Presbyterians and the Civil War than the opportunity the War offered this group — in 1860 small in numbers and often regarded with disdainful superiority by the larger, eastern faction — to emerge triumphant in 1865, having attained a position from which it was able proudly, (and somewhat vindictively, it must be admitted), to commit the whole Church to its policy.   How its members managed, by taking advantage of human frailty during a period of flagwaving patriotism, to enlist the most cautious of eastern leaders in support of their program of drastic discipline for border-state political doubters, and to convert all but the most deep-dyed conservatives to their reunion scheme, is a story that

[25] The clergyman was Rev. James Smylie.   *Cf.* Stanton, R. L., *The Church and the Rebellion*, (New York, 1864), pp. 468-469.

[26] *Cf.* Palmer, B. M., *Life and Letters of James Henley Thornwell*, (Richmond, 1875), pp. 479-483.

[27] *Cf.* letter of Dr. Charles Hodge of Princeton, to his brother, Hodge, *op. cit.*, p. 445.

[28] *Cf. post*, pp. 158-160; *passim*.

calls forth admiration of their skill, if not always of their spirit. Throughout the period of 1860-1869, the interplay of the three forces of sectional jealousy, anti-slavery agitation, and propaganda for reunion of the two great bodies divided since 1837, forms the key to the explanation of the stand taken by individuals and groups on the great problems facing the Old School denomination. Illustrations of the activity of these influences will appear frequently in these chapters on the Old School Church.

Presbyterians are accustomed to pride themselves on the position of equality of their clergy. They boast that, unlike the Episcopalian and the Methodist, their Church tolerates no hierarchy — in their governing bodies all ministers are on the same footing. While this is true, it is but natural that in a denomination placing so much emphasis on education, and revelling to such an extent in fine-spun theological argument, there should always be individuals who stand out in importance. Certainly this was the case in 1860. Thornwell, Palmer, Hodge, Spring, Rice, Breckinridge, Thomas, MacMaster, Lord, Anderson, Boardman, Schenck — these and many others were names of leaders familiar to every Old School Presbyterian. When, therefore, the exciting political events of the winter of 1860-1861 threatened the integrity of the denomination, leadership was not wanting.

Though the Old School General Assembly in the early summer of 1860 had proved to be exceptionally harmonious, the feeling aroused by the presidential election of that year almost immediately gave evidence of the precarious state of Old School unity. On November 21, the day appointed as a State Fast Day in South Carolina, Dr. James H. Thornwell preached a sermon in Columbia in which he declared, " The Union, which our fathers designed to be perpetual, is on the verge of dissolution. . . . Even though our cause may be just, and our course approved of Heaven, our path to victory may be through a baptism of blood. . . . Our State may suffer; she may suffer grievously; she may suffer long. Be it so: we shall love her all the more tenderly and the more intensely, the more bitterly she suffers." [29] The standing of the preacher made the position he had taken particularly important. Without question, he was the leading Old School clergyman of the South. A man of brilliant intellect, of wide educational training in Europe as well as in America, his genius was very early recognized. As President of the College of South Carolina, he had been " confessedly the only man who . . . could govern the proud and turbulent South Carolinians." [30] Now he was a professor in the Columbia Seminary, universally admired for the depth of his theological learning as well as for the brilliance of his logic and the clearness of his argument in the pulpit. In his own section of the country, he was called the " Calhoun of the Church." [31] In 1847, at the age of thirty-four, he had held the coveted position of Moderator of the General Assembly. Admired for his intellect, loved for his warm-hearted, generous nature, an intense South Carolinian who " took great delight in propagating and defending the peculiar doctrines of that pompous and pragmatical people upon all the great moral and political questions of the day," [32] it is not remarkable that contemporaries later said of him that " many were led into war . . . by his eloquent pleas." [33] To have him so outspoken a secessionist immediately after the election of Lincoln presaged ill for the chances of South Carolina remaining in the Union.

That the Old School Church in South Carolina was behind Dr. Thornwell in his stand, was evident from the fact that the Synod of South Carolina, meeting before the secession of that state, deliberately resolved to cast its fortunes with those of South Carolina, in case it should secede from the Union. In a great ratification meeting to endorse the action of the South Carolina Convention, three of the professors of the Columbia Seminary, as well as other Old School preachers, were among

---

[29] Stanton, *op. cit.,* p. 157.
[30] Editorial, *Presbyterian,* August 23, 1862, on the death of Thornwell.
[31] Stanton, *op. cit.,* p. 156.
[32] Editorial, *Presbyterian,* August 23, 1862.
[33] *Ibid.*

the speakers.[34] The succeeding weeks saw the leaders of this denomination active in working up secession sentiment in other states. It is said that Robert Toombs, unable to arouse the people of New Orleans to a secessionist point of view in November, 1860, called upon Dr. B. M. Palmer for the purpose of enlisting his assistance. Dr. Palmer responded by preaching a Thanksgiving sermon in which secession was advocated, and resistance, if necessary, " till the last man has fallen behind the last rampart." [35] Dr. Palmer, the intimate friend of Dr. Thornwell, was the only Presbyterian clergyman in the South who approached him in leadership. His eminence as a theological scholar had been recognized by his election to a chair in Princeton Theological Seminary by the General Assembly of 1860, without a dissenting vote, a position which he declined. Later it was said of him that he had done more for the Confederate cause than a regiment of soldiers. [36] The Old School press in the Cotton States also argued powerfully for secession during the winter of 1860-61.[37] It is not surprising that an informed Southern observer should declare in April, 1861, " This revolution has been accomplished mainly by the churches." [38]

With Old School leaders in the South so actively engaged in the secession movement, their brethren farther north became increasingly anxious concerning the future of the Church, as well as the State. The influential *New York Observer,* conservative undenominational religious weekly with an Old School Presbyterian editor,[39] advocated that the Moderator of the

[34] Stanton, *op. cit.,* pp. 161-162.

[35] *Ibid.,* pp. 163-167.

[36] *Cf.* statement quoted from a "Secesh lady's" letter, *Presbyterian,* August 16, 1862.

[37] Stanton, *op. cit.,* p. 174.

[38] *Ibid.,* p. 197. The statement was made in a communication to the *Southern Presbyterian* which was published April 20, 1861. The writer, who is described by the editor of the *Southern Presbyterian* as a "gentleman occupying a high civil position in the Confederacy," is supposed to have been Thomas R. Cobb, afterward a general in the Confederate army.

[39] Rev. Samuel I. Prime, D. D.

1860 General Assembly name a day of prayer for the country. This suggestion was " concurred in and urged by so many," [40] that the Moderator, Dr. J. W. Yeomans, sent out a circular to the " Ministers, Ruling Elders, and Churches connected with the General Assembly of the Presbyterian Church in the United States of America " earnestly recommending that they observe January 4, 1861, which had in the meantime been appointed by President Buchanan as a national day of prayer.[41]

On December 15, 1860, the *Presbyterian,* leading denominational weekly, gave editorial expression to the anxieties disturbing members of the denomination:

[There is a] probability that our national confederacy . . . may be riven asunder. . . . [It behooves us to] ponder the effects which a political separation may have on the Presbyterian Church. While other branches have unhappily suffered their councils to be invaded by the bitter animosities which political rivalries have engendered, and have hopelessly been severed, our own Church has presented the Christian example of ' brethren dwelling together in unity '. . . . appreciating the peculiarities of each other's position . . . and heartily co-operating in measures for extending the kingdom of the Lord. It has more than once been remarked by sagacious politicians that as long as the Presbyterian Church remained united in its wide ramifications North and South, there was hope for the country amidst the turbulence of political feeling. . . . [Whether or not it helps avert disunion], we feel assured that it should be preserved for the higher purpose of securing the sacred interests of Christ's cause. . . . The religious may be separated from the political question, and in long settled opinion, it should be. . . . Let the world have at least one example before it of the power of a religious faith in cementing hearts together which have so many causes, in principle and association, to be fraternally one.

In the critically eventful opening weeks of the New Year a circular letter, addressed to pastors in the South, was being signed by some thirty distinguished divines — half of them Old School Presbyterians — in New York City, Philadelphia, and New Jersey. It deprecated the misrepresentation which had been going on in both North and South — particularly that for which the pulpit had been responsible. Suggesting that the office of peace-maker is the particular work of the Church, it

---

[40] *Cf.* letter, J. W. Yeomans to R. J. Breckinridge, Dec. 8, 1860, in *Breckinridge Papers,* Mss. Division, Library of Congress.

[41] *Cf.* single-sheet printed pamphlet, "A Day of Prayer," dated Dec. 21, 1860, in *Breckinridge Papers,* Mss. Div., Library of Congress.

cautioned against the demoralizing influences of war, and advocated a prompt return to the spirit and requirements of the Constitution, wherever they might have been departed from. There is little evidence that this letter produced much of an impression in either North or South. In fact, its statements were too general to arouse enthusiasm or excite opposition. About the only clear-cut recommendation was that for " a strict regard for truth and the rights and feelings of men . . . [in] press and pulpit." [42]

What Presbyterians were looking for was not generalizations but rather a frank statement of the issues and principles involved, to serve as a sort of platform for the Church. Tremendous interest was, therefore, displayed in an article entitled " The State of the Country " which appeared about the same time as the Circular Letter, in the January number of the *Biblical Repertory and Princeton Review*. The editor of this quarterly, who had founded it some thirty-five years before, was Dr. Charles Hodge, whom probably no man in the Old School Church surpassed in influence. For forty years, since his appointment at the age of twenty-three, he had been a member of the faculty of the Princeton Theological Seminary.[43] Fully 2000 students had received training under him,[44] and the greater number of them, of course, were still laboring in the Old School Church. His *Review* exercised a more potent influence upon the clerical portion of the Church than any other periodical. Impressive in appearance, with two years of European study to his credit,[45] closely related to the Bayards of Delaware and to other influential families,[46] immensely popular with his students and fellow-preachers,[47] clear and forceful

[42] For a copy of the Circular Letter and the signatures attached, *cf. Presbyterian*, January 19, 1861.

[43] Hodge, *op. cit.*, is the best source of information regarding Dr. Hodge.

[44] This estimate, which is conservative, is based upon the statistics on the enrollment of Princeton Theological Seminary as given *ante*, p. 22.

[45] Hodge, *op. cit.*, pp. 100-107.

[46] *Ibid.*, pp. 5-10.

[47] *Cf., e. g.*, letter of Dr. Thornwell to his wife, Palmer, *op. cit.*, p. 299.

in his writing — here was a man whose word carried tremendous weight.

His conservative temperament made it but natural that he
should be found a leader in opposition to the Abolitionists:
" If . . . the Scriptures under the Old Dispensation permitted
men to hold slaves, and if the New Testament nowhere condemns slave-holding, but prescribes the relative duties of masters and slaves, then to pronounce slave-holding to be in itself
sinful is contrary to the Scriptures." [48]   Two articles by him
had very recently been published in the formidable collection
Cotton is King.[49]   He was as much out of sympathy with the
pro-slavery men who considered the institution divine, as with
the Abolitionists who regarded it as sin,[50] but his activities
against the Abolitionists caused him to be regarded as a strong
pro-slavery man.

The essay, " The State of the Country," appearing during
that anxious month of January, 1861, in a conservative religious periodical commonly alleged to be pro-slavery,[51] was
widely read.   In order to meet the demand of the public, it
was separately printed, and widely distributed as a pamphlet.[52]
Readers could have no possible doubt as to where its writer
stood on the question of the preservation of the Union.   Dr.
Hodge undertook, first, to prove that the complaints of the
South against the North were either unfounded, or did not
constitute just cause for the dissolution of the Union; second,
to prove that secession was not constitutional.   On the other
hand, with regard to the Abolitionists, he tried to prove to the
satisfaction of the South that the mass of Northerners were
not Abolitionists, and to prove to Northerners that the program

---

[48] Hodge, *op. cit.*, p. 334.

[49] Elliott, E. N., *ed., Cotton is King*. . . . (Augusta. 1860).

[50] Hodge, *op. cit.*, p. 333.

[51] *Biblical Repertory and Princeton Review*, April, 1861, vol. xxxiii, p. 328.

[52] Hodge, Charles, *The State of the Country*, (New York, 1861).   The
pamphlet, containing 32 pages, according to an advertising statement on
page 1, sold at the rate of 6 cents per single copy; 60 cents a dozen; $4.00
per hundred.   Thousands of copies were distributed in this country and
abroad.   Hodge, *Life of Charles Hodge*, p. 467.

of the Abolitionists was unjust and unscriptural. The essay calls the spirit, language, and conduct of the Abolitionists an intolerable grievance;[53] declares that "tampering with slaves is . . . a grievance that would justify almost any available means of redress,"[54] and that all opposition to the return of fugitive slaves is immoral.[55] It admits that the South has the same rights to the territories that the North has, and calls for an even division of them.[56] But the writer insists that the South's grievances cannot justly be charged against the North; that the Abolitionists, who are really responsible, are very few in numbers.[57] He deprecates coercion, and urges a convention of the States, so that if disunion must come, it may at least be effected peacefully.[58]

The editorial response to the article was immediate and widespread. But there was evident a significant contrast in its reception, North and South. In the South, to the writer's surprise, it met with universal condemnation. The Presbyterian journals of the seceded states were particularly severe.[59] In the North, on the other hand, it was generally praised by the religious and secular press, except those journals which were of abolitionist persuasion. Presbyterian papers as far apart in their views on slavery as the pro-slavery *Presbyterian* and the stormy anti-slavery *Presbyter* united in praise of the views set forth.[60] The divergence of opinion between North and

[53] Hodge, Charles, "The State of the Country," in *Biblical Repertory and Princeton Review*, January, 1861, vol. xxxiii, p. 10.

[54] *Ibid.*, p. 15.

[55] *Ibid.*, pp. 19-22.

[56] *Ibid.*, pp. 23-24; 36.

[57] *Ibid.*, p. 15.

[58] *Ibid.*, p. 35.

[59] *Cf.* Hodge, *Life of Charles Hodge*, p. 462; also account of the reception of the article, in editorial in the *Presbyterian Banner*, February 9, 1861.

[60] Hodge, Charles, "The Church and the Country," in *Biblical Repertory and Princeton Review*, April, 1861, vol. xxxiii, p. 330. It should be added, however, that through the columns of the *Presbyter* the abolitionist Dr. E. D. MacMaster denounced the article in unmeasured terms. *Ibid.*, p. 331. The *Presbyterian Banner* commented favorably, editorially, on December 29, 1860, and February 9, 1861. The *Presbyter* copied large portions of the article in its issue of January 3, 1861.

South boded ill for the cause of Old School unity. The essay is of unique interest in connection with the history of the General Assembly of 1861, for its arguments were then used to controvert the stand taken by their writer.[61]   There can be no doubt that in the winter of 1861 it must have converted many to anti-secession sentiments, and confirmed many others in their pro-Union convictions. The great Dr. Hodge had spoken.

An equally important, and a more picturesque, Old School figure in the controversy over the preservation of the Union was Robert J. Breckinridge of Kentucky. Although not so profound a scholar as Dr. Hodge and not so popular in the Church as a whole, Dr. Breckinridge's antecedents, his long career of leadership, and his peculiar hold on the Presbyterians in the border state of Kentucky, made his stand in the crisis of 1861 of vital importance. Son of the author of the Kentucky Resolutions of 1798, member of the Kentucky bar, a former state legislator and state superintendent of public instruction, professor in the Danville Theological Seminary, the varied experiences of his sixty years illustrate in a striking manner the close association which then so often existed between Church and State. Delighting in controversy, he lectured and wrote on a wide variety of topics.[62]   Although an early advocate of emancipation, he was bitterly opposed to the Abolitionists. During the trying months of the winter of 1861, when border-state men were making up their minds, he was watched with peculiar interest, for there were few public men whose families were more evenly divided in sentiment on

---

[61] Cf. post, pp. 70-71.

[62] The facts regarding Breckinridge's life have been taken largely from Johnson, Allen, ed., Dictionary of American Biography, (New York, 1928—); National Cyclopaedia of American Biography, (23 vol., New York, 1893-1927); and Thomas, Alfred A., ed., Correspondence of Thomas Ebenezer Thomas, mainly relating to the Anti-Slavery Conflict in Ohio, especially in the Presbyterian Church, (n. p., 1909). The Breckinridge Papers, Mss. Division, Library of Congress, throw interesting light upon the personality and career of Robert J. Breckinridge.

the political situation. John Cabell Breckinridge, candidate for the Presidency in 1860, was his nephew. His sons shortly found their way into opposing military camps, and literally hosts of other relatives were lining up on either side. Too controversial in his tastes, too extreme in his statements, too ready to express his opinion upon all occasions, to be particularly attractive to one who reads his writing seventy years later, there must have been — in spite of the fact that he was considered by his contemporaries difficult to handle — [63] something very winning in his personality. He was showered with honors: Moderator of the General Assembly in 1840; recipient of the LL.D. degree from Harvard in 1862; [64] Temporary Chairman of the Republican National Convention in 1864. Editorial references to him usually paid tribute to his erudition, forcefulness, and courage.

It did not take him long to make up his mind on which side he stood, in the fall of 1860. On Thanksgiving Day, 1860, he preached a Union sermon in Stanford, Kentucky, which attracted wide notice.[65] Another address, delivered on the National Fast Day, January 4, 1861, reëmphasized his stand for the Union.[66] About the same time, he undertook the writing of an essay on "Our Country — Its Peril — Its Deliverance," for the first issue of a new quarterly which he and some of his colleagues were about to launch — the *Danville Quarterly Review*. Fairness to his co-editors, he believed, required his first obtaining their consent to the publication of the article. "No man in Kentucky will rejoice more than I," wrote one of them in reply, "if you will either in the Review or out of it expose that miserable Compound of Jesuitry and Black Republicanism

[63] *Cf.* George H. Stuart's story of Dr. Breckinridge's attitude at the Reunion Convention of 1867, Thompson, *Life of George H. Stuart*, pp. 211-214.

[64] *Presbyterian*, July 26, 1862. John Stuart Mill was similarly honored at the same commencement.

[65] *Cf.* letter, S. S. McRoberts to R. J. Breckinridge, Dec. 3, 1860, *Breckinridge Papers*, Mss. Div., Library of Congress.

[66] *Cf.* letter, Stuart Robinson to R. J. Breckinridge, January 24, 1861, *Breckinridge Papers*, Mss. Div., Library of Congress.

from the Princeton Review." [67]   As Breckinridge proposed to
do quite the opposite, this editor along with two others of like
persuasion, withdrew before the publication of the first number. [68]

When the *Review* appeared, the sentiments of the article
proved to be all that the staunchest Union man could desire.
The loyal press universally commended it, and rejoiced to have
so prominent a man from the doubtful state of Kentucky taking
so pronounced a position.   That the article buoyed up Breckinridge's friends and strengthened their faith in the Union,
there can be no doubt.   On the other hand, there is equally
clear evidence that the bitter feeling resulting from the personalities indulged in by Breckinridge toward his former editorial colleagues who opposed him, did much to increase the
bitterness of the Kentucky citizens whose adherence to the
Union was not so close. [69]   Dr. Breckinridge's article, like Dr.
Hodge's, was printed as a pamphlet and widely distributed. [70]
The third Old School quarterly, the *Southern Presbyterian Review*, in its January number presented a long and able defense
of secession, by its editor, Dr. Thornwell.   The three most influential writers in the denomination had now expressed themselves unequivocally.

Of the Old School periodicals having a wide circulation
among the laity, there were several of considerable importance.
The *Presbyterian*, (Philadelphia), conservative, of pro-slavery

[67] *Ibid.*

[68] *Cf. ibid.*, and letters of John H. Rice and Thomas A. Hoyt to R. J.
Breckinridge, both under date of January 25, 1861, *Breckinridge Papers*,
Mss. Div., Library of Congress.

[69] The controversy between Dr. Breckinridge on the one hand, and Dr.
Stuart Robinson and Rev. Thomas A. Hoyt on the other, occupied considerable time, and was the subject of special action, in the General Assembly
of 1862.   Dr. Breckinridge introduced the matter.   The course of the controversy may be followed through communications of interested parties to
the *Presbyterian* during the winter and spring of 1862.   *Cf.* also *Minutes
of the General Assembly*, vol. xvi, pp. 599-601; 604-609; 631-633.   At their
face value, the sentiments expressed by his opponents breathe much more
of forbearance and Christian charity than those of Dr. Breckinridge.

[70] Editorial notes, *Presbyterian*, January 18 and March 15, 1862.

traditions, after expressing itself strongly for the Union in December and January, determined to confine itself to statements of fact only, on the subject of the political crisis, evidently fearing that statements of opinion would tend to promote division in the Church.[71] The *Presbyterian Herald,* (Louisville), found its position especially difficult, as the foremost Old School churches in Louisville were under the care of outspoken pro-Southern men.[72] It took the position that the Church should not interfere in the political crisis. On the other hand, the *Presbyterian Banner,* (Pittsburg), and the *Presbyter,* (Cincinnati), the former not strongly attached, and the latter bitterly hostile, to slavery, were now consistently emphatic in their pro-Union sentiments. At the opposite extreme were the New Orleans *True Witness,* the *Central Presbyterian,* the *Southern Presbyterian,* and the *North Carolina Presbyterian,* all published in the Old South, and all strongly supporting secession.[73]

With the leading clergymen and the influential periodicals of the Church aligned on one side or the other, the public waited with particular interest to see what attitude the General Assembly of 1861 would take on the great question. Superficially, it might seem that just one outcome was possible: the division of the Church. This was far from true. There was a large element — probably in the early spring of 1861 the majority in the Church — who believed that, while individuals might express their opinions on the subject of dispute, the Church neither should, nor rightly could, take a stand. Unlike

---

[71] *Cf.* editorials, Feb. 2, 1861 and March 16, 1861.

[72] Dr. Stuart Robinson and Rev. Thomas A. Hoyt.

[73] The *Presbyterian Expositor,* (Chicago), edited by the conservative Dr. N. L. Rice, who was the protégé of Cyrus McCormick, (*cf.* Dodd, *loc. cit.,* p. 782), had strong pro-slavery traditions. With the resignation of its editor from a professorship in the Seminary of the Northwest, and from the pastorate of the North Presbyterian Church in Chicago, to take the pastorate of a leading Presbyterian Church in New York City, this paper was suspended in the early spring of 1861. Incidentally, the Seminary of the Northwest was renamed " McCormick Theological Seminary " in 1871; not at the time of its removal to Chicago, as Professor Dodd states. *Cf.* Thomas, *op. cit.,* pp. 132-133.

those of some other denominations, the church periodicals were Old School Presbyterian only in the sense that their editors, and to a large extent their readers, were of that faith; they had no formal connection with the Church, and could not officially speak for it. They were expressing themselves on the political situation, it is true, but like individuals, they might state their own opinions freely without compromising the Church as an organization. Some Old School individuals and periodicals most outspoken in their own opinions were the staunchest defenders of the theory that the Church must remain silent.

Those who held this theory were becoming increasingly alarmed by the campaign that was going on in their midst for obtaining a decisive stand from the General Assembly at its next meeting, in May.[74]   The *Presbyterian,* as the date for the Assembly meeting approached, though it extolled patriotism as " a sentiment which God approves," though it deplored the "unjustifiable course of the extreme Southern States" and maintained that " war has now become a *necessity* not to be evaded," [75] still believed that the dispute was essentially a political one, and cautioned against the introduction into the General Assembly of controversial subjects:

> Since the appointment for the meeting of the approaching General Assembly, great and fearful changes have occurred in the state of the country, which will, without doubt, affect its general aspect. The arrival of many commissioners will be prevented. War has obstructed the great highways of travel. . . . While we do not doubt that there is a general desire to preserve the unity of the Church unbroken, there may be insuperable difficulties in the way of a full representation. . . . Peculiar responsibilities will rest on those who may be present. Our own settled conviction is that it would be prudent and wise in the Assembly to confine its attention to routine business requiring their [sic] annual revision, and to avoid all other questions which may engender difference of opinion and debate. A short session will be best. The state of the public mind requires this. . . . Let Christians earnestly pray for heavenly wisdom. . . . Let us also hope that

---

[74] *Cf., e. g.,* letter marked "Private and Confidential," from Dr. S. J. Baird to John L. Nixon, January 8, 1861, *Baird Papers,* Mss. Division, Library of Congress.

[75] Editorial, *Presbyterian,* April 27, 1861.

the meeting together of such a body of the friends of our Redeemer may be the means of pouring oil on the troubled waters.[76]

However this advice may have been regarded by the readers of the *Presbyterian,* it must certainly have stimulated interest in what the Assembly would do.

[76] Editorial, *Presbyterian,* May 11, 1861.

CHAPTER II

THE OLD SCHOOL ASSEMBLY MEETS THE CRISIS

THE General Assembly of the Old School Presbyterian Church convened for its annual session in Philadelphia on May 16, 1861, less than five weeks after the fall of Fort Sumter and Lincoln's call for volunteers. Those five weeks, however, had been ample to produce an emotional patriotism such as no one had dreamed possible. No battles had yet been fought, but the newspapers were daily reporting the progress of the amassing and equipment of troops in both North and South. The tenseness of the political atmosphere was evident in the nervous, irritable tone of newspaper editorial comment — an irritability relieved only by bitter attacks on the South. The killing of the immensely popular Colonel Ellsworth on May 24 furnished the press with an outlet to relieve its pent-up feelings. Here was the opportunity it craved for exploiting the romantic and valorous side of war, and throughout the remainder of the sixteen-day session of the Assembly, the members were each day presented by the daily papers with details of the life-history, the tragic death, the love affair, and the dying words[1] of the picturesque leader of the New York Zouaves. At the same time, editors were anxiously pondering what the attitude of Europe toward our conflict was likely to be. These, too, were times to try men's souls! What were the possibilities for dispassionate decisions in such a state of emotional ferment?

The names of the commissioners enrolled by the Permanent Clerk on the opening day of the session revealed the fact that

---

[1] Actually, according to an eye-witness, Col. Ellsworth was killed instantaneously. *Cf.* account of New York *Tribune,* May 26, 1861, as given in Moore, Frank, *ed., The Rebellion Record, a Diary of American Events* . . . . (2 vol., New York, 1861), vol. i, pp. 277-281.

but 264 had reported, as contrasted with 336 the previous year. Representation in the General Assembly was by presbyteries. The following table [2] shows the extent of representation of the presbyteries of Southern synods:

Synod	Presbyteries represented	Unrepresented
South Carolina	0	4
Georgia	0	5
Alabama	0	3
Mississippi	6	1
Texas	2	2
North Carolina	0	3
Nashville	2	2
Memphis	2	2
Arkansas	0	4
Virginia	1	5
Baltimore	4	1
Kentucky	6	0
Missouri	5	0
Upper Missouri	3	1
	31	33

It will be noted that but two of the unrepresented presbyteries lay in Border State synods.

More discouraging to those who still hoped that the Church might remain united, than the fact that thirty-three Southern presbyteries were unrepresented, was the absence of the two greatest Southern Presbyterian leaders, Dr. J. H. Thornwell and Dr. B. M. Palmer. A communication from Dr. Thornwell explained that a trip to Europe and illness had at first rendered it impossible, and that political troubles had since rendered it "inexpedient, if not impracticable" to complete certain committee work: "Other issues, much more pressing, and much more solemn, are upon us. . . . Brethren, I invoke upon your deliberations the blessing of the Most High.

[2] For statistics with regard to the membership of the General Assembly in 1861, *cf. Minutes of the General Assembly*, 1861, vol. xvi, pp. 289-380. The Synod of Wheeling is not included in the above list because three of its four presbyteries lay wholly in Ohio and Pennsylvania, and less than one-half of the churches of the fourth presbytery lay in Virginia. The four presbyteries were all represented in the Assembly of 1861.

STATISTICS OF SYNODS OF THE OLD SCHOOL PRESBYTERIAN CHURCH, 1861 [1]

Synods	Organized	Presbyteries	Ministers	Churches	Communicants	Total Amount Given for All Purposes
Albany [2]	1803	5	100	66	9,761	$128,669
Buffalo	1843	4	56	46	4,978	83,629
New York	1788	11	196	139	21,857	376,619
New Jersey	1823	11	200	195	23,823	224,058
Philadelphia	1788	7	200	203	27,941	240,025
Baltimore [3]	1854	5	104	137	11,680	195,891
Pittsburgh	1802	5	104	150	18,812	86,592
Allegheny [4]	1854	4	62	95	10,620	43,913
Wheeling [5]	1841	4	90	131	14,141	67,835
Ohio	1814	7	92	161	11,721	65,831
Sandusky [6]	1860	4	28	60	3,032	22,454
Cincinnati	1829	5	89	116	10,533	88,666
Indiana	1826	5	56	95	6,682	39,926
Northern Indiana	1843	5	60	100	5,620	42,138
Illinois	1831	7	89	143	6,817	52,370
Chicago	1856	3	77	101	6,644	79,207
Wisconsin	1851	3	38	50	1,896	15,651
St. Paul	1860	4	25	29	669	9,824
Iowa	1852	4	41	83	2,932	24,041
Southern Iowa	1858	5	40	68	3,112	19,204
Upper Missouri	1858	4	49	88	3,090	31,086
Missouri	1832	5	78	102	6,260	63,680
Kentucky	1802	6	104	164	11,229	141,270
Virginia	1788	6	117	151	11,628	123,173
North Carolina	1788	3	93	180	15,709	101,908
Nashville	1826	5	47	58	3,999	46,892
South Carolina	1813	4	97	128	13,746	111,131
Georgia	1845	5	87	143	7,318	68,810
Alabama	1835	3	60	110	5,907	107,222
Mississippi [7]	1829	7	97	133	7,136	146,612
Memphis [8]	1847	4	58	99	4,760	47,366
Arkansas	1852	4	38	63	3,381	15,408
Texas	1851	4	47	69	2,103	38,624
Pacific	1852	5	26	20	1,010	47,188
Northern India	1841	3	22	8	267	......
Total 35		176	2,767	3,684	300,814	$2,996,913

[1] Compiled from statistical tables, *Minutes of the General Assembly*, 1861, vol. xvi, pp. 402-403; *Presbyterian Historical Almanac*, 1862, p. 130. Some significant contrasts in geographical distribution of denominational strength may be discovered by comparing the above table with a corresponding table for the New School Church, *post*, p. 342.

[2] Including 11 churches in Massachusetts and New Hampshire.

[3] Including one presbytery in Pennsylvania.

[4] In northwestern Pennsylvania.

[5] Three of the four presbyteries lay in Ohio; 22 of the 40 churches in the other presbytery were in Pennsylvania; 18 in western Virginia.

[6] Three presbyteries in northern Ohio; one in Michigan.

[7] Three presbyteries wholly, or largely, in Louisiana.

[8] Two presbyteries in Mississippi.

I sincerely pray that . . . He may save the Church from every false step; that He may make her a messenger of peace in these troublous times, and that He may restore harmony and good will between your country and mine." It is to be feared that whatever good effect this pious wish might otherwise have had was wrecked by the concluding phrase, for the reporter in the Philadelphia *Press* commented, " The last part of the letter created great laughter."[3] Thus in a burst of merriment perished the influence of one who in less troubled times had been respected as had few others in the Old School Church. As for Dr. Palmer, from him there was no word at all.

The two authors of the widely read essays on the " State of the Country," already referred to,[4] had both been appointed[5] commissioners to the Assembly, but Dr. Breckinridge, due to extreme illness, was unable to attend.[6] Dr. Hodge was destined to play a role demanding a hero's courage — a role that was bound to tax heavily the feelings of love and loyalty borne toward him by so many of his fellow-commissioners.

The non-Presbyterian[7] reporter of the Philadelphia *Press* found the members of the Assembly a striking group: " The majority of them are well stricken in years. A large proportion of them were provided with spectacles, and gray crowns dotted the house. The white neckcloth common to clergymen was adopted by a sparse representation, and rough, indurated, weather-hued faces looked out from all the pews. A sturdy individuality, characteristic of the Presbyterian, was evidenced in the countenances of several, and the great mass were of features more marked and intellectual than classic or handsome. . . . There were few bronchial, consumptive, attenuated bodies, but on every hand evidences of strong earnestness and

---

[3] For the letter and an account of its reception, *cf.* report of proceedings of Assembly, Philadelphia *Press,* May 21, 1861.

[4] *Cf. ante,* pp. 33-38.

[5] Commissioners were chosen by the individual presbyteries, and were apportioned, to some degree, according to the size of the presbytery.

[6] Ed. note, *Presbyterian,* May 25, 1861.

[7] *Cf. post,* p. 52, note 40.

zeal, high ecclesiastical abilities, and rare bodily power.   Many of these were the pioneers of Presbyterianism, whose names have been heard wherever the Church is known." [8]

The election of a border-state man, Dr. John C. Backus [9] of Baltimore, as Moderator, seemed to augur well for the cause of a conservative stand on political problems.   The opening sessions were marked by a policy of extreme caution.   Considerable opposition was raised, for example, against the suggestion that one of the commissioners from Kansas should be "invited to state the condition of that State," even though the commissioner himself "thought that he could exercise discretion enough to avoid saying anything on the matter which would tend to distract or be unpleasant to any of the brethren. . . ." [10]   When several members objected to "anything being introduced here in regard to the temporal affairs of any section," a philosophically humorous brother pointed out that bodies and souls in Kansas, as well as in Philadelphia, were closely connected. [11]   The full significance of this remark must have dawned on many of the members before the 1861 Assembly came to a close.

Indeed, the advocates of a policy of silence on temporal matters were doomed to early disappointment.   On the third day of the session, the blow fell.   The more fiery element in the Assembly demanded action on "the state of the country."   To the amazement of many, the spokesman of this element proved to be Dr. Gardiner Spring, since 1810 pastor of the Brick Presbyterian Church of New York City.   Although his orthodoxy had once been suspected, [12] Dr. Spring had long been a respected leader in the denomination.   He opposed the division

[8] Philadelphia *Press,* May 28, 1861.

[9] Since 1835 the pastor of the First Presbyterian Church of Baltimore. Gillett, *op. cit.,* vol. ii, p. 15, note.

[10] Account of second day of the sessions of the General Assembly, *Presbyterian,* May 25, 1861.   Rev. J. G. Reasor, pastor of the Westminster Presbyterian Church, Leavenworth, Kansas, was the Kansan quoted.

[11] *Ibid.*

[12] Gillett, *op. cit.,* vol. ii, p. 219.

THE ASSEMBLY MEETS THE CRISIS 47

the constitutionality of the exscinding acts,[13] although keeping
his church in the Old School organization. Under his pastorate the Brick Church became famous for its scenes of revival, its general usefulness, and particularly for the success
of its philanthropic efforts, " reaching across the continent and
around the world." [14] In 1843 he had been Moderator of the
General Assembly. For years he had been regarded as one
of the staunchest of conservatives. An old man now, the pastor
of a conservative congregation, of all the leaders in the Old
School Church he seemed about the least likely to cause the
conciliatory element trouble. If not an out-and-out friend of
the South, he was certainly regarded as a bitter opponent of the
Abolitionists. In 1842 he had been singled out by James G.
Birney as a minister whose utterances and printed sermons
caused him to be " looked on by the pro-slavery party as highly
serviceable to their cause." [15] Such a man would not be expected to be a radical now. In fact, some of the members of
the Assembly asserted that he had been chosen a commissioner
with the distinct understanding that he would stand for a policy
of silence on the part of the Assembly with regard to the political crisis.[16]

To expect silence from Dr. Spring at this time, however, was
to overlook one important factor in his make-up — his intense
nationalism. Dr. Spring was the son of a Revolutionary officer, and experienced no difficulty in remembering that fact.
As " his father's son," he could not refrain from urging decisive action on the part of the Church, he declared.[17] The Assembly was to prove in case after case that when a man's

[13] *Ibid.*, vol. ii, p. 551.
[14] *Ibid.*, vol. ii, p. 244.
[15] " An American," [James G Birney], *The American Churches the Bulwarks of American Slavery*, (2nd American edition, revised, Newburyport,
1842), pp. 36-37.
[16] *Cf.* account of speech of Rev. W. M. Baker of Texas, in report of proceedings of Assembly, Philadelphia *Press*, May 28, 1861.
[17] *Cf.* account of sixth day of Assembly session, *Presbyterian*, May 25, 1861.

nationalism conflicted with his natural conservatism, it was the conservatism that had to give way.

On the third day of the session, Dr. Spring rose to offer a resolution "that a Special Committee be appointed to inquire into the expediency of making some expression of their devotion to the Union of these States, and their loyalty to the Government; and if in their judgment it is expedient to do so, they report what that expression shall be." [18]   This resolution was promptly tabled, by a vote of 123 to 102.   Realizing that the weight of public opinion was on their side, the advocates of the motion demanded that the *yeas* and *nays* be recorded, but the Moderator ruled that since the members had already begun to vote by rising, this demand could not be recognized.   Not content to be so summarily silenced, the Spring supporters demanded that the tabled resolution be taken from the table, and that the *yeas* and *nays* be recorded on this motion.   A large portion of the remainder of the morning session was taken up in debating the points of order involved, and the resolution remained on the table, without the matter being put to a vote.[19] To the student of history this failure to record the *yeas* and *nays* is extremely disappointing, for the record of the individual vote on this proposition before outside pressure had come to be exerted on the commissioners would have given a true picture of the real sentiment of this important body.

At the close of this Saturday morning session occurred the first of the many dramatic scenes which were to make the 1861 Assembly historic.   Dr. Spring offered one of the two prayers which marked the end of the first week's deliberations.   A correspondent of the Philadelphia *Press* gives the setting: "The Prayer of the venerable Dr. Spring . . . will not soon be forgotten.   His resolution, looking to some patriotic expression of the Assembly in this time of the country's peril, had been under consideration.   Every technical difficulty in the shape of points of order, for some reason unexplained, had been in-

---

[18] *Minutes of the General Assembly,* 1861, vol. xvi, p. 303.
[19] *Ibid.*

terposed against its adoption. The significance of the earnest invocation of this aged man of God is thus seen." Dr. Spring knew how to make the most of the dramatic possibilities of the occasion. He closed his prayer with the petition that "our great chieftain [alluding to the aged Scott] who for so many years has carried in triumph our national flag, might yet, before his eyes closed in death, have the joy of seeing that flag re-established, and waving in its beauty and glory at every point, from the Lakes to the Gulf, and from Eastern shore to Western." [20]

The publicity given to the activities of this veteran preacher in attempting to get the Assembly to take action on the political crisis was beginning to attract the interest of the public. When he preached in one of the Philadelphia churches the following day, an unusually large crowd came to hear him. The size of the audience, according to journalist opinion, was to be attributed to the part he had been playing in the deliberations of the Assembly.[21]

The ensuing sessions of the Assembly were to prove that the tabling of Dr. Spring's resolutions had not discouraged him. On the following Wednesday, having obtained recognition from the chair, he sarcastically "presumed that, having the floor, he would have it till he was done, and that no motion to lay on the table, to postpone, or other motion, should interrupt the remarks he had to make, after reading the resolution he had in his hand." [22] Evidently not satisfied with the Moderator's statement that he "could only assure him of protection under the rules," Dr. Spring took the liberty to make his remarks *before* the reading of his resolutions. Declaring that the tabling of his resolution of five days before had "placed the Assembly in a false position before the Church and the Country," and that he was well-informed by advices received from both the North and the West that the influence of the tabling action

---

[20] Philadelphia *Press,* May 22, 1861.

[21] *Ibid.,* May 20, 1861.

[22] *Cf.* account of sixth day of session, *Presbyterian,* May 25, 1861.

had been most unfortunate in its effect upon the " friends of the Govermnent," [23] Dr. Spring insisted that the Assembly should take some action, and offered the following resolutions:

> Gratefully acknowledging the distinguished bounty and care of Almighty God toward this favored land, and also recognizing our obligations to submit to every ordinance of man for the Lord's sake, this General Assembly adopt the following resolutions:
>
> *Resolved*, 1. That in view of the present agitated and unhappy condition of this country, the first day of July next be hereby set apart as a day of prayer throughout our bounds; and that on that day ministers and people are called on humbly to confess and bewail our national sins; to offer our thanks to the Father of light for his abundant and undeserved goodness towards us as a nation; to seek his guidance and blessing upon our rulers, and their counsels, as well as on the Congress of the United States about to assemble; and to implore him, in the name of Jesus Christ, the Great High Priest of the Christian profession, to turn away his anger from us, and speedily restore to us the blessings of an honorable peace.
>
> *Resolved*, 2. That in the judgment of this Assembly, it is the duty of the ministry and churches under its care to do all in their power to promote and perpetuate the integrity of these United States, and to strengthen, uphold, and encourage the Federal Government.[24]

These were the famous " Spring Resolutions," destined to become historic in the annals of the Old School Church. The party of silence evidently realized that sentiment had changed and the matter could not be stifled, for on motion of Dr. Hodge the paper was made the first order of the day for the following Friday. Dr. Hodge himself, in his brief autobiographical sketch, explains the reason for this change of attitude: " Dr. Spring's resolutions [that is, the original resolution of the first week], when first introduced, were promptly laid on the table by a decisive vote. But the next morning, there was such a burst of indignation from the secular press of Philadelphia, and such a shower of threatening telegrams fell upon the mem-

---

[23] *Ibid.*

[24] *Ibid. Cf.* also *Presbyterian Historical Almanac*, 1862, p. 69. Note the inconsistencies, in this and subsequent statements of the various resolutions, with regard to the practice of the capitalization of terms referring to the Deity.

bers, that the resolutions were taken up and ultimately passed." [25]

With the public apprised, through the press, that the first order of the day on Friday was to be the consideration of the Spring Resolutions, it is not surprising that the church at Broad street and Penn Square was filled to its utmost capacity, (something over 1200),[26] at an early hour in the morning.[27] Those who came expecting the Assembly to reach a decision on Friday were doomed to disappointment. The discussion continued, with a few brief interruptions, through Friday, Saturday, Monday, and Tuesday, and was concluded by a final vote on Wednesday evening at eight o'clock.[28] Interest by no means lagged, however. On Friday, during the eloquent speeches, "the crowd thronging under the portico was striving to gain entrance." [29] On Monday, when an evening session was held, many remained in their places during the interim between afternoon and evening meetings,[30] in order to insure themselves seats, while, when the Wednesday afternoon session was "protracted until a late hour of the evening . . . the immense audience, manifesting throughout the liveliest interest in the debate, maintained their seats and standing positions" until, at eight o'clock, the report was passed.[31]

Indeed, the frequency with which the accounts of reporters were interspersed with notations of "applause," "sensation," "laughter," "hisses and applause," "great confusion," in spite of the fact that the Moderator had several times forbidden all such forms of demonstration, and that at one point he felt com-

---

[25] Hodge, *Life of Charles Hodge*, p. 22. I have found no evidence of the secular press of Philadelphia becoming aroused *immediately*, but it is possible that this was true of some of the papers to which I did not have access.

[26] *Presbyterian Historical Almanac*, 1862 (vol. 4), p. 136. A historical sketch of this Seventh Presbyterian Church of Philadelphia is given, pp. 133-143.

[27] Philadelphia *Press*, May 25, 1861.

[28] *Cf.* account of General Assembly, *ibid.*, May 30, 1861.

[29] *Ibid.*, May 25, 1861.

[30] *Ibid.*, May 28, 1861.

[31] *Ibid.*, May 30, 1861.

pelled to threaten to adjourn the Assembly and close the house
if the applause continued,[32] leaves no doubt that the audience
was having an exceedingly good time. All witnesses agree that
the meetings were orderly and dignified, but even staid Presbyterians could grow fiery with indignation over their mouths
being "gagged"[33] by the tabling of resolutions, insinuate
unfair motives on the part of their opponents,[34] glowingly describe the pleasure with which they "unfurled the Stars and
Stripes of the old Government,"[35] refer eloquently to their
ancestors' patriotism,[36] and cry that "Treason, full-armed is
abroad . . . !"[37]

Other qualities besides enthusiasm and eloquence contributed to the interest of the occasion. Some of the speakers
were exceedingly skilful in arousing the sympathies of their
auditors. One Tennessee speaker[38] "looked very honest, and
no doubt felt so," says the reporter in the Philadelphia *Press*,
momentarily departing from his usual admirably maintained
policy of impartiality, "but his manner indicated the presence
of pressure which a lawyer evinces in making the best of a weak
side. . . . With considerable adroitness, however, he succeeded in enlisting the sympathy of the audience before fairly
showing his hand."[39] One should not be too hasty in concluding from the un-Presbyterian figure with which this quotation ends that the reporter was not of that faith,[40] for the same

[32] On Saturday, May 25. *Ibid.*, May 27, 1861.
[33] Dr. Thomas, of Dayton, Ohio. *Ibid.*, May 25, 1861.
[34] Dr. Spring did not believe the truth of the Bates dispatch before he had
heard it actually read in the Assembly (*cf. post*, pp. 60-61), or at any rate,
thought that "influences had been employed to secure it." Philadelphia
Press, May 25, 1861.
[35] Dr. Matthews of Kentucky, (later a Union chaplain). *Ibid.*, May 25,
1861.
[36] Dr. Spring. *Cf.* account in *Presbyterian*, May 25, 1861.
[37] Rev. L. H. Long, of Urbana, Ohio. Philadelphia *Press*, May 27, 1861.
[38] Rev. James H. Gillespie, of Denmark, Tennessee.
[39] Philadelphia *Press*, May 25, 1861.
[40] Incidentally, there is a good deal of evidence that he was not a Presbyterian. His evident unfamiliarity with certain denominational terms and
with denominational history, ("John Calvin of Genoa" may perhaps be

figure was used by an eloquent clergyman during the Assembly debate.[41] The audience was responsive. The Moderator was fairly successful in checking the frequent bursts of applause, says the same reporter, "but it was impossible to check the feeling — an event was in progress which is to become historic! "[42]

Although the party of silence had won the first round with the tabling of the original motion of Dr. Spring,[43] all hope of stopping the discussion of the state of the country had died with the introduction of the Spring Resolutions. Now, during the five days of discussion, they bent their energies in desperate attempts at substitutes for these resolutions, which they considered much too radical. No doubt Dr. Hodge's reason for moving the postponement of consideration of the resolutions from Wednesday to Friday [44] had been to gain time for the preparation of substitute resolutions. On Friday he presented as a substitute for the Spring Resolutions a paper which had been adopted the previous day at a meeting of the Southern commissioners, with a few Northerners.[45] This paper asserted that Presbyterians were ready at all suitable times, and at whatever personal sacrifice, to testify their loyalty to that Constitution under which " this goodly vine has sent her boughs into the sea, and her branches into the river," but declared that it was impossible at the present time to put forth a more extended and emphatic deliverance, giving the following reasons for this stand:

blamed on the typesetter, but there are many other slips in terminology), and his statement that the scene was " exciting, even to a disinterested observer," (issue of May 30, 1861), point to his being a non-Presbyterian, and therefore more likely to be impartial, so far as his account of the Assembly is concerned. He is, of course, strongly pro-Union, but manages, for the most part, to deal fairly with both sides.

[41] Dr. W. C. Anderson, of San Francisco. Philadelphia *Press,* May 29, 1861.
[42] *Ibid.,* May 25, 1861.
[43] *Cf. ante,* p. 48.
[44] *Cf. ante,* p. 50.
[45] *Minutes of the General Assembly,* vol. xvi, p. 315. *Cf.,* also, account of General Assembly in Philadelphia *Press,* May 25, 1861.

1. The General Assembly is neither a Northern or Southern body.

2. "Owing to Providential hindrances," nearly 1/3 of the presbyteries are not represented here. [46]

3. All other Evangelical denominations have been rent asunder. "We alone retain, this day, the proportions of a National Church." United in all questions of doctrine and discipline, "we are not willing to sever this last bond which holds the North and South together in the fellowship of the Gospel. . . . For the present, both religion and patriotism require us to cherish a Union which, by God's blessing, may be the means of reuniting our land." [47]

This "milk and water: one gallon of milk and five barrels of water," [48] evidently proving unpalatable to the majority of commissioners, Dr. Hodge on Monday was allowed to withdraw his paper.[49] Meanwhile, several other substitutes, of varying degrees of mildness, had been moved.[50] They "all breathed the spirit of patriotism," [51] but none was seconded. The proponents of action wanted nothing short of Dr. Spring's paper. In spite of the fact, however, that Dr. Spring had endeavored to make his resolutions more acceptable to anti-Lincoln men by agreeing that his second resolution be modified by the addition of a phrase which made it read "to strengthen, uphold, and encourage the Federal Government in the exercise of all its functions under our noble Constitution," [52] his supporters evidently did not yet dare to venture a demand for a vote. Things seemed to have reached an impasse.

Three days of argument had brought the Assembly no solution of its problem. In this situation the party of silence saw a new ray of hope. Perhaps a majority of the commissioners,

[46] It is puzzling to find the basis for this fraction. Actually, about 1/6 of the total number of presbyteries were unrepresented; about ½ of the Southern presbyteries. It is true that the 31 Southern presbyteries which were represented did not, for the most part, send their full quota of commissioners. One might accurately have said, "Fully one-third of the presbyteries are unrepresented, or not fully represented."

[47] Philadelphia *Press,* May 25, 1861.

[48] Dr. W. C. Anderson of San Francisco. *Ibid.,* May 25, 1861.

[49] *Minutes of the General Assembly,* 1861, vol. xvi, p. 321.

[50] Philadelphia *Press,* May 27 and 28, 1861.

[51] Rev. D. J. Waller of Pennsylvania. *Ibid.,* May 28, 1861.

[52] *Cf.* account *ibid.,* May 27 and 28, 1861.

discouraged, would be willing to drop the entire subject. Accordingly, Dr. Hodge moved that the whole matter be laid on the table.[53] Anyone who hoped that Dr. Spring's resolutions would suffer the same fate as his original motion (which, it will be remembered, had been tabled by a vote of 123 to 102), was doomed to disappointment. Whatever the causes, the past nine days had wrought a tremendous change in sentiment as to the necessity of Assembly action. The motion to table was decisively rejected by a vote of eighty-six to one hundred fifty-three.[54] On this motion, the *yeas* and *nays* had been ordered — a fact that may in part account for the heavy adverse vote. Of the eighty-six votes in favor of the motion, thirty-one came from commissioners of the eastern presbyteries, forty-four from presbyteries south of the Mason-Dixon line, while only eleven came from the presbyteries of western Pennsylvania and the Northwest. Not a single Southern vote was recorded against the motion. Far more significant, however, is the fact that so few *yeas* came from the Northwest. From eight of the fourteen synods of the Northwest, not a single vote was cast for tabling.[55] It is also interesting to note that of the forty-two Northern commissioners who voted for tabling, twenty-nine were ministers, and only thirteen ruling elders, in spite of the fact that the representation of clergy and laity in the Assembly was equal. It is not surprising that the clergy should be more reluctant to commit the Church to a radical policy. At any rate, the first show of colors had been called for and met. " The scene during the . . . ballot, was marked and interesting. Men with tears in their eyes . . . voted for

[53] *Minutes of the General Assembly,* 1861, vol. xvi, p. 321.

[54] In the *Minutes,* the vote is given as 87 to 153, but only 86 *yeas* are named. The Philadelphia *Press* gives the vote as 74 to 139. (Issue of May 28, 1861.) This discrepancy may be accounted for by the fact that special permission was given to commissioners not present to record their votes later. (*Minutes of the General Assembly,* 1861, vol. xvi, p. 322.)

[55] The geographical distribution of the vote may be determined by comparing the recorded *yeas* and *nays* with the list of commissioners for 1861, *Minutes of the General Assembly,* 1861, vol. xvi, pp. 293-297.

Dr. Spring's resolution, [this is inaccurate — the vote was on the question of tabling the whole business, although no doubt nearly all who voted against the tabling motion intended to vote for Dr. Spring's resolutions, if possible,] and the resolution alone was a test of the feeling in the Assembly." [56] That body was now virtually committed to take some definite action on the state of the country.

The next morning a proposition which had in an earlier session been first ignored [57] and later voted down by a vote of one hundred two to ninety-five,[58] was renewed and adopted by a vote of one hundred thirty to eighty-nine: the proposition that a committee be appointed to consider all the papers before the house on the subject of Dr. Spring's resolutions, the committee to report in the afternoon at four o'clock.[59] The Moderator almost immediately announced the names of the nine men who were to compose the committee.[60] The five members who were ministers, and two of the four ruling elders, had all taken prominent parts in the debates. It has been asserted that the border-state Moderator packed the committee.[61] This contention is not borne out by the evidence in the debates. Dr. Spring, who would, of course, normally have been a member, had the previous day obtained a leave of absence from the Assembly.[62] Of the seven members of whose views we have a record, two [63] had declared themselves emphatically for the Spring Resolutions, another [64] had been a consistent advocate of action by the Assembly, and the chairman of the committee, Dr. Musgrave, had expressed himself only a short time before his appointment as ready to vote for the Spring Resolutions,

[56] Philadelphia *Press,* May 28, 1861.
[57] Cf. account of Judge Ryerson's motion, *ibid.,* May 28, 1861.
[58] *Ibid.*
[59] *Minutes of the General Assembly,* 1861, vol. xvi, p. 322. *Cf.* also Philadelphia *Press,* May 29, 1861.
[60] *Minutes of the General Assembly,* 1861, vol. xvi, p. 322.
[61] Thompson, *op. cit.,* p. 152.
[62] *Minutes of the General Assembly,* 1861, vol. xvi, p. 326.
[63] Dr. W. C. Anderson of California and Judge Ryerson of New Jersey.
[64] H. K. Clarke of Michigan.

and unwilling to vote for resolutions not expressing such senti-ments.[65] Three of the nine members,[66] it is true, including the powerful Dr. Hodge, had expressed themselves as opposed to the Spring Resolutions, but this number does not show dispro-portionate consideration of the anti-action faction.

It is a tremendous tribute to the sagacity and diplomacy of Dr. Hodge that when the majority report of the committee, em-bracing his own sentiments, and drafted, no doubt, by him,[67] was presented, eight of the nine members of the committee en-dorsed it. The committee reported on Tuesday afternoon. The chairman, in offering the report, made some explanatory remarks. Dr. Spring's resolutions, he said, had been modified and softened so that, while the Government of the Union was endorsed, the antipathies of the extremists might not be di-rected toward the Assembly and Southern presbyters.[68] The report was as follows:[69]

Gratefully acknowledging the distinguished bounty and care of Almighty God towards this favored land, and also recognizing our obligation to sub-mit every ordinance of man for the Lord's sake, this General Assembly adopts the following resolutions:

Resolved, 1. That in view of the present agitated and unhappy condi-tion of this country, Monday, the first day of July next, be hereby set apart as a day of prayer throughout our bounds, and that on that day ministers and people are called upon humbly to confess and bewail our national sins, to offer our thanks to the Father of lights [sic] for his abundant and undeserved goodness to us as a nation, to seek his guidance and blessing upon our rulers and their counsels, as well as upon the Congress then about to assemble, and to implore Him, in the name of Jesus Christ, the Great High Priest of the Christian profession, to turn away His anger from us, and speedily restore to us the blessings of a safe and honourable peace.

Resolved, 2. That the members of this General Assembly, in the spirit of that Christian patriotism which the Scriptures enjoin, and which has

---

[65] Philadelphia *Press*, May 29, 1861.

[66] Dr. Hodge, Dr. J. W. Yeomans of Pa., and Dr. E. C. Wines of Mo.

[67] Dr. Hodge assumed the responsibility for the defense of the report, in the debates on it, and was the author of the most effective protest against the Assembly's final action with regard to it.

[68] Philadelphia *Press*, May 29, 1861.

[69] The report is given in *Minutes of the General Assembly*, 1861, vol. xvi, p. 325.

always characterized this Church, do hereby acknowledge and declare their obligation, so far as in them lies, to maintain the Constitution of these United States in the full exercise of all its legitimate powers, to preserve our beloved Union unimpaired, and to restore its inestimable blessings to every portion of the land.

Resolved, 3. That in the present distracted state of the country, this Assembly, representing the whole Church, feel bound to abstain from any further declaration, in which all our ministers and members faithful to the Constitution and Standards of the Church, might not be able conscientiously and safely to join, and therefore, out of a regard as well to the interests of our beloved country, as to those of the Church, the Assembly adopts this minute as its deliverance upon this subject.

Dr. William C. Anderson of California, the single dissenting member of the committee, after referring to the unpleasantness of being in a minority,[70] read as his minority report the resolutions of Dr. Spring, with some verbal alterations in the second resolution, and the substitution of the first for the fourth of July as the day of prayer. In order that it may be readily compared with the majority report, Dr. Anderson's minority report is given below: [71]

Gratefully acknowledging the distinguished bounty and care of Almighty God toward this favored land, and also recognizing our obligations to submit to every ordinance of man for the Lord's sake, this General Assembly adopt the following resolutions:

Resolved, 1. That in view of the present agitated and unhappy condition of this country, the first day of July next be hereby set apart as a day of prayer throughout our bounds; and that on this day ministers and peoples are called on humbly to confess and bewail our national sins; to offer our thanks to the Father of light for His abundant and undeserved goodness towards us as a nation; to seek his guidance and blessing upon our rulers, and their counsels, as well as on the Congress of the United States about to assemble; and to implore Him, in the name of Jesus Christ, the great High Priest of the Christian profession, to turn away his anger from us, and speedily restore to us the blessings of an honourable peace.

Resolved, 2. That this General Assembly, in the spirit of that Christian patriotism which the Scriptures enjoin, and which has always characterized this Church, do hereby acknowledge and declare our obligations to promote and perpetuate, so far as in us lies, the integrity of these United States, and to strengthen, uphold, and encourage, the Federal Government

---

[70] Philadelphia *Press,* May 29, 1861.

[71] *Minutes of the General Assembly,* 1861, vol. xvi, pp. 329-330. The *Minutes* give the minority report as it stood after being amended by the addition of another paragraph. The content of this paragraph is given *post,* pp. 62-63.

in the exercise of all its functions under our noble Constitution: and to this Constitution in all its provisions, requirements, and principles, we profess our unabated loyalty.

It will be noted that, in their first resolutions, the two reports are practically identical; it is in the second resolution of the majority report that the "modifying" and the "softening" of the original Spring Resolutions has taken place. Both reports acknowledge the obligation of the Church to support the Constitution and to preserve the Union. But while the minority report (which, as it left Dr. Spring's resolutions almost unchanged, was usually referred to as the "Spring Resolutions"), declared the obligation of the General Assembly to *strengthen, uphold, and encourage, the Federal Government in the exercise of all its powers under our noble Constitution,* the majority of the committee in their report satisfied themselves with a general statement of loyalty to the Constitution and the Union. And to emphasize the conciliatory nature of their report, they added a third resolution pledging abstinence from further declaration in this time of crisis.

For another full day the debate continued. Now, however, the issue was more clear-cut. It had proved impossible to stifle any and all discussion of the question of action,[72] as well as to table the whole matter after several days of discussion;[73] a choice between two alternatives remained: the majority and minority reports. The opponents of the Spring Resolutions did not relax a particle, but the body of the Assembly proved far harder to convert than the members of the committee. At a distance of seventy years, the two reports may not seem so different. But Dr. Musgrave, who declared he could vote for either,[74] in this respect stood alone among the members of the 1861 Assembly. When a veritable "hurricane of patriotism and loyalty" was making deliberate action almost impossible, when the editor of the leading secular newspaper of Philadel-

[72] *Cf. ante,* p. 48.
[73] *Cf. ante,* p. 55.
[74] Philadelphia *Press,* May 30, 1861.

phia could declare, " In times like these patriotism is Christianity," [75] it is not surprising that a difference in degree of professed loyalty could be misconstrued into a distinction between loyalty and treason: " for one of the oldest denominations in the land, which has preserved itself intact, amidst agitations and convulsions that have severed not churches alone, but states and nations, had presented before it the plain question of Church or country, patriotism or treason, silence which meant cowardice, or speech which meant loyalty and allegiance. " [76] To those who had followed the arguments, it was apparent that the majority of the members so regarded the alternatives before them, or at least believed that the public so regarded them. Such being their opinion, the result of the vote was inevitable.

The proponents of the minority report would take no chances, however. Early in the discussion the previous week, Dr. Hodge had asserted that a member of the President's Cabinet had said, " the best you, [referring to the Old School Assembly], can do for the Union is to keep unbroken the unity of your Church. " [77] Another commissioner added that it had been learned by telegraph that other members of the Cabinet wished the Church to preserve its unity.[78] Dr. Spring's declaring that he did not believe that dispatch — that the circumstances were not understood in Washington,[79] prompted the production of copies of two telegrams before the Assembly the following morning: [80]

[75] Both quotations are from an editorial in the Philadelphia *Press,* May 30, 1861. The term " hurricane " was not used to indicate disapproval.

[76] From the reporter's account, *ibid.,* May 30, 1861. From internal evidence it appears that a different man reported this final meeting of the Assembly. *Cf., e.g.,* first paragraph of account of afternoon meeting, with accounts of previous sessions.

[77] *Ibid.,* May 25, 1861.

[78] *Ibid.*

[79] *Ibid.*

[80] *Cf.* account of General Assembly, *ibid.,* May 27, 1861. The diary of Edward Bates, covering the years 1859-1866, which has been deposited in the Mss. Division of the Library of Congress, was not, at the time this study was made, open to investigators, and could therefore not be consulted with regard to this incident. The diary is now (1932) in the course of publication.

Hon. Edw. Bates,
Washington City.
    Have you said that in your opinion, and that of other members of the
Cabinet, the best thing our Assembly can do to sustain the Government
is to preserve the unity of the Presbyterian Church by abstaining from
any deliverance on our present troubles; it is so stated by what claims
to be good authority. If consistent with your views, please answer
immediately.

E. C. Wines.

Washington, May 24th.

Rev. E. C. Wines, D.D.
    Yes; for myself, decidedly; and I believe for other members of the
Cabinet.

Edward Bates.

Now, just as the vote on the two reports was about to be
taken, the following message was produced by the other side:

    Cannot properly advise, but perceive no valid objection to unequivocal
expressions in favor of the Constitution, Union, and freedom.

S. P. Chase.

This message was greeted with loud applause.[81] The pro-
Spring faction had got even with their opponents!

The climax of the long-drawn-out dispute was now at hand.
" Much confusion here ensued, as the hour for voting had arrived. Motions and counter-motions were made on every hand,
and an effort was made on the part of each wing to bring their
respective report before the Assembly prior to the other. . . .
Efforts were made to adjourn until this [Thursday] morning,
and avoid a vote. Loud cries of 'vote,' 'vote,' were made,
and there was great confusion. The Assembly refused to adjourn."[82]

When the majority report was put to a vote, it was defeated,
eighty-four to one hundred twenty-eight.[83] A reversal of
twenty-two votes would have balanced the count. In the Border State synods, the sentiment was seventeen to eight in favor
of the majority report; in the synods of the South, two to four-

[81] *Ibid.,* May 30, 1861.
[82] *Ibid.,* May 30, 1861.
[83] *Minutes of the General Assembly,* 1861, vol. xvi, p. 329.

teen against it.[84]   Thus the commissioners from the slave-holding states voted nineteen to twenty-two against the majority — the milder — report.   There were therefore enough votes in the Border States, counting the vote of the Moderator in case of a tie,[85] to have carried the majority report.   That the twenty-two adverse votes were largely due to the feeling that even the majority report went too far, is indicated by the fact that twenty of these twenty-two votes were later cast against the minority report.[86]   It will be remembered that the commissioners from slave-holding states had voted almost unanimously for a policy of silence, on the propositions of tabling the whole matter.[87]   On the other hand, among the delegates from the region which may be termed the West and North-west — the territory west of central Pennsylvania and north of the Mason-Dixon line — the vote stood twenty-three to eighty-eight against the majority report.   As an effort to conciliate the West and the South, the majority report was a distinct failure. Only in the conservative East, comprising the five synods of Albany, Buffalo, New York, New Jersey, and Philadelphia, did the majority report have a balance of the vote in its favor. There the record stood forty-two to thirty.[88]

With the majority report disposed of, the minority report was then considered.   To conciliate the anti-Lincoln men, the following paragraph was added:

And to avoid all misconception, the Assembly declare that by the terms " Federal Government," as here used, is not meant any particular

---

[84] *Cf. ibid.*, vol. xvi, p. 329, for a record of the vote, and pp. 293-297 for the list of commissioners and of the presbyteries they represented.   It should be noted that the Synod of Wheeling, covering almost exclusively Ohio and Pennsylvania territory, should not be included with the synods of slave-holding states; while the Presbytery of Carlisle, in the Synod of Baltimore, being almost entirely a Pennsylvania presbytery, should be classed as a Northern unit.

[85] That the Moderator was in favor of the majority report is indicated by his later signing the Hodge Protest. *Cf. ibid.*, vol. xvi, p. 341; also *post*, pp. 64-70.

[86] *Minutes of the General Assembly*, 1861, vol. xvi, p. 330.

[87] *Cf. ante*, p. 55.

[88] *Minutes of the General Assembly*, 1861, vol. xvi, p. 329 and pp. 293-297.

administration, or the peculiar opinions of any particular party, but that central administration, which being at any time appointed and inaugurated according to the forms prescribed in the Constitution of the United States, is the visible representative of our national existence.[89]

The minority report was then carried by a vote of one hundred fifty-six to sixty-six.[90] Forty-four of the adverse votes came from men who had voted for the majority report. This decision was thus even more sectional than that on the majority report. Thirty-two of the sixty-six votes adverse to the minority report came from below the Mason-Dixon line; only three favorable votes came from south of that line, [six commissioners from the South did not vote], and these were from the Border State presbyteries. Twenty-two votes on the adverse side came from the East; twelve from the West.

A comparison of the vote on the two reports shows that the greater number of the Southern commissioners were opposed even to as conciliatory action as the majority report proposals, while the opposition to a strong pro-Union stand was practically unanimous. On the other hand, it will be noted that the North and East vote against the minority resolutions was only about one-half of the vote for the majority report. In other words, some thirty commissioners from the North and East, when they discovered that the Hodge majority report resolutions had been voted down, decided to transfer their allegiance to the minority report. Some may have been actuated by the desire to be with the crowd; some may have feared the wrath of their constituents in case they did not join the larger group; probably the greater number were motivated by the feeling that the Assembly should take some action, and that, with the milder resolutions ruled out, the more decisive stand was the only remaining alternative.[91]

[89] *Ibid.*, pp. 329-330.
[90] *Ibid.*, p. 330.
[91] *Cf., e.g.*, the reasons given by Dr. E. C. Wines, (a member of the committee majority which presented the majority report), for his final vote in favor of the minority report, as stated in his communication to the *Presbyterian*, June 29, 1861.

At any rate, the final vote was decisive: the Spring Resolutions, having survived a bitter five-days' attack, had been adopted by a seventy per cent majority. The die had been cast. The conservative element waited apprehensively to see what the effect upon the unity of the Church would be. On the other hand, the flag-waving faction was jubilant: the Church would probably be divided, it is true, but at least the majority had taken their stand with the denominations of the North on the side of the Union.[92]   Gratified this group must have felt to have the Philadelphia *Press* comment: "[We] feel proud to know that a united Church worships under a united Republic; and that whatever the liturgy, or the litany, or the catechism may teach, they teach nothing incompatible with loyalty to the Constitution, and inculcate no sentiments but those which do honor to the American people and American Christianity." [93]   The visitors who packed the galleries and the aisles [94] sensed to the full the importance of the Assembly's action.   "All seemed to feel that a great issue depended upon the result of the final ballot, and when it was announced, the audience could scarcely restrain itself from giving demonstrations of its satisfaction.   From that day the audience has grown smaller and smaller, until Saturday morning [the final session] there were not, all told, more than a dozen spectators in the gallery. . . ." [95]

Outside visitors may have lost interest in the General Assembly as soon as its great decision on the Spring Resolutions had been made; within the Church, and even within the General Assembly itself, the whole matter was by no means dead. Partly to vindicate their own stand, and partly, no doubt, with the hope of still placating southern members, immediately after the vote Dr. Hodge and others gave notice that they protested

[92] For the stand taken by other northern denominational groups at this time, *cf. post*, pp. 73-79.

[93] Editorial, Philadelphia *Press*, May 30, 1861.

[94] *Cf.* account of General Assembly, *ibid.*, June 3, 1861.

[95] *Ibid.*, June 3, 1861.

against the action of the Assembly for reasons to be given.[96] The following day, letters of protest were presented by various individuals and groups. The protest read by Dr. Hodge had been signed by fifty-eight commissioners.[97] The papers were all admitted to record and referred to a special committee appointed to answer them.[98] These papers of protest — six in all — and the answer prepared for the Assembly by the special committee[99] furnish a compact summary of the principal arguments on both sides, in the long-drawn-out battle on the Spring Resolutions.

In the first place, all of the protestants emphatically declared their loyalty to the Constitution, laws, and government of the United States. In fact, however many secessionists there may have been among southern Old School Presbyterians, not a single states' rights speech was made in the Assembly. Probably everyone realized only too well that the expression of such sentiments would be dangerous. On the other hand, as virtually all the Southerners who spoke declared themselves strongly for the Union, it may be that such commissioners as had anti-Union feelings had stayed at home.

Nor did the matter of the Church expressing loyalty to a civil government prove a stumbling-block to more than one or two.[100] On the other hand, Dr. Hodge and his fifty-seven fellow-protestants explicitly acknowledged "loyalty to our country to be a moral and religious duty, according to the word of God, which requires us to be subject to the powers that be."[101]

[96] *Minutes of the General Assembly,* 1861, vol. xvi, p. 330.
[97] *Ibid.,* p. 341.
[98] *Ibid.,* vol. xvi, p. 333.
[99] For these papers, *cf. ibid.,* pp. 336-344.
[100] The only explicit objection of this kind expressed, is in the protest of Dr. A. G. Hall. Dr. Hall, fully recognizing his duty to do all as a citizen to sustain the Government against rebellion, held it to be "the duty of the Assembly by the Constitution of the Church, to abstain from all political deliverances, and to confine itself exclusively to ecclesiastical action." *Ibid.,* vol. xvi, p. 338.
[101] *Ibid.,* vol. xvi, p. 339.

Nor did Dr. Hodge and his party deny the right of the Assembly to enjoin loyalty and all other like duties on the ministers and churches under its care. But the Spring Resolutions, they asserted, assumed for the Assembly " the right to decide the political question, to what government the allegiance of Presbyterians as citizens is due, and . . . to make that decision a condition of membership in our Church." This the Assembly did, they alleged, by promising in the name of all the churches and ministers whom it represented, to do all that in them lay to " strengthen, uphold, and encourage the Federal Government." Since many Old School ministers and members conscientiously believed that the allegiance of the citizens of this country was primarily due to the states to which they belonged, it followed that they believed that when a state renounced its connections with the United States, the citizens of that state were bound by the laws of God to continue loyal to their state. Therefore, the protestants asserted, in adopting the Spring Resolutions, " the Assembly does decide the great political question which divides and agitates the country " — the question whether allegiance was primarily to the state or to the Union. Thus the Assembly assumed a particular interpretation of the Constitution — a matter clearly beyond its jurisdiction.[102] This was the first great source of objection to the Assembly's action, expressed by the Hodge Protest.

But the action of the Assembly not only decided a political question, the Hodge Protest continued, but made that action a term of membership in the Church. It was one thing, Dr. Hodge pointed out, for the Assembly to issue a recommendation of a religious or benevolent institution, which the members might regard or not at pleasure; it was quite a different thing to put into the mouths of all represented in the Assembly, a declaration of loyalty and allegiance to the Union and the Federal Government. Such a declaration, for those living in what were called the seceding states, was treasonable. Presbyterians living in those states were consequently forced to choose

[102] *Ibid.*, vol. xvi, p. 339.

between allegiance to their states and allegiance to the Church. The Assembly in thus deciding a political question, and in making that decision practically a condition of membership in the Church, had, it was claimed, "violated the Constitution of the Church, and usurped the prerogative of its Divine Master."

Another charge brought against the action of the Assembly, in the Hodge Protest, was that it was a departure from all previous actions of the Assembly:

The General Assembly has always acted on the principle that the Church has no right to make anything a condition of Christian or ministerial fellowship, which is not enjoined or required in the Scriptures and Standards of the Church.

We have, at one time, resisted the popular demand to make total abstinence from intoxicating liquors a term of membership. At another time, the holding of slaves. In firmly resisting these unscriptural demands, we have preserved the integrity and unity of the Church, made it the great conservative body of truth, moderation, and liberty of conscience in our country. The Assembly have now descended from this high position, in making a political opinion, a particular theory of the Constitution, however correct and important that theory may be,[103] the condition of membership in our body, and thus, we fear, endangered the unity of the Church.

Again, the action of the Assembly was not needed — either to instruct or to excite Presbyterians in the northern states. "Old School Presbyterians everywhere out of the so-called seceding states, have openly avowed and conspicuously displayed their allegiance to the Constitution and the Government, and that in many cases, at great cost and peril." (This was an exaggeration: the statement would have been generally true, had it been applied to Old School Presbyterians in the non-slave-holding states. The exaggeration is pardonable, considering that the statement was made early in the war period, when the pro-Union men had made themselves much more conspicuous than the Southern sympathizers.) Nor was such action required by duty to country: "We are fully persuaded that we best promote the interests of the country by preserving

[103] Dr. Hodge had voted for Fremont and Lincoln. Hodge, *Life of Charles Hodge*, p. 230.

the integrity and unity of the Church. We regard this action of the Assembly, therefore, as a great national calamity, as well as the most disastrous to the interests of our Church which has marked its history."

Then too, it was alleged that the action of the Assembly was cruel and unjust in its bearing on Southern Old School Presbyterians. It was unfair to entertain and decide so momentous a question "when the great majority of our Southern Presbyterians were, from necessity, unrepresented in this body," and unchristian to expose the Southern churches that remained in connection with the Old School Church to loss of property and to personal danger. Finally, the Hodge Protest asserted that "the act of the Assembly will not only diminish the resources of the Church, but greatly weaken its power for good, and expose it to the danger of being carried away more and more from its true principles, by a worldly and fanatical spirit." [104]

Comprehensive as the Hodge Protest was, it did not include all of the anti-Spring arguments advanced during the great debate. Almost all of the speakers declared themselves stout adherents of the Union; much had been made by a very few of the opponents of the Spring Resolutions of the so-called "right of revolution." Declaring that it was "a sad day for the Church of Jesus Christ and [when?] the Gospel herald must hoist the stars and stripes to be heard at all," one of the commissioners [105] proceeded to argue the right of revolution, not deterred by the interruptions of a gentleman who declared he would not remain in the church to hear treason preached. [106] Several speakers and writers took pains to refute the "right of revolution " theory as applied to the struggle then going on. [107]

The same man who argued the right of revolution emphasized the difficulty of carrying out the Spring Resolutions in slave

---

[104] The text of the Hodge Protest is given in the *Minutes of the General Assembly*, 1861, vol. xvi, pp. 339-341; also in Thompson, *History of the Presbyterian Churches*, pp. 380-384.

[105] Rev. S. A. Mutchmore of Missouri.

[106] Philadelphia *Press*, May 30, 1861.

[107] *Ibid.*

states, declaring that he should have to order several regiments of troops from General Harney to protect one poor preacher if he attempted to enforce the will of the Assembly.[108]

Another member emphasized the constitutional position of the Assembly in the Church: it was not a legislative body but rather entirely a judicial body. The same speaker — a Mississippian — opposed the minority report because it committed the Church to the "administration of Abraham Lincoln, William H. Seward, and Salmon P. Chase. . . . If passed, it will gratify every Abolitionist in the country — William Lloyd Garrison, Wendell Phillips, and the like." The gentleman was evidently obsessed with the fear of gratifying his enemies, for he also declared that he was "opposed to being counseled by the New School Church."[109] "From the days of Constantine," declared a Kentuckian, "the State has nearly always preserved the unity of the Church." Was the Presbyterian Church now going to act the tyrant to preserve the unity of the State? Such would resemble the action of the Roman Catholic Church, which made kings and emperors bow to it.[110]

But the Hodge Protest, with its fifty-eight signatures, twenty-four of which were those of commissioners from the North,[111] naturally drew more attention than the other papers of protest or the oral arguments in the Assembly, and furnished a basis of protest against action on political matters in subsequent assemblies.[112] In fact, although as pointed out above, in the oral arguments some points had been made which were not included in the Hodge paper, the other formal protests offered no arguments not to be found in the Hodge document,[113] and

[108] Speech of Rev. S. A. Mutchmore of Missouri, *ibid.*
[109] Speech of Rev. Thos. A. Ogden of Mississippi, *ibid.*
[110] Speech of Rev. George Fraser of Kentucky, *ibid.*
[111] But 8 of the 24 were from the West.
[112] *Cf. post,* pp. 116 and 123.
[113] Except for the Protest of John D. Wells and Thomas S. Childs, signers of the Hodge Protest, who offered a separate paper protesting against the fact that no opportunity was offered for a vote on the first resolution of the majority and of the minority reports, (virtually the same in wording), separately from the other resolutions. *Minutes of the General Assembly,* 1861, vol. xvi, p. 338.

the six principles of the Hodge Protest were made the basis for the answer of the Assembly committee.

In answer to the first charge, that the Assembly had virtually decided the question, to what government the allegiance of Presbyterians as citizens was due, the committee offered a paragraph from Dr. Hodge's own article in the January *Princeton Review*:

" There are occasions," says the author of an able article on " The State of the Country," in the January number of the *Princeton Review,* " there are occasions when *political* questions *rise into the sphere of morals and religion;* when the rule of political action is to be sought, not in consideration of State policy, but in the law of God. . . . When the question to be decided turns on moral principles; when reason, conscience, and the religious sentiment are to be addressed, *it is the privilege and duty of all who have access in any way to the public ear,* to endeavor to allay unholy feeling, and *to bring truth to bear* on the minds of their fellow-citizens." The General Assembly heartily approve these principles, and doubt not that if there ever was an occasion when political questions rose into the sphere of morals and religion, the present circumstances of our beloved country are of that character.[114]

One looks in vain for some explicit statement as to just what phases of the political situation made it so decidedly one of morals and religion; certainly the Assembly had maintained a most cautious silence on the whole matter of slavery.

The committee continued its refutation of the first argument of the Hodge Protest by calling attention to the fact that the Assembly was the Assembly of the Presbyterian Church *in the United States of America.* The organization of the General Assembly was contemporaneous with that of the Federal Government. " In the seventy-four years of our existence, Presbyterians have known but one supreme government, one nationality, within our widespread territory." [This is hardly a fair statement, since, though Presbyterians had been united for only seventy-four years under one general assembly, Presbyterianism had existed for nearly two hundred years on this continent.] " We know no other now. . . . No nation on earth recognizes the existence of two independent sovereignties

[114] *Ibid.,* p. 342. The italics are the committee's.

within these United States." [A dangerous argument in May, 1861!] "Would they [the protestants] have us recognize, as good Presbyterians, men whom our own government, with the approval of Christendom, may soon execute as traitors? . . . In the language of the learned Reviewer above cited, 'Is disunion morally right? Does it not involve a breach of faith, and a violation of the oaths by which that faith was confirmed? We believe, under existing circumstances, that it does, and therefore it is as dreadful a blow to the Church as it is to the State. If a crime at all, it is one the heinousness of which can only be imperfectly estimated.'" [It is only fair to Dr. Hodge to remind the reader that Dr. Hodge had written his article before the secession of South Carolina,[115] and that his article had to do with the stand of *individuals* on the question of disunion, rather than with the right of the Church to determine the matter of allegiance after a *de facto* secession government had been set up.]

The Hodge Protest had said that the Spring Resolutions set up a new term of communion. This the committee answer denied, asserting that the action taken was simply a faithful declaration by the Assembly of Christian duty towards those in authority, which added nothing to the terms of communion already recognized. "Surely the idea of the obligation of loyalty to our Federal Government is no new thing to Presbyterians." [Here again, it must be pointed out that for the General Assembly to demand a recognition of the supremacy of the Federal Government over the states *was* a distinctly new thing to Presbyterians.]

In answer to the statement that the action of the Assembly was not necessary, either to instruct or to excite the loyalty of Northerners, the committee's answer declared that at a time "when thousands of Presbyterians are likely to be seduced from their allegiance by the machinations of wicked men . . . when every national interest is in jeopardy, and every spiritual energy paralyzed . . . when it remains a question, whether our

[115] *Cf. ante*, pp. 33-36.

national life survives the conflict, or whether our sun sets in anarchy and blood—is it uncalled for, unnecessary, for this Christian Assembly to renew, in the memories and hearts of a Christian people, respect for the majesty of law, and a sense of the obligation of loyalty?   Let posterity decide between us."

So far as the matter of the South not being fully represented in the Assembly was concerned, the committee maintained that the presence of delegates from Virginia, Kentucky, Missouri, Louisiana, Tennessee, Mississippi, and Texas,[116] was adequate proof that all might have been as easily represented. Furthermore, to have waited for a full Southern representation, would have been to lose forever the critical moment when action would be productive of good.   As to the final ground of protest, the committee felt that it was enough to record its simple denial of the opinions expressed.   Far from proving to be a source of weakness to the Church, " this action of the General Assembly will increase the power of the Church for good; securing, as we humbly trust it will, the favour of her exalted Head, in behalf of those who testify for a suffering truth." [117]

To an impartial observer two generations distant in time from the 1861 Assembly, the arguments of the protestants— at least on the matter of the *right* of the Assembly to act—are more convincing than those of the majority.   One cannot escape the feeling that the majority were on the defensive.   While the arguments of the Hodge paper are characterized by calm, dispassionate logic, those of the answering committee reflect— at least to a degree—the hysteria of the time.   A generation whose church-goers each Sunday since the World War have seen national emblems conspicuously displayed in the meeting-houses of the " Church Universal " [118] need not be surprised

[116] Maryland was not mentioned.
[117] The text of the answer of the special committee is printed in the *Minutes of the General Assembly*, 1861, vol. xvi, pp. 341-344; also in Thompson, *History of the Presbyterian Churches*, pp. 384-388.
[118] It will be recalled that individual preachers during the years of the World War who had the courage to point out that national emblems had no place in houses of the " Church Universal," usually suffered short shrift.

that a generation slavishly devoted to proof-texts should find in the injunction, "Render unto Caesar the things that are Caesar's," not simply an injunction to respect the civil government, but also a command to be faithful in the support of nationalism.

There is little evidence of insincerity on the part of the members of the Assembly. Certainly there are abundant signs of a self-sacrificing sincerity in many of the commissioners. In so large and varied a group, however, when the question at issue was so peculiarly complex, it was inevitable that many should have been influenced — often probably unconsciously — by various ulterior factors. Without a doubt, love for the Union and for the Church was practically universal among those present. Now both were in danger. Was it the duty of the Church to be silent on the great political issue, or to take an open stand for the Union? Passing over the question of duty, could the Church best be served by a policy of silence or by one of open declaration? Did the Union need the Church's expression of opinion, or would the silence of the Church best serve it? If there was a conflict of interests, where did one's first duty lie? With such a tangle of vital questions, a variety of influences were bound to play a considerable part in individual decisions. Besides the war-time hysteria which was convulsing the nation, three influences in particular were evidently of considerable weight in determining the stand of individual members: the action taken by other religious denominations; a strong feeling of sectionalism dividing the Northerners into rival eastern and western factions; and pressure from the people "back home."

Practically every religious group of importance which had met in the spring of 1861 had taken some action with respect to the political controversy; in the South, expressing allegiance to the Confederacy; in the North, to the Union. Of greatest importance to the Old School Presbyterians was the action of the New School Presbyterians, convening in General Assembly at Syracuse, New York, on May 21, 1861. At the very time when

Old School Presbyterians were in the thick of their fight, the unanimous endorsement of the Federal Government by the New School Assembly in resolutions which were to be sent to the President of the United States, was being given publicity in prominent newspapers.[119]   Furthermore, the attitude of the New School press made this contrast particularly galling. During the trying days of the great debate, New School journals were exhibiting sentiments not far removed from gleeful satisfaction at the difficulties of the rival denomination.   The *Christian Herald*, (Cincinnati), pointed out the " striking contrast" between the positions of the two churches on the political situation.[120]   Similarly, the renowned Dr. Theodore Cuyler, commending, in the New York *Evangelist*, the political sentiments of members of the New School Assembly, asserted that the Old School had made a great mistake in cutting off the New School men: " It was just about as wise an act as it would be in a railway engineer, if he were to practise ' excision ' on the locomotive and tender of the train." [121]   True to the philosophy of its faith, the *American Presbyterian*, (Philadelphia), saw the spectre of retribution stalking the Old School Assembly. Reminding its readers that the Old School Assembly was meeting in the same church[122] as the famous Assembly of 1837, which had divided the Church, the journal found it most significant that the commissioners in 1861,

should be called upon to witness and realize a practical sundering of their body by the act of Providence, as extensive as that which they accomplished by violence, in the same Seventh Church twenty-four years ago. The only way in which their church can now be saved from downright immediate disruption, is by such humiliating concessions to the dictation of rebels in arms against the government, as will crush them under the weight of the loyal public opinion of the North, and so work in another,

---

[119] *Cf., e.g.,* front-page report in the Philadelphia *Press*, May 28, 1861; also report in New York *World*, May 24, 1861; also *post*, pp. 344-346.

[120] Editorial, " The Assembly at Syracuse," *Christian Herald*, May 30, 1861.

[121] Article, " The General Assembly [New School], — How it Looks," in New York *Evangelist*, May 23, 1861.

[122] The editor mentioned that the Church was now on Penn Square, instead of Ranstead Street, as in 1837.

and perhaps slower way, their overthrow. Whichever way they take, their glory as a great imposing, national Church, is departed. Their great artificial scheme of suppressing opinion in their ecclesiastical councils [the extensive use of the " previous question "]; their boundless concessions to the South for the sake of denominational unity; their boastings of conservatism loudly re-echoed by secular journals who admired that trait — all these have not saved them from the deplorable fate of discovering within their denominational limits, members, officers, ministers of the Gospel, even, armed against each other with the weapons of death. . . .[123]

This New School journal then assumed the role of adviser to the Old School Assembly. Since a large number of Synods and a whole section of the Church were charged with the gravest infractions of duty to the rightful authorities of this country, and since their extent made it impossible that proper discipline should be administered in the constitutional way, the *American Presbyterian* suggested that it might be desirable for the Assembly itself

promptly to *cut off* the offending Synods, and enact that no representative from their constituent Presbyteries be allowed a seat in future Assemblies, without *first taking the oath of allegiance to our Government.* This might seem a little revolutionary, but the place in which the body is now meeting, to say nothing of the extraordinary exigencies of the case . . . would materially aid the successors of the men of '37 and '38 in overcoming any constitutional scruples they might cherish on the subject. Certainly, the excision of the rebellious Synods of '61 would be a far clearer vindication of the loyalty of the church to the government, than the excision of the four Synods in '37 was of loyalty to the Confession of Faith.[124]

Can there be any doubt that sarcasm like this from the leaders of the New School brethren played a significant part in stirring the Old School men to action?

There was no national meeting of Episcopalians in 1861. Individual dioceses, North and South, however, had been prompt to act. Southern dioceses seceded with the States. A pastoral letter of Bishop Polk of Louisiana had explained the point of view of Southern Episcopalians: " We must follow our

[123] Editorial, " The Assembly in Philadelphia," *American Presbyterian,* May 23, 1861. This editorial was copied in full by the New York *Evangelist,* May 30, 1861.
[124] *Ibid.*

nationality. . . . With us it is a separation, not a division —
certainly not alienation. . . . Our relations to each other
will hereafter be the relations we both now hold to the
men of our mother church of England."[130]   On the other
hand, Bishop Whittingham of Maryland was emphatic in his
caution regarding the omission of the prayer for the President
of the United States.   Current events, he pointed out, had
settled any question of citizenship and allegiance: Maryland
belonged to the United States, and the clergy must pray for the
President of the United States.   "We of the clergy," he declared, "have no right to intrude our private views of the questions which are so terribly dividing those among whom we minister, into the place assigned for us that we may speak for God,
and minister in His worship. . . ."[131]   The annual convention
of the Protestant Episcopal Church of Pennsylvania, meeting
at the same time as the Old School General Assembly, had no
difficulty in taking a stand for the Union.[132]   This loyalty,
which was to be so much in evidence among individual groups
of northern Episcopalians in church action during the summer of 1861, must already have been evident in the actions of
individual persons of that denomination by May of that
year.[133]

[130] *Cf.* copy of letter in the *Presbyterian*, March 2, 1861.

[131] From letter of May 15, quoted in New York *World*, May 21, 1861.

[132] *Cf.* report of annual convention, (2nd day), Philadelphia *Press*, May 30,
1861.

[133] *Cf., e.g.,* "Southern and Northern Episcopalians and the War," Philadelphia *Press*, June 3, 1861; "A Patriotic Bishop — Letter of Bishop Polk of
Pennsylvania," New York *Evening Post*, June 4, 1861; "A Patriotic Bishop
— What Bishop Lee of Delaware . . . ," *ibid.*, June 6, 1861; Report of Rhode
Island Protestant Episcopal Annual Convention, (Note especially the protest of the bishop addressed to the Committee in Charge of General Domestic Missions "against the further payment of any of our funds to missionaries in the Diocese of Alabama. . . .") Newport *Mercury*, June 15, 1861;
Article, "Division of the Episcopal Church," (Note reference to projected
convention of bishops of the seceded states), *Presbyterian*, June 29, 1861;
"Seceding Episcopacy" (an account of the Episcopal Convention in the
seceded states, at Montgomery, July 3—note that the Bishop of North
Carolina, not present at the convention, in his diocesan address denied that
secession of necessity occasioned a disruption in the Church), *ibid.,* July

The Evangelical Lutheran Synod of Pennsylvania, meeting at the same time as the Old School Assembly, took a decisive stand for the Union.[134]   Subsequently, the Lutheran Church divided—North and South.[135]   While the quadrennial General Conference of the Methodist Episcopal Church did not convene in 1861, the hostile attitude toward slavery by members of the General Conference of the previous year, left little doubt in men's minds that that great church would be strongly anti-Confederacy in 1861.[136]

The Baptists, long since divided into northern and southern wings, took special delight in emphatic statements on the political situation in 1861.   The Southern Baptists deplored "the reign of terror at the North," with its "violence . . . committed upon unoffending citizens."   The North, they asserted, "threatens to wage a warfare upon the South of savage barbarity, to devastate their homes and hearths with hosts of ruffians and felons, burning with lust and rapine."[137]   Such statements were but a challenge to their Northern brethren.   The temper in which the challenge was accepted may be judged by

13, 1861; Account of Episcopal Convention of New Hampshire, and denunciation by Bishop Burgess of Bishop Polk for taking up arms, *ibid.*, September 7, 1861; Statement that the new assistant bishop of the diocese of Pennsylvania "was distinctly vouched for as loyal, before he received the votes of the laity," editorial note, *ibid.*, Nov. 2, 1861.

[134] *Cf.* account in Philadelphia *Press,* May 29, 1861.

[135] *Presbyterian,* Sept. 21, 1861; *cf.,* also, Heathcote, Charles W., *The Lutheran Church and the Civil War* (New York, 1919), pp. 70-79.

[136] *Cf.* for action of General Conference of 1860, McPherson, Edward, *Political History of the United States During the Great Rebellion. . . .* (Washington, 1876), pp. 494-496. For action of state conferences, *cf.* Sweet, William Warren, *The Methodist Episcopal Church and the Civil War* (Cincinnati, 1912), chapters ii, iii, iv.

[137] From the report of the Committee on the State of the Country, unanimously adopted by the Southern Baptist Convention. *Cf.* Moore, Frank, ed., *The Rebellion Record. . . .* (New York, 1861), Document 139, pp. 237-239. "It will be seen from this how thoroughly these Southern evangelists mistake the spirit and temper of the free, civilized North for the semi-barbarism of their own section," scornfully comments a correspondent of the Philadelphia *Press,* after quoting the above statements. *Cf.* column, "Religious," edited by "Graybeard," Philadelphia *Press,* June 1, 1861.

the resolutions adopted by the American Baptist Union at a meeting in Brooklyn. The news of the Baptist action could scarcely have reached Philadelphia before the final vote on the Spring Resolutions, but here again, the voice of the representative body simply echoed what was well known to be the sentiment of Northern Baptists:

Resolved, That the doctrine of secession is foreign to our Constitution, revolutionary, and suicidal, setting out in anarchy, and finding its ultimate issue in despotism.

. . . .

Resolved, That the wondrous uprising in strangest harmony and largest self-sacrifice, of the whole North . . . is cause of grateful amazement and grateful acknowledgement to God . . . and that this resurgent patriotism . . . may, in God's judgment, correct evils that seemed growing chronic and irremediable in the national character.

. . . .

Resolved, That what was bought at Bunker Hill, Valley Forge, and Yorktown, was not, with our consent, sold at Montgomery; that we dispute the legality of the bargain, and in the strength of the Lord God of our fathers still hope to contest, through this generation, if need be, the feasibility of the transfer.[138]

Such pungency naturally attracted wide attention. All over the North, the newspapers copied the resolutions,[139] quoting the last one with particular glee. Adopted on the same day as the Spring Resolutions, their language in emphasis contrasts sharply with that of the Old School pronouncement. One wonders how the members of the Old School Assembly regarded them. Some probably envied their decisiveness. Others no doubt regretted the fact that the Old School had been so much slower in taking a stand. Of course the more conservative element must have looked upon them with some scorn. Probably even most of the Spring supporters were comforted by the reflection that their resolutions were just as wholeheartedly expressed, and that certainly their language

[138] Quoted, *ibid.,* June 4, 1861; also in McPherson, *op. cit.,* pp. 474-475; Moore, *op. cit.,* Document 211, pp. 307-310.

[139] *Cf., e.g.,* Providence *Journal,* May 31, 1861; Detroit *Daily Advertiser,* June 1, 1861; besides New York and Philadelphia newspapers, and religious journals.

was much more in keeping with Presbyterian conservatism and dignity!

Individual groups of Congregationalists, as might be expected from their traditions, were prompt in expressing their loyalty to the Union.[140] Certain of the minor denominations had also been prompt in taking a stand for the Union. The Synod of the Moravian Church on May 30 adopted resolutions strongly endorsing the Federal Government,[140a] while the General Assembly of the United Presbyterian Church on May 15 had vigorously attacked slavery as the cause of the war, and pledged its allegiance to the administration at Washington.[141] As far as the Roman Catholic Church was concerned — the church which with the Old School Presbyterian Church, as the members of the General Assembly were told by one of their number, alone remained undivided,[142] or, as another put it during the course of the great debate, alone had " refused to recognize the Government " [143] — this denomination, too, had been heard from. For while no action had been taken by the Church as a whole, individual dioceses had declared their loyalty, so that the Philadelphia *Press* was able to remind its readers that " the highest point [in Philadelphia] from which our flag floats, is the pinnacle of a Papal cathedral." [144] Thus on all sides sister denominations, either through their central bodies or through influential units, were declaring for the Union. As a force impelling the Old School Presbyterian Church to do likewise, the influence of their action must have been tremendous.

[140] *Cf., e.g.,* action of the General Association of Congregational Churches of Michigan, referred to in editorial, Detroit *Daily Advertiser,* May 31, 1861.
[140a] McPherson, *op. cit.,* p. 483.
[141] *Ibid.,* p. 474; also, *post,* pp. 356-358.
[142] Speech of Rev. W. M. Baker of Texas, quoted in report of General Assembly, Philadelphia *Press,* May 28, 1861. Mr. Baker overlooked the Lutheran and Christian churches, (*cf. ante,* p. 17), though neither was in the same class, as far as numbers are concerned, with the Roman Catholic and Old School churches.
[143] Speech of Dr. Anderson of California, Philadelphia *Press,* May 29, 1861.
[144] Editorial, " The Church and State," *ibid.,* May 30, 1861.

The sectionalism displayed in the vote on the various loyalty resolutions before the Assembly,[145] was not the only evidence of rivalry and even antagonism between East and West in the Assembly proceedings. Over and over again in the debate, speakers referred to the conflict of interests between the two sections — a conflict which the Cincinnati *Presbyter* and the Pittsburgh *Presbyterian Banner,* for the " West," did their best to stir up in opposition to the interests represented by the conservative eastern Philadelphia *Presbyterian.* Fearful lest inaction on the part of the General Assembly would exhibit that body " in the aspect either of disloyalty, imbecility, or indifference," the *Presbyterian Banner* in an issue which appeared during the meeting of the Assembly, urged that a special convention be held, and suggested Pittsburgh or Columbus as good places because centrally located, and because of " hopes " of " many of our eastern friends uniting with us." [146]   Dr. Anderson of California, ardent supporter of the Spring Resolutions, declared that the Northwest would refuse to sustain the unity of the Church if the Assembly refused to stand by the country and its Constitution: " If we desert our national flag, the backbone of our Church, the Scotch-Irish element, the ' blues ' of the West and Northwest, will leave our Church in a body and join the nineteen hundred ministers of the New School Church — together with the Associate Reformed Church. If we now care for expediency instead of *right,* not a man of them will pass the doors of our Church again." [147]   [The eloquent doctor was evidently unconscious of the fact that he himself was advocating expediency in another form.]   A further remark of Dr. Anderson regarding the faithfulness " we Westerners " had shown Dr. Hodge and the editor of the *Presbyterian* — a remark that provoked much laughter [148] — by its obvious sarcasm prompted a protest from a later speaker: " Remember the handle our Cali-

---

[145] *Cf. ante,* pp. 55, 61-62, 63.
[146] Editorial, *Presbyterian Banner,* June 1, 1861.
[147] *Cf.* speech of Dr. Anderson, reported in account of General Assembly, Philadelphia *Press,* May 25, 1861.
[148] *Ibid.*

fornia brother made of Dr. Hodge's resolutions, to ridicule our
Philadelphia brethren and to ridicule Princeton." [149]   When it
was proposed to refer to a committee all of the papers of the
Assembly relating to the Spring Resolutions, the author of the
proposal, a former Moderator of the General Assembly,[150] suggested that the membership of the committee be apportioned
geographically — three from the North, three from the South,
and three from the West.[151]   A westerner, Dr. Lord of Chicago,
declared that non-passage of the resolutions would result in the
prostration of the Church in the great North and West.[152]

Southerners regarded the Northwestern brethren as the instigators of a policy of severity toward them.[153]   Some delegates
from the Northwest deprecated the threats made by men from
that section — one of them declaring that, as far as Wisconsin
was concerned, she would abide by whatever decision the Assembly made; she had no intention of withdrawing from the
Old School Church.[154]   To many the fiery spirit of the Northwest was indicative of the greater hold of Abolition there.   No
one regretted this more than Dr. Yeomans, a former Moderator
of considerable eloquence.   Alleging that an effort had been
made to establish a Northwestern sentiment, he said he wished
that the Northwest, and every other distinctive section, could
be forgotten.   The avidity with which members laid hold of
Dr. Spring's Resolutions to advocate sectional opinions, had
been an evidence of the existence of radical opinions upon the
question of involuntary servitude.   Let the Assembly still be
conservative, for division would make the Northern wing an

[149] *Cf.* speech of Dr. W. C. Matthews of Kentucky, Philadelphia *Press,* May
27, 1861.

[150] Dr. J. W. Yeomans of Danville, Pennsylvania.

[151] *Cf.* speech of Dr. Yeomans, reported in Philadelphia *Press,* May 28,
1861. The proposition of geographical distribution was voted down by the
Assembly. *Cf. ibid.,* May 29, 1861. The committee as appointed by the
Moderator, however, had virtually this distribution, (4-3-2).

[152] *Ibid.,* May 28, 1861.

[153] *Cf., e.g.,* speech of Rev. George Fraser of Kentucky, *ibid.,* May 30, 1861.

[154] Speech of Rev. George C. Heckman, *ibid.,* May 27, 1861.

anti-slavery body.[155]   But the opposition between the East and
the Northwest was too deep-rooted to be easily set aside. The
Northwest would not meekly accede to Eastern demands. However much Easterners might regret and Southerners might
threaten, the Northwestern brethren, " who," as one Southerner
put it, " wished to make the Southern Presbyterians traitors," [156]
continued steadfastly in the determination that the Spring
Resolutions must be passed.

The action of other denominations and the strong feelings
of sectionalism which permeated the Assembly were powerful
forces affecting the group as a whole. Of far more compelling
influence on individual members was the pressure of public
opinion. No one whose memory-span reaches back to the years
1917-1919 need be reminded of the well-nigh irresistible pressure of public opinion in war-time. And commissioners to the
General Assembly might well question, not to what degree they
might heed, but rather to what degree they might resist, public
opinion. As officials in the most representative of systems of
church government, duty seemed to dictate that the wishes
of the people " back home " be obeyed. " The people want the
Church to take this action," asserted one eloquent advocate of
the Spring Resolutions. " If we don't, they'll elect representatives next year who will." [157]   There is no doubt that to a great
degree his auditors agreed. Nor can the presence in the galleries of ministers of other denominations [158] have failed to promote the desire for loyal action.

The extended publicity given the proceedings of the Assembly by the press all over the North must have impressed the
commissioners with an exalted opinion of the importance of
their position, and made them particularly self-conscious. The
leading local newspaper, the Philadelphia *Press*, devoted important space to the daily debates, and described the membership and surroundings of the Assembly in considerable detail.

[155] *Ibid.*, May 28, 1861.
[156] *Cf.* speech of Rev. George Fraser of Kentucky, *ibid.*, May 30, 1861.
[157] *Cf.* speech of Dr. T. E. Thomas of Ohio, *ibid.*, May 25, 1861.
[158] Report of proceedings of Assembly, *ibid.*, May 25, 1861.

All of the important New York newspapers gave their readers daily reports of the progress of the debates — reports which were often acknowledged copies of the accounts in the *Press*. More important, wherever the Presbyterians had any hold on the country — and that meant every section west of New England — the daily and weekly press were telling their people of the doings of the historic old body in Philadelphia.[159]   And the commissioners were well aware of what their constituents were reading: "The afternoon papers were in the hands of all," writes a reporter, describing the scene just before the opening of a session, "and clusters of clergymen paused at times to discuss some current topic of political or ecclesiastical news."[160] Too much passion was "kindled in the Assembly by outside pressure, such as crowds, telegraphic despatches and letters," complained a conservative.[161]

"If the Assembly supports the Church in the North, the pastors can stand.   Without such resolutions, we will have discord in our congregations," Dr. Spring maintained.[162]   The masses in the East, the West, and the Northwest were in a mood that would cause tardy patriotism on behalf of this body to disconnect them from the Old School Church, declared another.   Presbyterianism had always been loyal, he continued, but now some places were doubtful.   The Spring Resolutions must be passed to put the Church in its true position.   Their motives the world would not remark; but their course would seem to be the index of their loyalty or disloyalty.[163]   The eyes

---

[159] *Cf.*, *e.g.*, reports in current issues of the New York *World*, New York *Herald*, New York *Evening Post*, New York *Times*, Detroit *Daily Advertiser*, Detroit *Weekly Tribune*, Ann Arbor *Journal*, etc., etc.   Practically every newspaper of the period which was consulted, carried news items on the Assembly, and in most of them there was also editorial comment.   Most of the news items were acknowledged as copies from the Philadelphia *Press*. Usually, even when not so acknowledged, it was evident that they came from this source.

[160] Philadelphia *Press*, May 28, 1861.

[161] Dr. Matthews of Kentucky.   *Cf.* account of his speech, *ibid.*, May 27, 1861.

[162] *Cf.* speech of Dr. Spring, *ibid.*, May 25, 1861.

[163] *Cf.* speech of Dr. Willis Lord of Chicago, *ibid.*, May 28, 1861.

of the world were upon the Church at this time, asserted another speaker; would it stand up for the Union? If the Church withheld its loyalty, the land would disown it. The eyes of our soldiers were upon the Church. Some of them had stood in the corner of this very room a few days before, curious lookers-on. Would the Assembly sustain these brave soldiers, thousands of whom were Presbyterians, in the noble cause of defending the Government? [164] "The theological leaders of the Church," commented the reporter of the Philadelphia *Press* in his final account of the session, "were enlisted for silence under the guise of conservatism; but the clergy, acting under home pressure, stood fast by Dr. Spring and the support of the Government, until, after painful embarrassments and inter-ferences, the Union triumphed, and the denomination stood true. The result of counter-action would have weakened, if not destroyed, the denomination in the north." [165] The temper of the reporter of this conservative daily incidentally affords an excellent explanation of why the Assembly voted as it did.

The "home pressure" was likely to be uncomfortable. A correspondent of the *Presbyterian* wrote that he hoped to be present at the 1862 Assembly, and then added, evidently with the Assembly of 1861 in mind, "—not as a delegate, for these are ticklish times in which to leave one's record, but as a mem-ber of that flourishing and highly respectable fungus known as ' the lobby.' I wish to be a ' looker-on.' " He thought it too bad that the Assembly could not devote more time to voting, " if for no better reason than to afford further entertainment to the galleries." [166]

It is rather significant that of the twenty-three Northerners who voted against the Spring Resolutions, six were without regular pastoral charge. Ten of the twenty-three had the title of " Doctor of Divinity " — indicative of a certain amount of maturity and standing to serve as a defense against adverse

---

[164] *Cf.* speech of Dr. W. C. Anderson of San Francisco, *ibid.,* May 29, 1861.
[165] *Ibid.,* May 30, 1861.
[166] *Cf.* communication, " Some Thoughts about the Meeting of the Assem-bly," by "A. E.," in *Presbyterian,* April 19, 1862.

criticism. Dr. Hodge tells of the dilemma of an acquaintance of his with regard to the Spring Resolutions — a dilemma that was probably experienced by many: " He came to me repeatedly, and asked ' What shall I do? I am opposed to these resolutions, but if I vote against them, I can never go home.' I told him that I was sorry, but I could not help him. It was easy for me to act, as I had nothing to fear from giving a negative vote. When his name was called in taking the final vote, he arose and said, ' Mr. Moderator, I want to say no, but I must say yes.' That saved him." [167]

To say that the pressure of public opinion was largely responsible for the change in the attitude of the members of the Assembly which occurred between the decision to table the original resolution and the final decisive vote for the minority report, is not to accuse the commissioners of cowardice. No one who recalls the hysteria of World War years would be disposed to speak unkindly of one whose deliberate judgment is temporarily swept aside by a " hurricane of patriotism and loyalty."

Whatever the reluctance of some loyal commissioners to vote for the resolutions, the result of the final vote was enthusiastically acclaimed by the secular press of the North. " The Presbyterian Church is true to its eldest and noblest traditions," exulted the New York *Times*,[168] and the New York *World* declared emphatically that the cause of the Union had " a right to the testimony and the sanction of all exponents of righteousness who have any public relations whatever. If such testimony confuses rebels or rebel sympathizers, it is all the more to be valued." [169] The violently patriotic Detroit *Daily Advertiser* could see no cause for hesitation " while traitors are in arms against the Government." [170] Alleging that he had never enter-

---

[167] The incident is related in Hodge, *Life of Charles Hodge,* pp. 22-23. The man quoted was Dr. J. G. Bergen of Illinois.

[168] Editorial, May 28, 1861. The editorial anticipated by two days the final action of the Assembly. It may actually have been of some influence in that decision.

[169] Editorial, May 30, 1861.

[170] Editorial, May 31, 1861.

tained a single doubt of the ultimate triumph of patriotism in
the Assembly — "because there are few Northern Presbyterians who would have worshipped God under an ecclesiastical
banner which was capable of being translated into a standard
of treason," the editor of the Philadelphia *Press* commended
the stand taken by the Assembly, and then, becoming a little
confused in his genders, rejoiced that the Old School Church
was now enabled to take its place "with its brother denominations, proudly forward on the side of Union."[171]

The endorsement of the Old School newspapers was not so
unanimous.   In fact, on the subject of the adoption of the
Spring Resolutions, the variation in opinion among them was
decidedly sectional.   The distinctly southern papers were violently condemnatory; the border-state *Presbyterian Herald*
was firm but dignified in its opposition; the conservative eastern
Presbyterian, though originally opposed to action, gracefully
accepted a decision which it considered morally right, but
inexpedient; the "western" *Presbyterian Banner* and *Presbyter*
could scarcely restrain their joy that the Assembly's action had
been so decisive.[172]

July 1 had been appointed in the Spring Resolutions as the
special day of prayer.   The *Presbyterian,* after some investigation, found that it had been generally observed for that purpose.[173]   As the circulation of this journal was predominantly
Northern,[174] it is to be taken for granted that its conclusion was
based on information from that section of the country.   At any
rate, there is no evidence of the spirit later displayed in a circular addressed to "Christians of Missouri" by one who styled
himself a "pastor and a patriot," [it is not stated whether or
not he was a Presbyterian], in which all were entreated to absent themselves from the churches on the Fast Day appointed
by President Lincoln, and celebrate, rather, a day of thanks-

[171] Editorial, May 30, 1861.
[172] For a more extensive account of the attitude of Old School newspapers,
cf. post, pp. 148-182.
[173] Editorial, *Presbyterian,* July 6, 1861.
[174] Editorial, *ibid.,* July 13, 1861.

giving for abundant harvests.[175]   Wherever their sympathies
may have lain, Old School Presbyterians were evidently all still
sportsmanlike enough in their attitude toward the enemy, at
least to let him pray unmolested.   Dr. Spring preached in his
own church, July 1, on a text that must have appeared particularly appropriate to the word-minded Christians of that day,
from Isaiah viii, 12, 13: "Say ye not a confederacy. . . ."[176]

With the passing of July 1, the special Day of Prayer, the
first stage of the battle in the Old School Church on the question of endorsement of the Union may be said to have ended.
The fight in the Assembly had been won; the secular press had
given the Assembly its hearty approval; the balance of opinion
on the part of Old School newspapers was decidedly favorable,
though the minority element of disapproval boded ill for the
cause of harmony in the Church; the day of prayer itself was
generally observed.   But, after all, it was but the first stage of
the conflict that had ended; with the return of the Assembly
commissioners to their individual presbyteries, the consideration of the vital issue at stake was transferred from the great
central body of the Church to some 140 individual local representative units of the denomination.   Would the presbyteries
sustain the action of the General Assembly?   This question
attracted lively attention in the summer of 1861.

[175] This circular received editorial notice in the *Presbyterian*, September
28, 1861.

[176] Editorial, *ibid.*, July 6, 1861.

CHAPTER III

THE RESPONSE OF THE CHURCH

In the early summer of 1861, Old School Presbyterians were awaiting with apprehension the effect upon Old School unity of the adoption of the Spring Resolutions. To the commissioners returning home from the General Assembly, no doubt a matter of much more immediate concern was the question as to whether their individual constituencies would endorse the stand they had taken. Many of the delegates probably anticipated with some dread the day of reckoning which must come to each of them with the meeting of their local presbyteries, for in the Presbyterian General Assembly the commissioners represent their respective presbyteries, by whose members they are also appointed; and it was but natural to expect that the presbyteries should take some notice of the action of their representatives on the momentous question which had confronted the Assembly. While the commissioners would be less interested in the action of the various synods at their fall meetings, the decision of these larger bodies was also vital to the cause of church unity. The meeting of the presbyteries occurred during the summer or early fall — before that of the synods. In scores of cases, particularly in the West and South, special resolutions on the Assembly action were passed by local bodies of both types.

It is exceedingly interesting to observe to what degree the commissioners reflected the sentiment of their territory. In not a single recorded instance in the North and West was favorable action by a commissioner on the Spring Resolutions repudiated by his constituency. On the other hand, five of the twenty-two adverse votes in the East,[1] and nine of the twelve

---

[1] *Cf.* action of Presbytery of Troy (N. Y.), *Presbyterian,* June 22, 1861; of Presbytery of Buffalo City (N. Y.), *ibid.,* July 6, 1861; of Presbytery of Northumberland (Penna.), *ibid.,* July 6, 1861.

in the West,[2] were disowned by resolution of the home presbyteries. Similarly, the Border State presbytery of Wyaconda (Missouri) disapproved of the favorable vote of one of its commissioners, and condemned the Resolutions as unconstitutional, inexpedient, unjust, and cruel.[3] Occasionally, these local bodies specifically reproved their misguided commissioners; sometimes in a gentle and forgiving tone,[4] more often by sharply reprimanding them;[5] but in every one of the cases recorded they were emphatic in their sentiments on the Resolutions. On the other hand, the adverse votes of commissioners from the presbyteries of the Border States and the farther South pleased these bodies, but did not always satisfy them. In some cases the Southern presbyteries insisted upon expressing sentiments far more hostile than those of their representatives.[6]

Thus the presbyterial action would indicate that each section of the country was more extreme in its stand than its representatives. The line of sectionalism was sharper in the Church than in the Assembly. This fact is more readily understood when it is recollected that in the choice of delegates, the older — and hence usually the more conservative — men were likely to be honored. Then, too, the presbyterial action came from one to four months after the meeting of the Assembly, and during the intervening period patriotic feeling had an opportunity to crystallize in both sections of the country.

---

[2] *Cf.* action of Presbytery of Clarion (western Penna.), *Presbyterian Banner,* June 22, 1861; of Presbytery of Washington (western Penna.), *ibid.,* October 26, 1861; of Presbytery of St. Clairsville (Ohio), *ibid.,* July 6, 1861; of Presbytery of Marion (Ohio), *Presbyter,* October 3, 1861; of Presbytery of Coshocton (Ohio), *Presbyterian Banner,* June 29, 1861; of Presbytery of Vincennes (Ind.), *Presbyter,* October 3, 1861.

[3] *Presbyterian Herald,* September 26, 1861.

[4] *Cf., e.g.,* action of Presbytery of Washington (western Penna.), *Presbyterian Banner,* October 26, 1861; also action of Presbytery of Clarion (western Penna.), *ibid.,* June 22, 1861.

[5] *Cf., e.g.,* action of Presbytery of Coshocton (Ohio), *ibid.,* June 29, 1861; of Presbytery of Wyaconda (Missouri), *Presbyterian Herald,* September 26, 1861; of Presbytery of Buffalo City (N. Y.), *Presbyterian,* July 6, 1861.

[6] *Cf. post,* pp. 93-95.

The action of the synods even more clearly illustrates the sectional divisions of the Old School Church. Of the five large conservative synods of the East, only one took occasion to commend the Assembly's stand.[7] In the West, nine of the eleven synods of which we have records for these years took such action.[8] Two of the Border State synods did not meet in 1861.[9] The other two [10] were decisive in their condemnation of the Assembly. The synods of the South saw in the Spring Resolutions a cause for secession from the Church.

The language of the reports of the presbyteries and synods often revealed the depth of feeling which animated the local bodies when the action of the Assembly was considered. Not satisfied with endorsing the Spring Resolutions, and expressing regret " that any of our Commissioners from Western New York should have voted with the minority," the Presbytery of Buffalo City also

Resolved, That we consider the revolt of the so-called seceding States a crime against God and the Church, no less than an offense against the Government, and that we can have no fellowship with those Presbyterian ministers or members who have given it their countenance and support, until by repentance and public confession of their sin, they purge them-

---

[7] The Synod of Philadelphia. *Cf.* report in *Presbyterian,* November 2, 1861.

[8] The two not taking such action were the Synod of Iowa and the Synod of Southern Iowa. The latter, however, passed strong resolutions in support of the Federal Government. (*Cf.* account in a " Letter from Iowa," *ibid.,* November 2, 1861.) It should be noted that it is impossible to make an entirely comprehensive statement of presbyterial and synodical action in 1861, as the records are not complete. The available *minutes* of the presbyteries and synods are very helpfully supplemented by reports of the actions of these bodies, published from time to time in Presbyterian newspapers.

[9] The Synod of Baltimore did not meet, " owing to the state of the country." (*Minutes of the General Assembly,* 1862, vol. xvi, p. 596.) In its meeting in 1863, this synod *"Resolved,* That we . . . concur with the last three Assemblies of our Church, in the expression of their sympathy with the Government, in this time of trial . . . ," *Minutes of the Synod of Baltimore* (Baltimore, 1864), pp. 13-14. Note that this is *not* an endorsement of the Spring Resolutions. The Synod of Upper Missouri also did not meet. *Minutes of General Assembly,* 1862, vol. xvi, p. 596.

[10] The Synods of Kentucky and Missouri. For action of these bodies, *cf. post,* pp. 98-101.

selves from the stain of a connection with this unholy conspiracy against our Union, our laws, and our liberties.[10a]

The Synod of Philadelphia, superlatively incensed by the "infatuation and wickedness of a portion of our fellow-citizens . . . [in seeking] to destroy this Government, which is the noblest monument of statesmanship and patriotism the world has ever seen, or is ever likely to see," urged its people to "pray for the suppression of the most groundless, cruel, and wicked rebellion in the history of any people."[11] Not content with resolutions pledging support to the Federal Government, the Synod of Chicago sent a pastoral letter to the churches under its care, exhorting them to pray for their country.[12]

In view of the frequent charges of extreme pro-slavery sentiments on the part of the Old School Presbyterians, it is noteworthy that individual presbyteries and synods were already willing, in the summer and fall of 1861, to commit themselves against slavery. The 1861 Assembly, it is true, had equivocated on that subject. When the Presbytery of Chillicothe (Ohio) presented a memorial alleging that the Act of 1818 condemning slavery[12a] had been abandoned, the Assembly blandly voted "that the memorialists be referred to all the deliverances of the General Assembly on this subject, from 1818 to the present time"![13]

Nevertheless, the Assembly of 1861 did take exception, in its approval of synodical records, to a statement of the Synod of South Carolina to the effect that the Act of 1818 had "been virtually rescinded." It made this exception on the ground that the General Assembly had "already in 1846 decided to the contrary; on which deliverance all the members from the South then in the Assembly voted in the affirmative."[13a] This adher-

[10a] *Cf.* report of proceedings in *Presbyterian,* July 6, 1861.
[11] *Cf.* report of proceedings, *ibid.,* November 2, 1861. The report is also given in the *Presbyterian Banner,* November 2, 1861.
[12] *Cf.* report of proceedings, *ibid.,* November 30, 1861.
[12a] *Cf. ante,* p. 25.
[13] *Minutes of the General Assembly,* 1861, vol. xvi, pp. 335-336.
[13a] *Ibid.,* pp. 332-333.

ence to the Act of 1818 — in spite of the lukewarmness and caution of its wording — was made the basis for protests against
slavery by several local bodies. In all, five presbyteries and
three synods voiced such sentiments. It is significant that all
of them were western. The Presbytery of Logansport (Indiana), unanimously expressed its earnest hope that the time
might soon come " when our church and country may be delivered from this enormous system of iniquity." [14] In the opinion
of the Presbytery of Highland (Kansas), slavery was the radical cause of the war.[15] The Synod of Wisconsin — evidently under the impression that resolutions could make facts — resolved
that the Church for nearly a century had been against slavery.[16]
The Synod of Allegheny unanimously looked forward to the
time when the sin of slavery should be removed from the church,
the country, and the world.[17] Similarly, the Synod of Southern
Iowa declared that,

while the one object of this war, on our part, is the preservation of government itself, we shall rejoice if we find that God, in his far-reaching
and merciful designs, is opening the way for the final removal of the
curse of American slavery, with all its attendant evils.[18]

The Synod of Chicago, on the contrary, argued against any
ulterior objectives in the war. Borrowing the words of a recent
resolution of Congress on the political crisis, the Synod after
full discussion resolved, *nem. con.,* that:

"The present deplorable civil war . . . is . . . waged . . . to defend
and maintain the supremacy of the Constitution, and to preserve the Union
with all the dignity, equality, and rights of the several states, unimpaired,
and that as soon as these objects are accomplished, the war ought to
cease." [19]

---

[14] *Presbyterian,* September 21, 1861. Besides the Presbytery of Logans-
port, the five presbyteries included: Richland (Ohio); Chillicothe (Ohio);
Washington (western Penna.); Highland (Kansas). The three synods were:
Wisconsin, Allegheny, Iowa.

[15] *Presbyter,* October 2, 1861.

[16] *Presbyterian,* October 26, 1861.

[17] *Presbyterian Banner,* October 19, 1861.

[18] *Cf.* "A Letter from Iowa," *Presbyterian,* Nov. 2, 1861.

[19] *Minutes of the Synod of Chicago.* . . . (Galesburg, 1861), pp. 13-14. The
resolution quoted by the Synod was one which had been passed by both

The importance of local action on the Assembly's adoption of the Spring Resolutions, however, lay neither in the matter of approval or non-approval of commissioners, nor in the anti-slavery actions of a few presbyteries and synods. It lay rather in the extent to which such action determined the future career of the Church. Would the Church remain intact? If it lost its synods in the states of the secession, would the Border State presbyteries and synods go, too? To what extent could it rely upon the support of the North and West? The general answers to these questions have already been suggested; more specific statements will illustrate the seriousness of the crisis the Church was passing through in the summer of 1861.

As far as the North and West were concerned, the hearty endorsement of so many presbyteries and synods and the fact that not a single unit voiced opposition to the Assembly's action, speedily made it clear that these sections were safe. Almost as speedily was it evident that the synods in the seceded states were lost — at least temporarily — to the Church. With them the verdict seems to have been practically unanimous that the Assembly had behaved unwisely, unjustly, and unconstitutionally. Certainly the sentiment for the separation of the Southern synods from the Church was everywhere in that section vehemently urged. As early as June, papers were in circulation among Presbyterians in Virginia advocating the calling of a convention at Richmond to ascertain the sense of the Presbyterians in regard to the formation of a General Assembly of that Church in the South. The circular charged that the Assembly had sustained the Government of the United States "in waging the most unchristian, criminal, and atrocious warfare of modern times upon the free and sovereign States known as the Confederate States of America. . . ."[20]

Presbyterian papers in these states were advocating immediate steps for the division of the Church and reflecting bitterly

houses of Congress by July 25, 1861. *Cf. Journal of the House of Representatives* . . . ," 37th Congress, 1st session, 1861, p. 123.

[20] The *Richmond Enquirer,* quoted in the *Presbyterian,* June 29, 1861.

on the fact that, in their speeches in the Assembly, their commissioners had not taken bolder ground for the South.[21]   The *Presbyterian Herald* (Louisville) reported, " As far as we have been able to learn, there will not be a voice raised against immediate separation in any of the presbyteries lying within the seceded States. They all seem to feel that they have been virtually exscinded by the Assembly, and that the action was intended to cut them off." [22]   *"And whereas,"* declared the Presbytery of Memphis, " This action virtually excommunicates the Presbyterian Church in the Confederate States — consisting of ten synods" containing 45 presbyteries, 706 ministers, 1,089 churches, and 75,000 communicants, "all of whom are cut off without a trial," it was deemed proper that an Assembly be invited to meet in Memphis the following May.[23]

The Presbytery of Charleston, finding that Dr. Spring's resolutions disregarded the rights and privileges of Southern states, seceded from the Assembly.[24]   Similarly, the Presbytery of East Alabama, regretting that the action of the Assembly had compelled its members to assume a position either of traitors to the actually existing government of their country, or else to differ hopelessly with the Church; and asserting that they could not remain in union with anyone who made political questions either the test of faith or the cause of dissensions and divisions in Christ's body, made plans to send commissioners to a Southern Assembly.[25]   The Presbytery of Western Tennessee on July 18 dissolved her connection with the Assembly and unanimously decided to be represented at a Southern Assembly in Augusta, Georgia, in December.[26]   Other presbyteries rapidly followed.

[21] *Presbyterian Herald,* " which still receives most of the Presbyterian papers from the seceded States," quoted in the *Presbyterian,* July 13, 1861.

[22] *Presbyterian,* July 13, 1861. The *Herald,* which the *Presbyterian* is here quoting, would be likely to see this situation darkly, having prophesied it as a result of General Assembly action.

[23] *Cf.* editorial, *Presbyterian,* July 6, 1861.

[24] *Presbyterian Banner,* August 17, 1861.

[25] *Presbyterian,* July 20, 1861 ; *Presbyterian Banner,* July 27, 1861.

[26] *Presbyterian Herald,* August 1, 1861.

The Presbytery of Tuscaloosa voted that not only the General Assembly, but the group of Southern members in it as well, deserved condemnation: "While some remained silent while the South was aspersed . . . others totally misrepresented the sentiment . . . of the southern people . . . [and] churches."[27] The Presbytery of Nashville took special care to sever all of her relations with the Old School Church, and unanimously cut off her connection with Danville Theological Seminary.[28] The small presbytery of Holston, in the extreme northeastern corner of Tennessee, apparently not yet ready to cut loose from the Assembly, decided to postpone action. It had no hesitation, however, in censuring the Assembly, citing Section 4 of Chapter xxxi of the Confession, which says, "Synods or councils are to handle or conclude nothing but that which is ecclesiastical, and are not to intermeddle with civil affairs which concern the Commonwealth unless by way of humble petition in cases extraordinary. . . ."[29] Before long it, too, had left the Church.[30]

All was not yet harmonious among the Presbyterians of the seceded states, however. One member of the Synod of Mississippi, which of the ten southernmost synods had been the most nearly completely represented in the Assembly of 1861, complained of the attitude of Presbyterians of other Southern states: "The Presbyteries of our Synod have been badgered and insulted in the newspapers printed outside of our own bounds, for being represented at the late General Assembly; and our delegates have been abused and misrepresented *ad nauseam,* and even Dr. Adger[31] . . . ventures to say . . . 'Southern men had no business to be in any such Assembly!'"[32] East-

[27] *Ibid.,* August 15, 1861.
[28] *Ibid.,* August 29, 1861.
[29] *Ibid.,* September 12, 1861.
[30] 1861 was the last year in which its churches made reports to the General Assembly.
[31] Dr. J. B. Adger was a member of the faculty of the Theological Seminary at Columbia, South Carolina.
[32] Letter of Dr. E. T. Baird of Mississippi to the New Orleans *True Witness,* quoted in the *Presbyterian,* August 31, 1861.

west sectionalism also disturbed Southern Presbyterians. The places suggested for the special convention of Southern Presbyterians were not pleasing to all: " Nor will we go in at the tail of a convention called for the convenience of the sea-board, but without reference to the convenience, or the wishes, of the western and weaker parts of the Church." [33] Yet hostility toward the North proved to be of far greater weight than divisions in the South, and the process of secession from the Old School Church went on apace in the presbyteries of the Confederate States.

It was to the Border State presbyteries that the passing of the Spring Resolutions brought the greatest problem. Here, in contrast to the virtual unanimity of feeling in the North and in the South, it was an extremely difficult matter to determine what the attitude of the presbyteries should be. The Presbytery of Paducah (Kentucky), though approving the action of its commissioners in opposing the Spring Resolutions, found its special committee divided on the wording of their report, and therefore was forced to postpone definite action.[34] The Presbytery of West Lexington was in session for three days before it could come to an agreement on the phrasing of its report. Then it finally adopted unanimously [35] a series of resolutions which, according to the *Presbyterian*, were " well considered, and were written, we judge, by one whose position in Church and State, is an enviable and honourable one — we mean Dr. Robert Breckinridge." [36] Mindful that general deliverances of the Assembly are entitled to respect and consideration, it respectfully voiced its objection to the Assembly's departing

[33] *Ibid.*

[34] Report of proceedings of Presbytery of Paducah, *Presbyterian Herald*, September 12, 1861.

[35] Thirteen ministers and thirteen elders were present. *Cf.* report of Presbytery of West Lexington, *Presbyterian*, September 28, 1861. The Assembly *Minutes* show that there were twenty-three ordained ministers in the presbytery.

[36] Editorial note, *Presbyterian*, September 28, 1861.

THE RESPONSE OF THE CHURCH

from the course required . . . by requiring of a great number of the office-bearers and members of the Church, the performance of acts, which had no other formal obligation but the order of the Assembly, and which could not be performed without danger to life, to character, to property, and to usefulness, on the part of many thousands of pious persons— members of the Presbyterian Church. . . . The Assembly had no right to require, or even advise, the tens of thousands of Presbyterians who are citizens of the States which had seceded from the United States, and are at war with them, to revolt against the actual governments under which they live; nor should it, under the pretext of a general fast, have required them to perform acts, which the Assembly could not fail to know, would subject them to criminal prosecutions, and . . . probably destroy the Presbyterian Church throughout considerable portions of at least ten States. . . . The Assembly ought, by no means, to have taken any action that necessarily involved the idea that it required any members of the Church, as a Christian duty, to revolt against any *actual* government under which they lived.

Yet, though sure of the injustice of the Assembly's action, the Presbytery of West Lexington was just as certain that this action was insufficient ground for separation from the Church. The reason given is interesting:

. . . we are equally clear in the conviction that the schism threatened in large portions of the seceded States, and actually accomplished in certain parts of them, finds no sufficient justification in anything done by the Assembly. For no one ought to suppose that any attempt would be made by the Church to enforce the erroneous principles of the particular minute of the Assembly which gave offense; nor has any one the right to assert that the Church will not, after due consideration, adopt and utter principles which are true on the whole subject.[37]

The Presbytery of Louisville was less pacific:

This Presbytery, therefore, utters this testimony against these errors of doctrine and principle and solemnly rejects the action of the Assembly— the premises as unconstitutional and of no binding force upon us.

The Presbytery, believing that the Kingdom of Christ is not to be limited by civil bounds, will cordially unite with all true and conservative men in our beloved Church, North and South, in defending and preserving the purity, unity, and prosperity of the Presbyterian Church in the United States of America.[38]

It is thus clear that the Presbytery of Louisville, in spite of

[37] Report of proceedings of Presbytery of West Lexington, *ibid.,* September 28, 1861; *Presbyterian Herald,* September 26, 1861.
[38] Quoted in editorial, *Presbyterian,* September 14, 1861.

its vigorous disapproval of the Assembly's alleged errors of doctrine and principle, was not yet ready to secede from the Church.

The *Presbyterian Herald* found the sentiment in Kentucky unanimous in opposition to the adoption of the Spring Resolutions, declaring that it had not discovered a single man who approved of the action of the Assembly in adopting them. Those who thought the resolutions right in themselves regarded it both unwise and inexpedient in the Assembly to pass them.[39] All apparently approved the main principles of Dr. Hodge's Protest.[40]

The action of the Synod of Kentucky in its fall meeting proved this estimate to be correct. The Synod found the requisition of the Assembly on all members and office-bearers of the Church living in the seceded States " to disregard the hostile governments which had been established over them, and in defiance of the actual authority of these governments, pray for their overthrow," incompetent to the Assembly, and neither wise nor discreet. It discovered no necessity for radical action on the part of the Synod, however:

> The action of the Assembly being exhausted by the occurrence of the day of prayer recommended,— and no ulterior proceedings under the order of the Assembly being contemplated — this Synod contents itself with this expression of its grave disapprobation of this action of the General Assembly, which the Synod judges to be repugnant to the Word of God, as that word is expounded in our Confession of Faith.

On the other hand, the Synod deplored the schism which had occurred in the states to the South. Although seeing in the schism a proof of the lack of wisdom of the General Assembly's action, the Synod decidedly condemned the schism itself as being without sufficient justification, and clearly stated its own position: " This Synod, it seems timely to declare . . . adheres

---

[39] *Presbyterian Herald,* quoted in the *Presbyterian,* July 13, 1861.
[40] *Ibid.* This statement represents the opinion of the *Presbyterian,* based upon the statements of the *Herald.*

with unshaken purpose to the Presbyterian Church in the United States of America. . . ." [41]

That the Synod refrained from more drastic action was probably due to the influence of Dr. Breckinridge, who, thoroughly opposed to the Spring Resolutions, was strongly in favor of preserving the unity of the Church, to which he had a deep sentimental attachment. He now pointed out that Presbyterian ministers, " a hard-headed set of men who do and think pretty much as they please, no matter what the circumstances may be which surround them," were not of so much importance; they could move, but their churches must stay. For this reason, he urged eloquently the necessity of the churches clinging together. [42]

There had been charges that all the Presbyterian newspapers in the non-seceding states except the *Presbyterian Herald* had closed their columns to opposition to the Assembly. [43] It was probably with this in mind that the report of the action of the Synod of Missouri was sent to the *Presbyter* with this explicit request:

Messrs. Editors:
  Please publish the following action of the Synod of Missouri adopted at Mexico, Mo., 11th inst., *unanimously and without debate*: "Resolved that the action of the General Assembly was unscriptural, unconstitutional, unwise, and unjust. We, therefore solemnly protest against it, and declare it of no binding force upon this Synod or upon members of the Presbyterian Church within our bounds." [44]

Explanatory communications later appearing in various Presbyterian papers indicate that the feeling was not so unanimous

---

[41] *Presbyterian*, November 2, 1861.
[42] Account in *Presbyterian Herald*, quoted in *Presbyterian*, November 2, 1861.
[43] *Cf.*, *e.g.*, communication from Owensboro (Kentucky) to the *Presbyterian Herald*, September 26, 1861.
[44] *Presbyter*, November 28, 1861. Another copy of the Missouri resolution may be found in a letter written on November 15, 1861, by Rev. J. J. Porter to the *Missouri Democrat*, printed in the *Presbyterian*, November 30, 1861.

as the report of the action itself might indicate.[45]   It was alleged that the only interest in the mind of the author of the
resolution, according to his own statement, was to assail the
constitutionality of the Assembly's action, not to touch its substance.[46]   Be that as it may, it was not likely so to be interpreted. As far as unanimity is concerned, one writer declared,
" From all the information at my command, my belief is that
a poll of the Church in the Synod of Missouri, either by ministers, ruling elders, or private members, would show a large
majority of loyal elders and members, if not of ministers. May
God forgive some of the last, for the pernicious example of open
disloyalty by which they may have led the young and the
inconsiderate into disaffection of their country!" [47]

One member of the Synod asserted that proof that the Synod
had no thought of the sin of schism lay in the fact that it proposed to ask for missionary funds from the Louisville Board
of Missions, and in case of failure there, to request the Board
in Philadelphia to take the Synod of Missouri under its
care.[48]   One church in the Synod,[49] as well as several individuals,[50] protested against the Synod's action on the Spring Resolutions. Missouri Presbyterians seem to have had much the
same feeling towards the General Assembly as those in Ken-

---

[45] *Cf., e.g.*, letter referred to in Note 44, above, in which the writer states
that illness in his family prevented his being present and casting a negative
vote; another letter, printed in the *Presbyterian,* December 7, 1861, alleges
that the Missouri resolutions were not intended to express disloyalty — had
they been, the vote would certainly not have been unanimous. *Cf.* also two
letters, *ibid.,* December 21, 1861; others, *ibid.,* January 18, 1862, January
25, 1862, February 8, 1862, all from Missourians, declaring their loyalty to
the Church and to the Government.

[46] *Cf.* communication of " D " to *Presbyterian,* December 7, 1861.

[47] *Ibid.*

[48] *Cf.* communication of Rev. A. P. Forman of Hannibal, Mo., in the
Presbyterian, December 5, 1861. Mr. Forman declared that the lateness of
the hour, combined with great fatigue on his part, caused him to neglect to
give the resolution proper attention. He did not vote at all on the matter.
Many others, he thought, felt the same.

[49] That at Kirkwood, Mo. *Cf. Presbyterian,* December 21, 1861.

[50] *Cf., e.g.,* the letters cited in note 45, above.

tucky, but their Synod was less felicitous in expressing it. In both states the feeling that the Assembly had acted unwisely was practically universal, that it had acted unconstitutionally was believed by many, but the element who held that its action constituted just cause for separation from the Old School Church was numerically very small in each state.

A third Border State synod, that of Baltimore, did not meet in 1861. Possibly because of this fact, possibly because Maryland was so soon definitely won for the Union, possibly because of the age, traditions, wealth, and standing of the Old School Church in her territory,[50a] and largely, no doubt, because of the wisdom of Old School leaders here,[51] this Synod avoided a serious crisis in 1861. The largest of her five presbyteries lay almost wholly in Pennsylvania; a much smaller one in Virginia. There were many ministers and laymen in this Synod whose loyalty was questioned.[52] Nevertheless, throughout the war, there was little anxiety displayed over the safety of the Synod of Baltimore in the Church. Attention in the matter of the Border State problem throughout the war period focussed on Kentucky and Missouri rather than on Maryland. In its 1863 meeting, the Synod of Baltimore *"Resolved,* That we, ministers and elders of this Synod, do concur with the last three Assemblies of our Church, in the expression of their sympathy with the Government, in this time of trial. . . ."[53] While this was scarcely a hearty endorsement of the various deliverances of the Assemblies of 1861, 1862, and 1863, it was so much more nearly favorable than the expressions of the Synods of Kentucky and Missouri that it placed this older, more conservative Synod in the light of a loyal adherent of the Assembly.

The fourth Border State Synod, that of Upper Missouri, had no meeting in 1861.[54] With three of its presbyteries in western

---

[50a] *Cf.* table of synods, *ante,* p. 44.

[51] The most prominent was Dr. J. C. Backus, pastor of the First Presbyterian Church of Baltimore, who had been Moderator of the 1861 Assembly.

[52] *Cf. post,* chapter 6.

[53] *Minutes of the Synod of Baltimore,* 1863 (Baltimore, 1864), pp. 13-14.

[54] *Minutes of the General Assembly,* 1862, vol. xvi, p. 596.

Missouri and the other in Kansas Territory, this small synod was bound to be torn by dissension in the matter of allegiance to the Federal Government. Two of its presbyteries ceased reporting to the General Assembly after 1861, and in 1864 the remaining presbyteries were joined to the Synod of Missouri.[55] While the small Synod of Upper Missouri was thus divided on the matter of loyalty to the General Assembly, with the definite decisions of the Synods of Kentucky and Missouri to stay in the Old School Church, and the extreme improbability that the Synod of Baltimore when it was again able to meet would take contrary action, the three more important Border State Synods appeared, in the fall of 1861, to be saved — for the time being, at least — for the Old School Church.

Meanwhile, the secession of the units of the Old School Church in the Confederacy had been virtually completed, and the organization of the Presbyterian Church in the Confederate States of America was effected at Augusta, Georgia, on December 4, 1861. Ten Synods and forty-five presbyteries constituted the new church, which numbered some 840 ministers and 72,000 communicants.[56] The geographical line of division between the two churches corresponded almost exactly with that between the seceding and the non-seceding states. In a paper prepared by Dr. Thornwell[57] and adopted at its first General Assembly, the new organization set forth its reasons for forming a separate denomination. This "Address of the Southern General Assembly to all the Churches of Jesus Christ throughout the Earth . . . ,"[58] disclaiming any desire to rend the Church, declared that the new Assembly was persuaded that the interests of true religion would be more effectually subserved by two independent Churches, under the circumstances in which the

[55] *Ibid.*, 1864, vol. xvii, p. 317.
[56] *Presbyterian Historical Almanac*, 1865, p. 333. The figures are from the *Minutes* of 1865, the first year in which statistics for the new church were printed. *Cf.* also *American Annual Cyclopaedia*, 1862, p. 707.
[57] Thompson, *History of the Presbyterian Churches*, p. 157, note 1.
[58] The Address is given, *ibid.*, Appendix xix, pp. 388-406.

two countries are placed." [59]   Had the General Assembly at
Philadelphia refrained from attempting to determine a political
question, it was possible that the ecclesiastical separation of the
North and South might have been deferred for years to come.[60]
But, "like Pilate, it obeyed the clamor of the multitude, and
though acting in the name of Jesus, it kissed the sceptre and
bowed the knee to the mandates of Northern phrenzy [sic]." [61]
Frankly admitting that "the mere unconstitutionality" of the
proceedings of the last Assembly was not in itself considered a
sufficient ground for separation, the address asserted that the
consequences of these proceedings rendered it impossible that
if the members North and South should attempt to continue to
meet together, "they could be . . . constrained from smiting
each other with the fist of wickedness." [62]

A second reason for the establishment of the separate church
was found in the fact that the bounding of churches by natural
lines had ever seemed a most natural and useful practice.   Such
a separation by the Southern churches would permit a richer,
fuller development of Presbyterian principles among them than
they could possibly receive "under foreign culture." [63]   One
fundamental difference between North and South accentuated
this desirability of separation along national lines: the antagonism of sentiment on the subject of slavery.   This hostility on
the part of the Northern element would handicap the Church
in its efforts for the slaves.   The Southern section of the Church,
"while even partially under the control of those who are hostile
to slavery, can never have free and unimpeded access to the
slave population. . . . This is too dear a price to be paid for a
nominal union.   We cannot afford to give up these millions of
souls and consign them, so far as our efforts are concerned, to
hopeless perdition, for the sake of preserving an outward unity
which, after all, is an empty shadow."   Dr. Thornwell, in thus

[59] *Ibid.*, p. 390.
[60] *Ibid.*, p. 393.
[61] *Ibid.*, p. 394.
[62] *Ibid.*, p. 394.
[63] *Ibid.*, p. 396.

presenting to the members of other churches " throughout the
Earth " this touching evidence of the interest of Southern Presbyterians in the spiritual welfare of the slaves, omitted mention
of the fact that in 1861 of the estimated 465,000 colored church
members of the South, less than three per cent were in the Old
School Church.[64] The document closed with a lengthy defense
of slavery.[65]

From the arguments of the address, it is thus evident that the
Southern Presbyterians themselves stressed as their reasons for
separation, not the action of the Philadelphia Assembly, but
rather the difficulty of avoiding political controversy in the Old
School Church, the desirability of national boundaries as church
boundaries, the divergence of opinion on slavery, and the
greater effectiveness of a Southern church in promoting the
spiritual welfare of the slaves.[66] It may be pertinent to add

[64] The *Presbyterian Banner,* February 18, 1861, quoting the *Educational
Journal* of Forsythe, Georgia, gives the above estimate of church membership, and presents interesting figures on the number of slaves in connection
with Christian churches:

Methodist Church, South	200,000
Methodist Church, North (Va. and Md.)	15,000
Missionary and Hard Shell Baptist	157,000
Old School Presbyterian Church	12,000
New School Presbyterian Church (supposed)	6,000
Cumberland Presbyterian Church	20,000
Protestant Episcopal Church	7,000
Campbellites, or Christian Churches	10,000
All other sects	20,000
Total	447,000

(Presumably the difference of 18,000 between this total and that given
above is accounted for by free colored membership in the South.)

[65] Thompson, *History of the Presbyterian Churches,* pp. 398-406.

[66] Similarly, the Synod of Mississippi, meeting in October, 1861 under the
moderatorship of Dr. B. M. Palmer, in adopting the report of a committee
on the action of the various presbyteries in separating from the General
Assembly of the United States, explained the reason for their separation
as follows: " They have severally, on the ground of inexpediency and impos-
sibility of maintaining, under existing circumstances, their previous relations with the General Assembly of the Presbyterian Church in the United

that, although the Southern Assembly in its address emphasized the contention that the provinces of the Church and State " are perfectly distinct," [67] it is recorded that the Assembly at one of its sessions " spent the first half hour in special prayer for the blessing of God upon the cause of the Confederate States, according to previous order." [68]

Would the Old School Church have divided, had there been no Spring Resolutions? The conservative *Presbyterian,* which before the convening of the 1861 Assembly had pleaded so earnestly for silence in the Assembly on the political situation,[69] by the fall of 1861 had concluded that a division was inevitable, regardless of Assembly action:

> Whatever may have been our desire, our hope of a different result had become enfeebled long before the last meeting of the General Assembly. It required no great sagacity to foresee a crisis approaching; extreme opinions on the slave question were begining to be entertained. . . . The Church to the North were prepared as a majority to adhere to the former deliverances of the General Assembly in regard to the agitating question, while wholly unwilling . . . to regard slavery as a morally good . . . institution. . . . No sooner did the politicians of the South broach the heresy of secession, than a large portion, at least, of the Church South seemed to acquiesce in the necessity of distinct ecclesiastical organization.
>
> We may err in the opinion, and yet we think we do not, when we say that the action of the last General Assembly had really little to do with the division of the Presbyterian Church. It would have come, had that Assembly never met. Politics and religion had become so mixed up that their hates and antagonisms were interchanged, and friendly relations and intercourse in the latter could scarcely have been maintained, while in the former the sword was drawn.[70]

The Old School Assembly's adoption of the Spring Resolutions may have hastened the breaking away of the Southern element — it was not the cause of that defection. On the other

States . . . dissolved those relations. . . ." Nothing was said of the Spring Resolutions. *Minutes of the Synod of Mississippi,* 1861 (Jackson, 1880), p. 6.

[67] Thompson, *op. cit.,* p. 391.

[68] *Minutes of the General Assembly of the Presbyterian Church in the Confederate States of America* (Augusta, 1861-1862), 1861, p. 12.

[69] *Cf. ante,* pp. 40-41.

[70] Editorial, *Presbyterian,* September 21, 1861.

hand, the debate of 1861 did have some far-reaching effects upon the history of the Old School Church. Though the Spring Resolutions were decisive in their statements, the terms employed were those least calculated to give offense to Border State men — far different from the violent language of the reports of most of the other religious groups.[71] There is evidence to indicate that the Hodge Protest, supported as it was by some of the great leaders of the Church, was effective in holding the Border State element in the fold,[72] even though very few commissioners from the Border States supported Hodge by their votes.[73] There was some basis for encouragement for them in the fact that more than one-fourth of the commissioners had voted against the Spring Resolutions. To be sure, this is ascribing a negative influence to the debate, but this does not minimize its importance.

Of more significance is the fact that the action of 1861 paved the way for a more emphatic and radical stand in each successive General Assembly during the war years. Once having taken the decisive step of pledging support to the political authorities, it was inevitable that similar action must be taken in every similar gathering as long as the political crisis continued. How far this policy, once embarked upon, was to carry this most conservative of churches, will be revealed in the next chapter.

Enough has already been said [74] of the tremendous pressure coming from the people "back home" to make it clear that without some such stand as was taken in the 1861 Assembly, the Church in the North — certainly at least the western portion of this section — would have been torn with dissension. The Assembly had to choose between a program of support of the Union which would wound a section of the Church prone

---

[71] Dr. R. E. Thompson, in his *History of the Presbyterian Churches* emphasizes this as an important factor in holding the Border States in the Old School Church. *Cf.* p. 205. *Cf.,* also, *ante,* pp. 73-79.

[72] Editorial, *Presbyterian,* July 13, 1861.

[73] *Cf. ante,* pp. 61-62.

[74] *Cf. ante,* pp. 82-85.

anyway to break away, and a policy of silence which would alienate an element, aggressive, fast-expanding, and otherwise loyal to the Church. When it chose the former alternative, the support and continued expansion of the important West was assured.

Similarly, the action of the Assembly was a distinct triumph for those advocating reunion with the New School Church. To what extent the passage of the Spring Resolutions mollified the New School leaders is illustrated by the complete change of attitude of the least friendly of the three leading New School papers — the *American Presbyterian*. How bitterly sarcastic this organ had been during the course of the debate, has already been told.[75] Yet in its first issue following the momentous decision of the Assembly, the friendliest sentiments were displayed. The *American Presbyterian* now expressed its " relief " and " gratification " over the Old School action, asserting that the Assembly in Philadelphia had increased the sense of security and of confidence in the ultimate triumph of the great cause of the Union.[76] Assuredly, the cause of reunion had been fostered by the Spring Resolutions.

Finally, the effect upon the public mind was of tremendous significance. The keen interest of the press in the attitude of the Assembly has been described, as well as its response once the Assembly had acted.[77] May, 1861, was an anxious month in the North, when it was of the utmost importance that sentiment should be aroused in universal support of the Federal Government. Yet thus early, when the war had scarcely started, nationalism had triumphed over conservatism in the Old School Assembly and the greatest Protestant denomination having a nation-wide membership — the largest non-political organization of national scope — had thrown the tremendous weight of its influence on the side of the Union.

[75] *Cf. ante*, pp. 74-75.
[76] Editorial, " The Assembly in Philadelphia," *American Presbyterian*, June 6, 1861.
[77] *Cf. ante*, pp. 85-86.

CHAPTER IV

THE ADVANCE OF THE OLD SCHOOL ASSEMBLY, 1862-1864

THE Old School General Assemblies of 1862 to 1864 were much freer to act on the matter of support of the Union than that of 1861 had been. In the earlier meeting there had been the apparent necessity of considering the rights and interests of the Southern wing of the Church. By 1862 the situation in this regard had completely changed. Although the reports of the General Assembly continued to include the names of Southern ministers until 1862, and of Southern synods and presbyteries until 1867, very few Old School Presbyterians suffered any illusions with regard to the *de facto* separation of the Southern wing of the Church.[1] Certainly the years 1862 to 1865 saw a steadily mounting spirit of enthusiasm for the Union cause. The more cautious leaders, having abandoned their solicitude with regard to the feelings of the Presbyterians of the seceded states, now stressed the importance of conciliating Border State men.[2] They succeeded in arousing the anxiety of "several prominent ministers and laymen in our church in the Northwest" lest the Border State leaders should be able to carry through in the 1862 General Assembly a repeal of the famous action of 1861.[3] As the *Presbyter* pointed out, however, by the spring of 1862 Kentucky's loyalty was no longer questioned, and while the editors of the *Danville Review* were having some serious difficulties with certain ministers "whom they are trying to prove disloyal," not enough opposition to

[1] *Cf., e.g.,* editorials, "Would the Church have divided, anyway?", *Presbyterian,* September 21, 1861; and "Southern Churches," *ibid.,* February 27, 1864.
[2] *Cf., e.g.,* arguments of Dr. J. M. MacDonald, Rev. J. L. McKee, Rev. A. P. Forman, and others, as given in reports of the proceedings of the 1862 General Assembly, seventh day, *Presbyterian,* May 31, 1862, p. 86.
[3] Editorial, *Presbyter,* April 17, 1862.

thwart a pro-Union policy in the Assembly was likely to be found in the Border States.[4]

The 1862 Old School General Assembly convened in Columbus, Ohio, on May 15. While not a commissioner from the states of the Confederacy was present, all except two of the fifteen presbyteries of the Border States were represented.[5] At its first session the Assembly accepted the invitation which the Ohio House of Representatives had unanimously and without outside prompting tendered, allowing the use of their hall in the capitol for the sessions of the General Assembly.[6] Perhaps this political setting had its influence upon the speakers. At any rate, there were frequent references to the political situation of the country: the battle of the *Merrimac* and the *Monitor*, " a conflict that . . . has placed us, in regard to self-defense in a position to defy the hostility of all creation [sensation] "[7]; Richmond, " the mausoleum of the rebellion," where one could read " in sombre capitals, this epitaph — *Hic jacet secesh*. [Applause] "[8]; Abraham Lincoln, whom history would place " not above, not along side, but not very far below the father of his country. [Applause] "[9] A statement from the Cincinnati *Gazette* alleging that the name of the President had not been mentioned in the prayers of the first two days' sessions, and that there had been no supplication for soldiers and for the Union cause, was very fiercely — and apparently justly [10]— attacked as false.[11] One of the eldest and most influential of the members in speaking on the cause of foreign missions wandered from the subject and " went into a lengthy and somewhat dif-

---

[4] *Ibid.* For the Robinson-Breckinridge controversy, *cf. post*, pp. 168-169; 174-177; 189-195.

[5] *Minutes of the General Assembly*, 1862, vol. xvi, pp. 585-589.

[6] *Cf.* report of proceedings of first day, *Presbyterian*, May 24, 1862, p. 82.

[7] Speech of Dr. Septimus Tustin, *Presbyterian*, May 24, 1862, p. 83.

[8] *Ibid.*

[9] *Ibid.*

[10] *Cf., e.g.*, report of the " loyal " prayers at the first day's sessions, as given on that day by the special correspondent, " W. M. F.," *Presbyterian*, May 31, 1862, p. 82.

[11] Report of sixth day of session, *Presbyterian*, May 31, 1862, p. 85.

fuse disquisition on the state of the country, denouncing rebellion. . . ." [12] Evidently many of the leaders were determined
that the Assembly should put itself on record as strongly patriotic, not only in its official actions, but also in the general tone
of its debates.

On the fourth day of the session Dr. R. J. Breckinridge read
a paper on the State of the Church and the Country, which he
proposed to be adopted as the General Assembly's deliverance
on that subject. " This paper was in the Doctor's vigorous and
unique style, and was listened to with the most profound and
silent attention. . . ." [13] When the paper was considered for
action, a two-days' debate ensued. " The debate was conducted
with great spirit and decorum, and in the midst of remarkable
surroundings. . . . Every part of this great hall, galleries and
all, was filled to overflowing with a deeply interested audience." [14] The paper had been published and handed to the
commissioners in pamphlet form. To Dr. Breckinridge's embarrassment, his enemies had seen to it that it was accompanied
by another pamphlet bearing generous quotations from the
resolutions the Synod of Kentucky had adopted the previous
autumn in opposition to the Spring Resolutions. [15] The source
of the embarrassment lay in the fact that Dr. Breckinridge had
written the Kentucky Synod's paper.

In content, Dr. Breckinridge's paper, " somewhat wordy and
violent like its author," [16] had little that was different from the
Spring Resolutions. In some 1500 words it said what had
been stated in 400 in 1861. The form of expression, however,
avoided a distinct declaration of the Church's duty of allegiance
to the civil government. Its author explained his apparent
change of front since the Synod of Kentucky's condemnation
of the 1861 General Assembly action, on the basis of this change

---

[12] Report of speech of Dr. George Junkin, *ibid.*
[13] Report of fourth day of session, *Presbyterian*, May 31, 1862, p. 88.
[14] Report of eighth day of session, *Presbyterian*, May 31, 1862, p. 86.
[15] *Ibid. Cf.* also, *ante*, pp. 98-99.
[16] Account of the Columbus correspondent of the New York *Evangelist*
[New School], quoted in *True Presbyterian*, June 19, 1862.

of form in which the deliverance appeared.[17]   Instead of asserting that the Church had obligations to strengthen, uphold, and encourage the Federal Government in the exercise of all its functions,[18] the General Assembly of the Church now through the Breckinridge deliverance declared it to be " the clear and solemn duty of the National Government to preserve, at whatever cost, the national Union and Constitution, . . . and . . . the bounden duty of the people who compose this great nation, each one in his several place and degree, to uphold the Federal Government. . . ."[19] Declaration of the duty of the Church to the Government had thus given way to declaration by the Church of the duty of the people toward the Government. Whoever owed the obligation, there was no doubt in 1862 as to its extent:

> To the Christian people scattered throughout those unfortunate regions, and who [sic] have been left of God to have any hand in bringing on these terrible calamities, we earnestly address words of exhortation and rebuke, as unto brethren who have sinned exceedingly, and whom God calls to repentance, by fearful judgments. . . . There is hardly anything more inexcusable connected with the frightful conspiracy against which we testify, than the conduct of those office-bearers and members of the Church who, although citizens of loyal States, and subject to the control of local Presbyteries and Synods, have been faithless to all authority, human and divine, to which they owed subjection.[20]

The Breckinridge paper was not equivocal on the question of the duty of allegiance!

Remembering that the Federal Government in its fight to preserve the Union was finding slavery an increasingly trying problem, one is curious to discover whether the Old School Church was ready to commit itself on that question in 1862. Although this General Assembly subsequently commended the work of the American Colonization Society in settling free

---

[17] Report of seventh day of session, *Presbyterian,* May 31, 1862, p. 86; also report of tenth day, *ibid.,* June 7, 1862, p. 89.

[18] *Cf.* resolutions of the Assembly of 1861 on the State of the Country, (Spring Resolutions), *ante,* pp. 50; 57-59; 62-63.

[19] *Minutes of the General Assembly,* 1862, vol. xvi, pp. 624-626.

[20] *Ibid.*

people of color in Liberia, "the land of their fathers' sepul-
chres,"[21] (evidently not to be taken literally in either the geographical or the anthropological sense), the deliverance on the
State of the Church and the Country avoided all mention of
slavery and the negroes.

That some action on slavery was contemplated by an element
of the Assembly's membership is indicated by a mysterious
blunder of the press in recording the action of the Assembly.
The New York *World,* the *Independent,* and other papers,
printed as the deliverance adopted by the Assembly on the State
of the Country a paper strongly condemning slavery.[22] The
Presbyterian hastened to explain that this was simply "a memorial of some irresponsible parties outside,"[23] but others
hinted that it was probably the "worse paper" which, it was
alleged, would have been offered had not the Breckinridge paper
— probably as a compromise between the anti-slavery men and
some of the "silence" men — superseded it.[24]

The debate on the Breckinridge paper was long and ardent.
Dr. Breckinridge himself did a good share of the talking.
Thanks also to the appeal to the Assembly of a dispute with a
rival editor in Kentucky, (Dr. Stuart Robinson),[25] the fighting
editor of the *Danville Review* was having a delightful time: "as
much on his feet as the Colossus of Rhodes," one New School
observer put it — adding that "his papers and his utterances,
his appeals and protests, his position as Professor, his opinions
and his quarrels, have certainly occupied little less than half
the time."[26]   In justice to the Doctor, (though he himself would
probably have regarded these charges as conferring a compli-
ment rather than demanding vindication), it must be said that

[21] Report of tenth day of session, *Presbyterian,* June 7, 1862, p. 90.
[22] Editorial, "Mysterious Blunder of the Press . . . ," *True Presbyterian,*
June 19, 1862.
[23] *Ibid.*
[24] *Ibid.*
[25] *Cf. post,* pp. 189-195.
[26] Columbus correspondent of the New York *Evangelist,* quoted in an
article, "The Assembly from a New School Standpoint," *True Presbyterian,*
June 19, 1862.

as one of the chief instruments in bringing about the division in the Church in 1837,[27] he was not likely to be popular with New School men. At any rate, that he was hugely enjoying his prominence there cannot be the slightest doubt:

> Now I will agree to this . . . I will take unto and upon myself all the blame that may attach on this account before men, if, when we have all gone up above, they will not claim the glory of it there! [Laughter]. . . . One very hot day a West India lady directed her servant to take some ice, and some water, and some lemon, and mix them for her to drink. "And if you please, mistress," said the servant, "shall I put in a little nutmeg?" "Begone, you beast," screamed the mistress, "*do you think I would drink punch?*" [A laugh] So now, when I would put in the "nutmeg" and make the question unequivocal, the brethen manifest abhorrence of the whole matter. [Continued merriment.] [28]

Dr. Breckinridge's supporters in the debate were emphatic. Far more wicked than the conspiracy of Catiline or the treason of Absalom — in fact, with no parallel in wickedness in all the records of the past — they found this Southern rebellion.[29] No wonder Dr. Stuart Robinson solemnly appealed from the judgment of 1862 to that of 1870! [30]

While the opponents of the Deliverance occasionally alleged that it was unconstitutional,[31] the vast bulk of their argument was leveled against it on the grounds of inexpediency: it would place the Presbyterians of the Border States in an unnecessarily embarrassing position. Commissioners from Missouri, from Kentucky, from Maryland, reiterated this charge. Dr. J. C. Backus, Moderator of the 1861 Assembly, declared that from one-third to two-thirds of the various congregations of the Synod of Baltimore sympathized with the South.[32] There

---

[27] Gillett, *op. cit.*, vol. ii, pp. 503-514; Thompson, *History of the Presbyterian Churches*, pp. 115-128.

[28] Report of ninth day of session, *Presbyterian*, June 7, 1862, p. 89.

[29] *Ibid.*

[30] *Cf.* article, "The Assembly from a New School Viewpoint," *True Presbyterian*, June 19, 1862; also, report of ninth day of session, *Presbyterian*, June 7, 1862, p. 89.

[31] *Cf., e.g.*, argument of Dr. S. B. McPheeters, report of ninth day of session, *ibid.*, June 7, 1862, p. 89.

[32] Report of ninth day of session, *ibid.*, June 7, 1862, p. 89.

is no record of a single Border State commissioner defending the Breckinridge paper in the debate.[33]

All of the argument must have seemed rather futile, for there could not possibly have been any doubt from the start what the outcome of the vote on the paper would be. Nevertheless, when the time for the vote arrived, the house became excited, and it was with some difficulty that the Moderator could keep order.[34] The decision was overwhelming: 206 *yeas*, 20 *nays*.[35] Of the 20 *nays*, 12 came from the Border State Synods of Baltimore, Kentucky, and Missouri. Eleven *yeas* came from these synods.[36] Much the same factors apparently prompted this vote as had motivated the action of 1861.[37] There was evidence of a similar self-consciousness with regard to the opinion of the world; a similar show of East-West sectionalism; [38] a similar regard for the sentiments of the people back home. " To have refused to make any declaration," asserted a New School observer, " would have been construed into practical disloyalty, and would have been followed by a wild revolt, especially in the Northwest." [39] Dr. Breckinridge had in his arguments stressed the day of reckoning when the commissioners should return home: " You dare not go home and face your congregations if you do not speak out. . . . Are you fearful of excitement? Well, there are ' dumb dogs ' that ought to be made to bark. This rebellion is the wickedest thing that ever cursed God's

[33] This statement is based on the account given in the *Minutes* and on the full reports of the General Assembly in the *Presbyterian*. The *Presbyterian* records numerous speeches by 11 Border State men in opposition to the Breckinridge paper.
[34] Report of ninth day of session, *Presbyterian*, June 7, 1862, p. 89.
[35] *Minutes of the General Assembly*, 1862, vol. xvi, pp. 623-624.
[36] Not including 4 *yeas* from the Presbytery of Carlisle in the Synod of Baltimore — a presbytery lying almost wholly in Pennsylvania. *Cf. ante,* p. 44.
[37] *Cf. ante,* pp. 73-85.
[38] *E.g.,* in the choice of a Moderator. *Cf.* report of first day of session, *Presbyterian*, May 24, 1862, p. 82. Dr. Charles C. Beatty of Steubenville, Ohio, was chosen.
[39] Article, " The Assembly from a New School Viewpoint," *True Presbyterian,* June 19, 1862.

earth. [Can the good Doctor have forgotten the story of the Garden of Eden?] Will you sit still and not denounce it?" [40] Dr. Stuart Robinson's *True Presbyterian*, in reviewing the action of the Assembly, declared that many voted contrary to their first expressed intentions,[41] and that a large number, if not a large majority, were at heart opposed to any further deliverance by the Assembly, but were compelled to vote for the paper only because the circumstances under which it was presented would have made their vote against it mean what it did not mean.[42] Public opinion required, he said, if such a minute was offered, that it should not be voted down in the Assembly.[43]

Nevertheless, though the elements of public opinion, sectionalism, and home pressure played their part in bringing about the action of 1862, it is noteworthy that the struggle was much less severe than that of the previous year. The two-days' debate, in spite of the fact that over ninety per cent of the votes were ultimately to be on the Breckinridge side, proved to be largely monopolized by anti-action Border State men, except, of course, for the "ubiquitous and sempiternal Breckinridge,"[44] and one or two long-winded old gentlemen from the North. The vast majority, content as long as they could cast their own votes for the measure, were willing to let the Border State men talk themselves out. Certain powerful leaders who had been more or less undecided in 1861, it is true, now came out emphatically for action.[45] But even Dr. Stuart Robinson — hostile as he was to the action taken — declared that "with the exception of the temporary furor that seemed to reign supreme"

[40] Report of seventh day of session, *Presbyterian*, May 31, 1862, p. 86.
[41] Editorial, "Mysterious Blunder . . . ," *True Presbyterian*, June 19, 1862.
[42] Editorial, "The General Assembly — Its Action," *ibid.*, June 5, 1862.
[43] Editorial, "Impressions of the World Without . . . ," *ibid.*, June 12, 1862.
[44] New York *Evangelist*, quoted in an article, "The Assembly from a New School Viewpoint," *True Presbyterian*, June 19, 1862.
[45] *Cf., e.g.,* speech of Dr. George W. Musgrave, report of ninth day of session, *Presbyterian*, June 7, 1862, p. 89. Dr. Musgrave was chairman of the famous committee of nine in 1861, and had been one of the signers of the Majority Report. *Cf. ante,* p. 56.

during the discussion of the Breckinridge paper, he had never seen a General Assembly characterized more peculiarly by the dignity, manliness, and good sense of its discussions. " It made us feel proud of our Church, in spite of all its novel tendencies to the heresies of Erastianism." [46] Nevertheless, the reaching of a decision just before a Saturday adjournment brought a feeling of relief to the members. "How sweet and needful is the coming Sabbath," sighed the special reporter of the *Presbyterian,* " May it bring peace *and rest to every* soul!" [47]

The generally conciliatory attitude of Northern members of the Assembly is well illustrated in the action taken on the hostile memorial which the Synod of Missouri had adopted [48] with regard to the Spring Resolutions. In spite of the fact that the resolution recommended by the Committee on Bills and Overtures merely expressed regret at the action of the Synod of Missouri as likely to encourage insubordination to ecclesiastical authority, the report of the committee was laid on the table, and no other action was taken on the matter. [49] Four formal protests against the Breckinridge deliverance, with a total of fourteen signatures, were entered upon the minutes. [50]

In general, the action of the Assembly on the Breckinridge deliverance met with widespread approval. Presbyteries and synods endorsed the action — in fact there is no record of any such body outside of the Border States expressing any disapproval. In several of the local meetings, resolutions stronger than the Breckinridge sentiments were adopted. The Presbytery of Chippewa (partly in Minnesota, partly in Wisconsin), for example, after endorsing the Assembly stand also took occasion to "hail the new call of the President for 300,000 additional volunteers as an omen of the successful conclusion of the war, and promise to use their influence in all lawful ways, to induce our able-bodied young men to give an early response

[46] Editorial, *True Presbyterian,* May 29, 1862.
[47] Report of ninth day of session, *Presbyterian,* June 7, 1862, p. 89.
[48] *Cf. ante,* p. 99.
[49] Report of eleventh day of session, *Presbyterian,* June 7, 1862, p. 90.
[50] *Minutes of the General Assembly,* 1862, vol. xvi, pp. 636-640.

to the call. . . ."[51] Here was a Presbyterian body not only acting on matters political, but undertaking military functions as well!

Almost as extreme was the resolution of the Synod of Buffalo which declared that it was a religious duty " to support the government by our influence, our treasure, by our prayers, and if called thereto, by laying down our lives in its defence."[51a]

It was particularly on the subject of slavery, however, that certain individual units were ready to forge ahead of the Assembly. Three presbyteries and three synods in 1862 demanded action by the Church on that subject. The Presbytery of Highland (Kansas) had already, several weeks before the Assembly of 1862, demanded that that body adopt a full and complete deliverance on slavery — " now everywhere recognized as the cause of secession in the States and schism in the Church."[52] The Presbytery of Chillicothe (Ohio) in its summer meeting resolved that it was glad to see more unanimous views on slavery among various denominations of Christians, "especially in our branch of the Church," and recommended action, in the form of collections and so forth, for the freed slaves of the District of Columbia.[53] The Presbytery of Madison (Indiana) was prepared to express one sentiment omitted in the Breckinridge paper — that slavery was the chief, if not the sole, cause of the war: " The war has now reached the point which presents the direct issue — the destruction of the Government or of slavery. . . ."[54] The Synod of Indiana by a vote of about 50 to 7 passed resolutions to the effect that since God would not turn away his judgment while the sin of slavery persisted, therefore it was the duty of all citizens to urge the government to do away with slavery.[55] Similar resolutions were passed by the

[51] Report of proceedings of Presbytery of Chippewa, *True Presbyterian,* August 14, 1862.
[51a] Report of Synod of Buffalo, *Presbyterian,* September 6, 1862.
[52] Report of Presbytery of Highland, *Presbyter,* May 8, 1862.
[53] Report of Presbytery of Chillicothe, *ibid.,* September 4, 1862.
[54] Report of Presbytery of Madison, *ibid.,* September 25, 1862.
[55] Resolutions of Synod of Indiana, *ibid.,* October 30, 1862. The resolutions were offered by Dr. E. D. MacMaster.

Synod of Northern Indiana.[56] The meetings of these two synods occurred after the issue of Lincoln's preliminary emancipation proclamation of September 22. No doubt it was of influence in gaining votes for action of this kind. The Synod of Southern Iowa specifically approved of Lincoln's proclamation, and added that, if emancipation was to be a by-product of the war, they were thankful.[57]

The Synod of Illinois, however, meeting a month after Lincoln's first proclamation on emancipation, was not yet ready to take a stand against slavery. By a vote of 26 to 21, it rejected a paper condemning that institution. It may well be that the drastic nature of the resolutions proposed was fatal to their passage, for besides declaring that the whole nation should individually and collectively confess the sin of slavery, they demanded that the members and ministers who had failed in the past to maintain a clear, unequivocal stand against slavery, "with grief and sorrow . . . confess this their sin against God, and . . . implore His forgiveness." To cap the climax, they maintained that it was "the duty of the pastors of our churches to instruct all to whom they minister, in the principles embraced in this action."[58] The wonder is, not that the resolutions did not pass, but that the vote was not more adverse! It was clear that anti-slavery sentiment was rising in the local units of the Church—particularly in the West. While there was no disapproval of the Breckinridge deliverance in the North and West, in Kentucky and Missouri that paper had a most disturbing influence, and played a vital part in the crisis through which the Old School Church in those states passed during the years of the war.[59]

The secular press of the North was not as unanimous in its approval as the Old School presbyteries and synods. The *Crisis* (Copperhead Democratic, Columbus) was emphatic in its opposition:

[56] *Presbyter,* November 6, 1862.
[57] *Ibid.,* October 16, 1862.
[58] *Ibid.,* October 30, 1862.
[59] *Cf. post,* chapter 6.

With thousands of others, we express our deep regrets, that this body of ancient [probably a case of misplacement of adjective!] and respected Christians . . . should have fallen into the snare of the evil one, and made politics instead of Christ's Gospel the great *I Am* of their proceedings.

The *Crisis* discounted the importance of the size of the vote on the Breckinridge paper: " Men do not go to Heaven by majorities; St. Peter does not sit at the gate to count up election returns." [60]

The Breckinridge paper did not " drive off the Border State Synods," as some had anticipated.[61] They " have only to stand boldly by the truth," asserted Dr. Robinson in his *True Presbyterian,* " just as they did last year, until some attempt shall be made to coerce them or their members in judicial form; which attempt will not be made shortly. . . . Better days, we trust, are yet ahead." [62] Perhaps it is just as well that Dr. Robinson did not realize how far ahead these better days were.

Political events of tremendous importance in the relation of the Old School Church to the war and its problems took place during the year which intervened between the Assemblies of 1862 and 1863. The proclamations of September 22, 1862, and January 1, 1863, on the subject of the emancipation of the slaves, it was clear to all Old School Presbyterians, would force the General Assembly of 1863 to take some action on the problem of slavery. Carefully as that vexing question had been avoided in the deliverances of 1861 and 1862, it could not be dodged in 1863. What would the answer be?

A month before the 1863 Assembly, the slavery-hating *Presbyter* thought it saw grounds for alarm. Danger of a retrograde action it thought not impossible:

Let men strong and true and sound be sent. . . . Let the Presbyteries of the free States select men who will not inquire what border States men

---

[60] *Cf.* quotations from the *Crisis* in an article, " Impressions of the World . . . ," *True Presbyterian,* June 12, 1862.

[61] *Cf.* argument of Dr. Cyrus Dickson, report of ninth day of session, *Presbyterian,* June 7, 1862, p. 89.

[62] Editorial, " The General Assembly — Its Action," *True Presbyterian,* June 5, 1862.

think or wish, in order to know what to do. . . . We have men in the East of high standing and position, who, as a matter of policy, would do more and yield more to conciliate the Synod of Baltimore than the whole of the Northwest. . . . Our Church stands on a proud eminence of loyalty to Christ and loyalty to the State. Let it not come down.[63]

Peoria, a little city of 15,000 [64] in the Illinois prairie-country, had been chosen for the place of meeting of the 1863 Assembly. The Northwest was becoming more important in the eyes of Old School Presbyterians!

There is no doubt that a large number of the commissioners hoped that having taken decisive action in 1861 on the state of the country and uttered a more formal and comprehensive statement on the same subject in 1862, the Assembly would not be required to repeat its testimony of sympathy with the Federal Government in 1863.[65] The Assembly had " ever been . . . content to abide calmly by its recorded deliverances." [66] Reiteration in 1863 was prompted by a motion coming from the flag-waving element. It was proposed that a committee be appointed to cause the national flag to be raised over the church edifice in which the Assembly was convened.[67] A motion to table was immediately met by a call for the *ayes* and *nays*. The motion to table was then lost by a vote of 93 to 131. One can readily understand that to some of the 93 the raising of a national emblem over an edifice devoted to a world religion may have seemed incongruous — even sacrilegious. If, however, this was the main motive influencing the vote, the latitude of men's consciences must be strangely affected by geographical longitude; for here, too, as in the previous votes, East seemed to be pitted against West. Western Pennsylvania and the Northwest voted 30 to 83 against tabling; but in the East, while the majority voted the

[63] Editorial, " The Next Assembly," *Presbyter,* April 8, 1863.

[64] Its population in 1860 was 14,045. *Cf. Population of the United States in 1860, compiled from the Original Returns of the Eighth Census* (Washington, 1864), p. 98.

[65] *Cf.* opening statements of Lowrie and Humphrey papers, *Minutes of the General Assembly,* 1862, vol. xvii, pp. 57, 60.

[66] *Ibid.,* p. 57.

[67] *Ibid.,* p. 26.

same way, the margin was very narrow: 34 to 40. In the Border State synods, the vote was 29 to 8 in favor of tabling.[68]

The move to table having been defeated, it was decided to refer the whole subject of action on the state of the country to a committee of seven. After a three-day interval, the special committee in its report offered a carefully worded paper, mentioning the general reluctance of the Assembly to repeat its testimonies and the completeness of previous deliverances in expressing the horror of the Assembly at the wickedness of the rebellion, its conviction of the guilt of those responsible for the fratricidal strife, its insistence on the duty of the government and the people to uphold the civil authorities, its rebuke of ministers and members who had aided the rebellion. Similarly, the Assembly had emphatically stated its sympathy for those guiltlessly suffering, its reproof of all wilful disturbers of the public peace, and its exhortation to those subject to the Assembly's care to discharge every duty tending to uphold the Government. On the other hand, the report recognized the desirability of reaffirming these statements in a manner free from all imputations of haste and excitement, the entire harmony between the duties of a citizen to the government and the duties of a Christian to the Great Head of the Church, and the inappropriateness of Christians seeming to stand back from their duty. The Church must uphold the constitutional authorities; indeed, the sphere of the Church is wider and more searching in matters of public interest than the sphere of the civil magistrate *in this important respect,* that the civil authorities can take cognizance only of overt acts, while the law of the Church of God is the interpreter, searches the heart, makes every man subject to the civil authority for conscience's sake, and declares that man truly guilty who allows himself to be alienated in sympathy and feeling from any lawful duty, or who does not conscientiously prefer the welfare and especially the preservation of the government to any party or partisan ends. Asserting that the Assembly was ready to declare its attachment to all

---

[68] The *ayes* and *noes* may be found *ibid.,* pp. 26-27.

of these principles, the Committee's report recommended that the particular action contemplated in the original resolution (that is, the raising of the flag over the church edifice in which the Assembly was meeting), be no further urged upon the attention of the body.[69]

As the report was submitted on Saturday, it was decided by the Assembly to postpone action until Monday.[70] In the meantime a curious incident prompted a change in the final wording of the report. On Sunday morning the members of the Assembly and the citizens of Peoria were amazed to see a flag floating over the Assembly church; their amazement changed to horror, however, when they discovered that the flag was not the Stars and Stripes, but the Stars and Bars! Some wag was evidently having a good time at the Assembly's expense. The rebel flag was quietly taken down, and on Monday morning the trustees of the church hoisted the national ensign, which continued to be displayed to the end of the Assembly's sessions, "to the satisfaction of all but a portion of 'the disloyal 90' . . . ."[71]

As a result of this episode, when the report of the committee was debated on Monday morning, the Assembly found an additional reason for not taking action on the original resolution, and inserted in the report the clause, "as the trustees of this church, concurring in the desires of many members of this Assembly, have displayed from this edifice the American flag, the symbol of national protection, unity, and liberty."[72] Thus amended, the report of the committee was passed, after brief debate, by the decisive vote of 180 to 19.[73] Thirteen of the nineteen adverse votes came from the Border States; four of the other six, from the East.

The Assembly then demonstrated its conciliatory temper by

[69] The report of the committee may be found *ibid.*, pp. 57-59.
[70] *Ibid.*, p. 47.
[71] The incident is told under the title, "The Flag," in the *True Presbyterian*, July 30, 1863.
[72] *Minutes of the General Assembly*, 1863, vol. xvii, p. 56.
[73] *Ibid.*, p. 57.

adopting with but one dissenting vote a paper prepared by Dr. E. P. Humphrey of Kentucky — a paper which had been originally introduced as a substitute for the greater portion of the committee report. The Humphrey paper, asserting that the loyalty of the Assembly as a body to both the Church and the civil government was assured, declared that the Assembly on this subject contented itself by enjoining upon all people the authority of the Constitution and laws of the land. It then urged upon the people the inculcation of the duty of confessing the many sins of the people of the land and the determination to walk more uprightly.[74] Having already adopted more clear-cut and emphatic resolutions, the Assembly had no objection to endorsing also this milder paper. It is significant that in contrast to action at the two previous Assemblies,[75] but one commissioner [76] entered a formal protest against the action of the 1863 Assembly on the State of the Country. The obviously conciliatory tone of the committee report had had its effect.

The Assembly had not been able to avoid a deliverance upon the State of the Country; it was no more successful in the matter of action on the subject of slavery. The Presbytery of Saline (Illinois) had requested that the General Assembly solemnly reaffirm the testimony of 1818 in regard to slavery.[77] The Committee on Bills and Overtures, to which this request was referred, reported as follows: [78]

The Assembly has, from the first, uttered its sentiments on the subject of slavery in substantially the same language. The action of 1818 was taken with more care, made more clear, full, and explicit, and was adopted unanimously. It has since remained that true and scriptural deliverance on this important subject, by which our church is determined to abide. It has never been repealed, amended, or modified, but has frequently been referred to, and reiterated in subsequent Assemblies. And when some

---

[74] *Ibid.*, pp. 60-61.

[75] *Cf. ante*, pp. 64-70; 116.

[76] Rev. Lewis C. Baker, of New Jersey. *Minutes of the General Assembly*, 1863, vol. xvii, pp. 67-68.

[77] *Ibid.*, p. 55. For the nature of the actions of 1818, 1845, and 1846, *cf. ante*, pp. 24-26.

[78] *Minutes of the General Assembly*, 1863, vol. xvii, p. 55.

persons fancied that the action of 1845 in some way interfered with it, the Assembly of 1846 declared, with much unanimity, that the action of 1845 was not intended to deny or rescind the testimony on the subject, previously uttered by General Assemblies; and by these deliverances we still abide.

This masterpiece of equivocation and indefiniteness was passed by the Assembly with little debate. When a Kentucky member [79] moved to amend by inserting the word " all " before "deliverances," in the last line, the amendment was lost. Perhaps the Assembly did not want to go on record as considering the action of 1845 as of equal weight with that of 1818. The same member unsuccessfully tried to have the report tabled; [80] the Assembly would not remain silent. What the committee report actually meant probably no one knew. Had the committee members been trying solely to be ironical, they could scarcely have improved on their first sentence. But how easily they themselves, after making a few seemingly direct statements about the action of 1818, fell into "substantially the same language" when dealing with the actions of 1845 and 1846! The Old School Assembly was indeed living up to its reputation for conservatism when, five months after the Emancipation Proclamation, it chose to abide by its former deliverances on slavery. Forced to take a stand, it cautiously chose an inconspicuous attitude. Perhaps, however, the emphasis should rather be placed on the fact that the Assembly took any action on slavery at all; certainly in this it was going far beyond the Assemblies of 1861 and 1862.

The 1863 deliverance on the State of the Country, like its two predecessors, met with widespread approval among the local units of the Church in the North. Occasionally a synod or presbytery discovered unique phrases to express the patriotism which was becoming more and more extreme in its utterances among them. The Synod of Chicago, for example, endorsed the 1863 paper in language that taxes the imagination: " Resolved that . . . we do, with our right hands on the tombs

[79] Dr. E. P. Humphrey. Ibid., p. 55.
[80] Ibid., p. 56.

of our fathers and our left on the heads of our children, solemnly pledge ourselves to the task of transmitting to the latter, unimpaired, the rich inheritance bequeathed to us by the former. . . ."[81] Though the form of expression used by other synods and presbyteries was not always so picturesque, their statements, where action was taken, was uniformly loyal to the Assembly deliverance.

When the General Assembly of 1864 convened in Newark, New Jersey, in May, a new note of optimism with regard to the state of the country was immediately apparent. On the second day of the session, when a resolution that the Assembly set aside a day " for fasting, humiliation, and special prayer " was proposed, a substitute resolution voiced in a decidedly different tone was promptly offered and unanimously adopted:

Whereas, There is enough in the recent operations of our army to claim our especial gratitude to God, and whereas, what remains undone demands our most sincere prayers to and reliance upon Him, (without whom all human effort is vain), therefore,

Resolved, That the Assembly, in view of the condition of our country, will spend Wednesday afternoon next in thanksgiving to Almighty God for past mercies, and in prayer for his continued blessing upon our country.[82]

Copies of this resolution were then sent to other religious bodies convening at the same time: the New School General Assembly, in Dayton, Ohio; the General Conference of the Methodist Episcopal Church, in Philadelphia; the General Assembly of the United Presbyterian Church, in Pittsburgh; the General Synod of the Reformed Presbyterian Church, in Philadelphia.[83] These bodies were cordially invited to join with the Old School Assembly in devoting this particular afternoon to a Thanksgiving service. Those in session on the day specified accepted the invitation and complied with the request.[84]

---

[81] *Minutes of the Synod of Chicago,* 1863, p. 6.

[82] *Minutes of the General Assembly,* 1864, vol. xvii, pp. 267, 270.

[83] *Ibid.,* pp. 270, 275.

[84] *Ibid.,* pp. 275; 284-285; 287; 294; 306. The New School and the Methodist Episcopal bodies accepted the invitation; the General Assembly of the United Presbyterian Church was not yet in session on the day specified;

The changed temper of the General Assembly of 1864 was apparent not only in its optimistic attitude on the state of the country; this Assembly, in contrast to that of 1863, made a frank, extended, and emphatic pronouncement on the subject of slavery. The plaintiff in this case was the Presbytery of Newton [85] (New Jersey), which addressed to the General Assembly a memorial asking the Assembly to " take such action as in their wisdom seems proper to meet the present aspects of human bondage in our country." [86] Judge Stanley Matthews, a ruling elder representing the Presbytery of Cincinnati, prepared for the Committee on Bills and Overtures, of which he was a member, a lengthy report on slavery, which was, after a few amendments, " with almost entire unanimity, adopted." [87]

Beginning with the statement that " From the earliest period of our Church,[88] the General Assembly delivered unequivocal testimonies upon this subject, which it will be profitable now to reaffirm," the report quoted the emphatic condemnations of slavery made by the Synod of New York and Philadelphia in 1787, and by the General Assemblies of 1795, 1815, and 1818.[89] No mention was made of the actions of 1845 and 1846.[90]

Such were the early and unequivocal instructions of our Church. . . . Whether a strict and careful application of this advice would have rescued the country from the evil of its condition, and the dangers which have since threatened it, is known to the Omniscient alone. Whilst we do not believe that the present judgments of our Heavenly Father . . . have been inflicted solely in punishment for our continuance in this sin; yet it is our judgment that the recent events of our history, and the present condition of our Church and country, furnish manifest tokens that *the time has at length come, in the providence of God, when it is His will that every*

---

the General Synod of the Reformed Presbyterian Church was no longer in session on that day. The messages of acceptance of the first two bodies named may be found *ibid.,* pp. 275; 284-285.

[85] *Ibid.,* p. 276.

[86] *Presbyterian Historical Almanac,* 1865, p. 47.

[87] *Minutes of the General Assembly,* 1864, vol. xvii, pp. 288, 296.

[88] It is interesting to note that before amendment the report began, " In our early days our Church in America delivered. . . ." *Ibid.,* p. 296.

[89] For the early stand of the Assembly on slavery *cf. ante,* pp. 24-26.

[90] *Cf. ante,* pp. 26; 123-124.

vestige of human slavery among us should be effaced, and that every Christian man should address himself with industry and earnestness to his appropriate part in the performance of this great duty.

Whatever excuses for its postponement may heretofore have existed, no longer avail. . . . Under the influence of the most incomprehensible infatuation of wickedness, those who were most deeply interested in the perpetuation of slavery *have taken away every motive for its further toleration.* The spirit of American slavery . . . threatens not only our existence as a people, but the annihilation of the principles of free Christian government; and thus has rendered the continuance of negro slavery incompatible with the preservation of our own liberty and independence.

. . . the highest executive authorities have proclaimed the abolition of slavery within most of the rebel States, and decreed its extinction by military force. . . . It is the President's declared policy not to consent to the reorganization of civil government within the seceded States upon any other basis than that of emancipation. In the loyal States . . . measures of emancipation . . . have been set on foot . . . and propositions for an amendment to the Federal Constitution, prohibiting slavery . . . are now pending in the national Congress. So that . . . the interests of peace and of social order are identified with the success of the cause of emancipation. The difficulties which formerly seemed insurmountable, in the providence of God, appear now to be almost removed. The most formidable remaining obstacle, we think, will be found to be the unwillingness of the human heart to see and accept the truth against the prejudices of habit and of interest; and to act towards those who have been heretofore degraded as slaves, with the charity of Christian principles in the necessary efforts to improve and elevate them.

In view, therefore, of its former testimonies upon the subject, the General Assembly does hereby devoutly express its gratitude to Almighty God for having overruled the wickedness and calamities of the rebellion, so as to work out the deliverance of our country from the evil and guilt of slavery; its earnest desire for the extirpation of slavery, as the root of bitterness from which has sprung rebellion, war, and bloodshed, and the long list of horrors that follow in their train; its earnest trust that the thorough removal of this prolific source of evil and harm will be speedily followed by the blessings of our Heavenly Father, the return of peace, union and fraternity, and abounding prosperity to the whole land; and recommend to all in our communion to labour honestly, earnestly, and unweariedly in their respective spheres for this glorious consummation, to which human justice, Christian love, national peace and prosperity, every earthly and every religious interest, combine to pledge them.[91]

At least there was nothing equivocal about this pronouncement! Although the Old School Assembly was somewhat tardy

[91] *Minutes of the General Assembly,* 1864, vol. xvii, pp. 296-299. The report may be found also in the *Presbyterian Historical Almanac,* 1865, pp. 47-50.

in endorsing the Federal Government's policy of emancipation, once it did take action, it did so emphatically. That the paper could be adopted with "almost entire unanimity," was indeed a triumph for the southern Ohio group that for over twenty years had been fighting to get the Assembly to adhere to its 1818 stand.[92] For some months there had been evidences of a change of attitude toward slavery on the part of the more conservative element in the Old School Church. Much to the delight of the strongly anti-slavery *Presbyter,* its more conservative rivals, the *Presbyterian Banner* by the summer of 1863, and the *Presbyterian* by the spring of 1864, had "made progress" toward a distinctly anti-slavery stand.[93] Prominent leaders in the Church announced a similar conversion in themselves. Referring to his earlier stand on slavery, Dr. Spring confessed, "I was wrong, sir," while another pillar of the Church, Dr. George W. Musgrave, declared in the same connection, "Moderator, this rebellion has converted me."[94] Even the redoubtable Dr. R. J. Breckinridge, originally an exponent of "gradualism," and for some time opposed to Lincoln's emancipation policy, was now in favor of emancipation.[95] With the conversion of leading men and leading journals of the Church to the anti-slavery cause, the way had been paved for decisive action against slavery in the Assembly of 1864.

While the report on slavery was the only "deliverance" of the Assembly on the state of the country, other problems connected with the war occupied considerable of the Assembly's time. Elaborate plans were made for promoting the welfare of the freedmen.[96] Large portions of twelve sessions were de-

---

[92] *Cf., e.g.,* account of Overture of Oxford Presbytery in 1842. Thomas, *Anti-Slavery Correspondence,* p. 36.

[93] *Cf.* editorials, "The Banner on Slavery," *Presbyter,* July 8, 1863; and "Plain Words — But True," *Presbyter,* May 18, 1864; also *post,* pp. 155; 157; 159; 162-163.

[94] Editorial, "Position Defined," *Presbyter,* July 13, 1864.

[95] *Cf.* editorial note, *Presbyter,* June 1, 1864; editorial, *ibid.,* March 23, 1864; also Thomas, *op. cit.,* p. 10.

[96] *Minutes of the General Assembly,* 1864, vol. xvii, pp. 321-323. *Cf.,* also, *post,* p. 440.

voted to the case of Dr. Samuel B. McPheeters, a Missouri pastor whose firm refusal to regard the war as anything but a secular matter had involved him in charges of disloyalty.[97] Although with the passing of the war years the Assembly was finding it increasingly easy to take a stand of outspoken loyalty to the government, these same years were bringing the Church a steadily mounting number of problems of social readjustment and internal discipline.

In 1864, as in previous war-years, the Assembly in its paper on the state of the country apparently interpreted rightly the sentiments of its constituents. The action of 1864 on slavery was almost universally approved. Indeed, some of the Old School synods and presbyteries were determined to go far beyond the position of this Assembly. The Presbytery of Cincinnati at its fall meeting voted " that any person teaching and maintaining that American slavery is not a sin, and is justified by the word of God, is justly liable to censure." [98] The Presbytery of Wooster (Ohio) resolved to give no funds to young men studying for the ministry, to license no candidates, to receive no ministers from another presbytery, who held views contrary to those of the General Assembly.[99] Again Ohioans were leading the Old School Presbyterians in their change of stand on slavery.

On the other hand, Dr. Stuart Robinson's *True Presbyterian*, representing ultra-conservative Border State opinion, was despondent over the degradation suffered by the Old School Church. Quoting approvingly a communication from " a highly intelligent and earnest Presbyterian lawyer of New York " who questioned, " Could the Church go further in its adulterous

---

[97] *Minutes of the General Assembly,* 1864, vol. xvii, pp. 261-330, *passim. Cf.* also, *post,* pp. 305-324.

[98] *Cf.* editorial, " The New Rule," *Presbyter,* November 9, 1864. This editorial defended the above-quoted action, maintaining that it was but carrying out the principles of 1818 and 1864, and did not, as the *Presbyterian* had insisted, establish a new term of ministerial communion and a new condition of church membership.

[99] *Ibid.*

intercourse with the State? ", Dr. Robinson asked, "What are Conservative men to do now?" The New York lawyer thought there would be found "at least 7,000" who would endure any trial for the truth's sake, but Dr. Robinson doubted whether there remained so many uncontaminated by Baal-worship. Such a remnant of the faithful as still existed should, he believed, "stand aloof from the General Assembly" and "wait and watch for an opportunity to reconstruct our wasted temple out of the ruins of the old." Inclined to think that the time was not yet ripe for any positive action on the part of the conservative element, he saw in the tendency toward reunion and the "taking back of the testimony of 1837" a possible opportunity for this class. He believed that surely there would be some who would not tolerate the idea of reunion with the New School church. They could then become the nucleus of a conservative church.[100] "Ichabod" must now be written upon the name of the Old School Presbyterian Church, said another correspondent in Dr. Robinson's paper, mourning the readiness of the Church to "belie its glorious history, and tarnish its garments with politics. . . ."[101]

The Old School Presbyterian Church had indeed gone a long way in the four Assemblies since the outbreak of the War. Step by step it had moved from a position of ultra-conservatism to one of outspoken endorsement of the position of the United States Government in its relations toward the South and slavery. Inclined at first toward a policy of silence in 1861, the Assembly had, after a long period of hesitation, and in the face of a minority opposition of considerable strength, decided to pass resolutions supporting the Federal Government. In 1862, with the party of opposition much smaller, the Assembly had issued a more formal and comprehensive statement of its position in 1861, but had still maintained a policy of silence on the subject of slavery. In 1863 it had broken silence on the slavery issue,

---

[100] Cf. editorial, "What are Conservative Men to do Now?", *True Presbyterian*, June 9, 1864.

[101] Cf. communication signed, "A Soldier of the Cross," *ibid.*, June 23, 1864.

but only to put forth a short and equivocal statement to the effect that the Assembly abided by its former pronouncements on that subject. Now in 1864 at last it was ready to pass, with almost entire unanimity, a full and frank deliverance in opposition to the institution of slavery and all that it stood for. Throughout this metamorphosis, the same factors were ever apparent as the incentives spurring the Church on to a wider and wider departure from its old position: fear of the opinions of the people; the example of other denominations, especially the New School Church; a decided East-West sectionalism, which incited the West to act as a unit in forcing the East to a more radical position; the desire of a large element in the Old School Church to seek favor in the eyes of their New School brethren, in order to promote the cause of reunion of the two great branches of the Presbyterian Church.[102] Four years of pressure on the part of these factors had indeed brought about a tremendous change in the Old School Presbyterian Church.

[102] More will be said of each of these factors, in subsequent chapters.

CHAPTER V

THE VOICE OF THE OLD SCHOOL PRESS

IT is natural that a denomination placing emphasis upon extensive training for its ministers should be well supplied with church journals. The Old School Presbyterian Church was no exception to this rule, and its many journals played a significant part in influencing the attitude of the Church and in shaping developments within it during this crucial period in its history. In any consideration of the position and influence of the Old School journals, however, it must not be forgotten that they were all private enterprises, and in no sense the official publications of the denomination.[1] The Old School Church, in contrast with some of its sister-denominations, had no official journalistic organs of opinion. In previous chapters the action of the highest governing body of the Church has been considered; in this chapter a study will be made of the important part played by the Old School journals in influencing — both directly and indirectly — Assembly action, and in serving as media for conveying the news of such action to the Presbyterian public. The Assemblies furnished the occasion for an annual crystallization of Church sentiment; during the intervening months, the Church periodicals were constantly engaged in the process of developing that sentiment to the point where crystallization was possible.

Not one of the many specific problems which the war brought the Old School Church could be satisfactorily solved by the choice of one of two alternatives; in every case several different positions were possible. It was this fact that made the editorial comment of Old School journals during the war years so controversial in character. On the matter of the proper sphere of the Church, for example, three distinct positions were taken

---

[1] *Cf. ante,* pp. 39-40.

by Old School leaders. Dr. Hodge and the conservative group he represented claimed that the sphere of the Church was easily determined: the Church was instituted to teach, maintain, and propagate the truth; everything, therefore, to which that teaching applied was " within her legitimate cognizance "; everything which was without the sphere of the Divine teaching was foreign to the Church. As the Bible commands obedience to the powers that be, it was clearly within the scope of the Church's authority to enjoin on all her members obedience, allegiance, and loyalty. But as no rules were to be found in the Scriptures by which it could be determined what form of government was best, or which of contending parties was the legitimate claimant to power, or how the commercial or other civil affairs of men should be conducted, such matters were distinctly beyond the sphere of the Church. In other words, the Scriptures were to be taken as defining the limits of its activity.

On the other hand, a large number of Old School Presbyterians in the North stood for a much broader interpretation of the scope of the Church. Nominally agreeing with Dr. Hodge that the limits were set by the Bible, they were inclined to construe the wording of the Scriptures less directly. To them the Spring Resolutions, for instance, clearly did not exceed the Scriptural limitations upon the sphere of the Church. Men of this group were rather susceptible to the demands of nationalism.

Very recently a third position had come to be advocated. In 1859 Dr. Thornwell in the General Assembly had presented this " new theory," urging that " the Church was in such a sense a spiritual body, clothed only with spiritual powers for spiritual ends, that all intermeddling with anything not directly bearing on the spiritual and eternal interests of men was foreign to its office and derogatory to its dignity." [2] The Thornwell theory

[2] Article, " The Princeton Review on the State of the Country and of the Church," *Biblical Repertory and Princeton Review*, October, 1865, vol. 37, p. 645. Pp. 641-651 contain a brief summary of the various theories on the proper sphere of the Church.

thus advocated the restriction of the sphere of the Church to what pertained exclusively to the religious element of man's nature. Coming at a time when the slavery controversy was at its height, this theory had all the appearance of an attempt to rationalize the opposition which the Thornwell faction had been directing against any consideration, in the deliberative bodies of the Church, of such problems as slavery. These three positions on the matter of the proper limits of the Church's activities each had strong supporters among the Old School journals.

On slavery four different theories had long been held. In the South strongly pro-slavery philosophy was prevalent. In the North many men accused of being pro-slavery were actually so only relatively; that is, there were many who believed that slavery itself was not sinful, that in fact it was recognized by the Bible, but that as carried out in parts of the South it was an abomination. Thus this group distinguished between "slavery" and the "slave system"; the latter, in so far as it denied the slaves education, religious training, marriage, and so forth, was sinful. A third group went a long step farther. To them slavery was always a sin, and they called themselves "anti-slavery" men. They were ever ready, however, to recognize that there might be circumstances under which the emancipation of a slave would work an actual hardship upon him; but slavery as an institution they mercilessly condemned. Thus while slavery was always a sin, slave-holding was not necessarily so. To them "anti-slave-system" men seemed pro-slavery; on the other hand, although calling themselves "anti-slavery" men, to the "anti-slave-system" men they appeared to be rank abolitionists. In the Old School Church there were very few indeed who belonged to the fourth class — the extreme class that could correctly be called abolitionists; that is, those who regarded slave-holding as always sinful. No Old School journal was abolitionist, although the *Presbyter* was frequently assailed as such; and in fact, while stopping short of this most extreme philosophy, it often employed the language and tactics of the Abolitionists. The other three theories on slavery — pro-slavery, anti-slave-system, and anti-slavery—all had their devotees among Old School editors.

As far as secession is concerned, it might seem that just two positions were possible: *for* and *against*. Actually, the Thornwell theory made possible a third position, and Old School journals fell into three categories on the matter of the justification of the action of the Southern states: *for, against,* and *silent,* on the question of the right of secession.

The specific problem of the endorsement of the Spring Resolutions also aligned the Old School journals into three groups: those which had favored such action before the 1861 Assembly met; those which were, and remained, opposed to such action; and those which, though at first opposed, became converted to the Resolutions. The war stimulated discussion of the advisability of reunion of the Presbyterians. But the problem of reunion was complicated by the fact that, with the recent break in the Old School Church, there were three great diverse Presbyterian groups to be considered: the New School, the Old School, and the Southern Church. The Old School journals came thus to be much divided on this problem: some opposed reunion; some favored reunion of the Old and New Schools in the North; others, of the Old School North and South; still others saw in a reunion of the Old School and the New School an opportunity for the more conservative wing of the Old School Church to set up independently as a "true" Presbyterian Church.

With such a wide variety of problems, complicated by such a multiplicity of possible solutions, the periodicals of the Old School Church had remarkable opportunities to mould sentiment, and to guide the Old School Presbyterian public out of the maze of war difficulties. Before the secession of the Southern element, the Church boasted three quarterlies and some ten important weeklies. Of the quarterlies the *Southern Presbyterian Review* was lost with the secession of the Southern wing of the Church. While the other two quarterlies—Dr. Hodge's *Biblical Repertory and Princeton Review,* and Dr. Breckinridge's *Danville Quarterly Review* — were both very prompt in vigorously defending the Union during the anxious winter of 1860-1861,[3] the succeeding years sometimes found them far apart on the question of the endorsement of the war policy of the Federal Government and on the problem of the relation of the Old School Church to the activities of the state.

The *Princeton Review*, as Dr. Hodge's journal was usually called, was very much interested in the political situation throughout the war. During the first three years, each issue contained at least one article bearing on this subject.[4] Dr. Hodge was always interesting, always well-informed, always cogent in his reasoning. Whether writing on " The Church and the Country," " England and America," " The History and Theory of Revolutions," or " The Natural Grounds of Civil Authority," his essays, even when they ran to fifty or sixty pages in length, were never boring. The most remarkable characteristic of this whole body of writing is the consistency of its principles throughout the whole course of the war. Other journals might be swayed by the hysteria of the times; the *Princeton Review* stood firm. To its contemporaries this did not always appear to be a virtue. The rabidly anti-slavery *Presbyter,* for example, observing that other pro-slavery men by 1864 had openly confessed a change of heart, could see in Dr. Hodge's careful distinction between opposition to "the slave system " and to " slavery," only a lack of frankness in admitting conversion.[5]

Dr. Hodge was not impervious to the attacks upon the policy of the *Review.* In October, 1865, he published a summary of the stand his quarterly had taken throughout the four years of the war.[6] After restating the principles enunciated in the vari-

[3] *Cf. ante,* pp. 33-38.

[4] There were usually six " articles " in each issue. These, together with a few pages of book reviews, made up the content of each *Review.*

[5] Editorial, " The Biblical Repertory," *Presbyter,* August 3, 1864.

[6] Article, " The *Princeton Review* on the State of the Country and of the Church," *Biblical Repertory and Princeton Review,* October, 1865, vol. 37, pp. 627-657.

ous essays which had come from his pen during these years, he declared that neither recantation nor apology was necessary.[7] Briefly, these principles as they concerned the justifiability of the war were as follows: the right of secession did not exist; the rebellion of the southern states was therefore unjustifiable and a great crime; hence the war undertaken for the suppression of this rebellion was a righteous war.

On the matter of slavery, Dr. Hodge asserted that his policy had been thoroughly consistent in adhering to the doctrine first set forth in his journal in 1836: "We are not aware that there is a sentence printed in the article in that year, which we would desire to retract or modify."[8] This doctrine defined slavery to be a "state of involuntary bondage"; it might be right or wrong, just or unjust, beneficent or cruel, according to circumstances. Abolitionism, therefore, was false and unscriptural. But the slave laws of the South which kept the slaves ignorant, forbade marriage, or justified cruelty, were an abomination. In so far as people understood by the term "slavery" this "slave system," they were right in regarding it as sinful. The sudden and general emancipation of the slaves would prove disastrous to whites and blacks alike; the scriptural method of dealing with the subject was the repeal of the unjust slave laws, the recognition of the claim of the slaves to a just compensation for their labor, provision for their intellectual, moral, and religious welfare, and liberty to acquire their freedom by payment of money to their owners. Instead of progressing in this direction, the South had been retrograding, and eventually had risen in rebellion. This altered the whole case, and slavery assumed the posture of an avowed enemy of the nation. When, therefore, it became evident that either our national life or slavery must be extinguished, and the General Assembly of 1864 declared unanimously[9] that the time had come when slavery should be

---

[7] *Ibid.*, p. 656.
[8] *Ibid.*, p. 637.
[9] *Ibid.*, p. 641. The *Minutes of the General Assembly*, 1864, vol. xvii, p. 296, state that this action was taken "with almost entire unanimity."

at once and forever abolished in the United States, the *Princeton Review* fully concurred in the sentiments expressed, although taking care to insist that in the deliverance of the Assembly the term " slavery " was used to denote the " slave system."

Indeed, it is significant that, although the Assembly of 1862 had taken no action on slavery,[10] by July of that year the *Princeton Review* was ready to declare that " if the overthrow of slavery is necessary to the preservation of the Union, slavery ought to be, must be, and inevitably will be overthrown." [11] The editor could not refrain from adding, however, the assertion that " abolitionism is contrary to the word of God, and contrary to the faith and practice of our church, and of the church universal." [12]   The following January, after Lincoln had announced his policy of emancipation, the *Review* took occasion to warn its readers that emancipation was being employed by the Federal Government only as a means to an end, and that the sole object of the war remained the preservation of the Union.   " If the abolition of slavery be made, either really or avowedly, the object of the war, we believe we shall utterly fail," [13] declared Dr. Hodge.   In other words, the *Review* held that slavery should be done away with, not because it was itself necessarily an evil, but because it had proved to be an obstacle to the winning of the war.   In July, 1864, the *Review* was still maintaining that it was not true that slavery, in the sense of involuntary bondage, was morally and universally wrong; [14] the doctrine of the abolitionists, it still claimed, was palpably in opposition to the Scriptures, both in the Old and the New Testament.[15]   At the same time it declared that only by defining

---

[10] *Cf. ante*, pp. 111-112.

[11] " The General Assembly," *Biblical Repertory and Princeton Review*, July, 1862, vol. 34, pp. 520-521.

[12] *Ibid.*, p. 522.

[13] Article, " The War," *Biblical Repertory and Princeton Review*, January, 1863, vol. 35, pp. 150-151.

[14] Article, " The General Assembly," *Biblical Repertory and Princeton Review*, July, 1864, vol. 36, p. 546.

[15] *Ibid.*, p. 547.

the term "slavery" as denoting the "slave system" could the recent deliverances of the Church be reconciled with its previous pronouncements and with the word of God.[16]

Similarly, the stand of the *Princeton Review* on the matter of the proper sphere of church action remained the same throughout the controversial war period. In 1861, it presented to its readers in amplified form the arguments of Dr. Hodge's Protest against the Spring Resolutions, emphasizing particularly the charge that the Assembly was here deciding a purely political matter, and was determining where the allegiance of all Old School Presbyterians — in the seceded as well as in the loyal states — was due.[17] On the floor of the Assembly, Dr. Hodge had declared that he would cheerfully vote for the Spring Resolutions if introduced into the Synod of New Jersey, though constrained to vote against them as decisions of the Assembly.[18] In 1862, therefore, the *Princeton Review* could consistently argue that, in principle, Dr. Breckinridge's paper on the State of the Church and the Country was not unsound, for the 1862 Assembly represented only the non-seceding states.[19] From the point of view of expediency, however, the Breckinridge paper was to be condemned.

Finally, in the matter of relations with the Southern Presbyterians, the *Princeton Review* followed a consistently conciliatory policy. Particularly in 1865 it urged that the Southern brethren be treated in an amicable spirit. Reunion of all Presbyterians it declared to be highly desirable, "provided they agree in adopting and carrying out our constitutional standards of doctrine and order."[20] The *Review* was here prescribing a

---

[16] *Ibid.*, p. 546.

[17] Article, "The General Assembly," *ibid.*, July, 1861, vol. 33, pp. 511-568. The arguments against the Assembly action are given, pp. 542-568. *Cf.*, also, *ante*, pp. 64-70.

[18] Article, "The General Assembly," *Biblical Repertory and Princeton Review*, July, 1862, vol. 34, p. 515.

[19] *Ibid.*, pp. 515-518.

[20] *Cf.* article, "The *Princeton Review* on the State of the Country and of the Church," *Biblical Repertory and Princeton Review*, October, 1865, vol. 37, p. 657. Unless otherwise noted, the statements made above with regard

platform which could be reached much more easily by the Southern Presbyterians than by the New School branch; there was little doubt which of the two groups the conservative Dr. Hodge most desired to conciliate. The *Review* had little faith in the feasibility of a satisfactory reunion of Old School and New School churches.[21] Undoubtedly from Dr. Hodge's point of view a reunited Old School Church promised much more harmony and unanimity and usefulness than a reunion of the two great branches in the North.

Consistency was thus the key-note of the *Princeton Review* in its policy on problems relating to the war. It was consistent in its loyal support of the Federal Government; it was equally consistent in abiding by its original views on the sphere of the Church, on slavery, secession, and church reunion. When its loyalty to the Union seemed to demand a modification of its former stand, as in the case of slavery, the *Review* was quick to assert that the change was not one of principle: it was simply a concession to the necessity of employing the most effective means of bringing the war to an end. No wonder this die-hard policy angered the journal's old opponents! If some of them hoped, however, that the *Review's* conservatism had cost it support in the loyal states, they were doomed to disappointment. While three hundred subscribers in the seceding states were lost at one blow when the hostilities commenced, the list in the loyal states was as large in 1865 as in 1860.[22] Consistency did not prove to be a costly policy for the *Princeton Review*.

to the policy of the *Princeton Review* during the war years were taken from this article (pp. 627-657).

[21] *Cf., e.g., Biblical Repertory and Princeton Review*, July, 1862, vol. 34, p. 497: " . . . we are persuaded that the peace and purity of the church would suffer by any attempt to unite the two bodies"; *ibid.*, July, 1864, vol. 36, pp. 537-538: [later naming six arguments against reunion], " . . . all efforts for an immediate general union would probably produce much more evil than good"; *ibid.*, July, 1865, vol. 37, pp. 490-491: " We are satisfied that any attempt to bring the two bodies together at the present time would . . . but increase the difficulties already existing. . . ."

[22] Article, " The *Princeton Review* on the State of the Country and of the Church," *Biblical Repertory and Princeton Review*, October, 1865, vol. 37, p. 657.

The demands of consistency did not trouble the vociferous Dr. R. J. Breckinridge, editor of the *Danville Quarterly Review*. The lifetime of this quarterly virtually coincided with the period of the duration of the war, the first issue appearing in March, 1861, and the last in December, 1864. According to the original plan [23] the contents of the publication were to be under the exclusive control of the members of an association of editors, which was to be limited to twelve persons. Each of the editors was to have complete freedom under the terms of the " Prospectus " to publish articles, provided they bore his signature or some other mark of identification. Such an arrangement virtually precluded the possibility of consistency. The number of members of the editorial association never reached the limit of twelve. There were nine in 1861,[24] seven in 1862, and only five at the close of 1864. Actually, throughout the period Dr. R. J. Breckinridge was very evidently the dominating personality, and it was obviously his views on political matters that caused the shrinkage in the membership of the editorial association.[25]

Of the ninety-four articles which appeared in the *Danville Quarterly Review* during the four years of its existence,[26] twenty-nine were concerned with the subject of the war. Like the *Princeton Review,* this quarterly was always ready to take a decided stand on the political issues of the day; unlike its older contemporary, its views sometimes changed radically with the passing of the war years. Consistency was not so easily maintained in Border State Kentucky, particularly under a multiple editorship. On the question of secession, however, the *Danville Review* was violently pro-Union from the outset. In its first issue Dr. Breckinridge asserted that secession imperiled

[23] *Danville Quarterly Review,* March, 1861, vol. 1, p. ii.
[24] *Cf.* account of withdrawal of three members of the editorial association, before the publication of the first number, *ante,* pp. 37-38.
[25] *Cf.* printed statements of Dr. Breckinridge and Dr. Stuart Robinson, *Danville Quarterly Review,* March, 1862, vol. 2, pp. 140-145; also, *ibid.,* December, 1864, vol. 4, pp. 632-634.
[26] Omitting book reviews.

American civilization, and in this point of view his journal never wavered. Not only was the theory itself untenable, " the method of secession, by *separate* state action, is founded on illusions utterly fatal and absurd, that the American people are not *a nation* — the Federal Constitution not a government . . . ," [27] declared the son of the author of the Kentucky Resolutions of 1798.[28] This position the quarterly steadfastly maintained.

The fact that the *Danville Review* was essentially a Southern journal, and that its near neighbor, the *True Presbyterian*,[29] was a powerful exponent of the Thornwell views [30] on the limitation of the sphere of the church, caused Dr. Breckinridge's journal to be especially sensitive to this peculiarly Southern theory. Here, too, the *Review* was thoroughly consistent in its teachings. Taking as its thesis

> That it is within the true province of the pulpit and of church courts, to examine and determine all questions, upon all subjects, in their religious bearings, which affect the moral, social, and civil well-being of society; the Bible being their guide as to topics and the views of them, and the providence of God in the exercise of a wise discretion determining the occasions on which they shall be presented,[31]

the *Review* produced a formidable array of argument from the Scriptures, from the creeds and confessions of the Church in all ages, from its deliverances in past times, and from the writings of churchmen of various branches and periods to prove that its emphatic advocacy of the cause of the Union was in accordance with the Scriptures and with Presbyterian constitutional theory.[32]

[27] Article, " Our Country — Its Peril — Its Deliverance," *Danville Quarterly Review,* March, 1861, vol. 1, p. 81.

[28] *Cf. ante,* p. 36.

[29] *Cf. post,* pp. 167-177.

[30] *Cf. ante,* pp. 133-134.

[31] Article, " Politics and the Church," *Danville Quarterly Review,* March, 1863, vol. 3, p. 63.

[32] *Cf.* articles, " Jurisprudence, Sacred and Civil . . . ," *ibid.,* March, 1862, vol. 2, pp. 168-195; " Politics and the Church," *ibid.,* December, 1862, vol. 2, pp. 611-640, and March, 1863, vol. 3, pp. 62-121.

The *Danville Review* condemned the Spring Resolutions, it is true, but not upon the ground that the Assembly had no right to decide the question of allegiance in general. Here the *Review* differed sharply from the point of view of the Hodge Protest and that of the *Princeton Review*. Dr. Hodge had asserted that the Assembly had no right to decide the political question, to what government the allegiance of Presbyterians as citizens was due;[33] the *Danville Review* maintained that when such a question came fairly before the Assembly, it lay within the province of that body to determine the answer.[34] But in the Assembly of 1861 the question did not come fairly before it, for at that time ten of the states were actually under a government which claimed to be independent of that at Washington:

It had the officers, appliances, and power of a government. Its authority was acknowledged, or at least acquiesced in for the time being, by the people of those States. The power of no other common government was in exercise among them. Such was the actual state of the case; and such being the case, we do deny the scriptural or constitutional right of the Assembly to say to Presbyterians in those States, you ought to overthrow this government; for "to strengthen, uphold and encourage the Federal Government," is tantamount to that.[35]

This attitude was similar to that revealed by Dr. Hodge when he said that he could have supported the Spring Resolutions, had they been introduced in the Synod of New Jersey, though he could not vote for them in the General Assembly.[36] It also explains why the *Danville Review* could heartily endorse the action of later Assemblies on the state of the country, after the presbyteries in the seceded states had withdrawn from the Church.[37]

It was the question of slavery that the *Danville Review*

[33] *Cf. ante*, pp. 66-67.
[34] *Danville Quarterly Review,* September, 1861, vol. 1, p. 514.
[35] *Ibid.*
[36] *Cf. ante*, p. 139.
[37] *Cf.* articles, "The General Assembly of 1862," *Danville Quarterly Review,* September, 1862, vol. 2, pp. 301-370; "The General Assembly of 1863," *ibid.*, September, 1863, vol. 3, pp. 370-453.

found most difficult of solution. For more than thirty years Dr. Breckinridge had been an ardent advocate of the gradual extirpation of slavery from the state of Kentucky.[38] But he was just as ardent in his hatred of abolitionism. In the first issue of the *Review*, he attributed the political crisis as due in large measure to the doctrine of the abolitionists, " which is the essence of lawlessness and anarchy." [39] Loyal as he was to the Lincoln administration, therefore, Dr. Breckinridge was profoundly convinced " that the anti-slavery policy and principles of the President's proclamation of September 22, 1862, can have no beneficial effect whatever, of the kind which he designed." [40] Furthermore, he declared that " neither *the Constitution as it is,* nor yet *the Union as it was* is compatible with the state of things which the effectual working of the President's proclamation would produce," that is, the state of things that would result if the Federal Government allowed itself to be " used to enforce the principles and aims of the Abolitionists." [41] Victory, he admitted, might come that way, " but even victory is not *all* that we need." [42] There was still a way out, he urged:

And we venture to add, if the peril to his administration and his party, which his proclamation has unquestionably produced, and his respect for public sentiment which has strongly pronounced against it, and which is steadily organizing in that direction; should lead him to abandon altogether — or even to omit for the present — the enforcement of his proclamation; he would do more for his own fame, for the triumph of the national cause, for the future peace and glory of his country, and for securing a fair, and to a certain extent, perhaps, a favorable consideration of his other plans of slave emancipation, than he can ever achieve by any use he can make of that proclamation.[43]

Dr. Breckinridge had no doubt that " God, in his own good time

[38] Article, " Negro Slavery and the Civil War," *ibid.*, December, 1862, vol. 2, p. 709.
[39] Article, " Our Country — Its Peril — Its Deliverance," *ibid.*, March, 1861, vol. 1, p. 74.
[40] Article, " Negro Slavery and the Civil War," *ibid.*, December, 1862, vol. 2, p. 672.
[41] *Ibid.*, p. 673.
[42] *Ibid.*, p. 696.
[43] *Ibid.*, p. 704.

and way, will give to the human race that freedom, which it lost before the dawn of history. . . . But we believe in the providence of God; and it seems to us a folly, if not a sin, to attempt to frustrate the course of Providence. . . ." [44] Asserting that neither the President nor Congress had any power to abolish slavery in any state in time of peace, Dr. Breckinridge was just as sure that a state of war could not confer such a power upon either of them, and least of all upon the President.[45] The efforts of the nation should be directed solely toward the restoration of the Union as it had been:

> Great as is our confidence that this rebellion can be conquered — it does not exceed the strength of our conviction, that a failure, afterward, to restore the Union as it was, would be attributable at least as much to our own folly, as to the phrensy [sic] of the Southern people.[46]

But the difficulty of winning the war finally brought about Breckinridge's conversion. By the end of March, 1864, the *Presbyter,* ever sensitive to its colleagues' changes in sentiment on slavery, thought it saw signs of progress in the attitude of the editor of the *Danville Review.*[47] Six weeks later, Dr. Breckinridge wrote Senator Reverdy Johnson, congratulating him upon his speech in the Senate advocating a constitutional amendment for abolishing slavery, and declared that his own feeling was that the Federal Government should either restore slavery conditions as they had been before the war, or extinguish slavery; having always been opposed to slavery, he favored the latter policy.[48] Certainly his speech in May before the Union State Convention in Louisville left no doubt as to the completeness of his conversion.[49] It is reported that as temporary chairman of the Union Convention in Baltimore, in June, 1864, he

[44] *Ibid.,* p. 709.

[45] *Ibid.,* p. 711.

[46] *Ibid.,* p. 713.

[47] Editorial, "Dr. Robert J. Breckinridge's Mistakes," *Presbyter,* March 23, 1864.

[48] *Cf.* letter of R. J. Breckinridge to Reverdy Johnson, *Reverdy Johnson Papers,* Mss. Division, Library of Congress.

[49] Editorial note, *Presbyter,* June 1, 1864.

declared, " They tell us what we will do is unconstitutional. We will change our constitution if it suits us to do so." [50] This changed point of view on the matter of emancipation was reflected in the *Danville Review*. In December, 1864, the *Review* declared, " Slavery has proved a burden too heavy to be borne by our country any longer. . . . The time so long hoped and prayed for, when the blot on our holy religion shall be effaced, has fully come." [51] Thus the conversion of the *Review*, though tardy, was complete.

As Dr. Breckinridge had taken a prominent part in the exscinding of New School synods in 1837,[52] it was but natural that he should not be enthusiastic over the proposition of speedy reunion. His opposition to the adoption of the Spring Resolutions had been in part due to his fear of a hasty reunion:

> Movements are already hinted at, and perhaps in progress, for uniting the Old and New School on the basis of a common anti-slavery sentiment. Intimations, by no means obscure, are thrown out that the mighty North-West must be respected; that the young giant is waking up to a sense of its growing power and importance, and will make the other portions of the Church give heed to its behests. Serious differences of doctrine, and everything else distinctive of the parties, are to be ignored or compromised away; and a comprehensive union of diverse Presbyterial elements, is to be cemented by the cohesive power of a common and unscriptural opposition to slavery and the " *slave power.*" The attempt to carry into effect this scheme, will be resisted unto the death, by the conservative part of the Church, all over the land.[53]

---

[50] Thomas, *Anti-Slavery Correspondence*, p. 10.

[51] Article, " Slavery in the Church Courts," *Danville Quarterly Review*, December, 1864, vol. 4, p. 556. This article (pp. 516-556), as was the practice in the *Review* after 1861, was not signed or initialed. It has some evidences of having been written by Dr. R. L. Stanton, of the Danville Theological Seminary, who was the author of *The Church and the Rebellion* (*cf. ante,* p. 28, note 25). The authorship, from the point of view of this paper, is not important, as the abandonment of the practice of signing articles threw the responsibility for the content of the *Review* upon Dr. Breckinridge, and after 1861 the journal was a Breckinridge journal from cover to cover.

[52] *Cf. ante,* pp. 112-113.

[53] Article, " The Late General Assembly — Church and State," *Danville Quarterly Review*, September, 1861, vol. 1, p. 517.

In 1862 he regarded the inauguration of correspondence between the Assemblies with a high degree of favor, but believed
that the time was not yet ripe for further progress toward union.
He was fully persuaded that the differences, in nearly all respects, between the two bodies were too great for them to constitute one denomination sufficiently harmonious to work together with great efficiency or great comfort. New School
Presbyterianism was "a type to itself," he declared, and he was
confident that "the Presbyterian Church can never recall or
regret what she did in 1837 and 1838, while she continues faithful. . . ."[54] In 1863 he reiterated that reunion was a "step
for which the church, as a whole, seems not prepared."[55] Local
unions would be greatly facilitated by a general move toward
reunion, he readily admitted, "but the general good should not
be sacrificed to local convenience."[56] Thus Dr. Breckinridge
kept his *Danville Review* a consistent opponent of reunion.

Despite difficulties with the members of his editorial association and with his publisher,[57] the *Danville Review's* leading
editor made it an interesting and an apparently successful journal during the four years of its existence. Its influence was
not limited to Presbyterians. When the affairs of the quarterly
were in a particularly critical condition in the spring of 1862,
and friends of the *Review* were asked to solicit subscriptions,
one minister reported that of the twenty-six subscriptions he
had secured in two days, eleven were taken by Episcopalians,
fourteen by Presbyterians, one by a Friend.[58] (One wonders
about that Friend. What impression was made upon him by
the fiery writings of the man about whom an ardent admirer
once wrote: "The Rev. Dr. Robt. J. probably never had peace
on any subject, with any person, at any place, during a long

---

[54] Article, "The Late General Assembly," *ibid.*, June, 1862, vol. 2, p. 322.
[55] Article, "The General Assembly of 1863," *ibid.*, September, 1863, vol. 3,
p. 399.
[56] *Ibid.*, p. 400.
[57] Article, "In Memoriam. A Tribute to Rev. Stuart Robinson and
Others," *ibid.*, March, 1862, vol. 2, pp. 140-167.
[58] Editorial note, *Presbyterian*, March 15, 1862.

and tempestuous life "? [59]) In general, the *Review* was strongly supported by other Presbyterian journals in the non-seceding states. Northern editors were willing to overlook the tardiness of its conversion to emancipation, in the light of its emphatic loyalty to the Union. This friendliness was to be found in New School as well as in Old School papers.[60] In spite of his opposition to reunion, Dr. Breckinridge could not prevent the patriotism of the *Review* from conciliating New School opponents!

The influence of the *Princeton Review* and the *Danville Quarterly Review* in moulding ministerial opinion must have been tremendous. There were probably few self-respecting Old School clergymen who did not regularly read at least one of these journals. To read the cool, dispassionate logic of Dr. Hodge's argument or the incisive, colorful rhetoric of Dr. Breckinridge, is — even today — to be strongly influenced, if not convinced. One can readily believe that the *Presbyterian,* which was always well-informed, was right when it declared, " Presbyterianism, in the persons of Dr. Hodge and Dr. Breckinridge, furnishes two of the ablest writers who have discussed the great topics to which the rebellion gave rise." [61]

The influence of the quarterlies upon the laity was largely indirect — through the medium of the ministers. Of far greater direct importance to laymen were the Presbyterian weeklies.[62] Four of the important journals of this class supported the Southern presbyteries in their withdrawal in 1861, and hence may be regarded as out of the Old School Church after that date; in fact, all but one had been suspended before the war had long continued.[63] These four were the *Central Presbyterian* (Richmond, Virginia), the *North Carolina Presbyterian* (Fayetteville), the *Southern Presbyterian* (Columbia, South

[59] A. A. Thomas, in his *Anti-Slavery Correspondence*, p. 10.

[60] The New School *American Presbyterian* (Philadelphia) and *Evangelist* (New York) became particularly friendly. *Cf.* quotations in the *True Presbyterian*, April 10, 1862.

[61] *Presbyterian*, January 25, 1862.

[62] *Cf.* table of Old School periodicals, *post*, p. 149.

[63] Editorial, " Religious Papers and the War," *Presbyter*, January 21, 1863. The one surviving was the *Southern Presbyterian.*

PERIODICALS OF THE OLD SCHOOL CHURCH DURING THE YEARS OF THE WAR

Name	Date [1] Founded	Place	Frequency of Issue	Price per Year [2] in 1861	in 1865	
Biblical Repertory and Princeton Review	1825	Philadelphia	Quarterly	$3.00	$3.00	
Danville Quarterly Review	1861	Danville, Ky.	Quarterly	$3.00		Suspended in 1864
Presbyterian	1831	Philadelphia	Weekly	$2.50	$2.50	
Presbyter	1841	Cincinnati	Weekly	$2.00	$3.00	In 1869 united with the *Christian Herald* [3]
Presbyterian Banner	1852	Pittsburgh	Weekly	$1.50	$2.00	
Presbyterian Herald	1831	Bardstown, Ky.	Weekly	$2.00		Sold in 1862 to the *True Presbyterian*
Presbyterian Expositor	1857	Chicago	Weekly	$2.00		Given in 1861 to the *Presbyterian Standard*
Presbyterian of Our Union		St. Louis	Weekly	$2.50		Sold in 1862 to the *True Presbyterian*
Presbyterian Standard	1861	Philadelphia	Weekly	$2.00		Discontinued in 1864
True Presbyterian	1862	Louisville	Weekly	$2.00 [4]		Discontinued in 1864

[1] In several instances the journals were founded under different names.

[2] It was commonly specified that the price would be higher (usually 50 cents) if not paid in advance. Often subscribers were many years in arrears, according to frequent complaints in the editorial columns. The subscription price to clergymen was commonly about 50 cents less than to laymen.

[3] A New School paper. The combined journal was called the *Herald and Presbyter*.

[4] This was the price at the time of founding — 1862.

Carolina), and the *True Witness* (New Orleans). Six Old
School weekly journals of more or less influence remained in
1861: the *Presbyterian* (Philadelphia), the *Presbyter* (Cincinnati), the *Presbyterian Banner* (Pittsburgh), the *Presbyterian
Herald* (Bardstown, Kentucky), the *Presbyterian Expositor*
(Chicago), and the *Presbyterian of Our Union* (St. Louis).
While, during the war years, the three last-named went out of
existence, three new journals succeeded them: the *Presbyterian
Standard* (Philadelphia), the *True Presbyterian* (Louisville),
and the *Western Presbyterian* (Louisville; Danville). Besides
these distinctly Old School periodicals, the venerable New York
Observer, undenominational weekly with an Old School editor,
was usually associated in the popular mind with the Old School
Church. Several of these weeklies were destined to play major
roles in the dramatic developments in the Old School Church
during the 1860's. Individually, they reflected the influences
which moulded these developments.

The most influential of the weeklies was the *Presbyterian,*
the "mother of us all," one of the other journals termed it.[64]
Founded in 1831, it had had thirty years in which to develop a
degree of prestige which was evidently a source of envy and
exasperation to some of its younger sister-journals. Western
Presbyterians accused it of exerting undue influence in church
politics,[65] and the General Assembly subjected the Board of
Publication to annual attacks on the ground of too close alliance
with the *Presbyterian.*[66] To the present-day reader, the *Presbyterian* of the 1850's and 1860's seems a very worthy sheet:
impressive in dignity, orderly and interesting in its presentation
of the news, intelligent and judiciously critical in its opinions.
It was ultra-conservative, but frankly so.[67] To its literary con-

---

[64] *Cf.* editorial, "The Spirit of the Press," *Presbyter,* July 10, 1862.

[65] Editorial, "The General Assembly," *Presbyterian,* June 8, 1861; also
editorial, "Work of the Presbyterian Board of Publication," *ibid.,* June 21,
1862.

[66] *Cf.* editorials referred to in Note 65, above.

[67] The *Presbyterian* was constantly referring to the conservatism of the
Old School Church, and to its own support of that conservatism.

temporaries, however, it evidently appeared smug and self-sufficient, for hostile criticisms by other religious periodicals — Presbyterian and non-Presbyterian — were frequently reflected in its pages.[68] In the absence of definite evidence regarding the circulation of journals of this period, the attention the *Presbyterian* received from its rivals is interesting testimony as to the extent of its influence.

One source of opposition to the *Presbyterian* was its conservative policy regarding slavery. Dr. Hodge wrote in 1861,

> Of all the journals at the North in any way connected with our church, the New York *Observer*, the Philadelphia *Presbyterian*, and the Princeton *Review*, have been considered the most "pro-slavery" and southern in their proclivities. They have been so stigmatized at the North, and so regarded at the South. They have generally been joined together by anti-slavery men and journals, as illustrations of subserviency to the South.[69]

The attitude of the *Presbyterian* on the proper policy of the Church with regard to slavery had been based on the theory that the deliverances already given by the Assembly covered the whole ground. Alleging in 1857 that the hostility of the *Presbyterian of the West*, (later the *Presbyter*), amounting almost to a "monomania," was due simply to the *Presbyterian's* discountenancing "the efforts that paper has been assiduously making to reopen the agitation of the slavery question in the General Assembly," the *Presbyterian* insisted such efforts would "tend to distract a harmonious Church, and turn it aside from the great work it is accomplishing . . . , [and] would in no way benefit the slave. On the last mentioned point we have the example of other denominations to serve as a beacon. . . our Church has gone on to prosper to a degree which has excited

---

[68] *Cf., e.g.,* criticisms mentioned in issues of the *Presbyterian*, as follows: November 7, 1857, by the *Western Presbyterian* (accusation: unmoral attitude on slavery); June 19, 1858, by the *American Presbyterian* (accusation: inaccuracy of the *Presbyterian* in confusing two periodicals of the same name); August 7, 1858, by the *Presbyterian Banner;* June 19, 1858, by the *Congregational Herald* (accusation: want of candour); August 7, 1858, by the *Independent* (accusation: vindictiveness toward the dead). *Cf.,* also, quotations from rival journals in this work, *passim.*

[69] *Biblical Repertory and Princeton Review,* April, 1861, vol. 33, p. 328.

the admiration, and perhaps also the jealousy of others. . . ." [70]

The prestige and conservatism of the *Presbyterian*, as well as its tolerant attitude toward slavery, made it an object of special interest with regard to its policy during the trying months of the winter of 1860-1861. On December 15, 1860, the *Presbyterian* issued an editorial appeal for preserving the unity of the Old School Church in the face of probable political division.[71] "The Church is a 'kingdom not of this world' . . . composed of spiritual membership . . . ,"[72] the journal reminded its readers. In another editorial in the same issue, it urged the necessity of political compromise and demanded the repeal of the Personal Liberty acts. In fact, its program of compromise seemed to consist largely of concessions to be made by the North.[73] Throughout the months of January, February, March, and early April, 1861, its editorials were strongly pro-Union, although the editor refrained more and more from plunging "into the partisan feelings which so frightfully agitate the public mind." Each person, he urged, should ask himself, "How can I be instrumental in averting the threatened catastrophe?"[74] Regretting that religious journals were rushing "into the melee," the *Presbyterian* complacently called attention to "our own course of neutrality." With other churches divided, the policy of political parties, it asserted, was to see the Old School Church divided, too.[75] Admitting that its own course was charged with being timid and time-serving, it denied that it was being motivated by ambitious denominationalism. It would "rejoice to see [the Church] maintain its spiritual elevation amidst political convulsions. . . ."[76] More and more, during this period, the *Presbyterian* confined itself to the *facts* of the news in its comments on political matters.

[70] Editorial, "A Word of Explanation," *Presbyterian*, November 7, 1857.
[71] *Cf. ante*, p. 32.
[72] Editorial, "The Position of the Presbyterian Church," *Presbyterian*, December 15, 1860.
[73] Editorial, "Threatening Clouds," *ibid.*
[74] Editorial, *ibid.*, March 16, 1861.
[75] Editorial, "Position of Our Church," *ibid.*, April 13, 1861.
[76] *Ibid.*

Of course Fort Sumter demanded a change of policy. Even so, the issue of the *Presbyterian* which appeared on the Saturday following that fateful Sunday of April 14, had but the briefest of editorials on the political situation. The editor was still preaching caution:

> Christians must deplore the present state of things, but they cannot contest it. They can but watch and pray, imploring the Great Arbiter of events to overrule all things for his glory, and restore our excited people to their wonted peaceful pursuits.[77]

By the following week he was ready for far more emphatic expressions:

> . . . war has been precipitated upon the nation by the assault on Ft. Sumter . . . but the government must and will be sustained, and the issue we must leave with God. . . .[78]

This attitude was consistently followed in succeeding numbers of the journal, and its editorials strongly endorsed the moves of the Lincoln administration.

The *Presbyterian* was an advocate of the doctrine that a private journal was at liberty to express its opinions on political matters, but that for the General Assembly a policy of silence was highly desirable.[79] When the General Assembly of 1861 abandoned such a policy in the adoption of the Spring Resolutions, the *Presbyterian,* though at first it had thought the churches of the South lost, soon came to hold hopes that, due to the Hodge resolutions and protest, that section might still be saved. It insisted that the public should understand that the cause of hesitation on the part of the Assembly had been the question of expediency — not of loyalty. On the matter of loyalty, the members of the Assembly, "with few exceptions," were, it asserted, of one mind.[80] Believing that the introduction of the Spring Resolutions was inexpedient, the *Presbyterian* was inclined to place the blame for their passage upon

[77] Editorial, "The War Commenced," *ibid.,* April 20, 1861.
[78] Editorial, "The State of the Country," *ibid.,* April 27, 1861.
[79] *Cf. ante,* pp. 40-41.
[80] Editorial, *Presbyterian,* June 8, 1861.

the West and the Northwest: " Some of the brethren from that section did not hesitate to assign as the reason of certain votes given in the late Assembly, their determination to let the Eastern portion of the Church feel that ' there is a North-West.' " [81]

By mid-summer, 1861, the *Presbyterian* had been disillusioned with regard to the likelihood of the Southern brethren remaining in the Church. It had also become convinced that all hope of compromise, as far as secession was concerned, had been lost, and it was ready to declare that " a more causeless, suicidal, and criminal procedure is not to be found in the world's history. . . . There is no more pestilential political heresy than that every State . . . has a reserved right of withdrawing . . . ." [82] This stand cost the *Presbyterian* the loss of one of its editors, Dr. John Leyburn, who now returned to his native Virginia.[83] Before long, however, his place was taken by Rev. M. B. Grier, a native of Pennsylvania, who had been a pastor in Wilmington, North Carolina. The secession troubles had " rendered it desirable for him to seek his Northern home. . . . We need scarcely add," the *Presbyterian* explained, " that Mr. Grier is a patriot, and a very strong advocate for the integrity of the Union. . . ." [84]

It is interesting to see the patriotism of this staid, conservative weekly carrying it farther and farther, as time elapsed, in its condemnation of secession and the war. The attempt to liken this uprising to the revolution by which independence from England was gained, it found " simply preposterous." [85] By the spring of 1862, it was proclaiming:

We owe a profound debt of gratitude to our country and its institutions; it has conferred upon us unspeakable blessings, and to prove recreant to it, in this its righteous struggle, would be to prove recreant to God, who has conferred on us such national distinction.[86]

---

[81] Editorial, *ibid.*, June 22, 1861.
[82] Editorial, " The Address from Tennessee," *ibid.*, August 10, 1861.
[83] Editorial notice, *ibid.*, August 10, 1861.
[84] Editorial notice, September 28, 1861.
[85] Editorial, *ibid.*, May 17, 1862.
[86] *Ibid.*

With the Thornwell doctrine of the ultra-spiritual character of the Church, it had no patience:

> When rebellion, a worse sin than witchcraft, is endeavoring to strangle out our national life, it will not do for Christians to excuse themselves from interference, lest they should be found soiling their hands with politics.[87]

This was indeed a great departure from its advice of the previous year.[88] By the summer of 1862, it was even becoming a little impatient with the Federal Government's policy of forbearance, which, it believed, reassured the rebels and afforded encouragement to domestic traitors. It welcomed the cheering prospect of the war being henceforth prosecuted " with less misplaced kindness." [89]

Meanwhile the *Presbyterian* had also been undergoing a change of heart on the problem of slavery. By the summer of 1862, even the critical *Presbyter* found occasion for rejoicing in the course of its rival in the direction of anti-slavery sentiments.[90] The following year the same observer reported further progress.[91] By 1864, the *Presbyterian's* stand on slavery was quite acceptable to the *Presbyter,* though the latter somewhat ungraciously could see no reason for its rival's change of attitude, " but the change that has occurred within the bounds of its circulation, or because its bounds have been somewhat changed by the loss of Southern territory." [92] These factors probably played their part, but the careful reader is more likely to see as the primary cause of the transformation, the growing tendency in the North to regard slavery as responsible for the horrors of the long war.

Indeed, for all its enthusiastic patriotism, the *Presbyterian* was never blind to the great evils of war. For a time, in the spring of 1861, its articles on religion employed military terms

---

[87] Editorial, *ibid.,* May 24, 1862.
[88] *Cf. ante,* pp. 40-41; 153.
[89] Editorial, " The Situation," *Presbyterian,* August 16, 1862.
[90] Editorial, " Spirit of the Press," *Presbyter,* July 10, 1862.
[91] Editorial, " Progress," *ibid.,* Oct. 7, 1863.
[92] Editorial, " Plain Words — But True," *ibid.,* May 18, 1864.

in figures of speech,[93] but as the reality of war came to be felt, that practice was abandoned. Over and over again, the dangers of war, the disproportionate emphasis it received in men's thoughts, its baleful effect upon men's religion, its promotion of carping criticism, its waste of life and treasure, its depreciation of the value of human life, received due emphasis.[94] On the other hand, the war had scarcely begun before the *Presbyterian* came forward with some practical suggestions for Christian service which might partially offset its evils.[95] For all its good sense on the subject of war, even this conservative journal lost its balance over Southern "inexcusable cruelties." To be sure, it would not have believed them, "except for the source." Inasmuch as the source was the Committee of Congress on the Conduct of the War, the lapse remains unpardonable. At any rate, the readers of the *Presbyterian* learned of the bodies of Federal soldiers after Bull Run being stripped of their clothing, buried face-downward, the heads of many cut off, their skulls kept as relics and manufactured into drinking-cups, "while other bones were converted into spurs, rings, and other *ornaments,* to be sent to friends, and even *ladies!* "[96] Thus even the editors lost their heads! But aside from this single instance, the tone of the *Presbyterian* remained remarkably sane.

Nowhere was its sanity more conspicuous than in its attitude toward the possession of Old School church buildings within the territory reconquered from the Confederacy. Recognizing the duty of the Old School Church to preserve them as Presbyterian churches during the period of occupation, the *Presbyterian* insisted that as soon as the war was over, if the Southern church remained separate, the church buildings must be returned to that body.[97] Throughout the period of the war, its

[93] *Cf.* editorials, " The Other Warfare," and " Mustering In," *Presbyterian,* May 4 and May 11, 1861.

[94] *Cf., e.g.,* editorials, *Presbyterian*: " The Excitement," April 27, 1861; " What We Read," May 25, 1861; " A Temptation," June 21, 1862; " Thoughts in War Times," June 27, 1863; *etc.*

[95] Editorial, " The Times of War," *ibid.,* May 4, 1861.

[96] Editorial, " Inexcusable Cruelties," *ibid.,* May 10, 1862.

[97] Editorial, " Southern Churches," *ibid.,* February 27, 1864.

contemporary, the *Princeton Review,* never gave up hope of the Southern wing of the Church returning to the fold after the conflict had ended, and hoped that any Presbyterian reunion which might take place, would be with this body.[98] The *Presbyterian* had no illusions with regard to the likelihood of an immediate return of the Southerners; nevertheless it did not embrace the alternative which was now more and more frequently being mentioned: reunion with the New School Church. The *Presbyterian,* in close alliance with the Princeton Seminary leaders and the conservative faction in Philadelphia, was traditionally opposed to reunion. In 1858 and 1859, its editorial columns were filled with complaints of New School misunderstanding and unfair criticism. In 1861 and 1862, it was not yet ready for reunion.[99] In 1865, it still felt that " it is apparent that this is a step for which the great majority of our Church are not at all prepared." [100] The following year the plans for reunion met with its hearty approval; [101] by 1867, it was ardently championing the cause.[102] The *Presbyterian* could change its mind! [103]

The staid old *Presbyterian* thus underwent a complete change in attitude on three important issues which confronted the Old School Church during the Civil War period: the question of action by the General Assembly on the political crisis of 1861; slavery; and reunion. The change reacted upon the *Presbyterian* in several distinct ways: loss of circulation in the South; [104] a steady increase in the subscription list in the North; [105] and a more charitable attitude toward the *Presbyterian* on the part of rival journals. Hostile remarks did not entirely disappear, but they were as nothing in frequency com-

[98] *Cf. ante,* pp. 139-140.

[99] Editorials, *Presbyterian,* December 7, 1861, and February 1, 1862.

[100] Editorial, *ibid.,* May 20, 1865.

[101] Editorial, *ibid.,* July 28, 1866.

[102] Editorial, *ibid.,* January 26, 1867.

[103] The influences that brought about this change of position will be treated in the chapter on Presbyterian Reunion. *Cf. post,* Part VI.

[104] *Cf.* statement in *Minutes of General Assembly,* 1862, vol. xvi, p. 605.

[105] *Cf.* editorial statement, *Presbyterian,* August 31, 1861.

pared with the period before the war. There is no satisfactory method of determining, even approximately, the extent of influence of a periodical like the *Presbyterian*. Judging from internal evidence, and from the statements of rival editors, however, it was a potent agent of the Old School Church, and the influence of its stand on matters pertaining to the war must have carried great weight.

The *Presbyterian* was the most conservative of Old School weekly journals; the most radical was the *Presbyter*, published at Cincinnati. Founded in 1841 as the *Presbyterian of the West*,[106] it had from the outset been a journal of militant Westernism. If the Civil War years were years of transformation for the *Presbyterian*, for the *Presbyter* they were years of triumph, years when it saw realized, or at least approximated, every one of its pet ambitions for the Old School Church. The Church declared its loyalty to the Union; it moved to a radical anti-slavery position; it made distinct progress toward reunion with the New School Church; in influence within the Church, the West came to its own.

The *Presbyter* was neither so well edited nor so full of news as the *Presbyterian*. What made it interesting was its radical stand and its enthusiasm for its principles. The fact that during the decade of the 1860's there was no other strong Old School weekly in the Northwest, that the *Presbyter* was actually, during a considerable portion of this period, the only journal of the denomination in this section, gave it peculiar importance there. This journal never failed in frankness. In a period when other periodicals were suggesting compromise measures to meet the political crisis, the *Presbyter* announced in its issue of January 3, 1861, "The *Presbyter* is the only paper in the Presbyterian Church (Old School) that has taken and maintained decided and consistent ground in defense of the action of the General Assembly [of 1818], in opposition to

[106] The name was changed to "Presbyter" in 1858. In 1869, when the reunion of the Old and New Schools was consummated, this journal joined with the *Christian Herald* (New School) to become the *Herald and Presbyter*.

the extension of slavery, and in favor of emancipation. On this subject it will not falter."[107] About the same time, in condemning the anti-abolition sermon of a Brooklyn pastor, it warned its readers of the "influence of large cities which are deeply interested in Southern trade."[108] (It should be remembered, however, that even this most radically anti-slavery of Old School journals was not abolitionist. Slavery it regarded as always sinful; slave-holding, not necessarily so.[109]) Two months before the fall of Fort Sumter, the *Presbyter* advocated that "this rebellion be subdued with as little loss of life as possible."[110]

With regard to the question of action on the political situation by the General Assembly of 1861, it was at first inclined to be less radical. Although it deprecated the attempt of anti-action advocates to have men "of their own stripe" elected to the Assembly,[111] for a few weeks in the spring of 1861 it was inclined to think silence better, if possible.[112] The stirring events of April completely reconverted it to its normal radicalism, and in an editorial on the next Assembly in the issue of May 2, it cautioned, "Let Northern Presbyterians be firm!" The action finally taken by the Assembly should, it declared, "fill every true Presbyterian with delight."[113]

This role of radical leader was maintained by the *Presbyter* throughout the war period. It assumed the responsibility of reporting on the progress made by other Old School journals toward an anti-slavery position;[114] urged presbyteries not to

[107] *Cf.* editorial announcing its own enlargement, *Presbyter*, January 3, 1861.

[108] Editorial, "Sermons of the Times," *ibid.*, January 24, 1861. The pastor was Dr. Henry J. VanDyke.

[109] Editorial, "Drs. MacMaster and Hodge," *ibid.*, February 14, 1861. *Cf.* also, *ante*, p. 134.

[110] Editorial, "Coercion," *ibid.*, February 7, 1861.

[111] Editorial, "The Next General Assembly," *ibid.*, March 28, 1861.

[112] *Cf.* editorials, *ibid.*, March 28 to April 18, inclusive.

[113] Editorial, *ibid.*, June 13, 1861.

[114] *Cf.* editorials, *ibid.*, July 10, 1862; October 7, 1863; March 23, 1864; May 18, 1864, *etc.*

fail to endorse Assembly action on the state of the country; demanded that they disapprove of the conduct of ministers who failed to pray for the success of the Government; [115] and never failed to grasp an opportunity to emphasize the importance of the West and the advantages of Presbyterian reunion.

These years were a period of prosperity for the *Presbyter*. The editor was able to enlarge the paper,[116] and thereupon commenced with the *Presbyterian* a lengthy and hardly dignified dispute as to which journal contained the greater amount of reading matter [117] — a dispute in which the *Presbyter* had, on the whole, the better of the argument; though had the contest turned on the question of the importance of the content, the palm would unquestionably have gone to the other party. The western journal's radical policy was evidently pleasing to its readers. Having appealed in December, 1862, for 1,000 new subscribers, six months later it could announce that it had received far more than it had asked or expected.[118] These were indeed years of triumph for the *Presbyter!*

The *Presbyterian Banner* (Pittsburgh), having been founded in 1852, was considerably younger than either the *Presbyterian* or the *Presbyter*. At $2.00 per year it was also a cheaper sheet, the subscription price of each of the older journals being $2.50.[119] Just as it lay half-way, geographically, between the Philadelphia and Cincinnati organs, so in policy it had taken a stand about half-way between the conservative East and the radical West. Originally much less well-rounded than the *Presbyterian*, much less colorful than the *Presbyter*, its interest in the progress of the war and its views on the proper relationship of the Old School Church to the national conflict made it

---

[115] Editorial note, *ibid.*, September 4, 1862.

[116] *Cf.* editorial announcement, January 3, 1861; also editorial announcement, December 31, 1862.

[117] *Presbyter*, December 31, 1862, and succeeding issues.

[118] Editorial, " Our Paper," *ibid.*, May 20, 1863.

[119] The price of the *Presbyterian Banner* rose during the war period from $1.50 to $2.00. During the same period the price of the *Presbyter* mounted from $2.00 to $3.00. *Cf.* table, *ante*, p. 149.

an increasingly readable sheet during the period of the war. Following months of silence on the political situation, it came out with a strong pro-Union editorial ten days after the election of Lincoln. " Disunion is treason," it asserted, " and treason must be suppressed at whatever cost. . . ." Commenting on the amazing political upheaval evidenced in the election, the *Banner* was convinced that Presbyterians had played a large part in the outcome of this event:

> We cannot but think that there is some moral feeling [sic] — some fundamental social principle, or principles, belonging to our religion and to the genius of our government, concerned in this change. . . . And Presbyterian ministers, though they talk less on politics, and write less, and hold fewer offices than their fellows, are yet among the first in *real* political influence. They give character and expression to the intellect of the community.[120]

That the political crisis called for a decisive stand on the part of the Old School Presbyterian Church, the *Banner* had not the slightest doubt. In January it was bitingly sarcastic with regard to the *Presbyterian's* attempt to shift responsibility by referring the matter " unqualifiedly and unreservedly to God." [121] When the fall of Fort Sumter stimulated war excitement, the *Banner* deprecated war, but regarded it as necessary for the preservation of peace.[122] Just as the *Presbyter* undertook the responsibility of reporting the progress of its contemporaries in the development of anti-slavery sentiment, so its Pittsburgh rival carefully noted the Union sentiments of members of the faculties of Old School theological seminaries.[123] The *Banner* never had any doubts about the necessity and the desirability of General Assembly action on the state of the country. The suggestion of the *Presbyterian* that the Assembly of 1861 should confine itself to routine business it regarded with scorn and derision:

[120] Editorial, " The Presidential Election," *Presbyterian Banner,* November 17, 1860.
[121] *Editorial, " The Presbyterian," Presbyterian Banner,* January 19, 1861.
[122] Editorial note, *ibid.,* April 27, 1861.
[123] Editorial note, *ibid.,* April 27, 1861; editorial, " Union Sentiment in Princeton Theological Seminary," May 4, 1861.

The Providence of God . . . calls for the consideration of a new question
. . . . Is the church of Jesus Christ in such a case as this, to be doomed
to inaction, her members being combatants and sufferers! . . . Has she no
instructions to give, no advice, no cheerings, no encouragements, no warnings! . . . Alas, mere routine business! What a thought! . . . When
good government and social joys and morality and religion are all deeply
involved we trust that the General Assembly of the Presbyterian Church
will not voluntarily consign herself to guilty silence.[124]

During the course of the Assembly sessions, it found the majority report sadly defective,[125] and expressed much regret over
the course followed by Dr. Hodge.[126] When the minority report
was finally adopted, the universal commendation of the press in
the North was a source of deep gratification.[127]

The *Banner's* course with regard to slavery had always been
far from satisfactory to the *Presbyter*.[128] The war had scarcely
begun, however, before signs of a transformation in the *Banner's* attitude became apparent. At the end of 1860, it had still
been assuring the South that with " rampant abolitionists " like
" *Garrison, John Brown,* or any of that crew," the great mass of
Northern people had no sympathy whatever; the vast majority
were " conservative people who would never incite a slave to
escape. . . ." [129] A little later, complaining that the only way
to satisfy the South was for the North to " *guarantee* to the
South the *perpetuity of slavery*," the *Banner* refused to sanction such a course.[130] By midsummer, 1861, the *Banner* had
come to the point of view that the " sin of slavery " was the
direct cause of the war. But if the South was overwhelmingly
guilty, the North was not innocent: " The whole land is involved. . . . The sin . . . is national." The whole problem

[124] Editorial, " What Will the Assembly Do? ", *ibid.*, May 18, 1861.

[125] Editorial, " Latest from the Assembly," *ibid.*, June 1, 1861.

[126] Editorial, " The Action of the Late General Assembly on the National
Crisis," *ibid.*, June 8, 1861.

[127] Editorial, " The Newspaper Press on the Late Action of the General
Assembly," *ibid.*, June 15, 1861.

[128] Editorial, *Presbyter*, July 4, 1861.

[129] Editorial, "A Word to our Southern Brethren," *Presbyterian Banner*,
December 29, 1860.

[130] Editorial, " The Christian and the Crisis," *ibid.*, January 5, 1861.

the *Banner* regarded as very difficult of solution, but it comforted itself by reflecting that the thought that " God has given us no right to interfere with slavery in States where it already exists, may relieve us greatly." [131] In other words, Providence, through the instrumentality of the Federal Constitution, had conveniently provided a means of relieving the consciences of Northerners on the problem of slavery. Nevertheless, having vigorously denounced slavery as a national sin, the *Banner* became steadily more and more opposed to a temporizing policy, and by the fall of 1863 it had won the hearty approval of even the exacting *Presbyter,* which now rejoiced that on this subject the *Banner* had been " completely revolutionized." [132]

As on other policies, so in the matter of reunion the *Presbyterian Banner's* position lay between that of its Philadelphia and Cincinnati rivals. It was neither an enthusiastic advocate of reunion, like the *Presbyter,* nor a sturdy opponent like the *Presbyterian* before the war. But when it appeared that the Southern wing of the Old School Church could be retained only at the price of silence on the political situation, the *Banner* did not hesitate in making a choice. Declaring that the South had for years been preparing to go, it pleaded for decisive action by the Assembly:

Presbyterianism cannot bear to be exhibited in the aspect either of disloyalty, imbecility, or indifference. . . . For the South to leave us would be comparatively a trifle; but to become divided among ourselves, presbyteries, churches, families, would be an immense calamity. . . . If the Assembly takes no action many will be disposed to leave that Assembly and go to the United Presbyterians or the New School Presbyterians.[133]

As the South seemed likely to leave, it might be possible that Old School, New School, and United Presbyterians could unite, the *Banner* suggested. Thus the dangers which the war brought the Old School Church were instrumental in breaking down the

[131] Editorial, *ibid.,* June 29, 1861.
[132] Editorial, " Progress," *Presbyter,* October 7, 1863.
[133] Editorial, " The Assembly and the Crisis," *Presbyterian Banner,* June 1, 1861.

indifference of the *Banner* toward the proposition of reunion. By 1867, it was a vigorous supporter of the project.[134]

The *Presbyterian Herald*, founded in the same year as the *Presbyterian*, (1831), received the respect which age inspires. Published at Bardstown, Kentucky, it was regarded as the organ of Old School sentiment in that region. Its influence was, however, limited to but one of the war years, for in 1862 it was sold to Dr. Stuart Robinson, and was superseded by the *True Presbyterian*. The *Herald* represented conservative middle-ground Kentucky opinion. It was loyal to the Union, but deeply grieved over the adoption of the Spring Resolutions. Had the Hodge Protest "gone a little farther," the editor declared, it would have expressed his views.[135] Nevertheless, he was vigorous in his contention that the action of the Assembly did not justify schism.[136] He deprecated the general misrepresentation of the action of those who protested against the Assembly vote,[137] and blamed the secular and the religious newspapers for the distracted condition of the country.[138] In almost its dying gasp the *Herald* expressed firm opposition to reunion of Old and New Schools.[139] Finally, in the spring of 1862, discouraged by the difficulties which war-time brought his paper, the editor suspended publication. For twenty years he had been trying to keep peace, he complained, and now all seemed to point to complete failure. He was particularly discouraged over a bitter quarrel in which five prominent members of the Kentucky Synod were then engaged.[140] A more specific reason for discontinuing was the announcement of a new paper to be started by Dr. Stuart Robinson (one of the five quarrelers); there was not room for two Old School papers in Kentucky.

---

[134] Editorial, *ibid.*, August 7, 1867.

[135] Editorial, *Presbyterian Herald*, June 20, 1861.

[136] Editorial announcement, *ibid.*, March 27, 1862.

[137] Editorial, "Misrepresentations of the Action of the Minority," *ibid.*, July 4, 1861.

[138] Editorial, *ibid.*, July 11, 1861.

[139] Editorial, *ibid.*, February 6, 1862.

[140] This quarrel centered about Dr. R. J. Breckinridge and Dr. Stuart Robinson. *Cf. post*, pp. 189-195.

The last number of the *Presbyterian Herald* appeared in March, 1862.[141]

The two other Old School weeklies survived but a short time after the outbreak of hostilities in 1861. But for the prominence of the editor of the one and the importance of the location of the other, they would scarcely merit mentioning. The *Presbyterian Expositor* (Chicago) was edited by Dr. N. L. Rice, the most prominent leader of the Old School Church in the West.[142] He and Dr. Hodge were considered the foremost defenders of slavery in the North, although both disliked the institution and hoped for its gradual disappearance in America.[143] " Dr. Hodge," declared the *Presbyter*, ". . . who is an anti-slavery man at heart, has done more (Dr. N. L. Rice, perhaps excepted) than any other man to stupefy the conscience and stultify the judgment of our church on the subject of slavery." [144] Cyrus McCormick had brought Dr. Rice to Chicago to become pastor of his (North Presbyterian) church, and had then made him editor of his newly-founded *Presbyterian Expositor*.[145] The *Expositor* turned out to be just what would be expected from such a background: a well-edited, conservative, pro-slavery (in the Hodge sense) sheet. Dr. Rice was a pessimist and bemoaned " the folly of the American people, which is greater than that of any other people under the sun. . . ." [146] Nevertheless he evidently believed their civilization worth saving, for he eloquently urged Presbyterians North and South to resist disunion.[147]

The *Expositor* did not have an opportunity to express itself on the momentous issue which confronted the 1861 Assembly,

[141] For notice of suspension and reasons therefor, cf. editorial announcement in last issue of *Presbyterian Herald*, March 27, 1862.

[142] Dodd, *loc. cit.*, p. 781.

[143] Stanton, *op. cit.*, pp. 89-90.

[144] Editorial, " The Assembly of 1863 on Slavery," *Presbyter*, September 23, 1863.

[145] Editorial, "A New Presbyterian Paper," *ibid.*, March 23, 1864.

[146] Editorial, " The Lord Reigneth," *Presbyterian Expositor*, November 22, 1860.

[147] Editorials, *ibid.*, November 29, and December 13, 1860.

for in the spring of that year Dr. Rice accepted a call from the
Fifth Avenue Presbyterian Church in New York City, and the
last issue of the *Expositor* appeared on May 16, after the journal had struggled through four years of none-too-prosperous
existence. The *Presbyter* later described its fate by saying that
"it was donated by its paymaster, Mr. McCormick, to the
Presbyterian Standard of Philadelphia in 1861." [148] The other
Old School weekly survived a little longer. In 1860 its title had
been changed from the *St. Louis Presbyterian* to the *Presbyterian of Our Union,* "though opposed to the Union," the *Presbyter* caustically commented. [149] This charge is not verified by
an examination of the paper, unless a policy of neutrality be
regarded as equivalent to opposition to the Union. The editor
declared that there was wrong on both sides, though most on the
side insisting on war and no compromises. [150] In February,
1861, he published an interesting and good-tempered editorial
on "The Two New Presidents," in which he expressed the trust
that "since the hot blood of South Carolina is no longer dominant," the conduct of Southern affairs would be more dignified. [151] On the matter of slavery, also, this journal attempted to
take a neutral stand; the Old School Church was neither for
it nor against it, was the contention of this Border State
paper. [152] However neutral the *Presbyterian of Our Union* may
have felt on the subject of the war, the war was not neutral
in its effect upon this journal. Starting out as a double-sheet
in 1860, by the spring of 1861 it had become a single sheet, and
before summer arrived it had suspended publication. [153] Its
subscription list was later taken over by the *True Presbyterian.* [154] Its suspension left the *Presbyterian Herald* (suc-

[148] Editorial, "A New Presbyterian Paper," *Presbyter,* March 23, 1864.
[149] *Ibid.*
[150] Editorial, "Modern Sauls in the Religious Press," *Presbyterian of Our
Union,* May 2, 1861.
[151] Editorial, "The Two New Presidents," *ibid.,* February 21, 1861.
[152] Editorial, *ibid.,* January 3, 1861.
[153] Editorial note, *Presbyterian,* June 29, 1861.
[154] *Cf. post,* p. 174.

ceeded by the *True Presbyterian* in March, 1862) the only Old School weekly west of Cincinnati.

When Cyrus McCormick turned over his *Presbyterian Expositor* to the new *Presbyterian Standard,* established in Philadelphia in the spring of 1861, he was — no doubt unsuspectingly — to this extent transferring his support from the ultraconservative to the more liberal wing of the church. An announcement by the editor of the new journal, Dr. Alfred Nevin, to the effect that his paper would stand for free discussion of controversial topics, was interpreted by the *Presbyter* as implying that the *Standard's* Philadelphia rival had not allowed such discussion. " To the last we say Amen! ", was the *Presbyter's* comment.[155] Certainly controversial topics were not wanting when the *Standard* made its appearance in the spring of 1861. From the outset of the long debate in the Assembly, the new paper was outspoken in its support of the Spring Resolutions.[156] In sharpest contrast to its predecessor it was also strongly anti-slavery,[157] rejoicing with the *Presbyter* over the conversion of the *Presbyterian.*[158] Similarly, from its beginning it agreed with the *Presbyter* in loyally supporting the cause of reunion of Old and New Schools.[159] Thus on all of the major issues it was a liberal journal. Perhaps its influence was a factor in the conversion of its Philadelphia rival. Evidently there was no room for another liberal Old School paper, however, especially not after the transformation of the *Presbyterian,* for in 1864 the *Standard* suspended publication. Its lifetime lay wholly within the war period.

The Old School quarterlies of the 1860's vividly reflected the personalities of their editors. In general this was not true of the weeklies. The one striking exception was the *True Presbyterian,* edited by Dr. Stuart Robinson. Stuart Robinson was

[155] Editorial, *Presbyter,* April 11, 1861.
[156] *Cf.* editorials, *Presbyterian Standard,* May 23, 1861; May 30, 1861.
[157] Editorial note, *Presbyter,* March 25, 1863.
[158] Editorial, " Plain Words — But True," *ibid.,* May 18, 1864.
[159] *Cf.* editorials, *Presbyterian,* February 15, 1862; *Presbyterian Standard,* June 18, 1863.

probably the most controversial figure in the Old School Church, unless one excepts his bitter enemy, Dr. Robert J. Breckinridge. Although born in the North of Ireland and educated in two Old School theological seminaries, in temperament and theology Robinson in many respects was closer to the ultra-conservative Scotch point of view than to either Scotch-Irish or American Presbyterianism. For a time, in fact, he had been the pastor of an Associate Reformed congregation, but he had found his way back into the Old School fold, where his gifts as an orator and thinker soon brought him into prominence. From 1856 to 1858 he was a member of the faculty of the Danville Theological Seminary, resigning to become pastor of the influential Second Presbyterian Church in Louisville. This charge he occupied until his death in 1881, with the exception of the period from the summer of 1862 until the close of the war — years which he spent in Canada.

In July, 1862, Dr. Robinson went to Canada to visit an invalid brother. Having received urgent warnings that because of his writings in the *True Presbyterian* the Federal authorities would cast him into prison if he should return to Louisville, he remained in Canada for the rest of the war period. Upon his return to his Kentucky pastorate he resumed the leadership of the conservative wing of the Old School Church in that state, and guided it through the various steps by which it eventually came to be a part of the Southern Presbyterian Church.[160] Brilliant, analytical, eloquent, "capable of interesting men in anything,"[161] Dr. Robinson would have been conspicuous in the Church at any time. His views on the relation of the Church to the war problems of the State made him distastefully conspicuous to the vast majority of Northern Presbyterians. As a defender of slavery he had become an ardent advocate of the Thornwell theory of the ultra-spiritual character of the Church. When, therefore, early in 1861 Dr. Breckinridge pro-

---

[160] *Cf. post,* pp. 203-264.
[161] White, Henry Alexander, *Southern Presbyterian Leaders* (New York, 1911), p. 417.

posed to publish an article on the state of the country in his new *Danville Quarterly Review* and requested the consent of his fellow-members in the editorial association, Dr. Robinson vigorously dissented from such a course, and withdrew from the association.[162] Thereupon began a lengthy controversy between these two fire-eaters, a controversy highly spiced with scornful ridicule, withering sarcasm, and devastating invective.[163] One suspects that among Dr. Robinson's motives in founding the *True Presbyterian* in 1862, not the least impelling was a desire to provide himself with a convenient medium for venting his spleen against his redoubtable opponent.[164]

In many respects the *True Presbyterian* was the most interesting of all the Old School journals during the war period. To be sure, its duration was very brief and its publication spasmodic; in all, but fifty-eight issues appeared.[164a] Other papers contained far more news and a much wider range of subject-matter, for the conservative Dr. Robinson was so staunch and consistent a believer in the Thornwell theory of the ultra-spiritual character of the church that he insisted even a private religious journal must refrain from the discussion of political matters. Yet this very insistence made the new journal unique and correspondingly interesting.

The *True Presbyterian's* non-committal position on political matters subjected it to charges of disloyalty; in fact, the assertion was made that it was alone in this disloyalty — one prominent Old School leader classifying it in 1864 as " the only paper of any denomination that we know of in all the loyal States that is not openly and decidedly sustaining the Government in its efforts to put down the rebellion." [164b]   It was without doubt a

---

[162] *Cf. ante*, pp. 37-38.

[163] *Cf. post*, pp. 173-177; 189-195.

[164] The facts with regard to the life of Dr. Robinson were taken from White, *op. cit.*, pp. 414-420; and from the *National Cyclopaedia of American Biography*, vol. i, p. 371.

[164a] The first issue appeared in April, 1862; the last, in November, 1864.

[164b] Stanton, *op. cit.*, p. 221.

paper of marked individuality. In editorial announcements in his first issue Dr. Robinson promised a paper which,

excluding from its columns secular and political news and discussions, shall be devoted entirely to articles on practical religion, ecclesiastical, theological and ethical discussions, and present, as a religious Eclectic, the completest possible view of the religious intelligence, and the current religious thought of the world.

[It purposes] to promote unity of action, and harmony of feeling among the churches of Kentucky in the present troubles.

It stands for separation of spiritual from secular matters. . . . the Scotch doctrine of the independence of the Church; the true American theory of the relation of Church and State. . . .[164c]

It only remains to add, that the title " True Presbyterian " has been selected simply as expressive of the idea, that one peculiar and distinctive feature of Presbyterianism as a Church Government, consists in that separation of the secular and spiritual order which this paper advocates against the non-Presbyterian tendencies of the times.[164d]

A third feature which made the new journal fascinating was the ruthless sarcasm of its editor, sarcasm which, probably as a result of Dr. Robinson's eagerness to stick closely to things spiritual, was often amusingly couched in Biblical terms. When Dr. Monfort, editor of the *Presbyter,* ventured to suggest ironically that the ten commandments and the asking of a blessing at meals were conspicuous examples of the mingling of things spiritual and things temporal, Dr. Robinson scathingly replied:

We fear that Dr. Montfort [sic] — in the prominent position to which accident has raised him — [thinks too highly of himself]. . . . We can remember him when he was known in the Church as the gentle creature, on which the brilliant and gifted Balaam of the New Albany Seminary [Dr. E. D. MacMaster] rode, when, in the interest of the abolition Moab, he sought to curse the Southern Israel. If ever known to break his natural silence, it was only, when goaded by his passionate rider, to remonstrate mildly, " Am I not thine ass? "

. . . in the general up-rising of tenth-rate-ism in the late revolutionary Assembly, he could even venture, as we are informed, to hector such men as Hodge and the signers of the Protest.[165]

These features of the *True Presbyterian* — abstention from discussion of things not spiritual, subjection to charges of dis-

---

[164c] " Prospectus," *True Presbyterian,* April 3, 1862.

[164d] Editorial note, " Prefatory," *ibid.*

[165] Editorial, *True Presbyterian,* April 3, 1862.

loyalty, and wholesale employment of stinging sarcasm — remained characteristic of it throughout its history. It was remarkably consistent in its avoidance of non-spiritual subjects. In looking over its files, occasionally one finds a heading which seems to betray a slip, such as, " The Dying Mozart." Upon reading farther, however, he discovers that the dying Mozart said to his daughter, " Take these, — my last notes — sit down to my piano here — sing them with the hymn of your sainted mother." [166] Invariably there is some connection with things spiritual. In fact, one is sometimes led to suspect that the clever Dr. Robinson occasionally put in worldly-sounding headings in order to trick his many hostile readers! Yet careful as his abstention from temporal things was, Dr. Robinson permitted himself some liberties in his journal which he would have denied himself in the General Assembly. When the *Presbyter* commended the spirit of humility he had displayed in the 1862 General Assembly, the fire-eating Doctor showed not the least evidence of humility in his reply:

> Now bearing in mind the warning, " Give not that which is holy to the dogs, neither cast your pearls before swine," we have no idea of explaining to the *Presbyter* how, with our views of a Spiritual Court of Jesus Christ, we felt less free to indulge in rebuke of folly and malignity in that Sacred Presence than through the press, before the great tribunal of public opinion.[167]

And yet this same editor remarked only a few weeks later, " Do any of our readers dislike controversy, especially personal controversy? If there be such, we can sympathize with them." [168] One shudders when he considers what this journal would have been like, had its editor not disliked controversy! The *Presbyterian,* which had greeted kindly the newcomer,[169] after looking over the first two numbers, judged that it aspired to be " the *Ishmael* of the religious press. It has ' run a muck '

[166] *Ibid.,* August 14, 1862.

[167] Editorial, *True Presbyterian,* June 5, 1862. The portion of the editorial above quoted was copied in the *Presbyter,* June 26, 1862.

[168] Editorial, "A Sign of Encouragement," *True Presbyterian,* August 28, 1862.

[169] Editorial note, *Presbyterian,* April 12, 1862.

[sic] against every Presbyterian newspaper extant, and, as far as we can see, nearly exhausted the vocabulary of vituperation."[170] Succeeding issues of Dr. Robinson's paper were to show how completely the *Presbyterian* had underestimated his verbal resources.

There is no evidence in the *True Presbyterian* as to where this paper stood on the question of secession. Opponents, it is true, accused it of being pro-Confederacy,[171] but no statement in the journal itself ever committed it to that position. Even the radical *Presbyter* at the end of four months could discover nothing "positively disloyal" in it.[172] Later, when some thought they saw signs of disloyalty in the editor's attacks on certain Northern preachers for their pro-Union sermons, Dr. Robinson replied that as his paper had no circulation in the South, he had no means of knowing about Southern preachers, but his impression was that they did not preach political sermons. He was careful to add that in attacking preachers of political sermons he was not condemning them for being loyal in the political sense, but rather for being "disloyal 'to Him.'"[173] He regarded with contempt much of the "patriotic" sentiment of the day, and characterized some of the ceremonies on the second anniversary of the United States Christian Commission as "Spread Eagle Charity, Piety and Oratory."[174] The war-time *Princeton Review* he found "flashy and Fourth-of-July-like in its style."[175] In the absence of any direct evidence of disloyalty, it must have been statements like these that caused Northerners to regard the *True Presbyterian* with so much fear. In the spring of 1864 a correspondent wrote to the *Presbyterian Banner*:

Men suspected of belonging to the Knights of the Golden Circle, are making great efforts to introduce the *True Presbyterian* into disloyal families

---

[170] Editorial note, *ibid.*, April 19, 1862.

[171] Editorial, *True Presbyterian*, July 31, 1862.

[172] *Ibid.*

[173] Editorial, *ibid.*, February 18, 1864.

[174] Part of title of editorial, *ibid.*, March 3, 1864.

[175] Quoted in editorial in *Presbyter*, May 1, 1862.

of every denomination. It is a scandal to the North that Stuart Robinson, a rampant secessionist, who dare not trust himself in Kentucky, should edit a paper at Louisville, professedly *spiritual*, but just as full of treason as it can hold. A few copies have been introduced into some of our congregations here, under a disguise.

Upon this communication the *Banner,* according to the *True Presbyterian,* remarked that

the man who would aid in its circulation is disloyal both to his Church and his country. Its editor, Dr. Stuart Robinson, is [the italics are the *Presbyterian Banner's*] *compelled to remain in the British dominions, because he refuses to take the oath of allegiance.* This refusal, of itself brands him as disloyal. . . .

To all of which the accused journal replied that Stuart Robinson did not know who the Knights of the Golden Circle were; that he had not been compelled to go to Canada, nor to stay there; that he had never refused to take oath, nor objected to any constitutional oath either to the government of the State or of the United States, " when properly required by the proper authority." [176]

Suspicions of Robinson's loyalty were strengthened by his firmly consistent defense of the institution of slavery throughout the period when war pressure was becoming more and more effective in converting men — notably Dr. R. J. Breckinridge — to radical anti-slavery sentiment. To be sure, some might regard slavery as a subject not to be touched upon by a strictly non-political journal like the *True Presbyterian.* Dr. Robinson's point of view on the matter was different: since slavery was sanctioned by the Scriptures, his weekly might very properly discuss it. Furthermore, while this paper might not discuss political subjects directly, its rivals were constantly expressing their opinions on such topics, and were thus guilty of actions which demanded reproof on the part of the *True Presbyterian.* In the process of reproof, the chiding journal was often conveniently obliged to give its own views on matters which it considered non-spiritual. At any rate, however its

[176] Editorial, " The Sort of Creatures that hiss at the *True Presbyterian* in Pennsylvania," *True Presbyterian,* May 26, 1864.

mention might be justified, Dr. Robinson's editorials frequently found occasion to uphold the institution of slavery.
When the Presbytery of Cincinnati declared in 1864 that " any
person teaching and maintaining that American slavery is not
a sin, and is justified by the word of God, is justly liable to
censure," [177] Dr. Robinson discussed the matter under the
heading, " Final Apostasy of a Presbytery. How should a
Pure Church treat it?" [178] In 1865, while still in Canada, he
published a lengthy defense of slavery, justifying it on biblical
grounds.[179] It is not surprising that so persistent a defender
of an institution to which Northern Old School men were becoming almost fanatically opposed, should have been regarded
with widespread suspicion.

It is unfortunate that there is no means of measuring the
extent of the subscription list of the *True Presbyterian*. There
is considerable evidence that many people read it — some perhaps surreptitiously. Dr. Robinson claimed that Dr. Breckinridge had " whispered " to him before he began his editorial
labors that he had power enough to have the new journal suppressed; whereupon Dr. Robinson had whispered back that
that would help bring people to their senses quicker than many
other things.[180] If the whispering episode actually took place,
Robinson's whispers were evidently the more effective, for in
spite of frequent reports that the journal had been suspended,[181] it appeared regularly for six months, and intermit-
tently for two years more, finally discontinuing publication in
November, 1864. Two-thirds of the issues were edited in
Canada, during Robinson's sojourn there. A few weeks after
its first appearance, the *True Presbyterian* augmented its subscription list by taking over the *Presbyterian of Our Union*.[182]

[177] *Cf. ante*, p. 129.

[178] *True Presbyterian*, November 10, 1864.

[179] *National Cyclopaedia of American Biography*, vol. 1, p. 371.

[180] Editorial, " The Theological Professor's New Political Party — His
Minions and Organs," *True Presbyterian*, August 4, 1864.

[181] *Cf., e.g., Presbyter*, July 17, 1862 (report retracted in issue of July 24);
ibid., September 25, 1862; editorial note, *Presbyterian*, October 4, 1862.

[182] Editorial note, *True Presbyterian*, May 15, 1862.

Evidently the circulation of Robinson's paper was wide enough to cause rival journals some alarm, because they universally took pains to condemn it, most of them laying particular emphasis upon charges that it was not as spiritual as it claimed to be.[183]

As for Dr. Robinson, attacks of this kind simply spurred him on to greater virulence, especially as he saw his rivals going farther and farther along the road to abolitionism. This evidence of "progress of apostasy" in the Church Dr. Robinson bitterly bemoaned since the advocates of emancipation were urging a step which "must inevitably lead to the indiscriminate butchery of thousands of wives and children of their own brethren in the slave-holding States."[184] Furthermore, abolitionism he regarded as deleterious in its effect upon the Church; it was "an atheistic humanitarianism which, unless kept out of the Church, will lead, step by step, to utter apostasy from the faith, as it has already done so extensively in New England and the North-west."[185] Not only were the *True Presbyterian's* rivals becoming more hostile to slavery; this increasing hostility, Dr. Robinson complained, went hand in hand with the demand for reunion with the New School.[185a] Such reunion he vociferously deprecated. When the General Assembly of 1864 adopted its outspoken condemnation of slavery, he felt that there was nothing for the conservatives to do but "wait and watch for an opportunity to reconstruct our wasted temple out of the ruins of the old"; though the time had not yet come for any "positive action by the conservative fragment" of the Old School Church, the tendency toward reunion and "taking back the testimony of 1837" might, he

[183] *Cf., e.g.,* editorial note, *Presbyterian,* April 19, 1862; also summary of comments of Old School, New School, and United Presbyterian papers, *Presbyter,* April 24, 1862.

[184] *True Presbyterian,* February 26, 1863.

[185] *Ibid.,* April 3, 1862.

[185a] Editorial, "Virulence and Malignity of New School Sectarianism," *ibid.,* April 17, 1862; also editorial, "We Are Marching On," *ibid.,* October 29, 1863.

thought, open the way for a step of that kind.[186]   Thus reunion might, after all, be of benefit to the faithful few.   It is evident that on the issues which the war produced or accentuated, the *True Presbyterian* and other Old School journals were drawing farther and farther apart.

Early in 1863, some ten months after its establishment, Dr. Robinson announced that he would be able to issue the paper only occasionally, but would try to keep it up.   He particularly regretted having to stop when his list was growing.[187] After appearing at very irregular intervals, the journal resumed regularity of publication in November, 1863, and from that date until November, 1864, was issued bi-weekly with extra issues occasionally thrown in.   Thus its activity continued almost up to the end of the war.   The influence of the paper was by no means confined to Kentucky.   The *Banner's* fears with regard to its promoting disloyal sentiment in Pennsylvania[188] may have been unfounded, but communications from readers in New York were frequently printed,[189] and Dr. Robinson took pains (though perhaps for advertising purposes) to decline through the columns of his paper the urgent invitation of "many kind friends in New York" to transfer the journal to that city.[190]   No doubt the frequent assaults of rival papers stimulated interest in it in the North, especially in the states which bordered Kentucky.[191]   To enemies of Dr. Breckinridge, Dr. Robinson's peppery attacks upon that individual would alone be worth the purchase price of the weekly.

[186] Editorial, "What are Conservative Men to do Now?", *ibid.*, June 9, 1864.

[187] Editorial, "Explanatory," February 26, 1863.

[188] *Cf. ante*, pp. 172-173.

[189] *Cf., e.g.,* editorial, "What are Conservative Men to do Now?", quoting such a communication, *True Presbyterian*, June 9, 1864; also communication from "one of the noblest and most widely known Presbyterian laymen of western New York," *ibid.*, April 17, 1862; *etc.*

[190] Editorial, "To Our Kind Friends in New York," *ibid.*, September 15, 1864.

[191] Many of the copies in the file of the Presbyterian Historical Society in Philadelphia bear the name "J. D. Shane." Rev. J. D. Shane was at this time a minister in Cincinnati.

As Dr. Robinson could say that he "never asked nor accepted pecuniary aid of anyone, toward the regular publication of the paper,"[192] it was particularly important that there should be a large subscription list. At any rate, considering the fact that Dr. Robinson was holding out against the pressure of change of point of view in the Church, that for two years he was directing his publication from Canada while it was being published in war-worried Kentucky, that rival journals were placing obstacles in his way, his *True Presbyterian* displayed amazing vitality. The question naturally arises, what proportion of the subscribers were sympathetic with the editor's sentiments? It would be highly interesting to know the answer.

The unsettled conditions in Church and State during the years of the war were reflected in sporadic attempts at founding new Old School papers. Dr. E. D. MacMaster, extreme anti-slavery leader, announced his intention of publishing a new monthly at one dollar per year, to be called the *Messianic Witness,* but the project was abandoned before the first issue had appeared.[193] When it was proposed to found the *Presbyterian Era* in Chicago in 1864, the *Presbyter,* evidently with the fate of Dr. Rice's *Presbyterian Expositor* in mind, commented, ". . . although the past offers little hope for it, especially as four thousand subscribers are asked to begin with, it may, nevertheless, struggle into life provided it takes decided loyal ground on the present state of the country."[194] The paper never appeared. To many, both in Kentucky and outside, it seemed desirable that there should be a journal to represent the views of the large number of Old School Presbyterians in that state for whom the sentiments of Stuart Robinson on the one hand, and Robert J. Breckinridge on the other, were too extreme. The *Presbyterian Guardian* which was announced in 1862,[195] having failed to appear, the monthly *Western Pres-*

---

[192] Editorial, "Explanatory," *True Presbyterian,* February 26, 1863.

[193] Editorial note, *Presbyterian,* July 12, 1862; also *Presbyter,* December 12, 1862.

[194] Editorial, "A New Presbyterian Paper," *Presbyter,* March 23, 1864.

[195] Editorial, *ibid.,* July 31, 1862.

byterian was established in January, 1864, at Louisville. At the beginning of the following year, it was removed to Danville. Much less colorful than the *True Presbyterian,* much less intellectual than the *Danville Review,* it was not particularly impressive, and its late establishment prevented its having much influence in the development of war sentiment. The Cincinnati *Presbyter,* which always delegated to itself the responsibility of passing judgment on things Kentuckian, complained of the "straddle position" taken on emancipation by the new *Western Presbyterian,* "which is published by the party of Kentucky Presbyterians who are on the fence between Dr. R. J. Breckinridge and Dr. Stuart Robinson. . . ."[196] Nevertheless, two members of the faculty of the Danville Seminary endorsed it as "the only Presbyterian monthly in the country, and distinguished by the character of its editors for intelligent orthodoxy. . . ."[197] At the end of the year 1864 a new and interesting project was anounced — the publication of the *Reunion Presbyterian,* a monthly magazine to be under the joint editorship of Old School and New School men.[198] It never appeared. Thus of all the Old School journals projected during the years of the war, only one — the *Western Presbyterian* — and that one established not long before the close of the conflict, lived on into the post-war period. The four long-established journals of the non-slave states survived and prospered, but very evidently the times were not propitious for the starting of Old School papers.

There was one distinguished religious journal which, although nominally undenominational, was so close to the Old School Church as to be commonly associated in the popular mind with the distinctly Old School periodicals.[199] This was the New York *Observer,* which, having been founded in 1823,

---

[196] Editorial, "Kentucky Progress," *ibid.,* July 20, 1864.

[197] Advertisement, *Presbyterian Historical Almanac,* 1865, p. 383. The theological professors who endorsed the new paper were Dr. E. P. Humphrey and Dr. Stephen Yerkes.

[198] Editorial announcement, *Presbyter,* December 7, 1864.

[199] *Cf. ante,* p. 150.

was now a veteran member of the religious press. In form it was strikingly different from the distinctly Old School papers in that it was divided into a religious sheet and a secular sheet — eight large pages in all. How far its reputation for ultra-conservatism[200] was justified may be estimated from its aims and purposes as set forth in the following advertisement in 1859:

The Aims and Purpose of the New York *Observer*
The New York Observer
The Largest Newspaper in the World
National, Conservative, Religious
Belonging to no party in politics, and to no sect in religion

One grand object of the New York *Observer* is to promote "peace on earth and good will among men." For this end it seeks to advance all those principles which make the *Union of the States* more firm and permanent; it cultivates harmony and good feeling among *all denominations* of Christians; and is a fearless defender of the rights of all men, under the Constitution of the United States and the Word of God.
. . . the New York *Observer* is determined not to be surpassed by any newspaper in the country. Resisting radicalism in Church and State, promoting revivals of pure religion and every wholesome moral reform, on Scriptural and rational principles, discarding and opposing all humbugs, fanaticism, and every scheme of infidelity, socialism and vice, the New York *Observer* designs to be a safeguard of virtue, law, and order, a champion of truth and righteousness in the earth.[201]

The extremely cautious policy followed by the *Observer* during the winter of 1861 exasperated the *Presbyter*. When the *Observer*, in printing in full Dr. Hodge's article on "The State of the Country," remarked that it was doing so "at some inconvenience to ourselves," taking care at the same time to make it clear that the article represented *Dr. Hodge's* opinion, the *Presbyter* was quick to observe that the same issue of the *Observer* gave a long account of horse-taming, and added:

We cannot withhold the expression of our admiration at the manliness of the *Observer* in boldly taking the risk of expressing itself on the important subject of taming wild horses, about which there are opinions diverse.[202]

---

[200] *Ibid.*
[201] Advertisement, New York *Observer*, January 13, 1859.
[202] Editorial, "Scylla and Charibdes [sic]," *Presbyter*, January 17, 1861.

When in January, 1861, the *Observer* failed to publish a communication entitled "A Word to the South" from a western Presbyterian elder, the *Presbyter* gladly printed it, "Though it will reach in our paper very few of the class for which it was intended."[203]   It was not surprising that the *Observer* should advocate a policy of silence for the 1861 Assembly,[204] nor that it should oppose the Emancipation Proclamation.[205]   Like the *Presbyterian*, however, it underwent a process of conversion, and by the fall of 1863 the *Presbyter* was pleased to announce that the New York journal was progressing in the right direction with regard to slavery.[206]   Before long the New York *Observer*, in keeping with the general trend, had become completely anti-slavery.   As war sentiment carried people farther and farther, this venerable, ultra-conservative weekly was keeping step with northern Old School journals.

As compared with the journals of most of the other religious denominations, the Old School periodicals — that is, those already established in 1861 — fared remarkably well during these years of trial.   By mid-summer, 1861, the *Presbyterian* had discovered that seventeen religious papers in the West and Southwest had already been suspended.[207]   Before two years had passed, the same fate had befallen three New School and four Congregational weeklies.[208]   Due to the abnormal economic conditions of the times, other journals had been forced to reduce their size or in some other way change to a less expensive form.[209]   The Methodist press, it is true, probably suffered less than that of any other denomination.   The *Presbyter* accounted for this by explaining that it was regarded to be the duty of Methodist ministers to circulate their papers, and they were required to report as to their faithfulness in the

[203] *Ibid.*, February 7, 1861.
[204] *Ibid.*, April 18, 1861, note, page 2.
[205] Editorial, "The New York *Observer* and the Proclamation," *ibid.*, October 23, 1862.
[206] Editorial, "Progress," *ibid.*, October 7, 1863.
[207] Editorial note, *Presbyterian*, June 29, 1861.
[208] Editorial, *Presbyter*, January 21, 1863.
[209] Editorial, *Presbyterian*, September 14, 1861.

matter.[210] Nevertheless, although denied, because of their
non-official status, the official denominational support with
which the Methodist Church could favor its church organs,
most of the private Old School journals were fully as well off
at the close of the war as they had been in 1860. In the case
of the *Princeton Review*, the *Presbyterian*, the *Presbyter*, and
the *Presbyterian Banner*, particularly, there was every evidence — in form, appearance, and statement — that their influence was enhanced by the war.

Certainly the war brought the Old School periodicals closer
together. Whereas in 1861 practically every conceivable solution of the various issues confronting the Church had had an
enthusiastic champion in one or another of the journals, by the
closing year of the war there was a marked similarity in the
platforms of all of the papers except the *True Presbyterian* and
the *Western Presbyterian*. All were enthusiastically pro-
Union; all at least admitted the right of the depleted General
Assembly to pass resolutions supporting the Union; all were
convinced that slavery must be immediately eliminated from
our country. To be sure, the *Princeton Review* was still firmly
maintaining that its earlier views on all of these matters remained unchanged, and that only because of the demands of
expediency had it come to alter its advice on some of them;
nevertheless the fact remains that its advice had changed.
Only on the question of reunion was there sharp difference of
opinion among them: while the *Presbyter* and the *Presbyterian
Standard* were enthusiastic exponents of this movement, the
Princeton Review, the *Presbyterian*, and the *Danville Review*
were still firmly opposed; the *Presbyterian Banner* — formerly
hostile — was showing signs of weakening. Two years later
the *Presbyterian* and the *Presbyterian Banner* had become
hearty supporters of this pet plan of the *Presbyter's;* only the
Princeton Review remained unconverted.[211] In sharp contrast

[210] Editorial note, *Presbyter*, January 28, 1863.
[211] The *Presbyterian Standard* and the *Danville Review* had been discontinued in 1864.

to this progress toward unanimity on the part of Old School journals, was the policy of the *True Presbyterian* and the *Western Presbyterian*. Both remained firm opponents of Assembly action on political subjects, of the trend toward anti-slavery, and of the agitation for reunion.[212] The ever-widening contrast in policy between these two Kentucky papers and the rest of the Old School press was evidence of a radical divergence of opinion which boded ill for the prospect of holding Old School Presbyterians of Kentucky within the fold of the Church. For there can be no doubt that the Old School papers both reflected and moulded Presbyterian public opinion.

[212] The *True Presbyterian* was discontinued in November, 1864, but its policies on the major issues in the Church were followed, though in a much milder form, by the *Western Presbyterian*.

CHAPTER VI

REVOLT IN THE BORDER STATES

In the decade of the 1860's the Old School Presbyterian Church, like the Federal Government, was engaged in a vital struggle to maintain its unity unimpaired. The situation which confronted the ecclesiastical body often bore a striking similarity to that facing the government to which it was pledging its hearty support. Each organization hoped to regain a southern wing lost in 1861; each, at first baffled by the question of negro slavery, moved toward a position of extreme hostility to that institution; each was immediately concerned with keeping the Border States loyal. In every case the Federal Government was more successful in its solution, or at least arrived at a solution more speedily. Particularly in the problem of the Border States, while the Lincoln administration was finding its solution becoming progressively simpler, the Old School Church was getting more and more deeply involved. No doubt the explanation of this contrast in success is to be found principally in the fact that the Federal Government could use force to keep its members loyal: conciliatory as it was in its policy toward the Border States, its military success was not the least convincing factor in holding them within the Union; the Old School Church, on the other hand, restricted to argument at a time when physical power was monopolizing men's respect, was indeed handicapped. Yet the problem was not insuperable; not only in Maryland (where the individual churches for the most part stayed with the denomination), but in Kentucky and Missouri as well, there was a strong traditional affection for the Old School Church, and the majority were not likely to break away from it without sharp provocation.

In Kentucky, where the trouble focussed, though they were outnumbered by the Baptists and the Methodists, as well as by the members of the Christian denomination,[1] Old School Presbyterians could rightly believe that membership in their venerable denomination helped place them in the front rank in prestige and influence.[2] One finds himself conjecturing whether the whole Border State contingent might not have been saved, had it not been for certain individuals and certain peculiar circumstances. Suppose there had been no Robert J. Breckinridge, no Stuart Robinson, would the Kentucky Synod have divided, and such a large number of Missourians been lost to the church? Suppose there had been no New School Church to conciliate, would not Old School leaders have taken a kindlier, less high-handed attitude toward their Border State brethren? Nevertheless the fact remains that there was a bitter Breckinridge-Robinson feud; and there was the necessity — from the point of view of leaders in the North-West — of conciliating the New School brethren. Such being the case, the break in the Border States was probably inevitable.

There were in 1861 four Border State synods in the Old School Church. In the cases of the Synod of Baltimore and the Synod of Upper Missouri, some of the constituent presbyteries lay outside of the Border States. The table given below[3] shows the Border State strength of each of the four synods in 1861 in comparison with corresponding numbers for the entire Old School Church in 1861 and in 1862:

Synods	Organized	Presbyteries Total	Presbyteries Border State	Ministers	Churches	Com-municants	Total Contributions
Baltimore	1854	5	3	57	63	5,174	$ 154,796
Kentucky	1802	6	6	104	164	11,229	111,270
Missouri	1832	5	5	78	102	6,260	63,680
Upper Missouri	1858	4	3	42	74	2,461	25,161
Old School Church 1861		176	17	2,767	3,684	300,814	3,040,824
Old School Church (*Active*), 1862		121	12	2,104	2,539	226,226	1,710,636

[1] Coulter, E. Merton, *The Civil War and Readjustment in Kentucky* (Chapel Hill, 1926), p. 398; *cf.*, also, tables, *ante*, p. 16.

[2] Coulter, *op. cit.*, pp. 398-399.

[3] Compiled from statistical tables, *Minutes of the General Assembly*, 1861-62, vol. xvi, pp. 402-403; 548-552; 832-836; *Presbyterian Historical Almanac*, 1862, p. 130.

Although the Synod of Baltimore had been but recently created, the Old School Church had long flourished in Maryland; several of the individual congregations of this synod were among the strongest and most highly respected in the denomination.[4] The synod was wealthy: the foregoing table reveals the fact that in 1861 its communicants contributed three times their share of the money raised by the whole Church. With several strong churches in the capital of the Republic — one of them attended by President Lincoln[5] — there was bound to be considerable pressure exerted to keep the synod loyal. Its wealth, traditions, and compactness all contributed to make it conservative — conservative in adhering to the organization as well as to the rigorous orthodoxy of the Old School Church. To be sure, the pro-Southern members of the synod were by no means negligible in numbers; one of the best-informed leaders in Maryland asserted in the General Assembly of 1862 that "from one-third to two-thirds of these various congregations sympathize with the South";[6] in several individual churches there were destined to be bitter war disputes before peacetime conditions were completely restored; nevertheless in general the Synod of Baltimore played the role of pacifier rather than of disturber during the war troubles.

The Synod of Upper Missouri was too weak and too completely overwhelmed by the war to take a leading part in the controversies in the Church; such activities it left to the Synods of Kentucky and Missouri. It was in Kentucky that the struggle was the fiercest. The Synod of Kentucky had nearly twice as many members as that of Missouri; centrally located within it was the growing Danville Theological Seminary; with the *Danville Review* and the succession of *Presbyterian Herald, True Presbyterian,* and *Western Presbyterian,* the extremely divergent views there prevalent on political mat-

---

[4] Gillett, *op. cit.*, vol. ii, pp. 14-17.
[5] The New York Avenue Presbyterian Church, of which Dr. P. D. Gurley was pastor.
[6] *Cf.* speech of Dr. J. C. Backus as reported in account of ninth day of session of the 1862 General Assembly, *Presbyterian,* June 7, 1862.

ters had, during most of the war period, organs of expression; and finally, with two such eager theological fighters as the editors of the *Danville Review* and the *True Presbyterian*,[7] the Synod could not possibly have avoided being a battle-ground. Throughout the war period, the eyes of the Old School Church were upon Kentucky.

In a hundred ways even the formal minutes of the presbyteries and Synod of Kentucky reflect the tense situation there and the extensive influence of the war upon all of the activities of the Church. Yet, considering the difficulties encountered, the church bodies assembled with surprising regularity. During the first three years of the war, presbyteries and Synod followed a consistent policy with regard to the deliverances of the General Assembly. In 1861, they all vigorously denounced the Spring Resolutions, though with equal emphasis they all declared their loyalty to the Old School Church.[8] In fact, throughout Kentucky sentiment seemed to be unanimous against the constitutionality and expediency of the General Assembly's action.[9] Having failed of a quorum in the regular fall meeting in 1862, the Synod adjourned to meet the following spring. Obviously some action on the Breckinridge Paper of 1862 [10] was to be expected from this meeting. No such unanimity as had prevailed in 1861 could be hoped for now, for Dr. Breckinridge in his paper had carefully avoided laying himself open to the charges that he himself had made against Dr. Spring's resolutions of the previous year.[11] Dr. Breckinridge's friends in the Kentucky Synod might thus be expected to endorse his deliverance, even though they had joined him in condemning the deliverance of 1861. On the other hand, his enemies — and they were many — would probably be more hostile than ever to General Assembly action, now that the particular action of the Assembly had been dictated by him. The

[7] *Cf. ante*, pp. 36-38; 141-148; 167-177; *post*, pp. 189-195.
[8] *Cf. ante*, pp. 96-99.
[9] *Cf. ante*, p. 98.
[10] *Cf. ante*, pp. 110-119.
[11] *Cf. ante*, pp. 142-143.

seventy men[12] who convened for the adjourned session of the Synod in May, 1863, were, however, apparently too evenly divided for either side to risk an argument, and it was agreed that

. . . the most proper course for this Synod to take, at its present sessions, with reference to the action of the Assembly, seems to be to content
itself with the preceding statements [that is, the statements of the 1861
session of the Synod]; to reserve, until its regular meeting in October
next, the consideration of any further decisive action, on the general subject, it may be its duty to take.[13]

When the time for the October meeting arrived, however, the Synod continued its policy of silence with regard to Assembly action. In this meeting perhaps a decisive factor in the Synod's determination to avoid an argument on the Assembly's stand was the amount of time it was found necessary to devote to the case of Rev. George Morrison, a Kentucky pastor who had quarreled with the pro-Confederacy majority of his congregation.[14]   Dr. Breckinridge's protest against the manner in which the West Lexington Presbytery had handled the case was sustained, but Mr. Morrison was rebuked by the Synod for using soldiers to recover the records and keys of the church.[15] The vigorous denunciation of slavery voiced by the General Assembly of 1864 produced a departure from the Kentucky Synod's policy of silence. By a vote of 75 to 10 the Synod at its fall meeting declared the action of the General Assembly "unnecessary, unwise, and untimely," but it still adhered "with unbroken purpose" to the Presbyterian Church of the United States of America.[16] About this time the *Presbyter*, Kentucky's close neighbor, could detect three distinct parties in the Old School Church in that state: the Robert J.

---

[12] Account of meeting of Synod of Kentucky, *Presbyterian*, May 16, 1863.
[13] *Minutes of the Synod of Kentucky*, May, 1863 (Cincinnati, 1863), p. 12.
[14] The communicant membership of the congregation was 35. *Minutes of the General Assembly*, 1863, vol. xvii, p. 220.
[15] *Minutes of the Synod of Kentucky*, October, 1863 (Cincinnati, 1863), pp. 20-30.
[16] Editorial, *Presbyter*, November 23, 1864.

Breckinridge faction, who were loyal anti-slavery men; a party of loyal men who wanted the state and the synod to go with the North, if there must be division; and the party of the *True Presbyterian.*[17] The vote in the 1864 meeting of the Synod of Kentucky showed unmistakably that the vast majority of the members still were strongly attached to the Old School Church.

From the outset of the troubles it had been apparent that the least tractable of Kentucky Presbyterians were to be found in the Presbytery of Louisville. As early as the summer of 1861 it had invited "all true and conservative men in our beloved Church, North and South" to unite with it "in defending and preserving the purity, unity, and prosperity of the Presbyterian Church in the United States of America,"[18] thereby showing itself ready for drastic action, though not yet prepared to depart from the Church. In the spring of 1864, when an order was issued from the office of the Assistant Adjutant General, permitting Old School ministers who bore a commission from the Board of Domestic Missions to exercise ministerial functions in the reconquered Southern territory, and directing that they be given "all the aid, countenance, and support . . . practicable,"[19] the incensed Louisville Presbytery passed a resolution calling upon the General Assembly to "disavow the said act," and followed this by another resolution to the effect that it did not design to cast reflections upon the War Department, since the latter was doing only "what it was improperly asked to do."[20] Instead of heeding the demands of the Louisville Presbytery, the General Assembly adopted its extended denunciation of slavery, thereby fairly inviting the defiant presbytery to go even farther in its hostile actions. The Presbytery did not equivocate in stating its attitude on this measure: "We decline to adopt the doctrine or

[17] Editorial, "Our Church in Kentucky," *Presbyter,* October 12, 1864.
[18] *Cf. ante,* p. 97.
[19] For a more extended account of this episode, *cf. post,* pp. 458-465.
[20] Editorial, "Our Church in Kentucky," *Presbyter,* May 4, 1864.

obey the duty enjoined in this deliverance. . . ." it declared.[21]
There could be little doubt that if a movement to leave the Old
School Church should be inaugurated in Kentucky, the Presbytery of Louisville would have a leading part in the undertaking.

Louisville was the seat of the bitterest hostility to Dr. Breckinridge. Presiding over the largest church of the Old School
denomination in that city when the war began was the pugna-
cious Dr. Stuart Robinson, who was shortly to found the *True
Presbyterian.* Rev. Thomas Hoyt, pastor of the second largest
church, shared with Dr. Robinson the bitterest portion of Dr.
Breckinridge's wrath. Although the quarrel had begun when
these two men withdrew from the association of editors of
the *Danville Review* shortly before the appearance of its first
number early in 1861,[22] it reached its climax in the General
Assembly of 1862. In March, 1862, Dr. Breckinridge published in leading secular newspapers a detailed statement of
his difficulties with five of his associate editors and with his
publisher. He called upon the readers of his advertisement
to assist him with their subscriptions.[23] Stuart Robinson, having been named as one of the withdrawing editors, immediately
replied to Breckinridge's charges by a lengthy statement of his
own — a statement that was bound to arouse in the hot-headed
Danville professor the direst sort of wrath:

> Now, granting the right of all literary enterprises to "drum" accord-
> ing to the adventurer's taste, no one will deny that it is of questionable
> taste, to say nothing else, for a venerable Professor of Theology, set to
> train and model the rising Ministry of the Church, to attempt the art by
> the rather unmanly and unchristian ruse of hounding on popular passion,
> already half frantic with excitement, against his brethren, merely because
> popular prejudices are just now in a condition to be easily roused, and
> credulous beyond degree in a direction to suit him. . . .
> As to the unworthy cry of "secessionist," I know of no ground for

---

[21] Editorial, "The Louisville Presbytery on Slavery," *Presbyter,* May 3,
1865.
[22] *Cf. ante,* pp. 37-38; 141.
[23] *Cf.* copy of advertisement, *Danville Quarterly Review,* March, 1862, vol.
2, pp. 140-142.

Dr. B's charge, except that I do not concur in Dr. B's despotic and intolerant spirit, nor in his Jacobinical contempt for courts and judges' decisions, nor in his judgment of the ability and the importance of his articles, in which I have discovered few important ideas, that the Louisville Journal and other papers had not presented before, though with less of the " *vox et praeterea nihil* " in the style of doing it. . . .

Neither I, as pastor, nor he, as professor, may take advantage of the pulpit or theological chair as a politician. The secular press is open to us as to other citizens. If that is not to his taste, Dr. B as a gentleman of wealth, has abundant means to publish his views in serial, or occasional form, without claiming the solemnity and dignity of a Theological Quarterly, and a Theological Seminary, to invest them with a fictitious solemnity. . . .[24]

Dr. Breckinridge devoted twenty-seven pages of the March number of his journal to the history of the controversy to date, directing his attack particularly against the charges in Dr. Robinson's communication, and hurling back counter-charges of deceit, malice, and hypocrisy.[25] But the other former associate editors were not neglected. Three of them, like Robinson, had published replies to Breckinridge. Each of these replies received an answer in the article in the March *Review*. Mr. Hoyt came in for particular personal abuse. Alleging that Hoyt's statements constituted a "gross and malicious personal attack," Breckinridge was sorrowful that a man who was a South Carolinian by birth could have been guilty of them: ". . . terribly as *Southern Chivalry* has run down of late, I would not have believed that a Presbyterian minister, whom I considered a gentleman, would — under any provocation — much less with almost none that was just — have put his name to a publication so completely disgraceful." [26] And all this furor had been stirred up by the simple question whether an article upholding the Federal Government should be published in the *Danville Review!* [27]

[24] *Ibid.*, pp. 142-145.
[25] " In Memoriam. A Tribute to the Rev. Stuart Robinson: With Notices of the Rev. J. M. Worrall, the Rev. T. A. Hoyt, the Rev. R. L. Breck, and some others," *ibid.*, pp. 140-167.
[26] *Ibid.*, p. 164.
[27] *Cf. ante*, pp. 37-38.

Apparently not at all disturbed over the questionable propriety of his action, Dr. Breckinridge submitted the whole matter of the quarrel — or at least his side of it — to the General Assembly of 1862. In a lengthy paper offering his resignation, he gave his version of the charges of Robinson and Hoyt against him. Mr. Hoyt had expressed regret that "a theological professor should use his position and the sacred funds [28] of his institution, as the means of hurling firebrands among the churches that raised him to that position, and contributed those funds." [29] Dr. Breckinridge chose to interpret this statement as meaning that he had abused his position, and "perverted sacred funds to the promotion of wicked and cruel ends, degrading both the pulpit and the theological chair, to the advancement of improper public objects, and unworthy personal aims." [30] The severest charges made in Dr. Robinson's statement were similarly summarized in Breckinridge's paper of resignation. This paper in turn called forth replies from the two gentlemen attacked. Dr. Robinson being a commissioner could defend himself orally from the floor of the Assembly; Mr. Hoyt's case was placed before the Assembly by his friend in the form of the communication which he had sent the week before to the *Presbyterian* and the *True Presbyterian*.[31]

Both statements categorically denied the Breckinridge charges, and Dr. Robinson further insisted that the Assembly had no higher obligation to protect the character of professors in its seminaries than that of pastors of its churches; that the resignation of a professorship according to the constitution of the Danville Seminary should first be laid before the Board of Directors of the Seminary on six months' notice, to be by them

---

[28] "To avoid any ambiguity" Mr. Hoyt had, when he sent his communication to the *Presbyterian* and *True Presbyterian,* substituted the word "prestige" for "funds." *Minutes of the General Assembly,* 1862, vol. xvi, p. 606.

[29] *Ibid.*

[30] *Ibid.,* pp. 599-601.

[31] *Ibid.,* pp. 604-607.

referred to the Assembly; that Dr. Breckinridge's assertion
that "Suddenly, and without any provocation on my part,
tending towards such accusations, but solely as the effect of
personal malignity and personal disloyalty on the part of
Thomas A. Hoyt and *Stuart Robinson* . . . I find myself accused of immoralities and crimes, by both of them, in the most
offensive terms, and in the most public manner, the bare suspicion of whose perpetration by me, would render it unfit that
I should hold my office of Professor. . . ." [32] was directly
contrary to the actual facts of the case. The statements of
both Hoyt and Robinson, though firm and vigorous, were respectful in tone and couched in temperate language. As Robinson later expressed it in his disrespectful reply to the editorial in which the *Presbyter* had commended his attitude in
the Assembly,[33] he was deeply impressed with the necessity of
being more moderate in the "rebuke of folly" in a Spiritual
Court than in a private — albeit a religious — journal.

The General Assembly now found itself in a difficult situation. It was being asked to take an extraordinary, if not unconstitutional, action in considering this quarrel, and the man
who was making this request was not only one of the most
powerful and most venerable ministers of the Church, but one
who in the eyes of the vast majority of the Assembly was
rendering the Church and the country invaluable assistance
by his forceful pro-Union labors. In 1862 of course the latter consideration far outweighed the former; it was soon agreed
that the Assembly must take some action in behalf of this
man who was even now assuming the lead in securing from the
Assembly a hearty endorsement of the Federal Government.[34]
The original report of the special committee to which the various papers in the case were referred consisted of a series of
resolutions which might easily have been interpreted as placing
the Assembly on Dr. Breckinridge's side of the controversy.

[32] *Ibid.*, pp. 599-600.
[33] *Cf. ante*, p. 171.
[34] *Cf. ante*, pp. 110-116.

After Dr. Robinson had protested — though "in no spirit of
threat, egotism, or bravado," he asserted — that if the resolutions were passed in this form it would be his deliberate conclusion that the Lord did not call him any longer to preach
the Gospel under the commission of the body who had pronounced such a decision, amendments were adopted which
made the report simply a statement of the constitutional rights
of the Assembly in such a case, an expression of confidence in
Dr. Breckinridge, and a denial that the acceptance of a chair
in the Seminary necessarily involved his yielding the right of
freely expressing his views "in relation to matters of great
national concernment" — matters on which "his bold and
patriotic stand . . . entitle him to the gratitude of the Church
and the country." [35]   So amended the report was passed, and
both parties were satisfied.[36]   The special correspondent of
the New York *Evangelist* (New School) was much impressed
by the amount of time the Assembly was willing to devote to
the Danville doctor:

Dr. Breckinridge has been the one conspicuous figure in the Assembly.
. . . Not to speak of the fact that in the general deliberations of the
body, he seemed to be always either speaking, or just about to speak, or
just through speaking . . . one might almost have imagined from the frequency with which his name was introduced that the Assembly had been
convened to listen to his particular case. Never have I seen a man assume
such prominence, or claim such high prerogatives in such a body. And I
confess to some quiet delight, when, toward the close of the long discussion
respecting his difficulties with Stuart Robinson, Dr. Hoge [venerable re-
tired pastor of the First Presbyterian Church of Columbus, which he had
founded some 55 years earlier, and which was now entertaining the General
Assembly] arose and intimated that, although he had voted for the resolution extolling his patriotism, &c., he was not prepared to see the Assembly
endorse and magnify any living man, even among the most eminent teachers of the Church, as they were called upon to do in this instance. At his
suggestion, the final resolution presented by the Committee, lauding the
Kentucky doctor as a professor of theology, was modified into a simple
request that he would withdraw his resignation; and so was passed — much

[35] For the report of the committee as finally adopted, *cf. Minutes of the
General Assembly*, 1862, vol. xvi, pp. 632-633.
[36] An account of this episode is given in the report of the sessions of the
Assembly, *Presbyterian*, May 31 and June 7, 1862.

to my satisfaction. I had grown exceedingly weary of the ubiquitous and sempiternal Breckinridge.[37]

Notwithstanding the fact that both Breckinridge and Robinson had professed satisfaction with the outcome of the episode in the Assembly, there was no diminution in the abuse which they heaped upon one another through the columns of their respective journals. On the whole, Dr. Robinson was the more expert at inventing and collecting epithets with which to designate his opponent. Robinson might be a "turbulent Professor of extra holiness"[38] as Breckinridge termed him, but that did not prevent him from applying some singularly unholy terminology to the editor of the *Review*, although usually he attributed its invention to others. Governor Bramlette was given the credit for "Reverend Maligner,"[39] while it was the Baltimoreans who "used to nickname [him] Hyena Bob, partly on account of his appearance and partly on account of his disposition," it was explained.[40] "Popular tradition in Kentucky," Robinson asserted, "attributes to some of his earlier friends [the reflection] 'That the conversion of Dr. Breckinridge was a curious instance of the marvellous [sic] grace of God to the individual, at the expense of judgment on the Church, and chastisement to his brethren.'"[41]

The settlement in the 1862 Assembly did not bring an end to charges of Breckinridge's misusing his position as theological professor. Under the title, "The Danville 'Stump' Theology and financial ethics," an editorial in the *True Presbyterian* claimed that he had taken his full salary of 1500 dollars for delivering only two lectures in his class-work, in spite of the fact that a considerable portion of his time was being devoted to political speaking.[42] So the quarrel raged on. Its

[37] The New York *Evangelist* quoted in article, "The Assembly from a New School Viewpoint," *True Presbyterian*, June 19, 1862.
[38] *Danville Quarterly Review*, March, 1862, vol. 2, p. 148.
[39] *True Presbyterian*, October 27, 1864.
[40] Louisville *Journal*, quoted in *True Presbyterian*, October 8, 1864.
[41] *True Presbyterian*, May 8, 1862.
[42] *Ibid.*, October 27, 1864.

influence extended far beyond the two contestants, for each had a whole army of ardent admirers. Dr. Robinson's intense loyalty to the truth as he saw it,[43] and the warmth and generosity of his heart inspired deep love for him on the part of his friends — a feeling that was intensified by his being regarded as "the object of a venomous and unrelenting persecution."[44] As for Dr. Breckinridge, his talents and attainments were so conspicuous that a well-informed student of Presbyterian history could write about him some thirty years after his death, ". . . he was a glory of a man; second to none, I believe, in the United States, of those who never held any official position."[45] The very fact that the General Assembly, never wanting in eloquent leaders, was always willing to listen to him, testifies convincingly to his importance. A persistent quarrel between these two powerful leaders was bound to divide Old School Presbyterians in Kentucky into two hostile camps. The Louisville Presbytery, of which both Robinson and Hoyt were members, quite naturally came to be regarded by the Breckinridge faction as the most troublesome unit in the Synod of Kentucky.

When the Presbytery of Louisville resolved, with regard to the action of the General Assembly of 1864, that "We decline to adopt the doctrine or obey the duty enjoined in this deliverance. . . ."[46], the *Presbyter* commented that the prospect seemed to be that a large part of the church in Kentucky would separate from the Old School Church and join the Southern General Assembly.[47] The climax in the relationship between the General Assembly and the obstreperous element in Kentucky came, however, a few months later, when it was

[43] *Cf.* statement of Dr. B. M. Palmer, quoted in White, *op. cit.,* pp. 419-420.

[44] *Cf.* statement of Dr. Thomas E. Peck (leader in Southern Presbyterian Church) quoted, *ibid.,* p. 418.

[45] Statement of Alfred A. Thomas, son of Dr. Thomas E. Thomas (*cf. post,* p. 228), Thomas, *op. cit.,* p. 10.

[46] Editorial, "The Louisville Presbytery on Slavery," *Presbyter,* May 3, 1865.

[47] *Ibid.*

precipitated by the action taken by the General Assembly of
1865. In the light of the disaffection which had been steadily
growing in Kentucky during the four years of the war, it was
inevitable that the attitude taken by the Assembly which convened almost immediately after the surrender of Lee should
have produced a permanent breach in the Church.

In many respects the circumstances under which the General Assembly of 1865 met in Pittsburgh were similar to those
of its predecessor four years before in Philadelphia.[48] Then
the recent attack upon Fort Sumter had stirred up a frenzy of
patriotism; now the North was beside itself with wrath over
the assassination of Lincoln. In both cases the major part of
the time, energies, and interest of the body was devoted to
problems which arose out of the political situation. In 1865
these problems were four-fold: Presbyterian care of the freedmen; the resumption of Old School activity in the states of the
former Confederacy; the matter of purging from the roll of
the Church the names of synods, presbyteries, and ministers
now belonging to the Southern Church; the course to be pursued with regard to the admission to any presbytery of ministers " known to be disloyal to the government of the United
States, or who may be suspected of disloyalty." Obviously
every one of these problems, and particularly the last-named,
was of immense concern to the Border States. That the solutions adopted would likely not be satisfactory to Presbyterians
in these states was indicated by the action taken early in the
session with regard to the records of the Synod of Kentucky.
The records were approved with the exception of the stand
taken by the Synod[49] on the General Assembly's 1864 deliverance on slavery, and the fact that " The Synod has wholly
failed to make any deliverance during the past year calculated
to sustain and encourage our government in its efforts to suppress a most extensive, wanton, and wicked rebellion, aiming

[48] *Cf. ante,* p. 42.
[49] *Cf. ante,* p. 187.

at nothing short of the life of the nation." [50]   Such words sounded ominous to those who had been sanguine of the growth of a spirit of tolerance on the part of the Assembly.

The policy the Old School Church chose to follow with regard to reëstablishing herself in the South [51] was clearly set forth in four of the eight resolutions submitted by the Committee on the Board of Domestic Missions — resolutions all of which were adopted *seriatim* after lengthy debate.   The four which dealt with the South were as follows:

> *Resolved,* 3. That the General Assembly direct the Board of Domestic Missions to take prompt and effectual measures to restore and build up the Presbyterian congregations in the Southern States of this Union by the appointment and support of prudent and devoted missionaries.
>
> *Resolved,* 4. That none be appointed but those who give satisfactory evidence of their loyalty to the national government, and that they are in cordial sympathy with the General Assembly of the Presbyterian Church in the United States of America in her testimony on doctrine, loyalty, and freedom.
>
> *Resolved,* 5. That special efforts be made to instruct and evangelize and gather into churches, on a credible profession of faith, the colored population.
>
> *Resolved,* 6. That in view of the extensive and urgent demand for pious and loyal ministers, elders and teachers, in the southern States, such be earnestly recommended to direct their course to that now opening and inviting field, as presenting a loud call from the Lord Jesus Christ to pass over and help to rebuild that part of the American Zion which has been so sadly laid waste by the rebellion and civil war.[52]

While the resolution demanding "satisfactory evidence of their loyalty" from all candidates for the work of the Church in the South caused a considerable amount of discussion, it did not arouse pronounced dissension.   It was subsequent measures of the Assembly which provoked the earnest protest of several members, the determined opposition of others, and which were responsible for bringing a large and important group in the Border States to a position of open defiance.

In reply to an overture from the Presbytery of Richland

[50] *Minutes of the General Assembly,* 1865, vol. xvii, p. 541.

[51] The action of the Assembly on the first of the problems named above, (Presbyterian care of the freedmen), is discussed *post,* pp. 440-446.

[52] *Minutes of the General Assembly,* 1865, vol. xvii, pp. 553-554.

(Ohio) and from members of the Presbytery of Madison (Indiana) asking the Assembly to "drop from its roll the names of certain ministers, Presbyteries, and Synods, in the so-called Confederate States," [53] the Assembly after due deliberation adopted a lengthy minute. Its principal provisions were:

Whereas, During the existence of the great rebellion . . . a large number of Presbyteries and Synods in the Southern States . . . have organized an Assembly denominated " The General Assembly of the Confederate States of America," in order to render their aid in the attempt to establish . . . a separate national existence, and to " conserve and perpetuate the system of slavery," therefore

Resolved, 1. That this Assembly regards the civil rebellion for the perpetuation of negro slavery as a great crime . . . and the secession of those Presbyteries and Synods . . . under such circumstances and for such reasons, as unwarranted, schismatical, and unconstitutional.

Resolved, 2. That the General Assembly does not intend to abandon the territory in which these churches are found, or to compromise the rights of any of the church courts, or ministers, ruling elders, and private members belonging to them, who are loyal to the government of the United States, and to the Presbyterian Church. On the contrary, this Assembly will recognize such loyal persons as constituting the churches, Presbyteries and Synods, in all the bounds of the schism, and will use earnest endeavours to restore and revive all such churches and church courts.

Resolved, 3. The Assembly hereby declares that it will recognize as the church, the members of any church, within the bounds of the schism, who are loyal to the government of the United States . . . the Confession of Faith, and . . . the several testimonies of the Presbyterian Church on the subject of domestic slavery. . . .

. . . . .

Resolved, 5. The General Assembly furthermore give counsel to the Presbyteries and churches which may be revived and restored under the provisions of the above action, to treat with kindness ministers and churches or parts of churches, who are disloyal, or who are not in sympathy with the former deliverances of the General Assembly on the subject of slavery, and to inform such persons of their readiness to receive them into ecclesiastical fellowship, when they properly acknowledge and renounce their errors.

Resolved, 6. The Board of Domestic Missions is hereby authorized and requested to give special attention to the Southern field. . . .[54]

Still more drastic was the Assembly's action on the matter of " disloyal " ministers, which was taken in response to an

[53] *Ibid.,* p. 549.
[54] *Ibid.,* pp. 560-561.

overture from the Presbytery of California inquiring what course ought to be pursued in regard to admitting to their body ministers "who are known to be disloyal to the government of the United States, or who may be suspected of disloyalty." [55] It was in its answer to this overture that the General Assembly of the Old School Church reached the climax of its rampant progress toward hyper-patriotism:

I. The right of every Presbytery to examine ministers asking admission into their body, as to their soundness in the faith . . . implies their right by parity of reasoning to examine them on all subjects which seriously affect the peace, purity, and unity of the Church.

II. The exercise of this right becomes an imperative duty, in the present circumstances of our country, when, after the crushing by military force of an atrocious rebellion . . . for the perpetuation of slavery, many ministers who have aided and abetted this revolt, may seek admission into Presbyteries located in the loyal States. Therefore,

III. It is hereby ordered that all our Presbyteries examine every minister applying for admission from any Presbytery or other ecclesiastical body in the Southern States, on the following points:

1. Whether he has in any way, directly or indirectly, of his own free will and consent, or without external constraint, been concerned at any time in aiding or countenancing the rebellion and the war . . . and if it be found by his own confession or from sufficient testimony, that he has been so concerned, that he be required to confess and forsake his sin before he shall be received.

2. Whether he holds that the system of negro slavery in the South is a Divine institution, and that it is "the peculiar mission of the Southern Church to conserve the institution of slavery as there maintained," and if it be found that he holds either of these doctrines, that he be not received without renouncing and forsaking these errors.

IV. This injunction to Presbyteries is in like manner applicable to Synods, and it is hereby ordered that upon the application of any Presbytery to be received into any Synod where such Presbytery is or has been connected with the Southern General Assembly, such Synod shall examine all the members of said Presbytery on the points above named . . .

V. Church sessions are also ordered to examine all applicants for church membership by persons from the Southern States, or who have been living in the South since the rebellion . . .

VI. The General Assembly gives counsel to the several church courts specified in these orders, that in discharging the duties enjoined therein, due regard be paid to the circumstances of the case, and that justice be tempered with mercy. Especially is this counsel given to churches in the

---

[55] *Ibid.*, p. 549.

border States, where many impulsive and ardent young men . . . have been led away by their superiors, or seduced from their loyalty by their erroneous interpretation of the doctrine of State rights. . . .

VII. It is further ordered, that if any minister or ministers belonging to any Presbytery or Presbyteries under the care of the General Assembly, have fled or been sent by civil or military authority beyond the jurisdiction of the United States on account of their disloyalty, or who may have gone for the same reason to any of the Southern States, and have aided in this rebellion, such Presbytery or Presbyteries shall take action on the subject, and unless they obtain satisfactory evidence of the repentance of such ministers, they shall declare and enter upon their records that they are henceforth suspended from the functions of the gospel ministry until their cases can be regularly issued. And if for two years they shall still remain beyond the reach of said Presbytery or Presbyteries, the names of such ministers shall be erased from the roll, and they shall thereupon be no longer deemed ministers of the Presbyterian Church.[56]

This report was adopted by the Assembly, but not without earnest protests being uttered during the debates which preceded the vote. Unfortunately for the cause of the protestants, the majority of the commissioners were not in a peaceful mood. Even among the delegates from the Border States were some who insisted that loyal members could not be blamed for refusing to take communion with Southern sympathizers until they had given " proper evidence that they feel the enormity of their sin, that they are humbled and truly penitent, and desire the forgiveness of their brethren." [57]   On the other hand, one Border State brother, calling attention to the fact that the report as presented required the special examination only of Southerners, proposed an elaborate amendment extending the investigation and test to all officers and members of the Church " who, while they retain all their sympathy for said rebellion, and are ready in any secure way to render any aid in their power, do yet abide in those places in the country and Church as . . . are not molested by any of the armies, or in danger of being arrested by any of the Provost-Marshals." [58]

[56] *Ibid.*, pp. 562-564.

[57] *Cf.* report of 10th day of session, *Presbyterian*, June 17, 1865. The speaker was Rev. John F. Coons of Kentucky.

[58] *Cf.* report of 11th day of session, *Presbyterian*, June 17, 1865. The speaker was Rev. A. B. Cross of Baltimore.

After reading his amendment, the speaker remarked, "What's sauce for the goose is sauce for the gander. What is good for us down South is good all over the country." His amendment was immediately laid upon the table.[59] When another speaker [60] suggested that the whole of the action contemplated was unnecessary, either for the direction of the presbyteries — which could be trusted to handle the matter satisfactorily by themselves — or to set the Church right before the country — which had been done by the deliverances of previous years, as well as by the adoption of other measures in the present Assembly — the editor of the *Presbyter* (who was serving as a commissioner from the Presbytery of Cincinnati) vigorously protested against this sort of argument. "There are Presbyteries and churches who will never do justice to the crime of rebellion," he cried, "unless their duties are defined by some such paper. They will greet rebels with a holy kiss, and settle down together." [61]

After the report had been adopted, one of the leaders of the Assembly,[62] evidently laboring under a curious misconception of the possibilities of parliamentary procedure, moved an amendment to the paper just adopted. In spite of strenuous objection, the Moderator declared the amendment in order. The change proposed was the insertion in the section defining the duties of church sessions of the words "and to take cognizance also of members of their own churches who have offended in like manner." [63] In spite of the fact that support of the amendment was actuated in part by a desire to see rules of the Church enforced uniformly throughout its membership, by many the proposal was regarded as a manifestation of a

---

[59] *Ibid.*

[60] Dr. William H. Green, Professor in Princeton Theological Seminary.

[61] Speech of Dr. J. G. Monfort, as reported in account of 11th day of session of the Assembly, *Presbyterian*, June 17, 1865.

[62] Dr. James Wood, President of Hanover College, Indiana. Dr. Wood's parliamentary error is the more conspicuous since he had been Moderator of the 1864 General Assembly.

[63] Report of 11th day of Assembly sessions, *Presbyterian*, June 17, 1865.

relentless vindictiveness.   One prominent lay commissioner [64]
gave utterance to a stinging rebuke:

> Moderator, I hoped we were done with this question.   I have been in
> many political conventions — and I wish you to understand they were
> Republican conventions, for I have never been in any other — yet I must
> say I have never before seen such a spirit of relentless persecution as is here
> manifested.   Have we not had enough of this talk about loyalty?   Are we
> not ready to quit and be done?   I have heard of nothing else since I came
> into this Assembly.   If the members of a church live in sin, it is the duty
> of the session to call them to account.   It will be done, if sessions are loyal,
> without this action.   If they are not, this action will do no good.   It is use-
> less — it is worse than useless — for its only tendency is to irritate and to
> drive away those whom we desire to see repent and return to the fold.
> Before asking them to come back, we prescribe the penance.   It is useless
> to pass this amendment.   Let the thing alone — let the thing alone, and give
> these brethren time.[65]

The amendment was lost by a vote of 64 to 83.[66] But the
report itself had been adopted, and through it the General
Assembly had gone on record as making its own deliverances
the test of orthodoxy and loyalty, declaring agreement with
this test to be a condition of ministerial and church fellowship.
" We are persuaded," wrote Dr. Hodge in reviewing the action
of the General Assembly, " that not a member of the body, when
he comes calmly to consider the matter, will hesitate to admit
that the Assembly, in so doing, transcended its power." [67] The
majority of the members, he thought, would admit on reflection that their action with regard to synods and presbyteries
was wholly unnecessary, since these bodies needed no action
of the Assembly to authorize them to handle such cases as
the report covered.[68] Furthermore, in demanding that all who
favored the rebellion should give evidence of repentance of that
sin and openly confess it, this paper was going beyond all
previous action of the Assembly and all demands of the civil

[64] Judge J. K. Ewing of western Pennsylvania.
[65] Quoted in article, " The General Assembly," *Biblical Repertory and Princeton Review*, July, 1865, vol. 37, p. 505.
[66] *Ibid.*
[67] *Ibid.*, p. 508.
[68] *Ibid.*, pp. 508-509.

government itself.[69] Certainly, it was hard to see why, if confession and repentance were demanded, they should not be required of Northern as well as of Southern offenders.[70]

Though firmly opposed to the action of the 1865 Assembly, Dr. Hodge could discuss it in temperate, dispassionate language; after all, it did not vitally affect him as an individual. Quite different was the point of view of Border State men. Those against whom the various resolutions were directed were men with whom they were intimately associated either as friends or enemies, depending upon the position they themselves had taken during the war. To those Border State men who had been staunch defenders of the Union, the measures taken seemed — at least in intent — highly essential to the safety of the Union and the Church. To those whose sympathies had been with the South or with a middle-ground policy, the action of the Assembly seemed to spell ruin to any possible hopes for peace and unity in the Church. In view of its previous record it was not surprising that the Presbytery of Louisville should take the lead in attacking the General Assembly's stand. But the bitterness of its attack created surprise and justified alarm throughout the Old School Church.

At its September meeting this Presbytery adopted a *Declaration and Testimony against the Erroneous and Heretical Doctrines and Practices which have Obtained and been Propagated in the Presbyterian Church in the United States during the last five years.* This *Declaration and Testimony* was printed and issued in pamphlet form. The length of the pamphlet was proportional to the extent of the title: the printed argument comprised some twenty-seven octavo pages.[71] The document was divided into three parts. In the first place, it

---

[69] *Ibid.*, p. 512.

[70] *Ibid.*, p. 513.

[71] *Declaration and Testimony.* . . . (2nd edition, n. p., 1865). This pamphlet is very rare. The Library of the Presbyterian Historical Society in Philadelphia possesses a copy. Compact, though lengthy, summaries of the document (with quotations) are to be found in the *Biblical Repertory and Princeton Review,* July, 1866, vol. 38, pp. 425-432; in the *Presbyter,* September 27, 1865.

testified against fourteen "errors in doctrine and practice" of which it charged the General Assembly had been guilty. Next, six reasons were given to justify the term "error" as applied to the fourteen points mentioned. This section concluded with the statement:

> We declare our deliberate purpose, trusting in God, who can save by a few as well as by many, to use our best endeavours to bring back the church of our fathers to her ancient purity and integrity, upon the foundation of the apostles and prophets, and under the banner of our only King. . . . we will never abandon the effort . . . until we shall either have succeeded in reforming the church and restoring her tarnished glory; or, failing in this, necessity shall be laid upon us, in obedience to the apostolic command, to withdraw from those who have departed from the truth. Compelled to this course, we will go bearing with us the true Presbyterian church, with her doctrines, order, worship, and freedom, as they have been given her by her divine Head, and transmitted from generation to generation by the hands of saints, and confessors, and martyrs.[72]

The third section of this momentous document dealt with the action its proponents had determined to follow. Their resolutions were as follows:

> 1. That we refuse to give our support to ministers, elders, agents, editors, teachers . . . who hold the preceding or similar heresies.
> 2. That we refuse to take any part in the discussion or decision by any ecclesiastical court, of those questions touching the policy and measures which do properly pertain to the civil commonwealth.
> 3. That we will recognize no authority in the decision of questions of Christian doctrine or morals, or concerning the rights of the church or the duties of its members, other than the written word of God.
> 4. That we will not take any oath prescribed by civil or military authority, as a qualification for sitting in a church court, or for worshipping God, or for preaching the gospel. . . . Nor will we sit in any judicatory thus constituted.
> 5. That we will extend our sympathy and aid . . . to all who in any way are subjected to ecclesiastical censure or civil disabilities or penalties, for their adherence to the principles we maintain. . . .
> 6. That we will not sustain, or execute, or in any manner assist in the execution of the orders passed at the last two Assemblies on the subject of slavery and loyalty; and with reference to the conducting of missions in the Southern states; and with regard to the ministers, members, and churches in the seceded and border states.

---

[72] *Biblical Repertory and Princeton Review,* July, 1866, vol. 38, pp. 427-428.

7. That we will withhold our contributions from the Boards of the church (with the exception of the Board of Foreign Missions) and from the Theological Seminaries, until these institutions are rescued from the hands of those who are perverting them to the teaching and promulgation of principles subversive of the system they were founded and organized to uphold and disseminate. And we will appropriate the moneys thus withheld, in . . . maintaining and defending the principles affirmed in this Declaration . . . and in assisting the impoverished ministers and churches anywhere throughout the country, who agree with us in these essential doctrines. . . .

8. We recommend that all Ministers, Elders, Church Sessions, Presbyteries and Synods who approve of this Declaration and Testimony, give their public adherence thereto in such manner as they shall prefer, and communicate their names, and when a church court, a copy of their adhering act.

9. That . . . we will unceasingly and importunately supplicate the Throne of Grace, for the return of that purity and peace, the absence of which we now sorrowfully deplore.

10. We do earnestly recommend that . . . a convention be held . . . composed of all such ministers and ruling elders as may concur in the views and sentiments of this testimony, to deliberate and consult on the present state of our church . . . and to adopt such further measures as may seem best suited to her prostrated standards, and vindicate the pure and peaceful religion of Jesus from the reproach which has been brought upon it, through the faithlessness and apostacy [sic] of its ministers and professors.

And now, brethren, our whole heart is laid open to you, and to the world. If a majority of our church are against us (as we have too much reason to apprehend it is), they will, we suppose, in the end, either see the infatuation of their course, and retrace their steps, or they will, at last, attempt to cut us off. If the former, we shall bless the God of Jacob; if the latter, we desire to stand ready for the sake of Christ, and in support of the testimony, now made, to endure whatever suffering may be required of us by our Lord. . . . It is our steadfast aim to reform the church, or to testify against its errors and defections until testimony will no longer be heard. And we commit the issue to Him who is over all, God blessed forever. Amen.[73]

The conflict was now on in earnest. It is difficult to see how defiance of the authority of the Assembly could have been more frankly and forcefully expressed. That the Old School Church was thoroughly alarmed is evident from the tremendous amount of attention which the Church periodicals devoted to the matter. The alarm increased as the number of signers

---

[73] *Ibid.*, pp. 428-430.

of the "Declaration and Testimony" mounted during the fall
and winter of 1865-1866. By the end of September, forty-one
had signed;[74] at the end of the year 1865, the number was
ninety-three;[75] when Dr. Hodge came to review the whole
struggle which the document had precipitated, he could report
that during the ten months which had passed since the paper
was first drawn up, forty-one ministers and seventy-eight
elders had attached their signatures to it.[76] It is no wonder
that, as the meeting of the General Assembly of 1866 approached, conservative men in the Church were apprehensive
for its continued unity.[77]

Meanwhile the "Declaration and Testimony" threw the Old
School Church in Kentucky into a furor. The Synod of Kentucky, which convened on October 11, sat for the unprecedented period of ten days[78] before the members had talked
themselves out to a sufficient degree to be willing to adjourn.
The redoubtable Dr. R. J. Breckinridge, determinedly vociferous as ever, continued throughout the sessions to make every
effort to have the "Declaration and Testimony" men punished
by the Synod. Shortly after the Synod had convened, he called
in question the right of the signers of the defiant document
to seats in the Synod. His motion to deny them that right,
after a long-winded debate in which lengthy passages of Scripture as well as documents famous in the history of the Church
were read to prove the rightness of the Louisville document,
was voted down by the decisive majority of 107 to 22.[79] In
due time Breckinridge read a protest which he announced
would be submitted to the next General Assembly, the purpose
of the protest being, in part, that the Assembly "may censure,
as its righteous judgment may deem proper, the sinful acts of

[74] *Presbyter,* September 27, 1865.
[75] *American Annual Cyclopaedia,* 1865, pp. 704-705.
[76] *Biblical Repertory and Princeton Review,* July, 1866, vol. 38, p. 430.
[77] *Cf. post,* pp. 219-220.
[78] It was unusual for a meeting of the Synod to ask for more than two
or three days.
[79] *Minutes of the Synod of Kentucky,* 1865 (Louisville, 1865), p. 17. There
were, besides, five members who did not vote.

the parties brought before the Synod, by a minute proposed to
it by the said Robert J. Breckinridge, and rejected by the
Synod, in part by the votes of the parties arraigned." [80]   Majorities — even five to one majorities — meant nothing to R. J.
Breckinridge if they did not agree with him.   A member of the
less extreme element then offered a paper which embraced the
following points:

1. The acts of the General Assembly of 1865 on Overtures 6 and 7, and
the 4th resolution on the Report of the Committee on the Board of Domestic Missions [81] " in the judgment of this Synod are unwise, as tending to
destroy the peace and harmony of the Church, and in some of their provisions unconstitutional and unscriptural. . . ."

2. But neither these acts nor the deliverances of the General Assembly
on the State of the Country in 1861, 1862, 1863, and 1864 justify a withdrawal from connection with the General Assembly.   The Synod would
" again assert " that it would adhere to the Church, and would oppose
every effort to interrupt ecclesiastical relations or to produce schism or
division.

3. The Synod in relation to the " Declaration and Testimony " expressed
its " disapprobation of the terms of this paper, and of its spirit and intent,
indicated on its face, as looking to the further agitation of the Church, if
not its division, at a time when great mutual forbearance is called for
among brethren to the end that we may have quietness and repose.   Where-
fore the Synod enjoins upon the Presbytery of Louisville, in particular,
and upon all Presbyteries and churches, Ministers and people subject to
it in the Lord, to forbear whatever tends to disturbance and alienation,
beseeching them in the name of our Lord Jesus Christ that ' they all
speak the same thing, and that there be no division among them; but that
they be perfectly joined together in the same mind and in the same judgment.' "

Finally, the Synod earnestly recommended to all under its care to " study
the things that make for peace," to exercise mutual forbearance, in order
that " a way may be opened for a reunion, under the General Assembly,
of all who profess the faith, adhere to the standards, and love the order
of the Presbyterian Church." [82]

Each of the four items was discussed and voted upon separately.   Of the 98 votes cast on the first item, but 22 were
recorded against it, and the list of members casting these
negative votes was almost exactly identical with that of the

[80] Ibid., pp. 20-21.
[81] Cf. ante, pp. 197-200.
[82] Minutes of the Synod of Kentucky, 1865, pp. 24-25.

supporters of Dr. Breckinridge in his attempt to exclude the
signers of the "Declaration and Testimony."[83]   Evidently
only one-fourth of the members of the Synod were willing to
stand back of the deliverances of the last five General Assemblies. Although 76 members had voted condemnation of these
deliverances, when the decision was taken on the second
item but 35 considered that they justified a withdrawal
from connection with the General Assembly. Yet it was significant that 10 members refrained from voting, and that the
adherents of continued connection with the Assembly numbered but 57. On the third proposition — condemnation of
the "Declaration and Testimony," — the vote was still closer;
by a 54 to 46 decision,[84] the Synod registered its disapproval
of the Louisville document. Inasmuch as both of the hostile
factions in Kentucky were opposed to reunion with the New
School,[85] the final item of the report could be interpreted only
as a move toward reunion with the Southern Church. Certainly from the point of view of both the Breckinridge and the
Robinson followers, Southern Presbyterians could be classified
among those who "profess the faith, adhere to the standards,
and love the order" of the Presbyterian Church; most New
School Presbyterians could not. Thus when the final item of
the report was unanimously adopted, the Synod was putting
itself on record as heartily favoring reunion of the Old School
Church with the Southern brethren. Having voted on each
item individually, the Synod acted on the report as a whole,
and adopted it by a vote of 53 to 47.[86]

Although twice thwarted in their attempts to have the "Declaration and Testimony" men punished, the "loyal" men now
made another attack. One of their number[87] who belonged

[83] *Cf. ante,* p. 206.
[84] Two members not voting.
[85] *Cf. ante,* pp. 146-147; 175-176.
[86] Two members not voting. For the record of the action of the Synod
on the various items, and on the report as a whole, cf. *Minutes of the
Synod of Kentucky,* 1865, pp. 26-29.
[87] Rev. J. P. McMillan of Shelbyville, Ky.

to the small minority in the Presbytery of Louisville read a complaint against the Presbytery in the matter of the offending document, and asked the Synod for redress. The majority of the Presbytery having entered vigorous protest against trial at this time, on the ground that the Synod was already exhausted and the issue twice decided, it was resolved that further hearing on this case be postponed until the next regular meeting of the Synod.[88] Thereupon Dr. Breckinridge promptly gave notice of his intention to make formal complaint concerning this action to the next General Assembly. The complaint, which he later read to the Synod, summarized concisely the middle ground that body had taken:

. . . Though it condemned, by the aid of those making this and the former appeal and complaint, the acts and proposals of that heretical and rebellious publication [the " Declaration and Testimony "] and its authors, it refused to do even this much, unless in connection with such manner of simultaneous action against the acts of the General Assembly for five years past, as was clearly indicative of the views and intentions which controlled the acts of the Synod which are the special ground of this appeal and complaint.[89]

From the actions of the Synod it is evident that in the fall of 1865 a majority — though a dangerously small majority — of Old School Presbyterians in Kentucky, in spite of widespread disapproval of the actions of the General Assemblies of the past five years, disapproved of the defiant conduct of the Presbytery of Louisville and was in favor of continuing in connection with the General Assembly of the Old School Church. The spirit of revolt which held the Presbytery of Louisville in its grip must be further stimulated if it was to take possession of the whole of the Synod of Kentucky.

Meanwhile men from the other Border State synods were signing the " Declaration and Testimony " and thus sharing in the defiance which it breathed. Eventually Northern men here and there registered their sympathy by the addition of their signatures.[90] By the end of the year 1865, nearly two-thirds

[88] *Minutes of the Synod of Kentucky*, 1865, pp. 29-31.
[89] *Ibid.*, pp. 31, 33-34.
[90] The most prominent Northern defender was Dr. Henry J. Van Dyke, later a Moderator of the General Assembly. *Cf. post*, pp. 227; 285-287.

of the names were those of Missouri men.[91]   While the number
of signers in the Synod of Baltimore was small, there too the
document created disturbance.[92]   Conditions in Maryland and
Missouri as well as in Kentucky had been developing, in varying degrees, discontent with the deliverances of the General
Assembly.   The crisis created by the memorial of the Presbytery of Louisville in 1865 afforded an opportunity for the meas-
urement of the extent of this discontent.

While there never was any real doubt with regard to the
Synod of Baltimore's maintaining its connection with the General Assembly,[93] there was always a degree of pro-Southern
sympathy to be found in the Synod, sympathy which " disloyal " leaders in the General Assembly were not slow to utilize
to their advantage.   Pro-Union Baltimoreans seized every opportunity to prove their loyalty; for example, one eager citizen
of this stripe, mentioning that probably not much less than
two hundred copies of the *Danville Review* were coming to
Baltimore, asked, " Is not that some proof of our loyalty? "[94]
The Presbytery of Baltimore in the spring of 1862 "after a
protracted debate" determined that when a day of fasting or
thanksgiving should be appointed by the civil authorities, and
the pastor should state and the session record the reason why
he would not officiate on that day, the reason assigned being no
denial of the power of the Executive, but rather the question
of "the propriety of and the Scriptural authority for a particular appointment at an inopportune time," the Presbytery
in passing upon the record was not committed to the sentiment
of that opinion.[95]

The rather luke-warm resolutions of loyalty of the Synod of
Baltimore in 1863,[96] during its first session in the war period,
were followed by a policy of silence in 1864.   The drastic

---

[91] *American Annual Cyclopaedia*, 1865, pp. 704-705.
[92] *Minutes of the Synod of Baltimore*, 1866 (Baltimore, 1866), pp. 8, 10.
[93] *Cf. ante*, pp. 101, 185.
[94] Correspondent in *Presbyterian*, March 29, 1862.
[95] *Cf.* communication of " C " in the *True Presbyterian*, May 1, 1862.
[96] *Cf. ante*, p. 101.

action of the General Assembly of 1865 called forth reproof from the Synod:

> With all due respect for the highest judicatory of our Church, this Synod would express its regret that the General Assembly should have felt it necessary at this time, and under the circumstances, to give this subject so large a share of its attention; and more especially to take action, which we fear, will be used still further to alienate rather than to reunite, our long distracted and divided Church. The war having closed, it would seem to be the special mission of all our ecclesiastical courts to heal breaches, rather than to widen and perpetuate them. The action referred to, however, was taken during a time of great excitement, and we cannot but hope that a calm and kind review of the subject, in the light of peace and returning good-will, will tend to more conciliatory measures in the next Assembly. In the meantime, this Synod, remembering the claims of that charity which " suffereth long and is kind," will study the things which make for peace, and things wherewith one part of the Church may edify another; and moreover, we embrace the occasion to assure the members of our Synod in Winchester Presbytery,[97] who have not met with us for the last four years, of our desire to welcome them to our fellowship and to cooperate with them in building up the Redeemer's kingdom.[98]

Thus the Synod of Baltimore was looking to the Assembly of 1866 to right what it considered to be the grievous errors of the Assembly of 1865. The Synod's action, coming as it did several weeks after the issuing of the " Declaration and Testimony," indicated that dissatisfied Presbyterians in Kentucky and Missouri might anticipate a considerable amount of sympathy if not open support from the Synod of Baltimore. This anticipation was strengthened by the fact that the Synod's action was taken " with only two or three dissenting voices." [99]

The unstable character of political and military conditions in the state of Missouri during the war years had a disastrous effect upon the interests of the Old School Church there. In the Synods of Missouri and Upper Missouri all was confusion. In December, 1863, a correspondent reported to the *True Presbyterian* that he believed there was no minister of the denomination left in Southwestern Missouri; he knew of but one in the Presbytery of Wyaconda, in the northern part of the state.

---

[97] *Cf. post*, p. 274, note 216.
[98] *Minutes of the Synod of Baltimore*, 1865, pp. 10-11.
[99] *Ibid.*

Of the four presbyteries of Upper Missouri, two (Lafayette and Platte) were almost entirely bereft of ministers. The Synod of Upper Missouri had failed to meet since the beginning of the war, and at the last meeting of the Synod of Missouri not one-fourth of the members were in attendance.[100] The picture painted was dark, but not exaggerated. Recognizing the necessity of readjustment in this region, the General Assembly of 1864 transformed the Presbytery of Highland (formerly belonging to the Synod of Upper Missouri) — which, located in Kansas, had continued to prosper — into the Synod of Kansas; and consolidating the remaining three presbyteries of the Synod of Upper Missouri into two, joined them with the Synod of Missouri.[101] The Assembly was thus frankly retrenching in Missouri.

In spite of the fact that the General Assembly of 1862 had been disposed to take a charitable view of the resolutions of the Synod of Missouri on its action of the previous year,[102] the spirit of hostility within the Synod steadily mounted. The Presbytery of St. Louis was torn with dissension over the case of Dr. S. B. McPheeters, whose policy of silence on political matters exposed him to charges of disloyalty. The intervention of the military authorities, a lengthy correspondence between the accused man on the one hand and President Lincoln and Attorney General Bates on the other, and a complete review of the case in the General Assembly of 1864, kept the affair in the limelight for a period of over two years.[103] The military trial of Dr. S. J. P. Anderson on charges of active sympathy with the rebellion brought another member of the Presbytery into a sort of prominence that was particularly distasteful to "loyal" men of that body.[104] By the summer of 1863 this element in the Presbytery had managed to rid it of

[100] *Cf.* communication "From Missouri," *True Presbyterian*, December 12, 1863.

[101] *Minutes of the General Assembly*, 1864, vol. xvii, pp. 313-314; 316; 317.

[102] *Cf. ante*, pp. 99-101; 116.

[103] For a more complete account of this case, *cf. post*, pp. 305-325.

[104] An account of this case is given, *post*, pp. 326-327.

members objectionable to themselves, although the process left it with but one-fourth of its former membership.[105] This rump element then adopted a paper expressing the loyalty of the Presbytery:

At a late meeting of this Presbytery, which has hitherto declined taking any action in relation to the rebellion, the following paper, offered by Gen. A. G. Edwards, was adopted:

. . . .

Resolved, that we . . . do hereby earnestly entreat and warn all members of our churches to abstain from all participation in the present rebellion, or from giving countenance and encouragement thereto by word or deed — as such participation, countenance, or encouragement involves sin against God. . . .

Ayes, 16; Noes, 0.[106]

Whatever opportunities existed for the pro-Union Presbyterians to control conditions in the Church, were offset by the effect of an order emanating from the military authorities:

Headquarters Department of the Missouri,
St. Louis, Mo., March 5, 1864.
Colonel:
In the opinion of the General Commanding, the interests of the country require that due protection should be given within the limits of this department to religious convocations, and other religious assemblages of persons whose function it is to teach religion and morality to the people. But at the present time he deems it expedient that the members of such assemblages should be required to give satisfactory evidence of their loyalty to the Government of the United States as a condition precedent to such privilege of assemblage and protection.
The Major General Commanding desires that you take such steps as in your judgment will best secure these objects.
I am, Colonel, very respectfully, your obedient servant,
O. D. Green
Assistant Adjutant General
To Colonel J. P. Sanderson, *Provost Marshal General, Department of Missouri.*[107]

---

[105] The membership in 1861 was 64; but 16 votes were cast at the 1863 meeting.

[106] *Presbyter,* June 24, 1863.

[107] McPherson, *Political History of the United States . . . during the Great Rebellion,* p. 538.

General Rosecrans, the Major General Commanding, undertook in a lengthy letter to defend this order, saying in part:

> If all who claim to meet for religious purposes can do so without
> question, a convocation from Price's army, under the garb of religion,
> may assemble with impunity and plot treason in our midst.
>
> If, on the contrary, religious assemblies, really such, are scrutinized with
> the same freedom as political meetings of unknown and doubtful charac-
> ter, not only would it be necessary to inquire into the ministerial character
> of its members, but their public and private proceedings must be so
> watched that treason could not be perpetrated without detection and pun-
> ishment, which would occasion a most irksome interference with personal
> privacy and the freedom of religious action.
>
> . . . my duty to the country and the people of the State required me
> to protect them from the machinations of enemies . . . while, as a Chris-
> tian, I felt bound to secure religion from the danger and disgrace of being
> used as the cloak of malice, and its freedom from a surveillance freely
> exercised over political meetings.[108]

To meet these peculiar needs it was provided that ministers
might assure the military authorities as to their loyalty in
either of two ways: by certifying on their honor that they had
sworn to support the Constitution and Government of the
United States and the provisional government of the State of
Missouri (as was required by the laws of the provisional government to enable ministers to solemnize marriage), giving the
time and place of such oath; or by taking a prescribed oath.[109]
Thus in either case an oath was necessary if a minister chose
to attend a church assemblage. Here was indeed cause for
excitement from the point of view of those who believed in the
extreme separation of Church and State, as well as those whose
sympathies were not wholly with the Union. On the other
hand vociferous supporters of the Union were now furnished
with an excellent means of testing the loyalty of the brethren
under suspicion. Sometimes, however, the system did not
function to their entire satisfaction, as in the case of the Presbytery of Palmyra (northeastern Missouri) the majority of

[108] Letter to Rev. J. B. [J. P.] Finley, Stated Clerk [of Presbytery of
Missouri] Westchester [Westminster] College, Fulton, Missouri, dated
April 29, 1864. *Ibid.,* p. 538.
[109] *Ibid.*

whose members, it was complained, had " evaded and virtually refused to take the oath of allegiance prescribed by the Military commandant of the Department to all members of such a court. . . . The private arrangement these Brethren made with the Provost Marshal of Hannibal does not carry with it the evidence of official sanction or authority. . . ." [110] When the Presbytery of Missouri convened a few weeks after the Rosecrans order, " The most, if not all the members, having, as citizens, taken the Convention oath, a few were willing to take their seats in Presbytery in virtue of that oath — this being graciously allowed by Gen. Rosecrans. Others of us contended that it was the same in principle, to sit as Presbyterians in virtue of that oath, or the oath prescribed by Gen. Rosecrans. We recognized Christ as the sole Head of the Church, and would not allow Caesar to usurp the place of Christ." [111]

As a result of the military order, conditions became worse and worse in the Synod of Missouri. The Synod's meeting in the fall of 1864 was described by Dr. Robinson in his *True Presbyterian* under the title, " The Late Meeting of the Synod of Missouri. A ' Rump ' Synod, organized by a Provost Marshal, expunging and falsifying its Records." The exscinding of the Synod's previous testimony,[112] Dr. Robinson declared, " was made by a meeting of Synod, organized by a Military Provost Marshal, taking *his place at the Clerk's table,* and composed of *one* pastor, *eight* other ministers, and *five* ruling Elders — fourteen all told — out of a Synod containing *seventy* ministers, and *one hundred and four* churches! — that is, one hundred and seventy odd members all told." [113] Dr. Robinson then described the difficulties the Synod encountered in dealing with two men who claimed seats, but who, although

[110] *True Presbyterian,* April 28, 1864, quoting the protest of Jacob R. Winters.

[111] Communication from a member of the Presbytery, *True Presbyterian,* May 26, 1864.

[112] *Cf. ante,* pp. 99-101 ; 116.

[113] Editorial, (title as given above), *True Presbyterian,* November 10, 1864.

they had evidently taken the Convention oath, refused to state that fact as a means of being recognized as entitled to seats in the Synod. One member, " evidently a ' half-breed' Yankee Presbyterian of the Strong School," moved that the men be denied seats. This motion occasioned some difficulty, as under the Presbyterian constitutional system every minister must be a member of a presbytery. It was finally decided that these men had permanent seats, but that they should be denied participation in the proceedings. This was accordingly done, but the next day, after the majority had had time for reflection, the two names were put back on the roll as of the previous day.[114] To force loyal men to proclaim their loyalty in presbytery in order that they might be entitled to participate in the proceedings was going a bit too far for even the most enthusiastic of Union adherents. But even though the authorities stopped short of this, to many members the oath was galling. In view of the steadily rising discontent in Missouri it is not surprising that there should have been a marked readiness among members of its Synod to endorse the " Declaration and Testimony." [115] Missouri was becoming more and more conspicuous as a center of disaffection.

It is clear that the Border State problem had been growing in complexity throughout the war period. The bitter rivalry between R. J. Breckinridge and Stuart Robinson had intensified the hard feelings between the hostile factions. If the evidence was read aright, there was a large element in the North which, becoming more and more interested in the possibility of reunion with the New School, was growing increasingly indifferent toward the Border State brethren — at least toward all who were not vociferously "loyal." Certain acts of the Federal Government through the War Department had stimulated discontent in the Border States: the order of the Assistant Adjutant General turning over Presbyterian churches in reconquered territory to those who bore commissions from the

[114] For an account of this incident, cf. ibid.
[115] Cf. ante, pp. 209-210.

Board of Domestic Missions had particularly angered Kentuckians; [116] the oath requirements in Missouri were extremely offensive to a large number of Old School Presbyterians there. The successive General Assemblies in their eagerness to prove their loyalty had become more and more unsympathetic in their attitude, until finally it seemed to Border State men that the General Assembly was deliberately trying to cast them off. Finally in 1865 the Presbytery of Louisville drew up its " Declaration and Testimony " — a document of open defiance. As the number of signatures attached to this challenge steadily mounted during the winter of 1865-1866, it became unmistakably evident that a crisis was at hand. The manner in which the General Assembly of 1866 chose to meet this crisis would determine the fate of the Old School Church in the Border States.

[116] *Cf. ante*, pp. 188-189.

CHAPTER VII

THE OLD SCHOOL ASSEMBLY OF 1866 AND ITS AFTERMATH

St. Louis had been chosen in 1865 as the place of meeting for the General Assembly of 1866. No doubt a principal factor in this choice had been the Border State location of the convention city, for it was certain even in the early days of the 1865 session[1] that the hold of the Church on that section was uncertain. Everyone realized that in each of the Border States there was an element (in 1865 people thought a majority element — at least in Maryland and Kentucky) which was sure to remain with the Church. Perhaps an Assembly held in a Border State city might prove to be effective in sustaining the faithful. As for the discontented, the feeling that they should be allowed to go was surprisingly general. In commenting on the 1865 General Assembly the *Presbyterian*, which was decidedly the most charitable of the Old School weeklies, declared:

> There is a feeling in the Church, which everyone must share in who loves the Church, that the men who are continually denouncing the Church as corrupt and apostate, should either voluntarily go out of it, or be cast out of it by the hand of discipline, and those who have warred against the government of the land, should be made to feel that in this they have sinned against God.[2]

And this statement was made before the Presbytery of Louisville had uttered its deliberate defiance, and while Stuart Robinson was still in Canada!

The course of events during the twelve months which elapsed between the Assemblies of 1865 and 1866 was not

---

[1] It was customary to choose the place of meeting of the next Assembly, early in the session. In 1865 the choice was made on the 3rd day of the 13-day session. *Minutes of the General Assembly*, 1865, vol. xvii, pp. 535-536.

[2] Editorial, "The General Assembly," *Presbyterian*, June 3, 1865.

likely to cause the *Presbyterian* to change its opinion. The "Declaration and Testimony" shocked Northern Presbyterians by the virulence of its language. The extent of the chasm which the war had cleft between Presbyterians of the North and those of the South was indicated by the promptness with which the Southern General Assembly decided, at its annual session in December, 1865, to maintain permanently its separate status. On this question there was no argument whatever, though there was considerable discussion as to what name should be given the Church.[3] The name "Free Presbyterian Church" was advocated by some, perhaps because of "having just been delivered from slavery," the *Presbyterian* suggested. At any rate, the Southern Church was determined to remain independent, and this fact, serving to sharpen the distinction between Northern and Southern church philosophy, suggested a parallel — though not so clear — distinction between Northern and Border State church thought. The welcome with which the "Declaration and Testimony" was received in Kentucky and Missouri — and to some degree in Maryland — emphasized the unique position of Old School men in those states. Furthermore, the trend of political reconstruction was making Northerners in general impatient with the Southern point of view. A particular event of ominous significance was the return of Stuart Robinson from Canada,[4] his welcome in Kentucky, and his election as a commissioner from the Presbytery of Louisville to the General Assembly of 1866.[5] "No selection could have been more unfortunate for the peace of the Church," asserted the *Presbyterian*.[6]

While antagonism toward the Border States was growing in the North, this sentiment came to be accompanied by a genuine fear as the extended popularity of the Presbytery of Louisville's document of defiance came to be recognized. This grow-

[3] Editorial, "The General Assembly at Macon," *Presbyterian*, December 30, 1865.
[4] Editorial, "Affairs in Kentucky," *ibid.*, April 28, 1866.
[5] *Ibid.*
[6] *Ibid.*

ing apprehension led to the call for a convention of ministers and elders who approved of the acts of the Assembly and decided to sustain them, to meet at the same time and place as the Assembly itself.[7] Over one hundred members attended this convention,[8] which became a powerful lobby for influencing sentiment in the Assembly.[9] Undoubtedly it played an important part in the choice of a Moderator for the more formal body it was seeking to direct. The election, occurring on the opening day of the Assembly sessions, clearly illustrated the dominance of the " Declaration and Testimony " issue, and the triple alignment which it prompted among the commissioners. Each of the three candidates nominated represented a distinct platform on the Border State question. Dr. R. L. Stanton, since 1862 a member of the faculty of Danville Theological Seminary,[10] as the candidate of the "bitter-enders" was in favor of an unyielding adherence to the deliverances of the preceding assemblies on the subjects of slavery and loyalty. Dr. P. D. Gurley, pastor of the Washington church at which President Lincoln had worshipped,[11] wished to sustain the deliverances of the former assemblies, but to construe and execute them with the greatest possible forbearance. Dr. S. R. Wilson, pastor of the First Presbyterian Church of Louisville, was one of the leaders of the Declaration and Testimony party.[12] The vote on these three candidates was significantly one-sided: of the 251 votes cast, Dr. Stanton received 158, Dr. Gurley 75, and Dr. Wilson 18.[13]

The commissioners who voted for Dr. Stanton could not possibly have had any doubt as to where he stood on the issues

[7] Article, "The General Assembly," *Biblical Repertory and Princeton Review*, July, 1866, vol. 38, p. 430.
[8] *Ibid.*, p. 431.
[9] *Cf. post*, p. 234.
[10] Nevin, Alfred, *ed.*, *Encyclopaedia of the Presbyterian Church in the United States of America. . . .* (Philadelphia, 1884), p. 854.
[11] Editorial, "Churches turned into Hospitals," *Presbyter*, June 19, 1862.
[12] For stand of each candidate, *cf. American Annual Cyclopaedia*, 1866, p. 621.
[13] *Proceedings of the General Assemblies . . . 1866* (St. Louis, 1866), p. 6.

which had so agitated the Church. In 1864 he had published
a 550-page treatise on "The Church and the Rebellion
. . . ." [14] in which he bitterly scored the Church for its responsibility for the conditions and philosophy which had made
the rebellion possible. Dr. Stanton found occasion to commend many Christian clergymen, North and South, for their
loyalty, but his book dealt primarily with those Protestant
and Catholic leaders whose utterances and actions he maintained had prevented a satisfactory solution of the slavery
problem and had so widened the gap between North and South
as to make the war inevitable. Perhaps because of his greater
familiarity with men of his own denomination, perhaps because
of pride in the importance of Presbyterians, Dr. Stanton believed them particularly responsible for the calamity which
had befallen the nation, quoting with entire approbation the
words of a venerable Old School colleague: [15]

"These Southern Presbyterians are either laughing at your simplicity
or pitying your stupidity. For, first, it is notorious that they held the
controlling power in their hands. I could name half a dozen of Presbyterian ministers who could have arrested the secession, if they had seen
fit. *Notoriously, the Presbyterian ministers of the South were the leading
spirits of the rebellion. It could not have been started without them.* . . .
But secondly, even in the Border States, the Presbyterian ministers alone,
if they had had a moiety of the heroic martyr spirit of Robert J. Breckinridge, could have shut up the sluices of treason and turned the battle
from the gates." [16]

If any proof had been needed, Dr. Stanton's book would have
made it clear that he belonged to the radically loyal group —
the group that believed that the Old School Church must be
"set right" in the eyes of the public. Early in the war period
it was said of him that he had declared in open Synod "that
he expected to meet such men as Thornwell and Palmer in

[14] Stanton, R. L., *The Church and the Rebellion*. . . . (New York, 1864).
[15] Dr. George Junkin, from 1848 to 1861 President of Washington College,
Virginia. For Dr. Junkin's own position on matters relating to the war,
cf. post, p. 291.
[16] Stanton, *op. cit.*, p. 202, note, quoting Dr. Junkin's work, "Political
Fallacies."

heaven; but first expected to see them hung upon earth, and he would rejoice in that hanging." [17]   While Dr. Stuart Robinson pointed out that this remark indicated either a taint of Universalism or the conviction that treason on earth was not wrong in Heaven,[18] Dr. Stanton's alleged declaration left no doubt as to what he thought of the earthly status of "disloyal" Old School clergymen. A radical of this stripe had now been elected to the highest position the Old School Church could offer.

The newly elected Moderator lost no time in putting himself on record as favoring prompt and decisive action with regard to the Declaration and Testimony men. After opening his speech of acceptance with a few statements as to his consciousness of his inability fully to meet the demands of the position, Dr. Stanton pointed out the highly critical nature of the Old School Church's position in 1866:

It has many times been said by members of this body and by others, as well as by the religious journals, that this would be one of the most important General Assemblies of the Presbyterian Church which has ever convened. While we ought not unduly to magnify our office as a Church Court, there may be some truth in the estimate thus put upon what may prove to be the result of our deliberations. Vital questions affecting the integrity of this Assembly, and the purity and peace of the Church at large, will claim from you a prompt and decisive solution. That rebellious defiance of lawful authority which has racked this Nation to its foundations during four years of war, still rages within the precincts where it was born, the Church of God! [19] It is the offspring of heresy, corruption, and all unrighteousness. To meet it promptly, courageously in the fear of God, and with the aid of His grace, is your manifest duty, as well as directly to deal with those who openly deride your most solemn injunctions. To settle all these questions upon principles so clearly right that they shall command the confidence of the Church and give it rest, while they shall advance the Saviour's glory and secure his favor, should be the aim of the prayers and the labors of every member. Then, those

---

[17] Quoted in editorial, "The Last Resort of an Editor," *True Presbyterian*, August 28, 1862. Dr. Robinson added the remark, "From what we know of said professor elect we suppose he said so in a moment of political excitement."

[18] *Ibid.*

[19] An interesting allusion to the thesis of Dr. Stanton's book. *Cf. ante*, pp. 220-221.

who have gone out from us upon vain and wicked pretexts may be left to their own chosen way, and if any still remain to revile they may know the cost of setting at defiance the authority which Christ has given to his Church. . . .[20]

It is evident that the Declaration and Testimony men could expect little favor from the presiding officer of the Assembly. Dr. R. J. Breckinridge was not a member of the 1866 Assembly. He was present, however, to carry before this highest Church Court his appeal from the action of the 1865 Synod of Kentucky,[21] and his enemies freely alleged that he was the directing force behind the bitter onslaught which was waged against the defiant Border State men.[22] The immediate perpetrator of the attack was Dr. D. V. McLean, pastor of a small church[23] in Red Bank, New Jersey. Dr. McLean appears not to have been prominent in the Church, although one of his enemies accused him of being a "general dealer in bogus stocks, ecclesiastical and financial."[24]—terminology which, in spite of its modern flavor, is not entirely clear in the significance of its application to the gentleman in question. Although the method by which Dr. McLean introduced the momentous subject of the treatment of the Declaration and Testimony men had every appearance of having been carefully prearranged,[25] it obviously did not follow the program which the special convention had devised for the handling of the issue in the General Assembly. That program would have allowed the whole matter concerning the Louisville Presbytery and the Declaration and Testimony to abide the issue of Dr. R. J. Breckinridge when he entered his appeal from the action

[20] *Proceedings of the General Assemblies . . . 1866*, pp. 6-7.

[21] *Cf. ante*, pp. 206-209.

[22] The New York *Evangelist*, June 14, 1866, quoting the *Free Christian Commonwealth*.

[23] *Minutes of the General Assembly*, 1866, vol. xviii, p. 210, give the communicant membership of Dr. McLean's church as 85.

[24] The New York *Evangelist*, June 14, 1866, quoting the *Free Christian Commonwealth*.

[25] Dr. McLean declared on the floor of the Assembly that "Long before he came here he had made up his mind just how he should act on this subject. . . ." (*Proceedings*, p. 48).

of the Synod of Kentucky.[26]   This method, as Dr. Hodge later
pointed out,[27] would have brought up the merits of the case,
given all parties a fair hearing, and secured a regular judicial
decision, against which there could be no appeal.   Once Dr.
McLean had launched his surprise attack, however, Northern
leaders for some reason felt it necessary to give him their
hearty support.[28]

The attack itself, coming almost immediately after the in-
stallation of the new Moderator, took the form of the following resolution:

> *Whereas,* It is understood that the Presbytery of Louisville has openly
> defied the General Assembly, and refuses to submit to its orders, in a
> pamphlet adopted by it, of which the following is a specimen, viz.,
> " We will not sustain or execute, or in any manner assist in the execu-
> tion of the orders passed at the last two Assemblies, on the subject of
> slavery and loyalty, and with reference to the conducting of missions in
> the Southern States, and with regard to the ministers, members, and
> churches in the seceded and Border States; " and
> *Whereas,* Said Presbytery has commissioned, and sent to this Assembly,
> at least one Commissioner, who, if the order of the last Assembly had been
> faithfully executed by said Presbytery, there is the strongest ground for
> believing would have been suspended from the functions of the gospel
> ministry: [29]   Therefore,
> *Resolved,* That until the Assembly shall have examined and decided
> upon the conduct of said Presbytery, the Commissioners therefrom shall
> not be entitled to seats in this body.[30]

It might have been supposed that so high-handed a proposal
would receive no consideration whatever from a dignified deliberative body.   On the contrary, an attempt to table this
resolution was defeated by a vote of 215 to 32, twenty-one

[26] Article, " The General Assembly," *Biblical Repertory and Princeton
Review,* July, 1866, vol. 38, p. 434.
[27] *Ibid.*
[28] *Ibid.,* p. 491. Dr. Hodge stated that " the leaders of the majority . . .
for some reason . . . felt constrained to adopt " the McLean action. That
his language was much too mild is apparent from the one-sidedness of the
votes on the various McLean proposals.
[29] Stuart Robinson was, of course, the man referred to.
[30] *Minutes of the General Assembly,* 1866, vol. xviii, p. 12.

of the minority votes coming from the Border States.[31] Having determined that the resolution should not thus be stifled, the Assembly adjourned for the day. At his first opportunity on the second day of the session Dr. McLean again obtained the floor, debated his resolution, and then moved the previous question.[32] By a vote of 206 to 56 the General Assembly adopted the resolution.[33] This time the Border State men had been aided by 25 votes from Northerners, but the fact remains that by a four to one decision the highest court of the Old School Church denied the Louisville commissioners seats without any opportunity for a hearing. To be sure, it was argued that this was merely a preliminary matter — that the merits of the case of the Louisville Presbytery would be considered as soon as the right to seats had been determined, but the record of the debates of the Assembly shows unmistakably that it proved to be impossible to prevent the discussion of the merits of the case, during the consideration of the matter of seating the Louisville commissioners. In other words, there can scarcely be a doubt that not a few members of the Assembly were guided in their decision more by their hostility to the sentiments of the Louisville men than by the question of title to seats in the Assembly.

Dr. McLean's next step was promptly taken. No sooner had the Assembly adopted his resolution that pending further investigation the Louisville men should be denied seats, than he moved the following:

Resolved, That a committee of seven be appointed, to be composed of four ministers and three ruling elders, to examine into the facts connected with the alleged acts and proceedings of the Louisville Presbytery; and whether it is entitled to representation in this General Assembly; and to recommend what action, if any, this Assembly should take in regard to said Presbytery.[34]

---

[31] *Ibid.,* vol. xviii, pp. 12-13. Three Louisville commissioners (Robinson among them) refused to vote, and much discussion ensued as to whether this fact should be recorded, and if so, in what form. *Proceedings,* pp. 9-10.

[32] *Proceedings,* p. 11.

[33] *Ibid.,* p. 12.

[34] *Minutes of the General Assembly,* 1866, vol. xviii, p. 16.

Naturally this proposal provoked much eloquent discussion. There were several unusual features about it. The resolution would place the case in the hands of a special committee and thus take it out of the hands of the judicial committee, where it already was on the appeal of Dr. Breckinridge.[35] Furthermore, the suggested action was directed solely against members of the Presbytery of Louisville and would ignore entirely the majority of the signers of the "Declaration and Testimony" who were not within the bounds of that Presbytery. This latter fact prompted Dr. James H. Brookes of St. Louis, who asserted that although he had not written it he had had "more to do with the origination" of the "Declaration and Testimony" than either Dr. Wilson or Dr. Stuart Robinson (the two Louisville pastors commonly held most responsible for the drafting and passage of the document), to offer the following amendment to Dr. McLean's last resolution: [36]

> *Resolved,* That the committee be also instructed to inquire into the truth of certain rumors charged upon other members of this body, and with the same offenses for which the Presbytery of Louisville has been arraigned before the Assembly, and to report what action should be taken in the premises.[37]

Dr. Brookes' speech stirred the house:

> Mr. Brookes. . . . I cannot remain silent and see them driven away and retain my place. . . . I will cheerfully suffer for what I believe to be God Almighty's truth and Christ's glorious kingdom. [Applause in various parts of the house.]
> A Voice. Clear the galleries.
> Another Voice. Never mind; they won't hurt you.

[35] Article, "The General Assembly," *Biblical Repertory and Princeton Review,* July, 1866, vol. 38, p. 492.

[36] Strictly speaking this was an amendment not to the original resolution, but rather to a previous amendment to the effect that the original resoluion should be made to cover the case of Rev. T. A. Bracken. *Proceedings,* p. 12. Mr. Bracken, though not a signer of the "Declaration and Testimony" had shown sympathy for its supporters, and was now being attacked on the ground of his title to membership as a commissioner from the West Lexington (Ky.) Presbytery while still technically a member of the Lafayette (Mo.) Presbytery.

[37] *Proceedings,* pp. 12-13.

The Moderator. I hope all such demonstrations, on either side, will not be manifested in this house.[38]

Another speaker who was impressed by the unfairness of limiting the proposed action to members of the Presbytery of Louisville was Dr. Henry J. VanDyke, pastor of the influential First Presbyterian Church in Brooklyn. Disapproving of the language of the " Declaration and Testimony," he had not signed that document,[39] but he now declared that " whatever of principle there is in it, I do now subscribe to, and practically will ever act upon it so long as God will give me strength so to do." [40] At any rate the Louisville Presbytery had simply given utterance to an opposition tacitly expressed against the orders of the 1865 Assembly by large numbers, particularly in the East. It was "perfectly notorious," according to Dr. Van-Dyke, that in the Synods of Baltimore and New York — especially in the cities — it had not been ever attempted to carry out the orders of the 1865 General Assembly.[41]

Other speakers declared their sympathy with the Louisville document and asserted that justice demanded that they be included within the scope of Dr. McLean's proposed investigation. The stated clerk of the Synod of Missouri called attention to the fact that that body " after a calm and thorough discussion of the principles involved " had adopted the main points of the much-discussed paper. "We wish to put ourselves, therefore," he said, " in the ranks with our brothers of the Presbytery of Louisville, and others who may fall under the action of the guillotine in holding these sentiments." The speaker then proceeded to relate an incident that had occurred at a recent meeting of his own church session. Two members had been received sitting side by side, one of whom had ridden in Merrill's horse on the Federal side and the other had

[38] *Ibid.,* p. 13.
[39] *Ibid.,* p. 13. Dr. VanDyke signed at a later date and was for this reason excluded from the Synod of New York at its fall meeting. *American Annual Cyclopaedia,* 1866, p. 622.
[40] *Proceedings,* p. 13.
[41] *Ibid.*

"bared his breast to the Union bayonets on the Southern side." They were neither of them asked any questions about their opinions with regard to one army or the other, but the church session had received them as Christians, "supposing that in their union with Christ there was a bond strong enough to bind them together across that gulf of blood that had for a time separated them." The speaker closed his remarks with the assertion that he would never obey an order that made him determine the political opinions or practices of any man who might come to him to be united in the fellowship of the Church of Christ.[42] Though few in numbers, the sympathizers with the Declaration and Testimony party were thus not timid in expressing their sentiments.

Of the anti-Louisville men the most conspicuous for eloquence was Dr. Thomas E. Thomas, pastor of the First Presbyterian Church of Dayton, Ohio. Dr. Thomas had for years been one of the most vociferous anti-slavery men in the Old School Church. Born in England in 1812, he had been brought to this country while still a very small child. At Miami University, from which he was graduated in 1834, he was much influenced by the dynamic leader then at its head, Dr. Robert H. Bishop, a man of strong anti-slavery sentiments. In 1836 he was licensed as a preacher by the Old School Presbytery of Oxford (Ohio). During the 1830's and 1840's anti-slavery sentiment in the Old School Church was concentrated largely in southwestern Ohio. Young Mr. Thomas came under the influence of a school of church thought which deprecated the division of 1837-1838[43] and was bitterly hostile to the institution of slavery. Throughout his career Thomas hated slavery; never a narrow sectarian, he was for years one of the foremost champions of Presbyterian reunion. The activities of his entire ministerial experience reflected the influence of the venerable church fathers with whom his early professional years had brought him into contact — such men as Dr. Bishop, who

[42] *Cf.* speech of Dr. S. J. P. Anderson, *ibid.*, p. 14.
[43] Thomas, *op. cit.*, pp. 44-45.

was rated by a worthy critic as "the strongest individual influence of his generation,"[44] and Dr. Samuel Crothers, who was "perhaps the first of the ministers in the Presbyterian Church to make the fight against slavery within the church, *and as a moral question alone.*"[45] It was not surprising that young Thomas, in close contact with at least half a dozen of these older Old School anti-slavery men,[46] should have regarded himself as a crusader commissioned to carry on the battle after the veterans had fallen. He had fought with them through the fierce struggles over slavery in the General Assemblies of 1845 and 1846;[47] by 1861 death or old age had removed all of them from the front lines, and he was left with younger — and for the most part weaker — colleagues to carry on the struggle.

The political crisis of 1860-1861 found Thomas — Dr. Thomas now — in a ready, even an expectant, mood. On January 10, 1861, after the *Star of the West* episode, he entered in his diary these words, "Yesterday, also, *the First Gun Fired in the coming Civil War!*"[48] Thus mistaken once, he was not quite so emphatic in April, yet on the thirteenth of that month he recorded, "Today's Gazette informs us that at 4 a. m. on yesterday, . . . the Rebels of South Carolina . . . *opened fire:* and so has begun the long-expected *war* between our Government, and the rebels of the slave-holding

[44] *Ibid.*, p. 41, quoting Sprague's *Annals.*

[45] Thomas, *op. cit.*, p. 22.

[46] This group included Dr. Robert H. Bishop (1777-1855), President of Miami University, 1824-1840, Professor, 1840-1845; Dr. Samuel Crothers (1782-1856), pastor at Greenfield, Ohio; Rev. James H. Dickey (1780-1856), from 1810 to 1837 pastor at Buckskin (later South Salem), Ohio, from 1837 to 1856 pastor at Union Grove, Illinois; Rev. James Gilliland (1769-1845), pastor at Red Oak, Ohio; Rev. A. B. Gilliland (1794-1885), pastor of various churches in Ohio. Among the younger men were Rev. Hugh S. Fullerton (1805-1864), Rev. E. D. MacMaster (1806-1866), and Dr. John M. Stevenson (born 1812). All of these men were active anti-slavery workers. *Cf.* Thomas, *op. cit., passim; Presbyterian Encyclopaedia* (under names of individuals mentioned above).

[47] Thomas, *op. cit.*, pp. 70-73; 83. For account of these struggles, *cf. ante,* p. 26.

[48] Thomas, *op. cit.*, pp. 109-110.

South." [49]   This time he really got the war started, and could begin his own campaign for patriotism and loyalty in church and state.   " Throughout the war," wrote his son a generation later, " he by voice and pen, led and held this whole Dayton community to the support of the war, which to him was a crusade." [50]   No wonder that he regarded the war with enthusiasm, for almost immediately it became evident that it would afford the small anti-slavery group which he typified — a group hitherto despised and rejected — the opportunity of dictating the policy the Church should take with regard to the political crisis.

Dr. Thomas is interesting because he was an exponent of the element which was now so rapidly forging to the front in the direction of church affairs; he is important because of the extremely significant part he and his group played in the memorable Assembly of 1866.   It soon became evident that the burden of the attack upon the Louisville Presbytery would have to be carried by him.   For years his program for the Old School Church, like that of the *Presbyter,* had been three-fold: anti-slavery, pro-West, pro-reunion.[51]   In 1864 the Assembly had taken as extreme an anti-slavery stand as even the most rabid hater of slavery could desire; [52] this Assembly of 1866, if its activities were properly directed, might well serve to augment the prestige of the West and bring the ideal of reunion definitely nearer fruition.   Here was Dr. Thomas's opportunity.   What was expected of him was indicated by a letter written him by his old friend Dr. William C. Anderson (who as the one dissenter on the famous Committee of Nine had presented the Minority Report which the epoch-making General Assembly of 1861 adopted as the expression of its sentiments on the State of the Country [53]) shortly after his first speech [54] in the Assembly of 1866:

[49] *Ibid.*
[50] *Ibid.*, p. 87.
[51] *Cf. ante,* pp. 158-160; also pp. 80-82.
[52] *Cf. ante,* pp. 126-128.
[53] *Cf. ante,* pp. 58-64.
[54] Extracts of this speech are given *post,* pp. 231-233.

We hold you, i. e., this General Assembly, responsible for the peace, progress, character, and general future of the old Presbyterian Church. You have begun nobly: all praise and honor to the stand taken in relation to the Louisville Rebels. Many thanks for your speech. . . . treason is right, or it is wrong. . . . I have Boardman's speech, in the St. Louis Democrat; and never read a more assailable effusion. . . . Now, Brother Thomas E. Thomas, we are looking to you, who have done so well in the preliminary fight, to maintain the great principle of the last five Assemblies, and give the argument, the appeal and all probable and possible sequences. Stand straight up to the last five Assemblies. Let all the Southern sympathizers go. Then urge on union with the New School Presbyterians. Don't be alarmed by the secession of the old Philadelphia-Princeton clique of pro-slavery men. Let them go: they have been the deep curse of the Old School Church since 1845. A union with our New School brethren, now in perfect sympathy with us, will give us the grandest organization, especially if we can clear of [out?] the Hodge-VanDyke-Boardman school of Presbyterians. God bless you. Finish up the work that we may have peace in the future.[55]

It is doubtful whether Thomas needed this urging. His whole previous career[56] had demonstrated that he loved a fight; never were the opportunities for victory better than in 1866.

The speech of Dr. Thomas which his friend lauded so highly had indeed produced a sensation in the Assembly. It had come during the debate on the McLean resolution to refer the Louisville case to a special committee, and was in part an answer to the contention of Brookes, VanDyke, and others that if there must be an investigation it should not be limited to the Louisville men. Dr. Thomas was exhilarated, triumphant. Anecdotes, poetry, witticisms, and personal remarks enlivened his argument and contributed to the interest, if not always to the good taste, of his speech:

You know very well, sir, that it is the nature of debate.to kindle that tingling in the blood which Sir John Falstaff declares was symptomatic of apoplexy. He had " read the cause of his effects in Galen ". . . . Shall there be appointed, under the second amendment, a smelling committee

---

[55] Letter from Wm. C. Anderson to T. E. Thomas, dated May 24, 1866. Thomas, *op. cit.*, pp. 127-128.

[56] For the facts of the career of T. E. Thomas *cf.* Thomas, *op. cit.*, *passim*, and *Presbyterian Encyclopaedia*, under "Thomas."

to investigate certain disagreeable odors that are said to be floating in the atmosphere. . . .

For five years this church, after a discussion that has reached every hovel in the land — a discussion that has been presented in religious periodicals and political papers, after a full and free debate, has four times repeated the testimony of 1861. Last year, sir, the General Assembly determined that the time had come when these principles should be carried into practical application.

. . . .

Moderator, we have in this case the deliberate and intentional defiance of the Presbytery of Louisville to the General Assembly. . . . We have it, sir, especially in the fact that they sent one representative, of whom, since he cannot reply to me, I will simply say that his presence here is the most marked affront to the dignity and loyalty of this house that the Presbytery of Louisville was capable of perpetrating. [Hisses.]

. . . .

Twenty years ago there was a solitary couple in this Assembly standing up to testify to what we thought to be the truth, and what the Church now, and the nation, and the world believe.

. . . .

Sir, when the National Government finds a State organized in armed resistance to its authority, does it send its scouts to search the portfolios of boarding school misses to ascertain what namby-pamby treason they may have written to their country cousins? I think not, sir. In this case, sir, we have a plain and distinct defiance. The paper of my friend, Dr. McLean, takes the bull by the horns, and, I mean no disrespect, sir, when I say that while we have the bull by the horns we need not trouble ourselves about the bleating of the calves. [Laughter.] It is natural, sir, that they should sympathize in the anguish of their sire. [Renewed laughter.]

. . . .

Why, sir, there are names on this very Declaration and Testimony, of brethren that I shall love while my heart beats. There is the name of one there, sir, with whom, if I ever reach heaven, I hope to walk arm in arm before God's throne and sing,
  "Amazing grace, how sweet the sound,"
as thirty-three years ago we sang it in our boyish days.

. . . .

Now, sir, there is a third aspect of this subject. I confess I felt for a moment a flash of admiration — if that is permissable [sic] — when I saw the gallant and almost martial bearing of some gentlemen who presented themselves yesterday for decapitation. [Laughter.] . . . And yet, alas, sir, age has accomplished for me that which was once given, I think, as a piece of advice to a young minister — it has torn away the plumage from the wings of my imagination and placed them in the tail of my judgment. [Laughter.] . . . Moderator, the age of martyrdom has passed, I fear, forever. . . . But, then, sir, consider the difference; martyrdom used to mean the sharp ax of Saint Paul; it used to mean the cross of Peter, with his head downward. . . . But, sir, what does this modern martyrdom mean? It means — applause in the galleries. It means a palatial mansion on Brooklyn Heights.[57] It means a trip to Europe. It means the smiles of an " innumerable company of angels " waving their cambric handkerchiefs. [Great merriment and sensation.]

Sir, when I want wine, give me the blood of the grape, and not your cider champagne. When the age of martyrdom comes, let it be martyrdom that means something and costs something — a martyrdom that empties a man's church and does not fill it — a martyrdom that drives a man from his pulpit and does not invite sympathizers.

. . . .

Well, sir, if it was intended to frighten this Assembly from its propriety, I beg leave to remind these gentlemen that they have been asleep these last five years. . . . Do they suppose, sir, that when we have met the hydra with his hundred heads, and those hundred heads lie bleeding around us, we are to be frightened from our propriety by the wriggling of his dying tail? [Sensation.] [58]

Dr. Thomas closed his argument with the assertion that the method of action proposed in Dr. McLean's resolution would afford the amplest opportunity for a full discussion of the whole matter. Having finished his speech he immediately moved the previous question. This motion prevailed, and the two amendments [59] which had been proposed to modify Dr. McLean's resolution were thus cut off. The Assembly then adopted the resolution as it was originally introduced, and thereby determined that a special committee should be appointed, to which the Declaration and Testimony matter should be referred.[60] Dr. McLean had reason to feel gratified: with remarkable promptness and but the slightest amount of opposition (so far as numbers went) his program had been carried through.

The motion to refer to a committee was passed on the first Saturday (the third day) of the session. As the committee

[57] A reference to Dr. VanDyke.
[58] *Proceedings*, pp. 19-22.
[59] *Cf. ante*, p. 226, and note 36.
[60] *Minutes of the General Assembly*, 1866, vol. xviii, p. 19. For the text of the resolution, *cf. ante*, p. 225.

did not submit its report to the Assembly until the following Thursday,[61] one might assume that the four intervening days were days of peace as far as the Louisville case was concerned. Quite the contrary was true: not a single session during that period was free from formal protests, bitter complaints, and acrimonious references to the stand the Assembly had thus far taken. First came the reading of an extended paper which had been submitted by the convention of ministers and ruling elders which had met to consider a program for Assembly action.[62] After a lengthy recital of the alleged errors of the Louisville brethren and the dangers they involved, three duties were pointed out for the Old School Church:

> The first is, to purify herself from the widely diffused poison of the times, which (in a form more or less virulent) is diffused through all the Churches; . . .
> The second is to hold out, and wide open, the arms of her love to every child of God in the Southern country who has been a victim — not the willing partaker of the sins against God, against His Church, and against their country, against which Divine Providence has testified by such severe and most righteous judgments.
> The third is to proceed, at once, and with a zeal proportioned to the urgency of the necessity, to redeem the solemn promise made by the first Assembly, after the schism organized in 1861 — that she would wholly disregard its existence, and as God might enable her, would strive to recover all she might lose by it, and to extend and establish, more and more, throughout the whole South, the precious system of Divine Truth, unto the liberty and power of which God has called her by His grace.
> Let the revenge we will ask of God be a double share in the work of saving those who have cast us out as doubly vile.[63]

With the one hundred and eleven members of the convention agreeing unanimously[64] upon this radical program, it is not surprising that the Assembly they sought to direct should be inclined toward extreme action.

Among the several papers of protest entered against the Assembly's action was one from the four Louisville commis-

[61] *Minutes of the General Assembly,* 1866, vol. xviii, pp. 33-34.
[62] *Cf. ante,* pp. 219-220.
[63] For the text of this paper, *cf. Proceedings,* pp. 25-27.
[64] *Ibid.,* p. 27.

sioners who had been prevented from taking their seats in the Assembly. Announcing that from a hasty reading it "seemed to be respectful,"[65] the Moderator suggested it be read to the Assembly. The paper alleged that the right to judge of the qualifications of commissioners was inherent in the presbyteries; the claim of any Assembly to judge of the qualifications of its own members must be limited in the nature of the case to the question whether the credentials were in accordance with the provisions in the constitution. The protestants also asserted that the action of the Assembly was in its nature judicial, and was therefore in effect a judicial sentence in disregard of all the provisions for a fair trial, and without any opportunity for the accused to be heard. This unfairness was aggravated by the singling out of the Louisville Presbytery alone for punishment. Finally it was but an intensification of the wrong done, the four complainants maintained, that the Assembly had resolved not absolutely and finally to exclude them, but to deny them seats until the Assembly "should have examined and decided"; this made it all the more manifest that the action of the Assembly was, in effect, pronouncing and executing sentence first and afterward proceeding to examine and decide. Having thus stated their grievances, the four commissioners announced the course they proposed to follow:

With these views and convictions there is but one course left open to us, viz.: To take our appeal at once upon the issue as it has been made for us and forced upon us, from this General Assembly to the Presbytery of Louisville in particular, in so far as it concerns ourselves and that body, and to the whole Church, in so far as it is an issue involving the great principles of her Constitution, and, indeed, her continued existence as a free Christian Commonwealth in the enjoyment of the franchises and immunities conferred upon her by her adorable Head.

We therefore respectfully inform the Assembly that we shall not attend further upon its sessions.[66]

---

[65] *Ibid.,* p. 27.

[66] The paper of the Louisville commissioners is printed in full in the *Proceedings,* pp. 27-29. It was signed by all four commissioners: Dr. Stuart Robinson, Dr. S. R. Wilson, Mark Hardin, and C. A. Wickliffe (the latter two being ruling elders).

Although it was proposed to refer this paper to the special committee, the Assembly took no action whatever with regard to it.[67]

For years there had been a strong feeling in the West that the more conservative East tried to dominate the Old School Church. The accusation had been made with particular frequency against a certain Philadelphia-Princeton group. The alleged pro-slavery leanings and the frank opposition of this group toward the movement for church reunion marked its members as likely targets for western radicals. One of the leaders, Dr. Henry A. Boardman, had been sent to the 1866 Assembly as a commissioner from one of the Philadelphia presbyteries.[68] A former student and an intimate friend of Dr. Hodge,[69] Dr. Boardman in many respects illustrated Hodge's philosophy and ideals. Since 1833, when he first began his ministry, he had been pastor of the Tenth Presbyterian Church in Philadelphia. His long service in that capital of Old School Presbyterianism had given him a truly remarkable hold on the leadership of the denomination. Dr. Boardman was eloquent; even today, fifty years after his death, one is swept along by the fluency of his recorded speeches. Very conservative in temperament and uncompromisingly orthodox in his doctrinal beliefs, Dr. Boardman was frequently engaged in controversy. In this sort of activity he was recognized as a most worthy foeman. Much of his power was attributable to a fineness of feeling and to an innate sense of dignity: " He was so high-toned and courteous in his controversial character that he commanded the respect and admiration of opponents." [70]

When, after several futile attempts, this man finally obtained the floor in the General Assembly of 1866, all present realized

---

[67] *Minutes of the General Assembly,* 1866, vol. xviii, p. 21.

[68] There were three presbyteries in Philadelphia and its immediate environs.

[69] Hodge, *op. cit.,* pp. 582, 584, and *passim.*

[70] *Presbyterian Encyclopaedia,* p. 83. Most of the facts cited with regard to Dr. Boardman's life have been drawn from this source, pp. 82-83.

that they were about to hear an impassioned but clear and logical defense of the rights of the Louisville commissioners. Dr. Boardman began by asserting that the operation of the " previous question " had unfairly prevented him from speaking earlier. For this he blamed Dr. Thomas, whom he also charged with want of good taste and unseemly satire in the lengthy speech he had delivered before the Assembly. The rebuke Dr. Boardman administered was dignified, but stinging. It is significant that when Dr. Thomas again had occasion to deliver a long address in the Assembly, there was nothing in the least indecorous about his remarks.[71]

The feature of the whole proceeding that most impressed Dr. Boardman was the spirit the majority were displaying toward the Louisville men. During the session of the previous day,[72] the visiting representative from the New School General Assembly [73] had addressed the Old School body. The kindly nature of his remarks, together with the warmth and friendliness of the Moderator's reply, contrasted, in Dr. Boardman's opinion, most painfully with the vindictive spirit displayed toward the Louisville brethren:

> We have said to our brethren from abroad, we are willing to overlook and forget many a hard thing you have said, and many an unsound doctrine you have cherished, and many a conflict in which we have met; and so, while we are glad to see them sailing down the broad stream of oblivion, we have taken the errors and mistakes of these men: every false step they have made, every unkind sentiment that in their moments of passion may have fallen from their lips, we have taken and visited upon them a rhadamanthine justice. Why is this, sir? Why is this? I will not answer the question.[74]

It is not surprising that arguments of this kind were not to the liking of western friends of Dr. Thomas, like Dr. Anderson.[75]

---

[71] For the second long speech of Dr. Thomas, *cf. Proceedings,* pp. 59-65.

[72] That is, Saturday, May 20. Dr. Boardman spoke on Monday, May 22. There were no Sunday sessions of the Assembly.

[73] The practice of sending delegates to each other's Assemblies had been inaugurated by the Old and New School Churches in 1863. *Minutes of the General Assembly,* 1863, vol. xvii, p. 36.

[74] *Proceedings,* p. 30.

[75] *Cf.* pp. 225-226.

To Dr. Boardman the whole proceeding was characterized by bad taste, unfairness, ungenerosity, and disregard of constitutional principles.[76]

Dr. Thomas's and Dr. Boardman's arguments had been in the nature of long addresses. There was a third extended speech at this stage of the proceedings, which, but for two facts, would perhaps not require mention. First, it was marred by taste fully as bad as Dr. Thomas's; second, largely because of this character, it prompted an unfortunate episode which led to the summary expulsion of a member from this most turbulent of Assemblies. The speaker was the Hon. Samuel Galloway, a ruling elder representing the Presbytery of Columbus (Ohio). This gentleman, who seemed to experience some difficulty in forgetting that he had formerly been a member of Congress and in remembering that the General Assembly was not the House of Representatives, had a delightful time orating, undisturbed by any consideration for the feelings of the Border State brethren or the citizens of the city which was entertaining the Assembly:

Why, Mr. Moderator, I did not expect to please certain ladies and gentlemen of this locality by any allusions to the triumphs of our arms and our testimonies. "Oh ye generation of vipers," it might not have been so well for you, but perhaps a little better for the purity and permanency of our freedom, if our testimonies had received a fuller development by a longer continuance of this war. [Sensation and merriment.] . . . I say to all in rebellion against the National Government or the loyal of Christ's Church, seek the communion of those who are your kindred in faith and practice; go your own way; and if that shall end as in the case of Judas — in hanging yourselves — you must take the responsibility. [Renewed merriment.]

. . . .

As I have not been led into the temptation of hospitality by any sympathiser with disloyalty [this statement follows a reference to the "bread and butter" argument of Dr. Boardman], I cannot appreciate the feelings of those whose principles, whilst in this city, are influenced by what they shall eat and drink.

. . . .

Bro. Boardman says this is an hour when we ought not to manifest unkind feelings towards these erring brethren. Sir, we are ready to re-

---

[76] For Dr. Boardman's speech, *cf. Proceedings,* pp. 29-34.

ceive repentant rebels, when they come to us washed with the washing of a regeneration, which shall be exemplified by a sincere sorrow for a participation in that terrible crime of treason, which has slain the beloved of many of the households of members of this Assembly."

The speaker was continually interrupted by " applause," " merriment," "sensation," "hisses." The more frequent the interruptions, the more fiery became his rhetoric.

The manner and content of Mr. Galloway's speech were more than some on the other side could bear. One member, Rev. W. M. Ferguson, of the Presbytery of Zanesville (Ohio), expressed his disgust in a letter to the Columbus (Ohio) *Statesman* in language that was decidedly strong:

The debate in the Assembly ran higher to-day, or rather *lower* than ever. It was reserved for Mr. Galloway, of Ohio, to cap the climax of vulgarity and demagogism. . . . His manner was monstrous! A dancing monkey's motions were graceful to it. Indeed it was awful! Sublimely ridiculous. His twistings and bodily contortions, could they have been photographed, would have furnished comic almanac-makers with an almost limitless number of grotesque samples for all time to come. Besides his disgusting egotism — his self-righteous laudations — his canting use of Scripture — his boasting, dirty insinuations — in a word, his scurrility and blackguardism exceeded anything of the kind it was ever my painful misfortune to hear.

. . . . Some who had no personal acquaintance with him thought he had a " Highland gill " in his cheek.[78] But it is declared that he is a radical temperance man. . . . Mr. G. boldly affirmed . . . that " Dr. Boardman was a traitor, and his speech yesterday treason, and till he washed his hands of the blood of this hellish crime, he (Mr. G.) would never sit down with him at the Lord's table." These were his words.[79]

. . . .

---

[77] *Proceedings*, pp. 46-47. For entire text of the speech, *cf. Proceedings*, pp. 37-41; 46-48.

[78] An allusion to Dr. Thomas's address. Dr. Thomas had offended the sensibilities of many of the members by quoting the lines of a " bacchannalian [sic] song " of Robert Burns:

" But bring a Scotsman from his hill,
    Clap in his cheek a Highland gill," and so forth.
Proceedings, p. 20.

[79] The *Proceedings* as recorded by the *Missouri Democrat* contain no such statement, but Mr. Ferguson alleged that this sheet — " the only one that pretends to give verbatim reports phonographically taken " — was " exceedingly radical " and perhaps guilty of some omissions. *Proceedings*, next-to-last page (not numbered).

Thus we go — *go to pieces* as a Church of Christ. It is alarming to witness how rapidly and superficially the legitimate business of the Assembly is passed over, and how eager many are to "take up the unfinished business" relating to Louisville Presbytery, &c. It is painful to say it, but many think and say that this Assembly has done far more against the interest of true religion in this city since it convened last week than the big horse races that have been in progress here for some time. What a curse Radicalism is!

But I weary you. So, for the present, I close, sorry that the great State of Ohio has been disgraced by the only two [80] really unsufferably [sic] Radical and disgustingly vulgar speeches in this Assembly so far.[81]

When Mr. Galloway brought the matter of this letter to the attention of the Assembly, it threw the house into an uproar. The excited body refused to refer the affair to a committee,[82] but insisted that Mr. Ferguson must at once retract his statements and make ample apology to the satisfaction of the house, or be immediately expelled. The Moderator then requested the offending member to make an explanation; when no response from him was forthcoming, the motion to expel Mr. Ferguson immediately was carried "by an overwhelming vote." No sooner had this step been taken, however, than the gentleman came forward and attempted to speak. Some confusion ensued, but finally the same member who made the motion for expulsion now moved that the vote be reconsidered in order that the man might have an opportunity to explain. Although the Moderator was very loath to put this second motion, several voices demanded it, and it was almost unanimously carried. But all in vain, so far as the final outcome was concerned. Mr. Ferguson was willing to express regret for having written the letter, but would not make a retraction of its contents in the manner demanded. Although several members made earnest pleas for more deliberate action, a second motion for immediate expulsion prevailed, "with a very light vote in the negative." The attitude in the galleries probably did Mr. Ferguson no good, for in that portion of the house there were persons who "listened with much satisfaction" to the reading of the letter, "particularly the more gross and scandalous portions of it," and a "tendency to merriment, almost breaking out into applause, was plainly audible." [83]

The episode reflects the excited character of the Assembly. One defender of Mr. Ferguson stated that he supposed no such action as that contemplated had ever been taken since the founding of the Presbyterian Church. There can be no doubt that the whole proceeding was most unusual. But the Assembly was in the awkward position of one called upon to prove that he really has dignity, at a time when he is all too conscious of being guilty of unbecoming conduct. Had Mr. Ferguson's charge been wholly unfounded, he would probably have escaped with a much lighter sentence. As it was, his accusers orated eloquently on the letter as a "monstrous libel," "one of the grossest outrages ever offered to a deliberative body," and an "insult to this Assembly." Since 1788 (the date of the founding of the General Assembly) there had never been, it was declared, such an outrage perpetrated on the Assembly. These speakers omitted any comparison of the dignity of the 1866 Assembly with that of its predecessors.

At the beginning of the second week of the Assembly sessions, the special committee of seven which had been appointed to consider the whole Declaration and Testimony matter rendered its report. To a body which for six days had been debating, in one form or other, the case of the Louisville men, the length of the report — some 5000 words — must have seemed appalling. As for the content of the report, the character of the committee's membership had left no doubt what its nature would be. The persistent Dr. McLean [84] had been appointed chairman, and the "radical" Moderator had taken care to include Dr. Thomas and Mr. Galloway in the personnel. Two of the four other members had early in the session clearly

[83] For an account of the episode, cf. *Proceedings*, pp. 86-89. For the offending letter, cf. *ibid.*, next-to-last page (not numbered).

[84] *Cf. ante*, pp. 223-227.

aligned themselves with the radicals;[85] the other two by their votes on the several motions of the first two days had shown themselves hostile to the Louisville commissioners.[86] The report drawn up could not have been a disappointment to the radicals. After a long review of the action of the offending brethren, the report recommended five measures for adoption:

1. That the Presbytery of Louisville be, and hereby is, dissolved. . . .

2. That a new Presbytery is hereby constituted, to be known by the same name . . . ; said Presbytery to be composed of the following ministers (together with so many elders as may appear), to-wit, [here follow the names of such ministers of the old Presbytery as had not signed the "Declaration and Testimony"] or so many of them . . . as shall, before their organization, subscribe the following formula, viz., "I do hereby express my disapproval of the Declaration and Testimony . . . and my obedience in the Lord to the General Assembly. . . ."

3. That so many ministers belonging to the late Presbytery of Louisville as are not herein named, are hereby directed to apply for admission to the Presbytery now constituted, . . . and they shall be received only on condition of acknowledging before the Presbytery their error in adopting and signing the Declaration and Testimony. . . . If at the expiration of two months . . . these ministers shall not have made such application, or shall not have been received, their pastoral relations, so far as they may exist with the churches under our care, shall thenceforth be *ipso facto* dissolved.

. . . .

5. That this General Assembly, in thus dealing with a recusant and rebellious Presbytery, by virtue of the plenary authority existing in it for "suppressing schismatical contentions and disputations," has no intention or disposition to disturb the existing relation of churches, ruling elders, or private members; but rather to protect them in the enjoyment of their rights and privileges in the Church of their choice, against men who would seduce them into an abandonment of the heritage of their fathers.[87]

In concluding its report the Committee recommended that on the hearing of the matters therein presented, the commissioners from the Presbytery of Louisville be heard, subject

[85] Rev. D. J. Waller (Pennsylvania) and Ruling Elder H. K. Clarke (Michigan).

[86] Rev. T. W. Hynes (Illinois) and Ruling Elder R. P. Davidson (Indiana.)

[87] *Minutes of the General Assembly,* 1866, vol. xviii, p. 39. The whole report comprises pages 34-39.

to the rules of order which governed the house.[88]   When Dr. McLean had finally ended his reading, the Assembly accepted his report together with the recommendation for the hearing of the offending commissioners, and requested Dr. Brookes, one of their fellow-signers of the " Declaration and Testimony," [89] to inform them of the action of the Assembly.[90]   As the reading of the report had consumed a considerable share of the time of the afternoon session, it was decided to postpone its consideration until the evening session.   This would give the Louisville men an opportunity to be present at the hearings from the outset.

Thus after a week of Assembly sessions had elapsed, the accused men were at last to have an opportunity to present their case.   After several parliamentary skirmishes the real battle now was on.   In the preliminary encounters those on one side who had most at stake had been denied participation, and each engagement had resulted in decisive defeat for their partisans.   Now that the enemy had had ample time to perfect its strategy, arrange its tactics, and complete its defenses, it was willing to concede the four offending men an opportunity to participate in the struggle.   If any members actually expected the Louisville men to appear, they were soon disillusioned.   When the Assembly convened for its evening session, the following communication was read:

The undersigned, Commissioners from the Presbytery of Louisville, who happen not yet to have left the city [91] — overlooking, in the spirit of Christian forbearance, the insult and seeming mockery of the Presbytery and themselves, in a proposition to appear and be heard before a court which has already condemned them unheard — in response to the resolution of this afternoon, transmitted to them by the Permanent Clerk of the General Assembly, most respectfully refer the Assembly to their letter

---

[88] *Ibid.*, p. 40.

[89] *Cf. ante*, p. 226.

[90] *Minutes of the General Assembly*, 1866, p. 40.

[91] A reference to a statement of Dr. Brookes on the floor of the Assembly (*Proceedings*, p. 54) to the effect that he thought some of them had left the city. As Ruling Elder Hardin (*cf. ante*, p. 235, note 66) did not sign the communication, it is probable that he had already left St. Louis.

of May 19th,[92] as containing very obvious and sufficient reasons why they could not, without further special instructions from their Presbytery, appear before the present Assembly in any capacity.

Samuel R. Wilson
Stuart Robinson
C. A. Wickliffe
by James H. Brookes [93]

The remainder of the debate on the case of the Presbytery of Louisville, like its earlier scenes, was to take place in the absence of the representatives of the body on trial.

The debate on the motion to adopt the Committee's report was opened by a two-hour speech by Dr. Thomas. As contrasted with his earlier speech, this address was moderate in tone and acceptable in taste. Occasionally, however, the orator lost his balance, as when he was discussing the punishment designed for the refractory Presbytery:

> It is indeed a summary method; yet sometimes short roads are the best. It was a very short method by which Pharoah [sic] and his hosts were put out of the house, when God moved upon the sea; a very summary process by which the lightning, fire and brimstone came down from Heaven upon Sodom and Gomorrah; and if you think the cases too far-fetched, then it was a very summary process by which, in the presence of a Church Court in Jerusalem, Ananias and Sapphira were sent to the Supreme Court in Heaven, to answer for their crimes. The speediest remedies are commonly the best.[94]

Yet in spite of the degree of wickedness suggested by these shocking parallels, but a few minutes later in referring to the attitude of the Synod of Kentucky on the Declaration and Testimony matter [95] as being "to say the least, hesitating," Dr. Thomas declared that he did not impugn the motives of the Synod's members and admitted that he did not know how he might have acted under the influences they might have felt.[96] Evidently not all of his emphasis was to be taken at its face value. But despite his occasional lapses into gross

[92] *Cf. ante*, pp. 234-236.
[93] *Minutes of the General Assembly*, 1866, vol. xviii, p. 41.
[94] *Proceedings*, p. 63.
[95] *Cf. ante*, pp. 206-209.
[96] *Proceedings*, p. 63.

exaggeration, the speaker's arguments were effectively presented. His peroration reflected significantly one of the dominant motives impelling his party to urge such drastic action:

> Moderator and brethren, we are called to vindicate ecclesiastical authority, the power of the keys, not only in our own Church, but for all the churches of the land. This thing is not done in a corner. The eyes of America are upon you. To every city, village and hamlet in the country the news of your decision will be carried on the wings of the lightning. Thousands and tens of thousands who have offered prayers for your guidance by Divine wisdom, are waiting to hear that the Church has sealed the doom of ecclesiastical rebellion. Let us meet our responsibility like men, like Christians. The Presbyterian Church expects every man to do his duty. [Applause.] [97]

As in 1861 [98] so too in 1866 the eyes of the world were impelling the Assembly toward drastic action.

Dr. Thomas's speech exhausted the entire time of the evening session of the Assembly. At the session of the following morning it was decided to postpone further consideration of the Louisville case until the appeal of Dr. R. J. Breckinridge against the Synod of Kentucky [99] had been heard, as it was thought that in the trial of this appeal some light might be thrown upon the Louisville affair.[100] In fact it had earlier been determined that the Breckinridge appeal was to be the order of the day,[101] and to have proceeded with the Louisville case as was proposed would have involved a departure from the regular order of business. Those who hoped for light from the Breckinridge appeal were doomed to be disappointed. The judicial committee and Dr. Breckinridge both desired that the two complaints of the Doctor against the Synod be tried together.[102] The request that this arrangement be made led to an involved and highly technical argument as to whether the parties in the two cases were the same; finally, however, the

---

[97] *Ibid.,* p. 65.
[98] *Cf. ante,* pp. 82-85.
[99] *Cf. ante,* pp. 206, 209, 223.
[100] *Proceedings,* pp. 65, 75.
[101] *Ibid.,* p. 65. *Cf.* also *Minutes of the General Assembly,* 1866, vol. xviii, p. 43.
[102] *Proceedings,* pp. 66-67.

request was granted.[103]   After a half-day had been consumed in wrangling over points of procedure, a determined effort was made to get the Breckinridge matter out of the way by having it recommitted to the judicial committee.[104]

In the debate as to whether this step should be taken Dr. Breckinridge was well-nigh helpless from the fact that he was not a member of the Assembly.   It was no doubt galling to a man of his temperament to have to ask permission to address the Assembly, especially since it seemed to him that his former Danville colleague,[105] the Moderator, was not as considerate of him as he should have been.   Dr. Breckinridge, as usual, was not always orderly in his behavior:

Dr. Breckinridge asked to be permitted to make a personal explanation.

The Moderator decided that he was not in order, not being a member of the Assembly.

Dr. Breckinridge remarked that the Moderator had a singular facility of deciding one way at one time and another way at another time.

Rev. Dr. Anderson.   I rise to a point of order.

Dr. Breckinridge.   *You* rise to a point of order!   [The point of the emphasis here was that Dr. Anderson had been tried before a military commission for disloyalty to the Federal Government, and convicted, although the commanding general had disapproved of the proceedings because of a defect in the orders convening the commission.[106]]

The Moderator stated that he had already decided that Dr. Breckinridge was not entitled to the floor.

Dr. Breckinridge.   Well, sir, when I am browbeaten in the Assembly, first by the Moderator, and then by a traitor, I have nothing more to say.

The Moderator.   I should have made this decision in respect to any other member.

.   .   .   .   .

Rev. Dr. Anderson.   I rise to a privileged question. . . .   I was called a traitor.   I stand here, sir, to say — and I wish to be heard by every person in this Assembly — that I here pronounce that statement as false and slanderous.

[103] *Ibid.*, p. 69.

[104] *Ibid.*, pp. 69-70.

[105] Dr. Stanton had, a few days before, offered his resignation as Professor in the Danville Theological Seminary. (*Minutes of the General Assembly,* 1866, vol. xviii, p. 29.)   He became President of Miami University. (*Presbyterian Encyclopaedia,* p. 854.)

[106] McPherson, *op. cit.,* pp. 537-538; *cf.* also *post,* pp. 326-327.

The Moderator. I am requested to state on behalf of Dr. Breckinridge that he wished to make a personal explanation. The vote was taken and the motion to permit Dr. Breckinridge to make a personal explanation was lost.[107]

Things were not going so well for the Doctor. The attempt to shelve his case failed, however, and his appeal was once more taken up. This meant that the Assembly was sitting in a judicial capacity; hence Dr. Breckinridge as a complainant could again come before it. But now another misfortune befell him. Dr. Stanton, who had formerly been a member of the Synod of Kentucky, was one of the appellants in Dr. Breckinridge's case. This of course involved his vacating the chair while the Assembly sat in a judicial capacity to hear the Kentucky cases. It had originally been agreed that three of the appellants should divide among themselves the task of presenting the case. Dr. Stanton was to have come first and to present an analysis of the "Declaration and Testimony," giving the chief arguments against its content.[108] Now when the time for his part arrived, Dr. Stanton explained that he had concluded, as there were four persons present as appellants, besides himself, "to take no part in the case for reasons which may appear obvious."[109] Dr. Breckinridge was furious and not entirely dignified in giving expression to his fury:

Dr. Stanton has declined to do his part, and I think for very obvious reasons, but not the reasons that he alludes to. . . .

I do not mean to say who are traitors. In regard to my brother who took such high dudgeon in regard to a plain truth, there are some other small matters of much more recent date, which I may take occasion to allude to hereafter. I understand that fighting means death and therefore I never fight if I can help it, and I never give unnecessary offense, which everybody will tell you that has quarreled with me, and that ain't a few. [Laughter.] . . . I was extremely anxious to preserve that Synod in peace, so that when we were done with war we might go and do our work, no matter which party triumphed. I reckon I erred in that respect, for I stood where I ought not to have stood. I found I had finally to perish or fight somewhere; then as far as I could by myself, I commenced this

---

[107] *Proceedings,* p. 70.
[108] *Ibid.*
[109] *Ibid.*

fight which I see is being lost here today, and which, if lost, I shall hold this Assembly responsible to the country and God for its being lost — lost by the mismanagement of its friends, and by the betrayal of its cause by the Moderator. Now interrupt me if you like [addressing Dr. Anderson].

Rev. Dr. Anderson. I do not intend that the dignity of this house shall be insulted.

Dr. Breckinridge. I beg pardon. I would as soon think of boxing the jaws of my venerable mother, after calling her back from the grave, as to insult this Assembly. . . . Well, sir, I want to go on with what little voice I have left. I am a very bad subject to be browbeaten. I am done, and will now take back as much as possible. . . . So far as this case is concerned, as I understand it, it is now in a posture that it cannot be issued. . . . when I got up merely to make a personal explanation, I was told that I could take no part in the case in that condition of it. . . .

Dr. Breckinridge continued at some length in vindication of his course, and at the conclusion of his remarks, the Assembly adjourned.[110]

Thus the Breckinridge cases were dropped, for the Doctor declined to proceed with them. The whole affair had turned out a fiasco after consuming the greater part of a day of the Assembly's time. The Assembly had been in session for nine days without a great deal of accomplishment to its credit, and was in no mood now to listen to a new case which promised to be exceedingly wordy. Mr. Galloway probably expressed accurately the sentiments of the commissioners when he declared that "they had had about enough of Kentucky before the Assembly. . . ."[111]

Having failed to receive any light on the Louisville problem from the Breckinridge appeals, the Assembly reverted to a consideration of the report of the Special Committee. For more than three days the debate continued.[112] Several long

---

[110] *Proceedings*, p. 71.

[111] *Ibid.*, p. 70. Dr. Breckinridge had advanced so many reasons for refusing to proceed with his cases that it became difficult to decide how their disposition should be recorded in the minutes of the Assembly, without doing an injustice either to the Assembly or to the complainant. After much discussion in the Assembly, and many motions, a satisfactory form was finally devised. *Proceedings*, p. 72; *Minutes of the General Assembly*, 1866, vol. xviii, pp. 49, 53.

[112] Some time was of course devoted to routine matters, but the Louisville case was always in the foreground.

speeches were made — the greater number of them in opposition
to the report. Earnestness and eloquence characterized the
addresses on both sides, but at this stage of the proceedings
the leadership of the opposition was decidedly more impressive
in personnel than that of the supporting party. Dr. W. L.
Breckinridge (distinguished brother of the notorious " Dr.
R. J."), who had long been respected as a leader in Kentucky,[113] pleaded effectively against the harshness of the report.[114] Dr. E. P. Humphrey, a native of Massachusetts,
whose long residence in Kentucky and whose position as fellow-
professor with Dr. R. J. Breckinridge in the Danville Theological Seminary entitled his opinions to a special degree of
respect, offered a series of much milder resolutions [115] as a substitute for the action proposed by the Committee's report.
Although the speech with which Dr. Humphrey urged his proposal " drew tears from many of the audience," [116] the Assembly would have none of this milder solution. Dr. VanDyke's
long argument against the Committee report produced a strong
impression.[117] Dr. Boardman also again entered the debate at
this stage, and spoke ably and convincingly.[118] But the greatest interest of all was evinced in the speech of Dr. James H.
Brookes,[119] for while the other speakers in opposing the Committee report all made it clear that they condemned the " Dec-

[113] Formerly pastor of the First Church, Louisville, President of Centre
College, and Moderator of the General Assembly (1859). *Presbyterian
Encyclopaedia,* pp. 97-98.

[114] *Proceedings,* pp. 76-79. For an estimate of this speech, *cf.* article,
" The General Assembly," *Biblical Repertory and Princeton Review,* July,
1866, vol. 38, pp. 460-461.

[115] *Minutes of the General Assembly,* 1866, vol. xviii, pp. 53, 59, 62.

[116] Article, " The General Assembly," *Biblical Repertory and Princeton
Review,* vol. 38, p. 467. Dr. Humphrey's speech is given in full (pp. 462-
467).

[117] *Ibid.,* pp. 467-468.

[118] *Ibid.,* p. 468. *Cf.,* also, *Proceedings,* p. 90.

[119] The speech is printed in full, *ibid.,* pp. 107-114. For an outline of the
argument, *cf.* article " The General Assembly," *Biblical Repertory and
Princeton Review,* July, 1866, vol. 38, pp. 468-470. For Dr. Brookes' record,
cf. ante, pp. 226, 243.

laration and Testimony" itself, Dr. Brookes as a signer of that fateful document not only condemned the Committee report but valiantly defended the paper which had caused all of the trouble.

Dr. Brookes' long address consisted largely in attempts to disprove the charges made against that document, and in the production of an interesting array of quotations from a host of synods and presbyteries which had at one time or another expressed opposition to the General Assembly's actions. He emphatically denied that the "Declaration and Testimony" party was responsible for the initiation of the difficulties in which the Church now found itself:

> Mr. Moderator: It has been asserted again and again on the floor of this house that the Declaration and Testimony party are laboring in the interest of secession, and are trying to to vitalize the dead body of slavery. . . . Sir, we had supposed that secession was ended by the war. We had supposed that slavery was done away with by the war, and what evidence have you that we refused to acquiesce in the stern decisions of the sword. . . . Do you desire to know who dragged these questions from the dead past to agitate our people with useless contentions? Do you desire to know who has thrown secession into our midst as the apple of discord? Do you desire to know who has gone about to vitalize the mangled body of slavery and make it a source of endless dispute and division? Sir, I believe before God it was the General Assembly. [Suppressed applause.] [120]

Whatever the attitude of individual commissioners toward Dr. Brookes' defense, there is no doubt whatever that he had the galleries with him. Early in his speech he found it necessary to appeal to the excited crowd to suppress their feelings and refrain from applause.[121] So far as the logic of his address was concerned, his arguments were cogently presented, but in comparing the "Declaration and Testimony" with previous statements of disagreement with the General Assembly, he failed to take into consideration the fact that the present paper was more than a protest; whatever its intent, its wording spelled defiance. Furthermore, he chose to overlook the fact

[120] *Proceedings*, p. 108.
[121] *Ibid.*

that to a large degree it was the previous record of some of the signers far more than the actual content of the document which had so stirred up the majority element in the Church. As Dr. Boardman pointed out,[122] individual quarrels in Kentucky and Missouri, where the war had been one of neighborhoods, had been brought into the Assembly. Stuart Robinson's name alone was probably responsible for much of the bitterness of the Assembly's hostility to the offending document. Nevertheless Dr. Brookes made out a good case for his side, and he was listened to with a great deal of interest.[123]

Evidently the eloquence of the defenders of the Louisville men had some effect, for after the debate had proceeded to some length the radical party switched its support from the Committee resolutions to a substitute series which had been offered by Dr. P. D. Gurley, who had been the middleground candidate for the position of Moderator of the Assembly.[124] Dr. Gurley's proposed action, while still severe, was distinctly less precipitous, and fairer in the sense that it applied to all signers of the "Declaration and Testimony," and not merely to the Presbytery of Louisville. The resolutions he offered were as follows:

1. *Resolved,* That this General Assembly does hereby condemn the Declaration and Testimony as a slander against the Church, schismatical in its character and aims, and its adoption by any of our church courts as an act of rebellion against the authority of the General Assembly.

2. *Resolved,* That the whole subject contemplated in this report,[125] including the report itself, be referred to the next General Assembly.

3. *Resolved,* That the signers of the "Declaration and Testimony," and the members of the Presbytery of Louisville who voted to adopt that paper, be summoned, and they are hereby summoned, to appear before the next General Assembly, to answer for what they have done in this

---

[122] *Ibid.,* p. 90.

[123] Article, "The General Assembly," *Biblical Repertory and Princeton Review,* July, 1866, vol. 28, p. 468.

[124] *Cf. ante,* p. 220.

[125] The Gurley paper was offered as a substitute for the resolutions recommended in the report of the Special Committee (*cf. ante,* p. 242), not for the entire report. The remainder of the report would stand.

matter, and that until their case is decided, they shall not be permitted to sit as members of any church court higher than the Session.

4. *Resolved*, That if any Presbytery shall disregard this action of the General Assembly, and at any meeting shall enroll, as entitled to a seat or seats in the body, one or more of the persons designated . . . , then that Presbytery shall be *ipso facto* dissolved. . . .

5. *Resolved*, That Synods, at their next stated meetings, in making up their rolls, shall be guided and governed by this action of the General Assembly.[126]

In support of his paper Dr Gurley read a series of eight reasons for adopting it, of which perhaps the most important was that it saved the Assembly " from even the appearance of taking action in this case which is too summary and severe." It was Dr. Thomas, the leader of the radicals himself, who on the thirteenth day of the Assembly's sessions moved that the resolutions of the Special Committee be tabled, thus making way for Dr. Gurley's substitute proposals.[127] After this motion had prevailed, a vote was taken on the adoption of the Gurley paper. By a vote of 196 to 37 (Dr. Brookes declining to vote) this paper was adopted by the Assembly. Twenty of the 37 adverse votes came from the Border States; 13 of the remaining 17, from the East. Only three Border State commissioners [128] — and they from western Missouri — voted for the Gurley paper. When it is remembered that the majority of the commissioners from this section were not signers of the " Declaration and Testimony," [129] the contrast between their attitude toward the offenders and that of the overwhelming majority of the brethren from the North is all the more striking.

[126] *Minutes of the General Assembly*, 1866, vol. xviii, pp. 60-61.

[127] *Ibid.*, p. 59. *Proceedings*, p. 93.

[128] More accurately, only three commissioners from distinctly Border State presbyteries. Dr. Gurley, from the Presbytery of Potomac, would have to be included if one were listing all Border State commissioners voting in the affirmative.

[129] It was impossible to find a list of the men who had signed the " Declaration and Testimony " up to May, 1866. (An earlier list is available.) From statements made on the floor of the Assembly it is clear that the above statement is a very safe one — undoubtedly less than half of the commissioners from the Border States had signed the document.

The Assembly had thus finally come to a decision with regard to the handling of the Louisville case and had decided that the action determined upon should cover the cases of all signers of the Louisville paper. Under the terms of the decision the offenders were virtually given a year in which to repent, but as in the meantime they were not to sit as members of any church court higher than the session, the Moderator pointed out that the effect of the Assembly action was to disqualify signers from sitting in the 1866 Assembly as well as in future bodies.[130] Upon this suggestion it was immediately resolved that the resolutions just passed should not take effect until the close of the current session.[131] The temper of the Assembly majority had changed since the beginning of the session: there seemed now to be a keen desire to maintain at least the appearance of generosity toward the erring ones. Perhaps the various votes by the Assembly had brought about a realization of the extreme smallness of the minority. Furthermore, as the ultimate action was not to come for a year, there could be no harm in letting the accused men participate in the proceedings of the remainder of the sessions. It must have been with mingled feelings, however, that the 1866 commissioners contemplated the postponement of final action. No doubt the satisfaction of having arrived at a settlement which provided time for repentance was at least partially offset by contemplation of the necessity of again engaging in the wearisome arguments which had consumed so many days of the 1866 session.

In a comprehensive and well-organized article in his *Princeton Review* Dr. Hodge considered the merits of the Assembly's action.[132] He suggested that three distinct points were involved: the right of the Assembly to exclude commissioners until their cases were decided, and to dissolve presbyteries; the

[130] *Proceedings*, p. 93.

[131] *Ibid.*, p. 94. The mover of this resolution was the editor of the radical *Presbyter*, Dr. J. G. Monfort.

[132] *Biblical Repertory and Princeton Review*, July, 1866, vol. 38, pp. 480-494. The whole article covers pp. 425-499.

sufficiency of the reasons for taking such steps; and the manner in which the Assembly had acted.[133] Dr. Hodge was probably the greatest living authority on the constitutional law of the Presbyterian Church; [134] when, therefore, after carefully weighing all of the arguments advanced, he decided that the General Assembly had the powers in question, his conclusion was convincing. Equally convincing was his verdict on the second point — he believed that there was no adequate reason for the action taken. He believed the penalty unduly severe, and decidedly inexpedient. Furthermore, the Assembly was inconsistent in its stand; by allowing signers of the " Declaration and Testimony " to retain their seats until the end of the sessions, it had virtually admitted that the signing of the document was not a sufficient reason for exclusion from church courts; yet it ordered that any presbytery which should admit one of the signers should be *ipso facto* dissolved for doing what the Assembly itself had done. Then too, as the dissolution of a presbytery did not suspend or depose its ministers, or separate them from the Presbyterian Church, or vacate their pulpits, the infliction of this penalty without further action would but bring confusion. After naming all of these reasons why the Assembly should not have taken this action, however, Dr. Hodge was careful to point out that they offered no justification for disobedience to the orders of the Assembly: a law was binding whether severe or otherwise.[135] As to the third point (the manner of the Assembly's action) he believed there could be little difference of opinion: the precipitate character of the whole proceedings, the high-handed methods followed by Dr. McLean, and the decision to refer the whole matter of the

---

[133] *Ibid.*, p. 480.

[134] He was frequently mentioned as such by other Presbyterian writers. He was the author of the standard treatise on the constitutional history of the Presbyterian Church in the United States. (His *Constitutional History of the Presbyterian Church in the United States,* in two volumes, had been published in 1839 and 1840. It carried the history of the Church to 1789. *Cf.* Hodge, *op. cit.*, p. 279.)

[135] *Biblical Repertory and Princeton Review,* July, 1866, vol. 38, p. 491.

Presbytery of Louisville to a special committee (thereby taking it out of the hands of the judicial committee, where it already was on the appeal of Dr. Breckinridge) — all of these features of the Assembly's action were extraordinary and extremely unfortunate.[136] It is difficult to see how any temperate man could seriously take issue with Dr. Hodge's conclusions, yet how far they were from representing the temper of the General Assembly may be judged from the one-sidedness of all of the votes on the Louisville case. Minority leaders referred with scorn to Dr. Thomas' boasts about his four to one majority.[137]

How did the Assembly come to take such drastic action? Apparently the factors prompting the votes of the majority were much the same as had motivated the supporters of the Spring Resolutions five years earlier,[138] but five years of war conditions had intensified their power so that the commissioners of 1866 were impelled to a position far more radical than would have been possible in the first of the war-time Assemblies. In 1861 the majority were anxious to prove to the public that the Old School Church was not disloyal to the cause of the Union; in 1866 a more revengeful public must be convinced that the Church would do its share in punishing rebels. Over and over again the commissioners were reminded that the world was tremendously interested in the attitude the Assembly would take toward the " disloyal " brethren; almost every whisper in the house was reported not only in the religious but also in the secular papers, it was asserted.[139]

Throughout the war period there had been a growing agitation for reunion with the New School Church,[140] and a tendency on the part of the promoters of this movement to govern their actions with an eye to New School approval. Their

---

[136] *Ibid.*, pp. 491-492.

[137] *Cf.*, *e.g.*, speech of Dr. Boardman, *Proceedings*, p. 29; also, speech of Dr. Brookes, *ibid.*, p. 113.

[138] *Cf. ante*, pp. 73-85.

[139] *Proceedings*, p. 89 (Speech of Dr. Nathaniel West of Brooklyn).

[140] *Cf. ante*, chapter 5, *passim;* also, *post*, part VI, *passim.*

cause seemed to be progressing;[141] it was therefore particularly desirable that the action of the 1866 Assembly should not only give no cause for offense, but should rather, if possible, be such as to make reunion seem all the more desirable. Whether or not the eyes of the whole world were upon the 1866 Assembly,[142] there can be no doubt that those of the New School brethren were cast in that direction. The fact that the Assemblies of the two branches convened at the same time in the same city[143] made it especially natural that the actions of the two bodies should be frequently compared. As usual the New School Assembly ended its work earlier than did its rival; but when it took the Old School body a full week longer to settle its problems, all the more interest was stimulated in what its solution would be. With their own Assembly out of the way, New School journals devoted their attention to Old School matters. The New York *Evangelist* approved of the Gurley Resolutions[144] because they afforded the erring Border State brethren of the other fold time to "decide to live in peace under the Government of the United States, or . . . cast in their lot and portion with their friends South."[145] The *Christian Herald* (a close friend of its Old School neighbor, the strongly pro-reunion *Presbyter*,[146] with which it was destined to unite in 1869) had special occasion for approving the action of the 1866 Old School Assembly, for just before the convening of the two bodies in St. Louis, this paper had stipulated the requirements of loyalty which the

---

[141] *Cf. post,* pp. 497-504.

[142] *Cf. ante,* p. 245.

[143] The New School sessions lasted from May 17 to May 28, inclusive; those of the Old School, from May 17 to June 4, inclusive.

[144] *Cf. ante,* pp. 251-252.

[145] New York *Evangelist,* June 14, 1866.

[146] It is possible that the editor of the *Presbyter* (Dr. J. G. Monfort), who was radically "loyal," may have suggested to the editor of the *Christian Herald* the possibility of stirring the Old School Assembly to take drastic action toward the Louisville Presbytery — and hence promoting the cause of reunion — by means of an editorial in the New School paper.

Old School Church must meet before reunion could be considered:

> Now there are three Assemblies in the land, instead of the *one* previous to 1837 — one Southern and two Northern; one thoroughly disloyal [in 1866!]; one loyal, with an active and belligerent disloyal element; and the third (our own) thoroughly loyal.
>
> Shall these three ever be reunited? If so, when and how? The three cannot unite. The New School and the Southern are too far apart on great moral issues to come together in this generation. The New School cannot unite with the Old School until it is delivered from the disloyal element. It will watch with interest the contest in that body between the friends and the foes of our National Union.
>
> If the Old School Assembly is true to the spirit of Presbyterianism; if it promptly repels the suggestion, even, of taking the viper of secession into its bosom, there will be few obstacles to a reunion of the loyal bodies, and Committees of Conference will, no doubt, be appointed.
>
> The interest at St. Louis centers first, therefore, upon the effort to modify the loyal action of the Old School Assembly, so that copperheads and traitors may nestle securely in it. If this is successful, reunion will not even be mentioned. If this fails, it may be near.[147]

It is not likely that dictation of this sort failed to have some effect upon the action of the Old School Assembly.

The triumphant enthusiasm of the radical leaders played its part in carrying the Assembly to a program of extreme measures. Dr. Thomas and his followers, long despised as extremists,[148] were now having their day of glory. It is not surprising that the dizzy eminence they had attained in church counsels should have distorted their better judgment. There was probably much truth in the estimate placed upon these men by a Border State ruling elder when he declared " they have imbibed the spirit of war . . . these Christian brethren, who have risen to their position of power in the downfall of those to whom they were once a contemptible minority, can see none but 'impenitent sinners,' nothing but heretics doubly damned for the guilt of the enormous sin of rebellion and of conserving an institution, secured to them by the Constitution of the Government and the Constitution of the Church under all dispen-

[147] Editorial, " The Two Assemblies," *Christian Herald and Presbyterian Recorder*, May 17, 1866.

[148] *Cf. ante*, pp. 228-230.

sations, in their conquered brethren of the South. . . . I can see no motive for their action than the fear that when brotherly love shall again prevail, they will fall back to the position they occupied before the war broke out."[149]   Certainly Dr. Thomas did not hesitate to make it clear to the Assembly that he enjoyed his new position far more than the one he had previously occupied.[150]

Although there is no direct evidence in the debates that the difficulties of political reconstruction influenced sentiment in the Assembly, there can be little doubt that the reports of the " black codes " of the Southern states, the frequent accusations of Southern " defiance," and the progress of the quarrel between President Johnson and Congress, all tended to make the commissioners more fervent in spirit, though at the same time rendering it more questionable whether they were actually serving the Lord.   It is surprising, however, that there was scarcely even mention of the existing political situation.   The speeches teemed with references to the war and its wickedness, but for the most part passed over current Republican difficulties and Southern confusion.   Exasperation seemed to be focussed particularly upon the Old School brethren in Kentucky.   It was not easy to forget some of the unpleasant things Stuart Robinson and his followers had been saying during the past five years [151] — things perhaps particularly unpleasant because in a measure justified.   Instead of directing their wrath against contemporary political offenses, therefore, the majority speakers concentrated their attack upon the sin of disloyalty, of which, among Old School members, Kentuckians seemed to be particularly guilty.   One speaker,[152] for instance, admitting that there were many great and good men in Kentucky, declared that it was also true that if there were mischievous men

---

[149] From a communication from " one of our oldest and best known, and most judicious ruling elders " which is quoted in an editorial, " The General Assembly is Over," *Missouri Presbyterian*, June 8, 1866.

[150] *Proceedings*, p. 21.

[151] *Cf. ante*, pp. 167-177.

[152] Mr. H. K. Clarke, of Michigan (Presbytery of Sandusky).

anywhere they were to be found in Kentucky.[153] Galled by years of Kentucky criticism and sarcasm, exasperated by the unwillingness of many Kentuckians utterly to despise their Southern brethren, Northern commissioners could scarcely be expected, perhaps, to let pass an opportunity for wreaking vengeance upon these Border State trouble-makers. After all, Old School Assembly commissioners were only human! It is not surprising if the desire for vengeance, along with the effects of popular clamor, New School demands, unrequited ambition, and political confusion carried them to extremes in their solution of the Declaration and Testimony problem.

The official minutes of the General Assembly of 1866 exceeded in length by fifty per cent those of any previous Old School Assembly. This excess was almost wholly due to the length and the number of papers dealing with the Louisville case and the Southern problem generally. Besides the extended report of the Special Committee,[154] there were papers of protest against the exclusion of the commissioners from the Louisville Presbytery; [155] against the refusal of the General Assembly to extend to the Southern Church the same expressions of fraternal affection and of desire for reunion as had been so freely extended to the New School branch; [156] and against the action finally taken by the Assembly on the Louisville case; together with a formal answer by the Assembly to the last-named protests.[157] There were also included various papers which had been offered as substitutes for the resolutions of the Special Committee, before the Gurley paper was finally adopted; [158] and also a series of resolutions which declared the Assembly's friendliness toward those in the South who had

[153] *Proceedings,* p. 85.

[154] *Cf. ante,* pp. 241-242.

[155] *Minutes of the General Assembly,* 1866, vol. xviii, pp. 91-93; 100-103; 104-105. The Assembly resolved that " the protest of Dr. Boardman and others is not respectful in language, and that it be returned to the author." (*Ibid.,* p. 104.) This protest, therefore, does not appear in the *Minutes.*

[156] *Ibid.,* pp. 51-53.

[157] *Ibid.,* pp. 91-93; 93-94.

[158] *Ibid.,* pp. 62-64.

" bowed before what they believed to be an irresistible necessity," and its absence of vindictiveness toward those who had
voluntarily aided the rebellion.[159]   The multitude of these various papers testified to the turbulence and confusion in the
Assembly over the Declaration and Testimony matter.   It was
no doubt with this confused state of affairs in mind that the
Assembly decided that a pastoral letter should be drawn up
and circulated among the churches.   The letter as drafted and
adopted undertook to give a review of the action taken on the
subjects of loyalty and freedom by the six Assemblies which
had met since the outbreak of the war.[160]   If the letter was
actually read aloud in the churches it added some 5500 words
to the services — already long enough in the Old School
Church of the 1860's.

So after fifteen days of wearisome debates, bitter quarreling,
censuring and counter-censuring, papers, protests, and answers,
the General Assembly of 1866 finally dragged to a close.   Certainly there had been much in the sessions to justify the statement that " while the soldiers were for peace, the ministers
were for war." [161]   The well-balanced *Presbyterian,* however,
was inclined to defend the belligerent body, admitting that
there had been some follies of speech, but asserting that, considering what the commissioners had had to listen to, they
had shown marked forbearance.   Remarking that it had been
bruited abroad that the Assembly had been " disorderly beyond
precedent," the veteran Old School weekly asked, " Who
started the disorder?" [162]   In spite of the challenging character
of this question, an honest and accurate answer might not have
been to the *Presbyterian's* liking.   Whoever was responsible
for the character of the proceedings, the fact remains that the
General Assembly, having in 1865 prescribed stringent rules

[159] *Ibid.,* p. 79.

[160] *Ibid.,* pp. 82-90.

[161] Dr. Boardman during one of his speeches quoted this remark as having
been made about the Assembly.   *Proceedings,* p. 92.

[162] *Cf.* two editorials on the General Assembly: " The General Assembly,"
Presbyterian, June 23, 1866; " The Late Assembly," *ibid.,* July 21, 1866.

for testing the loyalty of ministers and members — rules that provoked defiance — felt constrained in 1866 to prescribe drastic punishment for hostility to those rules and to summon before the bar of the next Assembly all offenders who had not in the meantime repented. The interest of the whole Church was therefore focussed upon these offenders. Would they repent before the meeting of the 1867 General Assembly?

Kentucky as the seat of the most intense hostility to the General Assembly absorbed the greatest amount of Presbyterian attention. When the Presbytery of Louisville met, shortly after the General Assembly had adjourned, the Declaration and Testimony wing was ready for decisive action. After approving, through the adoption of the report of Stuart Robinson, the action of their commissioners to the last Assembly, they disclaimed any connection with the General Assembly and called on the people of Kentucky to prevent the church property from falling into the hands of the opposing faction.[163] As more than three-fourths of the Presbytery belonged to the Declaration and Testimony wing,[164] the remnant loyal to the Assembly was virtually helpless.

When the Synod of Kentucky met at Henderson in October, the struggle was not so one-sided, as far as numbers were concerned. As a matter of fact, the battle of words was very brief. The task of organizing the body was rendered impossible by the fact that the retiring Moderator (whose responsibility it was to call the body to order) belonged to the Declaration and Testimony party, while the Stated Clerk was a "loyal" man. When the Moderator directed the Stated Clerk to call the roll,

[163] The Cincinnati *Gazette*, quoted in the *Christian Herald and Presbyterian Recorder*, June 28, 1866.

[164] But seven of the more than thirty ministers of the Presbytery adhered to the "loyal" Synod of Kentucky when it was organized in November. *Minutes of the Synod of Kentucky*, 1866 (No place; no date; published by James Davidson and Co.). These *Minutes* must be carefully distinguished from those of the same name, published by Harney, Hughes, & Co. The former are the minutes of the "loyal" Synod; the latter, those of the Synod who represented the Declaration and Testimony party and their followers.

the latter responded by calling the names of all except the Declaration and Testimony men. After futile efforts to get the Stated Clerk to include all of the names, the Moderator announced that he himself would call the roll according to the official records furnished the last Assembly, and would leave the question of membership to the body itself when organized. When Dr. R. J. Breckinridge and another member rose to protest, they were " cried down by the loud clamor in the house, and were not allowed to take an appeal to the Synod from the ruling of the Moderator." [165] The Moderator proceeding with the roll, Dr. Breckinridge called on those agreeing with him and adhering to the General Assembly not to answer. Meanwhile the Declaration and Testimony element completed their organization by the election of a Moderator and Clerk, and then adjourned. Thereupon the Stated Clerk of the original meeting resumed the calling of the roll at the point where he had been interrupted by the retiring Moderator, carefully omitting, as he had set out to do, the names of all signers of the " Declaration and Testimony " and of those who had sat in the dissolved Presbyteries (that is, the presbyteries which according to the Gurley Resolutions of the 1866 Assembly had been dissolved automatically through their having admitted to seats subsequent to the meeting of the Assembly, signers of the offending document).[166] After some difficulty in finding a place to meet for its next session, this rump Synod held one more meeting and then adjourned to meet the following month in Lexington.[167]

Thus at last the event so long feared had taken place: the Old School Church in Kentucky had been divided. Henceforth there were to be two Synods of Kentucky instead of one.

[165] Minutes of the Synod of Kentucky [General Assembly adherents], 1866, p. 18.

[166] Cf. ante, pp. 251-252.

[167] Minutes of the Synod of Kentucky [General Assembly adherents], 1866, p. 7. The minutes of the two Synods are in remarkable agreement with regard to the story of the proceedings which led to the break in the original Synod.

The distinction in size between the two organizations was significant: the new organization (composed of Declaration and Testimony sympathizers) numbered 100 ministers and ruling elders; the remnant remaining loyal to the General Assembly had but 60, of whom 32 were ministers and 28 ruling elders.[168] Even more significant is the distribution among the 32 ministers of the loyal Synod: 7 were pastors, 15 without charge, 9 stated supplies, and one an evangelist.[169] Thus but little over a fourth of the ministers adhering to the General Assembly were in regular charge of congregations. This fact is brought out sharply by the contrast in the number of communicants represented by the two Synods. Of the 11,250 communicant members of the undivided Synod, but 1800 were represented by the ministers remaining loyal to the General Assembly.[170] Undoubtedly there were many more whose sentiments were with that body, but they were not represented in the loyal Synod.

Even by the spring of 1867, after earnest efforts had been made to rehabilitate the Old School Church in Kentucky, there were but 18 regular pastors in the entire loyal Synod.[171] Among the ministers "without charge" were theological professors and members of the faculty of Centre College — men

---

[168] *Cf.* table of statistics, *Minutes of the Synod of Kentucky* [Independent], 1866. The *Minutes of the Synod of Kentucky* [General Assembly adherents], 1866, pp. 7-8, state that 31 ministers and 29 ruling elders convened for the meeting in Lexington.

[169] *Minutes of the Synod of Kentucky* [Independent], 1866, p. 21. The figures given leave one member of the 32 unaccounted for.

[170] *Ibid.* The *Minutes of the General Assembly*, 1867, vol. xviii, pp. 487-491, record the communicant membership of the Synod as 7400; but this figure is obviously reached by counting in all of the congregations to which the Synod had the least possible claim. For example, the statistics include the membership of some 52 churches listed as "vacant" (that is, without a regular pastor or a stated supply in charge). Probably a large portion of this membership favored the other Synod. It is significant that by 1869 the Synod had reduced its membership claims to 5400 (*Minutes of the General Assembly*, 1869, vol. xviii, pp. 1036-1040). Probably even this figure was considerably exaggerated. There were in 1869 only 13 regular pastors in the entire Synod.

[171] *Ibid.*, pp. 487-491.

whose prestige was great, but who did not directly represent the people in church courts.   On the other hand, the 70 ministers [172] who left to join the new Synod were mostly men who were in charge of congregations, and hence close to the people. The split in Kentucky had not been an even one: the sympathizers with the Declaration and Testimony group had — as far as membership went — come away with the greater part of the spoils, and left the remnant of the old Synod shattered and weak.   For years Robert J. Breckinridge had been fighting to keep the Synod of Kentucky loyal — here was his result.   One cannot help wondering what the outcome would have been had he not entered the struggle.   But after all, that is equivalent to conjecturing on the supposition that he was not in existence in the 1860's; one cannot imagine Dr. Breckinridge *observing* a battle.   Nor can one imagine him, when the smoke had cleared away and the tragic condition of the Church in Kentucky was fully revealed, ever entertaining the slightest doubt with regard to the wisdom of the course he had pursued.

The two Synods now set out upon their individual ways. Neither one found progress easy.   They were handicapped by mutual hostility and jealousy, by quarrels over church property, by financial and membership weakness.   Nor did either find complete unanimity within its own midst.   In the new and larger Synod the one common bond was opposition to the policy of the General Assembly on the subjects of loyalty and slavery, and more particularly to its rulings with regard to the Declaration and Testimony men.   This Synod at its first meeting had no difficulty in agreeing upon the adoption of the report of its committee on the minutes of the 1866 General Assembly — a report which condemned the McLean and Gurley papers, the appointment of a committee to arrange for reunion with the New School, and the spirit and affirmations of the pastoral letter.   Indeed about the only action of the General Assembly which the Synod could find to approve was

[172] *Minutes of the Synod of Kentucky* [Independent] 1866, p. 21.

the appointment of a week of prayer, and a day of prayer for the youth, schools, and colleges.[173]

When it came to its own policy of action, however, the Synod was not so unanimous. It rejected Stuart Robinson's proposal for the appointment of a committee to " confer with conservative men " at the next General Assembly and urge upon them the union of all who did not approve of reunion with the New School, also his suggestion that a committee be sent to the next General Assembly of the Southern Presbyterian Church to convey to that body the sympathy and good wishes of the Synod of Kentucky. In place of these proposals the Synod adopted a report which stated at some length the course which the new Synod of Kentucky proposed to follow:

1. It is not the purpose of this Synod to make any change of its formal ecclesiastical relations, but to continue to stand in its present position of open protest and resistance to the enforcement of the acts of the General Assemblies of 1861-1866, concerning " Doctrine, Loyalty, and Freedom " as unconstitutional, and, therefore, null and void.

2. This Synod stands in position for work of mediation between the Church of the North and of the South. [It] . . . stands in full sympathy with a large body of Conservative Ministers and people in the Northern Assembly, and with the Synod of Missouri, who like ourselves, have protested against the same unconstitutional acts. On the other hand this Synod has held that the Southern churches, being driven into a separation from us . . . are, therefore, not schismatical. . . . [This Synod has therefore the special duty of promoting reunion.]

3. The Synod hereby invites all Presbyterian Ministers, and people who concur with us in protesting against the present course of the Board of Domestic Missions in Philadelphia, to co-operate in the missionary work through the Synod's committee. . . .

5. This Synod also hereby expresses, on the one hand, its sympathy and its readiness to co-operate with such conservative brethren in the Northern Assembly as desire to return to the old paths; and on the other hand, its sympathy with, and readiness to assist to the utmost of its ability, the brethren of the Southern churches; and at the same time, expresses the hope that they will evince a readiness to co-operate with all Conservative men, North and South, in a common effort to restore the General Assembly as it was before the war, on the basis of those ancient conservative principles of Presbyterianism, for which this Synod is contending.[174]

---

[173] *Minutes of the Synod of Kentucky* [Independent], 1866, pp. 17-18.

[174] *Minutes of the Synod of Kentucky* [Independent], 1866, pp. 19-20.

Whether or not it would be possible for the Synod to maintain this middle-ground position depended of course upon the General Assembly of 1867. The Synod had acted in direct violation of the Gurley Resolutions in including signers of the "Declaration and Testimony" on its rolls. Its presbyteries having seated such men were, from the point of view of the Assembly, non-existent. Under the terms of the Gurley paper the signers of the defiant document and the members of the former Presbytery of Louisville who had voted for it must appear before the 1867 Assembly. With this body, then, rested the fate of the new Synod, as far as future relationship with the Old School Church was concerned. Few people could have doubted what the decision of the General Assembly would be.

Only two signers of the "Declaration and Testimony" responded to the summons to appear before the General Assembly and answer for what they had done,[175] but the division of the Synods of Kentucky and Missouri [176] had resulted in two sets of commissioners claiming seats from several of the presbyteries there, and the Assembly must settle the claims. The handling of the case was in tone in marked contrast with the proceedings of the previous year. The elaborate report which the Assembly adopted with almost entire unanimity,[177] though firm, was moderate and considerate. The report first carefully defined which synods and presbyteries were the true and lawful judicatories under the authority of the General Assembly, but explicitly asserted the complete jurisdiction of that body over the "unlawful" ecclesiastical organizations. Signers of the "Declaration and Testimony" might be readmitted to the lawful organizations upon their subscription to a prepared formula in which they were to disclaim that in the

---

[175] *Minutes of the General Assembly,* 1867, vol. xviii, p. 340. The two men were Rev. J. A. Quarles of Missouri, and Rev. William C. Handy of Maryland.

[176] For the division of the Synod of Missouri, cf. *post,* pp. 271-274.

[177] The vote was: *ayes,* 261; *nays,* 4; *excused,* 1. But one of the *nays* came from the non-Border States. The man excused from voting was from Kentucky. *Minutes of the General Assembly,* 1867, vol. xviii, p. 335.

signing of that fateful document they had had "any intention
to rebel against or renounce the authority of the General Assembly." (Evidently even abject repentance would not entitle
a man to forgiveness for *intentional* rebellion.) The report
stressed the point that the proposed action would sever no one
from the Church, but would leave the responsibility of final
separation upon the individual.

A more significant contrast between the reports of 1866 and
1867 lay in the fact that while the former cited offenders to appear before the General Assembly, the latter remitted the cases
to the lower church courts for final disposition. This change
in policy was made possible, the 1867 report maintained,
only by the fact that in the latter year the lower church courts
were uniformly faithful to the General Assembly, while in
1866 "such was notoriously the condition of the lower courts,
almost universally, in the Synods of Kentucky and Missouri,
as subsequent events have but too well shown, that it would
have been nothing less than vain trifling with sacred interests,
which were greatly imperilled, for that General Assembly to
have remanded the cases of these brethren to those courts." [178]

However moderate the tone of the Assembly's report, there
was an unmistakable air of finality about it. It virtually ended
the possibility of the new Synod of Kentucky finding its way
into an amicable relationship with the Old School Assembly,
for few of its members would be likely even to consider the
terms prescribed. Moreover, the steady progress of the movement for reunion of the Old School Church with the New
School branch,[179] as well as the constant quarreling going on
between the two synods in Kentucky during the years immediately following the division of 1866[180] made the new Synod
less anxious to return to the old fold. The progress which
had been made by 1868, on the other hand, toward a union
with the Southern Church is evident from the tone of the resolutions passed unanimously by the Synod in that year:

[178] *Ibid.*, p. 339. The whole report may be found *ibid.*, pp. 335-340.
[179] *Cf. post*, pp. 504-517.
[180] *Cf. post*, pp. 268-270.

Whereas, The General Assembly of the Presbyterian Church in the United States [181] received our commissioners with great kindness. . . .

And Whereas, This Synod are perfectly agreed that an organic union with said Assembly is most desirable, and will ultimately be consummated.

And Whereas, A highly respectable portion of this Synod believe that such an organic union at this time would be greatly injurious to a number of our churches, and perhaps jeopardize our other interests in the State,[182] Therefore

Resolved, That as the final action of this Synod, the whole subject be referred to the Presbyteries for such action as may be deemed most advisable, to send delegates to the next Assembly [that is, of the Southern Church] or not.[183]

It would appear that the Synod in this action was unnecessarily cautious, for it soon became evident that sentiment was overwhelmingly for union with the Southern Church, and in the following year (1869) the union was effected.[184]   Thus the same year that witnessed the reunion of Old and New Schools,[185] saw the majority of Old School Presbyterians in Kentucky casting in their lot with the Southern Church.   No doubt the *Presbyterian* was reminded of a statement it had made editorially in the summer of 1866.   Commenting on the existing troubles among Old School Presbyterians in the Border States, it had then remarked that it would have been easier to heal the difficulties after the war if the line of division earlier had been sharper, for some, it averred, had stayed " where their sympathies were not! " [186]   If that diagnosis was correct, the chief source of irritation had been removed in 1869, and healing might be expected to follow.

Meanwhile the loyal Synod of Kentucky had been having

[181] The name adopted by the Southern Church after the close of the war. The absence of the words " of America " alone distinguishes it from the one name by which the Old School and the New School bodies were both then known, and from the name of the Northern Church today.

[182] Probably a reference to Centre College, in which both Synods at that time were interested.

[183] *Minutes of the Synod of Kentucky* [Independent] 1868, pp. 8-9.

[184] Johnson, Thomas C., *History of the Southern Presbyterian Church* (American Church History Series, a part of vol. xi) pp. 358-359.

[185] *Cf. post,* pp. 515-517.

[186] Editorial, " The Condition," *Presbyterian,* August 4, 1866.

its troubles. That it was not, in spite of its faithfulness to the General Assembly, entirely satisfied with existing conditions in the Old School Church may be seen from the sentiments of the Synod's report on the minutes of the 1866 Assembly, particularly with reference to the latter body's action on reunion with the New School Church.[187] This movement it considered "hasty, untimely, not regardful enough of sound doctrine and scriptural order. . . . Should this measure be precipitated, instead of subserving the cause of Christian union, it would most assuredly promote dissension.[188] (Was the latter statement meant to sound like a threat?) On the other hand the Synod regarded the Assembly's condemnation of the " Declaration and Testimony" with entire approval: "These severe terms of censure meet the hearty approval of this body; they are discriminating and just." [189] As far as conditions within its own bounds were concerned, the Synod found cause for little but discouragement; the presbyteries had "little to report which does not call for sorrow and lamentation." [190]

In fact divisions and partisan strife dominated the history of Presbyterianism in Kentucky for several years after the break of 1866.[191] In 1867 the Presbytery of Louisville reported to the Synod that "never since Presbyterianism was planted in their region, have our people met so severe a crisis." [192] So serious were conditions that the Synod felt called upon to "beseech God to visit his [sic] languishing

---

[187] *Cf. post*, pp. 504-505.

[188] *Minutes of the Synod of Kentucky* [General Assembly adherents], 1866, pp. 16-17.

[189] *Ibid.*, pp. 17-18.

[190] *Minutes of the Synod of Kentucky* [General Assembly adherents], 1866, p. 20. Each presbytery reported annually to the Synod, and the gist of their reports was included in the " Narrative of the State of Religion " prepared each year by a committee appointed for that purpose. The Narrative for 1866 is printed *ibid.*, pp. 20-26.

[191] Coulter, *op. cit.*, pp. 395-399, gives a vivid picture of these conditions.

[192] *Minutes of the Synod of Kentucky* [General Assembly adherents], 1867, p. 38.

Zion with gracious outpourings of his spirit. . . ."[193] At about
the same time the Lexington correspondent of the Cincinnati
Commercial painted a gloomy picture of Presbyterian difficulties in his part of the state: the religious war between Robert
J. Breckinridge and Stuart Robinson was still going on,
churches were being split up, the ownership of church property was provoking particularly bitter strife. Sometimes both
parties amicably used the church property until the courts
could decide to whom it belonged, but in other instances the
church would be locked up by one party and broken open
by the other.[194] By 1869 the reports of the presbyteries indicated that "comparative rest" had come to their churches,
though a few "continued to be harassed by litigations, growing
out of the schism in our midst. . . ."[195] On the whole, however, unseemly strife and heated discussions were passing
away, and ministers and people were "enabled more and more
to devote their time and energies to the direct work of building
up the Kingdom of Christ. . . ."[196] Certainly during the past
few years the degree of directness in this work had not been
all that might have been desired! By 1871 the bad feeling
between the two Synods of Kentucky had been sufficiently
allayed to permit special committees of the two bodies to
meet in conference to consider coöperation in the control of
Centre College. The loyal Synod's committee, however, was
"surprised and pained" at the reticence of the other committee, and at the insistence they placed on all communications
being in writing.[197] Nothing came of the plan. Open hostility
and bitter strife had given way, not to friendly coöperation,
but rather to sullen and suspicious tolerance. Kentucky was
henceforth to be the seat of a divided Presbyterianism, with

[193] *Ibid.*
[194] Editorial, "The Separation in Kentucky," *Christian Herald and Presbyterian Recorder* (quoting the Cincinnati *Commercial*), August 8, 1867.
[195] *Minutes of the Synod of Kentucky* [General Assembly adherents],
1869, pp. 20-21.
[196] *Ibid.*
[197] *Minutes of the Synod of Kentucky* [Northern], 1871, pp. 6-8.

the Southern Synod steadily outstripping its Northern rival in numerical strength.[198]

Meanwhile the progress of events in the history of Old School Presbyterianism in Missouri following the close of the war was not unlike that in Kentucky. Like the Presbytery of Louisville, the Synod of Missouri came into direct conflict with the General Assembly of 1866. It too, the Assembly claimed, had defied the action of the General Assembly of 1865. The difficulties were directly traceable to the meeting of the Synod in 1864. The minutes of that body carefully recorded the expunging of previous "disloyal" testimony of the Synod,[199] but omitted any reference to the part that military intervention and the administration of an oath might have had in cutting down the attendance to less than one-tenth that of a full Synod.[200] These minutes were approved by the General Assembly of 1865, in spite of vigorous protest.[201] But the Synod at its meeting in October, 1865, pronounced the 1864 meeting of its own body "not a free Court of Christ, and its entire acts null and void and of no binding force." [202] This the Assembly of 1866 chose to regard as "an act of insubordination to the authority of the Church, which said Synod is required to reconsider and reverse," and the Synod was ordered to report to the next Assembly "what they have done or failed to do in the premises." [203] The defiant Synod of 1865 had

---

[198] The communicant membership of the undivided Synod of Kentucky in 1866 was 11,250. After the division it was a number of years before it became entirely clear just how this membership had divided. The decrease in the claims of the "loyal" Synod is significant: 1867, 7441; 1868, 6811; 1869, 5436; 1871 (after reunion with the New School), 5721; 1872, 6048; 1873, 5120. By 1873 most of the "deadwood" had been eliminated from the statistics, but even in this year "estimates" amounting to more than 250 were included in the total given. For these figures, *cf.* tables of statistics, *Minutes of General Assembly.*

[199] *Cf. ante,* pp. 99-101; 116.

[200] *Cf. ante,* p. 215.

[201] *Minutes of the General Assembly,* 1865, vol. xvii, pp. 545; 542-543; 561; 576-580.

[202] *Proceedings of the General Assemblies . . . 1866,* p. 103.

[203] *Ibid.,* p. 105.

gone beyond a nullification of the expunging act of its 1864 predecessor; it had taken pains to reaffirm its testimony of November, 1861, in which the Spring Resolutions had been declared "unscriptural, unconstitutional, unwise and unjust." [204] This deliberate reaffirmation the 1866 Assembly could scarcely be expected to overlook. It declared that "the repeated exhibition of such a rebellious spirit, on the part of any inferior court towards the supreme judicatory of the Church, should not pass without censure." [205]

Thus the Synod of Missouri was rebuked, yet the mildness of the reproof was in striking contrast to the action taken toward the Louisville Presbytery. The resolutions with regard to Missouri came very late in the session; [206] perhaps the Assembly was too weary to persist in the vindictiveness it had earlier displayed. Perhaps there was a hesitancy to offend unduly a community that for more than two weeks had been extending a generous hospitality to the visiting commissioners.[207] There may have been the feeling that as the defiant Presbyterians in Missouri would be reached through the operation of the Gurley Resolutions, there was no necessity for doubly penalizing them by proscribing them for the insubordination of their 1865 Synod. Probably the contrast between the treatment of the Louisville and Missouri problems was principally due to the personnel of the offending parties: Stuart Robinson and his Kentucky friends were regarded as the instigators of all the insubordination within the Church. The members of the Assembly were told by one eloquent Missourian [208] that the Synod of Missouri had adopted by a vote of three to one a paper which condemned the action of 1865

---

[204] *Cf. ante,* pp. 99-101.

[205] *Minutes of the General Assembly,* 1866, vol. xviii, p. 97.

[206] On the last (the fifteenth) day of the session.

[207] St. Louis was of course within the territory of the Synod of Missouri. The *Proceedings* were filled with references to the hospitality with which the commissioners were being entertained.

[208] Dr. James H. Brookes of St. Louis.

in terms as emphatic and explicit as those found in the " Declaration and Testimony "; [209] nevertheless they chose to overlook all defiance in this body except such as the submission of reports for approval forced them to consider. The Presbytery of Louisville had been picked out for punishment by the 1866 Assembly.

In August, 1866, a conference of ministers and laymen composed of Presbyterians dissatisfied with the action of the General Assembly on the questions which had been agitating the country met in St. Louis. Of the 65 members of this conference, all except four were from the Border States; 21 ministers and 27 ruling elders were from Missouri. It was resolved not to form a new church organization, but to prepare a popular warning against the errors of the General Assembly for five years back, and to appeal for coöperation in the correction of these errors. It appears that when a second conference (called to meet in November) failed to materialize, the leaders of this movement found their way into the Southern Presbyterian Church.[210] In the meantime the Synod of Missouri, like its Kentucky neighbor, had been divided as a result of the Gurley Orders. Here too the majority had been against the Assembly's action, and when it was resolved — contrary to the orders of the higher court — to enroll signers of the " Declaration and Testimony," 27 ministers and ruling elders withdrew and organized a synod in accordance with the decision of the General Assembly.[211] Both Synods sent commissioners to the 1867 General Assembly, but only those of the smaller body were given seats.[212] The larger Synod maintained an independent existence until 1874, when it became a part of the Southern Presbyterian Church.[213] As in Kentucky,

---

[209] *Proceedings*, p. 112.
[210] For an account of this movement, *cf. American Annual Cyclopaedia*, 1866, p. 623.
[211] *Ibid.*, 1866, p. 622.
[212] *Cf. ante*, pp. 266-267.
[213] Johnson, *op. cit.*, pp. 358-359; 452-455.

so in Missouri, the Southern Church obtained the larger share of the Old School following.[214]

The Old School's eastern Border State Synod — that of Baltimore — had expressed regret in 1865 that the General Assembly of that year had failed to realize that its special mission was "to heal breaches, rather than to widen and perpetuate them."[215] Nevertheless relatively few of its members signed the "Declaration and Testimony," and little anxiety was felt over its loyalty. The war had cost it the loss of one presbytery[216] which lay in Virginia, but the rest of this strong Synod seemed likely to adhere to the General Assembly. Its session of October, 1866, proved it to be as docile as any supporter of the Assembly could wish: it promptly ordered one of its presbyteries to refer to the next Assembly for adjudication the case of a member who had signed the "Declaration and Testimony" since the dissolution of the last Assembly, and directed that the accused man should not be allowed to sit as a member of any church court higher than the session.[217] The Synod's loyalty cost it the loss of a small minority of dissenters: the following month at a meeting at which four ministers and three ruling elders were present a new presbytery was organized in protest against the action of the General Assembly.[218] This presbytery soon found its way into the fold of the Southern Presbyterian Church.[219] Loyalty prevailed throughout the remainder of the Synod of Baltimore and this

[214] According to Johnson, *op. cit.* (p. 455, note 1), the Synod which joined the Southern Church brought 67 ministers, 141 churches, and 8000 communicants. In 1869 (before reunion with the New School), the loyal Synod had 71 ministers, 107 churches, and 4681 communicants. (*Cf.* table of statistics, *Minutes of the General Assembly,* 1869, vol. xviii, p. 1110).

[215] *Cf. ante,* p. 211.

[216] The Presbytery of Winchester. A few churches of the Presbytery of Potomac were also lost — that is, some of those lying in Virginia.

[217] *Minutes of the Synod of Baltimore,* 1866, pp. 8-10.

[218] The Presbytery of Patapsco. Johnson, *op. cit.,* pp. 438-439.

[219] According to Johnson, *op. cit.* (pp. 438-439, and p. 439, note 1), the Presbytery brought to the Southern Church "6 ministers, 3 churches, 576 communicants, much wealth and intelligence."

body retained its rank as one of the strongest and wealthiest of the synods of the Old School Church.

Outside of the Border States the action of the 1866 General Assembly with regard to defiance within the Church awakened remarkably little response from the synods and presbyteries. In contrast to the general endorsement or repudiation of the Spring Resolutions of 1861,[220] for instance, there was almost universal silence in Northern local bodies in 1866. Three western synods expressed their hearty endorsement; [221] a half-dozen scattered presbyteries gave their approval; [222] all except two others of the lower courts of the Church in the North evidently felt that no action was necessary or desirable. That there were, here and there throughout the North, individuals who disapproved of the relation of the Assembly to political matters during the war years there can be no doubt; but the Gurley Orders had been directed solely against signers of the "Declaration and Testimony," and of such the North was almost wholly free.

In the October (1866) meeting of the Synod of New York, however, a signer of the condemned document claimed a seat, and thereby raised the issue of whether the Synod would sustain the Assembly's orders. The claimant was promptly rejected by a vote of 111 to 7.[223] Thereupon the session of the church to which the rejected commissioner belonged (the First Presbyterian Church of Brooklyn, New York) unanimously declared that the various acts of the Assembly on the political

---

[220] Cf. ante, pp. 88-107.

[221] The Synods of Southern Iowa, Indiana, and Sandusky. *Presbyterian,* October 27 and November 10, 1866.

[222] The presbyteries of Luzerne (New Jersey), New Albany (Indiana), and Kaskaskia (Illinois) approved of the action of the Assembly. (*Cf. Presbyterian,* October 6 and October 27, 1866.) The Second Presbytery of Philadelphia and the Presbyteries of Huntingdon and Northumberland (Synod of Philadelphia) approved of affirmative votes on the part of their commissioners. (*Cf. Presbyterian,* October 20 and 27, 1866.) The Presbytery of Nassau (Long Island) expressed its approval of Assembly action, but with three members voting *no.* (*Cf. Presbyterian,* October 20, 1866.)

[223] *American Annual Cyclopaedia,* 1866, p. 621.

situation were null and void and of no binding force upon their church; that the session would continue as heretofore to receive members ,from Southern states upon the same conditions as other candidates, and would ask no questions whatever " in regard to their political opinions and conduct "; and that the session would appoint no other representative to the synod and presbytery until the right of the rejected commissioner to his seat was recognized or until his standing as a member of the session had been impeached by regular process of law.[224] The prominence of the Moderator of this session,[225] Dr. Henry J. VanDyke,[226] accentuated its defiance of presbytery, synod, and Assembly. It was evident that an active, if small, minority in the Synod of New York was prepared to stand out against the orders of the highest court of the Church.

The other eastern synod taking notice of the Gurley orders was the Synod of Philadelphia. In this body 29 out of 111 members voted against endorsing the action of the 1866 Assembly as the product of " an honest and enlightened zeal for the purity of our beloved Church " and as a step that would " ultimately appear healthful and happy in its results "; fifteen members signed a formal protest against the Synod's endorsement.[227] Evidently the conservative East was not as willing as the more radical West to acquiesce in the vindictive measures of the 1866 General Assembly. Yet the total Northern opposition to the Gurley Orders was slight; the General Assembly had evidently interpreted correctly the sentiment of the Old School Church when by an overwhelming majority it had determined upon a program of drastic punishment for " Declaration and Testimony " men.

The two years which followed the close of the war were

[224] " Resolutions of the First Presbyterian Church, Brooklyn, New York," *Presbyterian,* October 27, 1866.
[225] The pastor of the church is normally the moderator of the church session.
[226] *Cf. ante,* p. 227.
[227] *Cf.* record of fall meeting of the Synod of Philadelphia, as given in the *Presbyterian,* November 24, 1866.

indeed eventful ones in the history of the Old School Church. Stirred up by the confusion of political reconstruction, fired by a desire for reunion with the New School Church, eager to wreak vengeance upon the Border State disturbers, keen to test out their newly gained power, the radical element in control of the 1866 General Assembly had triumphantly carried through the adoption of a program which would bring about the repentance of the offending brethren or purge them out of the Church. Technically, there was that alternative; practically, few intelligent men could have expected the accused parties to regard the Assembly Orders as offering any alternative. Asked to choose between abiding by their principles and continuing in opposition to the Assembly's action, the great majority of them scarcely hesitated. By 1867 independent synods had been formed in Kentucky and Missouri, and an independent presbytery in Maryland — bodies which before long found their way into the Southern Presbyterian Church. Although by 1869 the Old School Church had regained sufficient foothold in the South to count some 1700 communicant members in five states of the former Confederacy,[228] this gain was but slight compensation for the thousands of members lost in the Border States, for the shattering of two synods — one of them in leadership, wealth, and tradition among the most powerful in the Church, and the other of great potential strength — and for the engendering of such bitterness of feeling[229] as

---

[228] The tables of statistics in the *Minutes of the General Assembly,* 1869, vol. xviii, pp. 995-1104, show 800 communicant members in Georgia, 71 in North Carolina, 142 in Texas, 468 in Tennessee, and 184 in Louisiana.

[229] The commonest source of bitterness was contention over the ownership of church property (*cf. ante,* p. 270). In scores of instances individual congregations in the Border States were divided over the question of which Synod should receive their allegiance. After a split occurred, there was usually argument as to the disposition of the property of the congregation. The most famous of the lawsuits arising from such arguments was the case of the Walnut Street Church in Louisville, Kentucky. In this case the courts of the state of Kentucky decided against the adherents of the Old School Assembly. As some of these adherents were citizens of another state, the case could be taken into the United States courts. Finally the Supreme Court of the United States decided in favor of the adherents of

two generations have not been able completely to eradicate. In 1867 by relaxing sufficiently to permit the cases of signers of the " Declaration and Testimony " to be tried in the lower courts of the Church instead of requiring that they be referred to the highest judicatory, the General Assembly had localized the punishment of the signers, though still requiring that they be punished.[230]   In 1868 it virtually closed the whole " Declaration and Testimony " matter [231] by resolving that, although it was not prepared to modify or repeal the action of the previous year, the whole business should be referred to the various synods concerned, " with liberty to take such action consistent with the honour and authority of the General Assembly, as may in their judgment secure peace and order to the Church." [232]

From the point of view of the majority in the Assembly, this relaxation had been made possible by the purging of the synods of most of their troublemaking members. Now that the synods were safely loyal they might be trusted to handle cases of local insubordination. That condition had been reached, however, by tactics and measures of the Assembly of 1866 which scarcely redounded to the glory of the Church or to the dignity of the General Assembly.   There is little occasion for disagree-

the General Assembly on the ground that " the courts of law must accept as final and conclusive the decisions of the General Assembly on subjects purely ecclesiastical, and must give full effect to these decisions in settling the property rights of litigants." This came to be recognized as a leading case. Southern Presbyterians — that is, adherents of the Presbyterian Church of the United States — resented the enthusiasm with which their Northern brethren acclaimed what to themselves appeared to be " the false and ridiculous principles adopted by the Supreme Court . . . — that of making the judgment of an accidental majority of the highest church court of final authority in interpreting the constitution of the church. . . ." For an account of this case, cf. Johnson, op. cit., pp. 465-466; 468; Thompson, op. cit., pp. 169-170.

[230] Cf. ante, pp. 266-267.

[231] Except for the rejection of some overtures from members of independent presbyteries, asking for the repeal by the Assembly of some of its previous acts on matters dealing with the political situation. These overtures were presented to the General Assembly in 1869. *Minutes of the General Assembly*, 1869, vol. xviii, pp. 924-925; 943.

[232] *Ibid.*, 1868, vol. xviii, p. 643.

ing with the opinion of a Presbyterian writing some thirty years later that "the acts of the Assemblies of 1865-67 are not those upon which Presbyterians generally look back with gratification." [233]   Perhaps the break with the Border States was unavoidable; perhaps Kentuckians, at least, were so constituted that in church as well as in state matters they should wait until after the war to secede; [234] be that as it may, if the break had to occur, it was unfortunate that it was accompanied by so much of the spirit of revenge and vindictiveness.

[233] Thompson, *op. cit.*, p. 170.
[234] Coulter, *op. cit.*, p. 396.

CHAPTER VIII

THE VOICE OF THE OLD SCHOOL PULPIT

THE Old School General Assemblies which met during the war period left no doubt regarding the marked degree to which loyalty to the Federal Government prevailed among the ministers of the denomination. This evidence was more than confirmed by the Old School press. Although it was not disputed that there was a minority of doubtful loyalty, neither was it denied that this minority was proportionally very small. Yet in spite of the prevalence of patriotic sentiment in the denomination, loyal sermons, if one may judge from the small number which survive, were comparatively few in number. From the point of view of the professional patriot it is fortunate that our estimate of Old School sympathy for the Union does not depend entirely upon the record of quantity of pulpit utterances upon political subjects during the war years. If such were the case, Old School Presbyterians would not fare well in comparison with their New School brethren; certainly they would be regarded as far outdistanced by their Congregationalist and Unitarian contemporaries.

Obviously, in the light of Assembly action and the position of the Old School press the limited output of political utterances on the part of the clergy cannot be ascribed to any deficiency in patriotism. It was rather due to the Old School conception of the proper functions of the pulpit. To be sure, within the Church there were widely varying points of view on what these functions were. At one extreme was Stuart Robinson, who believed so strongly in the non-secular character of the Church that he refused to express political views in a church journal as well as in the pulpit; at the other was Thomas E. Thomas, to whom the war was a " crusade." [1] The

---

[1] *Cf. ante*, p. 230.

majority of the Old School clergy, much as most of them despised Dr. Robinson's extreme philosophy, were actually nearer his position than that of Dr. Thomas.[2] Only when the political situation clearly involved a critical moral issue was it justifiable (according to their opinion) to bring the discussion of government problems into the pulpit.

In fact, Old School Presbyterians prided themselves that their Church had successfully resisted a tendency toward the secularization of the pulpit which had penetrated far into certain rival denominations. At the end of 1860 when the threatened dissolution of the Union was uppermost in men's minds, the *Presbyterian of Our Union* quoted with approval the sentiments of a St. Louis daily: " Political sermons are a great deal too common both at the North and the South, now-a-days. For a long time, the clergy of the New England States enjoyed a monopoly of the business and spit anti-slavery fire with what was thought at the time, inimitable unction." The approving journal rejoiced that, although the custom might be extending to the Southern portions of the country, there had not as yet been manifested " any such degree of outrage and fanaticism as has for so long characterized the ebullition of Beecher and several others of that genus at the North and East." [3] In the summer of 1862 the *Presbyterian,* itself a vigorous advocate of the Union cause, undertook to correct what it considered to be a prevalent impression that many of the pulpits in the Northern States were filled by men who had " turned aside from the preaching of the gospel, to preach about the exciting questions of the day." This leading Old School weekly assured its readers that — at least as far as Presbyterians were concerned — the impression was far from the truth. In proof of

[2] Even Dr. Thomas — perhaps " by voice and pen " the most active of all Old School preachers in advocating the cause of the Union — has left little evidence of pro-Union *sermons,* either in the collections or in the records of war-time sermons. Evidently even he confined his political efforts to non-pulpit activities.

[3] Editorial, *Presbyterian of Our Union,* December 27, 1860. The name of the " St. Louis daily " quoted is not given.

its assertion the *Presbyterian* quoted an extract from a letter of a Congregationalist correspondent writing from New York to the *Vermont Chronicle*:

> What I saw of the Congregationalist preachers of the city, leads me to class them as *reformers*, rather than evangelists. They talk and act as though they expected to save men by *reformation*, instead of *regeneration* — as though they believed in the perfectibility of human nature, instead of the need of a renewed nature, as the only sure basis of the true progress of society.
>
> The preachers in the Presbyterian churches whom I happened to hear, seemed to me to be possessed of a very different spirit, and to labour for very different ends. Their themes were, without exception, decidedly evangelical. . . . If the truth and justice of these views be admitted, . . . we see one reason why the influence of the pulpit in New England is waning. . . .[4]

Strongly as the *Presbyterian* commended these views, another editorial in the same issue asserted that there was a clearly defined limit to the muteness which the pulpit should ordinarily maintain on political matters:

> We should keep the sacred desk free from the discussion of ordinary politics, under conviction that, when it thus descends, it loses its commanding influence, and imperils its usefulness; and yet we have never wavered in the belief that there are national crises in which it is required to speak, and when its influence for good may be potent. If apostles thought it befitting in them to inculcate great general principles of politics, we cannot see the impropriety of ministers, under the present circumstances of our nation, in upholding the government which God has bestowed on us, and denouncing the wickedness of an attempt to subvert it.
>
> A great principle of religious morals is involved in such a crisis, which no minister can be justified in disregarding. We do not mean that the pulpit should be always resounding with this theme, but it should have its proportionate place, as any other doctrine should. . . . It may be well enough to assert that politics should be kept out of the pulpit, but it is carrying the principle too far, to shut out the revealed doctrine of government, as an ordinance of God, and the iniquity of causeless rebellion. . . .[5]

Thus while the pulpit must not be " always resounding " with the political theme, its trumpet must give forth no uncertain

---

[4] Quoted in editorial, " Political Preaching," *Presbyterian*, June 7, 1862.
[5] Editorial, " Dr. Rice's Sermon," *ibid.*

sound. The principles here set forth by the *Presbyterian* were apparently representative of the attitude of the great majority of the Old School clergy. Old School sermons on political themes during the war period were characterized rather by the vigor of their patriotism than by the extent of their number.

Several individual churches were thrown into the limelight during the war period either because of their previous record on slavery or because of the activity — or non-activity — of their preachers in the Union cause. The General Assembly of 1861 left little doubt as to the role which would be chosen by the venerable pastor of the Brick Presbyterian Church in New York, Dr. Gardiner S. Spring. Though Dr. Spring was considered to be strongly pro-slavery, the aggressiveness of his leadership in bringing the General Assembly to a position of outspoken loyalty showed that he was first of all pro-Union.[6] Indeed several weeks earlier he had made clear to his fellow-citizens at a great mass-meeting in Union Square his devoted attachment to the Federal Government.[7] Dr. Spring was safe, but what of his associate pastor, the Southern Dr. William J. Hoge? Dr. Hoge soon settled the answer to that question by praying for the rulers of the Confederate States as well as for those of the Union. His explanation that he was simply obeying the Biblical injunction to pray for those in authority was not satisfactory to his congregation, and he resigned in July, 1861.[8] Needless to say, his successor was thoroughly "loyal." [9]

A few blocks down the Avenue,[10] Dr. N. L. Rice,[11] the newly installed pastor of the Fifth Avenue Presbyterian Church, was having his difficulties. A Kentuckian by birth,

[6] *Cf. ante*, pp. 46-51.

[7] New York *Evangelist*, April 25, 1861. The meeting was held on April 20. (The date given in Moore, *op. cit.*, vol. i, Document 73½, pp. 82-83 — where the proceedings of the meeting are given — is May 20. This is obviously an error.)

[8] *Presbyterian*, July 27, 1861.

[9] The successor was Dr. Wm. G. T. Shedd.

[10] At that time the Fifth Avenue Presbyterian Church was at the corner of Nineteenth Street.

[11] *Cf. ante*, pp. 165-166.

by reputation one of the strongest defenders of slavery in the Northern wing of the Church, it is not surprising that his consistent observance of the principle of silence with regard to the discussion of political matters in the pulpit should have been interpreted as betraying sympathy with the Southern cause. Charges against him were so persistent in the secular and the religious press that Dr. Rice felt called upon to defend his position. This he did in a sermon entitled, " The Pulpit: Its Relation to Our National Crisis," delivered early in 1862. The speaker undertook to prove from his publications and from his recent acts that he had been uniformly a loyal subject, that he had never approved of the principle of slavery, that he had never sympathized with the existing rebellion, and that by no word or act had he countenanced those in arms against the Federal Government. He avowed that his silence had been due to his conviction that the pulpit was not the place for the discussion of political questions.[12] Dr. Rice's explanation did not entirely satisfy his critics. Acknowledging his loyalty, the *Presbyterian* found occasion to regret that he had adopted a " principle which others, whose antecedents have not been so clear, have practised to conceal their disloyalty." [13] The *Presbyter* was less generous: " No minister in our Church in the North needed more to explain himself on the great question of the day. . . . No one has been more willing to accede to the demands of the South, down to the fall of Sumter." [14] Nevertheless, Dr. Rice's congregation seems to have been reasonably well satisfied with his explanation; at least he continued as the pastor of the Fifth Avenue Church until 1867. On the other hand, there is considerable evidence that he was not as happy here as in previous pastorates, and the historian of the Fifth Avenue Church emphasizes the great strides made

---

[12] The sermon is summarized in an editorial, " Dr. Rice's Sermon," *Presbyterian,* June 7, 1862.

[13] *Ibid.*

[14] Editorial, " Dr. N. L. Rice," *Presbyter,* June 19, 1862.

by the congregation under his successor.[15]   The charges against
Dr. Rice's loyalty can scarcely have contributed to either the
happiness or the success of his ministry in New York.

Across the East River, in Brooklyn, on the other hand,
charges of pro-slavery sympathies against the energetic pastor
of the influential First Presbyterian Church of that city, Dr.
Henry J. VanDyke, seemed not at all to interfere with the
growth and prosperity of the congregation.   In December,
1860, Dr. VanDyke preached a sermon on "The Character
and Influence of Abolitionism"[16] which the near-Abolitionist
Presbyter termed "by far the most objectionable that we have
seen.   It is the result of breathing the atmosphere of the New
York cotton, sugar and rice trade."[17]   But however objectionable this preacher's views on slavery may have appeared to the
men of the anti-slavery wing of the Church, however pro-South
they may have seemed, no one could legitimately challenge
Dr. VanDyke's patriotism.   On Thanksgiving Day, 1859, he
had preached a sermon in which he insisted that resistance
against the civil government was in violation of the law of
God.[18]   The exponent of such views could scarcely be suspected of sympathizing with the rebellion of the South.

Yet as the war progressed, Dr. VanDyke exasperated a large
number of his fellow-Presbyterians by insisting that the Southern brethren be treated with forbearance.   In the October,
1864, meeting of the Synod of New York he introduced a
series of resolutions attacking the General Assembly for its
recent deliverances on the political situation — resolutions
which the Synod by a vote of 88 to 15[19] pronounced "a fire-

---

[15] Jessup, Henry W., *History of the Fifth Avenue Presbyterian Church
of New York City, 1808-1908* (New York, 1909), *passim.   Cf.* also *Presbyterian Encyclopaedia*, pp. 760-761.

[16] This sermon, preached on December 9, 1860, was published as a pamphlet (New York, 1860).

[17] Editorial, *Presbyter*, January 24, 1861.   *Cf.* also editorial, *ibid.*, January 17, 1861.

[18] *Cf.* speech of Mr. H. K. Clarke in the General Assembly of 1866, *Proceedings*, pp. 83-84.   Mr. Clarke quoted at length from this sermon.

[19] Eight were excused from voting, among them Dr. N. L. Rice.

brand in the Church and false and disloyal." [20]   Although in 1865 the threat of proceedings for slander brought satisfactory retraction from a trustee of Dr. VanDyke's congregation who had accused him of disloyalty, similar charges against him persisted.   It was asserted that he refused to read from the pulpit notices of meetings for the benefit of wounded soldiers, to preach in a church over which the flag floated, or to promote the objects of the Sanitary and Christian Commissions.[21]   That a man might find that his principles prescribed such a course for him, and still be loyal at heart, did not seem to occur to his accusers.   "A minister of the Gospel who has taken and maintained such a position should be fully known," commented the *Presbyterian Banner* in devoting more than a column of its editorial space to an account of the Brooklyn divine's alleged shortcomings in patriotism.[22]

Dr. VanDyke's strong plea in the 1866 Assembly for reunion with the Southern Church [23] and his able defense of the Declaration and Testimony men [24] branded him in the eyes of that violent body as a man dangerous to the Church, and invoked the vitriolic sarcasm of Dr. Thomas.[25]   When in 1870 the Northern Church was at last ready to take a somewhat more charitable attitude toward its Southern neighbor, Dr. VanDyke was one of the ambassadors sent to make overtures for the appointment of a joint committee of conference.[26]   The failure of this and similar later gestures finally convinced him that reunion in his generation was impossible; [27] never-

---

[20] Editorial, *Presbyter,* November 2, 1864, giving account of meeting.

[21] Editorial, " Rev. Henry J. VanDyke," *Presbyterian Banner,* June 21, 1865.

[22] *Ibid.*

[23] *Proceedings . . . 1866,* pp. 27; 77-78.

[24] *Cf. ante,* p. 227.

[25] *Cf. ante,* p. 233.

[26] *American Annual Cyclopaedia,* 1870, p. 622.

[27] In a letter sent to the writer, Dr. Henry VanDyke of Princeton, N. J., son of the Dr. Henry J. VanDyke who figures in this account, states that his father remained throughout his life (he died in 1891) hopeful of the ultimate reunion of the Northern and Southern Churches, but finding that

theless he remained one of the strongest advocates for the bringing together of the Northern and Southern Presbyterian Churches. In proportion to the degree in which animosity toward the South persisted, he continued during the war to be regarded as a man of questionable patriotism, and his congregation shared his reputation in this respect. Patriots asserted that before the rebellion was over, nearly every loyal family in the congregation had left, and that their places had been taken by those who were disloyal.[28] Whatever its complexion as to loyalty, the size of the membership of the First Church of Brooklyn, according to the official records, remained virtually unchanged throughout the period of war and reconstruction. Northern bitterness against its pastor for his kindly feelings toward the Southern brethren[29] gradually disappeared after the period of church reconstruction was over,[30] and in 1876 the General Assembly bestowed upon him the highest honor it could render by electing him Moderator. By that time Northern Presbyterians could forget the "unpatriotic" record of the First Church of Brooklyn under his leadership.

While the absence of an episcopal hierarchy in the Presbyterian Church means also the absence of cathedral churches,

the attitude of the Southern branch was rather irreconcilable, he concluded that " further public efforts in that direction would be provocative of little or no good, and that the much desired reunion . . . could hardly be brought about until some funerals had taken place." This letter was written under date of April 8, 1929.

[28] Cf. editorial, " Dr. Henry J. VanDyke," *Presbyterian Banner*, June 21, 1865.

[29] Dr. VanDyke was not only accused of too much friendliness for the South; some believed that the " Declaration and Testimony " was written in his office in Brooklyn. This is stated as a fact by a historian of the Southern Church. (Johnson, *op. cit.*, p. 443, note 3). Perhaps Dr. Thomas was referring to this charge in 1866 when he exclaimed, " What matters it to us, sir, whether a trio of confederates may have met on a Lee shore somewhere in New York? " etc. *Proceedings*, p. 21.

[30] During 1867 and 1868 Dr. VanDyke's church was virtually out the denomination on account of the defiant stand taken by its session in the fall of 1866. *Cf. ante*, pp. 275-276.

there have always been certain congregations and churches which stand out as leaders of the denomination. People thought of Old School Presbyterianism in New York largely in terms of the Brick and the Fifth Avenue churches. Dr. VanDyke's First Church was in the forefront in Brooklyn. In recent years the North Presbyterian Church in Chicago had seemed to typify the denomination's progress in that city and region. The North Church owed its reputation largely to two factors: it was the church of Cyrus McCormick, and it had just had a remarkable growth [31] under the brief but effective pastorate of the powerful N. L. Rice, who had left it in 1861 to take charge of the Fifth Avenue Church in New York. The reasons assigned by anti-slavery men for Cyrus McCormick's bringing Dr. Rice to Chicago in 1858 were effectively, if somewhat caustically, summed up by the New School *American Presbyterian* in 1862:

> When abolitionism was eating into the vitals of the Old School Presbyterian Church in the North-West four or five years ago, you remember that a certain Boanerges was sent for, and baited with a chance to " do a great work " in turning back the tide, and so came here walking on a good pavement of dollars, laid down in the track of a reaping machine. Obstacles yielded to the blows of the Son of Thunder most wonderfully. . . .[32]

However effective Dr Rice was in removing the obstacles, it is certain that anti-slavery men were dissatisfied with the record of the North Church for some time after his departure. In the summer of 1863 a correspondent of the *Presbyter* reported that the new pastor was taking a decided stand " for the Government " with the result that " the prejudices formerly against this church in the city " were giving way.[33] The inclusion of political topics in a Thanksgiving sermon, however, brought this man into serious trouble, and discovering that " some six families to whom God has given wealth " would leave in the

[31] *Presbyterian Encyclopaedia*, pp. 760-761.
[32] Quoted in *True Presbyterian*, April 17, 1862.
[33] *Cf.* communication of " Hoosier," *Presbyter*, June 24, 1863.

event of his remaining, he concluded to resign.[34] By the fall
of 1864 "loyalty" had evidently made considerable progress
in the congregation, for the new pastor then chosen had served
for three years as a chaplain in the United States Navy.[35]

From the cases cited it might be inferred that in all of the
leading churches of the Old School denomination the radical
patriots found ground for disapproving of the pulpit utterances.
This was not true. The First Church in Brooklyn had its
difficulties, and the congregation Dr. Rice left behind him, as
well as the one he took over when he went to New York in
1861, suffered the displeasure of the radical brethren for lack
of unanimity in sentiment on the subjects of slavery and the
Union — or at least for a division of opinion as to whether
these topics should be discussed in the pulpit. On the other
hand, in other conspicuous pulpits of the denomination in the
Northern states there was little to cause the Thomas crowd
anxiety. The renowned Dr. William B. Sprague[36] of the
Second Church of Albany; Dr. Henry A. Boardman of the
Tenth Church in Philadelphia; Dr. Spring and his associate
pastor, Dr. William G. T. Shedd, of the Brick Church in New
York; Dr. L. H. Christian, of the North Church in Philadelphia; Dr. William M. Paxton, of the First Presbyterian
Church, Pittsburgh; and Dr. Henry Steele Clarke, of the Central Presbyterian Church, Philadelphia, all identified their influential pulpits with the cause of the Union.[37] No doubt the

[34] *Presbyter,* February 24, 1864. The pastor was Rev. John B. Stewart.
Strictly speaking, he did not resign, but rather declined the call which the
church had tendered him some seventeen months before.

[35] This was Dr. D. X. Junkin. *Presbyterian Encyclopaedia,* p. 389.

[36] Author of *Annals of the American Pulpit.*

[37] Typical sermons preached by the men mentioned are named below,
together with the approximate date of delivery and a citation of sources
in which a summary or at least a brief reference may be found:

W. B. Sprague, "Glorifying God in the Fires," Thanksgiving, 1861,
Presbyterian, January 4, 1862.

H. A. Boardman, "Thanksgiving in War," Thanksgiving Day, 1861, *ibid.,*
January 4, 1862.

G. S. Spring, "State Thanksgiving during the Rebellion," 1861, *ibid.,*
February 1, 1862.

lesser pulpits of the denomination were similarly identified. But most of the Old School ministers stopped with one or two sermons, or perhaps a sermon a year. Having put themselves on record as loyal supporters of the Federal Government, they were inclined to confine the scope of their pulpit activities to the stricter limits prescribed by Old School theology and tradition.

Here and there among the less prominent churches of the denomination — as among their more illustrious neighbors — there was trouble over the pastor's position on the political crisis. One minister's name was struck from a presbytery's roll because of "sympathy with the existing rebellion, and serving in a military capacity under the so-called Confederate Government."[38] Sometimes it was considered necessary for the presbytery to send a committee to visit a pastor who refused to pray for the success of the Union armies.[39] Occasionally a presbytery felt constrained, for the good of all concerned, to dissolve the pastoral relations of a minister whose congregation had ceased to have confidence in his patriotism, even though the members of the presbytery themselves perhaps did not doubt his loyalty.[40] Cases of this kind were rare, however, among the 1900 Old School ministers in the Northern

W. G. T. Shedd, "The Union and the War," 1863, Patterson Library, Princeton University.

L. H. Christian, "Our Present Position," November 27, 1862, *Bib. Rep. & Princeton Review*, January, 1863, vol. 35, p. 175.

W. M. Paxton, "The Nation's Gratitude and Hope," November 27, 1862, *ibid.*, p. 175.

H. S. Clarke, (No title given), May 5, 1861, *Presbyterian Banner,* June 29, 1861.

The Patterson Library, Princeton University, has sermons by a number of Old School leaders during the war period.

[38] Rev. James H. McNeill. *Presbyter,* May 11, 1864. This pastor was expelled from the Presbytery of Elizabethtown (N. J.).

[39] Rev. David Teese, of White Plains, New York, was a man so visited. *Cf.* editorial, "Disloyal Prayers," *True Presbyterian,* January 21, 1864.

[40] *Cf.* case of Rev. D. O. Davis (Presbytery of Cincinnati), *Presbyter,* April 1, 1863; also that of Rev. Charles Axtell (Presbytery of Indianapolis) of whom the Presbytery, by unanimous vote, recorded "their confidence in his loyalty." *Presbyter,* April 20, 1864.

states [41] — remarkably rare considering the long period during which Old School ministers of the North and the South had worked side by side in a united Church, and the frequent interchange of pastors between the two sections.

Perhaps one reason why there were so few disturbances of this sort lies in the fact that there was a pretty general exodus from each section, during the opening weeks of the war, of the sympathizers of the opposite side. The exchange, for example, of the Southern Dr. Leyburn for the Northern Rev. M. B. Grier (who had virtually been forced to leave his Wilmington, North Carolina, pastorate) as junior editor of the *Presbyterian* [42] was but typical of dozens of sectional changes. The circumstances of these moves were often dramatic, involving danger, bravery, pathos, and sometimes lengthy suffering. There was the case of the seventy-year-old Dr. George Junkin, father-in-law of Stonewall Jackson,[43] who after twelve years as president of Washington College (Lexington, Virginia) resigned his position when his students hoisted the Secession flag over the College and insisted that he should perform his official duties under it.[44] Sometimes the inconveniences of forced removal were offset by agreements between interchanging parties, as in the reported case of two brethren — one Northern and one Southern — who, "not being able to remove their libraries to their new fields of labour, . . . have made the following arrangement, — each is to use that of the other till these troublous times are overpast!"[45]

---

[41] In 1865 there were 2301 ministers in the Old School Church, about 350 of whom belonged to Border State presbyteries.

[42] *Cf. ante,* p. 154. Dr. Leyburn subsequently became secretary of the Board of Domestic Missions of the Southern Church.

[43] Dr. Junkin was the father of Jackson's first wife. *Presbyter,* December 31, 1862.

[44] *Christian Herald,* May 23, 1861; *Presbyterian,* August 31, 1861.

[45] *Presbyterian,* July 19, 1862, quoting *Religious Herald.* The writer in the *Religious Herald* commented, "an interesting fact — if fact it be!" The two ministers were Rev. John E. Annan, who was "compelled to leave" Charlottesville, Virginia, and Dr. Wm. J. Hoge, formerly of the Brick Church in New York (*cf. ante* p. 283), who took Mr. Annan's place in Charlottesville.

There were charges of cruelty and persecution leveled against the South by some of the returning preachers. One of these men, for example, asserted that after eleven years of labor in the South, when the war broke out he had been imprisoned, heavily ironed, insulted, starved, and would have been hanged in a few days, had he not escaped. He had been charged with treason against the Confederate States.[46] A case that attracted widespread attention was that of Dr. Robert C. Grundy, pastor of the Second Church of Memphis, Tennessee. Dr. Grundy prayed God to let his people know if they were right, to convince them of their error if they were wrong. This sort of prayer, he was informed, was "not in accordance with the piety of many of his parishioners," and he was dismissed by his presbytery.[47] His friends then rented a hall for him; "and when the United States get possession of Memphis," declared one of them, "we are going to build him a church five stories high, and he shall preach in every story of it!"[48] Fortunately for the good doctor's powers of endurance, when the United States military forces came to occupy Memphis, the parishioners were virtually compelled to take back the ejected pastor,[49] and the five-story building was not necessary. A few months later Dr. Grundy grasped the opportunity of enjoying "the fellowship of kindred minds"[50] by accepting a call to the Central Presbyterian Church of Cincinnati. There he soon indicated his strong anti-slavery views[51] by asserting that for a Northern man to be in favor of "the

[46] *Cf.* letter of Rev. John H. Aughey printed in the *Presbyterian*, September 6, 1862. Mr. Aughey had been pastor of the church at Poplar Creek, Mississippi.

[47] *Cf.* editorial, *Presbyterian*, August 30, 1862.

[48] *Presbyterian*, June 21, 1862, quoting from the New York *Evangelist's* story of the visit of one of its editors to Tennessee.

[49] Editorial, *Presbyterian*, August 30, 1862.

[50] Quoted in the *Presbyter's* (December 25, 1862) announcement of the call of Dr. Grundy to Cincinnati.

[51] Dr. Grundy's presence in Cincinnati was highly welcome to the anti-slavery *Presbyter* published there. His views and his work were frequently the subject of favorable comment in that journal during the war years.

Union at it was and the Constitution as it is," (Dr. Breckinridge's original platform in opposition to emancipation),[52] "not only makes him a traitor, but makes the nation sinful in the sight of God."[53] A more northerly latitude than his native Kentucky[54] or his adopted state of Tennessee was quite evidently better suited to his sentiments.

Probably for every such "exile from the terrible scourge of secession"[55] there was a corresponding exile from "Yankee" domination. That the exiles themselves constituted something of a problem in the havens of refuge may be gathered from the appointment of a special committee by one Northern presbytery "to examine the credentials of travelling ministers." This was suggested by a request from one of the churches of the presbytery, asking leave to employ as minister a man "purporting to be a licentiate and refugee from Alabama."[56] Most of the flights naturally came during the opening months of the war; after the close of the year 1862 few cases were recorded. By that date the problem of "disloyalty" in Northern pulpits had largely disappeared.

The theological seminaries were the pride of the Old School Church. They were the symbol of Presbyterian conservatism and erudition, the safeguards of the future of the Church. Immediately upon the outbreak of the war, therefore, considerable interest — and perhaps some anxiety — was felt for the attitude the theological leaders of the denomination would take toward the problems of the political crisis. Were the new generation of ministers sitting at the feet of men whose loyalty was as unquestioned as their orthodoxy? While the synod-controlled Southern seminaries (Union Theological Seminary,

[52] *Cf. ante*, p. 144.
[53] *True Presbyterian*, June 4, 1863, quoting the Cincinnati *Enquirer*.
[54] *Presbyterian Encyclopaedia*, p. 285.
[55] Rev. Edward Cooper thus described himself in a letter published in the *Presbyter*, January 7, 1863. Mr. Cooper had been the pastor of a church in Brownsville, Tennessee, but had come North in the summer of 1861.
[56] *Cf.* report of the proceedings of the Presbytery of Schuyler (northern Illinois), *Presbyterian*, October 4, 1862.

at Prince Edward, Virginia; and Columbia Theological Seminary, South Carolina) had been lost with the division of 1861, the four Assembly-controlled seminaries (Princeton, New Jersey; Western, Allegheny, Pennsylvania; Danville, Kentucky; and Northwestern Theological Seminary, Chicago) had remained faithful to the Assembly. But the record of three of these four on the question of slavery may well have raised some doubt as to the attitude of their leaders toward a war which, though primarily concerned with the integrity of the Union, was closely associated in the popular mind with the issue of slavery. "Abolition does not even breathe here, let alone flourish," wrote a student in Princeton Theological Seminary in 1840.[57] The record, during the subsequent twenty years, of the most prominent member of its faculty, Dr. Hodge,[58] had surely given no indication of any relaxation in the hostility of the institution to radical anti-slavery propaganda. While Dr. Breckinridge, the leader at Danville, had been an exponent of "gradualism,"[59] he was known in 1861 as a bitter opponent of any radical program for the elimination of slavery. As far as the Seminary of the Northwest was concerned, for several years prior to the outbreak of the war it had been the focus upon which the bitterest slavery disputes in the Church had been concentrated. When the General Assembly of 1859 had by a large majority shown its preference for the "pro-slavery" Dr. N. L. Rice, rather than the strongly anti-slavery Dr. E. D. MacMaster, to be professor in the new seminary at Chicago, the election was interpreted by the Church and by the public as a decision that the Seminary of the Northwest should not be an anti-slavery institution.[60] Dr. MacMaster's good friend, Dr. Thomas, termed

[57] Letter of George W. Swan, quoted in Thomas, *op. cit.,* pp. 118-119. The date of the letter as printed is January 12, 1830, but the context indicates that it was probably 1840, instead.

[58] *Cf. ante,* pp. 33-35; 137-139.

[59] *Cf. ante,* pp. 143-146.

[60] For an account of this whole controversy, *cf.* Halsey, *op. cit.,* pp. 48-50; 100; Thomas, *op. cit.,* pp. 105-108.

this event "a wonderful triumph of ambition, injustice, dishonesty and pro-slavery." [61]

Curiously enough, the only serious charges of disloyalty directed against a theological professor during the war were made against a member of the fourth seminary — the only one that did not stand out as bitterly opposed to pronounced anti-slavery views. This was the Western Theological Seminary at Allegheny City, Pennsylvania, an institution that in attendance (158 in 1862) [62] closely rivalled Princeton. The accused man was Dr. William S. Plumer, who besides being a member of the Seminary faculty, was the pastor of the Central Presbyterian Church of Allegheny City. Though Dr. Plumer was born in Pennsylvania and received most of his formal education in the North, the twenty-eight years of his experience as a pastor prior to his acceptance of a professorship in the Western Theological Seminary in 1854 had been spent south of the Mason-Dixon line. Dr. Plumer had been a veritable Moses to the conservative wing of the Presbyterian Church in the crisis from which it had emerged in 1838 as the separate Old School denomination. When in the epoch-making General Assembly of 1837 an eloquent plea for continued union had swept the Assembly off its feet and it appeared that a division would be avoided, it was Dr. Plumer who brought a majority of the commissioners back to the conviction that the two wings of the Church must be separated. "His speech changed the fate of the question," [63] and he was thus responsible for "saving to our country the system of Calvinism in doctrine and the Presbyterian system in church government." [64] Dr. Plumer was rewarded with the honor of being

[61] *Ibid.* Dr. Rice was elected by a vote of 314 to 45. Dodd, *loc. cit.,* pp. 774-778, also gives an account of this election.
[62] *Cf.* statistics quoted in editorial, *Presbyterian,* August 16, 1862. The enrollment of the Princeton Seminary was 170; Danville, 11; Seminary of the Northwest, 11. The enrollment at Danville had been 53 in 1860. For the last-named figure *cf. Minutes of the General Assembly,* 1860, vol. xvi, p. 50.
[63] White, *op. cit.,* p. 289, quoting Dr. William H. Foote.
[64] White, *op. cit.,* p. 289.

chosen the first Moderator of the separate Old School Church.[65] It was this distinguished veteran of the Church who now became conspicuous as the only theological professor in the denomination to be seriously suspected of disloyalty.

It is possible that other theological professors with Dr. Plumer's views may have escaped censure, for most of them did not have regular pastoral charges. A man preaching only occasionally before a given congregation might escape suspicion, but one meeting the same congregation from week to week was likely to find his audience sensitive to his political sentiments and with a keen sense of their responsibility for his patriotism. It was Dr. Plumer's manner of conducting his church services rather than his activities as a professor that first got him into difficulty. In the summer of 1862 the *Presbyter*, vigilant guardian of pulpit patriotism, reported that trouble had arisen in the Allegheny City church because the pastor would not lead the congregation in asking " God's *blessing upon the Government of our country in its efforts to suppress rebellion*," nor would he "*give thanks to God for the victories which God has granted our armies*." The *Presbyter*, of course, quite approved of the decision of Dr. Plumer's presbytery that he should pray in the required way.[66] It also commended the strong resolutions on loyalty and patriotic prayers subsequently adopted by that body.[67] The Pittsburgh *Presbyterian Banner* was disposed to take a more charitable view of the man whose stand was creating such a disturbance in the neighboring city, and undertook to give Dr. Plumer's own explanation of his position:

He affirms that he is a Union man. . . . He desires the country to be as free as it was five or ten years ago. He cannot pray for the success of our arms, nor give thanks for our victories, because arms and victories produce alienations rather than fraternal feelings; men cannot be coerced

---

[65] *Ibid.*, pp. 289-290. The facts regarding Dr. Plumer's career were taken from White, *op. cit.*, pp. 286-292, and *Presbyterian Encyclopaedia*, p. 622.
[66] *Presbyter*, June 26, 1862.
[67] *Ibid.*, July 24, 1862.

to love; swords and bayonets can never piece together these states in a happy and enduring Union.[68]

The *Banner* added that in a " card " inserted in the Pittsburgh papers, the accused man had declared that he loved the Union, regarded it as his duty to sustain the government, and did not believe in the right of secession. The *Banner*, like the *Presbyter*, professed to be unable to understand his attitude.[69]

Dr. Plumer's point of view is particularly interesting because it was the nearest approach to pacifist sentiments reached by an Old School minister. It is amazing that amid all of the argument over the proper attitude of the pulpit toward the great conflict, this man should have been the only one to suggest a possible inconsistency between the teachings of Jesus and prayers for military victories, the only one to vouchsafe the opinion that men cannot be coerced to love. Perhaps there is no better argument for the sincerity of the disputants in this great struggle in the Church than this absence of pacifism from their pleas. Had the proponents of pulpit silence on political matters hypocritically been urging this practice in order to prevent the necessity of revealing their own sympathy for the Confederacy — as their enemies alleged — it is scarcely conceivable that at least a few of them would not have added the argument of pacifism to their plea that the pulpit was not the place for the discussion of political topics. The argument would have been a logical corollary of their original thesis, although (as the attitude of the *Presbyter* and the *Banner* toward Dr. Plumer's statements seems to indicate) it would probably have made little favorable impression upon the members of the radical camp. To the word-minded Presbyterians of that era a doctrine that opposed prayers for the success of arms and thanks for victories would seem like a repudiation of the God of Joshua and David and Hezekiah. At least, such seemed to be the point of view of those who settled

---

[68] *Presbyterian Banner*, July 31, 1862.
[69] *Ibid.; cf.* also long article from the *Banner* quoted in *Presbyter*, July 24, 1862.

the case of the one minister [70] of the Old School denomination who even approached the principles of pacifism.

The pressure upon Dr. Plumer became so great that he tendered his resignation as pastor of the Allegheny City church. This was accepted, but a large portion of the congregation sent a remonstrance to the presbytery against losing their pastor. The presbytery after " respectful delibera- tion" decided not to reverse the action of the church session.[71] Meanwhile the *Presbyterian Banner* had been demanding that he also resign his position on the faculty of the Seminary.[72] Before long the accused man acceded to the demand and sent a letter of resignation to the Board of Directors of that institution. Protesting that he loved his work, Dr. Plumer explained his reasons for giving up his post:

> But my peace is destroyed, my life is embittered, and my health is suffering from cruel calumnies which I have borne as silently and as patiently as I could, and from the line of conduct pursued toward me by some of the directors, and approved, as I fear by others of your number.[73]

The Board of Directors unanimously decided to accept the resignation.[74] Thus ended the only case of proceedings against a theological professor on the grounds of lack of patriotism. The affair attracted the attention of the secular as well as the religious press, though the *Banner* asserted that the accounts of students' disturbances as given in the daily papers were greatly exaggerated. The Pittsburgh weekly declared that the students respected Dr. Plumer as a man and a scholar, but that

[70] It is of course possible that there were other ministers in the denomi- nation who leaned toward pacificism, but with the majority element in the Church so sensitive to anything that savored of lack of loyalty, it is hardly likely that such cases would have escaped the notice of the Old School press — particularly not that of the *Presbyter,* which was ever on the look- out for things "disloyal." Dr. Plumer's are the only even near-pacifist views the writer has been able to discover.

[71] *Presbyter,* October 10, 1862, quoting the *Presbyterian Banner.*

[72] *Presbyter,* July 24, 1862, quoting the *Presbyterian Banner.*

[73] *Cf.* letter quoted in *Presbyter,* October 2, 1862.

[74] *Ibid.,* quoting *Presbyterian Banner.*

only a few, if any, sympathized with "his secession proclivities."[75]

The subsequent career of the man is interesting. After
three years without regular employment[76] he became pastor of
a church in Pottstown, Pennsylvania, whence in 1867 he went
to Columbia, South Carolina, to become a member of the faculty of the Columbia Theological Seminary, and incidentally to
cast in his lot with the Southern Presbyterian Church. With
the reunion of Old and New Schools fast approaching in 1867,[77]
the removal must have been a happy one to a man who had
played so important a part in the separation of the reuniting
branches. In 1871 he was made Moderator of the Southern
Assembly.[78] But what must have seemed like the climax of
his career came in 1877, when Dr. Plumer was seventy-five.
Happening to be in Chicago, he was invited to address the
Northern General Assembly, then in session there. A spectator
thus described the scene as the majestic figure of the handsome
old veteran moved down the aisle of the church in which the Assembly was gathered:

As the grand vision dawned upon the upturned faces of the assembly,
resistance to its charms was impossible; generous impulse overcame the
heat of prejudice, and courtesy paid voluntary tribute to the highest type
of manliness. The applause rose and swelled and waned again, then
waxed higher and more fervent as the royal form went on down the aisle;
and as the gallery caught the first glimpse of his advancing figure, ladies
and gentlemen rose *en masse* and cheered and cheered again.[79]

Considering that the subject of all of this excitement had,
some forty years earlier, with all the cocksure enthusiasm and
merciless rigor of a young conservative, taxed to the limit his
really remarkable resources of energy and eloquence to bring

[75] *Ibid.*
[76] During the winter of 1862-1863 he supplied the pulpit of the Arch St.
Church in Philadelphia.
[77] *Cf. post*, pp. 504-514.
[78] The facts here cited were taken from White, *op. cit.*, pp. 286-292, and
Presbyterian Encyclopaedia, p. 622.
[79] White, *op. cit.*, pp. 291-292, quoting a spectator of the incident.

about a division in the reunited body he was now to address; that he had been looked upon by the majority of its members as a man of questionable patriotism; that as the hour of re-union of the two Northern branches of the Church had approached, he had betaken himself to the unfriendly Southern Church; considering all of these things, perhaps the incident related was as much a tribute to the givers as to the recipient of the applause. Quite evidently by 1877 Northern Presby-terians were willing to forgive the theological professor who had refused to pray for the success of arms and to give thanks for military victories. There may even have been a few in this Northern Assembly twelve years after the close of the war who were beginning to doubt whether all of the right had been on the side of the North and all of the wrong on the side of the South.

Whatever harm Dr. Plumer's questioned loyalty might other-wise have done the Western Theological Seminary should have been largely offset by a speech made by another member of its faculty [80] at a mass meeting in Allegheny City. Extracts from this speech, which the *Presbyter* termed "a noble production," were as follows:

The hour we fail in this struggle, the sun goes back fifteen degrees on the dial. . . . If it must be so, let this land be deluged with blood, out of that red and clotted ocean, civil liberty will arise regenerated and repurified, and resplendent as Minerva leaped in full panoply from the brain of Jupiter. . . . While you were going on with your farming, your merchandise and your mechanic arts, perjured traitors were secretly plot-ting the destruction of the best government on earth. . . . At last came the consummation of the blackest villainy, perfidy and treason, in the records of all time. . . . [81]

The *Presbyter* reported that two other members of this faculty had been commissioners to war-time General Assemblies, "and their record is good," it commented.[82] Thus in spite of Dr.

[80] Dr. S. J. Wilson.
[81] Editorial, "Theological Seminaries and Loyalty," quoting Dr. Wilson, *Presbyter*, August 14, 1862.
[82] *Ibid.*

Plumer this Seminary could easily pass muster in a test of loyalty.

The Seminary at Princeton was viewed with more suspicion, in spite of the fact that there was no incident in its record corresponding to the Plumer case. When, however, a correspondent of the *Presbyter* asserted that Dr. Hodge's arguments against the Spring Resolutions in the 1861 Assembly were a "covert plea for the Princeton Seminary, much of whose support is derived from the South," the *Presbyterian,* remarking that Dr. Hodge was able to take care of himself, declared that the Seminary as a public institution of the Church should be defended against such attacks. The editor of this journal pointed out that the statistics of the last catalogue of the Seminary showed only 15 of the 156 students from south of the Mason-Dixon line, and 9 of the 15 were from Maryland and Missouri.[83] The figures may be regarded as proving that there was no desirability in a pro-Southern policy from the point of view of conciliating student sentiment; nevertheless the fact that the *Presbyterian* felt called upon to defend the record of the Seminary is significant. A more positive proof of the Seminary's loyalty was furnished by Dr. Alexander T. McGill of the faculty in the introductory lecture at the opening of the fall session in 1861. Taking as his theme the relation between religion and love for the State, he asserted that "true patriotism is born of Christianity, which also furnishes its principles and fixes its limits." While Dr. McGill maintained that to produce the truest patriotism, and every other social and civil virtue, religion must be kept distinct and engrossed with its own central theme, the salvation of souls, he made it clear that in these troublous times the call of the pulpit was not necessarily paramount, for he concluded his address to the young theologues with the declaration that if they could justify themselves

[83] Editorial, *Presbyterian,* August 24, 1861. The editor might have found further confirmation of his statement in statistics with regard to the class which had graduated from the Seminary in April, 1860. Of the thirty-six graduates, only one came from south of the Mason-Dixon line. *Cf. Presbyterian,* May 12, 1860 (account of graduation exercises).

in being there at all, and not in the camp, it could only be in the way of solemn industry, "which no call aside, less than that of the trumpet, could be suffered to interrupt or invade." [84]   Such statements must have helped to satisfy the doubtful regarding the loyalty of the Princeton Seminary.

In the summer of 1862 the *Presbyter*, faithful watch-dog of Old School patriotism, undertook to summarize the record made by each of the four seminaries during the first year of the war.   As the *Presbyter* was the organ of the anti-Philadelphia-Princeton faction of the Church,[85] its estimates were perhaps not entirely unbiased.   Princeton, it thought, had suffered much by the course of Dr. Hodge in the 1861 Assembly, "yet it has done nothing, through any of its Professors, which would justify a charge of disloyalty."   The Western Theological Seminary, while the difficulties between Dr. Plumer and his church had been very unfortunate, had been vindicated by the patriotic course of other professors.   The fact that every member of the faculty of the Danville Seminary was an editor of the *Danville Review* was enough to insure its record.   As for the Seminary of the Northwest, where the "pro-slavery" influence of Dr. Rice and Cyrus McCormick had prevailed in the years just before the war, the *Presbyter* felt that the presence of Dr. Willis Lord as a member of its faculty guaranteed its safety. Dr. Lord had been one of the most conspicuous fighters for loyal action in the 1861 Assembly; [86] his "course in the present crisis of public affairs," declared the *Presbyter*, "is a part of the history of the times." [87]   With this critical journal satisfied with the attitude of the theological seminaries, it is not likely that there was much in their record which could give offense to radical patriots.   That there continued to be misgivings with regard to some of these institutions, however, is indicated by the course pursued by the Presbytery of Oxford (southern

[84] Quoted in *Presbyterian*, September 28, 1861.
[85] *Cf. ante*, pp. 80-82; 158.
[86] *Cf. ante*, pp. 81; 83, note 163.
[87] Editorial, "Our Theological Schools," *Presbyter*, July 10, 1862; *cf.* also editorial, "Theological Seminaries and Loyalty," *ibid.*, August 14, 1862.

Ohio) at its fall meeting in 1862. "In view of the alarming prevalence of disloyalty in many parts of our country" this body urged that the greatest precautions be taken to safeguard the position of the Church, and resolved that, whereas the Western Seminary and the Danville Seminary had taken a stand of loyalty, young men under the care of the Presbytery should be recommended to pursue their studies at those institutions.[88] One surmises that this resolution was intended as much for a threat to the seminaries of more doubtful patriotism, as for the immediate welfare of the presbytery's candidates for the ministry. At any rate, there is nothing in the record of the seminaries during the war years to indicate that the advice was necessary. Whatever the motives actuating their stand, the seminaries were "loyal."

With the greater number of the cases of questionable loyalty in Northern pulpits disposed of during the first year of the war, and with the patriotism of the theological seminaries pretty convincingly established, the activities of traitor-seekers in the Old School Church came to be largely confined to the Border States. There all was confusion, and the percentage of loyalty was difficult to determine, even by experts of the radically patriotic crowd. Members of this faction experienced no difficulty in determining that certain conspicuous individuals like Stuart Robinson were traitors, but there was less certainty with regard to the degree to which such men typified Old School opinion in the Border States. In 1866 this question was eventually answered as far as Stuart Robinson's state was concerned, by the uneven division of the Synod of Kentucky,[89] but until that time no one knew how sentiment in Kentucky was divided. The most serious source of difficulty in determining the sentiments of the Kentucky preachers lay in the fact that the Robinson crowd refused to tolerate any reference to political matters in the pulpit. To what extent did this silence in

---

[88] Proceedings of the Presbytery of Oxford, as recorded in *Presbyter*, October 16, 1862.

[89] *Cf. ante*, pp. 262-263.

the pulpit represent secession proclivities; to what degree did it encourage anti-Union sentiments in the parishioners? No one, of course, could satisfactorily answer these questions. The casual reader of the Old School's pulpit record in Kentucky might readily conclude that Presbyterians there were uniformly loyal, for the members of the Danville Seminary faculty and their followers delivered many patriotic sermons and addresses; there were no disloyal sermons; except in the references to them in loyal sermons, there is no record of the scores of pulpits which refrained from political utterances. Nevertheless, Dr. George Junkin, himself an exile from the South,[90] was not satisfied with the number of loyal pulpits in the Border States. "Even in the Border States," he declared, "the Presbyterian ministers alone, if they had had a moiety of the heroic martyr spirit of Robert J. Breckinridge, could have shut up the sluices of treason and turned the battle from the gates."[91]

Stuart Robinson's voluntary exile in Canada[92] prevented his voice being heard in the pulpits of his native state after the first year of the war. Yet his *True Presbyterian* must have had a strong influence in the Border States; certainly he was regarded by the Northern Old School press as the most dangerous man in the Church, and his activities and reputed activities were carefully recorded from time to time. In the summer of 1865, the *Presbyterian* recorded Robinson's denial of having made profane remarks about the assassination of Lincoln (which Robinson in his denial asserted he regarded as "the most awful of calamities for the country, North and South"), and of any knowledge of a plot to introduce yellow fever into cities in the North. After publishing an account of these denials the *Presbyterian* expressed regret that a man of such ability should have placed himself in a position where he was regarded with distrust by nine-tenths of the Church to

[90] *Cf. ante*, p. 291.
[91] Stanton, *op. cit.*, p. 202, note.
[92] *Cf. ante*, p. 168.

which he belonged; "and we must say," the editor added, "that his career, since the rebellion broke out, seems to justify this distrust." [93] It must have been exasperating to the distrustful majority to be unable to adduce positive proof of any deed or word of actual disloyalty from the suspected Doctor or any of his Kentucky followers.

In Maryland, as well as in Kentucky, opponents of the General Assembly's loyalty measures followed a policy of silence on political matters, and whatever disloyalty there may have been among the Old School ministers of that state, their pulpit conduct furnished no direct proof of it; however much the radical loyalty men may have desired to "get something on" their doubtful brethren, that objective appeared to be impossible of achievement. In Missouri, on the other hand, conditions were more favorable to such enterprises, and the patriots were able — as they saw it — to force out into the open several ministers whom they regarded as disloyal. A peculiar set of circumstances brought into the limelight the most famous — or notorious — of these cases, that of Dr. S. B. McPheeters. The activities of military leaders, supplemented by those of patriotic informers, led to charges, punishments (with or without trial), and appeals, in the case of other Old School men. Old School Presbyterianism in Missouri was in a turmoil.

The case of Dr. McPheeters illustrates perhaps better than any other single incident how war-time hysteria blinded the better judgment and the sense of justice of Northern Old School leaders. Dr. McPheeters, a leader in the denomination [94] and a man of the finest character and the loftiest ideals, (his old-time teacher, Dr. Hodge, in criticising his arguments in 1862 took occasion to speak of him as "Dr. McPheeters, whom to know is to love" [95]), became the victim of a seemingly relent-

[93] Editorial, "Rev. Stuart Robinson," *Presbyterian,* July 15, 1865.

[94] He was, for example, made chairman of the important committee appointed to investigate the affairs of the Board of Publication in 1862. *Cf. Minutes of the General Assembly,* 1862, vol. xvi, p. 592.

[95] Article, "The General Assembly," *Biblical Repertory and Princeton Review,* July, 1862, vol. 34, p. 517.

less persecution, not for anything that he had done, but because
it was assumed that his silence on political matters made him a
traitor. In 1851, as a young man of thirty-one, Mr. McPheeters had come from Virginia to assume the pastorate of an
Old School church in St. Louis. While in Virginia he had
proved himself to be a man of courage by his persistence — in
the face of threatening opposition from a part of the white
population [96] — in evangelical work among the slaves on a large
number of plantations.[97] Not long after his arrival in St. Louis
his congregation was greatly strengthened by uniting with a
church which had been in connection with the New School
General Assembly.[98] It is possible that this New School leaven
may have been partially responsible for the later troubles
between the pastor and his congregation. Be that as it may,
for more than nine years he found his work with the St. Louis
church congenial and prospering.[99]

The news of the fall of Fort Sumter reached Dr. McPheeters [100] while he was serving as chaplain in an army post in
New Mexico, whither he had gone the previous summer in the
hope of improving his impaired health.[101] No secessionist, he
was shocked by the news, and when rumors reached him that
the Confederates planned to attack the fort in which he was
stationed, it is reported that he at once declared, "Though
the United States Government did not commission me to fight,
but to preach the Gospel, yet should this Fort be attacked I

[96] *Cf.* testimony of Mr. J. G. Jefferson, quoted in Grasty, Rev. John S.,
Memoir of Rev. Samuel B. McPheeters, D.D. (St. Louis. 1871). p. 88. Mr.
Jefferson states that "although the educated and genteel people did not
generally object to his scheme of preaching from house to house to the
negroes, yet quite a large number of the lower class were very resolutely
opposed, and some even threatened violence, which did not make him
hesitate."

[97] At one time he had as many as eighteen appointments at different
houses. *Ibid.*

[98] *Ibid.*, pp. 108-109.

[99] *Ibid.*, pp. 110-113.

[100] He had had the degree of Doctor of Divinity conferred upon him by
Westminster College in 1859. *Ibid.*, p. 109.

[101] *Ibid.*, p. 115.

shall be one of its defenders." [102] Troubled over the possible effect the civil conflict might have upon his Border State congregation, and unable, due to the confused state of affairs throughout the country, to return to them immediately, he sent his people a pastoral letter in which he urged them to be particularly careful to guard their tongues when discussing political matters. As far as he himself was concerned, he declared that he did not feel called upon, either as their pastor or as a minister of Christ, to discuss the purely civil and political questions which were then shaking the country. "I wish to address you," he wrote, "not as a friend or advocate of any party or section, but as an ambassador of One whose 'kingdom is not of this world.'" [103] Such words made it perfectly clear that when he returned to his fold he would follow a policy of silence with regard to the state of the country.

For about a year after Dr. McPheeters' return to St. Louis in the summer of 1861, all appeared to go well with him and his congregation — at least, as well as the troublous times would permit. His difficulties began when his conscience dictated that he should, as a commissioner in the General Assembly of 1862, pursue a course which ran counter to the program Dr. Robert J. Breckinridge had mapped out for that body. [104] When Dr. McPheeters opposed the adoption of Dr. Breckinridge's paper on the state of the country, the latter remarked that it was a well-known fact that all of the Presbyterian churches in St. Louis were loyal, and every minister there disloyal, in his (Dr. Breckinridge's) sense of loyalty. [105] For this statement the Kentucky professor was rebuked — albeit "very gently" — by the Moderator, [106] and Dr. McPheeters distinctly and emphatically denied "the right of any ecclesiastical body

---

[102] *Ibid.*, p. 116. *Cf.*, also, statement of Dr. Robert P. Farris in Leftwich, Rev. W. M., *Martyrdom in Missouri* (2 vol., St. Louis, 1870), p. 94.

[103] For this pastoral letter, *cf.* Grasty, *op. cit.*, pp. 117-120.

[104] *Cf. ante*, pp. 110-116; 191-194.

[105] *Cf.* speech of Dr. Breckinridge, as reported in account of seventh day of session of General Assembly, *Presbyterian*, May 31, 1862.

[106] Statement of reporter, *ibid.*

to question and challenge his political opinions on any subject."
He asserted that "no one could love this Government better
than he."[107] The Assembly, however, was in no mood to recognize as legitimate any sentiments short of enthusiastic endorsement of the Breckinridge paper. The arguments by which
Dr. McPheeters ably sought to justify his main thesis (the denial of the theory that the Church of Christ as such owes
allegiance to civil government[108]) fell on deaf ears, as far as
the majority of the Assembly were concerned. As for the ears
of his congregation, however, the effect was quite different.
The story of the accusations against their pastor and of his activity in opposition to the Breckinridge Paper reached them
through the press before his return from Columbus. The radically patriotic minority of the congregation were thus in a state
of mind which rendered them peculiarly sensitive to any evidences of disloyalty on the part of their pastor.

It was an absurdly insignificant incident which brought matters in the church to a crisis. One of the members of the congregation presented a child for baptism. When Dr. McPheeters leaned forward to ask the parents what name they had
chosen for the infant, he must have been startled by their
reply: "Sterling Price." Either the irony of fate or human
malice was forcing the high-minded minister, by compelling
him to mention the name of a famous rebel major-general,
to introduce a secular subject into his church service! For in
this matter he had no option: under the rules prescribed by
the Directory for Worship of the Presbyterian Church,[109] there
was certainly no authorization for declining to perform the
sacrament on account of the baptismal name chosen. As Dr.

[107] Speech of Dr. McPheeters, *ibid.*

[108] For Dr. McPheeters' arguments on this subject *cf.* his speech during
the ninth day of the session, as reported in the *Presbyterian,* June 7, 1862.

[109] Dr. McPheeters quoted chapter viii, section 5, of the Directory for
Worship to vindicate his stand. There seems to be no question of the cor-
rectness of his position in this matter. *Cf.* Thompson, *op. cit.,* p. 164. For
Dr. McPheeters' own statement *cf.* Grasty, *op. cit.,* pp. 126-127. For the
rules cited, *cf.* Moore, William E., *ed., The Presbyterian Digest.* . . .
(Philadelphia, 1886) p. 796.

N. L. Rice, in defending Dr. McPheeters, later pointed out, if the name had been Beelzebub it might hardly have been proper to falter.[110] Probably the assertion that the infant was dressed in rebel colors had no foundation in fact,[111] though one certainly hesitates to delete from the story so picturesque a detail. At any rate, the child was given the desired name and the patriots of the congregation chose to interpret the pastor's part in the ceremony as proof of his sympathy with the rebel cause.[112]

Declaring that "the baptism of the child of Samuel Robbins, in our Church, on the 8th instant, by the name of that arch rebel and traitor, Sterling Price, we regard as a premeditated insult to the government and all its friends in the Pine Street Church," a faction of the church addressed to Dr. McPheeters a communication making "minute inquiries" in regard to their pastor's loyalty.[113] These the man on principle refused to answer, although he mentioned that he had twice before coming to Missouri taken an oath of allegiance to the Constitution of the United States (adding, "To me that oath has not grown old") and had recently fulfilled the state Convention's requirement of an oath from those who solemnized the civil part of the marriage contract. Commenting on the dissatisfaction expressed with his practice of following literally the Biblical injunction to "pray for kings and all who are in authority" instead of making supplications specifically for the President of the United States, the pastor declared that to him it was very plain that "neither the Scriptures, the Church of God, nor Christianity *know anything of prayer as a means of showing loyalty, or of praying up to the requirements of some*

[110] *Ibid.*, p. 282. Dr. Rice made this statement in his speech in defense of Dr. McPheeters in the General Assembly of 1864.

[111] The chief accuser before the General Assembly of 1864 made this statement, though he admitted not having been present at the ceremony. Dr. McPheeters declared that he saw no rebel colors. *Ibid.*, p. 276.

[112] This incident is related in Grasty, *op. cit.*, pp. 123-129; also in Thompson, *op. cit.*, p. 164.

[113] Grasty, *op. cit.*, p. 123.

popular standard of loyalty."[114]   The patriot element at a special meeting unanimously resolved that the pastor's communication was not satisfactory, " for the reason that it entirely omitted to inform us whether Mr. McPheeters was a friend or an enemy of the Government of the United States," and that it should not be published, " as its publication would only confirm the opinion of his disloyalty " and thus for them intensify the " odium of being a secession church." They declared that they should feel constrained to abandon their church " until a cordial obedience to the lawfully constituted authorities of the State and opposition to treason are taught from the pulpit and by the private influence and example of the pastor." [115]

This action, however, was taken some three months after the receipt of the pastor's communication, and the eighteen or twenty who " unanimously " expressed their disapproval of his letter were but a fraction of the number who had signed the original request.[116] Evidently the " bitter-enders " in this affair represented but a small minority of the 300 communicant members of the congregation.[117] After Dr. McPheeters had sent a second communication to the dissatisfied group, his accusers changed their method of attack and published their next charges in a letter appearing in the *Missouri Democrat* in December, 1862.[118] Meanwhile a petition calling for a dissolution of the pastoral relation was being circulated among the parishioners [119] — a most extraordinary proceeding in the Presbyterian Church.

All of this activity bore fruit first in a remarkable order by

[114] Dr. McPheeters' letter is given *ibid.*, pp. 124-129.

[115] *Ibid.*, 129-130.

[116] For the history of the whole correspondence, *cf.* letter of Dr. McPheeters of November 3, 1862, *ibid.*, pp. 130-139.

[117] In 1862 the communicant membership of the church, as reported to the General Assembly, was 308. *Cf. Minutes of the General Assembly,* 1862, vol. xvi, p. 781. In a letter dated December 22, 1862, Dr. McPheeters asserted that four-fifths of his church continued to support him. *Cf.* Grasty, *op. cit.,* p. 146.

[118] In the issue of December 13, 1862. *Cf.* Grasty, *op. cit.,* p. 141.

[119] *Ibid.*, pp. 147-148.

the military, six days after the publication of the charges in the *Missouri Democrat*. The order was as follows:

Office Provost Marshal General,
Department of the Missouri,
St. Louis, Mo., December 19, 1862.

[Special Order No. 152]

Whereas, On account of unmistakable evidence of sympathy with the rebellion on the part of Rev. Samuel B. McPheeters, Pastor of the Pine Street Church, certain loyal members of his congregation, about six months since, urged him to avow his sentiments openly, and to take a stand in favor of the Government, which he has refused to do, and has also . . . failed to remove a widespread and increasing impression that he desires the success of the rebel cause; and . . . has used all the influence of his ministerial character to prevent the body of the Church . . . from declaring or manifesting its loyalty to the Government, and has refused to observe, in their obvious meaning and intent, the recommendations of the President of the United States to the various churches, and has allowed the influence of his wife, his brothers and intimate associates to seduce him from an open and manly support of the Government into active sympathy with the rebellion . . . ; and, whereas, in all his course of unfriendliness to the Government, and sympathy with, and favor to, rebels, the said McPheeters has been stimulated and encouraged, if not led on, by his wife, who openly avows herself a rebel; whereby the said McPheeters and his wife have forfeited the right to the protection and favor of the Government in their present position, and have become pro-moters of rebellion and civil discord. Therefore, it is ordered that the said McPheeters and his wife leave the State of Missouri, within ten days after the service of this order, and that they take up their residence within the Free States, north of Indianapolis and west of Pennsylvania, and remain there during the war, and that the said McPheeters cease from this date to exercise the functions of his office within the State of Mis-souri, and that he deliver to the Clerk of Pine Street Church all books, records and papers belonging to that Church.

It is further ordered, that the church edifice, books and papers . . . be placed under the control of three loyal members of Pine Street Church, namely . . . who shall see that its pulpit be filled by a loyal minister of the Gospel, who can invoke the blessing of the head of the Church upon the efforts of the Government to re-establish its authority.

By command of Major-General Curtis.
F. A. Dick,
Provost Marshal General Dep't of the Missouri.[120]

Quite apparently it was proving difficult to trump up evi-

---

[120] McPherson, *op. cit.*, p. 533. The order is also given in Grasty, *op. cit.*, pp. 148-149.

dence against the accused man. The order furnished excellent subject-matter for the anti-administration press. The New York *Express* pointed out that the order was unaccompanied by a single proof of any one of its allegations.[121] " Is it America? Is this the nineteenth century? Do men imagine that God is to be worshiped in compulsory forms in this country? ", exclaimed the *Journal of Commerce*, adding that if Mr. Lincoln approved the act he would do well at once to import a quantity of Chinese praying machines, put his proclamation in them, and set them at work with Provost-Marshals to grind out prayers for the nation.[122] The *Leader*, a British-Canadian journal, reminding its readers of the Virginia magistrate who in the old times had sentenced a man to receive twenty lashes because his wife stole wool, expressed its amazement that this novel sort of application of the husband's responsibilty was still current in American military courts. This journal suggested the propriety of a further military order " requiring every man and *his wife* and child to visit the praying machine, every Sunday at least, under pain of banishment; for, in the new theory of religion, of what use are the prayers if no audience is present to be made *loyal*, or preserved in their *loyalty*, by them?" [123]

Impressed with the importance of the principle involved in the military order, Dr. McPheeters almost immediately determined to present his case directly to President Lincoln, certain that he could procure an early interview with the Chief Executive through the agency of Attorney-General Bates, who was himself an elder in the Old School Church [124] and a warm personal friend of the accused pastor.[125] Determined to appeal to Mr. Lincoln against the authority of the military to con-

[121] Quoted in Grasty, *op. cit.*, p. 150. This editorial is also quoted in the *True Presbyterian*, February 26, 1863.

[122] Quoted in Grasty, *op. cit.*, pp. 150-151; also in *True Presbyterian*, February 26, 1863.

[123] Quoted in Grasty, *op. cit.*, pp. 151-152.

[124] Smyth, Thomas, *Complete Works* (10 vol., Flinn, J. W., *ed.*, Columbia, 1908-12), vol. vii, p. 573.

[125] Grasty, *op. cit.*, p. 159.

trol the Church, Dr. McPheeters courteously declined to accept from the Attorney-General's brother-in-law, Governor Gamble,[126] a letter asking for the alleged traitor's release on the ground that the writer knew him to be loyal and of perfect integrity and faithfulness in all obligations. Such a request, the appellant reasoned, would at once procure his release, but at the sacrifice of the opportunity of presenting to the President the arguments against military dictation to the pulpit.[127]

Upon the completion of the three-day journey to Washington,[128] accompanied by Mr. Bates he put his case before the President. Dr. McPheeters' picture of the visit reveals the sympathy, fair-mindedness, and common sense which characterized Mr. Lincoln in all of his interviews with people in trouble. He said that he did not know that the rebellion would be put down; he doubted if the Government had the power to suppress it — the means that were necessary, it seemed, the country would not allow. He remarked that if the order against the pastor should be revoked, it would be regarded as a secession triumph. " I presume if you were in Jeff. Davis' dominions you would preach and pray differently from what you do here? " he inquired, but Dr. McPheeters promptly replied that as a minister of the Gospel he " conducted the worship of God's house without reference to human government." The Attorney-General staunchly defended the principle for which his ministerial friend was contending. The President was perplexed, and walked back and forth across the room as he tried to think out the problem. Finally he decided to take the matter under further advisement, and having been reminded that the ten-day respite granted Dr. McPheeters and

---

[126] Hamilton Rowan Gamble, Provisional Governor of Missouri from July 31, 1861, until his death, January 31, 1864. *Presbyterian Encyclopaedia*, pp. 256-257.

[127] *Cf.* Mrs. McPheeters' account of this incident, Grasty, *op. cit.*, pp. 159-161.

[128] " Owing to not making the necessary connection," Dr. McPheeters and Capt. W. W. Greene, an elder in his church, who accompanied him, were delayed in their arrival. Grasty, *op. cit.*, p. 183.

his family had nearly expired, he immediately wrote a dispatch to General Curtis suspending the order against them until further instructions came from Washington.[129]

When the harassed pastor reached his home he found this message awaiting him:

> Office of the Provost Marshal Gen'l,
> Department of the Missouri,
> St. Louis, Mo., Dec. 28, 1862.
>
> Rev. S. B. McPheeters and Wife:
>
> The order made against you on the 19th of December, is modified until further orders, to this extent: that you are not required to leave the State.
>
> By order of Major General Curtis:
> F. A. Dick,
> *Lieut. Col., Provost Marshal General.*[130]

It looked to the parties most concerned as though the military authorities were interpreting the orders of the Chief Executive about as they pleased.[131] A few days later the President sent General Curtis the further instructions which his previous order had suggested would be forthcoming. Frankly admitting that he believed that Dr. McPheeters did sympathize with the rebels, he pointed out that the charges against him were all general in character, and expressed doubt whether a man of unquestioned good moral character who had taken such an oath as he had, and could be charged neither with violating it, nor with committing any other specific objectionable act, could "with safety to this government be exiled upon the suspicion of his secret sympathies." But he agreed that the question must be left to the authorities who were on the spot; "and if, after all," he wrote, "you think the public good requires his removal, my suspension of the order is withdrawn, only with this qualification, that the time during the supension is not to

---

[129] Dr. McPheeters' own interesting account of his interview with the President (upon which the above narrative is largely based), is given in Grasty, *op. cit.*, pp. 183-186.

[130] McPherson, *op. cit.*, p. 534.

[131] *Cf.* extract of letter of Dr. McPheeters to Attorney-General Bates, Grasty, *op. cit.*, pp. 186-187.

be counted against him. I have promised him this."[132] Then
the President added a suggestion expressed in one of those
homely phrases that his people were so fond of repeating:

> But I must add that the United States Government must not, as by this
> order, undertake to run the churches. When an individual, in a church
> or out of it, becomes dangerous to the public interest, he must be checked;
> but let the churches, as such, take care of themselves.
>
> It will not do for the United States to appoint Trustees, Supervisors,
> or other agents for the churches.[133]

The military authorities in Missouri, however, appeared not
to have such scruples against undertaking to "run the
churches." Some two months after the receipt of the President's letter the Pine Street Church building was released, but
the minister was still in bonds.[134] A little later General Curtis
showed a disposition to give him another chance and submitted
for his answer two specific questions as to whether he wished
the rebellion crushed and the success of the Federal forces.
The minister replied by reminding the General that before the
General Assembly of 1862 he had openly repelled the charge
of disloyalty and that he had taken the Convention oath in
Missouri; he then reiterated that he must decline on principle
to answer questions which required a minister of the Gospel to
express his views on political matters.

Even though the military authorities were indicating a will-
ingness to be placated, the "loyal" minority of the congrega-
tion were relentless. Discovering that they were urging the
Government to take action against such members of the St.
Louis Presbytery as refused to expel him, Dr. McPheeters de-
termined when this body convened, to hand in his resignation.
This, however, the Presbytery refused to accept, and the Pine
Street congregation by a vote of 91 to 56 requested their pastor

[132] At the opening of his letter, Mr. Lincoln acknowledged receipt of a
letter from General Curtis written on December 29, 1862, "by the hand
of Mr. Strong." Mr. Strong was the leading member of the minority in
the Pine Street Church which was opposed to Dr. McPheeters.

[133] President Lincoln's letter is given in full in McPherson, *op. cit.*, p. 534.

[134] Grasty, *op. cit.*, p. 187.

to withdraw his resignation. Yet he was still by military order prevented from preaching to them. Unwilling to accept his salary under these circumstances, he obtained employment in the office of a government official. No objection was raised on the part of government officials when he undertook to practice in the United States Court of Claims. He voted in political elections without challenge or objection. And yet, as he himself pointed out, it would have been a military offense for him to preach a sermon, to sit in an ecclesiastical court,[135] to administer the Lord's Supper, or to officiate at a funeral.[136] This anomalous condition was brought to the attention of Attorney-General Bates,[137] and by him referred to President Lincoln.[138]

About the same time the President received a number of petitions from friends of the St. Louis pastor, and on December 22, 1863, he sent a reply to one of the petitioners in which he reiterated his views on government interference in church matters. Quoting from his letter to General Curtis the sentences in which he had defined those views, he added:

This letter, going to General Curtis, then in command there, I supposed, of course, it was obeyed, especially as I heard no further complaint from Dr. McPheeters or his friends for nearly an entire year. I have never interfered, nor thought of interfering as to who shall or shall not preach in any church; nor have I knowingly or believingly tolerated any one else to so interfere by my authority. If any one is so interfering, by color of my authority, I would like to have it specifically made known to me.

If, after all, what is now sought, is to have me put Doctor M. back over the head of a majority of his own congregation, that, too, will be declined. I will not have any control of any church on any side.[139]

Attorney General Bates wrote directly to Dr. McPheeters, advising him to quietly resume the rights, duties, and functions

[135] General Curtis ruled that he might not attend meetings of his Presbytery. General Schofield, who succeeded General Curtis, permitted him to attend for the purposes of defending his character, but not to sit as a member. Grasty, *op. cit.*, p. 192.
[136] General Curtis ruled thus. *Ibid.*
[137] By Governor Gamble. *Ibid.*, p. 198.
[138] *Cf.* letter of Bates, *ibid.*, pp. 198-199.
[139] This letter is given in McPherson, *op. cit.*, p. 536.

of his office as if no interruption had occurred. He was writing, he explained, with the express permission of the President.[140]

Thus a little more than a year after the original order of banishment all military disabilities against the pastor were removed, and in January, 1864, at the earnest solicitation of a large portion of the Pine Street congregation, he again resumed his labors among his people. But although the military authorities had ceased interfering, the "loyal" agitators in the Church were far from giving up their campaign against him. Several of the disaffected members of the congregation, it is true, had taken pews in the New School Church,[141] but the leader of this element in the congregation was more active than ever, and had succeeded in obtaining support from other Old School Presbyterians in the state. In June, 1863, six months before President Lincoln's second letter had removed the military disabilities against the St. Louis pastor, the Presbytery of St. Louis at a *pro-re-nata* meeting [142] had dissolved the pastoral relation between Dr. McPheeters and his congregation.[143] An appeal against this action was carried to the Synod of Missouri at its October session; but the Synod, finding that certain interested parties were not able to be present, decided to postpone the matter until the next Synod.[144]

In the meantime came Mr. Lincoln's second letter and the resumption by Dr. McPheeters of the pastoral relations which military orders had for more than a year prevented him from performing. True, his Presbytery had six months earlier declared such relations dissolved, but he assumed that the dissolution was arrested until the appeal before the Synod of Mis-

---

[140] Attorney General Bates' letter is given *ibid.*, pp. 198-199.

[141] *Cf.* letter of Dr. McPheeters to Rev. A. Munson, dated February 17, 1864, *ibid.*, pp. 200-201.

[142] This was the third meeting of the Presbytery — and its second special meeting — in the spring of 1863. *Ibid.*, pp. 192, 203.

[143] *Ibid.*, p. 203.

[144] An extract from the minutes of the Synod of Missouri bearing on this subject is given *ibid.*, p. 206.

souri was decided.[145]   However, the eighteen men—out of
nearly sixty qualified members—who attended the meeting of
the Presbytery of St. Louis in April, 1864, thought differently.
Calling attention to its action of the previous year on Dr. Mc-
Pheeters' case, this body expressed regret at learning that he
was still officiating as minister of the Pine Street Church; it
resolved that "the peace and harmony and spiritual interest"
of that church, "as well as a proper respect for the feelings of
a large minority opposed to the ministrations of their former
pastor, require that Dr. McPheeters shall cease all connection
with that Church and no longer attempt to minister to that congregation."[146]

A number of the members of the Presbytery—Dr. Mc-
Pheeters among them—had refrained from attending this
meeting, being unwilling to comply with General Rosecrans'
famous "Order No. 61,"[147] though they assured the General
that they had taken the Convention Oath, would support the
Constitution and laws of the United States, and would not
give aid or comfort to the enemies of either Missouri or the
United States. They had protested that they could not "allow
any human authority to determine the qualifications of members who compose our Ecclesiastical Courts" as in their opinion the Rosecrans order required them to do, and they had
requested the General to allow them "as loyal citizens" to
assemble without let or hindrance.[148]   But as this request had
not been heeded, these conscientious objectors had stayed away
from the meeting.[149]   Obviously their absence was ruinous to
Dr. McPheeters' interests, and it is not surprising that after

[145] *Cf.* statement of Judge Wood before the General Assembly of 1864,
ibid., p. 203.

[146] The action taken by this April, 1864, meeting of the Presbytery of
St. Louis is recorded *ibid.,* p. 206.

[147] *Cf. ante,* pp. 212-216.

[148] The interesting petition which these objectors sent to General Rosecrans is given in Grasty, *op. cit.,* pp. 217-218.

[149] Fully one-fourth (a majority of the majority) of the members of the
Presbytery could not "conscientiously attend" the meeting of the Presbytery. *Ibid.,* p. 218.

the Presbytery had taken its hostile action in the spring of
1864, a seemingly paradoxical move was made — a majority of
the ministers and sessions of the Presbytery of St. Louis drew
up a formal protest against its decision. This memorial, together with a complaint signed by six of the seven elders of
the Pine Street Church and another complaint from Dr. Mc-
Pheeters, was forwarded to the General Assembly of 1864 and
became the basis of the appeal action.

In form the case was perfectly simple. It would seem to
present simply the two questions as to whether the Presbytery
of St. Louis had the right to prohibit Dr. McPheeters from
preaching in the Pine Street Church and whether the act by
which this was done was itself wise and just. But although
simple in form, the case was in reality, according to Dr. Hodge,
who gave it extended attention in his account of the General
Assembly of 1864,[150] " one of the most comprehensive cases
in facts and principles, and one of the most important in its
bearings that ever claimed the attention of the General Assembly." [151] There were intricate constitutional points as to the
technical status of the case — depending on whether the various actions of the Presbytery had been executive or judicial
in character and whether the case had come before the Synod
of Missouri as a complaint or as an appeal. There was the
peculiar circumstance that for the first time the accused man
was present at the consideration of his case: during the various hearings in 1863 he had been disqualified by the military
orders from attending ecclesiastical bodies as a member, and
in 1864 he had refused to attend the meeting of his presbytery
because of the Rosecrans' oath requirement. On the other

[150] Article, " The General Assembly," *Biblical Repertory and Princeton
Review*, July, 1864, vol. 36, pp. 506-574. Pp. 551-574 deal with the Mc-
Pheeters case and furnish an excellent summary of the whole affair. Because of the vast amount of documentary evidence given in Grasty, *op.
cit.*, most of the facts given in the present monograph have been taken
from that source, but all of the statements made are substantiated by Dr.
Hodge in his account.

[151] *Biblical Repertory and Princeton Review*, July, 1864, vol. 36, p. 552.

hand, his chief accuser (the one opposing elder of his congregation) had once been permitted to address the Presbytery even though not a member, and had at another time obtained by trickery election as a commissioner to a meeting of the Presbytery which was to decide on the pastor's case.[152]   Then there was the anomalous situation created by the opposition of a large majority of the congregation and of the Presbytery to the carrying out of what purported to be the action of the Presbytery.   Were the eleven members of the Presbytery who separated the pastor from his flock the Presbytery? " In a technical, legal, constitutional sense, they are entitled to be so regarded," wrote Dr. Hodge, " but in a fair, honourable, moral, and righteous sense, they are not." [153]   Some of the practices followed in the hearing of the case in the Assembly were irregular in character.   In his six-hour speech Dr. McPheeters' chief accuser was allowed to include a great deal of testimony — testimony not before the lower court, not on record, given without the sanction of an oath, without the opportunity of cross-examination or contradiction.   His very admission as " one of the original parties " was certainly open to question.   Surely the points of doubtful regularity in this case were many and involved.[154]

Considering the various elements involved in this case, soberminded men like Dr. Hodge " expected fully that his [Dr. McPheeters'] complaint would be sustained and his rights vindicated." [155]   The history of the case was marked by points of

[152] On May 27, 1863, at a special meeting to consider the resignation of the pastor, the Pine Street congregation by a vote of 91 to 56 declined to accept the resignation. When, near midnight, a large part of the meeting had withdrawn, Mr. George Strong, the one hostile elder, got himself elected by the minority remaining, as commissioner to the meeting of the Presbytery. At a subsequent meeting of the congregation, protest was made against his serving unless he would carry out the wishes of the majority. Mr. Strong went to the Presbytery and pleaded the cause of the minority. *Ibid.,* pp. 553-554; 573-574.
[153] *Ibid.,* p. 572.
[154] The statements of this paragraph are based upon Dr. Hodge's account, *ibid.*
[155] *Ibid.,* p. 559.

questionable regularity; Dr. McPheeters himself was universally respected and beloved; he had taken and kept a stringent oath of allegiance to the Government; the President and the Attorney General of the United States pronounced themselves so satisfied with his loyalty that they forbade interference with him on the part of the authorities; his conduct and the performance of his ministerial duties had been such as to retain for him the affection and confidence of the vast majority of his congregation and four-fifths of the members of his Presbytery.[156] In view of these conditions and circumstances it was certainly justifiable to expect Dr. McPheeters' complaint to be sustained. Such an outcome was rendered all the more likely by the clearness and power of the arguments of his supporters. Dr. N. L. Rice and Dr. W. L. Breckinridge, venerable ex-Moderators of the Assembly, were convincingly eloquent. If the pulpit conduct of the former [157] and the border-state home of the latter [157] detracted from their effectiveness before a Northern Assembly, such could not be true in the case of the vigorously pro-Union Dr. George Junkin [159] and the "zealously loyal" [160] President Maclean of Princeton College, or of the eminent lawyers who as lay-commissioners helped plead the case of the harassed pastor.[161] Yet when the wearisome arguments were finally ended and the Assembly after days of debate was ready to vote, the decision was overwhelmingly against Dr. McPheeters: 47 voted to sustain his complaints;

---

[156] This summary is based upon that of Dr. Hodge, *ibid.*, p. 574.

[157] *Cf. ante*, pp. 283-285.

[158] Dr. Breckinridge (brother of Dr. R. J. Breckinridge) was President of Centre College in Danville, Kentucky.

[159] *Cf. ante*, p. 291.

[160] Dr. Hodge termed him thus. *Biblical Repertory and Princeton Review*, July, 1864, vol. 36, p. 555.

[161] Among the distinguished lawyer members of the Assembly who defended the St. Louis pastor were Judge Martin Ryerson of New Jersey and Mr. H. Murray of the Presbytery of Carlisle (in Pennsylvania, with the exception of some three churches in Maryland). Judge W. T. Wood, an elder in Dr. McPheeters' church, presented his case.

322   THE PRESBYTERIAN CHURCHES, 1861-1869

2 to sustain in part; while 119 voted not to sustain.[162] However doubtful the procedure in the case, the Assembly was not doubtful as to how it should be decided.

Dr. Hodge's expectation that the complaint would be sustained was a perfectly reasonable one. Had he been in a position to listen to the debates and note the character of the arguments against Dr. McPheeters, he would no doubt have found his confidence rapidly slipping. In fact, after he had had an opportunity to read the great masses of irregular testimony admitted, Dr. Hodge concluded, " The form which the matter evidently took was — Here is a disloyal minister and a loyal Presbytery, whose side will you take? There could, of course, be but one answer to that question." [163] One speaker on the floor of the Assembly put the matter more baldly. Asserting that he had heard the facts in the case " by *common fame* " before he came to the General Assembly, he declared that " some had attempted to befog this subject by *quoad hocs, fiat justitias, delenda est Carthagos;* but they could not befog *him* with their Latin." Then, likening the present rebellion to that of Absalom, in which the tribe of Levi had remained faithful to the constituted authority, he hoped " that the tribe of Levi would now adhere to the country, and oppose rebellion, and therefore he went for sustaining the Presbytery." [164] The first consideration with the majority in this General Assembly of 1864 — the same Assembly that had unanimously adopted a violent denunciation of slavery and a fiercely loyal endorsement of the Government [165] — was not whether justice should prevail, but rather whether the Assembly should avoid any possible suspicion of disloyalty. Thus it was found necessary to sustain the action of a Presbytery which had decided to punish for disloyalty a man in whom the highest Federal authorities

[162] *Minutes of the General Assembly,* 1864, vol. xvii, p. 312.
[163] *Biblical Repertory and Princeton Review,* July, 1864, vol. 36, p. 568.
[164] *Cf.* speech of Rev. William F. Kean (pastor of the Presbyterian Church at Freeport, Pennsylvania), report of twelfth day of session of General Assembly of 1864, *Presbyterian,* June 25, 1864, p. 2.
[165] *Cf. ante,* pp. 125-128.

could find no fault. Dr. Hodge, who, like many of Dr. Mc-
Pheeters' ablest supporters on the floor of the Assembly, was
vigorously opposed to the principles which motivated the accused man's actions (the " exaggerated doctrine as to the spir-
ituality of the church," [166] opposition to the taking of an oath
as a condition of membership in a church court,[167] and adherence to a policy of neutrality with regard to the war) nevertheless regarded the punishment meted out to him as "an
injustice which has few, if any, parallels in the history of our
church." [168]   But the General Assembly's action revealed that
a majority of the Old School Church had come to the position
that anything short of a positive declaration of loyalty in the
pulpit was justly punishable by the dismissal of a minister,
even though he might have the faithful adherence of a large
majority of his congregation.

The condemnation of Dr. McPheeters for refraining from
positive assertion of his loyalty in the pulpit [169] was but the
natural outcome of a spirit which had been growing in the Old
School Church during the war.   A year before the St. Louis
pastor met his fate at the hands of the 1864 Assembly, the
Presbyter in commenting on "disloyal" ministers had asked,
"Ought not the Church to purge herself from all complicity
with such conduct and rescue congregations from the supervision of men whose patriotism is at so great a discount? " [170]
A few months later the same journal declared:

[166] The " Thornwell theory." *Cf. ante,* pp. 133-134.
[167] Specifically, the " Rosecrans Oath." *Cf. ante,* pp. 212-216.
[168] *Biblical Repertory and Princeton Review,* July, 1864, vol. 36, p. 574.
[169] Dr. R. L. Stanton, a radical anti-slavery and pro-Union man (*cf. ante,*
pp. 220-222), and a strong supporter of the position taken by the Assembly
on the McPheeters case said, in his *The Church and the Rebellion* (pp.
260-261), after remarking that the Doctor regarded himself as *virtually*
on trial for disloyalty, " This is the aspect given to the case by the proceedings of the Assembly, by the arguments on both sides, though not of
course by the judgment."
[170] Editorial, " The West Lexington Presbytery," *Presbyter,* March 11,
1863. The question was asked with regard to disloyalty in the North.

The man who cannot pray for the efficient prosecution of the war, for the success of our armies, and for the destruction of the rebellion; and who fails to express his sentiments in favor of these ends . . . is a traitor at heart, and the churches and the educational institutions, which are encumbered by such men, are justly liable to the imputation of giving their influence for the destruction of the country. Such will be held to a fearful account for their action or inaction in such cases.[171]

The home presbytery of the *Presbyter,* that of Cincinnati, also usually in the forefront of radical sentiment on slavery and political questions, in answer to overtures from some of its church sessions, declared that people staying away from church because of difference of opinion on loyalty should be dealt with by the session of the church according to the "usual course prescribed in all cases of failure in Christian duty." [172] Nor were all of the radicals satisfied with President Lincoln's policy of non-interference with the churches. The patriot Grundy,[173] himself a victim of persecution in the South, was uneasy because a corresponding policy was not carried out with greater rigor in the North, and diagnosed the difficulties in the North with disloyalty as follows:

Here, sir, is the secret and true cause of all that you call "copperhead-ism" — in the North and South. *It is the miserable and lamentable fail-ure of our President to comprehend the nature and power of the ecclesi-astical element of this rebellion.* Treason is bad enough in its civil dress, but in its ecclesiastical garb it is ten fold more potent and dangerous. *And yet Mr. Lincoln has so fallen in love* with the foolish aphorism that "it will not do for the General Government to run churches" that he will punish treason in its civil garb and let it run riot with an ecclesiastical dress! [174]

With sentiments of this type abroad in the Church, it is not surprising that Dr. McPheeters' case was decided against him.

Dr. McPheeters was by no means the only Old School min-

---

[171] Editorial, "Disloyal Ministers," *ibid.,* August 12, 1863.

[172] *Cf. True Presbyterian,* October 29, 1863.

[173] *Cf. ante,* pp. 292-293.

[174] Communication of Dr. Grundy to the Memphis *Bulletin* [?] of August 20, 1864, copied in *True Presbyterian* (in article, "Indications of the Failure of the Cincinnati Presbytery's Modest Embassage to President Lincoln"), September 15, 1864.

ister in Missouri who suffered for alleged " disloyalty," though his case was the most important because of the widespread attention that it received and the peculiar principles that it involved. Ministers in that state were especially likely to get into difficulties not only because of the widespread adoption there of the Thornwell theory of the ultra-spiritual character of the Church, but also because of certain governmental obstacles: the state " Convention Oath " of 1861,[175] the " Rosecrans Oath " of 1864,[176] and the famous " Test Oath " of 1865. After that of Dr. McPheeters, the most conspicuous case was concerned with Dr. Robert P. Farris, pastor of the Presbyterian Church in St. Charles, Missouri. Dr. Farris' refusal to take a special oath of allegiance and to give bond in the sum of two thousand dollars led to his arrest and a hearing before the General then commanding the District.[177] The General decided that this was a clear case of " general disloyalty " and sentenced Dr. Farris to be confined in a military prison during the war.[178] Later the sentence was commuted to banishment to any point north and east of St. Louis. The intervention of Judge David Davis of the Supreme Court of the United States brought a General Order covering all such cases,[179] together with a special message from the President that Dr. Farris would be released under this order. When, however, the accused man showed this letter in the President's handwriting to the Provost-Marshal-General in St. Louis [180] (the same official who had " modified " the order of banishment in Dr. McPheeters' case), instead of being freed he was ordered to go into exile in Chicago. Judge Davis again intervened, and this time obtained from the President a special order for Dr. Farris' unconditional release.[181] So after four months' absence,

[175] *Cf. ante*, p. 309.
[176] *Cf. ante*, pp. 212-216.
[177] Brigadier General Lewis Merrill. *Cf.* Leftwich, *op. cit.*, vol. ii, p. 86.
[178] *Ibid.*, p. 87.
[179] *Ibid.*, p. 89.
[180] Franklin A. Dick. *Ibid.*
[181] *Ibid.*

the man was allowed to return to his family and his church. Yet his peace was not to last long. Charges of treasonable plots brought his arrest a second time, but a protracted interview satisfied the military authorities, and he was released without bond, oath, or parole. His next difficulty came in connection with the Rosecrans Oath. When he refused to take this oath as a means to being recognized as a member of his presbytery, he was arrested and put on parole "to appear when called for." He was never called for. Finally he was indicted for preaching the gospel without taking the oath required by the 1865 constitution of the state. This case was dismissed before coming to trial.[182]   In each of the troubles encountered by Dr. Farris, the immediate action was brought by either Federal or State authorities; the Church courts did not, as in the case of Dr. McPheeters, molest him. Nevertheless Dr. Farris and his friends were certain that behind each of the moves of the governmental authorities lay the unwearied activities of the patriot party in the Church.[183]

It was another Missouri clergyman, Dr. S. J. P. Anderson of the Central Presbyterian Church of St. Louis, who had the doubtful distinction of being the only Old School minister in the non-secession states to be formally tried before the military authorities on a charge of disloyalty to the Federal Government. The eleven "specifications" adduced to substantiate the charge listed a formidable array of alleged shortcomings and errors on the part of the pastor, but although he was accused of uttering disloyal expressions and openly denouncing Federal activities, it was not asserted that any of the objectionable statements had been made in the pulpit. Among the

---

[182] More correctly, when the case came up for trial Dr. Farris was not present. The judge and the circuit attorney were about to enter upon the records that he had forfeited his bail when this "cowardly trick" was prevented by the accused man's counsel's appearance with the word that his client was within call and ready for trial. Thereupon the case was continued until the next term, and then dismissed. *Ibid.*, p. 91.

[183] The account of Dr. Farris' trials is taken largely from *ibid.*, pp. 83-93. More than half of the story as there given is in the pastor's own words.

accusations were statements that Dr. Anderson had "asserted and maintained, avowed and admitted, that rebellion is not a sin; . . ." and that "loyalty had nothing to do with the qualification for membership in the church, Synod, and other religious bodies." The Military Commission "after mature deliberation and reflection" found the prisoner guilty of all of the specifications and of the charge and sentenced him to be "sent south of the lines of the Federal army at as early a day as practicable." The proceedings of the Military Commission were, however, disapproved by the Commanding General on the ground that there had been a defect in the orders convening the Commission, the number of members being below the minimum prescribed by the War Department's orders.[184] It is apparent from the specifications named that a chief source of Dr. Anderson's difficulties lay in his observance of the Thornwell theory of pulpit silence on political matters. Dr. Anderson was not further disturbed by the military authorities, but patriots in the Old School Church, like Dr. Robert J. Breckinridge, were not quick to forget the accusations made against him and persisted in regarding him as a traitor.[185]

The inclusion of the famous loyalty-oath requirement in the new Constitution of Missouri in 1865 barring ministers, among other classes, from continuing the practice of their profession if they failed to take a specified stringent oath to the effect that they had never been disloyal in deed, word, or thought,[186] called forth the bitter opposition of all who had objected to the Rosecrans oath. Among these non-juring Old School clergymen in

---

[184] For the proceedings in the Anderson case, *cf.* McPherson, *op. cit.,* pp. 537-538.

[185] *Cf. ante,* p. 246.

[186] The substance of this oath is given in Leftwich, *op. cit.,* pp. 228; 232-235. This oath requirement was declared unconstitutional on the ground of its being *ex post facto* in nature, by the United States Supreme Court in the case of *Cummings v. the State of Missouri* (4 Wallace, 277). Mr. Justice Field in delivering the opinion of the Court stated, "The oath thus required is, for its severity, without any precedent that we can discover."

Missouri the brilliant Dr. James H. Brookes,[187] pastor of the Sixteenth Street Presbyterian Church in St. Louis, became particularly conspicuous in his condemnation of the obnoxious constitutional provision. Before the sixty days allotted to ministers and others to take the oath had expired, Dr. Brookes published a pamphlet addressed to all of the ministers and members of the Presbyterian Church in Missouri.[188] Its "effect upon the Missouri ministry *at the time* can not be overestimated," declared a Methodist brother.[189] Dr. J. L. Yantis,[190] one of the pioneers of Presbyterianism in Missouri[191] was particularly active in "lifting up the weak hands and strengthening the feeble knees of his brethren"[192] in western Missouri by boldly preaching from place to place in that section without having taken the required oath.

There were many other Old School clergymen in Missouri who became conspicuous for alleged lack of loyalty.[193] There might be a great amount of potential disloyalty in Kentucky, but patriots were more successful — thanks to the actions of military and state authorities — in "detecting" it in Missouri. Dr. Brookes named a dozen men who, he asserted, "were 'in perils of robbers, and in perils by their own countrymen, and in perils among false brethren.'" Some of these were compelled to flee for their lives, some were banished from their

---

[187] Dr. Brookes later delivered the most effective speech in favor of the "Declaration and Testimony" men when action was being considered against the Presbytery of Louisville in the General Assembly of 1866. *Cf. ante*, pp. 249-251.

[188] Leftwich, *op. cit.*, p. 276.

[189] *Ibid.* Dr. W. M. Leftwich was a leading member of the Methodist Church, South, in Missouri.

[190] Of Dresden, (later of Westport), Missouri.

[191] *Cf. Presbyterian Encyclopaedia,* p. 1051.

[192] *Cf.* Dr. Brookes' statement in Leftwich, *op. cit.,* p. 221.

[193] Besides Dr. McPheeters, Dr. Anderson, and Dr. Farris, he named Rev. William H. Parks (pastor in Providence, Mo.); Rev. A. D. Madeira (pastor of the Park Ave. Church in St. Louis); Rev. James Morton (stated supply at Boonville, Mo.); Rev. T. C. Smith (pastor, Creve Coeur, Mo.); Rev. J. A. Quarles (pastor, Glasgow, Mo.); Rev. J. M. Chaney (pastor, Dover, Mo.); Rev. B. M. Hobson (pastor, Lexington, Mo.); Rev. R. S. Symington (without charge, Kansas City, Mo.). *Cf. ibid.,* p. 217.

homes, and nearly all were in prison for weeks or months. "Indeed," declared Dr. Brookes, "there was scarcely a Presbyterian minister of the Gospel in Missouri who attended only to the work which his Master had given him to do without being brought by it into great and sore troubles. Those who used their sacred office to further political schemes, and were willing to barter the kingly crown of Jesus for the smiles of human government, rode on the high places of the earth; but those who determined to know nothing but Christ and Him crucified were sure to be suspected and persecuted." Yet how difficult was the task of the Government authorities and the self-appointed Church patriots in this matter of determining the loyalty of Old School men in Missouri and deciding upon a mode of procedure with regard to them, is made clear by Dr. Brookes' further statements:

It is probable that all whose names I have given were in sympathy with the people of the South; but it is certain that some of them had no sympathy with the effort to divide the Union, and that they openly preached and personally practiced the duty of subjection to the powers that be, according to the plain teachings of God's Word. I do not believe that any of them ever said a word or performed an act that was inconsistent with their obligations to Government as good citizens and sincere Christians; but because they desired to stand aloof from the contest, and to discharge the trust committed to them by the Head of the Church, they were exposed to insult and violence every day for five long and terrible years.[194]

These words were written from the point of view of the "persecuted," but they probably reveal accurately the sources of the difficulties among Old School Presbyterians in Missouri.

The war years had demonstrated the dangers to be encountered by any Old School minister who showed any sympathy for the Southern cause or who remained too obviously silent on the political situation. For such the war period was one of personal disaster. Conversely, for such as had by their "radical" anti-slavery notions in the pre-war era come into disrepute in the Church, these were years of triumph. In no single

---

[194] From a chapter by Dr. James H. Brookes on "martyrdom" among Old School Presbyterians in Missouri. *Ibid.*, pp. 217-218.

instance was this more strikingly illustrated than in the case of Dr. E. D. MacMaster.[195]   Dr. MacMaster had for years been regarded as the most strongly anti-slavery man among the leaders of the Old School Church.   Years later the son of Dr. Thomas E. Thomas wrote of him as "first in ability, and first in the effort, and finally, in the sacrifice he made, in the anti-slavery contest in the Presbyterian Church."[196]   There is no doubt that Dr. MacMaster suffered for his anti-slavery convictions.   After having served successively as president of Hanover College (1838-1845) and of Miami University (1845-1849) and as professor in the New Albany Theological Seminary (1849-1859), when the last-named institution was taken under the control of the General Assembly and moved to Chicago to become the Seminary of the Northwest, Dr. MacMaster was decisively rejected for a professorship in the new institution, and the place was given to Dr. N. L. Rice.[197]

There is not the slightest question that the principal factor prompting the General Assembly in its choice was the anti-slavery record of Dr. MacMaster.   During the ten years of his professorship in the New Albany Seminary he had devoted his energies chiefly toward "maintaining, reviving, moderating, and directing the anti-slavery sentiment of the church."[198] Such a man was not to be entrusted with a position of responsibility in the new Seminary at Chicago — particularly not in view of the fact that the Seminary had just been promised a gift of one hundred thousand dollars by Cyrus McCormick.[199] The rejection of Dr. MacMaster amounted to virtual banishment from the Old School Church; for seven years he was without regular employment in the denomination, and was forced to depend upon farming to eke out a living.[200]   But the revolution which the war wrought in Old School sentiment

[195] *Cf. ante,* pp. 170; 294-295.
[196] Thomas, *op. cit.,* p. 55.
[197] *Cf. ante,* p. 294.
[198] Thomas, *op. cit.,* p. 56.
[199] *Presbyterian Encyclopaedia,* p. 580.
[200] Thomas, *op. cit.,* p. 56.

brought a compete change in this man's fortunes.[201]   In the
radical-controlled General Assembly of 1866 he was, by an almost unanimous vote,[202] elected to the McCormick Professorship of Didactic and Polemic Theology in the Seminary of
the Northwest.

It is easy to believe the statement made by the son of Dr.
MacMaster's good friend, Dr. Thomas E. Thomas, that nothing in his father's whole life had given him greater pleasure
than to be chosen to notify the professor-elect of his appointment.[203]   For the election was a triumph for the whole radical
party.   Dr. Thomas' note accompanying his formal letter of
notification clearly reveals this significance:

Mr. McCormick was soon aware that you would be chosen by a very
large majority.   Such was his displeasure at the proposed nomination of
Dr. Lord,[204] that he seemed disposed to accept Dr. MacMaster as a
compromise.   He was informed, however, very plainly . . . that he must
not expect to be consulted by the Assembly as to the selection of our
theological teachers. . . .   Divine providence has hastened the revolution
of these last days.   Who could have foreseen seven years ago so rapid
a change of situation as that which the North and South now present?
You predicted the issue, indeed as many of us anticipated it; but when
you promised to meet Thornwell and Palmer at Philippi, I think you
scarcely looked for so early and so radical a revolution of public sentiment
as that we now witness.

The eastern brethren, except a few ultra-conservatives, who are fast
finding their level, are heartily for you.[205]

---

[201] Dr. MacMaster had in the meantime not been entirely silent, though
his expressions of opinion were as a rule addressed to his friends, rather
than to the general public.   That he could wield a vitriolic pen is illustrated
by his remark about Buchanan, " the poor ' Old Public Functionary ' who
makes it so hard for us to obey the Divine precept, ' Thou shalt not speak
evil of the ruler of thy people.'   Perhaps we may find forgiveness of our
offenses in the plea, ' I wist not that *he* was the Ruler.' "   (Letter to T. E.
Thomas, January 1, 1861.   Thomas, *op. cit.,* p. 111.)

[202] Thomas, *op. cit.,* p. 129.

[203] *Ibid.,* p. 56.

[204] The Board of Directors of the Seminary had requested by a vote of
11 to 9 that Dr. Willis Lord (for whose pro-Union activities *cf. ante,* pp.
81 ; 83, note 163; 302) be transferred from another chair to this one, but
it was decided to keep Dr. Lord in his original position.

[205] Letter of T. E. Thomas to E. D. MacMaster, June 12, 1866.   Thomas,
op. cit., pp. 129-130.   Dr. MacMaster's period of triumph was brief.   He
died in December, 1866.   *Ibid.,* p. 56.

When a man could be elected by an almost unanimous vote to the very position for which, though recognized as a man of eminent qualifications, he had just seven years before been rejected by a vote of 314 to 45, the completeness of the revolution which had swept over the Old School Church cannot be questioned.

Old School Presbyterians in 1866 must have found it difficult to recognize their Church as the one whose General Assembly in 1861 had debated so long and so earnestly over the question as to whether the Church should endorse the Federal Government. When the vigorous Spring Resolutions had finally been adopted, the General Assembly had set out upon a triumphant course which was destined to carry it farther and farther from the bounds of its traditional conservatism. The Breckinridge Paper of 1862, the successful termination of the flag-raising controversy in 1863, the virtually unanimous condemnation of slavery in 1864, the rigorous program of Church reconstruction determined upon in 1865, and the harsh punishment meted out to defiant Border-State men in 1866 were the fruit of an ever-increasing anxiety to prove beyond the shadow of a doubt that the Old School Church was "loyal."

Originally it was the general public which must be satisfied on this score, but as the years passed there was an increasing tendency to play up to the New School Church, for with the loss of the southern third of the Church, reunion with the New School branch became both more feasible and more desirable. Partly leading and partly following public opinion, the Old School press, with the exception of the *True Presbyterian,* had become ardent advocates of anti-slavery principles, and more outspoken in their pro-Union views. Except in the Border States, the Old School pulpit was by the close of the war almost uniformly loyal: practically all of those ministers who had not given satisfactory evidence of their patriotism had during the early years of the conflict been forced to relinquish their charges. Preachers of doubtful loyalty in the Border States had, wherever possible, been pounced upon by the military or Church authorities, and been made "examples."

Perhaps most significant of all, by 1866 the Church had come under the domination of what had once been regarded a contemptible group of radicals — men who for years had been agitators against slavery, against control of the Church by the East, and in favor of reunion with the New School Church. With its first two objectives virtually accomplished, this group, firmly in the saddle in 1866, gave the New School brethren an illustration of the completeness of its patriotism by its drastic handling of the case of the Presbytery of Louisville. The completeness of its power was illustrated by restoring to one of its number a position which in its judgment had been wrongfully denied him seven years before. Sternly anti-slavery, vindictively aggressive in its patriotism, critically watchful of the "loyalty" of its ministers, openly currying favor with the New School brethren, distinctly Northern in its geography and Western in its control, the Old School Church of 1866 was a very different body from that to which the outbreak of the Civil War had brought such a serious crisis.

PART III

THE NEW SCHOOL PRESBYTERIAN CHURCH AND THE
CIVIL WAR

THE NEW SCHOOL PRESBYTERIAN CHURCH AND THE CIVIL WAR

In conspicuous contrast to the divisions in the Old School Church ever the problems of the endorsement of the Federal Government, slavery, loyal sermons, and Border State patriotism, was the unanimity in the New School Church. Instead of discord, all was harmony in this youthful branch of the Presbyterian Church.[1] In fact, such harmony in the event of any North-South crisis was foreshadowed by the withdrawal in 1857 of the six Southern Synods;[2] the New School Church had become a distinctly Northern denomination. This was no doubt the principal reason why there were no difficulties concerning patriotism within the denomination during the years of the war, yet certain marked differences in the personnel, temper, and outlook of the two branches of the Church rendered the problem of the proper relation to the State much less difficult of solution for the younger and smaller denomination.

In spite of the similarity in name, organization, and creed, the New School Presbyterian Church was very different from the rival with which it had parted company in 1837. With the New England, Congregational element looming large in its background, the New School Church seemed scarcely Presbyterian — and certainly of doubtful orthodoxy — to the right wing of the Old School; while the latter denomination was viewed by its rival as narrow and ultra-conservative. With its greatest strength in Pennsylvania, New Jersey, and southern Ohio, the Old School was dominated by the influence of the Scotch-Irish element; strong in New York (particularly cen-

---

[1] For the history of the division into Old School and New School denominations, cf. ante, pp. 13-15.

[2] Cf. ante, p. 15.

tral and western New York) and in northern Ohio, the New School Church was distinctly Yankee in personnel. The contrast — evident in a dozen ways — is aptly illustrated by a comparison of the lists of names of ministers and licentiates of the two denominations. In 1861, for example, there were nearly three times as many names, proportionally, beginning with " Mc " and " Mac " in the list of Old School preachers as in a corresponding list for the New School.[3] The Scotch-Irish influence carried with it conservatism in theology, in pulpit conduct and scope of pulpit activities, and in the management of the affairs of the denomination. The Yankeeized New School was freer in all of these respects.

Both Old School and New School men were keenly sensitive to the differences between the two Churches, though not always particularly tactful in their manner of pointing out the contrasts. The correspondent of the New York *Evangelist* (New School) who reported the meetings of the Old School General Assembly at Columbus in 1862 pictured the distinctions as he saw them in vivid, if not always kindly, terms:

> There is an evident difference between Presbyterianism in America and American Presbyterianism. . . . If we were to grade the various bodies in our country, bearing this common name, according to the degree or measure in which they have become *Americanized,* we must undoubtedly place the Old School branch quite below several other Presbyterian bodies.
>
> Thus in this Assembly, the sharp and clear and vivid Puritan face so prominent among us, gives way almost entirely to a physiognomy unmistakably Scotch or Irish.[4]

He went on to mention the " Milesian or Scottish " accent of Old School men, their imported forms and phrases, and the emphasis placed upon the views of the fathers of Presbyterianism *across the water.* Asserting that the Scotch-Irish were

---

[3] Of the 1694 names in the New School list, 42 began with " Mc " or " Mac "; while of the 3136 Old School names, there were 199. *Cf.* lists appended to *Minutes of the General Assembly* of each denomination.

[4] Article, " The Assembly from a New School Standpoint " (quoting the Columbus correspondent of the New York *Evangelist*), *True Presbyterian,* June 19, 1862.

slower to become Americanized than the Germans, or the Welsh, or the French, or the Italians, or the Irish, he declared that this characteristic was responsible for the extreme conservatism of Old School men, for their "unphilosophic adherence to the *ipsissima verba* theory," for their "narrow jealousy of New England," for their "inflexible boards and close corporations . . . and many other prominent peculiarities." [5]

The simultaneous meeting of the General Assemblies of the two Churches in St. Louis in 1866 furnished the editor of the *Christian Herald and Presbyterian Recorder* (New School, Cincinnati) with an opportunity to contrast the conduct of business and the forms of procedure of the two bodies. The Old School Assembly, he found, had more set speeches, with a few men taking up most of the time. The use of the "previous question" to close debate—frequent in the Old School Assembly—was never employed by the New School, where the more courteous methods of closing by common consent or by fixing the time for taking the vote, prevailed. The raising of technical points of order and appeals from the Moderator's decisions—very rare in the New School—were common in the other body. The Old School practice of direct management of the theological seminaries (instead of management by self-perpetuating corporations, as in the New School) added much to the heaviness of the docket. Both Assemblies had judicial committees, but while membership on this committee was a sinecure in the New School, it involved heavy work in the other branch. This, the New School editor claimed, was due to two factors: the presence of a "disloyal" element in the Old School; and the fact that while the New School relied upon moral power, the Old School placed its reliance in the settlement of cases upon ecclesiastical power. "They are High Churchmen and we are Low Churchmen," it was explained. Finally (and this is rather surprising), the daily devotional exercises in the New School Assembly were longer than in the

[5] *Ibid.*

Old School body, the former devoting one hour to such exercises, while the latter gave them but half of that time.[6]

While these writers of the New School were largely concerned with pointing out the characteristics of the Old School Assemblies, their estimates furnish interesting negative pictures of the New School Church. Certainly they reflect a consciousness — perhaps even somewhat exaggerated — of the differences between the two denominations. On the New School side this consciousness became particularly sensitive when men of the other branch hinted at a deficiency in their orthodoxy. For there were many unable to agree with the candidate who, when asked whether he was Old School or New School in theology, replied, "I can preach either, as I have studied both."[7] It was not until 1862 that the conservative Reformed Dutch Church, which for years had been on friendly terms with the Old School, was sufficiently convinced of the orthodoxy of the New School to send a delegate to the General Assembly of the younger body.[8] The term "progressive Presbyterians," which some of the New School men applied to themselves, was particularly offensive to the ultra-conservatives of the other side.[9] On the other hand, the superior attitude adopted by Old School men angered the New School brethren, as is evident from an editorial in the *Christian Herald*:

One reason why we have not been convinced that the two branches of our once united Church are not [sic: double negative] prepared for a reunion is, that we have no evidence that our Old-School friends are prepared to begin an expurgation of their denominational literature, and accept what little we have as just as orthodox as their own. Nor are we prepared to make the exchange.[10]

New School theology, the other side were maintaining, emphasized a humanitarian rather than a scriptural religion.

[6] Editorial, "The Two Assemblies," *Christian Herald and Presbyterian Recorder,* June 7, 1866.
[7] *Cf.* story copied from *Presbyter* by *Presbyterian,* April 12, 1862.
[8] *Cf.* editorial in *Presbyter,* July 3, 1862.
[9] *Cf.* editorial, *True Presbyterian,* June 12, 1862.
[10] Copied from *Christian Herald,* in editorial in *Presbyterian,* June 21, 1862.

To those people in 1861 who were familiar with the history and characteristics of the two great branches of the Presbyterian Church, there can have been little doubt that the New School Church would not be confronted with the difficulties which the political crisis was certain to bring to the older branch. It was not only Northern, geographically, but its greatest strength lay in the more northerly latitudes of the North.[11] Its New England traditions precluded any hesitancy about pulpit and Assembly discussion of political affairs of moment. With less rigid rules of Assembly procedure and less emphasis upon a literal interpretation of the Scriptures and the Constitution of the Church, the obstacles of formalism to be overcome were far less formidable than in the Old School Church. Finally, whatever there was in the charge that the New School tended toward humanitarian rather than scriptural religion was all to the advantage of prompt endorsement of the Federal Government — especially in the days when " scriptural religion " implied faithful adherence to the words of an earlier dispensation. For the literalist cannot allow himself to forget that the Old Testament is more than three times as long as the New! If the Old Testament throughout sanctioned slavery, and Paul preached obedience of servants to masters, was not the weight of scriptural evidence — in spite of Christ's teachings — decidedly on the side of slavery? Was not a war which was likely to upset the American slave system thus clearly lacking in scriptural sanction? From this sort of philosophy the New School Church was much freer than the Old School. Patriot members of the younger denomination need have no anxiety with regard to the position of their Church in a political crisis which threatened the destruction of the Union and was likely to involve the fate of American slavery.

The General Assembly which met in Syracuse, New York, in May, 1861, represented a denomination which, in spite of its youth, was strong and prosperous. When the four synods

---

[11] *Cf.* table of statistics, *post*, p. 342.

STATISTICS OF SYNODS OF THE NEW SCHOOL
PRESBYTERIAN CHURCH, 1861 [1]

Synods	Organized	Presbyteries	Ministers	Churches	Communicants	Total Contributions
Albany	1803 [2]	5	84	72	8,617	$ 11,801
Utica	1829	4	88	72	6,845	11,245
Geneva [3]	1812	6	105	93	9,102	11,028
Onondaga	1855	4	79	71	7,800	25,527
Susquehanna	1853	3	44	46	3,967	3,443
Genesee [4]	1821	6	125	105	12,463	21,777
N. Y. & N. Jersey [5]	1788	9	241	158	26,217	91,296
Pennsylvania	1838	5	105	83	13,366	45,325
West-Pennsylvania	1843	3	23	35	3,072	7,591
Michigan	1834	9	93	106	8,664	9,824
Western Reserve	1825	7	100	83	6,431	8,650
Ohio	1814	4	52	71	5,002	4,316
Cincinnati	1829	3	48	42	2,975	12,913
Indiana	1826	4	37	63	3,360	12,798
Wabash	1851	4	37	58	2,702	1,890
Illinois	1831	4	70	87	4,175	3,968
Peoria	1843	6	88	75	4,581	10,030
Wisconsin	1857	3	25	35	1,412	1,269
Iowa	1853	6	54	67	2,098	690
Minnesota	1858	3	21	21	551	653
Missouri	1832	4	19	19	928	1,822
Alta California	1857	3	20	16	432	569
Total 22		105	1,558	1,478	134,760	$298,068 [6]

[1] Compiled from statistical tables, *Minutes of the General Assembly* (New School), 1861, vol. xii, p. 633; *Presbyterian Historical Almanac, 1862,* p. 204. A comparison of the above table with the corresponding one for the Old School Church (*ante,* p. 44) reveals some interesting contrasts in the geographical distribution of the two Churches.

[2] It should be noted that the date of organization given is the original date of the founding of the synod; *not* the date of its beginning its career as a unit of a separate New School Church.

[3] One presbytery in Pennsylvania.

[4] The first six synods named were, with the exception of one presbytery (*cf.* note 3, above) of the total twenty-eight synods, wholly in New York State. Besides, six of the nine presbyteries of the Synod of New York and New Jersey lay wholly or almost wholly in New York State.

[5] Two presbyteries in New Jersey; one in Pennsylvania.

[6] This is the total given in the *Presbyterian Historical Almanac;* actually the figures for the individual synods total $298,425. The discrepancy is not great. The figures in the last column above were taken from the *Almanac;* all others from the *Minutes.* The *Almanac* is usually remarkably accurate in copying statistics from the *Minutes* of the various Presbyterian denominations.

which had been exscinded by the General Assembly of 1837 [12] decided to organize a new denomination, it seemed doubtful whether the infant organization — with a membership hetero- geneous in temperament, training, religious associations, and theological bias [13] — could long survive. " The Church . . . was sailing year by year between the deep sea of Congregation- alism and the rugged cliffs of a conservative Presbyterianism, and was at every moment liable to be engulfed by the one or shattered to pieces on the other," [14] yet during the first ten years of its independent existence the membership increased from 100,850 [15] to 139,047. The loss of some 16,000 members through the withdrawal of the six Southern synods in 1857 [16] a little more than offset the growth of the denomination during the second decade of its history; in 1861 its communicant membership was 134,760.[17] Yet the greater unanimity in the Church after the Southerners had left, easily compensated for the slight decrease in net membership. In entering upon the third decade of its history, the New School branch of the Pres- byterian Church could look back with complacency upon its previous record. It had reared up a capable and resourceful ministry; its pecuniary resources had been steadily growing; educational institutions had developed in number and matur-

[12] Cf. ante, pp. 13-15.

[13] Morris, Edward D., A Book of Remembrance, The Presbyterian Church, New School, 1837-1869, An Historical Review (Columbus, Ohio, 1905), pp. 112-113.

[14] Ibid.

[15] This was the figure for 1839, the first full year of the New School's independent existence. Dr. E. D. Morris, the historian of the New School, judged that the figure was probably excessive, since many ministers and churches were probably included "who never really cast in their lot with the excluded [that is, the New School] party." Cf. Morris, op. cit., p. 112.

[16] Cf. ante, p. 15.

[17] Pointing out that during the decade as many as 65,820 new communi- cants had been added, and some 47,728 had been received by letter (many of whom must have come from other denominations), Dr. Morris was at a loss to understand the falling off between 1849 and 1859. None of the possible explanations he suggested was satisfactory to him. Cf. Morris, op. cit., pp. 146-147.

ity; [18] many individual churches in the denomination had waxed strong. The New School Church had achieved in less than a quarter-century of independent existence a position of prominence and influence among the Protestant denominations in the United States.

When one recalls the long and bitter struggle which preceded the adoption of the Spring Resolutions by the Old School Assembly of 1861, the unanimity [19] characterizing the General Assembly of the New School Church, which convened in Syracuse, on the same day that its rival began its annual session in Philadelphia, is both interesting and significant. On the very day when Dr. Spring's first motion was tabled the New School Assembly accepted the report of its Special Committee on the State of the Country. At its next session, after brief discussion the report was adopted. There was nothing equivocal in its terms:

> *Whereas,* A portion of the people of the United States of America have risen up against the rightful authority of the Government; . . . the General Assembly of the Presbyterian Church in the United States of America cannot forbear to express their amazement at the wickedness of such proceedings, and at the bold advocacy and defense thereof, not only in those States in which ordinances of " Secession " have been passed, but in several others; and
> *Whereas,* The General Assembly,— in the language of the Synod of New York and Philadelphia, on the occasion of the Revolutionary War,— " being met, at a time, when public affairs wear so threatening an aspect, and when (unless God in his Sovereign Providence speedily prevent it) all the horrors of civil war are to be apprehended, are of opinion, that they cannot discharge their duty to the numerous congregations under their care, without addressing them at this important crisis . . . ; " therefore,
> *Resolved,* 1. That . . . we should be recreant to our high trust were we to withhold our earnest protest against all such unlawful and treasonable acts.
> *Resolved,* 2. That this Assembly . . . cherish an undiminished attachment to the great principles of civil and religious freedom, on which our National Government is based; . . . and, by the preservation of which,

---

[18] Three theological seminaries (Union, New York City; Lane, Cincinnati; Auburn, Auburn, N. Y.) had gone with the New School in 1837.

[19] Not mentioned in the *Minutes,* but explicitly stated in *Presbyterian Historical Almanac,* 1862, p. 174.

we believe that the common interests of evangelical religion and civil liberty will be most effectively sustained.

Resolved, 3. That . . . there is no blood or treasure too precious to be devoted to the defense and perpetuity of the Government in all its constituted authority.

. . . .

Resolved, 5. That it be recommended to all our pastors and churches, to be instant and fervent in prayer for the President of the United States, and all in authority under him; . . . for the Congress of the United States; for the Lieutenant-General commanding the Army-in-Chief, and all our soldiers; that God may shield them from danger in the hour of peril, and, by the outpouring of the Holy Spirit upon the Army and Navy, renew and sanctify them, so that whether living or dying, they may be the servants of the Most High.

Resolved, 6. That, in the countenance which many ministers of the Gospel and other professing Christians are now giving to treason and rebellion against the Government, we have great occasion to mourn for the injury thus done to the kingdom of the Redeemer; and that, though we have nothing to add to our former significant and explicit testimonials on the subject of slavery, we yet recommend our people to pray, more fervently than ever, for the removal of this evil, and all others, both social and political, which lie at the foundation of our present national difficulties.

Resolved, 7. That a copy of these Resolutions, signed by the officers of the General Assembly, be forwarded to His Excellency, Abraham Lincoln, President of the United States.[20]

In various other ways this Assembly recognized the disturbed political condition of the country. A special day of fasting, humiliation, and prayer was appointed.[21] After the visiting secretary of the American Temperance Union had addressed the Assembly, it was resolved to ask for extraordinary prayer and labor " that our noble young men who go, in the spirit of Lexington and Bunker Hill, to the defense of the Constitution and Laws, may be kept from the temptations of the camp and field . . . ."[22] The pride which the Assembly felt in the unanimity

[20] *Minutes of the General Assembly* (New School), 1861, vol. xii, pp. 447-448.

[21] It will be remembered that a similar proposition had been made the occasion for the Spring Resolutions in the Old School General Assembly. *Cf. ante,* pp. 48, 50. For the New School resolutions on this subject, *cf. Minutes of the General Assembly* (New School), 1861, vol. xii, p. 464.

[22] *Ibid.,* p. 445.

of the Church's patriotism was summed up in a flowery paragraph included in the annual "Narrative of the State of Religion" adopted by the Assembly.

> One element which has largely entered into the recent religious history of our Church is the spirit of Christian patriotism. The wave of patriotic feeling, which has poured over the North, has indeed lifted all upon its breast, or overwhelmed those whom it has not lifted, as a tidal wave at the same moment buries the treacherous rocks and floats the gallant ships. Large numbers of the members of our churches have enlisted to fight their country's battles, feeling that the time has come, when those of the followers of the Prince of Peace who have no swords should sell their garments and buy them. . . . Many instances of hopeful conversion in the camp or the garrison are reported. More than one has learned to make himself a living sacrifice to God, by first laying himself upon the altar of his country. Providentially our Church is free from those unhappy divisions which separate brethren of many denominations in this trying hour. Whatever the issue of the coming conflict, we shall share alike in its triumphs or its humiliations.[23]

Yet the Assembly was not completely swept off its feet by pride in its patriotism. That it still recognized that its business was not primarily civil is illustrated by the closing sentence of the Narrative:

> Whatever the feelings with which some may enter the field of strife, we are glad to know that from our churches have gone so many, who will ever keep the Cross above the Flag; whose courage will get its nerve from prayer rather than from passion; and who, if sent to the judgment-seat by the hand of violence, will have no account to render for shedding a brother's blood in an unholy wrath.[24]

It is just as well that this final sentence was added; one might otherwise have been left in doubt as to whether an Assembly which recommended that the followers of the Prince of Peace who had no swords should sell their garments and buy them really did believe in keeping the Cross above the Flag.

The General Assembly of 1862, meeting in Cincinnati, Ohio, found the New School Church still more fervent in its devotion to the Union. As in 1861, the report of the Special Committee

---

[23] *Ibid.*, pp. 472; 481-484.
[24] *Ibid.*, p. 484.

on the State of the Country was unanimously adopted.[25] Calling attention to the fact that the New School Church had inscribed upon its banner " ' The Constitutional Presbyterian Church ' — having never favored secession, or nullification, either in Church or State," the report offered several strong resolutions:

. . . .

Resolved, 2. That rebellion against such a government as ours . . . can find no parallel, except in the first two great rebellions — that which assailed the throne of heaven directly, and that which peopled our world with miserable apostates.

Resolved, 3. That whatever diversity of sentiment may exist among us, respecting international wars, or an appeal to the sword, for the settlement of points of honor or interest between independent nations, we are all of one mind on the subject of rebellion . . . ; that our vast army now in the field is to be looked upon as one great police force . . . ; so that the strictest advocates of peace may bear an active part in this deadly struggle for the life of the Government.

Resolved, 4. That while we have been utterly shocked at the deep depravity of the men who have planned and matured this rebellion . . . , there is another class found in the loyal States, who have excited a still deeper loathing — some in Congress, some high in civil life, and some in the ordinary walks of business, who never utter a manly thought or opinion in favor of the Government, but they follow it, by way of comment, with two or three apologies for Southern insurrectionists; presenting the difference between an open and avowed enemy in the field, and a secret and insidious foe in the bosom of our own family.

Resolved, 5. That in our opinion, this whole insurrectionary movement can be traced to one primordial root, and to one only — *African Slavery,* and the love of it, and a determination to make it perpetual; . . . and while, under the influence of humanity and Christian benevolence, we may commiserate the condition of the ruined rebels . . . — should the case occur — despoiled of all that makes the world dear to them, we must be at the same time constrained to feel, that the retribution has been self-inflicted, and must add, " *Fiat justitia, ruat coelum."*

Resolved, 6. That we have great confidence in Abraham Lincoln . . . ; and, while we bless God that he has stood by them [our armies, prosecuting a " holy warfare "], and cheered them on . . . and crowned them with many signal victories, . . . we will ever pray, that the last sad note of anarchy and misrule may soon die away, and the OLD FLAG OF OUR COUNTRY, radiant with stripes and brilliant with stars, may again wave over a great, and undivided, and happy people.

---

[25] The unanimity was not mentioned in the *Minutes,* but was specifically mentioned in the *Presbyterian Historical Almanac,* 1863, p. 281.

Resolved, 7. That we . . . lay ourselves, with all that we are and have, on the altar of God and our country; . . . that our Rulers . . . and our commanders . . . and the brave men under their leadership, may take courage under the assurance that " THE PRESBYTERIAN CHURCH IN THE UNITED STATES OF AMERICA " are with them, in heart and hand, in life and effort, in this fearful existing conflict.

. . . .[26]

These resolutions, as in the previous year, were forwarded to the President of the United States. This time they were accompanied by a letter expressing to Mr. Lincoln the New School's gratitude to God for the President's firmness, integrity, moderation, and wisdom; and pledging continued unstinted support to the cause of the Union:

We have given our sons to the army and navy; some of our ministers and many of our church-members have died in hospital and field; we are glad that we gave them, and we exult in that they were true even to death. We gladly pledge as many more as the cause of our country may demand.[27]

It was sentiments such as these that prompted Dr. Robinson's *True Presbyterian*[28] to remark that if " fear of driving off from our Church to the New School, many persons, or even churches " was a dominant motive in the adoption of the Breckinridge Paper by the Old School Assembly of 1862, even this fiery document was woefully inadequate. The effort to keep up with the New School in patriotic utterances was, declared Dr. Robinson, "obviously useless"; with the "pervading leaven of Erastianism" which the New School body from the first received in its three measures of meal, it would always keep ahead.[29] Certainly the pace set by the New School Assembly in 1862 was a strenuous one to follow.

There were several statements of rather unique significance in the resolutions of the New School Assembly in 1862. The third resolution's careful distinction between international war

[26] *Ibid.,* vol. xiii, pp. 23-25.
[27] *Ibid.,* pp. 25-26.
[28] *Cf. ante,* pp. 167-177.
[29] Editorial, " Action of the New School General Assembly on the State of the Country," *True Presbyterian,* June 5, 1862.

and the suppression of rebellion seems to indicate that in this Church — in contrast to the Old School [30] — there was a pacifist element to be placated. Such sentiments were to be expected among followers of a "humanitarian" religion. The drastic denunciation of slavery and the conclusion that the war must bring about its destruction have particular significance when it is recalled that they came four months before Lincoln's preliminary Emancipation Proclamation. The sixth resolution's commendation of God for being on the right side is rather amusing; while the second resolution's admission that in the Fall of Man history had furnished a case parallel to the present rebellion certainly placed the New School Assembly on sounder theological ground than that taken by the ultraorthodox Robert J. Breckinridge himself when he declared that the Southern uprising was the "wickedest thing that ever cursed God's earth!" [31]   Here was one case where New School vituperation of the rebellion was surpassed! As the Assembly had, however, placed the rebels in the same category with the fallen angels, it could not be fairly charged with having completely failed to do justice to the wickedness of the insurrection.

While the Old School Assembly of 1863 in Peoria was arguing over whether the flag should be raised over the church in which its meetings were being held, the sister Assembly meeting in Philadelphia was having no difficulties in endorsing the Government with its usual promptness and decisiveness. The New School body had evidently learned some lessons in moderation in statement during the preceding year, for the paper of 1863, though long, comprehensive, and firmly loyal, was characterized by common sense and good taste.[32]   After

---

[30] *Cf. ante,* pp. 297-298.

[31] *Cf. ante,* pp. 114-115.

[32] Perhaps the credit for the sensible tone of the document belongs largely to the chairman of the special committee appointed to draw it up, Rev. Albert Barnes. This veteran pastor of the First Presbyterian Church of Philadelphia was one of the most highly respected members of the New School clergy. *Cf. Presbyterian Encyclopaedia,* pp. 55-57; Thompson, *op. cit., passim;* Morris, *op. cit.,* p. 119.

solemnly reaffirming the principles and repeating the declarations of the previous Assemblies, the resolutions emphasized fully the religious duty of loyalty. No doubt with special gratification that its demand of the previous year[33] for the elimination of slavery had been at least partially met, the Assembly now declared that "in the Proclamation of Emancipation issued by the President as a war-measure . . . the Assembly recognizes with devout gratitude that wonder-working providence of God, by which military necessities become the instruments of justice, in breaking the yoke of oppression, and causing the oppressed to go free; and further, that the Assembly beseeches Almighty God in his own time to remove the last vestiges of slavery from this country. . . ."[34]

The Assembly's war enthusiasm, somewhat repressed by the moderate tone of the paper on the State of the Country, found another opportunity for expression. A number of the commissioners decided to make a trip to Washington to visit the President. Some sixty-five[35] made the journey from Philadelphia to Washington and presented in person to Mr. Lincoln the resolutions which the 1863 General Assembly had just adopted. The President showed his appreciation of the Assembly's paper by singling out particular points that especially met with his favor.[36] While the interview was evidently a brief one, it must have been effective in gratifying the visitors' desire to put their Church and themselves on record as vigorous supporters of the Government of the United States.

The paper on the State of the Country which was offered in the Assembly which met in Dayton, Ohio, in 1864 was unanimously adopted, "(the whole Assembly rising in expression of their approbation)."[37] Though much briefer than its predecessors and similar to the paper of 1863 in the moderation of

---

[33] *Cf. ante*, p. 347.

[34] *Minutes of the General Assembly* (New School), 1863, vol. xiii, p. 244. The whole paper is given *ibid.*, pp. 241-245.

[35] McPherson, *op. cit.*, p. 471.

[36] The reply of the President is given *ibid.*

[37] *Minutes of the General Assembly* (New School), 1864, vol. xiii, p. 465.

its tone, the 1864 document did not relax a particle in the vigor of its endorsement of the Government. Professing to "recognize the same good hand of our God in the disappointments and delays of the war, by which he has made more sure the complete destruction of the vile system of human bondage, and rendered less self-confident and more religious the heart of the nation," the Assembly took particular pains to "urge all Christians to refrain from weakening the authority of the Administration by ill-timed complaints and unnecessary criticisms. . . ." A special committee of six was appointed to convey the news of the action of the Assembly to the President. It was also resolved, as in 1863,[38] that the paper be read in all the pulpits of the denomination.[39] As 1864 was a presidential election year, the advice that all Christians refrain from "ill-timed complaints and unnecessary criticisms" of the Administration can scarcely have been unwelcome to the President, especially when it was accompanied by a request that it be repeated in all of the pulpits of the Church.[40]

The assassination of President Lincoln, occurring less than five weeks before the meeting of the 1865 Assembly, caused a reversion to the longer and more extravagantly worded type of paper on the State of the Country. As finally adopted (unanimously, by a rising vote) the report of the special committee appointed to draw up such a paper comprised some four thousand words.[41] It expressed the Assembly's pride in its war record:

> Our record as a Church we commit to the calm judgment of posterity, in the full assurance that there is neither a line nor a word the Christian patriotism of the future will desire to erase; not a single sentiment befitting our relation to this great conflict, it will find unexpressed.

---

[38] *Ibid.*, 1863, vol. xiii, p. 245.

[39] *Ibid.*, 1864, vol. xiii, p. 467.

[40] For the text of the paper of 1864, *cf. ibid.*, pp. 465-466.

[41] The report as originally adopted contained some two thousand five hundred words. The special committee also reported a second paper containing about thirteen hundred words. The Assembly unanimously adopted this second paper also, and directed that it be appended to the original report. Thus the report with the appendage came to contain some four thousand words.

It also recognized the war as an agency which had familiarized the people with the evils of slavery:

> We wonder at, and admire especially, the Divine wisdom manifested in educating the nation through the successive stages of defeat and victory, through the unparalleled atrocities perpetrated, and the amazing malignity illustrated, by the leaders of this Rebellion, up to the purpose of utterly rooting out and destroying a condition of society so utterly hostile to the elevation of man and the spirit of the Gospel.

How the death of the President intensified Northern hostility to the South was illustrated by the reflections upon that event:

> In the sad event which has clothed the nation in mourning . . . we recognize the same wise Providence, which, looking far above our feeble vision, permitted the existence of Slavery and the rise of this Rebellion, and which, in this last act of baffled and defeated despotism, has illustrated its debased and malignant spirit so as to excite the loathing, horror and abhorrence of the world.

Much as the Assembly mourned the death of Lincoln, it was determined that men should understand that the New School's loyalty was not limited to support of a single leader. The paragraphs which pledged the Church to sustain the new President indicate with how little restraint the young denomination embarked upon the consideration of political topics. Nowhere was the contrast with the sister-denomination more striking. One cannot imagine the Old School Church — even when, in 1866, the ultra-patriots within it had finally brought it around to a position of almost blatant loyalty — even considering the adoption of a lengthy pledge of allegiance to an incoming President, such as the pledge which was now so blithely taken by the Assembly of the younger denomination:

> In Andrew Johnson, so unexpectedly called to the chair of our martyred Chief, the Assembly recognize a man distinguished for a long course of earnest effort to elevate the masses, and for a steady, consistent patriotism. . . . We desire to pledge to him . . . our confidence and support in his efforts to vindicate the majesty of law; . . . inspire a just appreciation of the crime of treason, and a true loyalty to the Government, in the breasts of the masses of the white population of the South; and extend, to the colored citizens of that section, the practical enjoyment of those personal and political rights announced in the Declaration of Independence, but denied to them by a despotic aristocracy. And, while

this Assembly deem it not their province to counsel our rulers in respect to political measures, we possess both the right, and regard it as our duty, to state distinctly that, in our opinion, a nation like ours, whose corner-stone is equal rights, cannot permanently prosper, nor be exempt from future convulsions, unless the principles of civil and religious liberty are fairly carried out and fully applied, with only just and healthful limitations, without reference to class or color, to all people.

The Assembly recognized a special opportunity and responsibility for the Presbyterian Church in the condition of the freed negroes:

God's just doom has been wreaked on the giant hypocrite, who held in one hand the Declaration of Independence, and in the other the hammer and manacles of the slave auctioneer. And in doing this He has made noble thought freer under the sun. . . . He has imposed on us the responsibility of giving this free thought to these emancipated millions. As our Church — republican and apostolic in its order and its doctrines — is, in the main, best fitted to create a free, intelligent, stable, Christian manhood, in harmony with our civil institutions, and the progressive spirit of the nation, so it is for us to enter the field God has opened for our labors; to establish churches and schools, and thus assist the civil authority in bringing order out of chaos, while we secure for the people the higher influence that saves the soul.

Yet, having accused the Southerners of hypocrisy, the New School men could not afford to pass over in silence certain inconsistencies between ideals and practice in the North:

[This] war . . . has imposed on us responsibilities for the correction of wrong here at home. . . . The heart of the people has thus begun to beat with a desire to remove all such inconsistencies, wrongs, shams, and hypocrisies from our own legislation. If we fight, or ask justice, for the African in the South, we must act justly toward him at the North. Neither the law nor the gospel, when rightly understood, will permit us to exclude, from the rights and privileges of freemen, those who are citizens like ourselves. . . . Let it not be said that, as a Church, we have nothing to do with civil legislation. The day has gone by, when an intelligent Christian will affirm the doctrine, that what is wrong in religion is right in politics. . . . We wish all men to know that the members of our churches are bound to be Christians, in politics as well as in religion. . . .[42]

Having adopted so full and explicit a statement of New School sentiment and advice on political matters, the Assembly di-

[42] For the 1865 paper on the State of the Country, *cf. Minutes of the General Assembly* (New School), 1865, vol. xiv, pp. 36-41.

rected that authenticated copies of the paper be sent to the President of the United States, to the members of the Cabinet, and to the family of the deceased President. It also recommended that the ministers of the denomination read it from their pulpits " for the information of the people." [43]   The general public, and the Presbyterian public in particular, must know where the New School Church stood.

While the Special Committee on the State of the Country had been at work on its report, the Standing Committee on Bills and Overtures had been preparing an answer to a memorial which the Assembly had received from a group of ministers and elders who claimed that it was of the highest importance to the future religious, social, and political well-being of the land, as well as " in accordance with the law of righteousness, as expounded by God during the history of the Great Rebellion," that the Government should promptly adopt such principles and measures " in the reconstruction of society in the revolted States " as should " distinctly recognize the rights of citizenship as inhering in every man, of whatever class or complexion, who is and has been true to the country and the flag." The Assembly was asked to adopt such a deliverance " in regard to this great subject, as shall seem demanded by the circumstances of the country at this time."

In answer to this memorial the Committee on Bills and Overtures submitted a paper which the Assembly unanimously adopted and directed to be appended to the Report on the State of the Country.[44]   Admitting that on the specific question of bestowing upon the freedmen all the rights of citizenship in the great work of reconstructing society in the Southern states there might be an honest difference of opinion, the Assembly " without undertaking to define the ways and means most proper to be adopted for this purpose " heartily concurred in the demands of the memorialists, declaring that the sooner this

[43] *Ibid.,* p. 41.
[44] *Ibid.,* pp. 41, 43.

end was gained, the better it would be for all classes. Upon
this subject the New School Church had no doubts:

That the colored man should, in this country, enjoy the right of suffrage
in common with all other men, is but a simple dictate of justice. The
Assembly cannot perceive any good reason why he should be deprived of
this right on the ground of his color or his race. Why, then, should not
the black man " in the revolted States," who is and " has been true to the
country and the flag," thousands and tens of thousands of whom have
fought for that country and flag, be at once included among the loyal
persons, upon whom shall devolve the task of reconstructing Southern
society? This the Assembly thinks to be the shortest and safest method
of solving the problem, most certain to gain the result and prevent future
evils.

The Assembly found many arguments for such a course: the
freedmen could not long be kept contented without the enjoyment of common civil and political rights; these rights would
put them into a position to be their own defenders; their enjoyment would give the freedmen respectability, " dignify their
labor, elevate their desires, quicken their moral consciousness,
and waken in their minds those hopes and high aspirations, upon
which the proper development of humanity so largely depends."
Furthermore, possession of these rights would prove the quick-
est method of preparing men for their proper use [democratic
theory *par excellence!*]; if the freedmen were fit for the duties
of the camp and the garrison as soldiers, the presumption was
(the paper declared) that they were not less competent for the
duties of citizenship. Perhaps the most interesting, if not the
most convincing, argument advanced was that the loyalty of
the freedmen entitled them to the full rights of citizenship.
There could be no doubt of their loyalty, the Assembly declared, adding caustically " and in this they have shown more
wisdom than most of their former masters." Claiming that the
country must eventually grant full rights to the freedmen, it
was maintained that more would be lost than gained by a
postponement of such action:

It is better to meet the question at once, and settle it in accordance
with the rights of man, the principles of our political system, and the clear
indications of Divine Providence. Any proper efforts of those in author-

ity looking towards this result, will receive the warm sympathies of this Assembly; nor can the Assembly doubt that they will be ultimately sustained by the great majority of the American people.

Apparently not realizing that it was scarcely in a position to point out the wisest course to be followed in bringing about social reconstruction in the South, this ultra-Northern religious body concluded its report on the question of suffrage for the Southern negroes by explaining that it considered advice and encouragement to the Federal Government on this subject most timely:

> It is not the purpose of the Assembly, in this deliverance, to argue this question at length, but simply to indicate its conviction in respect to the point intended in the memorial, and, if possible, to say a word that may serve to encourage the Government in the discharge of its difficult duties. The prayer of the Assembly is, that the Government may be guided by wisdom and justice, applying these cardinal qualities to all classes and all men; and that all the people, disciplined by Providence, and instructed by the trials of the past, may learn to practise that " righteousness " which " exalteth a nation." [45]

"Our record as a Church we commit to the calm judgment of posterity," the Assembly had declared in the opening paragraph of its report on the State of the Country.[46] Forty years later Dr. E. D. Morris, who had been a leader of the New School denomination during the war years, could still speak of the series of war deliverances of his Church as "action which shines so brightly in the denominational records; " [47] although he did admit in a subsequent statement in his *Book of Remembrance* of the New School Church that the 1865 denunciation of the ministers who had encouraged and justified the rebellion was phrased in "terms now seen to be immoderate." [48] But Dr. Morris belonged to the Civil War genera-

[45] For the report of the Committee on Bills and Overtures on the subjects of the rights of the freedmen cf. *ibid.*, 1865, vol. xiv, pp. 41-43.

[46] *Cf. ante*, p. 351.

[47] Morris, *op. cit.*, pp. 160-161.

[48] *Ibid.*, p. 165.

tion; [49] perhaps the "posterity" of the Church would be willing, if not to acknowledge possible exaggeration in some of the
condemnation in the war-time utterances, at least to admit that
the Assembly's advice on the negro problem in the South was
not entirely sound. [50] Even to some of the Church leaders of
the time, the wordy deliverance of 1865 was perhaps a bit too
extreme, for the 1866 Assembly's paper on the State of the
Country was much less extended in length, if perhaps equally
emphatic in tone.

The Assembly of the New School Church in 1866 convened
in the same city and at the same time [51] as the corresponding
body of the sister Church. While the Old School evidently
regarded the cessation of the war as affording an opportunity [52]
for the Church to relapse into its normal attitude of silence
on political topics (an opportunity particularly welcome to a
body already torn with internal dissension [53]), the New School
Assembly again took occasion to offer its opinion and advice on
the problems which were confronting the country. In a re-

[49] Dr. E. D. Morris was born in 1825. During the Civil War years he
was pastor of the Second Presbyterian Church of Columbus, Ohio. In 1867
he became a member of the faculty of Lane Theological Seminary. Although not a commissioner to the Assembly during any of the war years
(*cf. Minutes, passim*), he was a recognized leader of the Church during
this period. *Cf. Presbyterian Encyclopaedia*, pp. 545-546.

[50] Dr. Morris evidently did not read the Assembly's report on this subject with sufficient care. His statement, " As to the freedmen it [the
report] advocated the recognition of the rights of citizenship . . . , yet
admitting that there might be honest difference of judgment . . . as to
the immediate conferring of such rights," (Morris, *op. cit.*, pp. 165-166) is
grossly misleading, as the admission *preceded* the emphatic advocacy of
conferring the franchise upon the freedmen. Placed where it was, the
admission strengthened, rather than weakened, the positiveness of the
Assembly's unanimous convictions in favor of the suffrage for freedmen.

[51] In fact it was the practice of the Assembly of each Church to convene
on the third Thursday in May each year. The Assemblies of all of the
other Presbyterian Churches in the North convened at approximately
the same time.

[52] Though the surrender of Lee had occurred a month before the meeting
of the Assemblies in 1865, those bodies had not regarded the war as completely over.

[53] *Cf. ante*, pp. 218-261.

port which was unanimously adopted, the Assembly recorded its gratitude to God for the gifts He had bestowed upon the nation through the outcome of the war: the restoration of peace; the preservation of the Union (so that "we remain, as we were intended to be, one Nation, with one Constitution, and one destiny"); the manifestation that the republican institutions of the country were "as well fitted to bear the stress and shock of war as to give prosperity and increase in times of peace;" the outlawry of slavery; the "spontaneous, impassioned, and unbought loyalty" of the people; the consciousness of sure retribution for national sin. Besides these benefits to the nation as a whole, the Assembly recognized certain particular blessings which God had given the New School Church: He had "bestowed such grace upon our churches and ministry, that with singular unanimity and zeal they upheld our rightful government . . . identifying the success of the Nation with the welfare of the Church"; above all these things, He had "watched over His Church and kept it safe during these troublous times; so that not only has our American Christianity been vindicated . . . , but our purpose and plans for the future have been also enlarged in some proportion to the needs and growth of our country; while . . . He has also, in these latter days, rained down spiritual blessings in abundant measure upon so many churches all over the land."

After enumerating these benefits which the war had brought the nation and the Church, the Assembly also bore testimony in respect to "our urgent needs and duties as a nation, in view of the new era upon which we are now entering." The platform it advocated was clearly outlined:

1. . . . Freed by the national arms, they [the freedmen] must be protected in all their civil rights by the national power. And, as promoting this end, which far transcends any mere political or party object, we rejoice that the active functions of the Freedmen's Bureau are still continued; and especially that the Civil Rights Bill has become the law of the land. In respect to the concession of the right of suffrage to the colored race, this Assembly adheres to the resolution passed by our Assembly of 1865 . . . : "That the colored man should in this country

enjoy the right of suffrage . . . is but a simple dictate of justice. . . ."
Even if suffrage may not be universal, let it at least be impartial.

2. In case such impartial suffrage is not conceded, that we may reap the legitimate fruits of our national victory over Secession and Slavery, and, that treason and rebellion may not enure to the direct political advantage of the guilty, we judge it to be a simple act of justice, that the constitutional basis of representation in Congress should be so far altered as to meet the exigencies growing out of the abolition of Slavery; and we likewise hold it to be the solemn duty of our National Executive and Congress, to adopt only such methods of reconstruction as shall effectually protect all loyal persons in the States lately in revolt.

3. As loyalty is the highest civic virtue, and treason the highest civil crime, so it is necessary for the due vindication and satisfaction of national justice, that the chief fomenters and representatives of the rebellion should, by due course and process of law, be visited with condign punishment.

4. . . . We earnestly exhort all our ministers and churches to constant and earnest prayer for the President of the United States . . . ; and for all persons intrusted with authority. . . .

5. And we further exhort and admonish the members of our churches to diligent and personal efforts for the safety and prosperity of the nation, to set aside all partisan and sectional aims and low ambitions, and to do their full duty as Christian freemen; to the end that our Christian and Protestant civilization may maintain its legitimate ascendency, and that we become not the prey of any form of infidelity, or subject to any foreign priestly domination. . . .[54]

In the 1861 Old School Assembly a large minority had opposed endorsement of the Federal Government on the ground that the Assembly had no right to determine the political question to which government — state or federal — a man's first allegiance was due.[55] Never in the least troubled by this question, the New School Assembly for five successive years had unanimously and without hesitancy taken a firm stand under the Union banner; now, in 1866, finding a quarrel on between the President and Congress, with its accustomed eagerness it chose its side. The New School resolutions of the previous year on the state of the country left little doubt on which side of the political quarrel of 1866 the denomination would be found. The twelve months intervening between the two As-

[54] For the 1866 report on the State of the Country, *cf. Minutes of the General Assembly* (New School), 1866, vol. xiv, pp. 262-264.

[55] *Cf. ante,* pp. 66-67.

semblies had rudely shaken New School "confidence" in the new President's determination to "inspire a just appreciation of the crime of treason, and a true loyalty to the Government, in the breasts of the masses of the white population of the South." The 1865 Assembly had told the President that the country could not permanently prosper "unless the principles of civil and religious liberty are fairly carried out and applied, with only just and healthful limitations, without reference to class or color, to all people; " it had decreed that it was "but a simple dictate of justice" that the colored man should in this country "enjoy the right of suffrage in common with all other men."[56] Yet, in spite of these instructions, the new President had seemed more interested in restoring Southern men their rights than in inspiring them with a just appreciation of the crime of treason; more considerate of constitutional limitations than of liberties for the freedmen. Hence it was only natural that in place of the lengthy 1865 pledge of support for Andrew Johnson (with a special exhortation to ministers and churches "to sustain him in the just exercise of his authority, to judge charitably his measures and acts"),[57] the New School Assembly in 1866 should, in counseling prayers for those in authority, specifically name as the subjects of such prayers not only the President and his counselors, but the Senate and House of Representatives in Congress assembled, the Judges in our National Courts, "those that bear rule" in our army and navy, and "all persons intrusted with authority." With a President so misguided as to veto the Freedmen's Bureau Bill and the Civil Rights Bill, it was desirable to extend as widely as possible the prayer-list of his counselors! There is significance in the fact that while previous reports on the State of the Country had been sent to the President of the United States,[58] in 1866 it was resolved that copies also be sent

---

[56] For these quotations from the 1865 report, cf. *ante*, pp. 352-355.

[57] *Minutes of the General Assembly* (New School), 1865, vol. xiv, p. 39.

[58] In 1865 the Assembly had directed that copies be sent to the members of the Cabinet, and to the family of the deceased President, as well as to the new President. Cf. *ibid.*, p. 41.

to the President of the Senate and the Speaker of the House of Representatives.[59] The Assembly evidently preferred to entrust Congress with its demands that the chief fomenters and representatives of the rebellion should be " visited with condign punishment," that the North be allowed to " reap the legitimate fruits of our national victory," and that treason and rebellion might not " enure to the direct political advantage of the guilty." Congress could be expected to welcome a demand for reapportionment on the basis suggested by the Assembly.

The historian of the New School who spoke of the action of the 1861 Assembly as preparing the way for " all the succeeding action which shines so brightly in the denominational records," [60] in his account of the meeting of 1866 omitted any reference to the political stand of that year. It is not improbable that he may have considered that it too was expressed in " terms now seen to be immoderate." [61] In fact, on several occasions during the 1860's the particular time of meeting was singularly conducive to immoderation of statement. In 1861 the country had not yet recovered its equilibrium after the fall of Fort Sumter; in 1865 it had been incensed by the assassination of Lincoln; in 1866 the recent passage of the Civil Rights Bill over the President's veto had made irreparable the break between the Chief Executive and Congress, while the attention of the whole country was focussed upon the attempts of the latter to draft a more rigorous plan of reconstruction than that which had been advocated by the President. From the point of view of well-balanced action, the month of May seemed to be, during the years of the war period, a particularly inopportune time for the meeting of the General Assembly. Certainly the conditions which existed during the meeting of the 1866 Assembly seem to have successfully tempted the New School body to give forth pronouncements upon specific political issues of very doubtful relationship to things spiritual. The *Presbyterian*, resentful of some harsh remarks made about the

---

[59] *Ibid.*, 1866, vol. xiv, p. 264.
[60] *Cf. ante*, p. 356; also Morris, *op. cit.*, pp. 160-161.
[61] *Cf. ante*, p. 356; also Morris, *op. cit.*, p. 165.

1866 Old School Assembly by a correspondent of the New York *Evangelist* (New School), reminded the offending gentleman that if the manner of procedure of the Old School had not been all that it might have been, the subject-matter of the New School deliberations had not in its entirety been appropriate to a Spiritual Court; then this leading Old School journal added:

> It would be well, we think, for all parties, in all the churches, to accept the conclusion that the time for deliverances on the state of the country is past. . . . Our General Assembly recognized this fact, and made no utterances on the state of the country.[62]

The New School seems to have reached the same conclusion by 1867. The previous year had seen its last paper on the state of the country. Can it be that the twelve months which intervened between the two Assemblies had occasioned some doubt in the minds of New School leaders as to the efficacy of the Assembly's services in the role of political adviser? Whether or not its advice had been heeded, Congress had certainly gone in the direction it had pointed out. Perhaps it was not entirely clear that any great benefit had ensued. At any rate, in view of the fact that political conditions remained disturbed throughout the rest of the Johnson administration, it is interesting — and to the history student a bit disappointing! — that the New School Assembly did not continue in the part of political adviser to the Federal Government. To what degree its change of policy after 1866 was due to dissatisfaction with its past course and determination to adhere more closely to things spiritual, to what degree it was the result of increased absorption in the movement for Presbyterian reunion,[63] is not entirely clear. The fact remains that the year 1866 marked the close of its political career.

As might be surmised from the unanimity — almost monotonous — with which the war-time Assemblies of the New School Church adopted action on the State of the Country, the stand taken by individual synods and presbyteries was uniformly

---

[62] Editorial, " Politics and Religion," *Presbyterian*, June 16, 1866.
[63] *Cf. post*, pp. 503-517.

loyal. In 1861 the strongest and most important single local unit of the denomination, the Synod of New York and New Jersey, unanimously directed that its report on the "wantonness and wickedness of the rebellion of the Southern States, and the duty of all Christians and all patriots in the crisis" be transmitted to the Secretary of State for submission to the President of the United States.[64] In September, 1863, the Synod of Missouri, previously unable to meet since the beginning of the rebellion, took advantage of its first opportunity to show its colors by a staunchly loyal paper on the political situation. In true New School style it sought to give instruction to the President directly:

> Especially do we earnestly entreat his Excellency, President Lincoln, to require of all whom he appoints to rule and defend us, that they shall indeed so wield the sword that they shall be a terror of evil-doers, and a safe-guard to them who do well. . . .[65]

Evidently Missouri New School Presbyterians shared with their Old School brethren the anxieties arising from the somewhat uncertain political authority in their state; [66] yet as far as the ultimate effect of the war upon denominational strength was concerned, the fate of the two Churches was quite different. To the Old School Church in Missouri the war brought division; [67] the New School Church not only suffered no recorded loss in membership, but here and there made distinct gains. Sometimes Old School members, dissatisfied with their denomination's political stand, transferred their allegiance to the other branch, as in the case of a number of the ultra-loyal of Dr. McPheeters' congregation; [68] occasionally a whole congregation made the transfer from some other fold. The New School Church was now in a position to regain part of the

---

[64] McPherson, *op. cit.*, pp. 467-468.

[65] For account of this action of the Synod of Missouri, *cf. Christian Herald and Presbyterian Recorder*, October 15, 1863.

[66] *Cf. ante*, pp. 211-216; 271-274; 305-329.

[67] *Cf. ante*, pp. 271-274.

[68] *Cf. ante*, p. 317.

element which had split off in 1857 over the slavery issue.[69] How the war affected one of the presbyteries (Osage, in southwestern Missouri) which had left the New School Synod of Missouri in that year, was graphically described by one of its members in 1863. After stating that all except two of the ministers who had broken away six years earlier were either dead or " in Dixie," he pointed out the contrast in the political sympathies of the two surviving members:

We are political antipodes — he a secesh from the beginning, and all his church with him, except one large family. Many others would have remained loyal, but for his influence.

I have no intention of having anything more to do with the United Synod; much less with the Presbyterian Church of the Southern Confederacy. The two will, I think, unite together,[70] if the Confederacy is able to sustain itself and its institutions. [Here follows a statement that he and his church are loyal and wish to get back into the New School fold.] We are *politically* loyal, and if the term be admissible — we wish to be *Ecclesiastically* so.[71]

With the war not only causing no defection among its members, but even bringing some of the erring brethren back into the fold, it is not surprising that the New School Church, contrasting its experience in this respect with that of its Old School rival, should complacently regard itself as being rewarded by Providence for unwavering loyalty to the Federal Union.

In contrast to the complete unanimity among the membership of New School Assemblies and the people of the denomination, among the journals of the Church there was some diversity of opinion with relation to the political crisis. To be sure, only one of the six New School journals in existence in 1861 showed any sympathy for the Confederacy, and this one speedily removed itself to Southern territory;[72] nevertheless it is with some relief that one discovers a departure — however

---

[69] *Cf. ante*, p. 15.

[70] This union actually occurred in 1864. *Cf.* Johnson, *op. cit.*, p. 436; *ante*, p. 15, note 31.

[71] *Presbytery Reporter*, December, 1863, vol. v, pp. 557-558.

[72] *The Christian Observer*. An account of this journal is given *post*, pp. 370-371.

slight — from the tiresome unanimity of New School sentiment on the war. Aside from this one exception, the journals of the New School were typical of the denomination in the extravagance of their patriotism. In 1861 there were one quarterly and five weeklies representing the interests of the denomination. The *Presbyterian Quarterly Review* (corresponding in the scope and appeal of its subject-matter to the *Princeton Review* and the *Danville Review* of the other branch of the Church) took its opportunity at the first occasion to avow the Church's loyalty to the Union. In his article on the " State of the Country," the editor,[73] it is true, devoted much more time and effort to the alleged inconsistencies and shortcomings in the logic of his chief rival of the Old School, Dr. Hodge, than to the state of the country itself; yet he pointed with great pride to the position the New School Assembly of 1861 had taken:

Rising to their [sic] feet, every man in the Assembly gave his vote for decisive measures to uphold the sovereignty of the Union and to suppress rebellion. We were a unit, as is scarcely another of the large Churches of the country. Thus we have been led on prosperously by simply doing right.[74]

At the end of the year 1862 the *Presbyterian Quarterly Review* was absorbed by the *American Theological Review,* a non-denominational quarterly edited by Dr. Henry Boynton Smith, of Union Theological Seminary in New York. Dr. Smith was the leading theologian of the New School Church; in fact, according to one of the foremost of his Old School contemporaries he was " the greatest theologian of the American Presbyterian Church." [75] The combined journal was called the *American Presbyterian and Theological Review.* That it would be no less loyal than the New School quarterly which it replaced was

[73] Dr. Benjamin J. Wallace.
[74] *Presbyterian Quarterly Review,* July, 1861, vol. x, p. 145. For the entire article on " The State of the Country," cf. pp. 118-146.
[75] This was the opinion of Dr. Archibald Alexander Hodge, who was Dr. Charles Hodge's " still greater son," (Thompson, *op. cit.,* p. 210). The opinion was quoted *ibid.,* p. 139.

evident from the tone of articles on the state of the country which had appeared in the *American Theological Review* before the consolidation took place — particularly an article on "The Moral Aspects of the Present Struggle," in October, 1861. The writer [76] maintained that the unscrupulous ambition of political partisans in the South forced the Union to choose between war and inevitable ruin:

> Thank God the booming of the cannon that shattered the walls and tore the flag of Fort Sumter, roused the nation from a dream that had well-nigh proved its death. It was a glorious experience. Strangely, God seemed to give to the nation another heart. . . . The Church awoke, too, and from all her pulpits sounded out the word of God, which declares, not in the Old Testament, but in the New, that the civil magistrate is "the minister of God, *an avenger to execute wrath* on him that doeth evil," and "that he beareth not the sword in vain." . . . If there ever was a sacred cause on earth, we believe this is one. It is just the cause for which the New Testament explicitly commands the unsheathing of the sword in God's name. . . . Peace is a blessing. . . . But who supposes we could have had peace, had this foul conspiracy been suffered to triumph? . . . Much as we love and long for peace . . . we believe the utter crushing of this fearful rebellion is the only hope of its permanent maintenance. [77]

Rejoicing over reports that Christians of the South were praying over the subject, the writer declared, "In God's judgment we have the utmost confidence." In this reliance he urged, "Let us do our duty, cost what it may, and let the righteous God do what seemeth him good." [78]   It is rather interesting that there was no suggestion that God be consulted as to what men's duty was; this was doubtless so evident that God's opinion was not required.   Add such enthusiastic nationalism to that of the *Presbyterian Quarterly Review,* and the combined quarterly was bound to be the safest of periodicals so far as patriotism was concerned.

The leading New School weekly was the New York *Evangelist,* which had been founded in 1830.   Equally well edited

[76] The article (unsigned) was probably written by the editor, Dr. H. B. Smith.

[77] *American Theological Review,* October, 1861, vol. iii, pp. 730-733.

[78] *Ibid.,* p. 733.

and somewhat more liberal in tone than its principal Old School rival, the *Presbyterian*,[79] this journal's opinion on the political crisis was worth careful consideration. Early in 1861 it took the position that disunion was not necessarily fatal to our national existence. Pointing out that even with the loss of the states that had seceded, our territory would still be twice as large as Austria, three times as large as France, seven times as large as Great Britain; and that our population would be larger than that of the whole country in 1840, it considered that alienation and hatred between the North and South were "almost worse than open separation." It wanted no "forced union," declaring that union would be bought at too high a price if it involved a sacrifice of principle.[80] After the fateful fourteenth of April, however, the advice of the *Evangelist* was quite different. Claiming that the North might find consolation in the reflection "that we did not begin it," this journal now asserted that it was the duty of every citizen to stand behind the Government in the coming war.[81] As civil war was better than anarchy, the Government must be supported at any cost.[82] How this position, so promptly taken by the *Evangelist* upon the outbreak of hostilities, was maintained throughout the conflict, the "prospectus" of the journal for 1866 proudly pointed out:

This long-established paper . . . is nearing the close of another year with its *circulation unimpaired* — a matter of special gratification, as showing that its course in these trying times has been generally approved, and that it has been more widely useful than ever the past year, by its firm and cordial support of the Government when assailed by a wicked Rebellion.

. . . .

While it has aimed never to overstep the limits of a Religious Journal, by violence of language, or the discussion of merely political questions, it has constantly held up the cause in which we are engaged as the cause

[79] *Cf. ante*, pp. 150-158.
[80] Editorial, "Does Disunion Involve National Shipwreck?" New York *Evangelist*, January 31, 1861.
[81] Editorial, "The Duty of the Hour," *ibid.*, April 18, 1861.
[82] Editorial, *ibid.*, April 25, 1861.

of OUR COUNTRY AND OF LIBERTY, and for which it was the sacred duty of every good citizen to be ready to sacrifice his property and his life. . . .[83]

With as much loyalty as the *Evangelist* and more extravagance in expressing it, the *American Presbyterian* (Philadelphia) was unquestioned in its patriotism. While the *Evangelist* before the attack on Fort Sumter was inclined to advocate peaceful disunion, its Philadelphia contemporary from the beginning of the secession movement which followed Lincoln's election, was bitterly denunciatory of all plans involving the division of the country.[84] It bemoaned the "unmanly weakness" of officials — municipal, state and national — and pleaded for the strict enforcement of the laws.[85] The war which broke out in April it considered "better than peace,"[86] and confidently prophesied that the New School Church would be "found to be an *American* church in this crisis, in a most peculiar and happy sense."[87] Most virulent of all the New School journals in its hatred of the Old School, the *American Presbyterian* throughout the war period took particular delight in contrasting the loyalty of its own denomination with the record of the Old School in this respect.[88] As this most radical of the weeklies of the younger branch of the Church remained obstinately opposed to Presbyterian reunion long after most others had been converted to that cause,[89] it is not improbable that the constant reiteration of its charges of disloyalty against

[83] *Cf.* "Prospectus" of New York *Evangelist* for 1866, *Presbyterian Historical Almanac*, 1865, p. 380.

[84] *Cf.* editorials, *e.g.*, as follows: against disunion, November 8, 1860; "Anarchy or Order," January 31, 1861.

[85] Editorial, "The Enforcement of the Laws," February 7, 1861.

[86] Editorial, "Better than Peace," April 25, 1861.

[87] Editorial, "Our Paper in the Crisis," May 2, 1861.

[88] *Cf., e.g.*, quotations from the *American Presbyterian* in editorial, "Virulence and Malignity of New School Sectarianism," *True Presbyterian*, April 17, 1864; also, *ante*, pp. 74-75; 288.

[89] *Cf.* editorials, "Peril of Admitting 'Old School' Peculiarities to Equal Rights in the Reunited Church," *American Presbyterian*, April 25, 1867; and "The Responsibility of our Branch to our own Principles," *ibid.*, May 2, 1867.

the Old School was prompted in part by a desire to make reunion seem undesirable.

The *Christian Herald* (Cincinnati) bore a closer relation to its denomination than any other New School or any Old School paper, for it was owned and controlled by the Synods of Ohio, Indiana, Cincinnati, and Wabash, by which it had been founded in 1853. In the fall of 1861 it absorbed the *Presbyterian Recorder*, a weekly which had been founded in Chicago some eight months before. During its brief lifetime this infant journal had shown itself consistently anti-slavery and pro-Union. It had rejoiced to see the persistence with which Dr. Spring worked for Old School endorsement of the Federal Government, for it declared that it " would blush for shame " if a Presbyterian body having a majority of its membership in the North should " prove itself untrue to Presbyterian history and American liberty." [90] The *Christian Herald* did not need the leaven of patriotism which was introduced by its taking over the Chicago paper, however; like its Old School neighbor, the *Presbyter,* it was thoroughly loyal from the outset of the secession difficulties. Like the *Presbyter* it was the self-constituted critic of the patriotism of all Presbyterians, and was itself still so hyper-patriotic in 1866 that of the three leading Assemblies then in existence, it found only one (its own, of course) " thoroughly loyal "; another (the Southern) was " thoroughly disloyal "; while the largest of the three (the Old School) was " loyal, with an active and belligerent disloyal element." [91] A year after Lee's surrender the *Christian Herald* was thus still fighting the war. After the Old School Assembly of 1866 had satisfactorily met the demands of this belligerent paper with respect to proving its loyalty,[92] the Cincinnati journal abandoned its hesitancy with regard to the desirability of Presbyterian reunion, and when

[90] Editorial, " The General Assemblies and the Country," *Presbyterian Recorder,* May 30, 1861.
[91] *Cf.* editorial, " The Two Assemblies," (*Christian Herald and Presbyterian Recorder,* May 17, 1866) quoted *ante,* p. 257.
[92] For these demands, *cf. ibid.* For the manner in which they were met, *cf. ante,* pp. 218-255.

the reunion was finally accomplished it united with its neighbor of the other School, the *Presbyter* — a journal of kindred tastes and principles — to form the *Herald and Presbyter*.[93]

When the short-lived *Presbyterian Recorder* merged with the *Christian Herald* in the fall of 1861, there was no New School journal left west of Cincinnati, for the *Presbytery Reporter*, a monthly published at Alton, Illinois, had been suspended in 1860. Largely to make up for this deficiency in the Northwest, publication of the *Presbytery Reporter* was resumed in the spring of 1863, the Presbytery of Alton (Illinois) resolving to secure the editor and publisher[94] against pecuniary loss.[95] At a subscription price of a dollar a year this magazine — a sort of cross between a religious review and a weekly journal — undertook to "identify itself largely with the interests of the Presbyterian Church in the region of its principal circulation, viz., — the Synods of Illinois, Missouri and Peoria."[96] The message that it carried to the people of these sections of the Church was always firmly anti-slavery and pro-Union,[97] besides being intensely loyal to the interests of New School Presbyterianism.[98]

The record for complete denominational unanimity on the issue of adherence to the Federal Government was ruined by the attitude of another journal styling itself a New School paper. This was the *Christian Observer*, a weekly published in Philadelphia. This periodical became notorious for the only recorded expressions of questionable loyalty anywhere in the New School Church. That the editor, Dr. Amasa Converse, had been born in New Hampshire made his position all the

---

[93] For an account of the steps by which the union of these two Cincinnati Presbyterian papers was brought about, cf. the editorial on the subject in the last issue of the *Christian Herald* (September 23, 1869).

[94] Rev. A. T. Norton.

[95] For an account of this action of the Presbytery of Alton, cf. *Presbytery Reporter*, May 2, 1863, vol. v, p. 382.

[96] Cf. advertisement in *Presbyterian Historical Almanac*, 1865, p. 390.

[97] Cf., e.g., *Presbytery Reporter*, July, 1860, vol. v, no. 11, p. 311; also *ibid.*, July, 1863, vol. v, p. 430.

[98] Cf., e.g., *ibid.*, p. 427.

more surprising. A dozen years of experience as a preacher and editor in Virginia had, however, developed in him a strong sympathy for pro-slavery views. Although originally one of the prime movers in the separation of the New School in 1837, when twenty years later the great issue of slavery caused the splitting off of the six Southern synods of the Church, Dr. Converse openly defended the seceding party. Opposition to the *Christian Observer* became so pronounced after the outbreak of war that the Federal Government was importuned to prevent its further publication.[99] Before the end of the year 1861 Dr. Converse had left Philadelphia. Subsequently he established his *Christian Observer* at Richmond, Virginia,[100] but publication of the journal was decidedly intermittent until after the close of the war.[101] Thus before the close of the first year of the war as complete unanimity prevailed among the journals of the New School denomination as among any other group in this most " loyal " of churches.

New School Churchmen, while recognizing that the great majority of the preachers of the other branch were thoroughly patriotic, looked with scorn upon the difficulties which the Old School was having in cases of individuals deficient in outspoken patriotism. When Dr. N. L. Rice of the Fifth Avenue Church in New York undertook to explain the silence of his pulpit on political matters,[102] the *American Presbyterian* commented:

We shall begin to believe that the leading minds of the " Old School " branch of the Presbyterian Church are thoroughly and incurably infected

---

[99] *Cf.* editorial, " The Christian Observer," *Presbyterian Recorder,* August 29, 1861; also communication of Samuel Sawyer in *Christian Herald,* September 26, 1861.

[100] *Presbyterian Encyclopaedia,* p. 155. The above account of the *Christian Observer* is based on statements regarding the career of Dr. Converse, *ibid.;* on an editorial, " The Christian Observer," *Presbyterian Recorder,* August 29, 1861; and on a communication of Samuel Sawyer to the *Christian Herald,* September 26, 1861.

[101] From January 7, 1864 to March 3, 1865 it was issued as a small " single sheet." After June 1, 1865, it was again a double sheet. *Cf.* files in Library of the Presbyterian Historical Society, Philadelphia.

[102] *Cf. ante,* pp. 283-285.

by their long subserviency to Southern dictation, and incapacitated utterly from rendering sincere and earnest support to their country, in its hour of need.[103]

Similarly, the writer [104] of a letter to the New York *Evangelist* complained of the unfortunate political effects of Old School influence in Delaware. Writing from Wilmington concerning the degree of loyalty of Old School churches, he reported:

In them all there are true and loyal men, but most of the ministers, and the majority of the members, have not, I am constrained to believe, stood for the right. Had they, the result of the last election, coming so near a triumph, would not have been a defeat.[105]

This charge brought a sharp retort from a member of the only Old School congregation in Wilmington. The writer would not accept the assumption of the New School critic that political sermons were an unmixed blessing:

. . . . I would like W. A.[105a] to look a little nearer home, and see how many of the best members have been driven from the New-school branch of the Church, because in going to the Church in expectation of hearing a sermon suitable for the quiet of the mind and soul, as every one who goes to church fully expects to hear, they were forced to come away entirely disgusted with hearing a politico-Abolition sermon, such as can be heard upon the street every day of our lives.

He also calls the only Old-school church in the city "an ambulance for sick and wounded Secessionists." I would like him to say what he means by that expression; if he means that it is a refuge for those who are tired and sick of hearing political sermons, it is so.

He then remarks about the dissensions arising in some of the churches where the minister and the Union party in the church have been over-powered by the secessionists. I would ask him, if he has not noticed

---

[103] Quoted in editorial, "Not Ready for Union," *Presbyterian*, December 7, 1861.

[104] He signed himself "W. A." Perhaps he was Rev. William Aikman, pastor of the Hanover Street Presbyterian Church (New School), Wilmington, Delaware.

[105] Quoted in communication entitled "Unjust Charges," *Presbyterian*, December 27, 1862.

[105a] These were the initials with which the communication to the New York *Evangelist* had been signed. *Cf.* note 104, above.

the same thing transpiring in the New-school church in Pencader Hundred, of which the Rev. Mr. Foote [sic] is pastor.[106]

Were political sermons allowed by the deed by which the property was given to the Trustees,[107] I dare say that the Rev. Dr. McIlvaine of the College at Princeton, who is at present supplying the pulpit, would give us a far more eloquent political discourse than the pastor of the New-school Presbyterian Church ever could, or ever did, write or speak.[108]

This literary controversy reveals a recognition on both sides that political sermons were much more common in New School than in Old School pulpits. Certainly that is the conclusion one would draw from the relative representation of the two denominations in collections of sermons on war-time subjects.[109]

[106] The church at Pencader (near Glasgow, Delaware) of which Rev. George Foot was the pastor, had a communicant membership of approximately 105 in 1862. *Cf. Minutes of the General Assembly* (New School), 1862, p. 150. As the church failed, from 1860 to 1863, inclusive, to submit to its presbytery the required annual report (*cf. ibid.*, vol. xii and xiii, *passim*, statistical tables), it is probable that conditions were not entirely harmonious in the congregation during that period. The condition described in the above communication is particularly interesting because it is the only recorded instance of division within a New School congregation over the war. In this connection, two facts should be noted: the church was in a slave state; the minister belonged to the Union party.

. [107] This interesting reason for pulpit silence on political topics cannot have been a very common one, as it was very seldom that a congregation had been given the property where it met for worship.

[108] *Cf.* communication, " Unjust Charges," signed by " A Member of the Congregation " under date of December 19, 1862, in *Presbyterian*, December 27, 1862.

[109] Among the printed war-sermons of New School ministers, the following may be mentioned:

Dr. G. L. Prentiss (Union Theological Seminary), " Lessons of Encouragement from the times of Washington," and " Some of the Providential Lessons of 1861."

Dr. William Adams (Madison Square Presbyterian Church, New York, N. Y.), " Christian Patriotism," 1863.

Dr. John Jenkins (Calvary Presbyterian Church, Philadelphia), " Thoughts for the Crisis," 1861.

Dr. George Duffield (First Presbyterian Church, Detroit, Michigan), " A Thanksgiving Service: The Rule of Divine Providence applicable to the Present Circumstances of Our Country "; and " Our National Sins to be

With a membership largely ultra-Northern in background, with no serious Border-State problem on its hands, no Stuart Robinson and Robert J. Breckinridge to stir up the denomination by their personal quarrels, no ministers with hypersensitive consciences on the matter of political preaching, no *True Presbyterian* to bring down charges of disloyalty upon the Church, no group of ministers subjected to the watchful suspicion of the military authorities, no necessity of General Assembly decisions on cases of " disloyalty " within the denomination, no theological professors involving their seminaries and their Church in meeting the disfavor of the patriots — with none of these obstacles to unanimity of political sentiment, the position of the New School Church during the period of the war was indeed very different from that of its Old School rival. With the Old School strongholds in Pennsylvania, southern Ohio, and southern Indiana serving as a buffer between the New School and the South, it is not surprising that the Yankeeized Presbyterians whose strength lay principally in more northerly latitudes should have been not only staunch

Repented of, and the Grounds of Hope for the Preservation of Our Federal Constitution and Union," 1861.

Rev. Horace C. Hovey (Presbyterian Church, Coldwater, Michigan), " The National Fast," 1861; and " Freedom's Banner," 1861.

Dr. Henry Darling (Without charge; later pastor of the Fourth Presbyterian Church, Albany, New York), " Slavery and the War: A Historical Essay," 1863.

Dr. S. G. Spees (Third Street Presbyterian Church, Dayton, Ohio), " A New Song . . . : A Thanksgiving Sermon," 1863.

Dr. John G. Atterbury (Second Presbyterian Church, New Albany, Indiana), " God in Civil Government," 1862.

Dr. Samuel T. Spear (South Presbyterian Church, Brooklyn, New York), " The Nation's Blessing in Trial," 1862; and " The Duty of the Hour."

Cf. also two-column abstract of a patriotic sermon preached by Dr. E. D. Morris (pastor of the Second Presbyterian Church of Columbus, Ohio), *Presbyter*, September 23, 1863. Dr. Morris was later an historian of the New School Church. (*Cf. ante*, pp. 343, notes 13, 15; 356-357; 361.

Cf. also an oration, " The State of the Country," delivered by Dr. Walter Clarke (pastor of the First Presbyterian Church of Buffalo, New York) at Buffalo, N. Y., July 4, 1862.

The sermons named above were no doubt typical also of the hosts of New School patriotic sermons which were never printed.

patriots during the war, but also vigorous and vindictive radicals after its close, insistent upon punishment of the rebels and supremely confident in their own peculiar fitness for determining just how the negro problem should be settled. Had all Northerners in the 1860's been New School Presbyterians, it is conceivable that the war might have been won sooner, though it is scarcely likely, if one may judge from the recorded opinions of this Church, that there would have been less of the spirit of injustice and intolerance which characterized the reconstruction settlement.

PART IV

THE MINOR PRESBYTERIAN CHURCHES AND THE CIVIL WAR

THE MINOR PRESBYTERIAN CHURCHES AND THE CIVIL WAR

OF the lesser Presbyterian denominations in 1861 the youngest was of the greatest strength in the North.[1] This was the United Presbyterian Church of North America, which had come into existence in 1858 through the union of the Associate Presbyterian and the Associate Reformed Churches.[2] The Associate Church had long since been "purged of the sin of slavery"[3] by the removal to the lands north of the Ohio of large numbers of Southern anti-slavery members and by the secession of the Presbytery of the Carolinas.[4] The Associate Reformed Church, though spared an internal conflict over slavery, had lost most of its Southern membership through the "pure mismanagement and criminal captiousness" of its leaders.[5] It was therefore to be expected that the United Church would have little sympathy for the institution of human slavery or for Southern agitation for its extension.

Of the eighteen declarations constituting the "Judicial Testimony" which was the most important element of the Basis of Union, two in particular gave evidence of the attitude this United Church might be expected to take in the event of a North-South crisis:

13. *We declare*, That the law of God, as written upon the heart of man, and as set forth in the Scriptures of the Old and New Testaments, is supreme in its authority and obligations, and that where the commands of the church or state are in conflict with the commands of this law, we are to obey God rather than men.

---

[1] *Cf. ante*, pp. 5, note 6; 7; 9-13.
[2] *Cf. ante*, pp. 10-11.
[3] Scouller, James B., *History of the United Presbyterian Church of North America* (American Church History Series, a part of vol. xi, New York, 1894), p. 179.
[4] *Ibid.*, pp. 177-179.
[5] *Ibid.*, pp. 215-216.

14. *We declare*, That slaveholding — that is, the holding of unoffending human beings in involuntary bondage, and considering and treating them as property, and subject to be bought and sold — is a violation of the law of God, and contrary both to the letter and spirit of Christianity.[6]

As an historian of the denomination later remarked in explanation of United Presbyterian opposition to slavery, " Plain people cannot comprehend that system of ethics which divides a man's identity and allows him to do as a citizen that which it forbids him to do as a Christian." [7] Whatever the philosophy underlying their feeling, the plain people [8] who made up the new Church had inherited from the parent organizations a vigorous hatred of the institution of slavery and all that it stood for.

The sixty-nine ministers and forty-three ruling elders [9] who convened on May 15, 1861, in Monmouth, Illinois, for the third General Assembly of the United Presbyterian Church, unanimously adopted the report of the Special Committee on the State of the Country.[10] The most unique feature of the report was its attempt to catalogue the sins that had brought on the rebellion:

The sins that have in an especial manner provoked the eyes of the Holy One seem to be these: 1. Pride and self-sufficiency; glorying in our supposed wisdom and greatness. 2. Inordinate and excessive ambition. 3. Contempt of the unspeakable grace of God in Christ. 4. Sabbath desecration. 5. Obstinacy under former providential rebukes. 6. Slaveholding, the great and immediate cause of the present trouble, though seldom thought of as an evil by those who are directly concerned in it.[11]

The report then expatiated on the magnitude of the sin of slave-holding. " To debase and trample on . . . the image of

[6] *Ibid.*, pp. 230-231. For the entire " Judicial Testimony," *cf.* pp. 229-231.
[7] *Ibid.*, p. 210. Dr. Scouller was here writing of the Associate Reformed Church, but his remark was equally applicable to the denomination which joined it to make the United Presbyterian Church.
[8] For this characterization of the personnel of the United Presbyterian Church, *cf. ibid.*, p. 242; also, *passim.*
[9] For a list of the members *cf. Presbyterian Historical Almanac,* 1862, p. 220.
[10] *Ibid.*, p. 227.
[11] *Ibid.*

God enstamped on man; " to tear asunder the tender ties of
nature and affection; to work a man and give him no wages;
"to forbid the great God to speak to his own creatures, that
they may be saved; " to deprive a people of the ordinance and
privilege of marriage — to do these things was to bid defiance
to the God of justice. "Slavery," the report declared, "must
be exceedingly flagrant in the sight of the Great Parent and
Ruler of men." Yet the Assembly was by no means willing
that the South should bear the entire burden of the guilt of
slavery:

It should not be thought that we, in the Free States, have nothing to
do with this monstrous iniquity. Have we not countenanced those who
practised it? Have we not contributed to extend, and establish, [and?]
fortify it? Paul was guilty of the murder of Stephen, though he did
not cast a single stone. With regard to the aboriginal inhabitants of the
land, it is to be feared that they also have had cause to complain of
injustice and cruel rapacity.[12]

In view of these sins, and the general responsibility for them,
the Assembly had no doubt regarding the necessity of fasting,
mourning, and supplication, and it passed a series of five resolutions urging the appointment of a special day of prayer for
the welfare of the people and the land. Two of these resolutions recognized explicitly the relationship between the United
Presbyterian Church and the United States:

Resolved. . . . . *2.* That the Clerk of the Assembly be directed, and
hereby is directed, to forward to the President of the United States a
letter in behalf of this Assembly; and, after assuring him of our earnest
sympathy, and the sympathy of our people, and our and their readiness
to co-operate with him, in his endeavors to maintain the Constitution
and integrity of the nation, to solicit him, in behalf of this Assembly,
by his Proclamation, to invite and call all the people of the United States
to fasting, humiliation, and prayer. . . .
3. That the Assembly earnestly recommend all the people under their
care to confess and bewail, not only their own sins, but the sins of the
land, and to be much in prayer in these times of trouble.[13]

If the United Presbyterian Assembly's report on the State of
the Country lacked the pungency of the corresponding paper

[12] *Ibid.,* p. 227.
[13] *Ibid.*

of the New School Assembly in 1861,[14] there was in it at least
a frank avowal of allegiance to the Union and its cause, although — in view of the emphasis the Federal Government
was placing on the preservation of the Union as the sole object
of the war — the attention devoted to the subject of slavery
was distinctly disproportionate. If the action contrasted with
that of the New School in the moderation of its expression, it
contrasted as sharply with the action of the Old School in the
unanimity of its adoption.

The General Assembly of 1862, meeting in Pittsburgh, again
placed the United Presbyterian Church unequivocally on the
side of the Federal Government. As in the previous year, the
report on the State of the Country prefaced its resolutions with
a lengthy condemnation of slavery and a history of our country's policy with regard to it. The United Presbyterian Church
was proud of its own record on this subject:

> God is pleading his controversy with our nation, because of the oppres-
> sions done in the land. Slavery has culminated in acts of high-handed
> treason and open rebellion. . . .
> For many years have the bodies composing the United Presbyterian
> Church boldly maintained their Testimony against this system of grievous
> oppression. It has now become a distinctive principle of the United
> Presbyterian Church. She refuses to have fellowship with slavery or its
> abettors. This testimony has, however, been disregarded by politicians
> and slaveholders, and by many professing the gospel. . . . Our testimony
> has been recorded on high. The tears of the oppressed, God has put into
> his bottle. Their cries have been heard. The storm has gathered. The
> bolts of destruction have been hurled abroad. . . .
> These results, too terrible to contemplate, we believe have flowed from
> this system of American slavery. . . . The struggle which is now con-
> vulsing our country is to maintain constitutional liberty.[15]

Having thus reiterated its previous condemnations of slavery,
the Assembly expressed its resolutions with regard to the war
in terms that suggest that the authors may, during the previous twelve months, have been reading denominational endorsements of the Federal Union which made their own action

---

[14] Cf. ante, pp. 344-345.
[15] Presbyterian Historical Almanac, 1863, p. 349.

of 1861 seem weak in comparison. At any rate the resolutions of 1862 were stated in less moderate terms:

Resolved, 1. That in the judgment of the Assembly, this wicked rebellion, which imperils the existence of the Government, which aims to found a confederacy upon the ruins of crushed humanity, and which brutally assassinates and murders our fellow-citizens, is pre-eminently the result of the practical workings of American slavery.

2. That the true remedy for the evils which now surround us and threaten our national existence, lies in turning to the living God . . . and in complying with the demands of his law, which requires that "liberty be proclaimed throughout all the land to all the inhabitants thereof; " "then shall our light break forth as the morning, and our health shall spring forth speedily."

3. That this Assembly has an abiding confidence in the national Government; bids it God-speed in suppressing this rebellion; and we pledge ourselves to its support in maintaining the principles of civil and religious liberty, by all scriptural means.

4. That a copy of this paper be transmitted to the President and Heads of Departments, . . . to urge upon them the necessity of taking immediate and effective measures to remove the causes of our national troubles, that we may be restored to the favor of God.[16]

In view of the persistent emphasis with which the Assemblies of 1861 and 1862 had asserted that slavery was the primary cause of the war and that true peace could not be expected until this evil was blotted out, it is not surprising that the first Assembly of the United Presbyterian Church to convene after the issuing of Lincoln's Emancipation Proclamation made elaborate provisions for missionary work among the " freedmen of our Southern States." The constitution adopted for the " Board of Missions of the United Presbyterian Church of North America, for the Freedmen of our Southern States " made extensive provision for the machinery by which the Board was to operate, though it was resolved "that such Presbyteries as may prefer it are hereby authorized to select their own mission field, procure their own laborers, and conduct their missions in their own way, provided that they report to the Board the location of their respective fields, the laborers employed and the amount of funds collected and dis-

[16] *Ibid.,* pp. 349-350.

bursed." [17] The activities of four presbyteries which had already been engaged in such work were specifically recognized and approved. Quite evidently the United Presbyterian Church was entering upon missionary work among the freedmen with all the enthusiasm which its anti-slavery traditions would naturally engender, and quite possibly with more understanding than accompanied the labors of its more northerly neighbors,[18] for the southern origin of a large portion of the United Church [19] must have given this element, at least, some knowledge of the negro problem. At any rate the 1863 General Assembly was preparing for the United Presbyterian Church an elaborate program of work among the freedmen. As the Federal Government had at last taken steps in the direction urged by the anti-slavery people, it was but logical that a traditionally anti-slavery Church should immediately respond by making provisions for meeting the new needs which the Emancipation Proclamation brought to the Southern negroes.[20]

In 1864 the General Assembly's Committee on Bills and Overtures reported on three papers dealing with the state of the country — papers which had been submitted to them for recommended action. In each case the report of the Committee was adopted by the Assembly. In response to a demand for an address from the Assembly to President Lincoln, the Committee recommended that a special committee be appointed to prepare at their earliest convenience, a paper expressing the Assembly's " deep sympathy and earnest co-operation " with the Government, its recognition of God's favor " in the successes which have attended the movements of our armies on the Potomac and in Georgia," and its hope that the Government would continue to recognize the necessity of dependence

---

[17] For this Constitution, *cf.* McPherson, *op. cit.,* p. 507.

[18] The strength of the Church lay very largely in lower Pennsylvania (particularly in the western part of the state), Ohio, Indiana, and Illinois.

[19] *Cf. ante,* p. 379.

[20] For the work accomplished by the Board set up by the United Presbyterian Church in 1863, *cf. post,* pp. 453-454.

upon Divine favor.[21] A second paper which had been submitted to the Committee asked "what advice should be tendered by this Assembly to our National Executive, touching the *morality of retaliation* as a means of preventing the continuance of the cruelty and barbarity which has been practised upon our soldiers by our rebel enemies." The Committee recommended that as this paper had been presented under the impression that President Lincoln was "*hesitating* on the question of retaliation," no action was needed by the Assembly, " as we have been informed that the President has already decided the course to be pursued by him, and that retaliation is being already practised to some extent by the Union army." The third paper upon which the Committee was asked to suggest action requested that the Assembly hail the Emancipation Proclamation as "a measure of high military importance and necessity, and statesmanlike in striking at slavery, the root, cause and strength of the rebellion. . . ;" also that the Assembly recognize in the Proclamation "the voice of God speaking as he did to his ancient people Israel, saying by it to us, 'Break every yoke and let the oppressed go free.'" The Committee presented this resolution in another form, and recommended that it be adopted as restated. The changes suggested were highly significant, as may be recognized from the resolution as it was recommended to the Assembly:

> *Resolved,* That without expressing any judgment on the military importance and necessity, or the statesmanlike character of the Proclamation, we hail it as obedience to the voice of God, calling us, as he did his ancient people, " Let the oppressed go free and break every yoke." [22]

Thus the Assembly recognized the Scriptural limitations upon its activities, and refrained from passing judgment on military and political moves; at the same time it was willing to take such liberties with Biblical phraseology as would contribute to the success of an activity which it considered entirely Scriptural — the elimination of slavery.

[21] *Presbyterian Historical Almanac,* 1865, p. 175.
[22] *Ibid.,* 1865, pp. 175-176.

In its paper on the State of the Country the General Assembly of 1865 reminded the Church that the war "which was characterized by many acts of inhumanity on the part of those who brought it on, — particularly in starving to death thousands of our soldiers taken as prisoners of war, — " had been brought almost to a close. Considering the tone of this opening sentence of the paper, it is not surprising that the Assembly, after expressing to President Johnson its "cordial sympathy and support, in the hope that, like a Joshua, he will do right and accomplish, under God, the object of our desire, namely, the reconstruction of our Government on the broad basis of universal freedom," should have declared that "As civil magistrates are designed to be a terror to evil doers it is the unanimous opinion of this Assembly that all punishments defined by the Constitution as deserved by traitors, should be visited upon the leading instigators and prosecutors of this rebellion." If this pronouncement betrayed a certain vagueness on the part of United Presbyterians with regard to the content of the Constitution, there was at least no vagueness concerning the deserts of Southern rebels. Citing Scriptural authority,[23] the Assembly emphasized its position by asserting that "Mercy to the great civil and military heads of this rebellion would be cruelty to coming generations." It was voted that a copy of the 1865 resolutions be sent to President Johnson with the assurance of the Assembly's "heartfelt desire for his success in the work of reconstruction, in establishing order and peace and in perfecting the emancipation of the African race in our land."[24]

The United Presbyterian Assembly of 1865 also adopted a thirteen hundred word report prepared by the Committee on Bills and Overtures with reference to the status of the emancipated slaves. The substance of the report — reiterated in various forms — was to the effect that the only means by which the

[23] Ezra vii, 26: "Whosoever will not do the law of thy God and the law of the king, let judgment be executed speedily, whether it be unto death or to banishment, or to confiscation of goods, or to imprisonment."

[24] *Presbyterian Historical Almanac*, 1866, pp. 252-253.

freedmen could be assured justice and opportunities for progress was by securing them the political franchise. As firm adherents of the theory defined in their Confession of Faith that "Synods and Councils are to handle or conclude nothing but that which is ecclesiastical. . . . " some of the members of the Assembly were somewhat embarrassed by the political character of the subject under consideration, and therefore the report asserted that it was "competent to the Church to pass her judgment on all questions affecting public morals or . . . respecting human rights upon which depend the peace and welfare of human society; " and that the Church was the "'light of the world' on questions of policy as truly as on the doctrines of grace." The status of the emancipated slave the Assembly regarded as "*the question* now before the country." For thirty years, this 1865 Assembly declared its adherents had urged the abolition of slavery from considerations of right and policy;[25] with this end now virtually attained, the next task was to assist the negro to a position "of security for himself and advantageous to us." Nothing less than political equality, it was urged, would bring peace; nothing less would "please God or satisfy the conscience of an enlightened Christian people." Nothing would so much contribute to his independence and self-respect as to place him under the responsibilities of a free man; with the responsibilities he should have the privileges of a free man.

Various arguments were adduced to prove that justice demanded the suffrage for the freedman. "The black man whose enfranchisement we advocate is a native born American

[25] As far as official action is concerned, this statement is not wholly true. In 1851 the Associate Reformed Synod of New York, one of the two synods which united in 1855 (*cf.* Scouller, *op. cit.*, p. 212) to form the Associate Reformed Church which in 1858, in turn, united with the Associate Church to form the United Presbyterian Church, by a majority of five decided not to issue a testimony against slavery. (*Cf. ibid.*, pp. 211-212.) It is only fair to add, however, that doubts as to the propriety of the pronouncement — not as to the iniquity of slavery — apparently defeated the proposition. There was also suspicion that its suggestion was prompted by Free-Soil politics. *Cf. ibid.*, pp. 211-212.

citizen," blithely announced the United Presbyterians, judicial doubts to the contrary notwithstanding. The next step in the argument came very easily to the plain Scotch and Scotch-Irish people who made up this denomination: " The right of suffrage is the natural right of every citizen." A third statement in the argument showed this Church already in 1865 ready for the suffrage policy followed during the ensuing years in the reconstructed states:

> In times of trial, the colored population of the country have proved themselves loyal. Treason is the highest crime known to the laws of any civilized country, and so far as there is taint of treason, by refusing to bear arms or otherwise support the government, exceptions may, and should be taken to the privileges of citizenship. If this policy were adopted, not the black man, but the man who takes exception to the enfranchisement of the black man, should fall under reprobation and be subjected to disabilities. In this way the magistrate would magnify his office in showing himself " a praise to them who do well."

The report was concluded with a series of declarations which summarized the lengthy argument and frequently reiterated demands for negro suffrage. " From what we have seen and known of prejudice against the colored race," the report stated, " we have reason to expect to this specific point of reformation determined and persevering opposition. . . ." The people of the Church were therefore carefully warned to take no part in such opposition " ' lest haply they be found fighting against God.' " Quoting the sentence from the Westminster Confession so often repeated by adherents of the various Presbyterian sects during the war years, " Synods and councils are to handle or conclude nothing but that which is ecclesiastical; and are not to intermeddle with civil affairs, which concern the commonwealth, unless by way of humble petition, in cases extraordinary," the report recommended that the United Presbyterian councils take advantage of the one means open to them and " petition Congress for such legislation as shall secure, according to the preceding declarations, the rights of the colored race." [26]

[26] *Presbyterian Historical Almanac*, 1866, pp. 244-246.

This action was a bit too much for some of the members of even this strongly anti-slavery Church. Three of the members of the Assembly entered their formal dissent from the sentiments expressed in the paper which the Assembly had adopted. The protestants argued that the paper contained advice contrary to the Confession of Faith, and that the Church was in danger of most deplorable consequences if it departed from the " just, the reasonable, and the Scriptural line of conduct " laid down in this Confession. The other reason advanced for this dissent must have come as a blow to the overwhelming majority supporting the paper. In spite of the fact that the sentiment it expressed might with some propriety have been applied to the majority element in any of the war-time Presbyterian Assemblies, the 1865 United Presbyterian gathering seems to have been the only one to hear it formally uttered. As stated by the three dissenting commissioners it was not phrased in doubtful terms:

. . . we believe ecclesiastical men, however learned, able, and faithful in their own province, are, neither by office, by education, nor by habits of life, competent to give judicial decision on such subjects as are included in the Assembly's action.[27]

A strange doctrine, that, in 1865 — or today, either, for that matter! To the majority element in the United Presbyterian Assembly it probably sounded woefully undemocratic. Certainly the Federal Government did follow the direction pointed out by this body. It would be interesting to know to what degree this fact resulted from the Assembly's advice; to what degree it proved that the feeling of the Assembly was simply typical of that of the American people. As far as the sentiment of the dissenting commissioners was concerned, perhaps upon sober reflection this increasingly commended itself to the Church, for 1865 marked the end of its policy of advising the Government on matters connected with the war and reconstruction. Its record of war-time pronouncements rivalled that of the New School Church: the language employed had been

[27] *Presbyterian Historical Almanac,* 1866, p. 246.

scarcely less extravagant, and only in 1865 — and then with but a very small minority — had it fallen short of the unanimity which so consistently characterized New School action.[28]

The most extreme Northern patriot could hardly have found occasion to disapprove of the position taken by the United Presbyterians on the war and its problems. From the Northern point of view their record in press and pulpit was as blameless as in Assembly conduct: there is no recorded instance of disloyalty on the part of any preacher or any journal of the denomination.[29] Whatever inhibitions the strictness of their theology may have raised against the expression of political opinions, they were evidently more than overcome by the bitterness with which the United Presbyterians hated slavery. To the sixty thousand members[30] of this religious group a war which promised to eliminate the curse of American slavery was without question worthy of their unstinted support.

The groups which joined in 1858 to form the United Presbyterian Church left behind them a minority of each of the two old organizations.[31] Thus, though much reduced in size, there continued to be an Associate Synod and an Associate Reformed Synod. With scarcely more than a dozen ministers apiece,[32] neither organization can have had much influence upon public opinion; nevertheless their attitude is interesting because of their independence and their extreme anti-slavery position. The Associate Reformed Synod of New York (to

[28] *Cf. ante,* Part III.

[29] The writer of this monograph has had no opportunity to examine United Presbyterian journals for the war period. From the attitude of Old School and New School journals, however, it is quite evident that the United Presbyterian journals — the *Evangelical Repository and United Presbyterian Review* (quarterly, Philadelphia); the *Christian Instructor* (weekly, Philadelphia); the *United Presbyterian* (weekly, Pittsburgh); and the *Presbyterian Witness* (weekly, Cincinnati) — were all of unquestioned loyalty. The *Christian Instructor,* for example, endorsed the *Danville Review* — " though its earlier numbers were, indeed, tainted with the *pestilent heresy that slavery is not a sin, per se.* . . ." (*cf. True Presbyterian,* April 10, 1862.)

[30] *Cf. ante,* p. 7.

[31] *Cf. ante,* p. 10.

[32] *Cf. ante,* p. 7.

give the organization its full title) took no recorded action on
the state of the country. Perhaps, since the denomination was
confined geographically to the single state of New York, and
since the anti-slavery views of the members were well known,
such action was deemed unnecessary. Perhaps the reason
ascribed by Dr. Stuart Robinson in his *True Presbyterian* was
the correct one: "The meeting was entirely harmonious," he
wrote of the annual gathering of this body in 1862, "no outside business occupied the members, and no matter of State
or National concern, was proposed. As an ecclesiastical court,
it did not pretend to discuss politics, or war measures, or any
other matter not relating to the Church." [33] Whatever the
cause, the Associate Reformed Church remained silent on the
political situation.[34]

Not so the other small Church that persisted in remaining
free from the union of 1858. The Associate Presbyterian Synod
of North America represented the essence of Presbyterian independence, for not only had its fourteen ministers (serving
pastorates in five states and in Canada) [35] determined to keep
their Church separate, but the very Church to which they were
now so faithful had itself been perpetuated by the refusal of
their grandfathers in 1782 to join in a merger by which the
majority element of the Associate Church had become part of
the then new Associate Reformed Church.[36] The remnant
which in 1861 constituted the Associate Presbyterian Synod of
North America, at its annual meeting on May 22 [37] after resolving to "disallow *repeats* in tunes when used in singing
praise to God in his worship," [38] turned its attention to the
state of the country. The report of its committee on that sub-

---

[33] *True Presbyterian*, July 3, 1862. The Synod had met on June 19, 1862.
[34] *Cf. accounts* of annual meetings of the Synod, *Presbyterian Historical
Almanac*, volumes for 1862 to 1868, inclusive. (A volume of the *Almanac*
for a given year actually contains the record of the previous year.)
[35] *Cf.* list of ministers, *ibid.*, 1862, p. 278.
[36] Scouller, *op. cit.*, p. 174.
[37] At Iberia, Ohio.
[38] *Presbyterian Historical Almanac*, 1862, p. 277.

ject [39] declared that "No individual in whose bosom burns a spark of love for country, for liberty and for human rights, can stand an unconcerned spectator of the events that are transpiring around us; " and pledged the members to stand by their rulers "in all their lawful endeavors to maintain and defend our blood-bought, heaven-born right — our right to civil and religious liberty." The maintenance of "a system of the foulest oppression " — and that in a "land boasting its enlightened and Christian character " — could only be expected to "call down the wrath of a sin avenging God upon a guilty people." Yet the Synod was willing to recognize that, while the abolition of slavery was "a most imperative duty," it was attended with many and serious difficulties, and would demand great care and Christian prudence that the rights of all concerned might be safeguarded, "and their present and eternal welfare duly provided for." The wide divergence in the slave-holders' sentiments on loyalty, the Synod felt, suggested a logical procedure with regard to abolition:

. . . a proper discrimination should be made between law-abiding, loyal States or citizens, and rebels and traitors. Being released by the act of treason from any claim on the part of slavery, for protection; the Government should not only not re-assume these obligations, but is most imperatively bound to take effective measures for the complete destruction of this deadly foe to civil and religious liberty.[40]

Considering their traditional hatred of slavery, the members of the Associate Synod were remarkably moderate and sensible in their 1861 paper on the state of the country. Having made an unequivocal deliverance in the opening year of the war, the Synod took no further action on this subject except to adopt an act for a Fast and one for Thanksgiving, in 1864.[41] In a

---

[39] The account given *ibid.* mentions that the committee reported, and gives the paper submitted, but does not state what action the Synod took with regard to it. From the fact that the report was included in the summary of the proceedings of the Synod, it may be assumed that it was adopted by that body. In fact, if the committee was of any size it must have been very nearly a majority of the Synod!

[40] For the report of the committee, *cf. ibid.*, pp. 277-278.

[41] *Ibid.*, 1865, p. 218.

Church of less than fifteen ministers it was no doubt thought unnecessary to keep repeating what had been so explicitly stated in 1861.

As in the case of the Associate Presbyterians, the independent spirit of the Reformed Presbyterians had twice withstood the demands for union with other denominations. When a majority of the latter sect in 1782 joined with the majority of the Associate Presbyterians to form the new Associate Reformed Church,[42] a minority of them determined to perpetuate the Reformed Presbyterian Church, in spite of the fact that the occasion for retaining the most distinctive tenet of their faith — "political dissent"[43] — had largely disappeared. "Political dissent" involved a refusal to profess allegiance to an immoral government. The minority who insisted on continuing the old organization evidently did not agree with the departing majority that the breaking of the political bonds with England had removed the necessity for the observance of "political dissent." So Reformed Presbyterianism continued in America, and with it its pet tenet. When the Federal Constitution of 1787 omitted from its provisions any reference to the Deity or the Christian religion, it seemed to the members of this strict sect that they could not do otherwise than refuse allegiance to the new government. In 1858 a movement for a general union of the stricter Presbyterian sects — a movement which the more liberal wing of the Reformed Presbyterians had itself started some years earlier[44] — culminated in the formation of the United Presbyterian Church. When the less strict Reformed Presbyterians were asked to join the new denomination, their leaders turned down the proposition, determining, as one of them expressed it, that "the Reformed Presbyterian Church should march into the millennium with banners displayed."[45] Thus the Reformed Presbyterians of the

[42] *Cf. ante,* p. 391.
[43] *Cf. ante,* p. 11.
[44] Thompson, *op. cit.,* pp. 147-148.
[45] Quoted, *ibid.,* pp. 148-149.

1860's were among the most individualistic of Presbyterians. Nevertheless, all had not been harmony among the Reformed Presbyterians. The more liberal element among them had many years earlier abandoned "political dissent"[46] and were a distinct denomination under the name of the "Reformed Presbyterian Church, General Synod," though often they were also called "New Side Covenanters." The more conservative wing was known as the "Reformed Presbyterian Church, Synod," or as "Old Side Covenanters." This latter denomination was the most rigidly strict of all the Presbyterian groups in the United States, with the exception of the Reformed Presbytery of North America. As this last body had some difficulty in maintaining the minimum of two ministers necessary to constitute a presbytery,[47] the palm for strictness may fairly be awarded to the Reformed Presbyterian Synod. Both wings of the Reformed Presbyterians were placed in a somewhat embarrassing position by the outbreak of the Civil War. Though the New Side had abandoned political dissent, its traditional inclination toward that theory was still strong; the Old Side was as enthusiastic as ever in its adherence. Political dissent would make it difficult for these people to give the Union whole-hearted support. On the other hand, few people hated slavery as did the Reformed Presbytrians[48] — it would be extremely difficult for them to refrain from vigorous assistance in any war which promised its eradication. The outbreak of the war in 1861 thus placed them in a dilemma.

Extrication from this dilemma was naturally easier for the more liberal wing of the sect. The General Synod of the Re-

---

[46] *Ibid.,* p. 147.

[47] In 1840 the Rev. Robert Lusk and the Rev. David Steele withdrew from the Reformed Presbyterian Synod and with three elders formed the Reformed Presbytery of North America. The death of Mr. Lusk in 1845, as it left Mr. Steele alone in its ministry, dissolved the organization. Later it was revived, but with the death of Mr. Steele it was again dissolved. *Ibid.,* pp. 104; 147; 279.

[48] *Ibid.,* p. 162.

formed Presbyterian Church which convened on May 15 in
New York City "after an earnest discussion" adopted a report
which was characterized as much by the moderation of its
statements as by the firmness of its loyalty to the anti-slavery
cause. Declaring that among the members of the Reformed
Presbyterian Church there glowed "a patriotic ardor not inferior to that which marked the heroic ages of our history," it
cautioned the people that there was "danger that the sinful
and degrading feelings of a fallen nature may be developed in
connection with its holiest and most noble aspirations [sic],
commingling with the pure incense a false fire which will pro-
voke the displeasure of God." Viewing as incidental the issue
of disunion, the long report was entirely devoted to a consideration of the best means for doing away with American slavery. "Whatever may be the incidental causes of the war, there
can be no doubt," it was alleged, "that the existence of slavery,
and the desire to continue and extend it, is the fundamental
cause." The main question then was, what could be done to
avert war, and abolish slavery? Although the numbers of
the Reformed Presbyterian Church were few, yet "her noble
position on this subject" indicated that she might be "called
upon to move in this matter." Therefore some eight principles
were suggested which should determine the solution of the
grave problem confronting the American people. The platform suggested was that of the moderate abolitionists, admitting that the North shared in the guilt of American slavery,
and advocating that the burden and loss which might be required by emancipation should be shared with the South. On
the other hand, while avowing that it was the duty of every
Christian to seek for the things which make for peace, the
General Synod asserted that "there are occasions when war
is not only lawful but dutiful," and that the present war was
one "which every Christian and patriot should be willing to
sustain." [49]

[49] For the 1861 report of the General Synod on the state of the country,
cf. *Presbyterian Historical Almanac*, 1862, pp. 247-248.

The paper on the state of the country which was unanimously adopted by the General Synod in 1862 [50] was again directed almost solely against the evil of slavery. In the opinion of the General Synod both the Declaration of Independence and the preamble of the Federal Constitution guaranteed the blessings of freedom to our people; yet "in open and flagrant violation of this covenant agreement, . . . this nation, through her representatives in Congress, has for many years perverted the powers of the Executive, Legislative and Judiciary Departments of the Government to crush the rights of man, and support and extend slavery." The early defeats and disasters of the Federal forces were recognized as "a deserved visitation of God's wrath" for complicity in the sin of slavery; and while there was reason to "fear further reverses," yet there was cause for gratitude to God in "the recent victories and advantages obtained over the enemy." With gratitude to God also for the deliverance of the District of Columbia from the curse of slavery, the General Synod "would hail with pleasure the proclamation of universal liberty," and cautioned the Federal Government against a "compromise with rebellion in behalf of slavery." Ministers were reminded that they were "particularly bound in the present perilous crisis of our country's history to declare the counsel of God regarding the sin and crime of slavery." Literalists though they were, these Calvinistic exponents of the right of interpretation were occasionally not averse to doing a little interpolating. An instance of this occurred in the advice to the ministers of the denomination that the people and the nation must be instructed in the great truth that "righteousness exalteth a nation, whilst sin (and especially the sin of human oppression) is a reproach to any people." The paper concluded with the pledge of continual prayer for the President of the United States, his Counsellors, the Congress, the Army and the Navy, and "especially . . . those who have enlisted in the cause of their country.

[50] Meeting in Princeton, Indiana.

. . ." [51]   Thus the General Synod could support with enthusiasm a war which offered an opportunity for destroying American slavery, while the Government was still maintaining that the sole purpose of the war was the salvation of the Union. As the authorities at Washington progressed farther and farther toward an anti-slavery policy, the General Synod became more and more explicit in its solicitude for the salvation of the Union. In 1864 one of the resolutions which this body adopted (unanimously) declared:

> That in the judgment of Synod the present war is one of defence against a criminal rebellion, commenced and carried on under the auspices of a slave-holding aristocracy, whose success would eventuate in anarchy and the destruction of God's ordinance of civil government among us. [52]

By 1865 the policy of adopting a special paper on the state of the country had been abandoned, though the General Synod of that year did sustain the action of one of its presbyteries in refusing to condemn members under its care for being connected with the National Union League. The General Synod's action took the following form:

> *Resolved,* That it always be distinctly understood by all whom it may concern, that Synod in giving this deliverance, acts upon the ground that she has no evidence that the Union League belongs to the category of those secret societies which the Reformed Presbyterian Church has so emphatically condemned. [53]

During the later years of the war and the period immediately following, the attention of the General Synod seems to have been largely taken up with the welfare of the freedmen and with the movement for inserting in the Federal Constitution a recognition of the Deity. [54]   Whatever qualms may have

[51] For the 1862 paper of the General Synod on the state of the country, cf. *Presbyterian Historical Almanac,* 1863, pp. 378-379.

[52] For the resolutions of 1864, cf. *Presbyterian Historical Almanac,* 1865, p. 217.

[53] *Presbyterian Historical Almanac,* 1866, p. 283.

[54] *Cf.* accounts of proceedings of the General Synod in 1864, 1865, 1866, 1867, in *Presbyterian Historical Almanac,* volumes for years 1865-1868, inclusive. (*Cf.* table of contents in each volume.)

been entertained at the beginning of the war with regard to the loyalty of the General Synod of the Reformed Presbyterians and their willingness to participate in the various enterprises of the conflict, the several utterances of that body had shown how groundless such misgivings were. Furthermore, these utterances were supplemented in a conspicuous way by the enterprise and energy displayed in war-work by a member of the denomination—the distinguished head of the United States Christian Commission, Mr. George H. Stuart.[55]   Mr. Stuart's activities alone—non-denominational though they were—helped to put his Church into the limelight of war-time publicity.   From the standpoint of patriotism the ten thousand [56] New Side Covenanters were eminently safe.

The position of the Synod of the Reformed Presbyterians was more difficult than that of the General Synod, for the Old Side Covenanters were still faithful adherents of the theory of "political dissent." Their position was concisely stated in the paper on the state of the country adopted [57] in May, 1861 in New York City. Perhaps taking their cue from the paper of the General Synod which had been adopted some two weeks earlier,[58] the Synod declared that it felt called upon to present the position of its Church "in view of the calamities brought upon this land by the iniquitous war now raging, *in the interest of slavery, against the United States.*" These Scotchmen, like their colleagues of the rival branch, felt that they could justify themselves in supporting an "immoral government" if it undertook a war of defense against the iniquitous slavery interests. Although the Synod would "heartily acknowledge" the numerous excellences of the civil institutions of this land,

---

[55] *Cf. post,* pp. 467-469.

[56] *Presbyterian Historical Almanac,* 1862, p. 249. This source gives the above number as an *estimate.*

[57] The account in the *Presbyterian Historical Almanac* for 1862 (p. 266) does not state that the committee's report was adopted. The New York *World* for May 31, 1861, however, says that the report was "presented and accepted." In view of subsequent action of the Synod, there is little doubt that the report was adopted.

[58] The General Synod met on May 15; the Synod, on May 28.

its code of laws, its privileges and protections; although they took a deep interest in this land which was their home, and the "scene of a noble conflict for national freedom and independence;" notwithstanding all this, they felt constrained in conscience "to maintain, as we and our fathers have heretofore done, a state of dissent from the Constitution of the United States," since there was in this instrument not even the mention of the name of God, no recognition of the supremacy of His law, no profession of subjection to the Mediatorial authority of the Son of God — the "King of kings and Lord of lords." On the other hand, these omissions were all the more flagrant since the Constitution contained certain "compromises" in the interest of slavery and slave-holders. "On these grounds," the Synod explained, "we are compelled to withhold from said constitution, our oath in its support, and thus to deny ourselves certain privileges which we would gladly enjoy could we do so with good conscience toward God." That their position might be fully and definitely understood, certain specific declarations were made:

1. That we disclaim all allegiance to the government of any foreign nation.

2. That we "consider ourselves under obligation to live peaceably with all men, to advance the good of society, and to conform to its order in everything consistent with righteousness."

3. That we disown all sympathy, even the least, with the traitors styling themselves "the Confederate States," now in arms against these United States.

4. That we will, as true patriots, defend this, our common country, against these and all like enemies.[59]

The Synod in 1861 thus put itself on record as unqualifiedly loyal in spirit to the United States, and willing to do anything in its defense which did not require taking an oath to a Constitution which failed to recognize the sovereignty of God.

As was the case with the deliverances of most of the other synods and assemblies, the Old Side Reformed Presbyterian 1862 paper on the state of the country was phrased in more

[59] For the 1861 action of the Synod on the state of the country, cf. *Presbyterian Historical Almanac,* 1862, p. 266.

severe terms than its predecessor of the year before. "The history of the past," the Synod now declared, "especially when taken in connection with the present war, proves that the South would, if she could, subject the masses of our population to the condition of serfdom, if not slavery." The rebellion itself was "causeless in its origin and atrocious in its character," and the abettors of slavery in the North, and all who sympathized with slave-holders in the rebellion, were "scarcely less criminal than the rebels themselves"; as such, they deserved universal condemnation. "It is seldom in the history of war," the Synod believed, "that right is so entirely on one side, and wrong on the other, as in the present case." Nevertheless, while this body sympathized most heartily with the Federal Government and cheerfully admitted that in many respects the Constitution of our country was excellent in character, it felt that it "must also recognize the hand of God in visiting the nation with the calamities of war, as a national correction, because of national sin." As far as the Constitution was concerned, the sin consisted in the unchristian character of this instrument and the oppressiveness of some of its provisions. One of its features which made it unchristian in character was its placing false religions on an equal footing with Christianity. Its oppressiveness consisted in its recognition of the lawfulness of slavery. In view of these "serious and painful drawbacks," the immediate duty of the nation and Government was repentance and reformation. Yet the Synod was careful to make it clear that the deficiencies of the Constitution would not justify failure to support the Government in the present crisis:

In this great struggle for the preservation of law and order, . . . we may readily distinguish between the welfare of the country on the one hand, and the sinful character of the Constitution, and its imperfect administration, on the other, and will cheerfully by our prayers and all other proper means within our power, promote the welfare of the nation, and sustain it in the conflict against the Southern Confederacy. But as Reformed Presbyterians, we may not compromit [sic] the church's testimony by identification directly or indirectly with the Constitution of the United States as it now stands, or by swearing entangling oaths.

The paper concluded with expressions of gratification over the abolition of slavery in the District of Columbia and the proposal of the President that the slave states with the aid of the National Government undertake to extinguish slavery within their borders.[60]

The action of subsequent war-time Synods of the Old Side Covenanters was quite in keeping with the sentiments expressed by the 1861 and 1862 gatherings. In 1863 the Synod, meeting in Sharon, Iowa, drew up a suggested oath to be taken by any one called into the military service of the United States:

> I do swear by the living God that I will be faithful to the United States and will aid and defend them against the armies of the Confederate States, yielding all due obedience to military orders.[61]

This oath was designed especially to meet the cases of those who might be drafted under the new conscription law.[62] (Later it was ascertained that under this law no oath of any kind was required of the soldier, and that those people who had felt it to be their duty to offer their services to the nation in special emergencies had been accepted without an oath.[63]) The Synod of 1863 also appointed delegates [64] to a meeting to be held on July 4 to consider and urge the amendment of the Constitution in such a way as to put into it a recognition of God and the Christian religion. "The attendance was not as large as expected, owing, no doubt, in part, to the confusion and anxiety that prevailed at that critical time in the war." [65] Nevertheless the convention agreed upon a form for the suggested amendment [66] and appointed a committee to present it to the President. The committee was encouraged by the President's inter-

[60] For the Synod's 1862 paper on the state of the country cf. *Presbyterian Historical Almanac*, 1863, pp. 395-396.
[61] Cf. *ibid.*, 1865, p. 227. (This is an 1864 account of the incident.)
[62] *Ibid.*
[63] *Ibid.*
[64] *Ibid.*, p. 226.
[65] *Ibid.*
[66] *Ibid.* This consisted of the insertion of a number of phrases into the preamble of the Constitution.

est and attitude, and especially by his statement that he approved of the general aspect of their request. He informed his visitors, however, that he would have to examine into the matter more fully before taking action upon it.[67]   The work of the 1863 convention is particularly significant, because out of it and similar meetings grew the National Reform Association, which began an active career in 1864 and was remarkably successful in enlisting outside support in what always remained essentially a Covenanter movement. As faithful adherence to the principle of political dissent involved abstention from taking part in political elections, and as the Association became interested in various reform movements, Old Side members of the organization found themselves in the rather anomalous position of urging others to vote for measures for which they themselves would not vote. This incongruity was, however, partially offset by the non-Covenanter element of the membership — which, though in the minority, comprised some of the leading members of the other large Protestant groups.[68] For its share in the beginning of this active organization, the action of the 1863 Synod in appointing delegates to the special convention was a noteworthy event.

When the close of the war arrived, the Synod of the Reformed Presbyterians placed itself in the van of those demanding " justice " for the perpetrators of the rebellion.   After congratulating the country upon the " utter overthrow of the slaveholders' rebellion," and after recognizing in the assassination of Lincoln " the legitimate fruits of that system of wrong and bloodshed which inspired and animated the late Southern conspiracy," the Synod resolved:

3. That inasmuch as it is a principle of the divine government that " he that justifieth the wicked, and he that condemneth the just, even they both are an abomination to the Lord; " it is our calm and deliberate judgment that it is the duty of the government to inflict the penalty of death upon the leaders of the late rebellion.

. . . .

---

[67] *Ibid.*
[68] Thompson, *op. cit.*, pp. 280-283.

5. That we heartily rejoice in every step which has been taken for the destruction of slavery, and urge the carrying forward of the work, until every man in the nation, without regard to color, stands upon a perfect equality before the laws.[69]

The report closed with the demand that the nation "abandon its rebellion against God" by acknowledging His name in the Federal Constitution.[70] Because the resolutions and enactments of previous sessions had "not proved satisfactory to many members of the Church" and because "the exhibition of reformation principles" had "never at any former period been so important as at this very time," resolutions were introduced reaffirming the traditional position of the Church with relation to the Federal Constitution, and stating that if anything done by the Synod had been construed as a departure from its principles, such interpretation was now disclaimed. The resolutions also disavowed any intention to depart from the previous action of the Synod disapproving of the army oath, yet "on account of the indefiniteness of Synod's action at different times" it was proposed

That Synod direct Sessions to take no further action in the case of returned soldiers, than to ascertain that they still adhere to our testimony against the sin of the nation, and maintain a practical dissent from the constitution of the government. But in cases where individuals have taken oath of naturalization or of civil and military office, which involves an approval of the constitution, or have voted at the polls, we direct that they be dealt with according to the usual practice of the Church.[71]

Although it is not recorded that these resolutions were adopted,[72] the fact that they were introduced is evidence that there was some doubt as to the correctness of the Synod's previous action with regard to political conditions.

[69] For an account of the Synod's 1863 paper on the state of the country, cf. *Presbyterian Historical Almanac*, 1866, pp. 290-291.
[70] For the action of the Synod in 1865, cf. *ibid.*, pp. 290-291.
[71] *Ibid.*, p. 291.
[72] The title "Resolutions in Reference to the Late Rebellion" (*ibid.*, p. 291) leaves the reader uncertain with regard to their adoption, though it is probable that the fact of their inclusion in the account of the Synod's proceedings means that the resolutions were adopted.

The years of political reconstruction saw no extension of the Synod's 1865 advice that capital punishment be meted out to the leaders of the rebellion and that the freedmen be admitted to perfect equality before the laws. During these years the attention of the Reformed Presbyterians of the Old Side was more than ever devoted to the proposition of an amendment to the Constitution which would make it possible for them to pledge allegiance to the Federal Government. The problem of the freedmen was also an absorbing one to the members of this denomination.[73] Sometimes the post-war problems in the North were such as to tempt Old Side men to forget their scruples with regard to political dissent. In 1866, in answer to the inquiry, " Is it wrong for Covenanters to vote for proper amendments to the State Constitution? ", the Synod suggested that while there might be instances when it would not be wrong to do so, yet as there were other ways by which countenance and approbation might be given to what was proper, " as by petition and by public and private expression," such a course was not recommended.[74] In 1867 came the more specific question, " Whether members of this Church may, consistently with their principles, vote for an amendment to a State Constitution granting to colored persons the right of suffrage? The simple question to be voted is this, Shall the word ' white ' be stricken from the constitution? " The answer was, " The Synod does not advise such a course." [75] Thus on the issues of the Reconstruction period as well as during the Civil War itself, the Reformed Presbyterian Synod consistently advised its people to refrain from participation in the political activities of an "immoral" government, even when the government was engaged in settling issues dear to the hearts of Old Side Covenanters. Individuals among the seven thousand [76] adherents

[73] Cf. post, pp. 439; 455-456.
[74] Presbyterian Historical Almanac, 1867, p. 386.
[75] Ibid., 1868, p. 382.
[76] Presbyterian Historical Almanac, 1862, p. 267. The annual report of the Synod here given places the communicant membership of the Church at 6,650. (Cf. also, ante, p. 7.)

of the Synod might falter, but no critic could justly accuse the denomination of inconsistency in its policy with regard to the difficulties of the Federal Government and the states during the decade of the 1860's.

The right wing of the Presbyterian host had thus placed itself unequivocally on the side of the Federal Government. With the exception of the small Associate Reformed Church, all of the five stricter Presbyterian denominations had adopted from year to year papers which vigorously urged that the rebellion be speedily crushed. The Old Side wing of the Reformed Presbyterians, it is true, had been prevented by its adherence to "political dissent" from participating in any activities which involved swearing allegiance to the Constitution; yet it was making every effort to have this instrument so amended as to remove the only impediment preventing the denomination from putting into more practical form the enthusiasm with which it regarded the war against the slave-holding Confederacy. In view of the headway made in the Old School Church by the theory of the ultra-spiritual character of the Church, the readiness with which the stricter Presbyterian groups protested allegiance to the Union is surprising. While the hesitancy of many in its ranks was holding back the Old School, the New School on the left and the ultra-Presbyterian groups on the right were rushing forward to take their places in the van of the loyalty movement. This lends color to the charge that the doctrine of the complete separation of the Church and State had been invented by the Thornwell group to enable the Old School denomination to avoid the pitfalls of the slavery controversy.[77] It is at least a striking coincidence that the only Presbyterian denomination in which that doctrine caused hesitancy during the war years[78] was one which

---

[77] *Cf.*, *e.g.*, *Biblical Repertory and Princeton Review*, July, 1864, vol. 36, p. 562 (in an article on "The General Assembly").

[78] The theory was universal among members of the Presbyterian Church of the Confederate States of America (later the Presbyterian Church in the United States). Practically, the Church supported the Confederacy, however: "The Assembly met and spent the first half hour in special prayer

was not confined geographically to a single section of the country. It would appear that, although no doubt sincere in their convictions, the Old School advocates of the ultra-spiritual character of the Church had reasoned themselves into the acceptance of a position which promised to prevent a disruption of their denomination over the slavery issue. If there were doubts among the stricter Presbyterian groups concerning denominational pronouncements on the great political crisis, they could be easily forgotten by these wholly Northern bodies as soon as an opportunity presented itself for banishing the much-hated institution of slavery.

If the problem of political allegiance was readily settled by the Churches of the right flank, for the denomination at the extreme left — the Cumberland Presbyterian Church [79] — its solution was far from easy. This denomination, with half of its membership in the Border States, and more than three-fourths of it in slave states,[80] was more vitally concerned than any other Presbyterian group in arriving at a satisfactory position on the political situation. The 1100 ministers and 103,000 communicants [81] of the Cumberland Church were represented by but forty-six commissioners in the General Assembly which met in St. Louis on May 16, 1861.[82] A motion was made early in the session that "in view of the state of the country" the Assembly adjourn, but "after a long discussion it was so apparent that it would be best for the Assembly to attend to the ordinary routine of business" that the motion was withdrawn.[83] Dr. Milton Bird, (one of the two Doctors of Divinity present), who was a man of great influence in

for the blessing of God upon the cause of the Confederate States, according to previous order." (From the *Minutes of the General Assembly of the Presbyterian Church in the Confederate States of America*, 1861, p. 12. *Cf.* also Dr. Hodge's statement in *Biblical Repertory and Princeton Review*, July, 1864, vol. 36, p. 562.

[79] *Cf. ante*, pp. 9-10.
[80] *Cf. ante*, pp. 5, note 6; 7; 9-10; 16.
[81] *Cf. ante*, p. 7.
[82] *Presbyterian Historical Almanac*, 1862, p. 281.
[83] *Ibid.*

the Church,[84] presented a paper on the state of the country. In adopting this paper the Cumberland Presbyterian Assembly succeeded in doing what was at the same time being vainly attempted in the Assembly of the only other Presbyterian denomination having strength both North and South (the Old School Church): [85] it passed resolutions on the war without endorsing the government of either of the contending parties. "Considering the controversy of God with the nation, that . . . the country is maddened with passion, ruptured, and sinking into fratricidal war, — the most terrible of all calamities, —. . . producing a reign of terror, before which that of the French revolution pales," the Assembly

> *Resolved,* 1. That we recognize the good providence and rich grace of Almighty God, in bringing our General Assembly together in the present fearful crisis, in the unity of the Spirit and the bond of peace. . . .
> 2. That while we regret the circumstances which have prevented the attendance of Commissioners from some of the Presbyteries, we do now and hereby record our sincere thanks to our heavenly Father, that brethren have met from North and South, East and West, and that brotherly kindness and love have continued from the opening to the close of our present meeting. . . .
> 3. That, the grace of God assisting us, we will always endeavor to cherish the true principle and pure spirit of Christianity, knowing that with this enthroned in our hearts, we can and will walk in love, and live in peace. . . .
> 4. That the Assembly do now and hereby recommend in every family and congregation composing our Church the observance of Saturday, June 22, as a day of humiliation, fasting, and prayer, to . . . God . . . for the deliverance of his Church out of her fiery trials, and for a peaceful solution of the troubles and fratricidal war that now curses our common country.[86]

However much the Cumberland Church might strive to avoid a rupture in its midst, the various Boards of any Border State denomination were certain to be severely impeded in their work. In September, 1861, the Old School *Presbyterian* reported that the Board of Missions of the Cumberland Church had taken the following action:

[84] *American Annual Cyclopaedia,* 1864, p. 683.
[85] *Cf. ante,* Part II, chapter 2.
[86] *Presbyterian Historical Almanac,* 1862, pp. 281-282.

The State of Tennessee, in which the Board is located as a corporate body, is now a member of the Confederate States of America, and, as such, at war with the United States of America; therefore, according to the law of nations it would be illegal to make remittances to missionaries in the bounds of States that are at war with the Confederate States.[87]

If the *Presbyterian's* source of information [88] was authentic and such an announcement was actually made, the General Assembly at its next meeting chose to ignore it. The report which the Assembly adopted, after remarking that the body was "without any official report from the Board," recommended that a committee be appointed to superintend the missionary activities of the Church, "and that this Committee be authorized and requested to correspond with said Board as soon as possible, and procure from them a full report to be presented with their report to the next General Assembly." [89] Thus, though the Church remained undivided, the General Assembly had come to recognize a division in the practical work of the denomination.

Resolutions on the state of the country — again drafted by a committee of which Dr. Bird was the chairman — were incorporated in the 1862 Assembly's report on the state of the Church, and as a part of that report were unanimously adopted. They met with the hearty approval of Dr. Stuart Robinson, whose stern opposition to the Church's consideration of anything except the purely spiritual [90] made him a severe critic of Church action on the state of the country. Dr. Robinson in his *True Presbyterian* declared:

The Lord in His wisdom seems to have given to the Cumberland Presbyterian body, the mission to stand fast and testify for the great principles of Presbyterianism, in this time of general defection.[91]

---

[87] *Presbyterian,* September 14, 1861.
[88] Not given.
[89] *Presbyterian Historical Almanac,* 1863, p. 412.
[90] *Cf. ante,* pp. 167-177.
[91] Editorial, "Ecclesiastical Action Touching upon the State of the Country. The Cumberland Presbyterian Assembly," *True Presbyterian,* June 12, 1862.

As the Kentucky editor had never been conspicuous for his tolerance of the more liberal Presbyterian Churches, his statement that a perusal of the Cumberland Assembly's resolutions had "taught us a lesson in charity, that perhaps we have been slow to learn," [92] is all the more impressive. As may be inferred from Dr. Robinson's enthusiastic endorsement, these 1862 resolutions avoided any statement that might be interpreted as a political pronouncement. They pledged careful observance of the separation of Church and State; deeply deplored "the carnage and demoralizing tendencies of a war of brothers"; called upon the Church and nation to "humble themselves before God for their many and grievous sins"; earnestly and affectionately advised the ministers and members "to avoid partisanship and sectionalism in Church and State, and to evidence their loyalty to Caesar by their loyalty to Christ in following his example and teaching. . . ." [93] When the report had been adopted, the Assembly "knelt and returned thanks to God that a unanimous vote had been given on this important report." [94]

The unanimity of the Assembly of 1863 was all but as complete as in the previous year. With but two dissenting votes it was *"Resolved,* That this General Assembly look with censure and disapprobation upon attempts from any quarter to dissolve the Union. . . ." [95] Thus four months after the Emancipation Proclamation the Cumberland Church — or at least that part of it in the non-secession states [96] — was still able to avoid a sectional pronouncement, though its avowed opposition to disunion was evidence of a marked recession from the firm stand it had in 1862 taken on the separation of Church and State.

[92] *Ibid.*
[93] *Presbyterian Historical Almanac,* 1863, p. 410.
[94] *Ibid.*
[95] *American Annual Cyclopaedia,* 1863, pp. 758-759.
[96] The records of the war-time Assemblies show that few commissioners attended from the states of the Confederacy. The committee which drafted the 1862 report was composed of commissioners from Kentucky, Missouri, Iowa, Illinois, Indiana, Ohio, and Pennsylvania. *Cf.* editorial cited above, *True Presbyterian,* June 12, 1862.

To Stuart Robinson it must have seemed that the Church he had so heartily commended the year before was now seriously backsliding. The compromise ground adopted in 1863 appeared ominous of further slipping, in case the war lasted.

Whatever fears of this kind existed were justified by the action of the Assembly which convened in Lebanon, Ohio, on May 19, 1864. Among the forty-one ministers and twenty-four ruling elders who composed this body there was anything but unanimity with regard to the attitude the Church should take on the troubles which the country was experiencing. The first difficulty arose over the question which had so vexed the Old School Assembly of the previous year: [97] "Should the national flag be hoisted over the church in which the Assembly was meeting?" The eighteen members who opposed such action entered a long protest upon the Assembly's minutes. Significant in the list of members of this group was the name of Dr. Milton Bird, who had played such a conspicuous part in securing unpartisan action in the Assemblies of 1861 and 1862.[98] The protestants avowed that they loved the flag of their government "as the ensign of the best civil organization on earth," an organization which they would most faithfully maintain "by any legally required pledge of their honor, their property, and their lives"; yet in the faithful discharge of what they realized as their duty "as ecclesiastics" to God, His Church, and their beloved country, they must vote against a proposition which they believed to be repugnant to God's desires for His Church.[99] On the other hand, seven of the commissioners who had voted *aye* presented a formal explanation of their stand. They had voted for this resolution not that they regarded this as "any of the legitimate business of this General Assembly," not that they would be any less loyal had they voted *nay*, but rather

1. Because the issue of *loyalty* or *disloyalty* is presented in the resolution and by its supporters, and although we might explain to the satis-

---

[97] *Cf. ante*, pp. 120-122.

[98] Dr. Bird was the Moderator of the Assembly of 1863.

[99] *Presbyterian Historical Almanac*, 1864, pp. 232-234.

faction of those present our reasons for opposing the resolution, it would still be liable to misconstruction by all who are not present.

2. Because the pastor of the church with which we meet thought it necessary for the good of his congregation.[100]

The pressure of public opinion was driving the Cumberland Church farther and farther from its neutral position.

Much more serious than the flag episode as a cause of division was the slavery question. The Presbytery of Indiana had memorialized the Assembly to "set forth more fully and clearly . . . the social and moral evils inherent in the system of slavery, as it exists in the Southern States; and that it urge upon our Southern brethren in all faithfulness, that the time has fully come, in the providence of God, when they can, and therefore should without delay abandon a system which is a reproach to our holy religion, and which has so imperiled our beloved Church, our free government, and our National Union."[101] The special committee to which this memorial was referred proposed the following deliverance:

> *Resolved,* That we regard the holding of human beings in involuntary slavery, as practised in some of the States of the American Union, as contrary to the precepts of our holy religion, and as being the fruitful source of many evils and vices in the social system; therefore,
> *Resolved,* That it be recommended to Cumberland Presbyterians, both North and South, to give countenance and support to all constitutional efforts of our government to rid the country of that enormous evil.[102]

Obviously a proposal of this sort threatened the peace of the Church. Dr. Bird, who was apparently a perennial commissioner, now came forward with the suggestion that the report of the committee be referred to the next Assembly. He was able to rally a majority of the Assembly to his side and the motion to refer to the next Assembly was carried by a vote of 31 to 26. On the next day, however, two commissioners from Missouri and two from Tennessee[103] were permitted to

---

[100] *Ibid.,* p. 234.
[101] *Ibid.*
[102] *Ibid.,* pp. 234-235.
[103] *American Annual Cyclopaedia,* 1864, p. 683.

change their votes from *aye* to *nay*, making the vote 27 to 30. The motion to refer the report to the next Assembly was thus lost. Some of the opponents of the committee's report, seeing that it was now likely to be adopted, left the Assembly.[104] A motion to adopt the report was then carried.[105] Twelve men who had voted against the deliverance now entered a formal protest against it. The protest has much of the tone of a rejected leader. As Dr. Bird's name appears first in the list of signers, it is likely that he was the author of the document. A few sentences from its wordy paragraphs suffice to reveal the chief grievances of the protestants:

We protest against the action adopting the report: — 1. Because the principle of action is erroneous, and its spirit secular and sectional. . . . it is erroneous in principle, and fanatical in spirit, producing alienation, division, and ruin.

2. [It is unfair to take such important action in so small an Assembly, for instead of an Assembly of 35 or 36 presbyteries and from 70 to 79 members, as in previous Assemblies when especially important action was taken, in the present year] twenty-six Presbyteries are represented in the Assembly, and there are only sixty-three members, and of this number thirteen left for home before the final action, leaving only fifty-six[106] when this action was had; . . .

3. Intelligence, order, piety, justice, and benevolence do not consist with agitation and violence, or the result thereof. Indulgence sharpens the appetite for agitation and makes it more craving. In the incipient stages of it few, if any, look to the final result. It is a chronic nightmare, varied with periodical spasms, until its normal state is convulsion, and it enters upon a revolution, the radicalness of which becomes every day more apparent. . . .

4. The agitation is . . . demanded . . . by a strange mania that is abroad, which seems to operate alike in scoffing infidels, corrupt and babbling politicians and such possessors of religion as are led or driven by the pressure of any peculiar circumstances which may surround them.

---

[104] *Ibid. Cf.* also paragraph number 2 of the protest, *ante*, pp. 410-411.

[105] *Presbyterian Historical Almanac*, 1865, p. 235. The *American Annual Cyclopaedia* (1864, p. 683) is obviously in error in stating that the report was adopted " unanimously," as the twelve protestants stated explicitly that they had voted against it. (*Almanac*, 1865, p. 235.)

[106] Probably " fifty " was intended. Obviously the mathematics of the above statement is not correct. According to the *Presbyterian Historical Almanac*, (1865, p. 230) the original number of commissioners was sixty-five.

They who would make the Church conform to the outside secular, sectional pressure of the times, under the idea that if they do not do so, that pressure will crush and kill the Church, take the most effectual course they could to destroy the spiritual life, strength, and moral influence of the Church. . . .

.   .   .   .

6. We protest against the adoption of the report, because we are opposed to that which in effect leads to secession in Church and State. It is a historical fact that Church secession opens the way to, and was auxiliary to secession and division in the State; that which carries forward the former aids the latter.

There is an *abolition type of disloyalty* as well as a secession type; the latter is the offspring of the former, and there is a sympathy between them, both operating as a unit in effect. . . . They do greatly deceive themselves who think to establish a character for extraordinary patriotism and loyalty, by delivering themselves of preambles, and resolutions, and wind, in ecclesiastical bodies. If they would take their position with the suffering soldier in the front ranks under the lead of the true and earnest Generals, then they would obtain credit for patriotism and loyalty, by showing that they had a heart to serve the country in its trials. . . .

7. . . . . In our judgment, its [the report's] advocates are under some bewildering influence, and strangely misconceive the question which they undertake to settle, and the bearing of their action upon it. . . .[107]

It is quite evident that the "brotherly kindness and love" which had characterized the 1861 and 1862 Assemblies had been largely dissipated by 1864. Dr. Stuart Robinson, in whose opinion the Cumberland Assembly of 1862 had contrasted so commendably with that of his own Old School Church,[108] was sadly disappointed to see so little contrast in 1864. The Cumberland Church had not yet been formally sundered, he reported, "but from its course in this Assembly we may look for a separation in it, as well as in ours. The more 'loyal' in this body, in order to give a practical illustration of their loyalty, voted to raise the flag of the country over the house in which the court of Christ met. . . ."[109] The anti-slavery report adopted by the Assembly would, he predicted, tend to divide the Church.

[107] *Ibid.,* pp. 235-237.
[108] *Cf. ante,* pp. 408-409.
[109] *Cf.* article on Cumberland General Assembly of 1864, *True Presbyterian,* June 23, 1864.

In this prediction Dr. Robinson was wrong. Except for the Protestant Episcopal Church, the Cumberland Presbyterian Church was the only Protestant denomination which, though having strength in both North and South, was not divided. It is true that conventions were called at various times during the war for the purpose of effecting a division, but they either failed to meet, or, if convened, failed to accomplish anything.[110] Yet, practically, the Church was dismembered during the war years, for when the Church boards at Nashville ceased communicating with the General Assembly, the latter body set up special organizations at Pittsburgh, Alton (Illinois), and Owensboro (Kentucky) to take over the activities of the Church which had previously been directed from Tennessee.[111] On the other hand, as the new agencies were specifically temporary, it would be easy, once the war was over, to return to the former arrangements.

To substantiate his prediction that the Cumberland Church would be divided, Dr. Robinson might well have mentioned, besides the strong anti-slavery resolutions, the Assembly's own action with regard to the future unity of the Church. In response to a memorial from Richland Presbytery (Tennessee) stating that that body did "not desire the dissolution of our Church, whether our government be permanently divided or not," the Assembly declared:

In this conflict we must stand by our Master, . . . and as this Assembly has twice declared that obedience to the civil magistrate is a Christian

---

[110] *American Annual Cyclopaedia*, 1864, p. 683. This source states that conventions were called at various times at Chattanooga, Selina, and Dalton, Georgia. The writer adds, " It is stated on what appears to be good authority that a large number of the Southern Cumberland Presbyterians have remained loyal to their former church connection." If this is true, they were apparently unable to keep in touch with it during the war period. Certainly after the war was over they manifested abiding loyalty, in large numbers. It is sometimes stated that a large number of Cumberland Presbyterians had been Whigs, and that this Whig element was responsible for perpetuating Church unity. The statement is an interesting one, and plausible, but the writer has found no authentic substantiation of it.

[111] *American Annual Cyclopaedia*, 1863, pp. 758-759.

duty, therefore, we must regard those who are or have been voluntarily in rebellion against the Government of the United States, as not only guilty of a crime against the Government, but also guilty of great sin against God, and with such, without repentance and humiliation before God and the Church, we cannot desire fellowship. But to all who have stood true to God and the Government of the United States, and proved their loyalty by their works, we extend the cordial hand of a brother's greeting and a brother's welcome. . . ."[112]

The Cumberland Assembly was thus anticipating by a year the insistence upon examination, repentance, and humiliation which the Old School (the only other Presbyterian denomination confronted with the problem of returning Southern members) was to demand in 1865.[113] Certainly the Cumberland Church had made remarkable progress, between 1862 and 1864, in acquiring the war spirit! Instead of pleading for Church unity, it was now determined to have no unity except such as could be achieved on the basis of common political philosophy and patriotism.

Aside from a series of resolutions on the assassination of President Lincoln,[114] the General Assembly of 1865 adopted no deliverance specifically on the state of the country. The report on the "State of Religion," however, was of necessity largely concerned with this subject. One of the six resolutions which comprised the report dealt with the subject of the reconstruction of Southern churches of the denomination. Its content was not prophetic of future harmony in the denomination, for its recommendation to those in charge of church reconstruction in the South was "to adopt the action of the last General Assembly, touching that matter, as a basis, believing that said action after showing true devotion to civil government, is according to the principles of God's holy word and our Confession of Faith, and that no further legislation is necessary on the subject."[115] Thus "repentance and humiliation before God and the Church" was confirmed as the first re-

[112] *Presbyterian Historical Almanac*, 1865, pp. 237-238.
[113] *Cf. ante*, pp. 199-200.
[114] *Presbyterian Historical Almanac*, 1866, pp. 300-301.
[115] *Ibid.*, p. 302.

quirement to be met by Southerners who desired to return to
the fold of the Cumberland Church.

Other statements in the 1865 report, on the other hand, had
a distinctly neutralizing effect upon the harshness of this requirement. As compared with the paper of 1864, the action
of 1865 was conciliatory in tone. No doubt the Northern
element in the Church realized the practical difficulties of continuing without the aid of the Southern brethren. Consistency
would scarcely permit failure to reaffirm the decision of the
previous year, nor could the Assembly refrain from declaring
that it felt "devoutly thankful to Almighty God that it [the
war] has terminated in the overthrow of the rebellion and the
reestablishment of the rightful authority of our beloved Government, over all its former domain;" nevertheless the report
staunchly avowed the intention of the Assembly to promote
reconciliation. Mentioning that many of the ministers and
members had been involved in the rebellion, the framers of the
report had been careful to add, "some perhaps willingly, and
many from force of circumstances." It was resolved that
"whatever may have been our honest differences of opinion,
we rejoice that the root of bitterness will no longer be a disturbing element in the Church, to alienate feelings or to divide
or distract the harmony of God's children." It was also
recommended that as there was "now opened up to us a field
large and inviting, which is ripe for the harvest," a Sabbath in
July be specified as the occasion for a special sermon on the
subject of a call to the Gospel ministry.[116] Thus while the
Assembly determined to maintain the standards of church
reconstruction as they had been set the previous year, it was
prepared to take a forgiving attitude toward the erring brethren of the South, and was looking forward with eagerness to
an ingathering from that field.

The conciliatory statements of the 1865 report seem to have
had a wholesome effect upon the Southern districts of the
Church. Of the presbyteries within the bounds of the former

[116] *Ibid.,* pp. 302-303.

Confederacy, but one had been represented in the 1865 Assembly.[117] In November a convention consisting chiefly of members of the Southern presbyteries met in Memphis to consider the question of Church unity and to discuss the action of the last Assembly.[118] "In accordance with the spirit generally pervading the Southern Churches," wrote a reporter for a secular work, "it was resolved that 'the whole proceedings of the Assemblies of 1863 and 1864, touching slavery and the state of the country, and so far as the same were endorsed by the Assembly of 1865, were extra-ecclesiastical, and therefore entirely nugatory; ' that in their charges of sin upon the Southern people 'they condemn what God does not condemn,' and in laying down terms of communion which the Bible does not lay down, they exalt themselves above, and assume to 'be more holy than God.'" Having relieved themselves of this scorching criticism of their Northern brethren, these former Southern sympathizers expressed their gratification at the continuing unity of the Church, and at "the existence of a large conservative element in the northern portion of it," and recommended to the presbyteries to send up their full quota of commissioners to the next General Assembly.[118a] Evidently the protest of the dissenting group in 1864 and the assurances of brotherly love in the report of 1865 had convinced them of the strength of the sympathetic element in the Northern portion of the Church; if the Southerners remained in the Church, by allying themselves with this element "conservative" control would be insured.

This anticipation was justified by the course of the General Assembly of 1866, which met at Owensboro, Kentucky. With the Southern presbyteries again represented, the membership was twice as large as that of any of the five war-time Assemblies.[119] Upon the suggestion of a ruling elder of a presbytery

[117] *American Annual Cyclopaedia*, 1865, p. 706.

[118] *Ibid.*

[118a] *Ibid.*

[119] The attendance of the war-time Assemblies was as follows: 1861, 46; 1862, 55; 1863, 79; 1864, 65; 1865, 79. The attendance in 1866 was over 150. (*Cf. Presbyterian Historical Almanac* for Assembly statistics.)

in Mississippi,[120] it was resolved that a committee consisting of one member from each synod be appointed "to take into consideration the various 'Deliverances' of former General Assemblies on the subject of war and the slavery question, and to make such report thereon as the harmony of the Church and the exigency of the times require." [121]   The committee submitted a majority and a minority report.   The majority report represented the Southern point of view:

> *Resolved,* 1. That it is the sentiment of the Cumberland Presbyterian Church that Church and State are separate and distinct institutions. . . .
>
> *Resolved,* 2. That as the politico-ecclesiastical deliverances of the Assemblies of 1864 and 1865, which are hereby disclaimed, were the utterances of a small minority in contravention of what we believe the honest conviction of the great majority of the Cumberland Presbyterian Church, that they can therefore have no binding force whatever on any, unless indeed upon those whose opinions may be in accordance therewith.
>
> *Resolved,* 3. That though Church and State are separate and distinct institutions, yet we, as individual members of the Cumberland Presbyterian Church, one and all, accept in good faith the results of the late war, and acknowledge our allegiance to the Constitution and Government of the United States.
>
> *Resolved,* 4. That as the institution about which unhappy differences have heretofore existed has been abolished by the power of the sword, it is the opinion of this General Assembly that all ecclesiastical legislation or preaching on that subject, except for the moral welfare of the African race, should, in the future, be carefully abstained from.
>
> *Resolved,* 5. That we are grateful to Almighty God for the unity of the Cumberland Presbyterian Church, that whilst other denominations have been rent in twain by political jargons the Cumberland Presbyterian Church still maintains her integrity, and, by the help of God, will stand like a rock, immovable in her principles among surrounding change and innovation.
>
> *Resolved,* That we as a Church will studiously avoid, in the future, any legislation calculated to engender strife and discord; that we will . . . labor together as a band of brothers cemented together by a common faith and a common religion. . . .[122]

The minority report, on the other hand, found "nothing in the deliverances of the former Assemblies touching these questions requiring modification or repeal;" and decided that "fur-

[120] Oxford Presbytery.
[121] *Presbyterian Historical Almanac,* 1867, p. 468.
[122] *Ibid.,* pp. 468-469.

ther action is not needed at this time, as it would, in all probability, tend only to disturb the peace and harmony of the
Church." [123]   The content of this brief report was so completely at variance with that of the majority that it appeared
unlikely that either could be adopted without bringing about
a division in the Church. At this point the influential Dr.
Bird,[124] whose leadership of the minority in 1864 [125] had given
proof of his sympathetic understanding of the position of the
Southern brethren, came forward with a set of brief resolutions calculated to satisfy the more conservative, both North
and South:

> *Resolved,* 1. That this General Assembly is opposed to every move-
> ment, coming from any quarter, that looks to a union of Church and
> State.
> *Resolved,* 2. That we are opposed to the prostitution of the pulpit, the
> religious press, or our ecclesiastical courts to the accomplishment of politi-
> cal and sectional purposes.
> *Resolved,* 3. That any expression of political sentiment, made by any
> judicatory of our Church, North, South, East or West, is unnecessary,
> and no part of the legitimate business of an ecclesiastical court.
> *Resolved,* 4. That nothing in the foregoing shall be construed as an
> expression of opinion upon slavery or rebellion.[126]

---

[123] *Ibid.,* p. 469.

[124] It was a practice among the various Presbyterian Churches that each
General Assembly should be opened by a sermon by the retiring Moderator. If he was absent, an ex-Moderator was usually chosen to perform
this service. During the war years Dr. Bird always preached the sermon
for an absent retiring Moderator in the Cumberland General Assembly.
Perhaps he was always chosen because of his position as Stated Clerk of
the Assembly, but more likely because of his prominence in the denomination. The texts from which he preached revealed the conciliatory spirit
of the man: 1861, Hebrews xiii, 1, "Let brotherly love continue"; 1862,
Philippians ii, 1-5, "If there be, therefore, any consolation in Christ, . . .
fulfil ye my joy, that ye be like-minded, having the same love, being of
one accord, of one mind"; 1864 (when Dr. Bird was himself the retiring
Moderator), John xviii, 36, and I Corinthians, xiii, 13, "My kingdom is
not of this world"—" . . . but the greatest of these is charity"; 1866,
Romans xii, 19, "Dearly beloved, avenge not yourselves, but rather give
place unto wrath; for it is written, Vengeance is mine; I will repay, saith
the Lord." (*Cf. Presbyterian Historical Almanac* for the war period.)

[125] *Cf. ante,* pp. 411-413.

[126] *Presbyterian Historical Almanac,* 1867, pp. 469-470.

How well Dr. Bird had measured the sentiment of the Assembly was indicated by the vote on his paper. By a decision of 112 to 40 it was adopted in place of either of the committee reports.[127] Repudiated in 1864, the Nestor of the Cumberland Presbyterian Church had regained his prestige now that the Church had recovered its full strength. In accordance with his policy in 1861 and 1862 [128] he was able to avert disaster for the denomination in 1866 by piloting the Assembly over a middle course.

Notwithstanding the heavy majority by which Dr. Bird's paper had been adopted, like most middle-course propositions it was severely attacked by supporters of the two extreme positions. Some of the Northern presbyteries were so dissatisfied that they urged a special convention — a move that had the approval of the *Cumberland Presbyterian* (Waynesburgh, Pennsylvania), but was opposed by the *Western Cumberland Presbyterian* (Alton, Illinois).[129] Nothing came of their agitation.[130] Meanwhile some of the extremists in the South were anxious to join the Southern Presbyterian Church, but in this case also the agitation gradually died away without any serious accomplishment.[131] Yet many were determined to obtain further action from the General Assembly.

When the General Assembly of 1867 convened in Memphis, the most troublesome question proved to be whether the deliverance of the previous year should be modified. Some of the commissioners were inclined to regard the Bird paper as re-

[127] *Ibid.*, p. 470.

[128] *Cf. ante*, pp. 406-408.

[129] In 1859 (information for war years not complete), besides the *Cumberland Presbyterian* (weekly), Cumberland periodicals included the *St. Louis Observer* (weekly), the *Banner of Peace* (Nashville, weekly), the *Ladies' Pearl* (Alton, Illinois, monthly), and the *Theological Medium* (edited by Dr. Milton Bird, Louisville, quarterly). The *Western Cumberland Presbyterian* (weekly, mentioned above) was evidently founded between 1859 and 1864 (for it was not included in the list published in the *Presbyterian Historical Almanac* for 1861, but was advertised *ibid.*, 1865, p. 389).

[130] *American Annual Cyclopaedia*, 1866, p. 624.

[131] *Ibid.*

versing the deliverances of preceding years, and as evidence of conversion to pro-slavery tendencies. So far as this Assembly was concerned, the problem was settled by the adoption of a resolution to the effect that the 1866 deliverance did not repeal the decisions of former Assemblies, and that neither this deliverance nor those of the earlier years could be set up as tests of membership unless they were referred to the presbyteries and approved by them. As a result of the 1867 action, the Synod of Philadelphia suspended connection with the General Assembly.[132]

The year 1868 found the General Assembly still troubled over its war-time record. A memorial was presented comprising the following points:

1. That things secular and civil belong to the State.
2. That things moral and ecclesiastical belong to the Church.
3. That in regard to things mixed, being partly secular and partly ecclesiastical — the secular and civil aspects belong to the State, but the moral and ecclesiastical aspects belong to the Church.
4. That it is the prerogative of the Church to express its views through the pulpit, the press, and the various judicatories, on all moral questions, regardless of civil codes or political creeds.[133]

The first of these propositions the Assembly considered to be in conformity with the Confession of Faith; the second was

---

[132] *American Annual Cyclopaedia*, 1867, pp. 629-630. There is no source available giving the size of the withdrawing Synod of Philadelphia. Mr. Joseph Wilson in his carefully edited *Presbyterian Historical Almanac* (1867, p. 476) stated that in 1861, 34 of the 1187 ministers of the Church resided in Pennsylvania. The following note by Mr. Wilson (*ibid.*) indicates the difficulty in obtaining statistical information with regard to the Cumberland Church: " It is a subject of regret that the Minutes of the Cumberland Presbyterian Church do not contain a complete list of the Ministers and Licentiates. In 1861 I prepared from a great variety of sources a list, which was published in the *Presbyterian Historical Almanac* for 1862. . . ." Perhaps there is some relation between the incomplete records of this denomination and its early failure to stress educational training for its ministers (*cf. ante*, p. 9). It should be remarked, however, that the Church was now making a vigorous effort to raise its educational standards. *Cf., e.g.*, action on the problem of education taken by the General Assemblies of 1865 and 1866, *Presbyterian Historical Almanac*, 1866, pp. 301-302; *ibid.*, 1867, pp. 471-472.

[133] *American Annual Cyclopaedia*, 1868, p. 637.

disrespectful to the State; with the third it agreed substantially. It also was in agreement with the fourth proposition, except for the expression "civil codes": while the Church should reprove, she should not put herself in an attitude of defiance or disregard for the civil laws of the land.[134] By thus following a policy of partially concealing its substantial agreement under cover of criticism of terminology, the Assembly successfully adhered to the middle position in which it had found safety during previous years.

While the period following the war had found the New School and the United Presbyterian Churches offering the Government unsolicited advice with regard to political reconstruction,[135] the Old School and the Cumberland Presbyterian Churches, each with a considerable following in the former slave states, had been concentrating their attention upon internal problems.[136] From the point of view of church unity the Cumberland Church had been much the more successful of the two. This greater success may be attributed to the expert leadership of Dr. Bird; to the greater necessity of preserving the Cumberland Church intact (for division would have left both branches weak — not only in numbers, but particularly in financial resources); and to an apparently deliberate desire on the part of many leaders in the Old School Church to let the Border State faction go, in order that reunion with the New School might be more readily effected.[137] On the other hand, the war was of more directly vital concern to the Cumberland Church, because three-fourths of its membership was in the slave states, and more than one-half of it in the states which seceded.[138] In the light of this fact, the preservation of its unity was a great accomplishment and its frank avowal of

[134] Ibid.
[135] Cf. ante, pp. 351-362; 385-389.
[136] For such activities on the part of the Old School Church, cf. ante, Part II, Chapters 6 and 7.
[137] Cf. ante, pp. 255-257.
[138] Cf. ante, pp. 7; 9-10; 16.

loyalty to the Union in 1866 [139] truly remarkable. When the history of action on the state of the country closed with the disposal of the memorial of 1868, from many points of view the Cumberland Church, of all the Presbyterian Churches, had the least occasion to be dissatisfied with its war record.

The action of the Cumberland Assembly on the memorial of 1868 closed not only its own, but the whole Presbyterian record of "politico-ecclesiastical" measures dealing with war-time problems. In fact, most of the Presbyterian denominations had ceased such activities in 1865 or 1866; only the two Churches having a mixed Northern-Southern membership continued after the latter date, and the Old School Church had pretty well settled her problem—as far as Assembly action was concerned—by 1867.[140] Only one of the eight Presbyterian denominations having strength in the North—and that a very small one whose members were not in the least under suspicion for disloyalty [141]—had failed to assert its loyalty to the Union. Although in the Old School Church there had been for three years a constant—though dwindling—party of opposition and although it was not until 1864 that the Cumberland Church had made a frank pronouncement of its loyalty, eventually both had clearly aligned themselves with their sister Churches on the Union side. Similarly, the seven Churches of avowed devotion to the Union had all condemned slavery— most of them anticipating Lincoln's Emancipation Proclama-

---

[139] Strictly speaking, this statement is inaccurate from two points of view. First, the declaration of loyalty was in the majority report—which was *not* adopted; second, the declaration pledged the loyalty of all the members *as individuals*, not as a Church. Nevertheless as the majority report was presented by representatives of the faction most under suspicion for disloyalty, and as it was the opposition of the faction least suspected of disloyalty which prevented the adoption of the majority report, and as the pledging *as individuals* and not as a Church was simply to avoid having the Assembly take political action, it seems fair to speak of the "frank avowal of loyalty to the Union in 1866." For the statement *cf. ante*, p. 418.

[140] *Cf. ante*, pp. 266-267.

[141] The Associate Reformed Church. *Cf. ante*, pp. 5, 7; 390-391.

tion, and some of them, in fact, using the issue of slavery as an excuse for action which might otherwise be regarded as too political for the Church. On this subject, also, the Old School and the Cumberland Churches had lagged behind. Geography had much to do with Presbyterian action on war-time problems. Yet, viewing the period as a whole, the important consideration is not that all were not equally prompt, but rather that all had, before the close of the war, come to a decidedly pro-Union and anti-slavery stand.

PART V

PRESBYTERIAN PATRIOTISM IN PRACTICE

PRESBYTERIAN PATRIOTISM IN PRACTICE

THE Civil War furnished the occasion — many at that time would have said the necessity — for elaborate protestations of patriotism on the part of Presbyterian preachers, editors, and assemblies. In a multitude of ways it also afforded opportunities for the practical demonstration of loyalty to the cause of the Union. Northern Presbyterians on the whole grasped these opportunities with promptness and enthusiasm. This was but natural, for the Churches soon came to feel the reality of the war in its vital effect upon their activities and their people. When the conflict had been in progress for a year, the Moderator of the 1862 Old School Assembly, in presenting the annual " Narrative of the State of Religion " (a comprehensive statement summarizing the reports of the various presbyteries) emphasized the close relationship between the war and the Church:

> Since, in our country, ministers and people are at once men and citizens; residents in the land, and shareholders and constituent parts in the government, it is impossible that the state of the nation should not tell with peculiar power upon both the external prosperity and the spiritual condition of the Church. Accordingly, of all the reports from the Presbyteries for the past year, scarcely one fails to make mention of the agony that has been upon the nation, since the Assembly last met: of churches called to send forth members, and households sons and fathers, to fill the ranks of war; of the mustering and marching of soldiers, and of the eager, all-engrossing interest of church and congregation, in the Government, navy, and army. . . . In our armies, five hundred thousand men mustered under the Church's eye, have presented touching, and not unheeded claims for special outlay of Christian sympathy, prayer, and labour. And on many a march the songs of Zion have been sung, and in many a camp even revivals of religion have been enjoyed. And from those camps and hospitals where the sick and wounded lay, appeals have reached the kind-hearted, and have been responded to in such a breaking-up of the fountains of true and almost boundless charities, as the world has rarely, if ever witnessed. And besides, . . . thousands of prisoners

of war have been constrained by an undiscriminating liberality to say: "I was in prison and ye came unto me."[1]

Although he deplored the distracting and secularizing influence which the more worldly aspects of the war exerted upon the mind and heart of the Church through "the crippling of her pecuniary energies, in the general commercial prostration," and the increase in intemperance, profanity, and Sabbath-breaking in the world around, the Moderator of the venerable old denomination was inclined to believe that these evils were more than offset by the new opportunities which the war brought the Church, and the new heights to which it caused her to rise.[2]

At first there was some uncertainty as to how broad the field of activity was to be. There were suggestions that the soldiers in the Southern armies be included among the beneficiaries of Presbyterian charity. "Would it not be well enough to inquire what we in the North can do, in this respect for the South?" asked a correspondent of the *Presbyterian* in June, 1861, pointing out that notwithstanding the inability of Northerners to visit camps and send missionaries, it would apparently be possible to furnish the Southern soldiers with Bibles and religious publications. Such acts, he asserted, might "soften the asperities which exist," and hasten reconciliation.[3] The difficulty of such a project was obvious, nevertheless the Old School Board of Publication authorized the distribution to Confederate soldiers and sailors of many thousand dollars' worth of its books and tracts which were in the South at the outbreak of the war.[4] Aside from this action and the attention paid to Confederate soldiers in Northern prisons, Presbyterian relief activities were confined mainly to Union soldiers and sailors.

As early as July, 1861, letters from Old School Presbyterian

---

[1] *Minutes of the General Assembly* (Old School), 1862, vol. xvi, pp. 642-643.
[2] *Ibid.* The whole Narrative comprises pp. 642-646.
[3] *Cf.* communication from "E——s," *Presbyterian*, June 29, 1861.
[4] *Presbyterian Encyclopaedia*, p. 644.

chaplains began to appear in the journals of the denomination.[5] The *Presbyterian* and other denominational papers presented in enthusiastic terms the opportunities of chaplains.[6] If the figures which the *Presbyterian* printed the following spring are correct, however, the Old School journals had not been very successful in their efforts to increase the number of representatives from their Church in the Union chaplaincies. These figures indicated that while the Methodists could claim one-third, the New School Presbyterians one-fifth, the Congregationalists and the Episcopalians each one-seventh, and the Baptists one-eleventh of all the chaplains in the Union army, the Old School Presbyterians and the Unitarians stood tied with but one-twentieth each. The Roman Catholics alone among the major denominations had less than one-twentieth.[7] Considering the size of the Old School Church, its failure to secure any considerable number of chaplaincies was particularly conspicuous. Presbyterian leaders were impatient to have the condition improved.

By an order emanating on May 4, 1861, from the office of the Adjutant General, each of the forty regiments called into service by the proclamation of the President on the previous day was to be provided with a chaplain. The chaplain was to be appointed by the regimental commander on the vote of the field officers and the company commanders. The appointee must be a regularly ordained minister of some Christian denomination.[8] This policy was continued as the army was increased in size.[9] In the case of the state troops, chaplains were usually appointed by the governor or by the regimental officers. While the *Revised Army Regulations* for 1861 stipulated that " the wishes and wants of the soldiers of the regiment shall be allowed their *full* and *due* weight in making the selec-

---

[5] *Cf., e.g., Presbyterian*, August 3, 1861, *ff*.

[6] *Cf., e.g., ibid.*, September 21, 1861, and December 31, 1861.

[7] " General Item," *Presbyterian*, April 12, 1862, quoting the *Independent*.

[8] Editorial, *Christian Herald*, May 30, 1861.

[9] Moore, *Rebellion Record*, vol. i, *Supplement*, no. 38, pp. 224-225.

tion," [10] in Union as well as in state forces there was often the charge of favoritism in the appointment of chaplains. The Governor of New Jersey endeavored to escape criticism on this score in his first selections by choosing five chaplains from as many denominations.[11]

Not all governors, however, had so enviable a reputation for impartiality. " It is interesting to see what a rushing there is of abolition ministers to the Governor to get the appointment of Chaplain to a regiment. These precious pimps want office," remarked the Niles (Michigan) *Republican* in June, 1861. Such a statement challenged reply. " This is the way the dirty blackguard who edits the treasonable sheet at Niles, speaks of the highly respectable clergymen who have become attached to our several regiments," the Detroit *Weekly Tribune* retorted. " The disgusting brute may yet presume too much upon the forbearance of the community where he lives, lies and is loathed," [12] the editor added, forgetting in his violently vituperative alliteration to state whether or not it was true, as insinuated, that abolitionists were favored in appointments by the Michigan governor.

The small proportion of abolitionists among the Old School Presbyterians, if a factor, was by no means the only one responsible for the small number of chaplains from that denomination. Speaking of regimental services one Old School chaplain wrote, " While I have felt, especially at the prayer-meetings, reproved for my coldness by the fervour of others, [I] have yet felt that it was good to be there." [13]   To those who controlled the appointments of chaplains, Old School Presbyterians may well have seemed too cold and too reserved. Probably, too, the financial opportunities of a chaplaincy

[10] *Danville Review*, June, 1863, vol. 3, pp. 255-256, quoting *Revised Army Regulations*, 1861.

[11] *Presbyterian*, June 29, 1861.

[12] Detroit *Weekly Tribune*, June 11, 1861. The statement given above from the Niles *Republican* was here quoted and answered.

[13] Letter from Chaplain " B. T. P.," dated Camp Atterbury, Harper's Ferry, July 26, 1861, and published in the *Presbyterian*, August 3, 1861.

would not be so appealing to a Presbyterian as to clergymen of denominations in which ministerial salaries were lower.[14] Nevertheless, before the close of the war a quite respectable number of Old School ministers had served as army and navy chaplains. Of the 2300 ministers [15] of the denomination, 152 were at one time or other during the war period designated in the denominational records as chaplains.[16] In the New School Church 118 were similarly listed among the 1700 ministers [17] on the Church rolls. Thus the older denomination had more than made up the four to one lead its rival had held during the first year of the war; in percentage, however, the New School was still slightly ahead at the close of the war. The Methodist Episcopal Church, with a membership over four times as large as that of the Old School and seven times that of the New School,[18] furnished some 500 chaplains.[19] Thus while the Presbyterians were somewhat slower in entering upon this sort

[14] There are no available statistics to prove that average salaries among Old and New School ministers were higher than those of other sects, but there is abundant evidence of a general nature to make it clear that the average salary of a Presbyterian pastor was higher than that of the average in several other denominations, at least.

[15] In 1865 the number of ministers in the Old School Church was 2301. *Minutes of the General Assembly,* 1865, vol. xvii, p. 763.

[16] *Cf.* statistical tables, *ibid.,* 1862-1865. The above number was arrived at by counting the names of ministers designated as chaplains. The writer has compiled a list of Old and New School men who served in this capacity.

[17] In 1865 the number of ministers in the New School Church was 1694. *Minutes of the General Assembly* (New School), 1865, xol. xiv, p. 216.

[18] The membership of the Methodist Episcopal Church (based upon returns taken from the Minutes of the Conferences for 1861 and 1862) was 984,933. *Cf.* Sweet, W. W., *The Methodist Episcopal Church and the Civil War* (Cincinnati, n. d.), p. 46. This did not include the membership of the Methodist Episcopal Church, South. In 1863 the membership of the Old School Church was 227,575; that of the New School Church, 135,894.

[19] Professor Sweet (*op. cit.,* pp. 189-195) lists 487 chaplains in the Methodist Episcopal Church. Including some chaplains from the M. E. Church, South, who served in the Union army (p. 196), he places the total number in the Union army at 510 (p. 139).

of work — or rather, in being chosen for it — their record[20] compared favorably with that of the denomination for which the soldiers had shown the greatest preference during the opening months of the war.

Occasionally ministers entered the United States forces as combatants. While there were cases of this type in both Old and New Schools, they appear to have been very rare. As to Presbyterian laymen in the military and naval service, there seems to be no means of ascertaining their number. From casual statements to the effect that a given Presbyterian chaplain had been serving a regiment "in which were many of his own congregations and acquaintances,"[21] and that another had "received, unsought,"[22] his commission, it may be gathered that individual regiments were sometimes composed largely of Presbyterians, though there is little evidence to reveal how often this was the case.

In the fall of 1861 various schemes were on foot among army chaplains to perfect some sort of Christian organization in the army. The central motive was always the desire to band together those men who were determined to lead a Christian life, regardless of their creed or denomination. The attempts never materialized in any general, permanent organization — partly, no doubt, because the scheme was too ambitious, and partly because of lack of communication between chaplains of the various sections of the great army which had so suddenly been brought together. To some degree the objects of such an association were accomplished by the United States Christian Commission,[23] which was founded in 1861. But while the projects were under consideration by chaplains of all denominations, Presbyterians — as was natural from Presbyterian love of organization and administrative detail — were particularly active in their promotion.[24]

[20] Statistics are not available for the minor Presbyterian Churches.
[21] Cf. note on Rev. David McKay, *Presbyterian Historical Almanac*, 1863, p. 190.
[22] *Presbyter*, July 31, 1862. (Note on Dr. James C. Brown.)
[23] Cf. post, pp. 467-469.
[24] Cf. "Religious Movement in the Army," *Presbyterian*, December 7,

Among the various Presbyterian Churches, the activities of each denomination as a whole were directed along five principal lines: domestic missions, foreign missions, church extension, education, and publication. In the Old School Church the agencies for carrying on this work were boards chosen annually, and administered by permanent officials.[25] The New School Church, more faithful to the Plan of Union of 1801,[26] for fifteen years after the separation of 1837 had relied principally upon voluntary societies of an interdenominational character, but in 1852 Church boards were established to take over the work of home missions and publication, though this reversion was partially concealed by calling the new agencies "committees."[27] The New School Committees were somewhat more directly under the supervision of the General Assembly than were the Old School boards. Of the minor Presbyterian Churches the stricter ones followed the Old School policy of working through boards; the Cumberland Church used permanent committees. The central activities of the Churches were all vitally affected by the war; particularly in 1861, all of the boards and committees found themselves working under very severe handicaps.

The central agency best adapted to be of immediate service in relieving war conditions was obviously that dealing with publication. The Old School Board of Publication bent itself at once to the task of preparing and distributing to the men in military and naval service reading matter which it considered suitable. Notwithstanding the fact that the Board was handicapped by the depression of business, "the unusual scarcity of money, . . . and the new numerous, and extraordinary

1861, describing an organization effected by a meeting of chaplains of which Rev. Thomas P. Hunt (an Old School Presbyterian) was the president; also a letter of Dr. Samuel J. Baird, published in *Presbyterian*, January 18, 1862, in which the writer (an Old School Presbyterian) enthusiastically described another organization of the same sort.

[25] *Cf.* Thompson, *op. cit.*, p. 80.
[26] *Cf. ante*, pp. 13-14.
[27] Thompson, *op cit.*, p. 138.

claims upon the sympathies and charities of our people," it was able to report to the General Assembly of 1862 that it had made considerable progress in special war work.[28] Its most important achievement had been the publication of the "Soldier's Pocket-Book." Of this "admirable little manual for the use of soldiers" containing Bible-texts, religious verses, and spiritual advice, some 90,000 copies had already been printed.[29] Before the close of the war more than 300,000 were gratuitously distributed.[30] Other publications of the first year included "The Soldier's Series" of tracts, "Hospital Cards," "The Soldier's Library," "The Sailor's Companion," and other similar booklets. These all, the Assembly was assured, "have . . . been extensively circulated and done a great amount of good."[31] The volumes given away amounted to 44,311, nearly double the record of any previous year, while the 3,275,825 pages of tracts gratuitously distributed were more than thirty-five per cent in excess over the amount of the previous year. "Encouraged and enabled to go forward by the contributions of individuals and churches made with especial reference," to the soldiers and sailors, the Board had supplied camps, military posts, and naval vessels with "suitable religious reading." It had stationed its colporteurs at Philadelphia, Baltimore, Washington, Cairo, and other hospital cities, to take especial care of supplying the sick and wounded with reading matter; others it had placed at strategic points where they might furnish regiments passing through toward the seats of war. Nor had the thousands of Federal prisoners been neglected. The prisoners in the forts in New York and Boston harbors sent a letter of earnest thanks to the Board for remembering them, while the hosts of prisoners

[28] For the 1862 report of the Board of Publication, *cf. Minutes of the General Assembly* (Old School), 1862, vol. xvi, pp. 677-681.

[29] *Ibid.*, p. 678.

[30] *Presbyterian Encyclopaedia*, pp. 217, 644. Dr. William Engles, editor of the *Presbyterian*, was the editor of the "Soldier's Pocket-Book," which was published anonymously. (*Ibid.*, p. 217.)

[31] *Minutes of the General Assembly*, 1862, vol. xvi, p. 678.

taken at Forts Henry and Donelson had also received " eagerly and thankfully " the supplies of religious reading. The Board believed that during this first year of the war not less than three hundred thousand soldiers and sailors had been the recipients of its religious books and tracts.[32]

Each succeeding year of the war saw an expansion in the war-time activities of the Board. In 1864 it reported to the Assembly that there was now a new important and numerous class of claimants for its benefactions — the freedmen. They were now found, it was explained, collected in villages at numerous points along the Atlantic coast and the Mississippi River. " Their eagerness to learn to read and to possess books," the Board declared, " is very remarkable." Supplies of suitable elementary books and tracts had been sent as an aid to those engaged in their instruction, and the Board assured the Assembly of its willingness to extend its efforts among this new class of beneficiaries.[33] The report of the following year mentioned the freedmen only casually, but otherwise recorded the same progress in the expansion of its war-work as had characterized the history of the previous years of the conflict.[34]

The New School " Presbyterian Publication Committee," still less than ten years old when the war broke out,[35] was too busily engaged in building up its regular work[36] to become as absorbed in war activities as was the corresponding agency of the rival branch of the Church. Nevertheless, dur-

[32] *Ibid.*, p. 680.

[33] *Cf.* the 1864 report of the Board, *Minutes of the General Assembly,* 1864, vol. xvii, pp. 362-367.

[34] *Cf.* the 1865 report of the Board, *ibid.*, 1865, pp. 632-636.

[35] *Cf. ante*, p. 433.

[36] *Cf.* earnest pleas for funds in reports of the Committee for 1860, 1861, 1862, *ibid.*, for the years indicated. So important a work as Rev. Ezra H. Gillett's *History of the Presbyterian Church in the United States* awaited publication for two years before the Committee's appeals (*cf.* reports of 1862 and 1863) for funds for this purpose were successful. There is no doubt that the Committee was not nearly so well established in its work as the much older Board of Publication of the Old School Church.

ing the first year of the war the Committee published and distributed a booklet edited especially for the use of soldiers by the Committee's editor. It was described as follows in the Committee's 1862 annual report to the Assembly:

> *The Soldier's Friend.* By Rev. John W. Dulles. 123 pages. 32mo. A small volume, prepared to meet the wants of the thousands of volunteers, mustered into the service of the United States. It contains thirty-one brief religious readings, thirty-one selected psalms, thirty-one hymns, the Ten Commandments, the Creed, prayers, and hints on preserving health.[37]

The Committee begged for donations of tracts and books to give to missionaries, to add to Sabbath-School libraries, and "to send through Chaplains, (of whom our own body has had more than ninety [38] in the field), the guidance and consolation of Bible teachings, to our myriads of soldiers in the camp and the hospital. . . ." [39]

The following year the Committee announced the publication of two tracts designed particularly for soldiers — one of them bearing the appealing title, "A Word to the Soldier. By a Lady." [40] The list of publications for soldiers was augmented in 1864 by the appearance of "The Soldier's Scrap-Book," a little volume of sixty-four pages. The Committee reported, "The Christian Commission show their appreciation of it by ordering 80,000 copies for distribution." [41] A forty-page tract, "The Young Soldier," reported in 1865,[42] completed the Committee's group of publications designed especially for soldiers. As compared with the work of the Old

---

[37] *Minutes of the General Assembly* (New School), 1862, vol. xiii, p. 93.

[38] If this figure is correct for the first year of the war, then the number (118) named *ante*, p. 431, would seem much too small for the whole war-period. The latter figure represents the number of ministers listed as chaplains during the war years. It is perfectly possible that some chaplains were not so listed in the *Minutes*. On the other hand, the term "Chaplains" as used above may have included various sorts of religious workers.

[39] *Minutes of the General Assembly* (New School), 1862, vol. xiii, p. 95.

[40] *Ibid.*, 1863, vol. xiii, p. 308. The other tract was entitled "Good Soldiers."

[41] *Ibid.*, 1864, vol. xiii, p. 540.

[42] *Ibid.*, 1865, vol. xiv, p. 82.

School Board of Publication its accomplishments along this line were limited, yet the appearance of at least one new work each year showed that the soldiers' needs were not forgotten. Perhaps the comparative poverty of the New School Committee was the principal factor preventing its record from being more impressive.

The publication agencies of the minor Presbyterian Churches apparently made no special efforts for the soldiers and sailors of the Union. The Board of Publication of the new United Presbyterian Church throughout the war period was clamoring for more funds [43] — evidently the people of this denomination were much more interested in the work for the freedmen which was started with great vigor in 1863.[44] At least two others of the stricter Presbyterian sects concentrated their energies upon the same object.[45] The confusion in the Cumberland Church on the other hand, resulting from the forced separation of a large part of its membership, rendered it well-nigh impossible for its agency of publication to undertake any special war-work. In fact when the Cumberland Assembly found that it could get no reports from its publication headquarters, it was deemed necessary to appoint a special Publishing Committee to carry on the work temporarily.[46] As the Church was having difficulty in securing the necessary funds for the publication of the minutes of the Assembly,[47] it was hardly to be expected that the Publishing Committee would undertake to extend the scope of its work. Probably the minor Presbyterian Churches felt that their soldiers would be taken care of in the wide distribution of literature on the part of the two larger Presbyterian denominations — especially the Old School Church.

The Old School Board of Publication was not only first

[43] *Cf.* reports of Board, *Presbyterian Historical Almanac,* 1863, p. 348; 1865, pp. 182-183.
[44] *Cf. post,* pp. 453-454.
[45] *Cf. post,* pp. 454-456.
[46] *Presbyterian Historical Almanac,* 1863, p. 413.
[47] *Ibid.,* 1865, pp. 231-232.

among Presbyterian agencies of its type, but also ranked very
high among all American church organizations of publication
in special war-time accomplishments. The *Presbyterian,*
whose editor [48] was an important member of the Board, published with pride an estimate of this organization which appeared in *The News of the Churches,* "one of the best, if not
the best, of the British religious journals":

> Several of our other Churches or Communions have Boards of Publica-
> tion, and are doing something in the way of furnishing their adherents
> and friends with a religious literature; but none of them rivals the Old
> School Presbyterian Church, excepting the Methodist Episcopal Church
> (of the North), which, in fact, greatly exceeds it in some respects, having
> accumulated a fund in houses, stock of books, and stereotypes and other
> plates, equal to half a million of dollars, which is, I apprehend, about
> equal to that of the London Tract Society.[49]

When this second largest Church publication agency had been
engaged in war-work for about a year, the *Presbyterian* recorded with satisfaction the reception with which the Board's
literature had been met in the camps:

> While other Societies are doing much, one thing is certain, that the
> books and tracts of our Board are received with extreme pleasure. It
> would seem as if the alleged prejudice against them among the masses,
> because of their clear and forcible statements of the doctrines of grace,
> does not, after all, exist. Those Societies which soften down, or keep
> back part of the truth of God's word, in order to make their publica-
> tions more acceptable, as they suppose, to the unconverted, have not
> gained any advantage over us in this respect.[50]

As the Board constantly expanded its soldier literature, it
must have remained convinced that Old School doctrine was
at least of interest to the men in the camps. There is no doubt
that the combined efforts of the Old and New School Churches
resulted in making Presbyterian literature available to the
great majority of Union soldiers and sailors, as well as to those
Confederates detained in Federal prison camps.

[48] Dr. William M. Engles.
[49] "The Presbyterian Board of Publication as Seen Abroad," *Presbyterian,* September 13, 1862.
[50] *Ibid.,* June 21, 1862.

As the progress of the war and the changing policy of the Federal Government led to the rapid growth of the class of freedmen, the condition of these people soon attracted the attention of the churches. As early as December, 1861, the Board of Domestic Missions of the Old Side Covenanters (Reformed Presbyterian Synod), the strictness of whose theology was matched only by the bitterness of their hatred of slavery,[51] having heard of the condition of the freed people of Port Royal, South Carolina, "at once secured the services of Rev. N. R. Johnston, of Topsham, Vermont, who set sail early in March, 1862, in a United States ship, having a free passage given him."[52] Within a week after Mr. Johnston's arrival at Port Royal he had begun to preach to the Contrabands and had opened a school for their benefit. In his report to the Board, the missionary expressed his impressions of the "appalling physical and moral destitution of the people," and the pressing need for teachers and preachers.[53] An appeal of this kind was scarcely necessary to start the denomination upon a career of strenuous activity for those being emancipated from the bonds of slavery.

Though one of the last of the Presbyterian Churches to undertake relief for the freedmen, the Old School Church partially made up for its tardiness by the elaborateness of its organization for the work. In December, 1863, the *Presbyter* published editorially a complaint concerning the slowness of the Old School denomination, in comparison with other branches of the Church. While synods and presbyteries and all the religious periodicals of the denomination had been urging the people to labor and to contribute, and reports had come of "large benefactions having been raised," the Church as a whole had done nothing. The *Presbyter* was of the opinion that the Old School Church should not undertake to carry on its work for the freedmen through the Board of Domestic Mis-

[51] *Cf. ante*, pp. 398-405.
[52] *Presbyterian Historical Almanac*, 1863, p. 396.
[53] *Ibid.*, pp. 396-397.

sions, nor should it establish a new board for the purpose, but it should rather coöperate with such existing agencies as the United States Christian Commission, the United States Sanitary Commission, the chaplains, the army, and the Federal Government.

When the Old School General Assembly had finally in 1864 been brought around to a position of unsparing condemnation of slavery,[54] it was free from any embarrassment it may previously have felt with regard to missionary efforts among the freedmen, and it proceeded to take action on that subject. It failed, however, to follow the advice of the *Presbyter,* and determined to establish two Committees for the Education of Freedmen, each to consist of two ministers and three ruling elders. The headquarters of the one were to be in Philadelphia, that of the other in Indianapolis. The committees were to appoint ministers and teachers for the work (upon the endorsement of the appointees' presbyteries), advertise for and collect and disburse funds, make a record of all facts gathered, and report to the next General Assembly. The Board of Publication was directed to furnish them gratis, at its discretion, such of its publications as might be used for the education and evangelization of the freedmen.[55]

When the General Assembly of 1865 met in Pittsburgh, members of the two committees provided for the previous year were asked to address the Assembly. The speakers were all enthusiastic over what had been accomplished and over the opportunities which the future offered. Frankly recognizing the faults of the black men, they were inclined to ascribe them to the effects of slavery, and named the changeableness of the negro as a strong reason for bending every effort to bring education to these people while they still retained their present enthusiasm for acquiring learning. There were strong protests against leaving the work entirely to voluntary aid societies, in spite of the fact that a representative of the Northwestern

[54] *Cf. ante,* pp. 126-128.
[55] *Minutes of the General Assembly* (Old School), 1864, vol. xvii, pp. 321-323.

Freedmen's Aid Commission was given fifteen minutes in which to address the Assembly on the work of his organization.[56] This gentleman urged the Old School body to unify Presbyterian efforts with those of his agency, but, discouraged at what he termed the "cut and dried" state of affairs in the Assembly, subsequently stated that his Society would canvass for funds among Old School Presbyterians, in spite of the determination of that body to carry on their work separately.[57] At the conclusion of the discussion on the subject,[58] the Assembly voted to adopt a plan which called for the substitution of one committee for the two of the previous year — the new committee to consist of nine ministers and nine ruling elders, and to have its headquarters at Pittsburgh. The committee was directed, as fast as was "consistent with the interests of the cause" committed to it, to transfer to the regular Boards of the Church such portions of its work as belonged to the specific objects of the several Boards. The Assembly also recommended a special collection for the cause of the freedmen on a given Sabbath in October, and resolved, finally,

That while this Assembly rejoices in all evangelical efforts of the various associations for the Freedmen, it affectionately urges all the churches under its care to make their contributions for the benefit of this class of people to the Assembly's own Committee.[59]

Debate-weary after the long arguments on the case of the Presbytery of Louisville,[60] the General Assembly on the fourteenth day of its 1866 session in St. Louis undertook the consideration of the report of its Committee on Freedmen.[61] On

[56] *Ibid.*, 1865, vol. xvii, p. 543.
[57] *Cf.* report of proceedings of sixth day of 1865 General Assembly sessions, *Presbyterian*, June 3, 1865.
[58] For report of this discussion *cf. ibid.*
[59] For the report and resolutions adopted by the Assembly in 1865, *cf. Minutes of the General Assembly*, 1865, vol. xvii, pp. 543-545.
[60] *Cf. ante*, pp. 218-261.
[61] That is, the Assembly's Standing Committee on Freedmen, who reported on the work of the Committee on the Education of the Freedmen — the latter Committee being the one charged with active work for the freedmen. The fact that both committees went by the name "Committee on Freedmen" is confusing.

the previous day the committee to which had been referred the
annual report of the Board of Domestic Missions had presented the results of its inquiries. This committee had expressed its dissatisfaction with the progress made by the
Board in carrying out the direction of the 1865 Assembly " to
secure a footing among our seceded southern churches." But
thirteen missionaries had been commissioned to labor in the
South. " Apparently, the only direct effort to reach our southern churches," the committee reported, " was made in Tennessee; but the attempt was a complete failure." This failure
was one of the main reasons for recommending that the Board
be directed to revise the whole system of Domestic Missions.[62]
The Committee on Freedmen made a much more cheerful report. Funds to the amount of $25,000 had been raised, fifty-
five missionaries had been commissioned, over three thousand
pupils were in the schools which had been established, and
over two thousand in the Sabbath-schools. In view of this
success the Assembly voted that the report be approved and
printed for circulation in all of the churches, commended the
cause to the prayers of the people, and again specified a given
Sabbath as a day of special prayer and collection for the
freedmen.[63]

The Old School's agency had come into conflict with the
Southern Presbyterian Church over the occupancy of a church
building in Charleston, South Carolina. When the Committee's agents had fully investigated the matter, they relinquished
at once all claim to the church, but a colored preacher instituted proceedings for the possession of the building under the
provisions of the Civil Rights Bill, and the Southern Church
still felt aggrieved toward the Northern body.[64] It was with
the purpose of preventing conflicts of this type that a Kentucky member of the Assembly [65] suggested that it be

[62] *Minutes of the General Assembly* (Old School), 1866, vol. xviii, p. 71.
[63] *Ibid.,* pp. 76-77.
[64] For an account of this incident, *cf. Proceedings of the General Assemblies . . . 1866,* pp. 96-97.
[65] Dr. E. P. Humphrey, Professor in the Danville Theological Seminary.

Resolved, That this General Assembly, deferring to what appear to be the manifest indications of the will of Providence in the matter, assure the Southern ministers and churches lately in connection with us of our desire to assist and co-operate with them in any judicious measures for the spiritual good of their coloured population.[66]

Such a suggestion was going much too far for men of the Thomas stripe.[67] The *Proceedings* of the Assembly report that

Dr. Thomas said he understood the resolution to be a recognition of their [the Southern Church's] separate existence as an organization with whom they could co-operate, and the corollary of that was, that being in the possession of that field they ought in all Christian courtesy to leave them undisturbed. He thought that was cutting it rather deep.[68]

To prove how dangerous such a policy would be, Dr. Thomas cited a recent discourse by a New Orleans pastor who declared that Southerners should still look for independence and that in one hundred years spiders would spin webs around the spindles of Lowell, and a Comanche Indian would sit on Bunker Hill Monument and sketch the ruins of Boston. Until this element was purged out, Dr. Thomas declared, he was "not willing to meet a direct or indirect proposition to co-operate with them." Upon his notion, the resolution for co-operation was laid upon the table.[69] The Old School would do its work for the freedmen independently.

In 1867 the Committee on Freedmen[70] reported that more than $40,000 had been appropriated for their work during the past twelve months, yet but 526 of 2,508 churches of the denomination had made any contribution. This apathy the Committee bemoaned. There had been 104 missionaries in the employ of the Board during the course of the year at an average salary of $365, but the difficulty of the work and the

[66] *Minutes of the General Assembly* (Old School), 1866, vol. xviii, p. 73. For the discussion on this resolution, *cf. Proceedings,* pp. 97-98.

[67] *Cf. ante,* pp. 228-233.

[68] *Proceedings,* p. 97.

[69] *Ibid.,* pp. 97-98.

[70] In this case, the Committee actively carrying on the work in the South. (*Cf. ante,* p. 441, note 61.)

peculiar trials — particularly the social ostracism — which it involved had resulted in one-third of them leaving the field before the expiration of the twelve months. "To be despised by a wicked world, through grace, leads the servant of Jesus to be strong; but to be disgraced in the eyes of those who profess to follow the common Lord, saps the strength and wounds the soul." Two members of a presbytery of the Southern Church[71] had taken commissions to work for the Old School Church (one for the Committee on Freedmen and the other for the Board of Domestic Missions), but had immediately been given the alternative of returning their commissions and refusing all aid from the North, or of leaving the presbytery. Choosing the latter alternative, they had organized a presbytery faithful to the Old School. This new presbytery, aided by a special donation, had established an institute for the training of negro catechists and ministers.[72] As far as the number in schools and Sabbath-schools was concerned, there was a slight increase over that of the previous year.[73]

During the two remaining years before reunion with the New School, the Old School work for the freedmen made moderate progress. By 1869 the annual appropriation for this cause amounted to about $80,000; the number of pupils in the schools was 3,208, and in Sabbath-schools, 4,723; while the whole number of communicants amounted to 5,634. The Secretary of the Committee reported that he had attempted to carry out the instructions of the previous Assembly that he ascertain whether coöperation could not be secured with the similar organizations of the New School and the Southern Presbyterian Churches, so that the work could be carried on "more harmoniously and efficiently by Presbyterians"; but his efforts to secure active coöperation with either of these

[71] The Presbytery of Concord (North Carolina).
[72] The Henry J. Biddle Memorial Institute, Charlotte, North Carolina.
[73] For an abstract of the Second Annual Report of the Committee on Freedmen, cf. *Minutes of the General Assembly* (Old School), 1867, vol. xviii, pp. 441-448.

bodies had thus far met with entire failure.[74] Actually, reunion of Old and New Schools was not of benefit to the cause of the freedmen. The total amount of money available for the use of the Committee of the combined Church steadily declined until in 1873 it was $59,000 (although the act of apportionment had recommended the sum of $75,000),[75] which was but three-fourths of the amount which the Old School alone had expended for the same object four years earlier.

From the outset the patriotic theme had been emphasized by the Old School Church as one of its chief objects in carrying on work for the freedmen. In 1864, when provision was first being made for this labor, the Assembly asserted that since the freedmen had been taught the use of arms they must also be given Christian education, for " no human foresight can assure us of safety from issues of this civil strife, when a people having such a history, and educated only in the school of war, shall be cast into a society with inveterate prejudices against them." [76] Similarly, the Assembly of 1865 recognized that " the elevation of that people among us is essential to the highest interests of our own race, and of our beloved country. . . ." [77] The danger of neglect was reiterated in 1866: " If they are not to become a disturbing and dangerous element in society, they must be educated to take care of themselves." [78] A statement in the 1867 report sent to the Assembly by those actively engaged in the Southern field may not have been entirely convincing to the " radical " element of the Old School body: " Again, under the sudden, unexpected demand for the exercise of the franchise, new issues and new duties, in the providence of God, are thrust upon them . . .

---

[74] *Cf.* abstract of Fourth Annual Report of the Assembly's Committee on Freedmen, *ibid.*, 1869, vol. xviii, pp. 987-994.

[75] *Cf.* report of the Standing Committee on Freedmen, *ibid.*, 1873, vol. 2 (new series), pp. 521-524; also abstract of report of Permanent Committee, *ibid.*, p. 629.

[76] *Minutes of the General Assembly* (Old School), 1864, vol. xvii, p. 322.

[77] *Ibid.*, 1865, vol. xvii, p. 544.

[78] *Ibid.*, 1866, vol. xviii, p. 76.

for which no thoughtful man can deny that they need instruction." [79] It was apparently believed that one of the best means of interesting the Old School Church in the cause of the freedmen was to appeal to the emotion of patriotism. Considering the history of the war-time Assemblies such a belief was not unjustified.

In view of the anti-slavery record of the New School Presbyterian Church and the liberality with which its Assembly had dispensed its advice on how the Federal Government should treat the negro,[80] the small effort made by this denomination for the freedmen is astonishing. Although every New School Assembly since the outbreak of the war had expressed sympathy for the cause of emancipation, it was not until 1864 that this body recognized any responsibility toward the freedmen. In that year it was

> Resolved, That the Standing Committee on Home Missions be directed to inquire as to the necessity and expediency of the General Assembly's adopting some specific arrangements, whereby the institutions of the Gospel may be given to the large and increasing number of Freedmen, who have been emancipated during the present civil war.[81]

The following year the annual report of the Committee of Home Missions [82] stated that "the Freedmen and Refugees constitute a new department of missionary work." [83] One missionary had been laboring among these classes in St. Louis "with great acceptance and success," yet the Committee was forced to add, "We have made some earnest attempts to inaugurate the work in other places; but the difficulties of the undertaking, and especially the lack of the right men for it, have rendered our efforts fruitless." Yet it was recognized that the close of the war offered new opportunities, and that

[79] Ibid., 1867, vol. xviii, p. 448.
[80] Cf. ante, pp. 341-362.
[81] Minutes of the General Assembly (New School), 1864, vol. xiii, p. 467.
[82] That is, the Committee in the field (to be distinguished from the Standing Committee on Home Missions, which was a committee of the Assembly).
[83] Minutes of the General Assembly (New School), 1865, vol. xiv, p. 77.

it was "a great duty of the Church" to give these people the Gospel, "to whose influence they seem particularly susceptible." [84] The Standing Committee to which this report was referred recommended that an agent or agents be appointed to investigate the spiritual needs of the freedmen, and that every effort be made "to institute such Christian relations with *them* as may be formed with the white population in the South, depending on the piety and liberality of our churches for the means of supporting such a work." [85]

In spite of these recommendations, all that the field Committee could report in 1866 was the organization of three "flourishing" churches. This department of labor, it was asserted, had been greatly crippled for want of men. In reviewing this report the Standing Committee considered the labors, as far as they had been prosecuted, "reasonably successful," but complained, "Here, again, it is our straitened faith that produces our limited efficiency." The inconsistency of neglecting wants at home caused the Committee to exclaim, "If the millions of China and Caffraria are to be evangelized, how much more these multitudes at our own doors!" Attention was called to the fact that while slavery had "depressed the adult negro population too low for even Christianity easily to elevate them," there were 1,150,000 of this race between the ages of five and fifteen, who were as "impressible" by educating and evangelizing influences as any class of the white population.[86]

Year after year the Committee of Home Missions reported the great need for work among the freedmen, but seemed to accomplish little for them. The Assembly's Standing Committee on Home Missions always enthusiastically echoed the statements with regard to the opportunities in this field, and appeared to be trying to spur the field Committee to definite accomplishment, but these efforts availed little. In 1868 the

[84] *Ibid.* For the Committee's report *cf.* pp. 76-81.
[85] *Ibid.*, pp. 26-27.
[86] *Ibid.*, 1866, vol. xiv, p. 268.

field Committee reported that the subject of the freedmen had "not ceased during the year to occupy their thoughts." There had been some uncertainty as to whether educational work should be undertaken along with evangelization, but the Committee had concluded that this combination was necessary.[87] There were signs of impatience in the Standing Committee's comments upon these reflections:

> In this view we heartily concur; and we therefore recommend that the Committee be fully authorized and urgently desired to go forward in this work boldly and swiftly; remembering that the opportunity for it is precious and fleeting; remembering, also, that no denomination of Christians has better opportunity to engage in this work advantageously; and that thus far we have only coöperated with agencies established by others, instead of taking our proper place by the side of others, with an appropriate agency of our own, for which we would be duly responsible.[88]

In order to insure the "vigorous prosecution" of this work, it was recommended that an Assistant Secretary be employed, and that special collections be taken to finance the Committee's activities along this line.[89]

This emphatic demand of the Standing Committee's report (which was adopted by the General Assembly)[90] at last brought results. A separate Freedmen's Department of the Presbyterian Committee of Home Missions was created. By the spring of 1869, nine preachers had been employed, the work of the Freedmen's Union Commission of Pittsburgh had been taken over, as well as twenty-nine schools which the Freedmen's Bureau at Washington was about to abandon. Yet as the first report of this Department pointed out, all of this was "only a beginning — experimental, nothing more." As the encouragements were abundant, as the enmity of the whites was relaxing, and as the Freedmen's Bureau and other agencies of a general character must soon pass away, it was hoped that the New School Church would accomplish much.[91]

[87] *Ibid.*, 1868, vol. xv, p. 94.
[88] *Ibid.*, p. 46.
[89] *Ibid.*, pp. 46-47.
[90] *Ibid.*, p. 45.
[91] *Ibid.*, 1869, vol. xv, pp. 318-320.

Through the adoption of the paper submitted by the Standing Committee which reviewed this report, the Assembly expressed its gratification that the work had been "fairly and successfully begun," and at the same time its "wonder and regret at the strange delay with which we were chargeable, as a Church, in entering upon a field of missionary labor whose claims were so peculiarly urgent and sacred, and which was at the same time, in all its aspects, so hopeful." It was a source of humiliation that "nearly every other denomination of evangelical Christians is in advance of us, in respect both to the promptness and the liberality with which they have entered upon this work of educating and evangelizing the Freedmen." Yet it was hastily added, "This remark applies, of course, only to our action as a Church; for, from the very first hour that opportunity was offered, the Christian people in our New-School Presbyterian churches have been contributing largely to this Cause." These gifts had been placed at the disposal of "numberless Societies," some of them working in the interest of other denominations, others without supervision by any evangelical denomination whatever. As there was no doubt that "the time has fully come for the New-School Presbyterian Church to do something in behalf of the emancipated slaves which shall be seen by the world to be correspondent with her wealth, her heart, and her history," and as it was felt that the provision of the previous year for an "Assistant Secretary only" was "likely to be misinterpreted," it was recommended that the executive officer of this department be known as the "'Secretary for the Freedmen;' it being understood, that the work which he is called to superintend takes its place fully abreast of the largest and most important schemes which we are carrying forward as a Church for the evangelization of the world." The churches were urged to raise during the coming year "no less a sum than $100,000 for the purpose of carrying forward, not feebly, but boldly, swiftly, and vigorously, the work of educating and evangelizing the Freedmen." [92]

Within a year the New School Church had merged with the

[92] *Cf.* report of Standing Committee on Freedmen, *ibid.*, pp. 295-298.

Old School,[93] and the ambitious program which it had outlined for itself was never tested out. Yet from the fact that the funds available for the welfare of the freedmen after the Churches had combined, dwindled from $77,000 in 1871 [94] to $65,000 in 1872 [95] and $63,000 in 1873,[96] while the Old School Church alone had had $79,000 for this work in 1869,[97] it would appear that New School Presbyterians never gave much support to Presbyterian agencies for the freedmen. While it is possible that some New School money found its way into the Old School funds before the reunion of 1869, there is no evidence among the Old School records that this was the case. Indeed, even with reunion fast approaching, most New School Presbyterians probably preferred to contribute through some other agency than the Old School Church. That they were willing to contribute to the cause was the unanimous testimony of the members of the Standing Committee in 1869:

> Probably almost every pastor in our body can testify, as those of your Committee certainly can, that no object, especially for the last four years, has enlisted such a quick and hearty sympathy in the bosoms of the people as the elevation and the thorough evangelization of the Freedmen. In some of our churches, as many as three or four collections, in the course of the year, have been cheerfully given for this Cause. No other Cause would have borne such a frequent presentation, and been met with such an unwearied and substantial welcome to the last. A word for the Freedmen has always been answered quickly and generously.[98]

If the Committee was right in attributing the smallness of the total contributions to the New School agency during the past year (less than $15,000) [99] to ignorance on the part of the

[93] *Cf. post,* pp. 515-517.
[94] *Minutes of the General Assembly,* 1871, vol. 1 (new series), p. 669.
[95] *Ibid.,* 1872, vol. 2 (new series), p. 156.
[96] *Ibid.,* 1873, vol. 2 (new series), p. 629.
[97] *Minutes of the General Assembly* (Old School), 1869, vol. xviii, p. 988.
[98] *Minutes of the General Assembly* (New School), 1869, vol. xv, p. 296.
[99] " One hundred and eighty-nine only of the more than 1600 churches of our body contributed last year to this Cause — less than one-eighth of the whole; $15,000 being the total of the receipts, and even this including sums of considerable importance contributed by the Freedmen's Bureau, benevolent persons in Great Britain and others." *Ibid.,* pp. 296-297.

churches that the New School had really begun work for the freedmen,[100] this explanation would scarcely suffice for the apparent indifference in later years. In 1873 it was reported that 3,195 churches of the 4,730 belonging to the reunited denomination had, during the previous year, made no contribution toward the denominational fund for the work for the freedmen.[101]

New School leaders were uncomfortably conscious of the discrepancy between the preaching and the practice of their denomination in its attitude toward the emancipated slaves. Having through the General Assembly's 1866 paper on the State of the Country declared that " our most solemn national trust concerns that patient race so long held in unrighteous bondage," [102] it is not surprising that the corresponding body in 1869 looked back " with wonder and regret at the strange delay with which we were chargeable." [103] This " strange delay " is no doubt partly attributable to the youthfulness of the New School Committee of Home Missions. This Committee had been created in 1861. Even if it be considered the natural outgrowth of the Church Extension Committee, whose work it took over in that year, it would still rank as a young organization, for the Church Extension Committee (the agency through which the New School Church first embarked upon home missionary effort independent of the interdenominational American Home Missionary Society) itself was founded as late as 1855.[104] Thus when the Standing Committee on Freedmen in 1869 mentioned the Committee of Home Missions as " that veteran Missionary Committee whom we know

[100] *Ibid.*, p. 296.

[101] *Minutes of the General Assembly,* 1873, vol. 2 (new series), p. 629.

[102] *Cf. ante,* pp. 357-359. This statement was quoted in a resolution which the 1866 Assembly later passed, urging collections for the freedmen. *Cf. Minutes of the General Assembly* (New School), 1866, vol. xiv, p. 278.

[103] *Cf. ante,* p. 449; also *Minutes of the General Assembly* (New School), 1869, vol. xv, p. 295.

[104] An interesting history of the founding of the Church Extension Committee and the Committee of Home Missions is given in the first annual report of the Committee of Home Missions, *ibid.*, 1862, pp. 80-89.

and trust," [105] it betrayed a somewhat defective time sense.

Had the New School Assembly entrusted its work for the freedmen to a wholly new organization, as did the Old School,[106] or had it possessed a truly veteran organization able to carry through with efficiency a heavy additional task, no doubt its endeavors would have been much more successful. Unfortunately, it saw fit to leave the responsibility for this important work in the charge of a Committee whose resources and experience were utterly inadequate, and whose interest and enthusiasm were devoted to the engrossing task of carrying Presbyterianism into the rapidly growing West. Absorbed in the work of nursing into a healthy and vigorous Presbyterianism the missionary enterprises in the West alleged to have been for years neglected by the American Home Missionary Society,[107] the youthful Committee of Home Missions had little time to devote to the case of the freedmen. In 1869 (after the work for the freedmen had been separately organized and the Committee was no longer obliged to include their case in the annual report), it was stated that

The Committee have employed every available man in the denomination, and taken many from other denominations, for their missionary work; and have needed, and would gladly have employed fifty more in the West, if they could have found them.[108]

With such a need for men in the West it is not surprising that the Committee should have been timid about entering with vigor upon the work in the South.

On the other hand, neither is it surprising that Presbyterian historians have done little boasting about the record of New School aid for the freedmen. There can be little doubt that many members of this denomination were interested in the cause of the emancipated slaves, but until 1868 the interest of the denomination itself did not advance much beyond

[105] *Ibid.*, 1869, vol. xv, p. 296.
[106] *Cf. ante*, pp. 440-446.
[107] *Minutes of the General Assembly* (New School), 1862, vol. xiii, pp. 82-83.
[108] *Ibid.*, 1869, vol. xv, p. 318.

wordy pronouncements upon the evils of slavery, the rights of
the negro, the merits of the Freedmen's Bureau and of the
Civil Rights Bill,[109] and the proper attitude for the Federal
Government to take toward the freedmen. In practical assistance to the negro the New School record contrasted sharply
with its preachments for nearly thirty years.

Quite different from the attitude of the New School Church
toward the problem of the freedmen was that of the other
Presbyterian denominations of anti-slavery traditions.   In
1864, before the Old School had started its creditable work,
and before the New School Assembly had even resolved that
something should be done, the United Presbyterian Church
Assembly in session at Philadelphia received from the Board
of Missions to the Freedmen its first annual report. Six "stations" had been occupied, fifty-four teachers had been employed, about 4,500 persons had been in schools and Sabbath-
schools conducted by the Board. Something over $8,000 had
been received for the work, besides special donations of books
and supplies, assistance from other Freedmen's organizations,
and special reductions in railroad fares. The Government had
been friendly to the mission and it was believed that a Freedmen's Bureau would soon be established which would save the
workers "from many annoyances now experienced." Some
interesting comments on the experiences of the workers were
expressed:

The work as conducted by this Board and the Presbyteries during the
year, encourages the belief that the colored people are not only intensely
anxious to learn, but have capacities which compare very favorably with
those of the whites. Also, they are eminently a devotional people, and
fond of religious excitement. . . . The age of the scholars ranges from
four to seventy years, and the general impression is that those of pure
African blood are more robust in constitution, and in a general way
more vigorous in intellect than those known as mulattoes. For the study
of arithmetic and penmanship they discover marked ability. But the
great desire of this people is to be able to read the Bible.[110]

[109] *Cf. ante*, pp. 358-359.
[110] *Presbyterian Historical Almanac*, 1865, pp. 187-188. For the complete
report, *cf.* pp. 183-188.

The Board urged an expansion in its activities during the coming year, and asked for denominational support.[111]

The United Presbyterian Church made steady progress in this work in spite of some opposition on the part of Southern whites — amounting in certain cases to mob violence.[112]   At certain "stations" the Board's plan of charging tuition of those who could afford to pay was frustrated by its being compelled "to compete with other associations occupying a part of these fields, who charged no tuition."[113]   In 1866 "the uncertain tenure" by which the Board could hold buildings furnished by the Freedmen's Bureau necessitated the building of schoolhouses and lodging-houses for teachers.[114]   By 1867 "some of the leading and more thoughtful citizens of the South" were beginning to exhibit an interest in the education of the freedmen, and it was thought that all opposition would soon die away. Tranquillity, the Board reported, prevailed in all the stations. The Church's policy of educating the freedmen to become educators of their fellows, was beginning to bear fruit.[115]   Altogether, the progress made by the United Presbyterian Church in its work for the emancipated slaves was quite in keeping with its record of consistent opposition to slavery.[116]

Of the four smaller denominations which with the United Presbyterians made up the stricter wing of Presbyterianism, the Associate Synod of North America and the Associate Reformed Synod of New York, having but about a dozen ministers each, were evidently too weak to undertake work for the freedmen, in spite of their anti-slavery bias.[117]   At least,

[111] *Ibid.*, p. 188.
[112] *Cf., e.g., ibid.*, 1867, p. 349.
[113] *Ibid.*, pp. 349-350.
[114] *Ibid.*, pp. 350-351.
[115] For the annual report of the Board in 1867, *cf. ibid.*, 1868, pp. 262-263. For an account of the activities of the United Presbyterian Church for the freedmen, *cf.* Scouller, *op. cit.*, pp. 245-247.
[116] *Cf. ante*, pp. 379-390.
[117] *Cf. ante*, pp. 390-393.

no such action on their part is recorded.[118] The Reformed Presbyterian Church, General Synod (or New Side Covenanters) and the Reformed Presbyterian Church, Synod (or Old Side Covenanters), on the other hand, each undertook to do its share in efforts to uplift emancipated slaves. The Old Side Covenanters, in fact, undertook to do more than their share. The work which they had so promptly begun in 1861 [119] was rapidly extended. Missions (concentrating their efforts largely upon schools and Sabbath-schools) were established in the city of Washington, and in Natchez, Mississippi.[120] In the city of Washington a method was discovered of rendering the mission partially self-sustaining. Upon finding that the freedmen were paying exorbitant rental charges, the Board of Domestic Missions, realizing that by this means not only could a source of income be obtained but the freedmen would also be " more directly and fully under [the mission's] influence," built tenements and rented them to the contrabands.[121] The Synod's missions prospered. In 1865 the Board reported that during the previous year over $6,000 had been raised for the freedmen's cause.[121a] The following year the Old School Presbyterian Church, with a communicant membership which was almost thirty times as great,[122] raised $25,000; [123] at the height of its activities for the freedmen this veteran denomination raised less than $80,000 [124] in any single year. In spite of its success in raising funds, however, the Board found that the amount collected was not sufficient. "We need funds," it complained in the same report which

---

[118] *Cf.* reports of annual proceedings of these bodies in *Presbyterian Historical Almanac* for the years 1862 to 1868.

[119] *Cf. ante,* p. 439.

[120] *Presbyterian Historical Almanac,* 1865, pp. 224-225.

[121] *Ibid.,* p. 224.

[121a] *Ibid.,* 1866, pp. 287-288.

[122] The communicant membership of the Old School Presbyterian Church in 1867 was 246,350; that of the Reformed Presbyterian (Synod), 8,323. *Cf. ibid.,* 1868, pp. 158 and 383.

[123] *Minutes of the General Assembly* (Old School), 1866, vol. xviii, p. 76.

[124] *Cf. ante,* pp. 444-445.

announced the \$6,000 raised the previous year; then it confidently added, "with these furnished, we could dot over the entire South with our schools and stations."[125] Evidently the Board felt that the entire denominational membership of 8,000 could be relied upon to carry on the work, were there but money enough to finance it. Finding its requests for greater funds unavailing, the Board in the fall of 1866 discontinued its mission at Natchez, and concentrated its efforts upon the one in the city of Washington, which continued to prosper.[126]

The New Side Covenanters (Reformed Presbyterians, General Synod) failed to make as impressive a record as their stricter brethren. At the 1864 session of the General Synod the Board of Domestic Missions reported that the freedmen in the South and the South-west had been visited, and that efforts were "in process to secure the blessings of the Gospel to this interesting class of our countrymen."[127] These efforts materialized in the establishment of a mission at Alexandria, Virginia. In 1865, at the time of its regular session, "a public meeting of Synod was held on behalf of this enterprise, and it was decided to enlarge their operations and increase the number of teachers."[128] In 1866 it was reported that the charges of the mission were "fast learning to read and many of them are quite proficient — being called upon to assume the duties of citizens, they are striving to be able to meet all its [sic] requirements."[129] The following year the treasurer of the General Synod's Board of Domestic Missions recorded that about five hundred scholars had received instruction in the mission's school, the average attendance being about two hundred. Some \$3,500 had been raised for the cause of the freedmen during the preceding year.[130] Thus while not so active as the non-juring branch of the Reformed Presbyterians, the New

[125] *Presbyterian Historical Almanac*, 1866, p. 289.
[126] *Ibid.*, 1868, p. 380.
[127] *Ibid.*, 1865, p. 216.
[128] *Ibid.*, 1866, p. 283.
[129] *Ibid.*, 1867, p. 395.
[130] *Ibid.*, 1868, p. 389.

Side Covenanters could present a record characterized by vigor and consistency.

While the Churches of the right flank of Presbyterianism in the loyal states were attacking with energy the problem of the freedmen, the left flank (the Cumberland Presbyterian Church) lagged behind. Separated in body from their Southern brethren by the war, and in spirit by divergent views on slavery, the Northern element were not in a position to undertake welfare work for the freedmen, in spite of their 1864 pronouncement against slavery.[131] When the war was finally over and the Church reunited, however, the General Assembly in 1866 had a committee appointed to report on the condition of the colored people. The views of the committee reflected the acquaintance of the Cumberland Church with the negro problem. The committee reported:

That the present condition of this people calls loudly upon every American Christian — not for the inconsiderate enthusiasm that would bestow honors which they cannot appreciate, and burden them with responsibilities which they cannot support — but, for the prompt and sober attention that will patiently and faithfully train them in their duties to God and their fellow-man in the new relation which they now sustain to society. We believe that their moral and religious destitution, take them as a whole, is perhaps greater at this time than it has been at any other period within the history of our Church. Whilst it is true that there are at this time in successful operation for their benefit many well-regulated schools, it is also true that they as yet only occupy the great centres of population, and cannot for a long time, if ever, reach the distant hamlets of honest labor or the children at the hut of the miserable vagrant. It is also true that the sudden violence of the stroke that severed the tie which bound them to their former masters, has likewise for the present dislocated the channel through which flowed to them not only many of the restraints of religion, but many of its duties and precepts.[132]

Convinced that no class of citizens were so " well prepared, nor . . . any more willing to aid them, than those with whom this people have always lived," the committee recommended that all the presbyteries of the Church take steps to organize Sab-

[131] *Cf. ante,* pp. 411–412.
[132] *Presbyterian Historical Almanac,* 1867, p. 471.

bath-schools for the freedmen, and to supply them with books and teachers; that they coöperate with the American Bible Society in sending them Bibles; "that they use every means, so far as they can, to afford them the means of grace and encourage them to sustain the same, as God may prosper them; " and that they aid them in obtaining houses "suitable for such schools and the more public worship of God." [133] These resolutions are in interesting contrast to those passed by some of the other Presbyterian Assemblies in the same year. The Cumberland Church realized that the demands of true patriotism as well as the needs of the negro required from the Churches immediate activity in behalf of the freedmen rather than elaborate instructions to the Federal Government with regard to the Civil Rights Bill and the right of suffrage. Unfortunately the scanty records of the Cumberland Church offer little evidence as to the completeness with which the advice of 1866 was carried out. Unfortunately, also, the opportunities for intimate understanding of the needs of the freedmen were considerably reduced by the formation in 1869 of the separate African Cumberland Presbyterian Church.[134]

The reconstruction work of the Churches was not unrecognized by the Federal Government. Not only did the agencies of the United States assist (through the donation of funds and the use of buildings) the efforts of the Churches for the

[133] *Ibid.* There is no statement with regard to the action of the General Assembly on this committee report, but as the reports of other boards and committees were entered in the same way, it may be inferred that the report was adopted.

[134] Dr. Scouller (*op. cit.,* p. 300), writing of his own Church (the Cumberland Presbyterian), quoted the editor of the *Cumberland Presbyterian* as follows: "' . . . in 1869 the colored people asked and received the consent of the General Assembly to the organization of a separate African Cumberland Presbyterian Church.'" Dr. R. E. Thompson (*op. cit.,* p. 193), writing on all of the Presbyterian groups, had this to say: "The Cumberland Presbyterians encouraged their colored membership to withdraw and, in 1869, to organize themselves as a separate denomination, now [1895] numbering 13,439 members."

freedmen,[135] but as early as the fall of 1863 the administration at Washington specifically authorized certain Church agencies to carry on reconstruction activities in the South. The Methodist Episcopal Church obtained such authorization in November and December, 1863; the Baptists in January, 1864. A few weeks later the following order was issued:

> War Department, Adjutant General's Office,
> Washington, March 10, 1864.

To the Generals commanding the Military Division of the Mississippi, and the Department of the Gulf, of the South, and of Virginia and North Carolina, and all generals and officers commanding armies, detachments, and posts, and all officers in the service of the United States, in the above mentioned Departments:

The Board of Domestic Missions of the Presbyterian Church and the Presbyterian Committee of Home Missions enjoy the entire confidence of this Department, and no doubt is entertained that all ministers who may be appointed by them will be entirely loyal.

You are expected to permit such ministers of the Gospel bearing a commission of the "Board of Domestic Missions" or of the "Presbyterian Committee of Home Missions" of the Presbyterian Church, as may convince you that their commissions are genuine, to exercise the functions of their office within your command, and to give them all the aid, countenance, and support which may be practicable and in your judgment proper in the execution of their important mission.

By order of the Secretary of War:

> E. D. Townsend,
> *Assistant Adjutant General.*[136]

It was this action which provoked the Presbytery of Louisville to demand that the General Assembly (Old School) "disavow the said act," and to follow this demand with the explanation that there was no intention to cast reflections upon the War Department, since this Department was only doing "what it was improperly asked to do." [137]

[135] *Cf. ante,* p. 453. The Church agencies for the freedmen frequently reported that buildings, funds, and supplies had been turned over to them by the agencies of the Federal Government. The Old School's Committee of Freedmen in 1869 recorded the receipt of $37,500 "from the Boards of Church Extension and Domestic Missions, and grants from Government." *Minutes of the General Assembly* (Old School), 1869, vol. xviii, p. 988.

[136] McPherson, *op. cit.,* p. 522.

[137] *Cf. ante,* p. 188; also McPherson, *op. cit.,* p. 522, note.

Whether or not the Old School authorities improperly requested the War Department to take this action, there is evidence that both the Old School Board and the New School Committee did solicit the authorities for such an order.[137a] No doubt it was felt that without it the Methodists and the Baptists would have too much of an advantage. Certainly the various orders of this type stirred up a tremendous amount of trouble. At the request of "loyal" Methodists of Missouri,[138] the War Department issued an explanatory order to the effect that the orders previously issued with regard to the rights of loyal Churches were "designed to apply only to such States as are by the President's Proclamation designated as being in rebellion" and not in loyal states.[139] In fact the orders which had preceded that of March 10, 1864, were far more offensive to Southerners than that which concerned the Old and the New School Presbyterians, for in the earlier cases the loyal denominations had obtained from the War Department an explicit order directing that houses of worship in which there was no loyal pastor should be placed at their disposal by the military authorities.[140] For example, the order with which the United Presbyterian Church was concerned (dated February 15, 1864) contained the following paragraph:

You are hereby directed to place at the disposal of the authorized Agent of the "Board of Home Missions of the United Presbyterian Church" all houses of worship belonging to the Associate Reformed Presbyterian Church [South],[141] in which a loyal minister who has been appointed by the Board of Home Missions of said church does not now officiate. It is a matter of great importance to the Government in its efforts to restore

---

[137a] Ibid., p. 522.

[138] Ibid, p. 522, note.

[139] Ibid., p. 522.

[140] This had been done in the case of the Methodist Episcopal, Baptist, and United Presbyterian Churches. Cf. ibid., pp. 521-522.

[141] Of course, if Northern denominations were to take over Southern churches, the similarity in creed and theological belief would give the United Presbyterians a good claim to the churches of the Associate Reformed Presbyterians of the South. The earlier orders all followed the policy of turning over Southern churches to the corresponding Northern denomination.

tranquillity to the community, and peace to the nation, that Christian ministers should, by example and precept support and foster the loyal sentiment of the people. The Board of Home Missions of the United Presbyterian Church enjoys the entire confidence of this department. . . .[142]

It is evident that, as compared with the Methodists, Baptists, and Associate Reformed Presbyterians of the South, the former members of the Old and New Schools in that section fared well in the matter of authorized military interference.

The necessity for the explanatory order, and a note written by President Lincoln on the subject probably convinced the War Department, when it came to issue its order of March 10 relating to the Presbyterians, that a more cautious policy was desirable. At the time of the issuance of the explanatory order, President Lincoln explained in a note to a Methodist clergyman in Missouri that he had learned from the Secretary of War that the original order concerning Methodist churches was never intended " for any more than a means of rallying the Methodist people in favor of the Union, in localities where the rebellion had disorganized and scattered them." He was quite evidently skeptical about the whole matter. " Even in that view," he added, " I fear it is liable to some abuses, but it is not quite easy to withdraw it entirely and at once."[143] In the light of these sentiments, it is significant that when the Presbyterian order was later issued, nothing was said about Southern Churches with disloyal ministers, but the military authorities were simply directed to give to Presbyterian ministers bearing the proper commissions " all the aid, countenance, and support which may be practicable . . . and proper in the execution of their important mission."[144]

The Old School Board of Domestic Missions made no immediate attempt to utilize the special opportunities which the War Department's orders placed at its door. In its report of 1864,

---

[142] *Ibid.*, pp. 521-522. This order came two days after the issuance of the " Explanatory Order." While the wording was virtually the same as that of the Methodist and Baptist orders, care was taken to explain that it applied only to states in rebellion.

[143] *Ibid.*, p. 522, note.

[144] *Cf. ante*, p. 459.

it is true, it called attention to the great task which confronted the Church in the South: "To reconstruct churches, to win back with the kind persuasions of the Gospel the deceived and the erring, to cast the mantle of Christian charity over the past, . . . will make demands upon the benevolence of the Church unknown before. For years the South will be a mission field, to be supplied by the kindness of the North."[145] A year later, when the war was at last over, the Board was not quite so sure of its opportunities in the South:

> The South in its desolations creates uneasiness — that we have a work to perform there, we doubt not, and by God's grace we will enter upon it when that seething caldron shall cease to boil, and when the quieted feelings of the people shall prepare them to receive the gospel of love and peace. For years the South will be a mission field, and the white and black population require the labour of love.[146]

The Board had not yet begun its work in the South, although with the cessation of the war the opportunity for military protection and assistance was fast disappearing.

The General Assembly of 1865 was not daunted by the implications in the Board's report that the "seething caldron" of the South had not ceased to boil, and that the feelings of the people had not yet quieted to a sufficient degree to "prepare them to receive the gospel of love and peace." Impatient to get started, the Assembly directed the Board "to take prompt and effectual measures to restore and build up the Presbyterian congregations in the Southern States of this Union by the appointment and support of prudent and devoted missionaries." Then, faithful to the trust of the War Department, which a year earlier had declared with respect to the Board of Domestic Missions that "no doubt is entertained that all ministers who may be appointed by them will be entirely loyal,"[147] the Assembly now resolved that "none be appointed but those who give satisfactory evidence of their loyalty to the national government, and that they are in cordial

---

[145] *Minutes of the General Assembly* (Old School), 1864, vol. xvii, p. 357.
[146] *Ibid.,* 1865, vol. xvii, p. 626.
[147] *Cf. ante,* p. 459.

sympathy with the General Assembly . . . in her testimony on doctrine, loyalty, and freedom." [148] This was one of the several "loyal" measures of the Assembly of 1865 which by the harshness of their terms called forth the "Declaration and Testimony" of the Presbytery of Louisville.[149]

In practice the rules prescribed for the Board proved very obnoxious to men in the Border States — particularly in Missouri. The brilliant Dr. James H. Brookes in his eloquent plea for the Declaration and Testimony men described to the 1866 General Assembly the hardships which the Board's policy had inflicted upon some of his friends. One "consistent man of God" who had "preached constantly during the war in a part of the State where suspicion was almost certain death," and had yet suffered no disturbance at the hands of the military authorities, had received the following reply to his request that the Board furnish him pecuniary aid "in the work of saving souls":

Dear Sir:

The General Assembly have enjoined the Board to commission no one except of loyal submission to the Government, and to the deliverances of the Church on the subject of slavery. We are informed your record is not fair, and we decline sending you a commission.

Yours, truly,

Thomas L. Janeway

Cor. Secretary, &c.[150]

Because of this denial of assistance, the applicant had been "driven to hard manual labor to obtain support for his wife and little ones." [151]

Another applicant who had received the unanimous endorsement of his presbytery " — a Presbytery, too, enrolling among its members some who are loyal to the highest possible degree, and according to the highest possible standard — " [152] was

[148] For the more important resolutions passed by the Assembly upon this general subject, *cf. ante*, p. 197.

[149] *Cf. ante*, pp. 203-205.

[150] Quoted by Dr. Brookes in his speech before the General Assembly. *Cf. Proceedings of the General Assemblies. . . 1866*, p. 111.

[151] *Ibid.*

[152] Dr. Brookes' statement, *ibid.*

doomed to disappointment, for "after awhile the decree came forth from the Secretary's office in Philadelphia: "

> Mr. Forman will hardly come up to the requisitions of the last General Assembly. His is a *quasi* loyalty, and he is hardly in accord with the Presbyterian Church in its declaims on freedom. It may be hard for him, but he reaps as he sowed. Such men have well nigh ruined the Church; and it is hardly to be expected that loyal men will contribute to support one in affiliation with rebellion.
>
> Yours, truly,
T. L. Janeway.[152a]

Actions of this type on the part of the Church's authorized agencies, Dr. Brookes alleged, left little doubt in Border State men's minds "what was the path of honor and the path of duty," and constituted a direct cause of the " Declaration and Testimony." [153]

The incidents about which Dr. Brookes complained were interpreted somewhat differently in the annual report which the Board of Domestic Missions submitted to the same Assembly as had listened to the St. Louis pastor's plea. The Board was confident that its course would appear justified in the eyes of the Church:

> Nor were we forgetful of the direction not to send any but loyal men to the country, and true to the deliverance of the Assembly. Few of the excepted class applied, and we were spared the pain of refusal. In a few cases we declined, as in duty bound, and great efforts were made to render the Board odious, and no small obloquy cast upon its officers. We have faith to believe the Assembly will justify our course. It may be sufficient to say the clamor came from men whose churches persistently, during the whole war, contributed not a dollar to our treasury — thus undertaking to control the managment of funds in which they had no share, and to direct a Board whose efforts they had done their best to cripple.[154]

Perhaps there were two sides to the story. Regarding the Board itself, however, there was a good deal of dissatisfaction in the Church, especially in the western wing,[155] and before two

---

[152a] Quoted by Dr. Brookes, *ibid.*
[153] *Ibid.*
[154] *Minutes of the General Assembly* (Old School), 1866, vol. xviii, p. 144.
[155] *Ibid.*, pp. 69-70; also *Proceedings*, p. 95.

more years had elapsed, the Board had been entirely reconstituted.[156]

The Board's work in the South did not prosper. In 1866 it reported that the "division of the Church has been made as permanent as the leaders could accomplish," and that "as far as their present leaders can continue it, the South is a sealed land to us."[157] There was an air of finality in the report of 1867, which stated: "After the war of rebellion ceased, men loyal and true, South, sought aid from the Board to carry on their work, amid the deep poverty which came upon them. Our missionaries, finding that their late flocks had turned from the gospel, were directed to find more pleasant success among the Freedmen."[158] As far as the Old School Presbyterians were concerned, military assistance during the war and patriotic surveillance of its domestic missionaries after the war had certainly not helped its cause in the South.

Nor had the New School Church fared better in this section of the country. In 1864, a few weeks after the War Department had issued its order concerning the Presbyterian Committee of Home Missions, that Committee announced with enthusiasm, "A great field of missionary operations is opening at the South."[159] By 1865 its confidence in success had been somewhat diminished:

> Both the labor and the expense will be very great. Prejudices will yield very slowly. It will be difficult to repair or build anew church edifices, and the requisite number of ministers of Christ to supply the wants of so wide a field, it may be impossible to find. But however slow, difficult, or costly the work, we must hold ourselves in readiness to aid all that need assistance.[160]

The following year "a very encouraging measure of success" was reported, but the work had been mostly confined — as

[156] *Cf.* " Report of Committee appointed by the Assembly of 1867, on the Board of Domestic Missions," *Minutes of the General Assembly,* 1868, vol. xviii, pp. 689-692.

[157] *Ibid.,* 1866, vol. xviii, p. 144.

[158] *Ibid.,* 1867, vol. xviii, p. 425.

[159] *Minutes of the General Assembly* (New School), 1864, vol. xiii, p. 545.

[160] *Ibid.,* 1865, vol. xiv, p. 77.

far as the whites were concerned — to East-Tennessee and Missouri. The real reason for the success, however, is explained in a subsequent sentence: "A people whose loyalty could not be crushed turn fondly to our Church and welcome laborers among them from the North." [161] In 1867 the Committee representing this most "Northern" of churches was feeling the full force of reconstruction hate in the South:

> The work at the South has been more encouraging among the freedmen, wherever they have been able to send missionaries, than among the whites. But the colored missionaries are very few, and the prejudices against all Northern men, among all the whites at the South, both loyal and rebel, is such as to hinder the usefulness and comfort of missionaries sent from the North.[162]

By this time the New School Church, like the older branch, was evidently ready to abandon the Southern field; at least the Committee's report in 1868 did not even mention that section of the country (except in connection with the cause of the freedmen),[163] and in 1869, the last year of the separate existence of this denomination, the entire emphasis of the report was placed upon opportunities in the West.[164]

As far as the United Presbyterian Church was concerned, the reports of its Board of Domestic Missions made no reference to any attempt to recruit white members for the denomination in the South.[165] Evidently the Board was not disposed to take advantage of the generous offer of the War Department to turn over to it the churches of "disloyal" Associate Reformed Presbyterian pastors in the South.[166] Thus none of the three denominations which had been the recipients of special concessions in the South from the War Department had profited from the Government's orders. The only Presby-

---

[161] *Ibid.*, 1866, vol. xiv, p. 314.

[162] *Ibid.*, 1867, vol. xiv, p. 555.

[163] *Ibid.*, 1868, vol. xv, pp. 92-96.

[164] *Ibid.*, 1869, vol. xv, pp. 317-318.

[165] *Cf.* abstracts of the annual reports of the United Presbyterian Board of Domestic Missions in *Presbyterian Historical Almanac*, 1865, p. 180; 1866, pp. 246-247; 1867, p. 347; 1868, p. 261.

[166] *Cf. ante*, pp. 460-461.

terian Church which attained (or reattained) considerable
strength in the South after the close of war was the Cumberland Presbyterian Church, which — not permanently divided
by the war [167] — after 1865 managed to keep its large Southern
membership and remained the only Presbyterian Church truly
national in its following.

Churches and church organizations were by no means the
only agencies endeavoring to bring relief to war sufferers, and
Presbyterian records contain many references to the works of
mercy being accomplished by other bodies. The one most
frequently mentioned was the United States Christian Commission, which was founded in November, 1861, at a convention of the Young Men's Christian Association. Mr. George
H. Stuart, wealthy Philadelphia merchant who presided over
this convention and had been active in the Association since
its establishment in America a few years earlier,[168] became
the Chairman of the Christian Commission.[169] Believing that
there was " a good deal of religion in a warm shirt and a good
beefsteak "[170] (a rather surprising statement from a prominent member of so strict a sect as the Reformed Presbyterians
— even though he belonged to its New Side wing),[171] Mr.
Stuart saw to it that the Christian Commission looked after
the temporal as well as the spiritual wants of the men in the
military and naval services.

As pains were taken to keep the Christian Commission non-
denominational, it is difficult to determine from the literature
dealing with this organization to what degree its support in
money and men came from Presbyterian denominations. Mr.
Stuart seemed to rely to a considerable degree upon Presbyterians and Presbyterian Church buildings in his raising of

[167] *Cf. ante*, pp. 406-424.
[168] Thompson, Robert Ellis, *ed., The Life of George H. Stuart, Written
by Himself* (Philadelphia, 1890), p. 94.
[169] *Ibid.*, pp. 129-131.
[170] *Ibid.*, p. 129.
[171] *Ibid.*, pp. 44-48.

funds,[172] but that may have been due to the fact that he himself belonged to the Presbyterian family and that in Pennsylvania, his home state, Presbyterianism was numerically and
financially very strong.   Among those prominent in the activities of the organization who either then were or later became
leaders in the Presbyterian Church were Mr. George H. Stuart,
Dr. Charles Hodge,[173] Mr. John Wanamaker,[173a] Mr. George
S. Chambers,[174] and Mr. Robert Ellis Thompson.[175] Both Old
and New School Presbyterians were well represented among
the authors of the stories related in Rev. Edward P. Smith's
*Incidents of the Work of the United States Christian Commis-
sion,*[176] and both furnished many of the names in the list of
more than five thousand delegates who, serving a minimum
of six weeks, did the field work of the Commission.[177]

The Christian Commission received the vigorous support
of most of the Presbyterian Churches through the action of
their central bodies.   In 1863, for instance, the General Assembly of the Old School Church dispensed with one of its
evening meetings so that its members might attend a special
meeting being held in the city (Peoria, Illinois) in the interests
of the Christian Commission.[178] Most of the central bodies of
the denominations regularly at their annual sessions endorsed

[172] *Cf. ibid.,* pp. 147; 157; 158, note.
[173] *Ibid.,* p. 131.
[173a] *Ibid.,* p. 130.
[174] *Ibid.,* p. 171. Later pastor of the Murray Hill Presbyterian Church
in the city of New York.
[175] *Ibid.,* p. 172. Later the author of the volume on *The Presbyterian
Churches in the United States,* in the "American Church History" series;
also editor of the *Life of George H. Stuart;* also for a time a member of
the faculty of the University of Pennsylvania.
[176] This work, published under the above-named title in Philadelphia in
1869, appeared in a later edition under the title, *Incidents with Shot and
Shell.*
[177] The list of delegates is given in Moss, Lemuel, *Annals of the United
States Christian Commission* (Philadelphia, 1868), pp. 602-638. As it includes the names of many laymen, it is not possible to determine how
many of the more than 5000 delegates were Presbyterians.
[178] "Side Work of the Assembly," *True Presbyterian,* June 4, 1863.

the Christian Commission.[179] In several instances Mr. Stuart
in person visited the meetings in the interest of his great
work.[180] Because of its predominantly Christian character
(and perhaps also because its chairman was a Presbyterian),
Presbyterian Churches distinctly favored it above other non-
denominational agencies. In 1864 the Old School Assembly
through the adoption of a special report on the Christian Commission declared:

> While the General Assembly has nothing to say, except in terms of
> cordial approval, of all properly conducted organized benevolent enter-
> prises . . . but would bid all such God-speed — for alas! there is work
> enough for all — they would, and hereby do, in a special manner, com-
> mend the United States Christian Commission to the liberal support and
> encouragement of all their churches and congregations, and of all the indi-
> viduals and families composing them; and invite their warm coöperation
> with it.[181]

If the Presbyterian people in the North were at all heedful of
the urgent solicitations of their General Assemblies and
Synods, the United States Christian Commission must have
had their generous support.[182]

[179] For these endorsements cf. Minutes of the General Assembly (Old
School), 1863, vol. xvii, p. 18; 1864, vol. xvii, p. 300; Minutes of the
General Assembly (New School), 1863, vol. xiii, p. 280; 1864, vol. xiii, p.
477; Presbyterian Historical Almanac, 1864, p. 346, and 1865, p. 191
(General Assembly of the United Presbyterian Church); ibid., 1864, pp.
364-365, and 1865, p. 217 (General Synod of the Reformed Presbyterian
Church). The absence of the Cumberland Presbyterian Church's General
Assembly from this list is especially striking in view of the fact that the
Presbyterian Historical Almanac records that body's endorsement of other
organizations. (Cf. notes 184, 185, and 186, below.)

[180] Cf., e.g., Minutes of the General Assembly (Old School), 1864, vol.
xvii, p. 287; Thompson, Life of George H. Stuart, pp. 152-154; Presbyterian Historical Almanac, 1865, p. 191; ibid. for 1865, p. 217. These
references report the facts of Mr. Stuart's addressing, in 1864, the Old
School Assembly at Newark, the United Presbyterian Assembly at Philadelphia, and the General Synod of the Reformed Presbyterian Church at
Philadelphia.

[181] Minutes of the General Assembly (Old School), 1864, vol. xvii, p. 300.

[182] The Presbyter (Cincinnati) complained that the Commission, having
its base in the East, supplied itself with Eastern papers for distribution.
This evidence of sectional opposition, however, was not evident in Assembly
action. For the complaint cf. Presbyter (editorial note), August 19, 1863.

Other organizations generously endorsed by Presbyterian
bodies were the United States Sanitary Commission,[183] the
American Tract Society,[184] the American Bible Society,[185] and
the American Colonization Society.[186]   As late as 1863 the
Cumberland Presbyterian Church commended the last-named
organization not only for the " grand and noble " character
of its " object and aims . . . originating in the hearts and
heads of some of the most devotedly pious men and true patriots of the nation," but also for its accomplishments.   The
Assembly declared that " its workings and results have shown
most freely that it is designed by the Almighty to be the rich-
est blessing to those colonized that has ever been conferred on
their race, and likely to be the most effectual means of civiliz-
ing and Christianizing Africa, as well as the most appropriate
and successful way of disposing of the free colored population
of the United States." [187]   The previous year the Old School
Assembly had resolved that the American Colonization Society
" and all others having in view the accomplishment of the same
benevolent object " be commended to the liberal support of
the members of the denomination.[188]   Coming from the General Assemblies of the only two Presbyterian Churches [189]
which had not before the outbreak of the war become anti-
slavery, these measures represented the dying gasps of the resistance to the abolitionizing influence which was fast taking

[183] Minutes of the General Assembly (New School), 1862, vol. xiii, pp.
26-27.
[184] Presbyterian Historical Almanac, 1864, p. 379 (Cumberland General Assembly).
[185] Minutes of the General Assembly (Old School), 1864, vol. xvii, pp.
323-324; Minutes of the General Assembly (New School), 1864, vol. xiii,
p. 510; Presbyterian Historical Almanac, 1865, pp. 191, 231 (United
Presbyterian Assembly and Cumberland Assembly).
[186] Ibid. for 1864, pp. 378-379; Minutes of the General Assembly (Old
School), vol. xvi, p. 633.
[187] Presbyterian Historical Almanac, 1864, pp. 378-379.
[188] Minutes of the General Assembly (Old School), 1862, vol. xvi, p. 633.
[189] Excluding, of course, the distinctly Southern Churches — the United
Synod and the Associate Reformed Presbyterian Synod of the South, as
well as the very small Independent Presbyterian Church. (Cf. ante, p. 7.)

possession of both denominations.[190] How futile these middle-ground tactics were in resisting the onslaughts of abolition was demonstrated by the drastic condemnations of slavery adopted by the General Assemblies of these two Churches in 1864.[191]

While the various Presbyterian denominations through the efforts of their chaplains, of their permanent boards and committees, of special agencies established, and through the support of non-denominational war-time organizations were endeavoring to ameliorate the evil effects of war and — with more or less success — to put their patriotism into practice, the war itself in a multitude of ways was having a reflex action upon the Churches. Not only did war-time problems occupy much of the time of assemblies, synods, and presbyteries, but the direct effects of the war were apparent in almost every Church activity. "Church extension" agencies were hampered by lack of funds; Boards and Committees of Domestic Missions suffered from want of men; fluctuating rates of exchange crippled the activities of foreign missionaries; denominational colleges and theological seminaries found their enrollments cut down, and to some extent their faculties depleted.[192] It was but inevitable that the agencies of the Churches should all " share largely in the disasters of the country." [193]

To the churches of the area swept by military strife the war was disastrous. In 1865 conditions in this territory were described in the annual Narrative of the State of Religion of the Old School Church:

[190] *Cf. ante,* pp. 126; 410-415.

[191] *Cf. ante,* pp. 126-127; 411-412.

[192] For the effect of the war upon the various agencies of the Presbyterian Churches, *cf.* the reports (and abstracts of reports) which each annually submitted. These may be found in the *Minutes of the General Assembly* of the Old and the New School Churches, and in the *Presbyterian Historical Almanac; cf.* also the annual Narrative of the State of Religion of each Church. (Most of these may be found in the *Minutes* and the *Almanac.*)

[193] An expression used in the annual report of the Board of Church Extension (Old School), *Minutes of the General Assembly,* 1862, vol. xvi, p. 681.

Silence . . . broods over that region of our ecclesiastical territory within whose limits was nurtured into life a crime of unparalleled enormity against the government and free institutions of our country — a solemn stillness which tells of the terrible retributions and judgments of God. We can only learn that, in many places, the " candle " has been quenched, the " candlestick " removed, and that the Lord hath " violently taken away his tabernacle ", " swallowed up the habitations of Jacob ", and " covered the daughter of Zion with a cloud in his anger." [194]

While the effect of the war was most calamitous to the Southern churches, the annual presbyterial reports in the Northern portion of the Church, too, spoke " with marked uniformity . . . of fresh graves and desolated hearts." [195] There was no part of the Church where the war was not distressingly real.

The far-reaching effect of the hate engendered by the conflict is interestingly illustrated by the experience of a Cumberland Presbyterian missionary who had begun his work in Turkey in the fall of 1860:

During the spring and summer of 1861, as the news of battles began to reach us, the fanaticism of the American missionaries ran so high that all their religious services abounded in political and war-like harangues. They greedily adopted the most extreme views of such men as Greeley, Cheever and Beecher of subjugation and utter annihilation. Of course, at a very early period we were compelled to absent ourselves from all religious meetings in which Americans participated in any part of the city. This led first to estrangement, and, as matters progressed, to an open rupture, all of which took place about the time our Southern ambassador left for America and our funds gave out.

The Americans refused all assistance, and the end came, the day arrived when we were to be ejected from our house, but deliverance was sent us by our heavenly Father, by the hand of one of the natives, a total stranger. Soon after the chaplain of the British embassy came to our relief; . . .

December 3, 1861, I was attacked by Asiatic fever. . . .

During my most severe illness we were treated with great kindness by Christians, of many nationalities, Americans included, who had entirely changed their course toward us. The money upon which we subsisted for some weeks prior to our departure, and with which, we started, was loaned us by the Treasurer of the American Missions, whose account is herewith appended.[196]

[194] *Ibid.*, 1865, vol. xvii, p. 594.

[195] *Ibid.*, 1863, vol. xvii, p. 75.

[196] This letter, dated at Nashville, Tennessee, April 16, 1866, was printed in the *Presbyterian Historical Almanac*, 1867, pp. 473-474. The author was Rev. J. C. Armstrong.

It is a relief to discover that among the Presbyterians in Turkey the American Civil War ended more speedily than in America.

In the Old School Narrative of the State of Religion in 1864 the special committee appointed to draw up this paper commented:

> The future historian of the Church of our country, will, we apprehend, inquire with special solicitude into the condition of the Church, during the years of the great civil war. He will ask, what were the effects of the war on the spiritual life of the Church? — what were the modifications of the Church's state wrought by the terribly strange and seemingly adverse providences of God? [197]

The effects of the war upon the spiritual life of the Church were by no means all adverse. While there were frequent complaints regarding the "distracting and secularizing influence" of the war upon "the mind and heart of the Church," [198] reports of its sobering effects were fully as numerous. Presbyterial reports and Presbyterian journals during the war period abounded with accounts of revivals. In the early months of 1862 not a single issue of the *Presbyterian* failed to mention revivals in individual churches. In 1864, twenty-two of the seventy-nine Old School presbyteries which had sent in annual reports for that year mentioned special "revivings and awakenings" in one or more churches.[199] In fact the years of war and reconstruction witnessed marked increases in the membership of the various Presbyterian Churches. The number of members in the New School Church rose from 134,760 in 1861 [200] to 172,560 in 1869.[201] The figures for the Old School Church are particularly interesting because of the divisions suffered by the denomination during these years. Of

[197] *Minutes of the General Assembly*, 1864, vol. xvii, pp. 331-334.
[198] *Cf., e.g.*, summarizing statements in the Narrative of the State of Religion of the Old School Church in 1862. Minutes of the General Assembly, 1862, vol. xvi, p. 642.
[199] *Ibid.*, 1864, vol. xvii, pp. 331-332.
[200] *Minutes of the General Assembly* (New School), 1861, vol. xii, p. 632.
[201] *Ibid.*, 1869, vol. xv, p. 462.

the 300,814 communicants in this Church in 1861,[202] 112,213 were residents of slave-holding states.[203]   Of the latter number, 25,610 belonged to the Synods of Kentucky, Missouri, and Upper Missouri, and to the Presbyteries of Baltimore, Lewes, and the Potomac (in the Synod of Baltimore) [204] — all of which remained (during the years of the war) loyal to the General Assembly.   Thus the membership of the Church after the secession of the Southern presbyteries in 1861 amounted to about 215,000.   Yet in spite of the fact that after the close of the war the greater portions of the Synods of Kentucky and Missouri were lost,[205] the statistics of the denomination in 1869 recorded the Church membership as 258,903.[206]   Notwithstanding the internal strife which the war had brought, the loss by secession was very nearly offset by vigorous natural growth, and the Church in 1869 was more than five-sixths as large as it had been in 1861.   When the unified condition of the Old School Church in 1869 is contrasted with its divided character in 1861, it is apparent that this venerable denomination had gained rather than lost power as a result of the civil conflict.

The United Presbyterian Church grew in membership from 57,567 in 1861 to 63,489 in 1867.[207]   Even the Old Side Covenanters (Reformed Presbyterian Synod) — strictest of all Presbyterians — in spite of public absorption in worldly topics, experienced during these years a remarkable growth, extending its membership from 6,650 in 1861 [208] to 8,323 in 1867.[209]   From the point of view of numerical strength the years of war and reconstruction were quite evidently far from disastrous to the various Presbyterian denominations.

[202] *Minutes of the General Assembly* (Old School), 1861, vol. xvi, p. 552.
[203] *Cf.* editorial, *Presbyterian,* August 16, 1862.
[204] *Ibid.*
[205] *Cf. ante,* pp. 261-279.
[206] *Minutes of the General Assembly* (Old School), 1869, vol. xviii, p. 1108.
[207] *Presbyterian Historical Almanac,* 1862, p. 236; 1868, p. 280.
[208] *Ibid.,* 1862, p. 267.
[209] *Ibid.,* 1868, p. 383.

Certainly there had been ample opportunity for these growing organizations to prove their effectiveness in meeting new problems. The readiness with which most of them had endorsed the policy of the Federal Government and the extravagance of the terms in which they had expressed their patriotism had suggested that they would undertake with equal promptness and vigor the great task of relieving those in distress and of lifting to a higher plane of social well-being the millions emancipated from slavery. If some of the Churches had proved disappointing in this respect, and had appeared to many of their adherents remiss in putting their preaching into practice, yet there was much in their record to afford consolation to friendly critics. Much had been accomplished for both soldiers and freedmen. As far as the record of shortcomings was concerned, perhaps the most comforting feature was their widespread recognition by the friends of the Churches.

To the Presbyterian Churches themselves the period had been one of remarkable development. It was not alone in numbers that Presbyterianism grew during these years of sectional conflict; war and reconstruction had brought it a new tolerance of spirit. Coöperation in hospital and on battlefield had broken through the barriers of rigid denominationalism [210] and stimulated a spirit of harmony and union among the Christian sects. To the Presbyterians, whose history had been characterized by so many denominational divisions, this influence was especially wholesome. It was not merely a coincidence that the reunion of the two greatest divisions of Presbyterianism should have followed so closely upon the successful outcome of the conflict which was fought to prevent the necessity for Federal reunion.

[210] For an interesting estimate of the effect of the United States Christian Commission in promoting a spirit of coöperation among all of the denominations, *cf.* Thompson, *Life of George H. Stuart*, p. 170.

PART VI

REUNION

REUNION

At the outbreak of the Civil War the division of the Presbyterian Church into separate Old School and New School denominations was twenty-four years old. The "Exscinding Acts" of 1837 by which it had been accomplished were readily remembered by the majority of the members of both Churches, for the controversies which occasioned them had been of absorbing interest to the laity as well as to the clergy. When a New School admirer of the dauntless fighter then occupying the White House attempted to condole with him over his political troubles, the President is reported to have replied, "To tell you the truth, Dr. Beman, these fellows don't bother me half so much as do the dissensions in the Presbyterian Church."[1] Most of the leaders of the quarrels which had proved so disturbing to President Jackson were still alive in 1861, and more active than ever in the Church. The three most prominent promoters of the Exscinding Acts[2] — Dr. William S. Plumer,[3] Dr. Robert J. Breckinridge,[4] and Dr. George Junkin[5] — were all destined to play prominent parts in the history of the Old School Church during the period of the war. On the other side, the men whose alleged unsound theology had provoked the more conservative wing of the Church to such drastic action in 1837 were still for the most part active in directing the policies of the New School. Dr. Lyman Beecher, who had been tried for heresy (though not convicted) in 1835,[6] had, it is true, ended his public labors in 1852,[7] but

---

[1] Thompson, *op. cit.*, p. 109, note 1.
[2] *Cf. ibid.*, pp. 102-128.
[3] *Cf. ante*, pp. 295-300.
[4] *Cf. ante*, pp. 36-39; 185-196; and *passim*.
[5] *Cf. ante*, p. 291.
[6] Thompson, *op. cit.*, pp. 108-109.
[7] *Presbyterian Encyclopaedia*, p. 65.

of the other three theologues whose doctrines had most frequently been called in question,[8] the saintly Rev. Albert Barnes was still pastor of the influential First Presbyterian Church of Philadelphia, and Chairman of the Presbyterian Publication Committee; Dr. George Duffield was at the height of his long pastorate (1838-1868) in the First Presbyterian Church of Detroit, Michigan; while Dr. Nathan S. S. Beman, the "War-horse of the New School,"[9] who had been the Temporary Moderator of its first Assembly,[10] had still a few years to serve as pastor of the First Presbyterian Church of Troy, New York.[11]

Other factors besides the continued presence of the leaders of the excision and the alleged heretics who had, it was charged, provoked it, kept alive the hostility between the two Schools. Charges and counter-charges of unsound theology, ultra-conservatism or ultra-liberalism, and unfair competition in the field of domestic missions, were constantly being made in the journals of the two denominations.[12] While the General Assembly of the Old School Church annually exchanged "corresponding delegates" with the Reformed Dutch Church, the Associate Reformed Synod of New York, and the Associate Reformed Synod of the South, and while, on the other hand, the New School General Assembly exchanged delegates in a similar manner with the Cumberland Presbyterian Church, the General Synod of the Reformed Presbyterian Church, the General Synod of the Evangelical Lutheran Church in the United States, and a host of Congregationalist bodies,[13] both Churches had failed to inaugurate the most natural correspondence of all—that with each other. After twenty-four

[8] Thompson, *op. cit.*, pp. 102-128.

[9] *Ibid.*, p. 127.

[10] *Ibid.*, p. 119.

[11] The *Minutes of the General Assembly* (New School) first reported him as "Pastor Emeritus" in 1863.

[12] *Cf. ante*, pp. 74-75; 135; 139-140; 146-147; 175-176; and *passim*.

[13] *Cf.*, e.g., lists of corresponding delegates, *Minutes of the General Assembly*, (New School), 1857, vol. xi, p. 374; 1860, vol. xii, p. 226.

years of separation the two Churches were not yet ready to
consider a practice which would involve an annual interchange
of cordial greetings.

In 1861 reunion of Old and New Schools seemed very re-
mote — if, indeed, ever possible at all. To be sure, there
were a few individuals in the Old School, like Dr. Thomas [14]
and the editor of the *Presbyter* (Dr. J. G. Monfort) [15] who
favored reunion at as early a date as possible, but the strength
of the ultra-conservative Southern and Eastern wings of the
Church rendered any such move impossible. To the New
School Presbyterians reunion would not be so difficult as to
the Old School, as the orthodoxy of the older denomination
was scarcely questioned, while to many of the latter body, New
School theological views could not pass muster. Yet even though
for them the step would not be so momentous, New School
Presbyterians — who considered themselves the injured party
in the division of 1837 — would hardly be likely to initiate
a reunion movement.

Yet while the hostility between the two denominations
seemed as bitter as ever in 1861, certain changes had taken
place which rendered reunion less impossible of attainment.
The quarrel in 1837 had been focussed on two issues: doctrine
and church organization. On both of these points the two
parties had been drawing closer together. The Old School had
been forced to relax considerably in the rigidity of its orthodoxy,[16] while "theologically the new-school church [sic] did
not fulfill any of the prognostications of its unfriendly critics." [17] Though the New School did not withdraw from the
position it had taken in its "Auburn Declaration" of 1837 [18]
(which was un-Presbyterian in the inferences which its hostile
critics drew from it, rather than in its statements), the period
from 1837 to 1861 saw a marked growth of Presbyterian feel-

[14] *Cf. ante*, pp. 228-233.
[15] *Cf. ante*, pp. 159-160.
[16] Thompson, *op. cit.*, pp. 139-141.
[17] *Ibid.*, p. 138.
[18] For the text of the "Auburn Declaration," *cf. ibid.*, pp. 357-362.

ing in the new denomination, while the distance between New School Presbyterianism and Congregationalism became steadily greater.[19]   This increasing divergence was stimulated by growing dissatisfaction with the management of home missions and the education of the ministry by voluntary societies of an interdenominational character.   With the establishment of "permanent committees" (very similar to the Old School boards) in 1852 to take over the work of publication and home missions,[20] a policy was inaugurated which within a decade resulted in every one of the Old School boards being duplicated by New School committees.[21]

Perhaps the more successful growth of the Old School Church in the decades following the division of 1837 was the most compelling factor in convincing the other Church that the Old School plan of carrying on denominational work was superior.   While the membership of the New School had increased from 100,850 in 1839 to 137,990 in 1859 (had the six synods which seceded in 1857 been included, the number would have been 147,664),[22] during the same period that of the Old School had risen from 126,583 [23] to 279,630.[24]   The New School increase, though in itself gratifying, was at best less than fifty per cent and thus in painful contrast to the one hundred twenty per cent growth to the credit of the Old School. The Old School Church alone was considerably larger in membership in 1859 than the combined Church had been in 1837.[25] Such a contrast might logically be attributed — at least in

[19] Ibid., p. 138.

[20] Ibid., p. 138. The Home Missions work was for several years carried on under the auspices of the Church Extension Committee. The Committee of Home Missions was established in 1861. Cf. Minutes of the General Assembly (New School) 1862, vol. xiii, pp. 80-82.

[21] Cf. annual reports of Committees, ibid., pp. 61-101.

[22] Presbyterian Reunion, A Memorial Volume (New York, 1870), pp. 500-504.

[23] This was the number in 1840.

[24] Ibid., pp. 493-499.

[25] The membership of the undivided Church in 1837 was 220,557. Ibid., p. 494.

part — to the differing methods of conducting denominational work.

While the New School was being converted to the committee (or board) system, certain Old School leaders (most conspicuous among them Dr. Thornwell) had with some degree of success been attacking the exaggerated importance attached to the board system by the older denomination, and the tremendous amount of discretionary power accorded to individual boards. Thanks to attacks of this kind the Old School by 1860 was "no longer of the mind that these organizations were implied in the apostolic succession." [26] Both denominations were approaching a middle-ground position with regard to the handling of denominational activities.[27]

Nevertheless, while the "progressive Presbyterians" [28] had sufficiently proved their orthodoxy so that the Reformed Dutch Church in 1862 inaugurated the practice of exchanging corresponding delegates with them,[29] while the "Congregational element [had] been almost entirely purged" [30] from their body, and while, on the other hand, the Old School Church had relaxed somewhat in its dogmatism on matters of doctrine and organization, these changes in themselves were not sufficient to bring the two Churches together again. For one thing, it was only the friendlier element of the Old School that was willing to do full justice to the essentially Presby-

[26] Thompson, *History of the Presbyterian Churches*, p. 181. *Cf.* also p. 141.

[27] Another point of disagreement in 1837 had been concerned with the necessity of the ruling eldership to the right constitution of a congregation, the New School admitting to seats in synod and presbytery men who had never been ordained to the eldership. As early as 1842-1844, however, Dr. Hodge declared himself for this "lower view of the office," refusing the elder ordination by laying on hands. *Ibid.*, pp. 140-141.

[28] Dr. Stuart Robinson sarcastically asserted that the New School men delighted to term themselves thus. *True Presbyterian*, June 12, 1862.

[29] Editorial, *Presbyter*, July 3, 1862.

[30] An expression used by Dr. R. L. Stanton, Moderator of the General Assembly (Old School) of 1866, in his reply to the speech of Dr. Henry A. Nelson, corresponding delegate from the New School Church. Dr. Stanton added, "I refer to the Congregational Church with no feeling of disrespect. . . ." *Proceedings . . . 1866*, p. 24.

terian character of the newer denomination. On their part,
the New School Presbyterians experienced a good deal of difficulty in forgetting their grievance against the Old School for
the alleged high-handed measures of 1837-1838.[31] Both organizations were stable and growing, and neither felt the need
of union. In fact, as the Old School — larger in 1860 than before the excision of 1837 — had become somewhat unwieldy,[32]
it might be argued that from the point of view of size reunion
was distinctly undesirable. Again, though to the less preju-
diced it was clear that both bodies were essentially Presbyterian in character, no one could deny that the Puritan,
slavery-hating members of the New School — to a large degree
the product of a " Presbygational " system [33] — were a different sort of people from the Scotch-Irish, slavery-tolerating Old
School brethren. If reunion were to be achieved in the near
future, it would take more to bring it about than the changes
which had taken place in the first twenty-four years of the history of the two Schools as separate denominations. These
changes might serve as a foundation for reunion, but only by
a severe jolt from the outside could the bitterness of the quarrels of the 1830's be sufficiently forgotten to make possible
reunion within the space of a generation.

Such a jolt was furnished by the Civil War. For four years,
while this struggle absorbed men's attention, religious and
ecclesiastical bickerings could be, if not forgotten, at least
relegated to a secondary place in men's thoughts. Furthermore, while the process was at first hesitating, and throughout
very gradual, by 1865 the Old School Church through her
annual deliverances on the State of the Country had taken a
firm pro-Union and anti-slavery position — a position highly
acceptable to the unanimously, vehemently Northern New
School Church. This stand had been possible for the Old

[31] *Cf. ante,* pp. 74-75.
[32] By 1860, for instance, it had become necessary for the Old School
General Assembly to remain in session for two weeks, in order to complete
its business.
[33] Thompson, *op. cit.,* p. 72.

School only through the withdrawal of the Southern section
of the Church — the section most thoroughly out of sympathy
with the New School.[34]   From the Old School point of view
the withdrawal of the Southern section eliminated one of the
arguments against reunion — the danger of unwieldiness. Naturally the change which the war produced in the reunion issue
was not at once apparent to all concerned, but those to whose
hearts the cause was dear wasted little time in taking advantage of the opportunities which the great civil conflict afforded
them.

The first step in the series of moves which led to the consummation of reunion in 1869 was taken in 1862. In that year
the Committee on Bills and Overtures reported to the Old
School Assembly memorials received from the Presbyteries of
Ogdensburg (New York), Madison (Indiana), and California, asking that measures be inaugurated to bring about a
union between the Old School and New School bodies.   The
Presbytery of Ogdensburg had previously held a joint meeting with the New School Presbytery of St. Lawrence, and the
minutes of this meeting were now read to the General Assembly.[35]   In view of subsequent developments, the attitude of the
General Assembly of 1862 toward these proposals is interesting.   Its Committee on Bills and Overtures recommended that
the following minute be adopted:

In the judgment of this General Assembly it is inexpedient at this time to
take any definite action with reference to a reunion of the New and Old-
school Presbyterian Churches, and that the consideration of the overtures
on this subject be postponed till the next meeting of the General Assembly,
with the assurance that that body will kindly consider any proposition
for such reunion as may then be properly before them.[36]

When the Assembly came to consider this minute, it was first
decided to strike out everything after the words, "with the
assurance"; then the section next preceding, and beginning

[34] *Ibid.*, pp. 115; 122; 135-136.
[35] *Cf.* account of proceedings of fourth day of Assembly, *Presbyterian*,
May 31, 1862.
[36] *Minutes of the General Assembly* (Old School), 1862, vol. xvi, p. 599.

with the words, "and that the consideration," was eliminated.
The amended minute adopted by the Assembly read:

In the judgment of this General Assembly it is inexpedient at this time
to take any definite action with reference to a re-union of the New and
Old-school Presbyterian churches.[37]

It is evident that there was not yet much enthusiasm in the
Old School General Assembly over the cause of reunion.

The friends of the New School were not beaten. On the
day after the reunion proposition received its rebuff, it was
proposed that the Assembly resolve that since "it is desirable
to cultivate amicable relations with our brethren of the Presbyterian family, even though a closer union may seem, for the
present, inexpedient," steps be taken to open a correspondence
with the New School Church similar to that in existence with
the Cumberland Church; that a member be sent to visit the
New School Assembly then convened in Cincinnati, carrying
the invitation for reciprocation on the part of the other body,
"to the end that we may maintain and exhibit the unity of
the spirit in the bond of peace, that the world may believe
in the mission of our common and exalted Head." After
frequent considerations of this proposal,[38] the Assembly finally
by unanimous vote adopted proposals for correspondence with
the United Presbyterian and the New School Churches. The
proposal sent to the New School Assembly mentioned that it
had "determined against" proposals for steps toward organic
union, and that it understood that the New School Assembly
had during its current session taken the same stand; the suggestion for an interchange of delegates was then made in very
friendly terms:

On its own motion, this General Assembly, considering the time to have
come for it to take the initiative in securing a better understanding of the
relations which it judges are proper to be maintained between the two
General Assemblies, hereby proposes that there shall be a stated, annual,
and friendly interchange of commissioners between the two General Assemblies; each body sending to the other one minister and one ruling

[37] *Ibid.*, p. 610.
[38] *Ibid.*, pp. 612, 616, 617, 620, 633.

elder, as commissioners, year by year; the said commissioners to enjoy such privileges, in each body to which they are sent, as are common to all those now received by this body from other Christian denominations.[39]

This proposal, forwarded to the New School Assembly with the "Christian salutations" of the Old School body,[40] was indeed epoch-making in the history of the relations of the two Churches.

While the proposal had been unanimously adopted by the Old School Assembly there were influential members of this body, as there were men in the New School, who, heartily endorsing such manifestations of friendliness, yet deprecated any suggestion of reunion. Dr. R. J. Breckinridge, for instance, was still insisting that "the Presbyterian Church can never recall or regret what she did in 1837-1838. . . ."[41] Similarly, the reporter of the New School New York *Evangelist* who had become so weary of the behavior of the "ubiquitous and sempiternal Breckinridge"[42] in the meetings of the 1862 Assembly, expressed himself as firmly opposed to any immediate steps toward union. Commenting on the "wise and dignified" proposal of the Old School Assembly, he expressed the hope that his own Assembly would cordially accept it, but that "such fraternal correspondence being established, all attempts at union will be indefinitely postponed." He felt sure that there was no need for such a union: "If we are but true to ourselves, and to the special functions we are called to sustain, we shall do better every way as an independent body, than if we and they were one. Let us be content with being what we are! "[43]

His own New School Assembly had shown somewhat the same attitude. Presented with overtures urging steps toward

[39] *Ibid.,* pp. 633-634.
[40] *Ibid.,* p. 634.
[41] *Cf. ante,* p. 147.
[42] *Cf. ante,* p. 194.
[43] *Cf.* article, "The Assembly from a New School Standpoint," *True Presbyterian,* June 19, 1862 (quoting the Columbus correspondent of the New York *Evangelist*).

reunion,[44] the Assembly resolved that the "temper of these
overtures" met with its approval; and that while it had "ever
regretted the divisive acts of 1837, deeming them at variance
alike with the Constitution of our Church and the Word of
God," it had "never cherished an unkind or exacting spirit."
The basis upon which it could consider union was particularly
significant:

> *Resolved*, 3. That it would give us pleasure to unite, in the closest
> fellowship, with all persons who can stand with us on the basis of our Con-
> fession of Faith and Book of Discipline; and who substantially agree with
> us on the great moral questions of the day — in the matter, especially, of
> loyalty to the Government, and in the views of slavery set forth, prior to
> the division, in the deliverance of 1818.[45]

On the day that the New School Assembly in Cincinnati was
adopting these resolutions, the Old School body in Columbus
passed Dr. Breckinridge's violently patriotic paper on the
State of the Country; [46] hence it could easily have met the
New School's demand for loyalty to the Government. As far
as slavery was concerned, however, it fell utterly short of New
School standards, for it remained silent on the subject.[47] It
was not until two years later that it came out with a vigorous
anti-slavery pronouncement.[48] Hence the New School Assembly's resolution amounted to a dictation on the subject of
slavery which the 1862 Old School Assembly's attitude quite
clearly showed it would not have been willing to obey.

Having defined its position with regard to union and stated
the basis upon which alone it would consider such a move, the
New School Assembly in conclusion

> *Resolved*, 4. That, while we bear in remembrance the prayer of our
> Lord, that his disciples may be one, and while we can see some special
> advantages to be derived from a reunion of the two branches of the Presby-
> terian Church; we do not perceive, that, beyond the preceding declaration

[44] *Minutes of the General Assembly* (New School), 1862, vol. xiii, p. 20.
[45] *Ibid.* For an account of the Deliverance of 1818, *cf. ante*, p. 25.
[46] *Cf. ante*, pp. 110-116.
[47] *Cf. ante*, pp. 111-112.
[48] *Cf. ante*, pp. 126-128.

of our views, any thing remains for us, at the present, but to await humbly and teachably the movements of Divine Providence.[49]

Clearly the New School Assembly in 1862 was as yet by no means enthusiastic over the proposition of reunion. Like the Old School, it was disposed to postpone indefinitely action upon the subject.

While no specific steps were taken by the 1862 Assemblies toward reunion, a very definite move had been made in the direction of greater friendliness between the two denominations when the Old School Assembly made its cordial suggestion for an exchange of delegates. The practice was inaugurated in the Assemblies of the following year. The Old School appointed Dr. Septimus Tustin, of the city of Washington — one of the most venerable of its members — as delegate to the New School Assembly in Philadelphia. The editor of the *Presbytery Reporter*[50] described with feeling the impression which Dr. Tustin's address and reception made: " His address . . . gave evident and great satisfaction. . . . The hymn, ' Blest be the Tie ' was sung by the Assembly. . . . Rev. Dr. Cox followed with the most remarkable prayer of thanksgiving and supplication which I ever heard. If there were any dry eyes in that house during these scenes, mine were not in a condition to observe it." That it was a more worthy emotion than mere sentimentality which prompted this display of feeling on the part of the reporter may be gathered from the critical character of his further comments. Noting that Dr. Tustin had said, " . . . so far as we are concerned, the strife is at an end," he asked, " Are we to infer from Dr. Tustin's authorized remark, that the Old School will cease thrusting their organizations into those small places where we have previously occupied the ground, and where everybody can see another Presbyterian organization is not only utterly useless, but deeply

[49] For these resolutions, *cf. Minutes of the General Assembly* (New School), 1862, vol. xiii, pp. 38-39.

[50] *Cf. ante,* p. 370.

harmful! We shall wait and see. Meanwhile, 'charity hopeth all things.'" [51]

Although it lacked the dramatic qualities of Dr. Tustin's reception by the New School Assembly, the welcome accorded to the New School delegate, Dr. R. W. Patterson of Chicago, by the Old School Assembly at Peoria was generous and hearty. There was no public reference to the subject of reunion during the sessions which Dr. Patterson attended, however, and while in private intercourse the Old School brethren " revealed a warm sympathy " toward the New School Church, there were " few if any expressions of a desire for a speedy reunion. . . ." As the New School delegate witnessed part of the discussion over the question of raising the flag over the church in which the Assembly was sitting,[52] it was natural that his report to his own Assembly should note that there were " evidently conflicting currents of feeling among its members, in respect to our national troubles, and the terrible curse by which they have been created." He added, however, " But the controlling sentiment was largely on the side of loyalty and human liberty." Perhaps it was chiefly this fact which prompted him to conclude:

We cannot doubt that a large majority of the churches and ministers, represented by that Assembly, are coming nearer to us, in relation to most of the grounds of difference and separation between us and them. And we feel assured, that the correspondence that has been inaugurated between the two Assemblies will be attended with happy results, tending, as it must, to foster the spirit of brotherly love and confidence where it has been so far interrupted.[53]

Meanwhile dissatisfaction with the policy of inaction adopted by the Assemblies of 1862 on the matter of reunion had resulted in both Assemblies of 1863 being memorialized with urgent demands for specific action. In response to these requests the Old School Assembly resolved that it was not

[51] *Cf.* " A Remarkable Scene," *Presbytery Reporter,* July, 1863, vol. v, no. 16, p. 427.
[52] *Cf. ante,* pp. 120-122.
[53] Report of Dr. Patterson to the New School Assembly of 1864. *Minutes of the General Assembly* (New School), 1864, vol. xii, p. 518.

expedient to take at this time "any decided action" with reference to reunion. Nevertheless, two further resolutions showed that progress was being made:

> *Resolved,* 2. That in the fraternal correspondence, now happily inaugurated, the General Assembly would recognise an *initiative* in the matter of securing a better understanding . . . which may serve to prepare the way for a union that shall be harmonious and permanently promotive of the interests of truth and vital godliness.
>
> *Resolved,* 3. That as a still further preparative to such a desirable union, the General Assembly deem it important, and this in reference to both these branches of the Presbyterian Church, that the ministers, the elders, and such as have the care and instruction of the young, be increasingly careful to exhibit clearly the distinctive principles of Christian doctrine and church polity as held by the Presbyterian Church; that the ministers . . . cultivate fraternal intercourse . . . and . . . encourage and aid one another in the appropriate work of the ministry; and that the members of the one or the other branch connect themselves with existing congregations of either, rather than cast in their influence and their aid with bodies whose principles and form of government are foreign to their own.[54]

The New School Assembly, on the other hand, deciding that the subject of the memorials which had been presented to it with regard to reunion had been "substantially before the Assembly" some days earlier and satisfactorily acted upon at that time, determined that no further action was now necessary.[54a] The previous action to which the Assembly now referred had consisted simply in a hearty endorsement of the Old School proposal regarding the interchange of delegates, and in the appointment of Dr. Patterson and a ruling elder to represent the New School at Peoria.[55] In taking no further step toward reunion the New School Assembly of 1863 fell considerably short of the progress made in this direction by the corresponding body of the other branch.

It may be that New School men came to feel that they had shown themselves too reluctant in 1863; at any rate, their Assembly took the initiative in the following year. Presented

[54] *Minutes of the General Assembly* (Old School), 1863, vol. xvii, p. 39.
[54a] *Minutes of the General Assembly* (New School), 1863, vol. xiii, p. 274.
[55] *Ibid.,* p. 230.

with a memorial from the Presbytery of St. Lawrence (New York), the Assembly met its request for the appointment of a special committee on reunion by unanimously adopting a declaration prepared by the Committee on Church Polity (Dr. Henry Boynton Smith, of Union Theological Seminary,[56] chairman):

1. That this Assembly cordially welcomes all signs of increased love and union. . . .

2. That the tendencies of modern society, the condition of Protestant Christianity, the increase of infidelity, the progress of Romanism, and the present and prospective state of our country, afford powerful arguments against further subdivisions, and in favor of that union and unity of the Church into which it is to grow, and which is to be its consummation; . . .

3. That in an especial manner are those Churches bound to foster this spirit, who adopt the same standards of faith and order, . . . and for whose reunion there is only needed a wise deference to each other's rights and a higher measure of Christian charity. Adopting the same formulas of faith and form of government, all that is needed is to receive them in the same spirit.

4. That as the churches represented by this Assembly did not inaugurate separation, so, too, they hold to no principles and views, and would impose no terms, inconsistent with a full and cordial reunion, . . . and that it is our united and fervent prayer to our common Master, that he would so remove all hindrances as to make a plain path for our feet, where we may walk together, being of one heart and mind, in the ways of the Lord.

5. That, while we do not deem it expedient now to appoint such a Committee as that asked for . . . , yet that this expression of our principles and convictions, with our heartfelt Christian salutations, be transmitted to the General Assembly of the Presbyterian Church now in session at Newark,[57] New Jersey.[58]

The constant progress which the Old School had for three years been making in the direction of the New School position on the "present and prospective state of our country" made

[56] Cf. ante, p. 365.

[57] In its endorsement of the proposal for the interchange of delegates, the New School Assembly of 1863 had suggested that in the future the two branches "designate each other respectively by the places in which their sessions are appointed to be held." Cf. Minutes of the General Assembly, (New School), 1863, vol. xiii, p. 230. This would obviate the necessity for using the objectionable terms "Old School" and "New School."

[58] Ibid., 1864, vol. xiii, pp. 479-480.

possible the New School's hearty declaration. Everyone anticipated the vigorous denunciation of slavery which was forthcoming in the Old School Assembly only a few days later.[59]

This time it was the Old School Assembly's turn to be reluctant. Although during its sessions a reunion conference was held which adopted a paper[59a] expressing confidence in the doctrinal soundness of both Churches and in the possibility of removing the hindrances to reunion by developing "a spirit of unity and fraternity,"[60] and although the New School delegate reported to his own Assembly that in the Newark body "There was a manifest desire in the great majority of the Assembly, especially with all the younger members, that the two bodies should be one . . . ; "[61] still the Assembly held back. In its answer to three Presbyteries requesting steps toward reunion, the Old School body declared that it did "not deem it expedient at present to propose any additional measure towards the consummation of the object contemplated. . . . ; " but recommended the "prayerful consideration" of the suggestions and counsels on this subject proposed by the Assembly of 1863.[62]

Six presbyteries and the Synod of the Pacific petitioned the Assembly of 1865 for action on reunion, but the reply was, "That in the judgment of this Assembly an attempt to force a general reunion, before there is evidence by the action of the Presbyteries, that the two branches of the Church are fully prepared for it, will be likely to retard this result, and incur the danger of the formation of three bodies instead of two." It is readily apparent why this Assembly, confronted with the necessity of Church reconstruction in the South and threatened by the defiance of a dissatisfied element, should

[59] *Cf. ante*, pp. 125-128.
[59a] Published with the signatures of seventy ministers and fifty-three elders. *Cf.* Thompson, *op. cit.*, p. 173.
[60] *Ibid.*
[61] *Minutes of the General Assembly* (New School), 1865, vol. xiv, pp. 64-65.
[62] *Minutes of the General Assembly* (Old School), 1864, vol. xvii, p. 326. For the "suggestions and counsels" referred to, *cf. ante*, pp. 490-491.

have hesitated to incur further danger of division. Recognizing that the matter of reunion was most vital to the weaker
sections of the Church, it recommended that "in order to
strengthen the feeble missionary churches belonging to each,
and enable them to become self-sustaining, the Presbyteries
under our care . . . take such action as to them may be
deemed wise and expedient." Another resolution defined "the
essential condition of organic reunion" to be "an agreement
in Scripture doctrine and ecclesiastical order, according to the
standards of the Presbyterian Church." [63] The inclusion of
this definition made it appear that the Old School Assembly
was not any too sure of the New School's standards.

Despite the eloquent pleas for reunion made by the minister
and the ruling elder who served as the Old School corresponding delegates to the 1865 New School Assembly held at Brooklyn, New York,[64] that body chose not to go beyond its former
stand on reunion. In reply to overtures on the subject from
two presbyteries and from the Synod of Iowa, it declared that
"Until Providence shall more fully develop the question, and
thus indicate the course to be pursued, this Assembly judges
it most expedient for itself to wait on Providence. . . ." In
adopting this convenient method of disposing of the matter, the
Assembly explained that it did not mean to imply any judgment either for or against the reunion proposed, but simply
to leave the question open for further consideration and light.
In reply to the suggestion that the presbyteries be invited to
express their opinions on the subject, the Assembly judged it
"most expedient to leave this point to their own spontaneous
action." [65]

It is an interesting fact that although the delegates from the
New School Assembly who appeared on the floor of the cor-

[63] For the Old School resolutions of 1865, cf. Minutes of the General
Assembly (Old School), 1865, vol. xvii, p. 568.
[64] For the speeches of these delegates cf. proceedings of the General Assembly as recorded in the Presbyter, June 14, 1865.
[65] Minutes of the General Assembly (New School), 1865, vol. xiv, pp.
43-45.

responding body of the Old School always expressed cordiality, not one of the first four who carried greetings from the younger Church was an advocate of reunion in the near future; three of them specifically pointed out reasons why such a move appeared disadvantageous to them.[66] The Old School delegates to the New School Assembly, on the other hand, were as uniformly enthusiastic as those with whom they exchanged positions were reluctant.[67] The fact seems to be that the New School Church, an extraordinarily homogeneous body, was in its membership uniformly lukewarm on the proposition of reunion, while the Old School, somewhat heterogeneous in composition (even after the secession of the Southern presbyteries in 1861) with its Eastern, Western, and Border-State factions, represented all shades of opinion on the matter of rejoining the younger body. As the Western, more radical faction, which in general favored reunion, was steadily rising in power during the war years, it was natural that men who held its views of friendliness toward the New School should be sent as its representatives to the Assembly of that Church.

The New School delegate to the Old School Assembly at Pittsburgh in 1865 took the attitude typical of his predecessors when, in his report to his own Assembly, he praised the body he had visited but advanced reasons why early reunion was undesirable. Nevertheless the things he saw to praise in the Old School Church were such as to make reunion much easier for the more " progressive " body. He declared that the Old School brethren " though perhaps less prompt than some in reaching their position, . . . in declarations of unfaltering, patriotic, and Christian devotion to the Government

[66] The delegates' reports of their own speeches may be found in the section entitled " Correspondence " in the " Appendix " of the *Minutes of the General Assembly* (New School).

[67] *Cf.* report of speech of Dr. S. Tustin in 1863, *Presbytery Reporter*, July, 1863, vol. v, no. 16, p. 427; reports of speeches of Old School delegates in 1865, *Presbyter*, June 14, 1865; report presented by Dr. P. D. Gurley in 1866, *Minutes of the General Assembly* (New School), 1866, vol. xiv, pp. 272-273; also speeches of Dr. Gurley and Mr. H. K. Clarke in 1866, *Proceedings,* pp. 38-40.

and institutions of the country . . . are now perhaps surpassed by none." From a New School man, praise could
scarcely be higher. It was to be expected that the extravagantly patriotic New School men would be pleased by the violent method chosen by the 1865 Old School Assembly for dealing with cases of " disloyalty " in the Church.[68] Of the vindictive " Pittsburgh Orders "[69] which defined that method the
New School delegate reported, " In firm adherence to a righteous and consistent policy of ecclesiastical reconstruction their
utterances are none the less clear, and are worthy of all
praise." Having evidently observed the dissatisfaction which
was shortly to find expression in the " Declaration and Testimony "[70] of the Presbytery of Louisville, he exclaimed, " May
God defend them against that treasonable and reäctionary
spirit, some indications of which began to appear even in the
sessions upon which we attended, which would recall these
noble and righteous deliverances, turn to shame the glory
which God has given to the standards which they blessed with
their prayers, dishonor the patriot graves of more than a hundred battlefields . . . , and which seeks to satisfy a vanquished and atrocious treason by dragging its offensive corpse
to the altars of religion, thereby enacting a crime which to the
heart of patriotism is doubly execrable, and to that of piety
little less than sacrilege."[71]

In phrases equally ornate this New School patriot commented on the change in attitude on slavery which had come
over the denomination whose Assembly he had visited, and its
present determination " to redress in some measure, the wrong
of past indifference and neglect toward the slave." In spite
of his firm opposition to reunion and his assertion that " the

[68] *Cf. ante*, pp. 196-203.

[69] This was the name commonly applied to the policy determined upon
by the Old School Assembly at Pittsburgh for the handling of the problem of " disloyalty."

[70] *Cf. ante*, pp. 203-205.

[71] For the report of this delegate, *cf. Minutes of the General Assembly*
(New School), 1866, vol. xiv, pp. 300-301.

agitation even of this question of organic union between these
two bodies is only mistaken and mischievous," [72] it is clear
that the New School's representative at the meeting of the
1865 Old School Assembly was strongly impressed by the rapid
convergence in recent years of the sentiments of the two
branches of the Presbyterian Church. His impressions were
probably typical of those of his denomination. Purged of its
extreme Southern element, evidently determined to deal drasti-
cally with those who did not conform to its recent pronouncements on loyalty and slavery, undertaking with enthusiasm an
elaborate program to aid the freedmen,[73] evidencing clear signs
of relaxation in theological rigor, the Old School Church of
1865 was certainly much closer to the younger branch than
it had been four years earlier.

The year following the close of the war was one of marked
progress for the cause of reunion. The trend of political conditions afforded new opportunities, through Old School and
New School expressions of sentiment on reconstruction, for
discovering how similar in thought the two bodies were becoming. The Old School did not, it is true, emulate the New
School Assembly in undertaking the role of coach to the Federal Government in the matter of political reconstruction,[74]
but journals of both sides expressed identical opinions on this
engrossing subject, though with differing degrees of violence
of language. The self-possessed *Presbyterian* in June, 1865,
pointed out that it was the peculiar province of the minister
to interpose for the purpose of preventing the display of too
vindictive a spirit, and declared that its own opinion from the
first had been that " the principal leaders . . . should, as a
measure of security as well as justice, be so summarily dealt
with as to stigmatize the crime of rebellion to all future time
. . . , while the masses of the people . . . should be merci-
fully and leniently regarded." As they had already suffered,
kindness would do most to bring them back. " We can afford

[72] *Ibid.*
[73] *Cf. ante,* pp. 439-446.
[74] *Cf. ante,* pp. 357-362.

to be generous in the hour of victory . . . ," it reminded its readers, though taking pains to add that it would never cease to call the rebellion wrong.[75]

A few weeks later this journal's spirit of generosity had somewhat cooled. It now recognized three groups in the South which required special attention. The fangs of the rebel politicians, "who, although vanquished are not conciliated," must be drawn; the loyal Union men in the South must be favored and protected and "entrusted with such authority as will be safe in their hands;" and the millions of freedmen must be "tenderly cared for, . . . protected against oppression and brutality, . . . and taught to use their liberty aright, for their own good, and the good of the country at large."[76] The *Presbyterian's* interest in the masses of the whites in the South seemed to have disappeared.

At the same time New School journals were also demanding the punishment of rebel politicians. The *American Presbyterian* (Philadelphia) was growing impatient:

> With the lapse of another week, we find no sensible program made by our Government in the administration of justice to the guilty authors of our troubles. We cannot suppress our feelings of disappointment at the seeming haste exhibited to pardon rather than to punish, when such enormous crimes are concerned.[77]

The *Christian Herald and Presbyterian Recorder* found Scriptural justification for its demand for blood:

> Men whose loyalty is of the Christian stamp, who take the whole Bible as the teacher of men and nations — who believe in the 13th chapter of Romans as well as in the 13th chapter of Corinthians have been grieved by the evident shrinking of our Government, and many of our people from the great duty of the hour — the vindication of the powers ordained by God and of His law by punishing traitors.[78]

[75] *Presbyterian*, June 24, 1865.

[76] *Ibid.*, July 15, 1865.

[77] *American Presbyterian*, quoted in *Christian Herald and Presbyterian Recorder* in editorial, "Punishing Traitors," July 6, 1865. The latter journal mentions that it is quoting the *American Presbyterian* "of last week."

[78] Editorial, "Punishing Traitors," *Christian Herald and Presbyterian Recorder*, July 6, 1865.

What protection could there be against treasonable plots in the future, this ultra-patriotic Cincinnati journal asked, "if we accept advice from abroad to shed no blood . . . ?"[79] Foreigners might recommend the charity that suffereth long and is kind, but the militant *Christian Herald,* vociferous organ of New School Americanism, insisted that a policy of true patriotism demanded that the Deity be assisted in hurrying rebels to the fate prescribed for them by St. Paul: "They that resist shall receive to themselves damnation."

Other factors besides the agreement of Old School and New School journals regarding political reconstruction brought the two Schools closer in the year following the close of the war. When the Pittsburgh Orders of 1865 were followed by the "Declaration and Testimony," the constantly mounting discontent in the Border States made it more and more likely that drastic steps would be taken by the next General Assembly to purge the Church of the disorderly element. In 1861 there had been four geographical factions in the Church: Eastern, Western, Border State, and Southern. The two last named were virtually unanimous in their opposition to reunion, but one of them had left the Church after the outbreak of the war. Now the more troublesome element of the Border State faction was likely to follow. This would leave the composition of the Church almost solely Eastern and Western. With the West strong for reunion and at least part of the East of like mind, the departure of Border State disturbers would render the reduced denomination proportionally more favorable to reunion and more acceptable to the New School in personnel and sentiments. The reduction itself would increase the desirability of combining forces.

Throughout the war period many Old School Presbyterians had hoped that with the return of peace the Southern Church would return to its former fold.[80] Even some weeks after the surrender of Lee, Old School journals were still suggesting

[79] *Ibid.*
[80] *Cf. ante,* pp. 135; 139-140.

plans for receiving back at least a portion of those who had left in 1861. Disapproving of the instructions of the Presbytery of Cincinnati that its commissioners to the 1865 Assembly vote for the purging of the names of Southern members from the rolls of the Church, the *Presbyterian* urged that the Old School Church should not abandon the entire Southern field, but should rather put forth " enlarged and most vigorous efforts in all parts of that vast region . . . the extinct Confederacy." [81] This journal even urged that full aid be given to Southern churches who proposed to " remain aloof," upon one condition: " they must fully consent to peace and reunion [Federal] upon the terms which may be presented to the South by the national authorities." If any refused Old School aid, there would still be work to do, since there would be many individuals in the South who would want to go back to their former denominational allegiance.[82]

A few weeks later the *Presbyter* in giving advice upon the same subject took it for granted that a large portion of the Southerners would seek readmission to the Old School Church. It foresaw for the Church the great task of passing upon requests of this kind. The applicants, it thought, might be grouped into three classes. Ministers who had been leaders of secession deserved " the penalty of the law, and should never be permitted to return to our church as teachers or rulers." Those less active and less guilty, " upon proper sense of their sins, and upon proper confessions and promises, might be restored." Those in heart loyal to the Government had, the *Presbyter* felt, " claims to be recognized as still in the church, with all their rights of church property and ecclesiastical position." The great difficulty would be to devise a " scheme of readjustment or reconstruction, that will separate from us those who were leaders of treason, and preserve those who ought to be with us. . . ." [83]

The superfluity of such an elaborate classification soon be-

[81] Editorial, " The Southern Churches," *Presbyterian*, April 29, 1865.
[82] *Ibid.*
[83] Editorial, *Presbyter*, May 17, 1865.

came apparent to all. With almost complete unanimity the Southern churches stayed Southern. Almost immediately after it became apparent that the war was over, the *North Carolina Presbyterian* urged that the ecclesiastical separation must continue:

> Better, far better, would it be for our future spiritual welfare, to be even subjugated by their civil power, if so be that we keep ourselves distinct in matters of faith and church government, than ever to strike hands with them again in common ecclesiastical association.[84]

Even in the face of such opinions some of the more sanguine Old School men hoped that when the General Assembly of the Southern Church met in December, 1865 (having been prevented by the condition of the country from convening at the regular time in May [85]) a decision would be reached to reunite with the Old School Church. The *Presbyterian,* for example, took pains in the fall of 1865 to give assurances that a large portion of the Old School Church desired such a modification of the action of the Assembly of 1865 (the Pittsburgh Orders) [86] as would " open the door to reunion at an early day." [87]

Cyrus McCormick — influential Virginia-born Old School layman — was also using his influence to restore the former unity of the Church by promises of revision of the objectionable decisions of the 1865 Assembly. In reply to a request for a donation, he wrote Dr. B. M. Smith of Union Theological Seminary in Hampden Sidney, Virginia, that he believed it to be the duty of every member of the Old School Church to exert whatever influence he might have in opposition to the action of the General Assembly. Mr. McCormick regretted "the first false step" made by the General Assembly with regard to political matters: " But for the error committed . . . in 1861 . . . what an influence and power might, and no doubt

[84] Editorial, " The Southern Churches," *ibid.,* May 3, 1865. The above quotation from the *North Carolina Presbyterian* was included in this editorial.

[85] *Presbyterian Historical Almanac,* 1866, p. 313.

[86] *Cf. ante,* pp. 196-203.

[87] *Presbyterian,* October 21, 1865.

would now be exerted by that Church for good, in reuniting the people North and South. . . ." The General Assembly in 1865, he pointed out, was perpetuating the disruption of the Church at the very time that President Johnson was declaring the status of the states to be the same as before the war. Evidently determined that he himself would do nothing to perpetuate the disruption, Mr. McCormick was careful to make it clear that any contribution he might make to Union Theological Seminary would be contingent upon the progress made toward a reunion of the Southern and Northern Churches. He declared:

[I would] most cheerfully make a contribution to . . . the Union Theological Seminary; but with my hope that the position of the [Old School] General Assembly will be set right at its next annual meeting, with reasons for believing that many able men in the Church contemplate a prompt and vigorous movement in that direction; and trusting that when that is done the churches South will as promptly return to their former connection with it, I should before contributing, prefer to see some indications to that effect.[88]

This letter was written in October, 1865. Mr. McCormick, like the *Presbyterian*, had not yet given up hope of a reunion with the Southern Church in the near future.

The attitude of the Southern General Assembly in December proved to be a decided dampener to such hopes. That body not only determined that the Southern Church should continue as an independent body, but adopted a special series of resolutions to define its relation to the Old School Church in particular, and to carpet-bag ministers in general:

Resolved, 1. That the Presbyterian Church of the North (Old School) is to be looked upon simply as a separate and distinct ecclesiastical body; and that the ministers and agents of that Church have no further or higher claims on our courtesy than any other Churches of the same section of the country, which hold to the same symbols of faith and order with ourselves.

. . . . .

3. That our ministers and churches be, and hereby are warned against all ministers, and other agents, who may come among us to sow the seeds of division and strife in our congregations, or to create schism in our

---

[88] For Mr. McCormick's letter, *cf. Presbyterian*, October 21, 1865.

beloved Zion. And owing to the peculiar reasons for prudence which now exist, we enjoin it upon our ministers and Sessions to exercise special caution as to whom they admit to their pulpits; and in case of doubt, to refer to the judgment of the Presbyteries the whole question of the nature and extent of courtesy or countenance they may extend.

4. That the Assembly would remind Sessions that in no case is it proper for them to invite ministers of other denominations statedly to occupy any of our pulpits without the consent of the Presbyteries, and the known purpose of such ministers, at the earliest suitable opportunity to unite with us in ecclesiastical relations.[89]

Even the *Presbyterian* was now convinced that for some time at least the issue of reunion with the Southern Church was closed.[90]

Thus as the time for the 1866 General Assemblies approached, reunion of Old and New Schools loomed up as a much more immediate issue than it had the year before. The like-mindedness of the journals of the two denominations on the subject of political reconstruction had indicated a close harmony of thought upon a patriotic issue. Conditions in the Border States had indicated that an element which had always been hostile to reunion was about to withdraw from the Old School Church. Such a movement would not only leave the Old School proponents of reunion a proportionally stronger element within that denomination, but by reducing the size of the Church would make reunion seem more desirable. At the same time the change effected would make the proposition more attractive to the New School. Finally, the action of the Southern General Assembly in December, 1865, had decisively dispelled any expectations which may have been held with regard to an early reunion of Southern and Old School Churches. The ultra-conservative element in the Old School Church could no longer urge such a movement as an alternative for reunion with the New School.[91] To the New School, on the other hand, the finality of the Southern Assembly's

[89] *Presbyterian Historical Almanac*, 1866, pp. 314-315. A brief summary of these resolutions may be found in the *American Annual Cyclopaedia*, 1865, p. 706.

[90] *Cf.* editorial, " A Question Settled," *Presbyterian*, December 30, 1865.

[91] *Cf. ante*, pp. 139-140.

action served as an additional guarantee of the patriotism and progress of the Old School. Thus 1866 was likely to be an eventful year in the history of the movement for reunion.

Both Assemblies met in St. Louis in 1866. The complete control of the Old School body by the Western "radical" element [92] insured favorable action on reunion. Having been overtured on the subject by six presbyteries (all Western),[93] the Assembly adopted resolutions endorsing reunion and calling for the appointment of a committee of nine ministers and six ruling elders (provided that a similar committee should be appointed by the other Assembly) "for the purpose of conferring in regard to the desirableness and practicability of reunion, and if, after conference and inquiry, such reunion shall seem to be desirable and practicable, to suggest suitable measures for its accomplishment, and report to the next General Assembly." [94] Dr. H. J. VanDyke immediately upon the presentation of the resolutions moved that they be amended to "include the eight hundred and fifty ministers in the Southern States," [95] but his motion was speedily (except for a long speech by the mover himself) tabled.[96] Considering the attitude displayed toward the Old School Church by the Southerners at their last Assembly, it is not surprising that the motion received so little consideration; considering the temper of the 1866 Assembly, it is surprising that it received any consideration at all. No opposition against the proposition calling for the appointment of a joint committee on reunion was recorded in the debates of the Assembly,[97] and the resolutions were passed by an almost unanimous vote.[98]

[92] *Cf. ante,* pp. 220-222; 228-233; 257-258.
[93] *Minutes of the General Assembly,* 1866, vol. xviii, p. 44.
[94] *Ibid.*
[95] *Ibid.*
[96] *Ibid. Cf.* also *Proceedings . . . 1866,* pp. 57-58.
[97] For these debates, *cf. ibid.,* pp. 57-58.
[98] *Cf.* speech of Dr. Gurley before New School Assembly, *Proceedings . . . 1866,* p. 39. (Note separate pagination for proceedings of the two Assemblies.)

When Dr. P. D. Gurley,[99] as corresponding delegate to the New School Assembly, presented to that body the suggestion of the Old School Assembly, his announcement was received with applause.[100] As soon as the response of the Moderator had been concluded, Dr. H. B. Smith[101] presented the report of the Committee on Church Polity in relation to memorials received from eleven presbyteries urging reunion. The Committee recommended that the Old School proposal for the appointment of a joint committee be carried out. The report of the Committee was unanimously adopted "amid applause and demonstrations of great satisfaction." [102]

The action of the two Assemblies of 1866 constituted an important turning-point in the history of Presbyterian reunion. With the appointment of a special joint committee on reunion, for the first time a step had been taken toward the practical achievement of that objective. An agency had been set up whose sole task, after satisfying itself with regard to the "desirableness and practicability" of reunion, was "to suggest suitable measures for its accomplishment. . . ." It was scarcely conceivable that once these two Churches, now so alike in theology and in organization, had begun to have actual conferences with regard to means of effecting reunion, they could fail to reach that goal. To be sure, this outcome did not appear so certain in 1866, and events proved that many harsh things were still to be said, many doubts still to be expressed, and many old scores still to be revived, before the end was finally attained in 1869. Yet these evidences of unfriendliness were rendered far less serious by the presence of a Joint Committee ready to soften the hard feelings displayed and to suggest methods of eliminating their causes.

Considering the contrasting backgrounds of Old School and

[99] *Cf. ante*, pp. *220; 251-252.* When Dr. Gurley was welcomed by the New School Moderator, mention was made of the fact that he (as the President's pastor) had been with President Lincoln during his dying hours. *Proceedings . . . 1866,* p. 40.

[100] *Ibid.,* p. 39.

[101] *Cf. ante*, pp. 365, 492.

[102] *Proceedings . . . 1866,* p. 41.

New School men, the comparative recentness of the division of
the Church, and the bitterness of the rivalry which had characterized so much of the history of the separate organizations,
the progress toward reunion which had been made since the
Old School in 1862 first proposed the interchange of delegates
was remarkable. There can be little doubt that the astonishing momentum gained during these brief four years was to a
considerable extent due to the effects of the Civil War. The
patriotic pronouncements which the war called forth had
taught the two Churches to respect one another as comrades
in holding up the arms of the Federal Government. Working
side by side in camp and on battle-field, contributing to the
same war-time causes, speaking from the same platforms at
patriotic rallies, ministers and members of the two denominations had developed a brotherly love for one another such as
before the war would have seemed impossible.

Both of the ministers who served as corresponding delegates to the Assemblies of 1866 recognized the importance of
the war as a factor in bringing the two Churches closer together. Dr. Gurley described this influence in phrases that
must have fully satisfied his flag-waving New School audience [103] that he was a truly "loyal" man:

> Moreover, recent events have brought us into a closer alliance and
> fellowship, than we have ever felt before. In the years of our country's
> peril we have rallied together round the dear old flag, and while the conflict
> was going on, we have sung and prayed together:
>> "The Star Spangled Banner — Oh, long may it wave,
>> O'er the land of the free, and the home of the brave."
> [Applause.] And when, at last, the rebel flag went down, and with it
> slavery, Oh! then we lifted our hands and hearts together unto God,
> and said: "Not unto us, Oh Lord, not unto us, but unto Thy name give
> glory, for Thy mercy and Thy truth's [sic] sake. Thy right hand and
> Thy holy arm have gotten Thee the victory."
> These are recent events, and they have brought us into the bonds of a
> nearer and a heartfelt fellowship.[104]

---

[103] This was the New School Assembly which gave the Federal Government such elaborate advice on problems of reconstruction. *Cf. ante,* pp.
357-362.

[104] *Proceedings . . . 1866,* p. 39.

The tenor of the New School delegate's remarks on this subject was much the same. Dr. Henry A. Nelson, pastor of the church in which his Assembly was sitting (the First Presbyterian Church of St. Louis) had been delegated to represent this body before the Old School Assembly convening in a neighboring church. Referring to the coöperation between the congregations of these two churches during the war period, Dr. Nelson said:

> Once I have seen this house crowded more than it is crowded now; I have seen the other crowded more than this is crowded now, within one week by the people of these two congregations, and of the Congregational Church with us, pouring out our tears together amid the dark drapery which sought to express our grief at the Nation's great loss, and for which the Nation's heart is still so sore. We mingled thus here on such an occasion. It is these great griefs, it is this deep experience, it is the conscious sympathy in these great interests, and in these tremendous issues, which have melted down the mountains of division, and they have disappeared at the presence of the God of Hosts.
> I take the attitude of these two congregations, and of their pastors . . . to be an adequate illustration of the present relations of these two great Churches. It cannot be wrong, I think, for me to advert to that great thing in the Providence of God which, more than all things else, has made this state of things possible; and as I ought to condense whatever I have to say here on this occasion, when time is so precious, it is all summed up and all told in these three words: " Slavery is dead." [105]

These remarks called forth the friendliest sort of response from the Moderator of the Old School Assembly, the slavery-loathing Dr. R. L. Stanton.[106] As a member of the radical group which had secured control of the 1866 Assembly, Dr. Stanton could not refrain from verbally parading the triumph this faction had achieved during the years of the war. In his reply to Dr. Nelson he said:

> In presenting your fraternal salutations to us . . . you have referred, and I regret that I cannot refer to it in the same eloquent and fervent words which you have used, to the union of sentiment, which is expressed before the Church and before the world, in regard to those great matters which have so agitated the hearts of this vast people during the years which we have recently passed through.

---

[105] *Ibid.,* p. 23.
[106] *Cf. ante,* pp. 146, note 51; 220-222.

I can, I think, express the thought that we may felicitate ourselves as an Assembly and as a Church that we have made some progress in regard to those subjects out of which these troubles have grown. . . ; so that for several years past our Assemblies successively have expressed before the Church and the world what I believe to be the sentiments of the word of God upon that great matter, and directly contrary to what had been entertained as being in accordance with the word of God in the Southern portion of our country. I rejoice in this fact, and I know a vast majority of this body rejoice with me. I am only sorry to say that the entire membership do not.[107]

Dr. Stanton could scarcely have failed to add this last sentence, as the New School delegate had just been listening to Dr. Thomas E. Thomas's vitriolic attack upon the "Declaration and Testimony" men; [108] nevertheless he made it clear that the "vast majority" of the Old School Assembly had become emphatically anti-slavery.

Thus the war had played an important part in bringing together — through their common loyalty to the Union, opposition to slavery, and interest in war-time religious and benevolent activities — the two great branches of the Presbyterian Church, until by 1866 the interest in reunion had become so great that the two Assemblies determined to set up a joint agency to devise means of bringing about organic unity of the two denominations. Reunion in the near future loomed up as a probability — at least if the negotiations were left to men of good judgment and tolerant philosophy.

Fortunately for the cause, the ministers chosen on each side to be members of the Joint Committee were not professional theologians, but rather "from the working pastors of the church." [109] There was only one "scientific theologian" among them.[110] After two meetings (with sessions covering a total of ten days [111]) the Committee submitted to the General As-

[107] Proceedings . . . 1866, p. 24.

[108] Cf. ante, pp. 231-233.

[109] Thompson, op. cit., p. 173.

[110] Ibid. This was Dr. Jonathan F. Stearns, pastor of the (New School) First Presbyterian Church of Newark, New Jersey.

[111] Cf. report of Committee, Minutes of the General Assembly (Old School), 1867, vol. xviii, p. 388.

semblies of 1867 a plan of reunion based upon "the doctrinal
and ecclesiastical basis of our common standards." The Confession of Faith, it was provided, should continue to be sincerely received and adopted, "and its fair historical sense,
as it is accepted by the two bodies in opposition to Antinomianism and Fatalism on the one hand, and to Arminianism and
Pelagianism on the other, shall be regarded as the sense in
which it is received and adopted. . . ."[112] Explicit provisions were made for the organization of the united Church,
and it was declared that the terms of the reunion should be
of binding force if ratified by three-fourths of the presbyteries
connected with each branch of the Church within one year
after submission to them for approval.[113]

When this plan of reunion was submitted to the Old School
Assembly of 1867, that body passed a series of resolutions
commending the work of the Joint Committee, continuing its
half of it in power for another year, and submitting the report
of the Committee to the consideration of the churches and
the presbyteries. The Assembly was careful, however, to state
that in thus submitting the report it was not called upon at this
time to express either approbation or disapprobation of the
terms of reunion presented, but only to "afford the Church a
full opportunity to examine the subject in the light of all its
advantages and difficulties, so that the Committee may have
the benefit of any suggestions which may be offered, before
making a final report for the action of the next Assembly."[114]

The report of the Joint Committee as presented to the New
School Assembly of 1867 was accompanied by a special report
from that Church's half of the Committee. This addition consisted of a particular plea for Church unity, citing among other
reasons for the worthiness of the Presbyterian Church its having been "intimately associated with civil and religious liberty
in both hemispheres, . . . its sympathy with our institutions,

[112] *Ibid.*
[113] *Ibid.*, pp. 388-390.
[114] *Ibid.*, p. 362.

its ardent patriotism in all stages of our history. . . ." [115]
These statements would necessarily have been different had it
not been for the war record of the Old School Church — yet
had the Old School's attitude toward the war been different,
there might have been no occasion for a Joint Committee report
in 1867. How completely the older denomination had met the
approval of the New School Church was demonstrated by the
action of the Assembly of the younger branch with regard to
the report of the Joint Committee. The vote in favor of its
adoption was unanimous; nor was its endorsement qualified,[116]
as had been that of the Old School body. Evidently the New
School denomination was rapidly coming to the point of view
of one of the presbyteries [116a] as quoted in the 1867 annual
Narrative of the State of Religion:

> We would not do evil to accomplish this Reunion, but we deem the
> separation *a great sin*. Worthy of reprobation only, in the present condi-
> tion of our country, is the attempt to revive in our churches a theological
> and philosophical controversy, which the *pulpit* can scarcely ever have
> occasion even to touch. We prefer that belligerency should be turned
> against Romanism, atheism, and other powers of wickedness, and the
> manifest practical evils which spring from them.[117]

That the Plan of Union, in spite of the friendliness displayed toward it by the New School and a large portion of the
Old School, still had some serious obstacles to overcome, was
forecast by the opposition immediately raised by the greatest
theologian in the older branch of the Church. In the July
number of the *Princeton Review* Dr. Hodge devoted some
twenty-five pages to an attack upon the Plan. The reunion
proposed, he claimed, was more than a mere change of name —
it called upon Old School Presbyterians "to renounce that in
which [their] special identity" consisted. To him the Old
School had distinct traditions which it could not rightly before

---

[115] *Minutes of the General Assembly* (New School), 1867, vol. xiv, p. 484.
[116] *Ibid.*, p. 480.
[116a] The Presbytery of Long Island.
[117] *Ibid.*, p. 526.

God sacrifice.[118] It is not difficult to understand the point of view of one who recognized that — in spite of growing similarity in theological beliefs and denominational administration — the two branches of the Church in temperament and outlook were quite different, although one might hesitate to agree with Dr. Hodge that the Old School " would be guilty of a great moral wrong should it accept of the proposed plan." [119] Another leading theologian of the Church, Dr. R. J. Breckinridge, asserted that any such plan of reunion was impossible; a Church could not be absorbed as a whole; the only method of union between the two bodies was for its members individually to come in through the presbyteries.[120] Apparently this veteran of the excision movement of 1837 [121] conceived of reunion only in terms of complete conformity on the part of the New School to Old School standards. With two such powerful leaders opposed to the Plan of Union, it was evident that all was not to be smooth sailing for its proponents.

The movement now, however, received an unexpected impetus from an outside quarter. The General Synod of the Reformed Presbyterians (New Side) under the leadership of Mr. George H. Stuart adopted at its 1867 meeting a series of resolutions calling a general convention of the Presbyterian Church of the United States (in all its various denominations) to meet in the First Reformed Presbyterian Church in Philadelphia the following September. It was recommended that the convention should consist of one minister and one elder from each presbytery, but that each denomination represented should have one vote, irrespective of the number of its delegates present.[122] Considerable interest in the project was shown by the various Presbyterian bodies, and when the convention assembled (on November 6, 1867 — the date originally specified

---

[118] *Biblical Repertory and Princeton Review*, July, 1867, vol. xxxix, pp. 502-503. *Cf.* also, Hodge, *op. cit.*, pp. 501-508.

[119] *Biblical Repertory and Princeton Review*, July, 1867, vol. xxxix, p. 521.

[120] *Ibid.*, p. 500.

[121] *Cf. ante*, pp. 36-39; 186-195; 479.

[122] For these resolutions, *cf. Presbyterian Historical Almanac* for 1868, pp. 386-388.

having been subsequently changed[123]) it was found that 263 clerical and lay delegates had appeared. Of these, 162 were from the Old School, 64 from the New School, 12 from the United Presbyterian Church, 12 from the Reformed Presbyterian Church, 6 from the Cumberland Presbyterian Church, 1 from the Southern Presbyterian Church, and 6 from the Reformed Dutch Church.[124]

Mr. Stuart was made president of the convention.[125] The most remarkable harmony prevailed throughout the sessions. To be sure, Dr. R. J. Breckinridge threatened to become a disturbing factor, but no one who knew the Doctor expected otherwise of him.[126] Illness prevented his attending any but the first session, however, and his methods in that session seemed to help rather than hinder the cause which he was so bitterly opposing. When he followed an assertion that none of the Old School members of the Joint Committee was a learned theologian[127] by declaring that he had not come to the convention to be lectured by its chairman, and then by shaking his first in Mr. Stuart's face and saying that the convention had made a great mistake in choosing a layman for its presiding officer, several former opponents of reunion took occasion to tell the chairman that if Dr. Breckinridge represented the spirit of the opposition, they were converted to reunion.[128]

The Breckinridge incident stood out especially because it

---

[123] Thompson, *Life of George H. Stuart*, p. 210. The September date would not have afforded many presbyteries an opportunity to choose delegates without calling a special meeting of the presbytery.

[124] Thompson, *History of the Presbyterian Churches*, p. 175.

[125] Thompson, *Life of George H. Stuart*, p. 213.

[126] Mr. Stuart in his autobiography (edited by Dr. R. E. Thompson) tells of a member rushing up to him at the beginning of the first session, saying, " It would have been better if this Convention had never been called. . . . Don't you see at the vestibule-door of the middle aisle Dr. Robert J. Breckinridge? That means fight! " Thompson, *Life of George H. Stuart*, pp. 211-212.

[127] Though not tactful, this statement was not untruthful. *Cf. ante*, p. 508.

[128] Thompson, *Life of George H. Stuart*, pp. 213-214.

was so entirely at odds with the harmony of the convention, where a most fraternal spirit prevailed. Dr. Hodge and Dr. Henry Boynton Smith, fresh from heated arguments on the subject of reunion, associated together on the friendliest terms, and Dr. Hodge, according to a letter written by Dr. Smith about this convention, "relented wonderfully." [129] A delegation from the Evangelical Knowledge Society of the Protestant Episcopal Church, which was then in annual session in a neighboring church, was appointed to present the salutations of that organization to the Presbyterian convention, while the Society as a body attended the session at which their greetings were presented. Although this got the Episcopalian speakers into difficulty later with some of their High Church brethren,[130] upon the Presbyterian assemblage it had the effect of heightening further the steadily mounting enthusiasm.

In fact the service which the convention rendered to the cause of reunion was to create an enthusiasm for it. Hitherto proceedings in the matter had been characterized by formal conferences and discussions; the 1867 convention was characterized by mass enthusiasm. It was not for nothing that its chairman had for four years devoted his time and energy to the production of this sort of emotion. How successful he and his friends were in the present instance was described by the *Presbyterian:*

The Convention for the purpose of furthering unity among the various branches of the Presbyterian Church in the United States, which met last week in Philadelphia, was certainly a remarkable body and has done a remarkable work. It was composed of representative men from various bodies which sent them up. . . . As we looked at them on the evening previous to the regular opening of the Convention, we judged them to be as little likely to be swept away by any gust of enthusiasm, or the soft words of sentimentalism, as any body of men we have ever chanced to see.

Yet it was manifest, to any one who watched the Convention, that enthusiasm was its special characteristic, and that the tide of feeling steadily rose from the commencement to the close of its sessions. The most obvious objection, indeed, to the Convention, was that it rapidly

---

[129] *Ibid.,* p. 223.
[130] *Cf.* letter of Bishop McIlvaine to Canon Carus, *ibid.,* pp. 219-221, note.

changed its character from that of a body calmly and soberly settling the
principles upon which a great movement is to be conducted, to that of a
mass-meeting, manipulated by hands skilful in the management of such
enthusiastic gatherings.[131]

A more approving account of the convention was written by
Dr. Henry Boynton Smith:

. . . . Manifestly a higher than human power presided in the Convention. . . . The spirit of prayer was poured out in an unwonted measure,
and in hallowed hymns the deepest feelings of faith and love found con-
cordant expression. It is not often that believers stand together on such
a mount of vision, and find the glory of heaven thus begun on earth.
And yet these high-wrought emotions did not lead to any rash conclusion, such as a cooler judgment might disapprove. On the contrary, the
spirit of love moved in unison with the spirit of wisdom. Men were still
cool and intent, and weighed their words. While points of controversy
were kept in the background, yet the differences were not neglected, but
rather harmonized. And the Convention . . . exceeded the most sanguine
expectations as to the conclusions reached, but it did not trespass on
ground not properly belonging to it. . . . It was good to be there.[132]

The enthusiasm thus created was needed to offset the determined activities of the opposition element in the Old School
Church. The influence of this element led by Doctors Hodge
and Breckinridge[133] was strong enough still — in spite of the
reunion party's determination not to be turned from its course
" by all the efforts of Princeton, Allegheny, and Danville "[134] —
to prevent reunion from being effected in 1868.[135] This fur-

[131] From an editorial in the *Presbyterian* for November 16, 1867, quoted
in Thompson, *Life of George H. Stuart*, pp. 221-222.
[132] Quotation from the memoir of Dr. Henry Boynton Smith, *ibid.*, pp.
222-223.
[133] *Cf. Debates and Proceedings of the General Assembly of the Presbyterian Church . . . 1868* (Philadelphia, 1868), pp. 17-18; 38-43; 53-56; 106;
109-111; and *passim*.
[134] *Cf.* speech of Rev. T. P. Hunt in Assembly of 1868. *Ibid.*, p. 55.
[135] The Plan of Reunion as elaborated by the Joint Committee between
the Assemblies of 1867 and 1868 was adopted by the Old School Assembly
by a vote of 188 to 70. In order to conciliate the large and powerful
minority, this Assembly (1868) resolved to propose to the other Assembly
the omission of certain definite doctrinal statements, and the substitution
therefor of a provision for reunion on the basis of " the standards pure
and simple." When this suggestion reached the New School Assembly
(sitting at Harrisburgh, Pennsylvania, while the Old School body was

nished another year for reviewing and advertising the alleged heresies of Rev. Albert Barnes and Dr. George Duffield.[136] It mattered little when friends of the New School pointed out that the fact that the attackers could name no new heretics was significant of the younger body's orthodoxy; [137] the ultra-conservatives answered that the Barnes-Beman-Duffield errors had never been specifically repudiated. Clearly it was necessary that the enthusiasm of 1867 be revived.

An opportunity for such a revival was furnished by the convening of the General Assemblies of 1869. As both bodies met in the city of New York, frequent conferences were possible, and union prayer-meetings of the two Assemblies " brought back the lost fervor." [138] A new Committee of Conference solved the difficulties of doctrinal statement by recommending that the two Churches, " each recognizing the other as a sound and orthodox body according to the principles of the Confession common to both," be reunited " on the doctrinal and ecclesiastical basis of our common Standards; " by this general statement of mutual confidence the pitfalls of theological definition were avoided. Reunion should be effected when two-thirds of the presbyteries of each denomination should have approved (providing such action was taken before November 1, 1869) of this Basis of Reunion. It was further recommended that the two Assemblies of 1869 should, after finishing their business, adjourn to meet in the city of Pittsburgh on the second Wednesday of the following November. If the two Assemblies should then find that the Basis

convened at Albany, New York) there was no longer a quorum present, and no action could be taken. The New School presbyteries proceeded to vote approval of the Joint Committee's Plan. The Old School presbyteries, on the other hand, gave their approval generally on the basis of " the standards pure and simple." Thus while the New School accepted the Joint Committee's Plan of Reunion, that Plan was rejected by the Old School Church. *Cf. ibid.,* pp. 111-116; *Minutes of the General Assembly* (Old School), 1868, vol. xviii, pp. 626-631; Thompson, *History of the Presbyterian Churches,* pp. 176-178.

[136] *Ibid.,* pp. 178-179.
[137] *Cf., e.g., Proceedings of the General Assembly . . . 1868,* pp. 27-28.
[138] Thompson, *History of the Presbyterian Churches,* p. 179.

of Reunion had been approved by the requisite number of presbyteries of each denomination, the reunion should be declared effected, and the two Assemblies should take action accordingly.[139]

These recommendations of the Committee of Conference were unanimously adopted by the New School Assembly;[140] in the Assembly of the other branch the vote was 285 to 9.[141] The Basis of Reunion was accordingly submitted for the approval of the presbyteries of each denomination. When the adjourned Assemblies convened in Pittsburgh on November 10, 1869, the Old School body found that of its 144 presbyteries, 126 had voted their approval; three, their disapproval.[142]

[139] For the report of the 1869 Committee of Conference and the Basis of Reunion suggested, cf. *Minutes of the General Assembly* (Old School), 1869, vol. xviii, pp. 912-917; *ibid.* (New School), 1869, vol. xv, pp. 275-279.
[140] *Ibid.*, p. 275.
[141] *Minutes of the General Assembly* (Old School), 1869, vol. xviii, pp. 912-914.
[142] The three presbyteries disapproving were Hudson (eastern New York), Rio de Janeiro (South America), and West Lexington (Kentucky). Eleven presbyteries (four of them in the states of the former Confederacy, and four in foreign mission fields) failed to report to the Assembly. Three (one in New Mexico and the other two in foreign mission fields) reported that they could not meet within the time specified. Another presbytery (in India), recently formed, had sent in its vote. The Stated Clerk of the Assembly asked — and received — permission to record this vote. (*Cf. ibid.*, p. 1158.) The vote of the presbyteries was thus overwhelming in its approval, yet within individual presbyteries there had frequently been a disapproving minority. Dr. Charles Hodge remained determinedly opposed to reunion, and cast his vote in opposition when the matter came before his own presbytery. In recording this fact in his *History of the Presbyterian Churches. . .* , Dr. R. E. Thompson has given a curious and unfortunate impression. Without citing the source, he quoted a statement that " Dr. Charles Hodge . . . ' rode nine miles . . . with the *anthrax malitiosissimus* on the back of his neck, for the purpose of casting his final vote against ' reunion." The uncited source was Dr. A. A. Hodge, who made this statement in his biography of his father (*Life of Charles Hodge*, p. 504). Dr. Hodge placed the words " anthrax malitiosissimus " in quotation marks (with no citation of source) in reference to a term used by Dr. Charles Hodge (in a letter written the day before the meeting of the presbytery) to describe a boil from which he was then suffering! (*Cf. ibid.*, p. 488.) From Dr. Thompson's account (*op. cit.*, p. 180) one would gather that the term referred to unusual stubbornness and malice. Actually, Dr. Charles Hodge was the mildest and most courteous of men.

From the New School Assembly came an account of the vote in that denomination: " In favor of the Overture for Reunion, and approving the same, One Hundred and Thirteen Presbyteries, being the whole number in connection with this body." [143] At last the *" great sin "* [144] of separation — so far as the Old School and New School Churches were concerned — had been removed. When the announcement of the approval of the New School Church was received, the Old School Moderator [145] quoted the words of the great Hebrew prophet:

Thy watchmen shall lift up the voice; with the voice together shall they sing: for they shall see eye to eye, when the Lord shall bring again Zion.

Break forth into joy, sing together, ye waste places of Jerusalem: for the Lord hath comforted his people, he hath redeemed Jerusalem.[146]

The joy was not entirely complete, however, for not all of Jerusalem had been redeemed: the minor Presbyterian Churches had not joined in the reunion. Though the more important ones had been represented in the Reunion Convention of 1867,[147] there was still too much dissimilarity in doctrine, or (as in the case of the Southern Presbyterian Church [148]) too great a want of brotherly love to render union practicable. Each of the minor Churches continued its separate way. To the New Side Covenanters (Reformed Presbyterians, General Synod), in fact, this period brought division rather than union. The General Synod, which in 1867 had suggested the Reunion Convention of that year, in 1868 by resolution suspended Mr. George H. Stuart from eldership and membership in the Church. The grounds for this action were that he had "sung hymns of human composition and communed with other than Reformed Presbyterians." [149] Mr.

---

[143] *Minutes of the General Assembly* (Old School), 1869, vol. xviii, p. 1162.
[144] *Cf. ante*, p. 510.
[145] Dr. M. W. Jacobs, of the Western Theological Seminary.
[146] Isaiah lii, 8, 9. *Cf. Minutes of the General Assembly* (Old School) 1869, vol. xviii (Supplement), p. 1162.
[147] *Cf. ante*, pp. 511-512.
[148] Technically, the " Presbyterian Church in the United States."
[149] Thompson, *Life of George H. Stuart*, p. 227.

Stuart had avowed both of these offenses before the General
Synod of 1856, but at that time this body had seen fit to
condone his actions by reëlecting him to important offices.[150]
His suspension in 1868, therefore, aroused a tremendous out-
cry both within and without his own denomination. He himself alleged that it had been brought about through fear that
if he remained in the Church he "might exert sufficient influence to cause it to be carried into the approaching union."[151]
As a result of the General Synod's action, four presbyteries
broke away. Three of them later joined the Presbyterian
Church, adding their strength to the reunited body; the other
found its way into the United Presbyterian Church.[152] The
years which saw the reunion of the Old and New Schools thus
also witnessed the reduction of the General Synod to less than
one-half of its former membership.[153]

Just as the war hastened the reunion of the two largest Presbyterian denominations, so the hard feelings it engendered
clove an ever widening breach between them and the youngest
of the Presbyterian bodies — the Southern Church. For many
years after the war had been ended, there were few signs of the
breach being healed. Inasmuch as the reuniting Churches had
decided that "no rule or precedent, which does not stand approved by both the bodies, should be of any authority, until
reëstablished in the united body . . . ,"[154] the Reunion nulli-
fied all of the Old School action with regard to the members
of the Southern General Assembly and of the independent
Synod of Missouri[155] (then not yet united with the Southern
body [155a]). But the hopes of many that this fact would hasten

---

[150] *Ibid.*

[151] *Ibid.*, p. 227.

[152] *Ibid.*, pp. 227-228.

[153] For the story of this division, cf. *ibid.*, pp. 227-230; Thompson, *History
of the Presbyterian Churches*, pp. 185-186.

[154] *Minutes of the General Assembly* (Old School), 1869, vol. xviii, pp.
915-916; *ibid.* (New School), 1869, vol. xv, p. 278.

[155] *Cf. ante*, pp. 196-200; 242; 251-252; 266-267.

[155a] *Cf. ante*, pp. 273-274.

the return of the Southerners to the old fold were doomed to early disappointment.[156]

Yet, in spite of the unwillingness of the lesser denominations to join in the union, there was abundant reason in 1869 to "break forth into joy." Two of the strongest Protestant bodies in the United States had merged to form a Church counting a membership of nearly a half million,[157] touching directly the lives of two millions of people. Within the span of a single generation the great break which in 1837 had seemed irreparable was healed. Ten years ago men had thought of reunion as possible only in the far distant future. But, as was said in the Old School Assembly of 1869, during those ten years "a change [had] come over the Church and the country . . . , a great and wonderful change, such as no man in the North, and perhaps few in the South, had any premonition of then, and which, hardly less in the Church than in the State, has revolutionized institutions and opinions."[158]

[156] Immediately after reunion steps were taken to bring about a reconciliation with the Southern Church, but they met with complete failure. (Thompson, *History of the Presbyterian Churches*, p. 184; Johnson, *op. cit.*, pp. 462-464.) In 1873, the General Assembly by unanimous vote specifically declared its previous actions (that is, those of the Old School Assembly) which had proved obnoxious to Southerners, null and void, and resolved to appoint committees of conference, if the Southern Assembly and the Synod of Missouri would do the same. (*Minutes*, 1873, new series, vol. 2, pp. 502-504.) But as there was still a great deal of opposition among Southern Presbyterians against joining an Assembly which "gloried . . . in having wheeled the church into the political fight" and which had perpetrated "wrongs such as no other evangelical church in modern times had dared to heap on another," the Southern committee of conference was not disposed to be conciliatory. *Cf.* Johnson, *op. cit.*, pp. 464-470. As Dr. Johnson's history was published in 1894, the statements here quoted would indicate that the spirit of conciliation had not made much progress in the more than twenty years which had elapsed since the meeting of the conference committee.

[157] The communicant membership of the Old School Church in 1869 was 258,903. *Minutes of the General Assembly* (Old School), 1869, vol. xviii, p. 1108. That of the New School was 172,560. *Ibid.* (New School), 1869, vol. xv, p. 462.

[158] From the report of the Special Committee on the Seminary of the Northwest, *Minutes of the General Assembly* (Old School), 1869, vol. xviii (Supplement), pp. 1145-1146.

This change had affected not only men's outward lives; it had transformed their thoughts. So far as Northern Presbyterians were concerned, the great war which had taken place had turned their minds from their ecclesiastical differences to their common interest in the salvation of the Union. Distinction between Old School and New School had seemed to fade away as it became increasingly clear that both bodies felt alike on the problems of loyalty and slavery. The withdrawal of the discordant Southern and Border State elements from the Old School had emphasized the convergence of the two great groups of Northern Presbyterians; while the drastic nature of the " Pittsburgh Orders " and the subsequent actions of Border State synods and of the Southern General Assembly had left little doubt as to the permanence of these war-time divisions. General agreement in views on political reconstruction had confirmed impressions with regard to the growing similarity in outlook between the two denominations. Meanwhile the practice of annual interchange of corresponding delegates, first inaugurated in 1863, had helped to crystallize the steadily increasing sympathy in political convictions, theological doctrine, and methods of ecclesiastical administration. When the veteran creator of mass enthusiasm, George H. Stuart, had in 1867 injected into the movement all of the energy and skill engendered by four years of war-time propagandizing, the success of reunion — in spite of the skepticism of but a half-dozen years earlier — seemed assured.

When reunion had formally been effected by the two adjourned Assemblies, it was decided that some fitting ceremony should mark the event, and arrangements were made for a Jubilee Convention to be held immediately after the close of the adjourned sessions. The ceremonies were to be initiated by a march to the meeting-place chosen for the Convention. Accordingly, members of the New School Assembly formed in order (with the officers of the Assembly and the members of the Reunion Committee at the head of the column) and proceeded to the church in which the other body had been sitting.

Here they found themselves stationed opposite the Old School Assembly, arranged in similar order. When the sign for the march was given, the two Moderators met in the middle of the street, shook hands, and joined arms. This was the signal for the other members following; the two columns merged into one, the New School arm in arm with the Old.

As the united column proceeded down the streets of Pittsburgh — that "most Scotch-Irish of American cities," a city that "had had its share in the troubles which had divided the church" [159] — crowds of people, undaunted by the chill November wind, thronged the sidewalks to witness this strange event. "The heart of the people was stirred. It was indeed, a spectacle altogether novel. Christian fraternity was holding Jubilee!" [160] The Presbyterian Church was marching from a divided past to a united future.

On the procession moved, "brethren unbosoming themselves to brethren at every step." [161] In the exchange of views with regard to the past and the future of the Church, mention must often have been made of the remarkable interplay of ecclesiastical and political history during the decade just past. How different both of the uniting bodies had become, as a result of the great struggle the nation had undergone! How deep

---

[159] Thompson, *op. cit.*, p. 180.

[160] *Presbyterian Reunion: A Memorial Volume*, p. 380. For an interesting account of these ceremonies *cf.* that written by the Moderator of the Old School Assembly of 1869 (Dr. M. W. Jacobus of Western Theological Seminary) *ibid.*, pp. 379-405. The "Additional Impressions" (pp. 406-414) of the Moderator of the New School Assembly of 1869 (Dr. Philemon H. Fowler, pastor of the First Presbyterian Church of Utica, New York) supplement Dr. Jacobus' account. This volume also gives biographical sketches of the members of the Joint "Reunion Committee." It is significant that two of the six lay representatives of the Old School Church were men who had become conspicuous during war years for their "patriotic" activities in the General Assemblies. Hon. George P. Strong of St. Louis, Missouri, had been the relentless persecutor of Dr. S. B. McPheeters in the General Assembly of 1864 (*cf. ante*, pp. 305-324); Hon. Samuel Galloway had the questionable distinction of having made some of the most extravagantly "radical" speeches of the 1866 Assembly (*cf. ante*, pp. 238-241).

[161] *Presbyterian Reunion: A Memorial Volume*, p. 382.

had been the interest of both in preserving the unity of the nation unimpaired! National unity had been saved, but — thanks to the war which had done so much to bring together Old School and New School — the reunited Church was a sectional, not a national body. Reunion had been hailed by the leading journals of the land as " a precious National boon," [162] but would the day ever come when the sectional breach caused by the war would be sufficiently healed so that the Presbyterian Church might be called a national Church within a national State? Time alone could tell. One thing was certain: the reunited Old School and New School were now marching to a common future and a common destiny. Perhaps the members of the uniting Churches were justified in priding themselves that their denominations had played some part in determining that the home of this greater Presbyterian Church should be an undivided Federal Union.

[162] *Ibid.*, pp. 371-372.

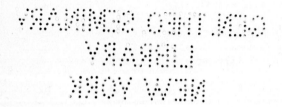

BIBLIOGRAPHY

I. BIBLIOGRAPHICAL AIDS

Allison, William Henry, *Inventory of Unpublished Material for American Religious History in Protestant Church Archives and other Repositories.* Washington, 1910.

Check List of Collections of Personal Papers in Historical Societies, University and Public Libraries, and other Learned Institutions in the United States. Washington, 1918. Compiled under the direction of the Manuscript Division, Library of Congress.

Handbook of Manuscripts in the Library of Congress. Washington, 1918. Supplemented by *Accessions of Manuscripts, Broadsides, and British Transcripts* (published yearly, Washington, 1921-1925).

List of Manuscript Collections in the Library of Congress to July, 1931. Compiled by Curtis Wiswell Garrison. American Historical Association *Annual Report* for 1930, vol. i, part iv. Washington, 1931.

Manuscripts in Public and Private Collections in the United States. Washington, 1924. A directory of the repositories of the more important manuscript collections in the United States.

Hurst, John Fletcher, *The Literature of Theology. A Classified Bibliography of Theological and General Religious Literature.* New York, 1900.

Jackson, Samuel Macauley, *comp., A Bibliography of American Church History.* (*American Church History Series*, vol. xii, pp. 441-513.) New York, 1894.

Mode, Peter G., *Source-Book and Bibliographical Guide for American Church History.* Menasha, Wisconsin, 1921.

II. PRIMARY SOURCES

I. UNPRINTED SOURCES

Baird, Samuel John, D.D., *Papers.* Over 600 pieces, dating from 1841 to 1875. Dr. Baird was a prominent preacher, editor, and writer in the Old School Presbyterian Church. The *Papers* consist mainly of correspondence between him and leading ministers of the Old and New School Churches. In the Library of Congress.

Bates, Edward, *Diary.* Covers the years 1859 to 1866. Not open to investigators at the time this study was made. In the Library of Congress. The *Diary* is to be printed by the American Historical Association. Attorney General Bates was an elder in the Old School Presbyterian Church, and much interested in the affairs of that denomination in Missouri.

Breckinridge Papers. Upwards of 30,000 pieces, consisting mostly of correspondence of various members of the Breckinridge family—especially of letters written to Dr. Robert J. Breckinridge. In the Library of Congress. The position of leadership in the Old School Presbyterian Church held by Dr. R. J. Breckinridge for over thirty-five years gives this collection considerable importance in Presbyterian history; the great diversity of his interests lends it fascination for the general historian.

Desha Papers. This collection consists mainly of correspondence between John R. Breckinridge and General Joseph Desha, 1812 to 1859. In the Library of Congress.

Johnson, Reverdy, *Papers.* Chiefly correspondence, covering the years 1826 to 1876. In the Library of Congress.

Letters of American Clergymen. 251 letters, 1719 to 1873, written by clergymen—mainly of the Protestant Episcopal, Presbyterian, and Congregational Churches. In the Library of Congress.

2. PRINTED SOURCES

A. *Official Church Records*

Minutes of the General Assembly of the Presbyterian Church in the United States of America, 1789- . [From 1838 to 1869 for the Old School Presbyterian Church, only.] Published yearly, with an appendix containing the annual "Narrative of the State of Religion" (based upon the reports submitted to the General Assembly annually by the individual presbyteries); comprehensive statistical records of the Church and its subdivisions; abstracts of the annual reports of the various organizations and institutions under the control of the General Assembly; and other papers. Philadelphia, 1789- .

Minutes of the General Assembly of the Presbyterian Church in the United States of America, 1838-1869. [New School Presbyterian Church.] Published yearly, in form and substance essentially identical with the above. New York, 1838-1869.

Minutes of the General Assembly of the Presbyterian Church in the Confederate States of America, 1861-1869. [After 1865 this Church was known as the Presbyterian Church in the United States.] Published yearly. Augusta, 1861-1862; 1865. Columbia, 1863-1864; 1866-1869.

Minutes and Phonographic Report of the Presbyterian National Reunion Convention Held in Philadelphia, November 6th, 1867. Philadelphia, 1868.

Minutes of the Synod of Baltimore, 1863-1867. Published yearly. Baltimore, 1864-1867.

Minutes of the Synod of Chicago, 1861-1868. Published yearly. Galesburg, 1861-1868.

Minutes of the Synod of Cincinnati, 1870-1875. Published yearly. Cincinnati, 1871-1875.

Minutes of the Synod of Kentucky [Undivided], 1861-1865. Cincinnati, 1861, 1863. Louisville, 1866.

Minutes of the Synod of Kentucky [Adhering to the General Assembly after the division of 1866,] 1866-1867; 1869; 1871-1874. Louisville, 1868; 1869; 1871-1874.

Minutes of the Synod of Kentucky [Independent of the Old School General Assembly after the division of 1866; adhering to the Southern General Assembly after 1869,] 1866, 1868. Louisville, 1866, 1869.

Minutes of the Synod of Michigan, 1861; 1863-1865. Published yearly. Detroit, 1861. Lansing, 1863-1865.

Minutes of the Synod of Mississippi, 1861-1867. Jackson, 1880.

Minutes of the Synod of New Jersey, 1865-1868. Published yearly. New Brunswick, 1865-1868.

Minutes of the Synod of Ohio [Old School], 1864, 1866. Zanesville, 1865; n.d.

Report of the Provisional Committee on Foreign Missions . . . presented to the General Assembly of the Presbyterian Church in the Confederate States of America in Augusta, Georgia, December, 1861. Columbia, 1862.

B. *Reports of Debates and Proceedings of Presbyterian Church Councils*

Reports of the Proceedings of the General Assembly of the Presbyterian Church in the United States of America . . . New York, May, 1856. Reported for the *Presbyterian.* Philadelphia, 1856. [Old School.]

Proceedings of the General Assemblies Old and New School Presbyterian Churches convened in St. Louis, May 17, 1866. St. Louis, 1866. Published by the Missouri Democrat Book and Job Printing House; thus probably a collection of the reports as they appeared in the *Missouri Democrat.*

General Assembly of the Presbyterian Church Annual Meeting, May, 1867, in the city of Cincinnati Proceedings. Cincinnati, 1867. [Old School.]

Debates and Proceedings of the General Assembly of the Presbyterian Church in the United States of America. A.D. 1868. Philadelphia, 1868. A collection of the reports as they appeared in the *Presbyterian.* [Old School.]

Similar collections of reports of debates and proceedings, if published for General Assemblies of other years or other Presbyterian denominations, are not now available in any of the larger Presbyterian libraries in the United States. As the leading journals of each of the Presbyterian denominations followed the practice of reporting very fully the proceedings of each General Assembly session, however, material of this kind is abundant, even though not in the form most convenient for the student's use. Reports of the proceedings of synods and presbyteries were also commonly published in the denominational journals, though naturally in a much more abbreviated form.

C. *Collections of Documents, Records, and Papers*

Baird, Samuel J., ed., *A Collection of the Acts, Deliverances, and Testimonies of the Supreme Judicatory of the Presbyterian Church in the United States of America.* [Old School.] Philadelphia, 1856.

The Congressional Globe . . . , 1861-1865. Washington, 1862-1866.

The Constitution of the Presbyterian Church in the United States of America: being its Standards Subordinate to the Word of God, viz., The Confession of Faith, the Larger and Shorter Catechisms, the Form of Government, the Book of Discipline, and the Directory for the Worship of God as Ratified and Adopted by the Synod of New York and Philadelphia in the Year of our Lord 1788, and as Amended in the Years 1805-1908; together with the Constitutional Rules adopted in 1893-1907, and Administrative Acts of the Assembly of a General Nature. Philadelphia, 1910.

The Journal of the House of Representatives . . . *37th Congress, First Session* . . . *1861.* Washington, 1862.

McPherson, Edward, *ed., The Political History of the United States of America, during the Great Rebellion, including* . . . *an Appendix containing* . . . *a Chapter on the Church and the Rebellion.* . . . *Third edition.* Washington, 1876.

——, *The Political History of the United States of America during the Period of Reconstruction.* . . . Second edition. Washington, 1875.

——, *Political Manual for 1866.* . . . Washington, 1866.

Moore, Frank, *ed., The Rebellion Record, A Diary of American Events, Documents, Narratives, Illustrative Incidents, Poetry.* . . . 9 volumes. New York, 1861 ff. Some material bearing directly upon the history of the Churches; much that is closely related to it.

Moore, William E., *ed., A New Digest of the Acts and Deliverances of the Presbyterian Church in the United States of America.* . . . Philadelphia, 1861.

——, *The Presbyterian Digest of 1886.* . . . Philadelphia, 1886.

The Public Laws of the United States of America . . . *1861.* Boston, 1861.

Richardson, James D., *ed., The Messages and Papers of the Presidents, 1789-1897.* Published by the authority of Congress. 10 volumes. Washington, 1896-1897.

Thompson, Robert Ellis, *A History of the Presbyterian Churches in the United States.* (Volume vi of the *American Church History Series.*) New York, 1895. Pp. 317-415 constitute an "Appendix of the Most Important Documents Illustrative of the History of the Presbyterian Church in America."

War of the Rebellion: A Compilation of the Official Records of the Union and Confederate Armies. 129 volumes. Washington, 1880-1900.

D. *Contemporary Works of Reference*

American Annual Cyclopaedia and Register of Important Events, 1861-1872. New York, 1862-1873.

Encyclopaedia of the Presbyterian Church in the United States of America: Including the Northern and Southern Assemblies. Edited by Alfred Nevin, D.D. Philadelphia, 1884. Although published nineteen years after the close of the Civil War, in content, emphasis, and point of view, this encyclopaedia belongs to the period of the 1860's. The studied avoidance of any reference to difficulties between North and

South, and between Old and New Schools indicates that sensitiveness on these subjects had by no means disappeared. Referred to in this work as *Presbyterian Encyclopaedia.*

National Handbook of Facts and Figures. New York, 1870.

Presbyterian Family Almanac for 1860. [Old School.] Philadelphia, 1860.

Presbyterian Historical Almanac and Annual Remembrancer of the Church, 1858-1868. Edited by Joseph M. Wilson. Philadelphia, 1859-1868. An invaluable supplement to the frequently meager records of the minor Presbyterian denominations; also an important source of biographical and statistical information with regard to Presbyterianism in Europe as well as in America. The later volumes are devoted more exclusively to the Presbyterian Churches in the United States.

Statistics of the United States . . . in 1860; compiled from the Original Returns . . . of the Eighth Census. . . . , " Miscellaneous " volume. Washington, 1866. Pp. 352-501 deal with the statistics of religious bodies. For an excellent digest of the information furnished by this volume on the subjects of religion and population, *cf. Presbyterian Historical Almanac,* 1866, pp. 417-460.

E. *Contemporary Histories*

Baird, Robert, *The Progress and Prospects of Christianity in the United States of America, with Remarks on . . . Slavery in America. . . .* London, 1851.

Baird, Samuel J., *A History of the New School and of the Questions involved in the Disruption of the Presbyterian Church in 1838.* Philadelphia, 1868. Carries the history of the New School movement to 1838. The intense hostility to the reunion movement betrayed by this Old School author in his preface at once makes it clear to the reader that the book was intended to serve as propaganda.

Billingsley, Amos Stevens, *Christianity in the War.* Philadelphia, 1872. The author was an Old School clergyman.

———, *From the Flag to the Cross.* Philadelphia, 1872. The same as the above, except for the title.

Cheeseman, Rev. Lewis, *Differences between Old and New School Presbyterians;* with an introductory chapter by John C. Lord, D.D. Rochester, 1848.

Gillett, Ezra Hall, *History of the Presbyterian Church in the United States of America.* Revised edition. 2 volumes. Philadelphia, 1873. Only one of the forty-two chapters deals with the period after 1838. The author, a New School Presbyterian clergyman, in this revised edition (which appeared after the reunion of the two Churches) softened considerably some of the judgments with regard to the Old School Church as they appeared in the original edition of 1864.

Greeley, Horace, *The American Conflict. . . .* 2 volumes. Hartford, 1866.

Hackett, Horatio B., *Christian Memorials of the War. . . .* Boston, n. d. A "collection of 130 scenes and incidents of the war and of the Christians in it."

Hill, William, *History of the Rise, Progress, Genius, and Character of American Presbyterianism.* . . . Washington City, 1839.

Leftwich, W. M., *Martyrdom in Missouri, A History of Religious Proscription, the Seizure of Churches, and the Persecution of Ministers of the Gospel, in the State of Missouri during the Late Civil War and under the "Test Oath" of the New Constitution.* 2 volumes. St. Louis, 1870.

Map of the Presbyterian Church in the United States. Taken from the New York *Evangelist.* New York, 1871.

Matlack, Lucius G., *The Anti-slavery Struggle and Triumph in the Methodist Episcopal Church.* . . . Cincinnati, 1881.

——, *The History of American Slavery and Methodism from 1780-1849 and the History of the Wesleyan Methodist Connection in America* . . . . In two parts. New York, 1849.

Moss, Lemuel, *Annals of the United States Christian Commission.* Philadelphia, 1868.

Nevin, Alfred, *Churches of the Valley . . . of Franklin and Cumberland Counties in Pennsylvania.* Philadelphia, 1852.

Norton, A. T., *History of the Presbyterian Church in the State of Illinois.* St. Louis, 1879. By the editor of the *Presbytery Reporter.*

Presbyterian Memorial Offering, 1870-1871. New York, 1871. An account of the success of the Presbyterian Church in raising the special offering of five millions of dollars voted by the reunited General Assembly in 1869 as a token of gratitude for the success of the movement for reunion. Largely statistical.

Presbyterian Reunion: A Memorial Volume. 1837-1871. New York, 1870. Containing an historical review of each branch of the Church since 1837; biographical sketches; a history of the reunion movement and of the General Assemblies of 1869; an account of the reconstruction of the Church; statistics of each branch of the Church; copies of documents relating to reunion.

Schaff, Philip, *Der Bürgerkrieg und das Christliche Leben in Nord-Amerika, Vorträge.* . . . Zweite Auflage. Berlin, 1866.

——, *Church and State in the United States.* New York, 1888.

Scott, William A., *The Church in the Army, or, The Four Centurions.* New York, 1862.

Smith, Edward Parmelee, *Incidents among Shot and Shell . . . under the notice of the United States Christian Commission.* . . . N. p., 1868.

——, *Incidents of the United States Christian Commission.* Philadelphia, 1869. Much the same as the above, except for the choice of illustrations, and the absence of an index. The author was the Field Secretary of the United States Christian Commission.

Stanton, Robert Livingston, *The Church and the Rebellion.* . . . New York, 1864.

United States Christian Commission. Facts, Principles and Progress. Philadelphia, 1864.

F. Contemporary Letters, Memoirs, and Biographies

Baird, Henry M., *The Life of the Rev. Robert Baird, D. D.* New York, 1866. The author was the son of the subject of the biography.

Boardman, E. B. and Mary A., *Memorials of Henry Augustus Boardman.* New York, 1882. Privately printed.

Gough, John B., *An Autobiography.* 31st edition. Boston, 1852.

——, *Sunlight and Shadow. . . .* Hartford, 1887.

Grasty, Rev. John S., *Memoir of Rev. Samuel B. McPheeters, D. D.*, with an Introduction by Rev. Stuart Robinson, D.D. St. Louis, Louisville, 1871.

Hodge, A. A., *The Life of Charles Hodge, D.D., LL.D., Professor in the Theological Seminary, Princeton, N. J.*, by his son. New York, 1880.

Hoge, Peyton Harrison, *The Life and Letters of Moses Drury Hoge.* Richmond, 1899.

Johnson, Thomas Cary, *The Life and Letters of Robert Lewis Dabney.* Richmond, c. 1903.

——, *The Life and Letters of Benjamin Morgan Palmer.* Richmond, c. 1906.

Junkin, D. X., *The Reverend George Junkin, D. D., LL. D. A Historical Biography.* Philadelphia, 1871.

Life and Times of David Bell Birney, Major General. Philadelphia, 1867.

Memorial Sketches of Zephaniah Moore Humphrey, and Five Selected Sermons. Philadelphia, 1883.

Nicolay, John G., and Hay, John, ed., *The Complete Works of Abraham Lincoln. . . .* 2 volumes. New York, 1894.

Palmer, Benjamin Morgan, *Life and Letters of James Henley Thornwell.* Richmond, 1875.

Prime, Wendell, *Samuel Irenaeus Prime. Autobiography and Memorials.* New York, 1888. Dr. Wendell Prime was the son of Dr. S. I. Prime. The latter was the editor of the New York *Observer* during the period of the Civil War and Reconstruction.

Princeton Theological Seminary. *Discourses Commemorative of the Life and Work of Charles Hodge.* Philadelphia, 1879.

Scottish Princetonian, A, [Rev. C. A. Salmond, M.A.], *Charles and A. A. Hodge, with Class and Table Talk of Hodge the Younger.* Edinburgh, 1888.

Smyth, Thomas, *Complete Works. . . .* Edited by J. W. Flinn. 10 volumes. Columbia, 1908-1912.

Spring, Gardiner, *Personal Reminiscences of the Life and Times of Gardiner Spring. . . .* 2 volumes. New York, 1866.

Thomas, Alfred A., *Correspondence of Thomas Ebenezer Thomas, mainly relating to the Anti-Slavery Conflict in Ohio, especially in the Presbyterian Church.* Published by his son. N. p., 1909.

G. *Sermons and Addresses*

Adams, William, *Christian Patriotism.* New York, 1863.

Anderson, S. J. P., *The Power of a Christian Literature.*

Atterbury, John G., *God in Civil Government.* Preached in the First Presbyterian Church of New Albany, Indiana, by the pastor of the Second Presbyterian Church, November 27, 1862.

Boardman, Henry Augustus, *The American Union.* . . . Sixth edition. Philadelphia, 1851. Preached December 12, 1850.

———, *The Federal Judiciary. A Thanksgiving Discourse.* Philadelphia, 1862.

———, *Healing and Salvation for our country from God Alone.* . . . Preached Thanksgiving Day, November 24, 1864. Philadelphia, 1864.

———, *The Low Value set upon Human Life in the United States.* . . . Philadelphia, 1853.

———, *The New Doctrine of Intervention, tried by the Teachings of Washington.* . . . Philadelphia, 1852.

———, *The Peace-Makers.* A sermon preached on Sunday, April 9, 1865. Philadelphia, 1865.

———, *The Peace We Need and How to Secure It.* Philadelphia, 1865.

———, *The Sovereignty of God, the Sure and Only Stay of the Christian Patriot.* . . . A sermon preached on September 14 and 28, 1862. Philadelphia, 1862.

———, *What Christianity demands of us at the Present Crisis.* . . . A sermon preached on Thanksgiving Day, November 29, 1860. Philadelphia, 1860.

Breckinridge, Robert J. *Two Speeches on the State of the Country.* . . . Delivered May 20 and 22, 1862. Cincinnati, 1862.

———, *Discussion on American Slavery between George Thompson, esq., . . . and Rev. Robt. J. Breckinridge, . . . holden in the Rev. Dr. Wardlaw's Chapel, Glasgow, Scotland, the 13th, 14th, 15th, 16th, 17th of June, 1836. With an appendix.* 2nd American edition, with notes by Mr. Garrison. Boston, 1836.

Clarke, Walter, *The State of the Country, an Oration delivered at Buffalo, N. Y., July 4, 1862.* Dr. Clarke was a New School Presbyterian minister. Buffalo, 1862.

Duffield, George, *Our National Sins to be Repented of, and the Grounds of Hope for the Preservation of our Federal Constitution and Union.* Preached on Friday, January 4, 1861, the day of Fasting, Humiliation and Prayer appointed by the President of the United States. Detroit, 1861.

———, *A Thanksgiving Discourse. The Rule of Divine Providence Applicable to the Present Circumstances of our Country.* Detroit, 1861.

Hovey, Horace C., *Freedom's Banner.* A sermon preached to the Coldwater Light Artillery and Coldwater Zouave Cadets. Coldwater (Michigan), 1861.

———, *The National Fast.* Coldwater, 1861.

Jenkins, John, *Thoughts for the Crisis.* Philadelphia, 1861.

Jones, Charles Colcock, *Religious Instruction of the Negroes. An Address delivered before the General Assembly of the Presbyterian Church, at Augusta, Ga., Dec. 16, 1861.* Richmond, n. d.

Moore, Thomas Vernon, *God our Refuge and Strength in the War. A Discourse before the Congregations of the First and Second Presbyterian Churches on the Day of Humiliation, Fasting and Prayer, appointed by President Davis.* Richmond, 1861.

Palmer, Benjamin Morgan, *The South: Her Peril and Her Duty. A Discourse delivered in the First Presbyterian Church, New Orleans, on Thursday, Nov. 29, 1860.* New Orleans, 1860.

Patterson, Robert, *A Plea for the Brethren of the Lord. Chicago, 1864.*

Prentiss, George L., *Lessons of Encouragement from the Times of Washington.* New York, 1863.

Rice, Nathan Lewis, *Lectures on Slavery . . . First Presbyterian Church, Cincinnati, July 1 & 3, 1845.* Cincinnati, 1845.

———, *Lectures on Slavery . . . North Presbyterian Church, Chicago.* Chicago, 1860.

———, *The Pulpit, Its Relation to our National Crisis. A sermon preached in the Fifth Ave. & 19th St. Presbyterian Church.* New York, 1862.

———, *Sermon on the Death of Abraham Lincoln . . . preached on the occasion of the national funeral. . . .* New York, 1865.

———, *Ten Letters on the Subject of Slavery: addressed to the Delegates from the Congregational Associations to the last General Assembly of the Presbyterian Church.* St. Louis, 1855.

Sermons on the Death of Abraham Lincoln. A Collection in the Library of the Union Theological Seminary, New York City. The collection includes the following sermons by Presbyterian preachers:

Bingham, Joel F., *National Disappointment. . . .* Buffalo, 1865.

Carey, Rev. Mr., *Discourse on the Death of Abraham Lincoln.* Freeport (Ill.), 1865.

Carnahan, D. T., *An Oration on the Death of Abraham Lincoln . . . before the Citizens of Gettysburg, Pa., June 1, 1865.* Gettysburg, 1865.

Chester, John, *The Lesson of the Hour . . . Capitol Hill Presbyterian Church.* Washington, 1865.

Dunning, H., *A Nameless Crime. . . .* Baltimore, 1865.

Farquhar, John, *The Claims of God to Recognition. . . .* Lancaster (Pa.), 1865.

Fowler, Henry, *Character and Death of Abraham Lincoln.* Auburn, 1865.

Hopkins, T. M., *A Discourse. . . .* Bloomington (Ind.), 1865.

Ludlow, James M., *Sermon Commemorative of National Events.* Albany, 1865.

Prime, G. Wendell, *A Sermon.* Detroit, 1865.

Sample, Robert F., *The Curtained Throne.* Philadelphia, 1865.

Stearns, Jonathan F., *Death of President Lincoln. . . .*

Sermon preached in the First Presbyterian Church of Newark, New Jersey, April 16, 1865. Privately printed. Champlain, 1919.

Sutphen, Morris C., *Discourse . . . Abraham Lincoln. . . .* Philadelphia, 1865.

Thomson, John C., *In Memoriam. . . .* Philadelphia, 1865.

Twombly, A. S., *The Assassination of Abraham Lincoln.* Albany, 1865.

Vincent, M. R., *A Sermon on . . . Abraham Lincoln.* Troy, 1865.

Williams, Robert H., *God's Chosen Ruler. . . .* Frederick (Md.), 1865.

Sermon-Collection in the Patterson Library, Princeton University. This collection includes the following sermons by Presbyterians on the State of the Country (besides a number of sermons named elsewhere in this Bibliography):

Breckinridge, R. J., *The Nation's Success and Gratitude.* 1864.

Crosby, H., *God's View of Rebellion.* 1864.

Prentiss, G. L., *Some of the Providential Lessons of 1861.* 1862.

Rice, N. L., *Our Country and Our Church.*

Stanton, R. L., *Causes for National Humiliation.*

Shedd, William G. T., *The Union and the War.* New York, 1863.

Spear, Samuel T., *The Nation's Blessing in Trial.* New York, 1862.

Spees, S. G., *A New Song. . . . A Thanksgiving Sermon preached . . . November 23, 1863.* Dayton, 1864.

Sprague, William B., *A Discourse addressed to the Alumni of the Princeton Theological Seminary, April 30, 1862, on the Occasion of the Completion of its First Half Century.* With an appendix. Albany, 1862.

Spring, Gardiner S., *State Thanksgiving During the Rebellion.* Preached on Thanksgiving Day, 1861.

VanDyke, Henry Jackson, *The Character and Influence of Abolitionism, A Sermon. . . .* New York, 1860. Preached in the First Presbyterian Church of Brooklyn on Sabbath Evening, December 9, 1860.

Warner, J. R., *Our Times and Our Duty: An Oration delivered by request of the Gettysburg Zouaves before the Citizens Civil and Military of Gettysburg and Vicinity. . . . July 4, 1861.* Gettysburg, 1861.

H. *Pamphlets and Tracts*

An American [William Birney], *American Churches, the Bulwarks of American Slavery.* Second American edition. Newburyport, 1842.

Boardman, Henry A., *The General Assembly of 1866.* Philadelphia, 1867.

Brainerd, Cephas, *Christian Work in the Army prior to the organization of the United States Christian Commission.* The Work of the Army Commission of the New York Young Men's Christian Association which led to the organization of the United States Christian Commission. A paper read before the Association at the monthly meeting, December 18, 1865. New York, 1866.

Brookes, J. H., [Title page missing] Argument in defense of the " Declaration and Testimony" before the 1866 Old School General Assembly. N. p., 1866. In the Library of the Presbyterian Historical Society, Philadelphia.

Dabney, Robert Lewis, *Letter of Rev. R. L. Dabney, D.D. of Union Theological Seminary of Virginia to the Rev. S. I. Prime, D.D., one of the editors of the New York Observer, on the State of the Country.* Republished from the *Central Presbyterian.* Richmond, 1861.

Declaration and Testimony against the Erroneous and Heretical Doctrines and Practices which have Obtained and been Propagated in the Presbyterian Church of the United States, during the last five years. N. p., 1865. Second edition. A copy of the original edition may be found in the *Presbyterian Historical Almanac,* 1867, pp. 69-78.

Forman, A. P., [Title page missing] A defense of the "Declaration and Testimony." N. p., 1867. In the Library of the Presbyterian Historical Society, Philadelphia.

Hodge, Charles, *The State of the Country.* An article in the *Princeton Review,* January, 1861, reprinted as a pamphlet. New York, 1861.

McCook, Henry C., *The Men and Measures of the Declaration and Testimony.* . . . St. Louis, 1867.

———, [Title page missing] *A Plea for the Freedom of the Churches in Missouri.* N. p., n. d. A paper on the Missouri Test Oath. In the Library of the Presbyterian Historical Society, Philadelphia.

Palmer, Benjamin Morgan, *A Vindication of Secession and the South from the Strictures of Rev. R. J. Breckinridge, D.D. in the Danville Quarterly Review. Reprinted from the Southern Presbyterian Review for April, 1861.* New Orleans, 1861.

The Supreme Court of Missouri and the Declaration and Testimony. The Lindenwood College Case. [Title page missing.] N. p., n. d. A reprint of the Court reports of the case. In the Library of the Presbyterian Historical Society, Philadelphia.

Thornwell, James Henley, *The State of the Country: an Article Republished from the Southern Presbyterian Review.* Columbia, 1861.

Tracts and Cards. About 120 contemporary tracts and cards in the collection of the Presbyterian Historical Society, Philadelphia. Many of these were used for war-time distribution.

I. *Contemporary Essays and Magazine Articles*

Aikman, William, "The Future of the Colored Race in America," *Presbyterian Quarterly Review,* July, 1862. Also reprinted as a pamphlet, New York, 1862. Mr. Aikman was the pastor of the Hanover St. Presbyterian Church (New School) of Wilmington, Delaware. (*Cf. ante,* pp. 372, note 104; 371-373.)

Alexander, J. W., "Sprague's *Annals of the Presbyterian Pulpit,*" *Biblical Repertory and Princeton Review,* July, 1858, vol. xxx, pp. 401-419.

Atwater, L. H., "Proceedings of the Late Assemblies on Re-Union," *Biblical Repertory and Princeton Review,* July, 1869, vol. xli, pp. 423-448.

Bacon, L., "The Pulpit and the Crisis," *New Englander,* vol. xix, pp. 140-160, January, 1861. A review of John Wingate Thornton's *Pulpit of the American Revolution* and J. H. Thornwell's "National Sins," (a Fast-Day sermon).

Breckinridge, Robert J., "The Civil War: Its Nature and End," *Living Age,* January, 1862, vol. lxxii, pp. 141-149. Extracts from the article on this subject in the *Danville Quarterly Review* of December, 1861.

"Condensed Statistical History of the Presbyterian Church in the United States, from 1828 to 1859," *Congregational Quarterly,* July, 1860, vol. ii, pp. 308-310.

Hall, W. T., "Religion in the Army of Tennessee," *Land We Love,* December, 1867, vol. iv, pp. 127-131. Deals with religious conditions in the Confederate army in Tennessee.

Hodge, Charles, "The Bible Argument on Slavery," an essay in Elliott, E. N., ed., *Cotton is King.* . . . Augusta, 1860.

——, "The Fugitive Slave Law," an essay in Elliott, E. N., ed., *Cotton is King.* . . . Augusta, 1860.

——, "The New Basis of Union," *Biblical Repertory and Princeton Review,* July, 1869, vol. xli, pp. 462-466.

Innes, Alexander Taylor, "The Church in its Relation to the State and Civil Law in Scotland and America," *Princeton Review,* January, 1878, new series, vol. i, pp. 24-48.

Musgrave, George W., "Exposition and Defence of the Basis of Reunion," *Biblical Repertory and Princeton Review,* July, 1869, vol. xli, pp. 449-462.

Wood, G. I., "Divine Guidance in the Civil War," *New Englander,* vol. xxiv, pp. 690-704.

J. *Newspapers*

The Ann Arbor Journal, 1861-1863. Weekly. Ann Arbor, Michigan.

The Baltimore Sun, 1861-1870. Baltimore, Maryland.

The Boston Evening Transcript, 1861. Boston, Massachusetts.

The Detroit Daily Advertiser, 1861-1866. Title varies: *Detroit Daily Advertiser,* 1861; *Detroit Daily Advertiser and Tribune,* 1862-1866. Detroit, Michigan.

The Detroit Weekly Tribune, 1861-1863. Detroit, Michigan.

The New Orleans Daily Picayune, 1861. New Orleans, Louisiana.

The New Orleans Daily True Delta, 1860-1861. New Orleans, Louisiana.

The Newport Mercury, 1861-1862. Newport, Rhode Island.

The New York Daily Evening Post, 1861-1865. New York, N. Y.

The New York Herald, 1861-1870. New York, N. Y.

The New York Shipping and Commercial List, 1861; 1863-1864. New York, N. Y.

The New York Times, 1861-1866. New York, N. Y.

The New York Tribune, 1862-1865. New York, N. Y.

The New York World, 1861-1863. New York, N. Y.

The Philadelphia Press, 1861-1870. Philadelphia, Pennsylvania.

The Philadelphia Public Ledger, 1862-1869. Philadelphia, Pennsylvania.

The Philadelphia Weekly Press, 1860-1861. Philadelphia, Pennsylvania.

The Providence Daily Journal, 1861-1866. Providence, Rhode Island.

K. *Periodicals*

The greater number of the periodicals listed below were Presbyterian journals. For an estimate of their individual historical importance, *cf. ante*, pp. 132-182; 364-371.

The American Presbyterian, 1861-1869. Weekly. Philadelphia.

The American Presbyterian and Theological Review, 1859-1868. Title varies: *American Theological Review*, 1859-1862; *American Presbyterian and Theological Review*, 1863-1868. Absorbed *Presbyterian Quarterly Review*, January, 1863. Quarterly. New York.

American Theological Review, 1859-1862. In January, 1863, absorbed the *Presbyterian Quarterly Review*, and became the *American Presbyterian and Theological Review*. Quarterly. New York.

The Biblical Repertory and Princeton Review, 1861-1869. Quarterly. Philadelphia.

The Christian Herald, 1860-1869. In 1861 merged with the *Presbyterian Recorder*, and became the *Christian Herald and Presbyterian Recorder*. In 1869 united with the *Presbyter*, and became the *Herald and Presbyter*. Weekly. Cincinnati.

The Christian Observer, 1861-1865. Weekly. Philadelphia, Richmond. This journal was published very irregularly during the war period. In 1861 it was moved from Philadelphia to Richmond, Virginia.

The Congregational Quarterly, 1860-1865. Quarterly. Boston.

The Danville Quarterly Review, 1861-1864. Title varies: *Danville Quarterly Review*, 1861; *Danville Review*, 1862-1864. Quarterly. Danville, Kentucky.

The Home and Foreign Record of the Presbyterian Church in the United States of America, being the organ of the Boards of Domestic Missions, Education, Foreign Missions, Publication, and Church Extension, 1861-1869. Title varies: changed in 1868 to *The Church at Home and Abroad*. Monthly. Philadelphia.

The Independent, 1861-1869. Weekly. New York.

The Land We Love, 1866-1869. Monthly. Charlotte, North Carolina.

The Living Age, 1861-1869. Monthly. Boston.

The Missouri Presbyterian, 1866. Weekly. St. Louis.

National Freedman, June, 1865. Monthly. New York.

The New Englander, 1861-1869. New Haven, Connecticut.

The New York Evangelist, 1861-1869. Weekly. New York.

The New York Observer, 1861-1869. Weekly. New York.

The Presbyter, 1858-1869. In 1869 merged with the *Christian Herald and Presbyterian Recorder* to become the *Herald and Presbyter*. Weekly. Cincinnati.

The Presbyterian, 1858-1870. Weekly. Philadelphia.

The Presbyterian Banner, 1861-1869. Weekly. Pittsburgh.

The Presbyterian Expositor, 1857-1861. In 1861 absorbed by the *Presbyterian Standard*. Weekly. Chicago.

The Presbyterian Herald, 1861-1862. In 1862 sold to the *True Presbyterian*. Weekly. Bardstown, Kentucky.

The Presbyterian of Our Union, 1861-1862. Weekly. St. Louis. Sold in 1862 to the *True Presbyterian*.

The Presbyterian Quarterly Review, 1861-1862. In January, 1863, absorbed by the *American Theological Review*, becoming the *American Presbyterian and Theological Review*. Quarterly. New York.

The Presbyterian Standard, 1861-1864. Title varies: March 21 to May 23, 1861, *Presbyterian Standard;* May 30, 1861 (when it absorbed the *Presbyterian Expositor*) to July 10, 1862, *Standard and Presbyterian Expositor;* July 17, 1862, to suspension in 1864, *Presbyterian Standard*. Weekly. Philadelphia.

The Presbytery Reporter, 1860-1866. Suspended publication, 1861-1862. Monthly. Alton, Illinois.

The True Presbyterian, 1862-1864. Weekly. Louisville. Publication very irregular.

The Western Presbyterian, 1865. Weekly. Louisville. Established in 1864.

III. SECONDARY SOURCES

Ambler, C. H., " The Cleavage between Eastern and Western Virginia," *American Historical Review*, July, 1910, vol. xv, pp. 762-780.

American Church History Series. Philip Schaff, H. C. Potter, Sheldon M. Jackson, editors. 13 vol. New York, 1893-1898.

American Nation: A History. A. B. Hart, editor. 28 vol. New York, 1905-1918.

Andrews, William Given, " A Recent Service of Church History to the Church," American Historical Association *Annual Report* for 1899, vol. i, pp. 389-427.

Bacon, Leonard W., *A History of American Christianity (American Church History Series*, vol. xiii), New York, 1898.

Blaikie, Alexander, *History of Presbyterianism in New England*. 2 volumes. Boston, 1881.

Brackett, W. O., " The Rise and the Development of the New School in the Presbyterian Church in the U. S. A. to the Reunion of 1869," *Pres. Hist. Soc. Jour.*, Sept.-Dec., 1928, vol. xiii, pp. 117-140; 145-174.

Briggs, Charles Augustus, *American Presbyterianism*. . . . New York, 1885. Carries the history of Presbyterianism to 1788.

Brown, William Adams, *The Church in America, a Study of the Present Condition and Future Prospects*. . . . New York, 1922.

Carroll, H. K., *The Religious Forces in the United States . . . Census of 1890 (American Church History Series*, vol. i). New York, 1893.

Casson, H. N., *Cyrus Hall McCormick, His Life and Work*. Chicago, 1909.

Channing, Edw., *History of the United States*. 6 vol. New York, 1909-1925.

Christie, Francis A., " The Field of Religious Development since the Civil War," American Historical Association *Annual Report* for 1921, vol. xxvii, p. 416. An abstract of a paper given before the American Historical Association at St. Louis, December, 1921.

Concise Dictionary of Religious Knowledge, Biblical, Doctrinal, Historical and Practical. Edited by Sheldon Jackson and others. New York, 1889.

Coulter, E. Merton, *The Civil War and Readjustment in Kentucky.* Chapel Hill, 1926.

Cutting, Robert Fulton, and Ledoux, Albert R., *The Brick Presbyterian Church of New York; Addresses . . . 150th Anniversary. . . .* American Scenic and Historic Preservation Society *Reports,* 1918, vol. xxiii, pp. 575-606.

Cuyler, Theodore L., *Recollections of a Long Life.* New York, 1902.

Davidson, Robert, *Historical Sketch of the Synod of Philadelphia.* Philadelphia, 1876.

Davis, William W., *The Civil War and Reconstruction in Florida.* New York, 1913.

Dictionary of American Biography. Allen Johnson, Dumas Malone, editors. In progress. New York, 1928-   .

Dodd, William E., " The Fight for the North West, 1860," *American Historical Review,* July, 1911, vol. xvi, pp. 774-788.

Dunning, William A., *Reconstruction, Political and Economic, 1865-1877 (The American Nation,* vol. xxii). New York, 1907.

——, *Essays on the Civil War and Reconstruction.* New York, 1904.

Eaton, S. J. M., *Memorial of the Life and Labors of the Rev. Cyrus Dickson, D.D. . . .* New York, 1882.

Encyclopaedia of Religion and Ethics. Edited by James Hastings. 13 volumes. Edinburgh and New York, 1908-1926.

Ficklen, J. R., *History of Reconstruction in Louisiana (through 1868).* Baltimore, 1910.

Fish, Carl Russell, *The Rise of the Common Man, 1830-1850 (History of American Life,* vol. vi). New York, 1927.

Fite, Emerson David, *Social and Industrial Conditions in the North during the Civil War.* New York, 1910.

Fleming, Walter L., *Civil War and Reconstruction in Alabama.* New York, 1905.

——, ed., *Documentary History of the Reconstruction.* 2 volumes. New York, 1906-1907.

Foster, Robert V., *A Sketch of the History of the Cumberland Presbyterian Church (American Church History Series,* vol. xi, pp. 257-309). New York, 1894.

Garner, J. W., *Reconstruction in Mississippi.* New York, 1901.

Halsey, Leroy J., *History of McCormick Theological Seminary. . . .* Chicago, 1903.

Hamilton, J. G. de R., *Reconstruction in North Carolina (Columbia University Studies,* vol. lviii). New York, 1914.

Hart, Albert Bushnell, *Slavery and Abolition (The American Nation,* vol. xvi). New York, 1907.

Hays, George Price, *Presbyterians: A Popular Narrative of their Origin, Progress, Doctrines, and Achievements. . . .* New York, 1892.

Heathcote, Charles William, *The Lutheran Church and the Civil War.* New York, 1919.

History of American Life. A. M. Schlesinger, D. R. Fox, editors. 12 vol. In progress. New York, 1927- .

Hosmer, James Kendall, *The Appeal to Arms (The American Nation,* vol. xx). New York, 1907.

———, *The Outcome of the Civil War (The American Nation,* vol. xxi). New York, 1907.

Hunter, Alexander, *The Women of the Debatable Land.* Washington, 1912.

Jenkins, H. D., "The History of Presbyterianism in Illinois," Illinois Historical Society *Transactions,* 1913, pp. 60-66.

Jessup, Henry Winans, *History of the Fifth Avenue Presbyterian Church of New York City, 1808-1908.* New York, 1909.

Johnson, Thomas Cary, *A History of the Southern Presbyterian Church (American Church History Series,* vol. xi, pp. 311-479). New York, 1894.

Johnson's Universal Cyclopaedia. Edited by Charles Kendall Adams. New edition. 8 volumes. New York, 1895.

Jones, F. D., and Mills, W. H., editors, *A History of the Presbyterian Church in South Carolina since 1850.* N. p., 1926.

Kelly, Robert L., *Theological Education in America: A Study of 161 Theological Schools in the United States.* New York, 1924.

Kirkland, Edward Chase, *The Peacemakers of 1864.* New York, 1927.

Knapp, Shepherd, *The History of the Brick Presbyterian Church. . . .* New York, 1909.

Local Histories of the progress of Presbyterianism in individual states and sections, in synods, presbyteries, and churches. Only a few of the vast number of works of this type are mentioned in this Bibliography. An extensive collection has been gathered in the Library of the Presbyterian Historical Society in Philadelphia. For the most part they are merely ecclesiastical annals and throw little light upon the relation of the Presbyterian people to the contemporary political problems.

Loetscher, Frederick William, *Fifty Years, the Reunion of the Old and New School Presbyterian Churches, 1870-1920 . . . .* Philadelphia, 1920.

Lonn, Ella, *Reconstruction in Louisiana after 1868.* New York, 1918.

Lyons, John F., "The Attitude of Presbyterians in Ohio, Indiana, and Illinois toward Slavery, 1825-1861," *Presbyterian Historical Society Journal,* June, 1921, vol. xi, pp. 69-82.

McClure, James Gore King, "Some Pastors and Pastorates during the Century of Presbyterianism in Illinois," Illinois State Historical Society *Journal,* April, 1920, vol. xiii, pp. 1-15.

The McCormick Theological Seminary. *Historical Celebration in Recognition of the Eightieth Year of the Origin of the Seminary, the Fiftieth Year of its Location in Chicago, and the One Hundredth Year of the Birth of Cyrus H. McCormick, November 1 and 2, 1909.* Chicago, 1909.

McMaster, J. B., *History of the People of the United States, from the Revolution to the Civil War.* 8 volumes. New York, 1883-1913.
———, *History of the People of the United States during Lincoln's Administration.* New York, 1927.
Morris, Edward D., *A Book of Remembrance—The Presbyterian Church, New School, 1837-1869.* Columbus, 1905.
National Cyclopaedia of American Biography . . . . 23 volumes. New York, 1927.
Nevins, Allan, *The Emergence of Modern America, 1865-1878* (*History of American Life*, vol. viii). New York, 1927.
New Schaff-Herzog Encyclopaedia of Religious Knowledge, Embracing Biblical, Historical, Doctrinal, and Practical Theology, and Biblical, Theological, and Ecclesiastical Biography from the Earliest Times to the Present Day. . . . Edited by Sheldon M. Jackson. 12 volumes. New York and London, 1908-1912.
Nicolay, J. G., and Hay, John, *Abraham Lincoln, A History.* 10 volumes. New York, 1890.
Norwood, John Nelson, *The Schism in the Methodist Episcopal Church, 1844: A Study of Slavery and Ecclesiastical Politics* (Alfred University *Studies*, vol. i). Alfred, New York, 1923.
Oberholtzer, Ellis Paxson, *A History of the United States since the Civil War.* 5 volumes. In progress. New York, 1917-   .
Patton, Francis L., *Caspar Wistar Hodge, A Memorial Address.* New York, n. d.
———, *A Discourse in Memory of Archibald Alexander Hodge, D.D., LL.D.* . . . Philadelphia, 1887.
Patton, Jacob Harris, *Popular History of the Presbyterian Church in the United States of America.* New York, 1903.
———, *The Triumph of the Presbytery of Hanover, or, the Separation of Church and State in Virginia.* New York, 1887.
Peirce, Paul S., *The Freedmen's Bureau—A Chapter in the History of Reconstruction* (State University of Iowa *Studies in Sociology, Economics, Politics, and History*, vol. iii, no. 1). Iowa City, 1904.
Perry, William Stevens, *The History of the American Episcopal Church, 1587-1883.* 2 volumes. Boston, 1885.
Pilcher, Elijah H., *Protestantism in Michigan, being a Special History of the Methodist Episcopal Church* . . . . Detroit, 1878.
Prentiss, George L., *The Bright Side of Life. Glimpses of It through Four-score Years.* . . . N. p., 1901.
———, *The Union Theological Seminary* . . . *Historical and Biographical Sketches of its First Fifty Years.* New York, 1889.
Princeton Theological Seminary. *The Centennial Celebration of the Theological Seminary of the Presbyterian Church in the United States of America.* . . . Princeton, 1912.
Ramsdell, C. W., *Reconstruction in Texas* (*Columbia University Studies*, vol. xxxvi, no. 1). New York, 1910.
Rhodes, James Ford, *History of the Civil War, 1861-1865.* New York, 1917.

———, *History of the United States from the Compromise of 1850.* . . . 7 volumes to 1877. New York, 1902-1912.

Rowe, Henry K., *History of Religion in the United States.* New York, 1924.

Schaff, David S., *The Life of Philip Schaff—in part Autobiographical.* New York, 1897.

Schlesinger, Arthur M., *New Viewpoints in American History.* New York, 1922.

Scouller, James B., *History of the United Presbyterian Church of North America (American Church History Series,* vol. xi, pp. 143-255). New York, 1894.

Smith, Edward Conrad, *The Borderland in the Civil War.* New York, 1927.

Smith, Mrs. Henry B., *Henry Boynton Smith, His Life and Work.* New York, 1881.

Stacy, James, *History of the Presbyterian Church in Georgia.* Atlanta, n. d.

Stearns, Lewis F., *Henry Boynton Smith (American Religious Leaders Series).* Boston, 1892.

Sweet, William W., *The Methodist Episcopal Church and the Civil War.* Cincinnati, 1912.

Thompson, Charles Lemuel, *An Autobiography.* Edited by Elizabeth Osborn Thompson. New York, 1924.

———, *The Presbyterians (The Story of the Churches).* New York, 1903.

Thompson, C. Mildred, *Reconstruction in Georgia (Columbia University Studies,* vol. lxiv, no. 1). New York, 1915.

Thompson, Robert Ellis, *History of the Presbyterian Churches in the United States (American Church History Series,* vol. vi). New York, 1895.

———, ed., *The Life of George H. Stuart, written by himself.* Philadelphia, 1890.

Twentieth Century Biographical Dictionary of Notable Americans. Rossiter Johnson and John Howard Brown, editors. 10 volumes. Boston, 1904.

Henry Jackson VanDyke. An anonymous memoir. New York, 1892.

Walker, Williston, *A History of the Congregational Churches in the United States (American Church History Series,* vol. iii). New York, 1898.

Weigle, L., *American Idealism (The Pageant of America,* vol. x). New Haven, 1928.

White, Henry Alexander, *Southern Presbyterian Leaders.* New York, 1911.

White, W. P., "The Evolution of a Presbyterian Religious Journal," *Presbyterian Historical Society Journal,* March, 1919, vol. x, pp. 36-41. An account of the background and history of the *Continent* (Chicago).

Wittke, Carl, "Religious Influences in American History," *California University Chronicle,* October, 1924, vol. xxvi, pp. 451-477.

INDEX

INDEX

Abolitionists, Charles Hodge and, 34-35; opposed by R. J. Breckinridge, 36, 144; accused of stirring up opposition in Old School Assembly, 81; *Presbyter* assailed as favoring, 134; *True Presbyterian* on, 175; H. J. Van Dyke opposed to, 285-287; N. L. Rice and, 288; Princeton Theological Seminary and, 294; United Presbyterian Assembly and demands of, 387; Associate Presbyterian Synod on demands of, 392; General Synod on program of, 395; Cumberland Church on, 413; Old School and Cumberland Churches offer last resistance to influence of, 470, 471; futility of resistance to, 471.

Act of 1818, on slavery, adopted by Old School Assembly, 25; referred to by 1861 Assembly, 91-92; 1863 Assembly requested to reaffirm, 123-124.

Adams, William, 373 n.

"Address of Southern General Assembly . . . ," 102-104.

Adger, J. B., 95.

Adventists, strength and wealth of, 5.

African Cumberland Presbyterian Church, 458.

Aikman, William A., 372 n.

Albany, Synod of, absorbs Middle Association of Congregationalists, 13.

Allegheny, Synod of (Old School), on slavery, 92.

Alton, Presbytery of (New School), and *Presbytery Reporter*, 370.

American Baptist Union, condemns secession, 78; action of, compared with Spring Resolutions, 78-79.

American Bible Society, 470.

American Colonization Society, 470.

American Home Missionary Society, 451.

American Presbyterian, New School weekly journal, quoted, 74-75, 498; changes attitude after Spring Resolutions, 107; on N. L. Rice, 288; and the Union, 368; on reunion, 368-369; quoted, 498.

American Presbyterian and Theological Review, on the Union, 366.

American Theological Review, nondenominational religious periodical, becomes *American Presbyterian and Theological Review*, 365-366; on the Civil War, 366.

American Revolution, Presbyterian Church and the, 22; and "political dissent," 393.

American Temperance Union, 345.

American Tract Society, 470.

Anderson, S. J. P., Old School minister, military trial of, 212, 246, 326-327; addresses Assembly, 227-228; and R. J. Breckinridge, 246, 248.

Anderson, William C., prominent Old School minister, 29; quoted, 54; presents minority report of special committee, 58-59, 230; a champion of the West, 80-81, 231, 237; on public interest in action of 1861 Assembly, 83-84; to T. E. Thomas, 230-231; on reunion, 231.

Anglican Church, establishment of, in America, 8.

Annan, John E., 291 n.

Antinomianism, Confession of Faith on, 509.

Arminianism, Confession of Faith on, 509.

Assembly. *See* General Assembly.

Church, 293-294; W. S. Plumer
and, 299.
Commercial, Cincinnati, on Presbyterianism in Kentucky, 270.
Concord, Presbytery of (Southern Church), two members of, organize new presbytery, 444.
Congregationalists, strength and wealth of, 5; establishment of, in America, 8; and Plan of Union (of 1801), 13; influence Presbyterianism, 13-14; influence the New School Church, 15, 483; essentially Northern, 15-17; attend Seminary at Princeton, 22; and the Union, 79; effect of War on press of, 180; ministers of, compared with Presbyterians, 282.
Congress of United States, Assemblies and, 359-360, 360-361, 388.
Connecticut Congregationalism, and Presbyterianism, 8; and Plan of Union (of 1801), 13.
Conservatism, of Old School Church, 23-24; of *Princeton Review,* 140; of *Presbyterian,* 150; of New York *Observer,* 178-180; of Old School Synod of Baltimore, 185; of Old School theological seminaries, 293; Old School Church carried away from, 332-333; in Cumberland Church, 417.
Constitution, Federal, and "political dissent," 10-11; Spring Resolutions and, 57-59; R. J. Breckinridge and, 144, 292-293; Reformed Presbyterians and, 393; General Synod of Reformed Presbyterians and, 396, 397; meeting to consider amendment of, 401; Synod of Reformed Presbyterians and, 393, 399, 400, 401-403, 404, 405; Cumberland Presbyterians on, 418.
Constitutional History of the Presbyterian Church in the United States, 254 n.
"Contrabands," condition of, 439.

Convention, recommended as a means of deliberating on state of Church, 205; called in 1866, 219-220, 234; meets to consider conditions in Missouri, 273; advocated to effect division in Cumberland Church, 414, 420; to consider troubles in Cumberland Church, 417. *See also* Reunion.
"Convention Oath," in Missouri, 318, 325.
Converse, Amasa, on war-time issues, 370-371.
Coons, John F., quoted, 200.
Cooper, Edward, quoted, 293 n.
Cotton is King, 34.
Covenanters, established in America, 10-11; and amendment of constitution, 402. *See also* Reformed Presbyterians.
Cox, Samuel H., 489.
Crisis, and Breckinridge paper, 118-119.
Cross, A. B., quoted, 200-201.
Crothers, Samuel, 229.
Cumberland Presbyterian Church, strength and wealth of, 5 n., 7, 9, 16, 406; origin and growth of, 9-10; a Border State church, 9-10, 406; slave membership of, 104 n.; and political allegiance, 406, 422; and the Civil War, 407-408, 409, 414, 416-424, 472, 473; conventions called for dividing, 414; movement in, to join Southern Church, 420; efforts of, to raise educational standards, 421 n.; war-time record of, 422-423; works through permanent committees, 433; special publishing committee of, 437; retains Southern membership, 466-467; and New School Church, 480; and Presbyterian convention, 512. *See also* General Assembly, Cumberland Presbyterian Church.
Cumberland Presbyterian, religious

Duffield, George, New School minister, preaches on the war, 373-374 n.; accused of unsound theology, 479-480, 515.

Dulles, John W., author of " Soldier's Friend," 436.

Dutch Reformed Church. *See* Reformed Dutch Church of North America.

East Alabama, Presbytery of (Old School), separates from Assembly, 94.

Edwards, General A. G., 213.

Ellsworth, Colonel E. E., death of, exploited by the press, 42.

Emancipation Proclamation, of Lincoln, influences Old School presbyteries and synods, 118; forces 1863 General Assembly to take action on slavery, 119; *Danville Review* on, 144-145; New York *Observer* on, 180; New School Assembly action preceding, 349; New School Assembly endorses, 350; United Presbyterian Assembly and, 383, 384, 385; Cumberland Assembly and, 409; most Presbyterian denominations anticipate, in anti-slavery pronouncements, 423.

Engles, William M., Old School minister, editor of *Presbyterian*, edits " Soldier's Pocket Book," 434 n.; member of Board of Publication, 438; publishes article on Board of Publication, 438.

Erastianism, New School and, 348.

Evangelical Knowledge Society, 513.

Evangelical Lutheran Church in the United States, and New School Church, 480. *See also* Lutherans.

Evangelical Lutheran Synod of Pennsylvania, and the Union, 77. *See also* Lutherans.

Evangelical Repository and United

Presbyterian Review, and the Union, 390 n.

Evangelist, New York, New School journal, quoted, 74, 112; on R. J. Breckinridge, 193-194; on Gurley Resolutions, 256; on Old School and New School types, 338-339; *Presbyterian* replies to, 362; and the Union, 367-368; communication in, quoted, 371-372; and reunion, 487.

Ewing, Judge J. K., 202.

Exscinding Acts of 1837, passed, 14; opposed by G. S. Spring, 46-47; referred to by New School journal, 75; R. J. Breckinridge and, 112-113; W. S. Plumer and, 295, 299-300; interest laity as well as clergy, 479.

Express, New York, anti-administration journal, on McPheeters case, 312.

Farris, Robert P., and oath of allegiance, 325-326.

Fatalism, Confession of Faith and, 509.

Federal Government, assists churches in efforts for freedmen, 458-459.

Federal Union. *See* Union, Federal.

Ferguson, W. M., Old School minister, comments on Galloway speech, 239-240; expelled from Assembly, 240-241.

Field, Stephen J., Associate Justice, 327.

Fifth Avenue Presbyterian Church, 283-285, 288.

Finley, J. P., 214.

First Presbyterian Church of Brooklyn, 227, 275-276, 285-287, 288.

Flag, raising of, Old School Assembly and, 120-122; Cumberland Assembly and, 410-411.

Foot, George, New School minister, 372-373.

Forman, A. P., Old School Presby-

bly, 115-116; quoted, 119; buys *Presbyterian Herald*, 164; and *True Presbyterian*, 167-177; early life of, 168, 173-174; career of, during and after Civil War, 168-177, 218, 304-305; on slavery, 168; on Thornwell theory, 168-169, 280; on controversy, 171; on Knights of Golden Circle, 172-173; on oath-taking, 173; on Abolitionism, 175; on action of 1864 Assembly, 175-176; on reunion, 175-176; attacks of, upon Dr. Breckinridge, 176-177; and division in Kentucky, 184; on Synod of Missouri, 215-216; returns from Canada, 219; elected commissioner to 1866 Assembly, 219, 224-236, 243-244; and "Declaration and Testimony," 226, 251; responsibility of, for extremes of 1866 Assembly action, 258-259, 272; and the Union, 303-304; on assassination of Lincoln, 304; on action of Cumberland Assembly, 408-409, 410, 413-414; on "progressive Presbyterians," 483 n.

Roman Catholics, strength and wealth of, 5, 16, 17; form of organization of, simplifies solution of problems (1861), 17; individual dioceses of, endorse Federal Government, 79.

Rosecrans, General W. S., defends his order regarding religious assemblages, 214; and oath-requirement, 214-217, 318, 323, 325, 326, 327.

Ryerson, Martin, 321 n.

St. Lawrence, Presbytery of (New School), holds joint meeting with Old School presbytery, 485.

St. Louis, city of, chosen as meeting-place of Assemblies, 218.

St. Louis Observer, Cumberland Presbyterian journal, 420 n.

St. Louis, Presbytery of (Old School), torn with dissension, 212-213; remnant of, pledges loyalty to Union, 212-213; and S. B. McPheeters, 315-323.

Saline, Presbytery of (Old School), requests reaffirmation of testimony of 1818, 123.

Sanderson, Colonel J. P., 213.

Sandusky, Synod of (Old School), commends Gurley Orders, 275 n.

Schenck, William E., 29.

Schuyler, Presbytery of (Old School), on exiled ministers, 293 n.

Scotch-Irish, promote rise of Presbyterianism in America, 8, 10; influence Old School Church, 337, 338.

Scouller, James B., author, quoted, 379 n., 380, 458 n.

Secession, theory of, championed by Old School leaders, 28; opposed by *Princeton Review*, 135-137; opposed by *Danville Review*, 141-142; opposed by *Presbyterian Banner*, 161; opposed by *Presbyterian Expositor*, 165; *Presbyterian of Our Union* on, 166; *True Presbyterian* silent on, 169, 172-177; denounced by Old School Assembly, 199-200; Cumberland Presbyterian protestants and, 413.

Second Presbyterian Church of Louisville, 168.

Sectionalism, in Old School Church, 54-56; revealed in vote on 1861 majority and minority reports, 61-64; evidence of, in Old School Assemblies, 80-82, 114, 120-122, 224-225, 252, 331; revealed in response of Church to adoption of Spring Resolutions, 88-105; in Southern Church, 95-96; *Presbyterian* on, 153-154; *Presbyter* an organ of, 160, 302; position of *Presbyterian Banner* on, 160; T.

School Church on, 341; New
School Assembly condemns, 347,
349, 351, 352, 358, 359; *Presbytery Reporter* on, 370; *Christian
Observer* on, 371; minor Presbyterian denominations and, 379,
387 n., 390-391; United Presbyterian Church on, 379-390; United
Presbyterian Assembly action on,
380-383, 384, 385, 388, 390; *Chris-
tion Instructor* reveals views on,
390 n.; condemned by Associate
Presbyterian Synod, 392; General
Synod of Reformed Presbyterians
and, 394, 395-397; Synod of Reformed Presbyterians and, 394,
398-399, 400-401, 403, 405-406;
Cumberland General Assembly on,
411-413, 414, 417, 419, 420, 424;
Presbyterian denominations approach common opposition to,
423-424.
Slaves, 1825 Assembly and education of, 25; as church members,
104 n.; work of S. B. McPheeters
among, 306.
Smith, Edward P., author, 468, 530.
Smith, Henry Boynton, editor, 365,
366 n.; on reunion, 492, 505; at-
tends Presbyterian convention,
513; quoted, 514.
Smith, T. C., 328 n.
Smylie, James, Old School clergyman, first advocate of most extreme pro-slavery theory, 28 n.,
27-28.
South Carolina, Synod of (Old
School), acts on secession, 30-31.
Southern General Assembly. *See*
Presbyterian Church in the Confederate States of America.
Southern Iowa, Synod of (Old
School), on action of 1861 As-
sembly, 90 n.; on slavery, 92;
commends Emancipation Proclamation, 118; commends Gurley
Orders, 275 n.

Southern Presbyterian, Old School
weekly journal, and the Union,
39; lost to Old School Church,
148, 150.
Southern Presbyterian Church. *See*
Presbyterian Church in the Confederate States of America.
Southern Presbyterian Review, Old
School periodical, on secession,
38; lost to Old School Church,
134-135.
Spear, Samuel T., 373-374 n.
Spees, S. G., 373-374 n.
Spiritualists, strength and wealth of,
5.
Sprague, William B., prominent Old
School minister, quoted, 22 n.;
and the Union, 289.
Spring, Gardiner S., prominent Old
School minister, 29, 46-48; intro-
duces resolutions in 1861 Assembly, 48-51; opponent of Abolitionists, 47, 283; quoted, 83; preaches
on Day of Prayer, 87; changes in
attitude toward slavery, 128; and
the Union, 283, 289.
Spring Resolutions, introduced in
1861 Assembly, 48-51; original
resolution tabled, 48; quoted, 50;
debates on, 51-64; modified, 54;
presented as report of minority
of special committee, 58-59; distinguished from majority report,
59; paragraph added to, 62-63;
adopted, 63-64, 332; protests introduced against, in 1861 Assembly, 64-70; opposed, as determining a political question, 66-67;
protests against, answered, 70-72;
compared with action of American Baptist Union, 78-79; character of Northern opposition to,
84-85; response of Old School
Church to adoption of, 88-107;
effect of, upon unity of Church,
93-107; condemned by Southern
Assembly's "Address," 103; effect

mony," 226; and seat in Assembly, 224-236, 243-244.

Winchester, Presbytery of (Old School), and Synod of Baltimore, 211, 274.

Wines, E. C., 61.

Winters, Jacob R., 215 n.

Wisconsin, Synod of (Old School), on slavery, 92.

Wood, James, 201-202.

Wood, Judge W. T., 321 n.

Wooster, Presbytery of (Old School), upholds 1864 Assembly, 129.

World, New York, quoted, 85; mistaken regarding Old School action on slavery, 112.

Worrall, J. M., 190 n.

Wyaconda, Presbytery of (Old School), on Spring Resolutions, 89; conditions in, 211.

Yantis, J. L., 328.

Yeomans, J. W., circularizes Old School ministers, 32; deprecates sectionalism in 1861 Assembly, 81-82.

Yerkes, Stephen, 178 n.

Young Men's Christian Association, founds United States Christian Commission, 467.

Zanesville, Presbytery of (Old School), W. M. Ferguson commissioner from, 239.

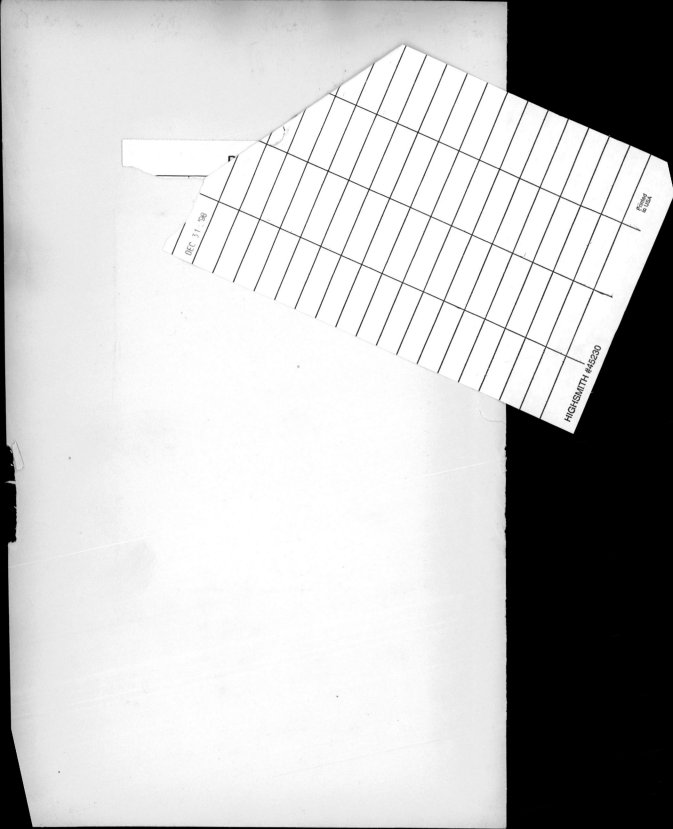